D1439186

Economic Factors in Population Growth

OTHER INTERNATIONAL ECONOMIC ASSOCIATION
PUBLICATIONS

Economic Factors in Population Growth

Proceedings of a Conference held by the International Economic Association at Valescure, France

EDITED BY
ANSLEY J. COALE

First published 1976 by
THE MACMILLAN PRESS LTD
London and Basingstoke
Associated companies in New York
Dublin Melbourne Johannesburg and Madras

Distributed in the United States
by Halsted Press, a Division of
John Wiley & Sons, Inc., New York

SBN 333 17955 2

Library of Congress Catalog Card No. 74-17375

Printed in Great Britain by
THOMSON LITHO LTD,
East Kilbride, Scotland

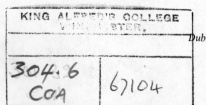

Contents

Contents

Acknowledgements

As in the case of an earlier conference on 'Public Economics', the conference recorded in this book was held in partnership with the French *Centre National de la Recherche Scientifique*. May we express to them our gratitude for their close collaboration through the good offices of Professor Henri Guitton? Our own contribution to the conference was again made possible by the grants received from the Ford Foundation and from UNESCO, our earliest sponsor. We wish also to thank Professor Ansley Coale and his programme committee for the work they put into the planning of the conference and Professor Douglas Hague and Mr Gordon Ibbotson for the essential record of our discussions. The rather Edwardian surroundings of the Golf Hotel at Valescure, among the pine trees and the wide spaces of a golf-course without golfers, with its swimming pool at whose side we continued our arguments, provided the perfect setting for intellectual argument.

Programme Committee

Professor Ansley J. Coale (United States), Chairman
Professor N. V. Sovani (India)
Dr Leon Tabah (France)
Dr E. A. Wrigley (United Kingdom)

Rapporteurs

Professor D. C. Hague
Mr Gordon Ibbotson

List of Participants

Sune Åkerman, Department of History, University of Uppsala, Sweden
P. Bauchet, Centre National de la Recherche Scientifique, Paris, France
Yoram Ben Porath, Falk Institute, Jerusalem, Israel
Bryan Boulier, Office of Population Research, Princeton University, U.S.A.
L. Bourcier de Carbon, Université de Paris, France
Ansley J. Coale, Office of Population Research, Princeton University, U.S.A.
Paul Demeny, The Population Council, New York, U.S.A.
J. C. Dischamps, Université de Nice, France
H. C. Eastman, University of Toronto, Ontario, Canada
Luc Fauvel, Secretary General, International Economic Association, Paris, France
Herbert Giersch, Institut für Weltwirtschaft, Kiel, German Federal Republic
Emre Gönensay, Bosphorus University, Istanbul, Turkey
P. Guillaumont, Université de Clermont, France
Henri Guitton, Faculté de Droit et des Sciences Economiques, Paris, France
D. C. Hague, Rapporteur, Manchester Business School, England
Albert I. Hermalin, Population Studies Center, University of Michigan, Ann Arbor, U.S.A.
Sir John Hicks, All Souls College, Oxford, England
I. M. Hume, IBRD, Washington, D.C., U.S.A.
Gordon Ibbotson, Manchester Business School, England
Gavin W. Jones, Lembaga Demografi, Universitas Indonesia, Djakarta, Indonesia
T. S. Khachaturov, Association of Soviet Economic Scientific Institutions, Moscow, U.S.S.R.
J. Lajugie, Faculté de Droit et de Sciences Economiques, Bordeaux, France
H. Leridon, Institut National d'Etudes Démographiques, Paris, France
Ron Lesthaeghe, Office of Population Research, Princeton University, U.S.A.
G. Létinier, Faculté de Droit et des Sciences Economiques, Toulouse, France
Fritz Machlup, President, International Economic Association, Princeton, U.S.A.
E. Malinvaud, Ministère de l'Economie et des Finances, Paris, France
Abdel-Fattah Nassef, Institute of National Planning, Cairo, Egypt
Goran Ohlin, University of Uppsala, Sweden
Kirit Parikh, Indian Statistical Institute, New Delhi, India
Mark Perlman, University of Pittsburgh, Pennsylvania, U.S.A.
André Piatier, Ecole des Hautes Etudes, Paris, France
P. Nørregaard Rasmussen, Vice-President, International Economic Association, Institute of Economics, University of Copenhagen, Denmark
Ronald G. Ridker, Resources for the Future, Washington, D.C., U.S.A.
Austin Robinson, Cambridge University, England
Alfred Sauvy, Institut National d'Etudes Démographiques, Paris, France
T. Paul Schultz, University of Minnesota, Minneapolis, U.S.A.
Frederic C. Shorter, Office of Population Research, Princeton University, U.S.A.
N. V. Sovani, Gokhale Institute of Politics and Economics, Poona, India
Richard Stone, Department of Applied Economics, University of Cambridge, England
Egon Szabady*, Demographic Research Institute, Budapest, Hungary
Léon Tabah, Division de la Population, Nations Unies, New York, U.S.A.
Michael P. Todaro*, Rockefeller Foundation, New York, U.S.A.
Victor L. Urquidi, El Colegio de Mexico, Guanajuato, Mexico

Etienne Van de Walle, Office of Population Research, Princeton University, U.S.A.
Pravin Visaria, Bombay University, India

Observers

Robert Black, O.E.C.D. Development Centre, Paris, France
Julien Conde, O.E.C.D. Development Centre, Paris, France
Lawrence Kegan, Population Crisis Committee, Washington, D.C., U.S.A.
Peter Lengyel, Department of Social Sciences, UNESCO, Paris, France

Interpreters

André Naudeau
Janine Yates

Secretariat

Mary Crook
Brenda Hague
Elisabeth Majid
Margaret Butler

* Presenting a paper but unable to attend

Introduction

Ansley J. Coale

The conference reported in this book was a discussion of the mutual interrelations between demographic conditions and trends on the one hand, and economic conditions and trends on the other. As background for the papers and comments that form the body of the book, this introduction provides a sketch of the demographic differences among parts of the contemporary world with different economic characteristics.

There is an easily visible link between economic conditions and trends and demographic characteristics and trends in different areas. The recent demographic history, the current demographic circumstances and the prospective demographic changes among the higher income populations of the world form a pattern quite different from the history, present circumstances and future trends characterising the lower income populations. If the countries of the world were arrayed in the order of the average duration of life implied by current mortality rates, or in the order of the average number of children each woman would bear according to current fertility rates, or in the order of the median age of the population, a point could be found on each continuum that would quite efficiently separate economically more developed (higher income) countries from economically less developed (lower income) countries.

The dividing line at present would fall at an expectation of life at birth for women of about 68 years, at a total fertility rate of some 3·5 births per woman, and at a median age of 24 years. The countries with greater durations of life, lower fertility, and greater median ages than these boundary points include the Soviet Union, Japan, the United States, Canada, Australia, New Zealand, Argentina, Uruguay, and every country in Europe except Ireland and Albania. On the other side are found all of Africa, Asia except for Japan and Siberia, Tropical Latin America, the Philippines and Indonesia.

There are, however, a few areas that have some but not all of the demographic characteristics of the more developed areas. For example, Hong Kong, Singapore, Taiwan and Puerto Rico have an average duration of life of more than 68 years, and a total fertility rate of less than 3·5 children per woman, but all have median ages less than 22 years, because recent high fertility has left a legacy of a high proportion of children and young adults in the population. Kuwait is particularly remarkable, with a female expectation of life at birth of over 70 years (as in developed areas), but a total fertility rate of 7·4 children per woman and a median age of 19·6 years (well within the less developed part of the spectrum). The economic classification of these countries is also borderline: Hong Kong, Singapore, Taiwan and Puerto Rico are candidates for designation as more developed, and Kuwait has recently attained the highest per capita income in the world.

There is a general pattern, characteristic of the modern demographic history of each category (less developed and more developed), with individual variations on the two themes – primarily variations in the extent and timing of the typical changes. In the developed countries, the characteristic pattern has been a decline in mortality and fertility, a decline that led from a starting point in the pre-industrial past when the average number of children per woman was double the present, and the average length of life only half as great as now, to the present low rate of child-bearing and extended average lifetimes. In some countries these changes began nearly two centuries ago; in others the fall in fertility and mortality has occurred since 1900.

One of the effects of low fertility is relatively few children in the population; if fertility was low during the period 20 to 50 years ago, there is also a low ratio of persons at early adult ages to those a generation older, and thus a relatively large proportion above the age of 65. Because all of the more developed countries have recently had low to moderate fertility, the population less than 15 years of age is less than 30 per cent in all but Ireland and New Zealand. The proportion over 65 is especially high (13 or 14 per cent) in the countries (such as France and Sweden) that had low fertility a long time ago, and is moderate (8 per cent), but rising, in countries (such as Australia and Canada) that had high fertility at the beginning of the century.

Demographers developed a set of generalisations that relate the decline in mortality and fertility to specified social and economic changes during modernisation or industrialisation, calling the process the *demographic transition*. That such a transition is an inevitable feature of development is a popular explanation of the differences between the high fertility and rapid growth of population in less developed countries, and the low fertility and more gradual increase in more developed countries. At the World Population

Conference in Bucharest in 1974, for example, 'Development is the best contraceptive' was a slogan frequently heard. Closer consideration of the evidence casts doubt on the existence of any simple list of social and economic conditions that are necessary and sufficient for the initiation of declines in mortality and fertility, especially the latter. Contrary to the implications of the simplest versions of the demographic transition, there are populations (such as that of Mexico in the 1960s or the United Kingdom in the 1870s) that had reduced mortality extensively, had become predominantly urban in residence, and enjoyed per capita incomes well above earlier generations, but had not experienced a decline in fertility; conversely, there are instances (such as certain *départements* in early nineteenth-century France, and certain sub-populations of mid-nineteenth-century Hungary) of greatly reduced fertility among rural and mostly illiterate populations in which mortality remained high.

Recent trends in mortality in the more developed countries are fairly uniform: the attainment of an average duration of life for females from about 70 to 75 or 76 years, with an average duration for males that is 4 to 8 years less. In most areas the recent declines in mortality have been gradual, with the exception of marked reductions in infant and child mortality where those rates were high relative to the developed country average. Reduction in death-rates for older males has been virtually absent in many populations.

Within the general pattern of declining fertility in the more developed countries there are complex recent variations. First, a recovery in fertility from a low point reached before the Second World War was shared by many but not all Western countries. In some countries this so-called baby boom was limited to a sharp peak in fertility just after the war; in others the upward trend in fertility continued until the late 1950s.

A contributing factor in the rise in fertility from before to after the war was a change in nuptiality that took place in many Western European countries, and in the United States, Canada, Australia and New Zealand. In Sweden, for example, there was a departure from a pattern of first marriage that had persisted with little alteration since early in the nineteenth century, to one of late marriage (mean age at first marriage for women, 25 or more years) and frequent celibacy (15 per cent or more still single at the age of 50). The change, which began in about 1930, was a steady decline in the mean age at first marriage and also a decrease in the proportion remaining celibate. In Norway, such a change in marriage customs was virtually the sole source of the increase in fertility; in the United States and Canada increases both in nuptiality and in marital fertility were important: in France there was little change in marriage, and the substantial increase in fertility in the 1940s and 1950s was the result almost wholly of increased child-bearing within marriage.

In the late 1960s and early 1970s in almost all of the more developed countries fertility fell to low levels attained previously by only a few during the 1930s. In the majority the current rate of child-bearing, if continued, is not sufficient to replace the parental generation; and in most of the remainder current fertility would yield only very gradual long-term growth. An interesting feature of declining fertility during the last decade is a new trend in marriage in some countries, most notably Sweden. In the mid-1960s the crude marriage-rate in Sweden began a steep decline, and by 1972 it was lower than the crude rate of *divorce* in the United States. When a well-substantiated model distribution of first marriage frequencies is used to estimate the future rates of marriage of cohorts that were past the modal age of first marriage by 1972, it is apparent that it is not the mean age at first marriage that has risen (the mean age has rather continued to decline, at least until the cohort that reached 20 in 1968 or 1969); the striking change is a sharp increase in the proportion destined to remain single – apparently more than 40 per cent will remain unmarried in the cohorts now at the peak ages of first marriage. The tendency towards avoiding first marriage has been accompanied by a marked increase in the avoidance of re-marriage. Remarriages per 1000 divorced women aged 15–49 declined by 80 per cent from 1966 to 1972.

The implications of this revolution in marriage for future changes in fertility are not easily determined, because there has been a concomitant increase in rates of child-bearing outside marriage, suggesting a substitution, to some extent, of other forms of sexual union for the conventional form of legal marriage. Nevertheless, greatly reduced proportions of those married among persons of parental age seem more likely to promote continued low fertility, or further reductions, than to cause a strong increase in child-bearing.

In the less developed world the recent past has been a period of rapidly accelerating growth of population, with current annual rates of increase ranging from two to nearly three and a half per cent, compared to rates generally less than one per cent in the more developed countries. This acceleration of growth has been the result of a fall in death-rates, rather than of any major increases in fertility. In fact, fertility in the less developed areas as a whole has declined somewhat in the last decade. The downward trend in mortality has been unmistakable. Since the Second World War death-rates have fallen in many less developed countries at a pace exceeding any previously experienced in the more developed areas. Innovations in medicine and public health and the effective transfer of appropriate medical technology seem to have been a major element in this rapid reduction. Such changes have been especially marked in areas that have also made the most rapid progress in overall economic development, and improvements in diet and living conditions have doubtless contributed to lower death-rates. The relatively small reduction in some areas can be accounted for in part by limited access to modern medicine and public health, and in part by poor nutrition and other effects of poverty.

The estimated average duration of life for major regions of the less developed world ranges from about 40 years in Tropical Africa to about 60 years in Tropical Latin America.

Fertility trends in the developing countries fall between two limiting patterns: in some areas fertility has remained at a high plateau, or even risen slightly; in others there has been a recent sharp decline, often at a faster pace than in the earlier experience of the more developed countries. In several countries in or bordering on the Caribbean, and in Mauritius, Singapore, Hong Kong, Taiwan and South Korea, total fertility has fallen by at least 25 per cent in the last 10 or 15 years. In other countries, including Egypt, Indonesia and the Peoples' Republic of China, there are indications of a major reduction, although reliable national records of births do not exist.

The recent history of trends in the more developed countries thus includes a convergence of mortality towards schedules of death-rates favourable enough to achieve the biblical three score and ten years, and fluctuations in fertility culminating in a contemporary move-ment to very low rates, insufficient, or barely sufficient, to replace the parental generations. The future prospects are for slow growth that may approach zero or negative rates within a generation, and for major changes in age composition towards still fewer children, still more old-age dependants, and an older labour force.

In the less developed areas the recent history is one of accelerated growth caused by sharp decreases in mortality, and fertility that has remained high or has declined well after a fall in death-rates occurred. The result of these trends is an age composition charac-terised by a larger proportion of children (more than 40 per cent under 15 rather than less than 30 per cent) and a smaller proportion of the aged (2 to 5 per cent over 65 rather than 8 to 14 per cent) than in the more developed countries. The future prospects for these areas is for continued substantial growth for two reasons: any downward movement of fertility will take time, and even when fertility reaches the low levels now found in the developed areas, an inertia that perpetuates growth for an additional generation is inherent in the age composition that is the legacy of past high fertility. Specifically, if by 2000 (in 25 years) fertility in the developing countries as a whole were to fall to the level that would insure mere replacement of each parental generation, the population of the developing areas would still be multiplied in the next 75 years by nearly 2·6.

The aggregate differences in population trends among areas in different economic circumstances just summarised are paralleled by individual differences within populations in fertility and mortality. Attempts to determine differences in mortality rates according to the income of the decedent before his death are complicated by the low income that is associated with illness, but strong differences in mortality for persons of different education and occupation make it clear that death-rates are higher, and the pattern of causes of death different, for persons in the same community but with different life-time incomes. There are also complex differences within the same population in the rate of child-bearing among couples with different economic characteristics.

The world-wide inventory of data on individual differences in fertility, although uneven in content, coverage and quality, is quite large. Many population censuses have included a question on the total number of children each woman has borne, and the responses have been tabulated by age, by duration of marriage, and by education, occupation and work-force status of husband and wife. In a number of developed countries extensive special surveys have been conducted to determine the intended, expected, and ideal number of children for each couple, and also to compile for each couple a complete fertility history, including a full record of contraceptive practice. These surveys are, moreover, designed to ascertain, for each couple, the social, economic, and psychological characteristics thought relevant to differences in fertility. In the less developed countries such extensive data are less frequent, although there have been many surveys to determine at least the fertility preferences, and the knowledge of, attitudes towards and practice of contraception. The earliest generalisation from this mass of data is that there is a tendency for lower fertility to be associated with higher socio-economic status, specifically, for example, with more education and with urban rather than rural residence. The relation to income (usually negative without statistical control for other variables) is a matter of dispute, as is the interpretation of observed differences in fertility associated with many particular characteristics of couples.

The purpose of the conference was for economists with an interest in demography, and some non-economist demographers, to examine together the effects of demographic trends on economic change, and conversely, the influence of economic factors on demographic trends and characteristics. In Part 1 of the volume that follows, there is a review of the attempts to incorporate demographic variables into economic thought, especially in accounting for the economic effects of population growth, and a discussion of how the classical concept of the optimum population can be generalised to the optimum rate of population growth. In Parts 5–8 particular implications of population change are explored – the effects of population growth on the environment and on the future availability of resources; the effects of rapid population growth and the demographic structure of the labour force on employment and unemployment in developing countries; the interrelation among population trends, economic conditions, and internal migration; and the effect of demographic variables on education, particularly in less developed countries.

In Part 2, there is a description of a micro-economic model of the determination of fertility, a model that puts the decision to have a child into the framework of the theory of consumer's choice; the application of such a model to the results of a survey conducted in Israel is also presented. In Parts 3 and 4 the role of economic factors in the decline of fertility in Europe, in Taiwan, and in certain areas of South East Asia is examined.

It is evident in the papers presented and in the ensuing discussion at the conference that economists have not yet formulated a general model of the determination of human fertility that is fully persuasive to non-economists; on the other hand, in their analysis of the causes of difference in fertility, demographers have taken inadequate account of economic factors and of modes of thought and techniques of analysis employed by economists. However, interchanges of ideas of the sort that took place at this conference are apparently having an effect on contemporary research, judging, for example, by the existence of an optional special 'module' of questions on economic factors in the World Fertility Survey that will ultimately be conducted in more than forty countries by the International Statistical Institute, and by the explicit attempt in the recent writings of Richard Easterlin and others to achieve a marriage of the sociologist's and the economist's approach to the study of human fertility.

It is also evident that no concise theory has yet been proposed that provides a satisfactory model of the aggregate economic effects of demographic variables. It is not that *particular* economic effects are always hard to discern. For example, the effects on higher education of the recent declining trend in the number of births in the United States (from a peak of 4·3 million in 1957 to 3·2 million in

1974) has been clearly analysed by Allan Cartter. Since the proportion of each cohort attending college has reached a high plateau of about 45 per cent, the declining number of births in the past 17 years implies that college enrolments will be smaller in the 1980s and early 1990s (when the reduced cohorts reach college age) than they are now. In short, the industry of providing college-level education in the United States will probably soon be a declining industry like the railroads, or coal mining, in earlier eras. A conspicuous form of capital goods for this industry is college teachers with Ph.D.s. According to the acceleration principle, the slackening rate of growth of college enrolments has reduced the demand for this capital good; the prospective cessation of growth and then shrinkage in enrolments implies that the need for new teachers will fall *below* the level of replacement. Replacement needs in turn will be minimal in the near future because recent high rates of new appointments have built up a faculty with only a small proportion near the age of retirement.

It is not likely that a macroscopic model of the effects of population trends on the economy as a whole, analogous to the clear picture of the effects of population trends on college education in the United States, will soon be found. Perhaps the more modest approach (adopted for most of this conference) of investigating the effects of population trends on specific elements such as rural–urban migration, on education, on employment and on the use of specific resources constitutes at the moment the best way of advancing.

Part One

The Concept of Optimum Population Growth

1 Economic Theory Confronts Population Growth

Goran Ohlin
UPPSALA UNIVERSITY

I. INTRODUCTORY

In spite of the abundant literature on the relationships between population movements and social and economic change it cannot be said that there is either a solid theoretical basis or hard empirical evidence for any grand interpretation of past experience or an assessment of the consequences of current rapid growth. There is an embarrassing gap between the confident assertions by prominent statesmen and international organisations which blame population growth for most of the evils of the world, and the hesitant and circumspect positions taken by those economists and demographers who have not turned crusaders.

In industrial countries like Britain and the U.S.A. recent commission reports have failed to find evidence that any serious social and economic problems would be less serious if population growth were slower. They reached the relatively tame conclusion that they could find no argument in favour of continued population growth either, which, however, is a far cry from the alarm voiced by many even in those countries (U.S., 1972; U.K., 1973).

In the case of the underdeveloped countries, where most observers agree that there are 'population problems' although they may differ on the nature and seriousness of these problems, many of the arguments put forward have been in the nature of special pleading, and a critic like Professor Bauer has had little difficulty in demolishing many of the assertions linking population growth and population pressure to the poverty of such countries (Bauer, 1972). In fact, one is tempted to say that the more rigorous the analysis and the more scrupulous the examination of the evidence, the smaller is the role attributed to population as an independent source of economic problems.

I shall make no attempt to survey the literature but shall try to focus instead on the question why the integration of population with economic thought, which was so natural for the classical economists, has been so unsuccessfully pursued since then, and whether recent contributions promise to make for a change in this respect.

For a long time we may simply have been putting the wrong questions. There has been a tendency to distinguish between the study of the determinants of fertility or population growth, which was left to sociologists, and the consequences of population growth, which were supposed to be explained by economists.

One would not consider it natural to make such a distinction between, say, the causes of the accumulation of capital and the consequences of it. It is surely reasonable to suspect that the consequences or implications of population growth will depend on the reasons for its growth and thus to try to weave demographic growth into the broader theme of economic growth and development.

Before resuming that discussion I shall briefly review some recent thought under the two traditional headings.

II. THE ECONOMICS OF FERTILITY

The empirical phenomenon which dominates the study of fertility and demographic growth is the 'demographic transition'. In all developed countries a decline in mortality has been followed by a drop in birth rates. Although the process has not been uniform and no clear relationship has been established between the movements in vital rates and various social and economic indices, the universality of this pattern is most impressive.

In underdeveloped countries, death rates have recently been dropping very much faster than they did in the countries that are now industrialised, and in those countries where a decline in birth rates has already set in, it too is steeper and has begun with a shorter lag than in the past. Thus observations so far make it reasonable to expect that the demographic transition will occur in at least part of the underdeveloped world and also that it will be foreshortened.

The questions arising in connection with the first stage of the demographic transition, i.e. the decline of mortality, have largely been whether the advance of medicine, public health measures, or generally improved living conditions were chiefly responsible. There being no clear-cut answer to such questions, the fall in death rates is often, both in historical and contemporary contexts, treated as an exogenous consequence of modernisation, much as the level and fluctuations of mortality in pre-industrial societies were determined by harvests and epidemics beyond anyone's control. It may well be objected that there is nothing exogenous about public health measures which reflect a political will to devote resources to the control of mortality and which in modern circumstances seem capable of remarkable success. But public health and its impact on mortality rest on public decisions; fertility decisions on the other hand have so far remained in the private and individual sphere.

The naive view of fertility has been that in traditional societies it fluctuated around a biologically or culturally determined level, and that it declined only as barriers of tradition and ignorance were broken down. Innumerable statistical studies have been devoted to the possible influence on differential fertility of such factors as income, occupation, urbanisation, education, the status of women, religion. Surprisingly often, fertility has even been studied with complete disregard of mortality, as if the two were independent, and low fertility or at least small families have been seen as a self-evident attribute of modernisation itself.

Demographic historians and anthropologists have demolished the conception of natural and immutable levels of fertility in pre-modern societies, and much attention has been given to possible links between economic conditions and fertility, particularly in the so-called 'European marriage pattern' which kept a large part of the population unmarried long after puberty or even forever and seems to have linked family formation with the accession to property or position (Hajnal, 1965). However, in the absence of a clear-cut conceptual framework, these observations remained fairly spurious. This is why the analysis of fertility as an aspect of the economic behaviour of households, which emerged in the 1960s, is of such major interest.

This 'micro-economic' approach to fertility, which evolved with contributions from Leibenstein, Becker, Schultz, Easterlin and others, assumes that the demand for children is influenced by such things as the preferences for a certain number of surviving children, by the cost of children, and of course by income variables. There is an expected return from child labour and old-age support which may make it reasonable to consider children as investments or 'producer goods'; there is also an intrinsic satisfaction from family formation and children as 'consumer goods' – a provocative term which, however, made the point that it was the theory of consumer choice that was being applied.

Among the principal elements in the net cost of children are the opportunity cost of the mother's time, the mounting pressure for education, and a consequent reduction of child labour. Cross-sectional studies of differential fertility have confirmed that low infant mortality, high female employment outside the home, and greater school attendance are all associated with lower fertility (T. P. Schultz, 1971).

Although this approach assumes that the motivation behind fertility behaviour has a strong component of economic rationality, it does not imply that people actually get the number of children they want or in retrospect might wish they had had.

In the first place, ignorance, uncertainty and risk mar all market performance. They are especially prominent when infant mortality is high; if the objective is to have a minimum number of surviving children (or sons) for old-age support or other reasons, parents may seek more births than would be necessary on the average. Ignorance of declining infant mortality is likely to be particularly important to explain the lag in fertility reduction; only after about a generation will it be evident that more children survive than used to be the case.

To the extent that parents do not assume the full costs of children, e.g. where the government provides free health care, education, and extensive maternal and child allowances, the number of children that parents wish to have may be enhanced over and above what they would be willing to pay for.

The historical record certainly suggests that fertility can be drastically reduced without access to modern contraceptives. The Western fertility decline began before such contraceptives could have had any demographic impact, and the fertility decline in places like Taiwan, Korea and Ceylon set in before the launching of family-planning programmes. But the cost of information about family planning and of contraceptive devices will enter into the economics of fertility, and it is probable that easy availability of family planning will accelerate fertility declines when the motivation is present.

Many of the problems for further research suggested by the new approach to the economics of fertility arise from the systematic disequilibrium which must be assumed to prevail if perceptions and expectations of, say, infant mortality lag behind actual changes. It seems likely that the decline in infant and child mortality which set in some two decades ago is now putting a very heavy strain on household resources in many countries. This is one reason to suspect that a fertility decline is latent even where birth rates have not yet begun to fall.

Other aspects of the process of modernisation and economic development would seem to work in the same direction where they have begun to touch significantly large groups of the population. The pressure on crafts and subsistence agriculture depresses the returns to child labour; the separation of family and economic activity raises opportunity costs of maternal care, and the growing returns to education or human capital induce parents to seek smaller families and provide them with more education (T. P. Schultz, 1971).

This analysis must thus reinforce the expectation that a fertility transition will occur in the underdeveloped countries, as it has anywhere else. But it obviously cannot rule out the possibility that in some places this will take a very long time, e.g. in Black Africa where fertility is more likely to rise than to fall in the near future. In the meantime, and even after the onset of fertility decline, populations will increase quite rapidly well into the next century.

III. ECONOMIC CONSEQUENCES OF POPULATION GROWTH

If a reasonably coherent picture, roughly concordant with empirical facts, may be said to exist with regard to the determination of fertility, the same can hardly be said with regard to the consequences of population growth. But it is only fair to emphasise that the role of population in economic growth cannot be expected to be very clear as long as the process of growth and development in general is so imperfectly explained and understood. In particular, it makes a great deal of difference whether economic growth is thought to be largely accounted for by the growth of conventional inputs, as capital formation may be a substitute for child rearing, or whether knowledge, technology, organisational improvement or other inputs which are not used up when they are employed are accorded a greater role.

Three basically different approaches to the assessment of consequences of population growth have become prominent and influential in recent years.

(i) One of them does not, strictly speaking, originate in modern economic or demographic work at all but has achieved greater renown than any population theory since Malthus. The M.I.T. model, whether in Forrester's *World Dynamics* version or in the Meadows report, *Limits to Growth*, has in fact updated and computerised the Malthusian vision (Meadows *et al.*, 1972). Except for the apparent complexity, the crude numerical character, and the addition of a few trendy variables such as pollution and the quality of life, the M.I.T. model is basically a gigantic elaboration on the famous dictum on geometric and arithmetic growth. A finite world does indeed offer limits to the growth of population and resource use.

There would be little reason to mention the M.I.T. model in this context were it not for the fact that it has dramatised something very much akin to the classical economists' view of population growth, found widespread and alarmed response in lay audiences, and been severely criticised by professional economists. Its reception vividly illustrates the gap between population alarmists and economists to which I have already alluded.

Apart from condemnations such as that of the *Economist* which called the Meadows report 'the highwater mark of an old-fashioned nonsense' (11 March 1972), the M.I.T. model has also called forth a number of efforts to explain why its threat of imminent disaster is not to be taken at face value. These exercises are certainly of great interest but for the most part they do not focus on the problem of population growth but on the sensitivity of the model to modest changes in the assumptions on technological growth, resource discovery, etc., which would, it appears, avert catastrophes, and on the lack of any built-in economic adjustment mechanism. (See e.g. Sinclair, 1972.)

(ii) More modest macro-economic models to illustrate or estimate the implications of different trends of fertility have been more influential in discussions of population policy. Starting with the seminal Coale–Hoover model, a great number of variants have seen the light of day. (For a detailed review, see Robinson and Horlacher, 1971.) In these models, the common feature has been that savings – and thus investment and capital formation – are depressed by high fertility and larger families, and that they are at the same time pre-empted for welfare investments related to population growth and supposedly yielding a lower contribution to output. In the Coale–Hoover model, labour was assumed to be initially in surplus and the growth of output was determined by an incremental capital-output which was, however, increased over time. Lower fertility was found to yield faster growth not only of per capita income but also of total income.

Later models have used Cobb–Douglas production functions and increasingly complex assumptions about savings and investment, all relatively easily handled by modern computers; but the results are similar.

When these studies focus on the impact of *changes* in mortality and fertility they bring out the interesting difference between short-run effects of changes in vital rates and the long-run effects of a transition from one quasi-stable regime to another.

Short-run effects arise from changes in the dependency burden, as the number of children starts growing faster or slower than the population of working age which remains temporarily unaffected. Whatever assumption is made about the possible second-run impact on the course of output during this period – e.g. as the result of increasing or declining investment – this primary effect is consider-able and does not rest on any hypothetical economies whatever. It is strictly a matter of age distribution.

At the onset of the demographic transition, therefore, rapidly declining child and infant mortality leads to a build-up, during two decades or so, of an increase in the dependency burden. As the new cohorts enter the labour force and mortality begins to stabilise there will be a gradual reduction of this dependency burden even if fertility remains constant. If and when a rapid fertility decline sets in, there will be a fairly quick short-run gain of the same character. There will suddenly be fewer children to take care of.

But in the longer run it is the consequences of the growth of the labour force that assert themselves. Even with a constant I.C.O.R. that rules out diminishing returns, the assumption that capital formation will be slower and welfare investments higher with high fertility suffices to guarantee that per capita output will grow faster the slower the rate of population growth.

The macro-models bear this out, and some of them add a great variety of detailed and numerical assumptions about other relationships, even extending to foreign trade and the balance of payments. Why is it, then, that even the best of them lack all conviction?

For one thing the results are inevitable, given the assumptions, and those are not the only ones that could be made. For another, the results seem to imply that the smaller population must always be preferable. McNicoll has derived the optimal growth patterns associated with the simple 'neo-classical' Solow model, maximising discounted welfare over the trajectory. As he notes, if the welfare function is specified as $u(c)$, i.e. as a function merely of per capita consumption, there may be no optimum path (McNicoll, 1973). Welfare at any point would be higher if the population were reduced. Excess population may not be instantly disposable as it is in Morishima's highly abstract economic-demographic growth model, but zero fertility and a dwindling population would be the best state of affairs, and this in any society, not just in very poor ones. It is impossible not to feel that some important aspects of the problem must have been left out of account. Which are they?

Two very different considerations immediately vie for attention. On the one hand the process of economic growth is not as simple as all that. There is the possibility that population may stimulate growth by economies of scale, by forcing men out of their natural torpor and inducing innovation and technical change (Colin Clark, E. Boserup, Hirschman), or by speeding up the replacement of the labour force with better educated cadres (Leibenstein). These have been called 'non-traditional' sources of growth to distinguish them from mere capital accumulation, and although it is difficult to assess the exact state of play in growth theory it is surely no exaggeration to say that both the econometric analysis of growth in industrialised countries and the practical experience of development policy in poor countries have left the impression that capital accumulation as such may be the least important element of growth, or at any rate that its role is very much more passive than suggested by the production-function approach.

Secondly, there is the objection that the conventionally measured per capita income, whatever its virtues or shortcomings in other contexts, is particularly irrelevant as a criterion in discussions of fertility and population growth. The family with four children under working age will have one-third the per capita income that the parents would enjoy if they had no children at all, but they may still prefer it that way. After all, it should not be necessary to point out that many people like children and are willing to bear the cost of having them.

This is not to say that it would not be interesting to know whether in fact different fertility patterns are associated with very different trends in per capita income. It simply means that as a criterion of welfare, on which to base population policies it cannot be sufficient. The same objection holds against the well-known attempts to assess the 'value of a prevented birth' in the ingenious manner pioneered by Enke.

A set of complex and ambitious models currently being elaborated at the I.L.O. under the name of BACHUE fall in a very different class from the macro-models so far discussed. They are primarily demand-oriented, and a number of constraints in a dual-economy context then determine employment, which is the focus of the exercise. The high level of disaggregation will, it is hoped, give a realistic insight into the process of employment generation and income distribution under alternative demographic trends (I.L.O., 1973). It remains to be seen whether this very disaggregation might not instead obscure the reasons for the results or give rise to spurious effects, but at any rate this is a new approach which can only be welcomed.

(iii)   The critique of the per capita income criterion takes us back to the micro-economic approach with its assumption that fertility is, in some sense and to some extent, determined by parents' assessment of the consequences. This is a salutary reminder that fertility is decided by parents and not by the makers of population policy. Moreover, there is the possibility that the parents may be right.

Nevertheless, it is only too evident that they are quite likely to be wrong – they may be wrong even in the assessment of the consequences for themselves, which is presumably what concerns them. In addition, they will ignore the consequences to others, and this may be a source of even more serious distortion.

As for the first possibility – that parents are mistaken in their private cost-benefit calculus – it is only too obvious that fertility decisions cannot be very precise. To a large extent they are guided by institutional patterns, e.g. with regard to the age at marriage. In the course of modernisation, rapid change with regard to important parameters such as infant mortality and the cost of children will make it almost impossible to have a very clear notion of how it is going to affect family welfare. The fact that these changes do make themselves felt and show fertility to be responsive to them does not mean that actual fertility decisions are at all optimal. Fertility regulation too has its costs, as already stated.

The conclusion from this approach to the demographic transition would seem to be that the scope for population policy is limited to such things as alerting parents to the implications of current social trends on their own life-time prospects, and making family planning as easy and costless as possible.

Such conclusions would aim at reducing the number of 'unwanted births' and they would probably not be widely contested. In so far as parents are assumed to bear the costs of parenthood this may also be as far as strictly economic advice can go.

But actually parents do not bear the whole cost of children. Even in poor countries government expenditures for child health and education, and for that matter for settlement and internal colonisation, will cause externalities. Extended family systems may also reduce parental costs and diffuse the link between fertility decisions and economic prospects. On these grounds alone one must recognise the possibility of serious discrepancies between the private and the social returns to population growth.

Another serious difficulty is one that is familiar from all attempts to formulate dynamic welfare theories. Is it adequate to see the problem exclusively from the point of view of the present generation of parents? The most serious externality may be found along the time dimension and imply that costs are thrown on the children which parents have not taken into account.

As far as the internal cost-accounting is concerned parental attitudes and time-horizons may be highly variable, but there is much to suggest, for instance, that a family system based on inherited property inculcates a strong concern with the welfare of the children as well. The documented eagerness to provide educational advantages to children may be described as an analogous ambition in the field of human capital.

Nevertheless, the next generation may be worse off for having, as it were, to share its patrimony among a greater number, whatever the benefits the parents derived from a large family. On the other hand, members of large families may obviously benefit both from sharing the support of their aged and from the mutual support which they presumably would extend in times of duress.

One can obviously imagine vicious circles in which poverty-stricken parents beget numerous children, this being the only pleasure they can afford, whereupon the point is reached where the marginal return to labour passes below the subsistence level and a situation of 'overpopulation' prevails. Such breakdowns, which are not at all inconsistent with the micro-economic analysis of fertility, have been suggested by various economic historians and theorists of overpopulation. (See e.g. Georgescu–Roegen, 1960.)

The micro-approach postulates, and its testing confirms, that fertility is indeed responsive to changes in the economic environment. The question remains as to how responsive it is, although our attention is now more firmly directed to the causes of possible market failures which may well occasion grievous population problems.

IV. INSTITUTIONAL RIGIDITY AND 'COHERENT GROWTH'

A study of economic and demographic history leaves one with a strong impression that the problems associated with rapid population growth in the past, or for that matter in the present, have not been of the Coale–Hoover type. In other words, it has not been a matter of the marginal attrition of growth in average per capita incomes. The problems which have been perceived and conceived as serious social maladjustments have originated in institutional rigidities of various kinds. Very largely they have concerned the redistribution of population and resources. The momentous struggles arising from adjustments of land tenure and internal colonisation reflect the rigidities affecting resource use, and the social dramas attendant upon short and long distance migration, the crowding of cities, etc., testify to the difficulties of moving people. Although one should not naively attribute all such phenomena to the evils of 'overpopulation' but should bear in mind the positive aspects of these agonising phases of history and the widening of opportunities which they entailed, there is no reason to think that they did not also involve great welfare losses which economic theory has difficulty in allocating. Population growth is not adequately represented by a movement along a smooth curve.

Kuznets has recently explored the association between population trends and modern economic growth in the developed countries and put much emphasis on the lags and the fitfulness of the process of institutional adjustment and change. The broad movements in mortality and fertility were not, he emphasises, closely associated in their timing with the onset of modern economic growth. To be sure, this raises the kind of controversy on which historical scholarship may feed, for what is 'modern' economic growth and when did it start? What is evident is that mortality in some cases declined before the beginning of industrialisation but in others only much later. Fertility in almost all cases declined only several decades later.

Yet, Kuznets suggests, there was a 'coherence' between the opportunities and requirements of modern economic growth on the one hand, and the response in population trends on the other (Kuznets, 1973). Economic growth, which Kuznets sees primarily as a matter of technological change, provided opportunities for reductions of mortality, but the structural changes wrought by migration, urbanisation, and education removed the need for a large family, raised the cost of children and depressed fertility. The process was far from prompt or smooth – 'like all processes of change in economic and social performance and institutions, it was subject to distortions and changes in pace'.

It is noteworthy that in Kuznets's interpretation, the impact of population growth on capital formation has no part. Historical evidence does not suggest any obvious association either way between population growth and savings ratios; moreover, as already suggested, there is little reason to believe savings to be instrumental in growth.

In the underdeveloped countries, as Kuznets points out, his 'coherence' is much less in evidence. That death rates have fallen is indeed a major achievement, but the institutional changes underlying the shift to a small-family fertility pattern seem slow. Political instability often hinders the institutional restructuring which would motivate parents in traditional or low-income groups to have fewer children.

On the other hand it has been argued that social and economic policies which have sought to reduce inequalities of income and wealth and to provide health, education and welfare to the large majority of the population have accelerated the fertility transition significantly. Thus William Rich (1973) argues that when the birth rate in Taiwan has dropped to 26 per thousand in 1970 while that in Mexico, with almost twice the per capita income, remained 42 per thousand, the principal explanation should be sought in the more equitable policies of Taiwan and the fact that the income of the poorest 20 per cent of the population was higher in Taiwan than in Mexico.

Although the demand theory of fertility still has difficulty in handling disequilibrium situations (Schultz, 1972), while it is precisely disequilibria that loom largest in the institutional and historical concern with population growth, there is obviously no conflict between the two approaches. They feed on one another and have the same aim. Both, however, seem to push us further away from simplistic conclusions about the consequences of population growth as such.

V. SOME CONCEPTUAL PROBLEMS

For a long time now, economic theory has evolved without much interest in population problems, and some of the difficulties in trying to force them back into economics may be due to this. Population has been treated as an exogenous factor of production, different from land and natural resources in being slightly more mobile and above all in consisting of consumers whose welfare is what economics should be all about. Capital, on the other hand, has been regarded as a man-made resource requiring for its formation a certain amount of abstinence from the consumption of the total product potentially available.

Capital theory has its own problems and the very concept of capital is hotly contested. Labour, too, becomes slightly muddled when fertility decisions are seen as economic. Labour is then an endogenous, man-made resource, yet part of the benefits derived from it do not arise from its future contributions but from the intrinsic pleasure afforded by children. The concept of human capital including investments in education, health, skills, etc., raises similar problems.

Another difficulty is that the 'household' or 'family' has rather fuzzy contours. Operating largely outside the market system it remains almost unexplored by economists. Usually it seems to be assumed that the nuclear family of parents and children represent a social unit in which parents support the children and the children, at some later time, support the parents. This norm may be contrasted with the extended or three-generation family. But actual kinship patterns are vastly more complex, both in traditional and modern societies, and the precise role of the family as a source of social security and other benefits is referred to in sweeping terms more often than it is carefully analysed.

Assuming, however, that parents make fertility decisions on certain economic grounds, the time-horizon would seem to be crucial. Historically, parents seem at times to have been strongly concerned with the future welfare of their children, at other times hardly at all. In the past, powerful institutions, above all that of property, seem to have served an important function in this respect. It is obviously a crucial question whether the process of modernisation, in the course of which the state comes to displace and replace the family in many respects, also results in the erosion or elimination of a vital steering mechanism, leaving society open to more capricious increases or decreases of fertility than in the past.

Finally, the phenomenon of migration seems to remain badly integrated in theoretical interpretations of population movements. There has been a fortuitous distinction between intranational and international migration which obscures the fact that migration is an aspect of all population growth. It would be too much to expect help from a body of economic theory in which the spatial dimension is virtually absent. In addition, there is the traditional question of 'push versus pull', which to be adequately answered requires a sharper focus on the resistance to move. And how would the prospects of future migration affect fertility decisions?

One of the most fascinating aspects of a subject which contains as many sources of wonder as population history is that some small islands stabilised their populations without emigration at a very early stage of the demographic transition. If the whole world is an island one has every reason to ask not only what the links might be between fertility and economic conditions but also how they could be rendered more effective.

REFERENCES

P. T. Bauer, *Dissent on Development* (London: Weidenfeld and Nicolson, 1971).

Nicholas Georgescu–Roegen, 'Economic theory and agrarian economics', *Oxford Economic Papers* (1960) 12, 1–40.

John Hajnal, 'European marriage patterns in perspective: The uniqueness of the European pattern', *Population in History*, ed. D. V. Glass and D. E. C. Eversley (1965).

I.L.O., 'Economic-demographic modelling activities of the World Employment Programme', stencil (1973).

Simon Kuznets, 'Population trends and modern economic growth – notes towards a historical perspective', paper prepared for U.N. Symposium on Population and Development, Cairo (4–14 June 1973).

Geoffrey McNicoll, 'On demographic turnpikes', paper prepared for the International Population Conference (Liège, 1973).

D. Meadows, *et al.*, *Limits to Growth* (Washington D.C., Potomac Associates, 1972).

William Rich, *Smaller Families through Social and Economic Progress* (1973).

W. C. Robinson and David E. Horlacher, 'Population Growth and Economic Welfare', *Reports on Population and Family Planning*, no. 6, The Population Council (1971).

T. Paul Schultz, 'An economic perspective on population growth', *Rapid Population Growth: Consequences and Policy Implications*, vol. II (1971), published for The National Academy of Sciences.

Theodore W. Schultz, 'The value of children: an economic perspective', *Journal of Political Economy*, Special issue (Mar/Apr, 1973).

Craig Sinclair, 'The work of the Science Policy Research Unit at Sussex University in the field of forecasting', paper prepared for the Third World Futures Conference (Bucharest, 1972).

U.K., *Report of the Population Panel* (1973).
U.S., *Population and the American Future*, final report of the U.S. Commission on Population Growth and the American Future (1972).

Discussion of the Paper by Professor Ohlin

Professor Bourcier de Carbon introduced the paper. Professor Ohlin's paper suggested a number of points for discussion, several of which had a bearing on subsequent papers in the conference. Professor Ohlin was somewhat sceptical about the actual value of models claiming to integrate population as a variable in theories of economic development: 'It cannot be said that there is either a solid theoretical basis or hard empirical evidence for any grand interpretation of past experience or an assessment of the consequences of current rapid growth'. Forecasts of population movements based on current information often differed. Commissions of enquiry in both the U.K. and the U.S.A. had shown that the economic and social problems raised for their countries would be less serious if demographic growth were slower. Economists and demographers could show both the nature and the seriousness of the consequences of present demographic developments. There was no shortage of alarmists, journalists rather than scientists, pointing to impending demographic catastrophe. Others, like Professor Bauer, denied the existence of any link between demographic growth and poverty. The population variable could not be left out of any study of economic development or of current world problems.

The paper, without examining the large literature on the relationships between population and development, was concerned principally with considering apparent obstacles to the integration of the demographic variable into economic thought.

Professor Ohlin would remit to sociologists a study of the factors which determined population growth, reserving for economists the study of the consequences of demographic changes. The latter were condemned for too frequently referring back the problem they were claiming to tackle. The causes and consequences of population change could not be separated from their effects. Professor Ohlin noted that the error committed was similar to that which separated the causes of capital accumulation from its consequences. One had to concern oneself simultaneously with predictions, and with judgements about predictions, according to the results.

First, at the micro-economic level, Professor Ohlin covered cost benefit analysis and the theory of consumption applied to fertility and family size. This method was wholly that of economics – the application of the theory of choice. It was a frequent basis for economic models which tried to link population growth with economic growth. However, Professor Bourcier de Carbon wondered whether the desire to have children really corresponded to a desire for food, clothing, accommodation, etc. For many couples, the arrival of a wanted child gave purpose to life which was not true of the satisfaction of other primary needs. As for food the accumulated wisdom was: eat to live and do not live to eat. However, with children, we gave life to others in living for ourselves.

Secondly, there was a macro-economic study of the cost of children and its relationship to potential economic growth. This opposed the dynamism of young populations to the mechanism and ended by describing the effects of a fall in productive savings, turning aside to examine the increase in the non-productive part of the population which resulted from the increase in fertility. This evoked the idea of the existence of a demographic period, capable of giving the necessary guarantees and realism to the calculation.

Thirdly, Professor Ohlin called attention to some of the tensions resulting from demographic growth and the dangers that they posed to balanced economic development.

Fourthly, he discussed some conceptual reconsiderations, aimed at integrating population as an endogenous and not exogenous variable in models of economic growth.

On the first point, the 'demographic transition', which took place through a reduction in mortality followed by a reduction in the birth rate, was a general phenomenon, but one which had specific features in particular cases and at particular times. The two phases were linked, and continued to be linked, in developing countries and this significantly increased the difficulty of reaching a new equilibrium. The reduction in mortality depended on various factors like medical progress, hygiene and public health, and the improvement in living standards, particularly nutrition. The reduction in mortality and child mortality could not be considered an exogenous element in modernisation. It resulted from general political action, resulting from public decisions, while fertility depended on private decisions.

In traditional societies, fertility appeared to result essentially from basic variables at the biological and cultural level. In developing societies, it was associated with income, profession, urbanisation, literacy, religion, the condition of the woman, etc. It was quite arbitrary to emphasise only one variable. To do so was to deny the complexity of the question, and led to uncertainty over the conclusions, as one saw in a good deal of research.

Professor Ohlin said that 'the lowering of fertility and the limitation of family size appeared to be intrinsic aspects of social modernisation'. Professor Bourcier de Carbon hoped that one might be able to make this more precise. Social modernisation depended on characteristics of various kinds, beginning with intellectual ability, but including private and public ability for forecasting, where statistical facilities were lacking in a state of underdevelopment. Forecasting them depended on action from the public authorities which was factual, programmed and anti-cyclical. Historians and anthropologists, said Professor Ohlin, emphasised economic factors among those determining fertility. What about economists? Perhaps this allowed us to point to the inadequacy of an analysis that was too exclusively Paretian. We had to look also at Marshallian conceptions, because the opposition between the two was as significant as ever.

In his *Cours,* in 1896, Pareto devoted a fifth of the book to the development of what he called 'personal capital'. He devoted only a tenth of his *Manuel,* written in 1906, to the problem of population. Pareto always restricted the field of pure economics to the rational and logical, rejecting sociological factors as suffering from the deficiencies of the human sciences. But it was pointless to separate the determinants of economic and social disequilibrium. For what would economic equilibrium be within a social (i.e. political and institutional) disequilibrium?

In his *Cours* Pareto wrote (§ 256):

As compensation for the cost of children there is the pleasure and advantage which parents derive from bearing and having children, i.e. the satisfaction of the genetic instinct, moral satisfaction given by children and of course the economic benefit by the numerically largest classes of society. (§ 266)   From the analysis of the population problem as a whole it follows that economic factors exercise a profound influence. For an advanced society population movements depend upon changes in economic conditions.

(§ 268)   There is good reason for pointing out that the optimum satisfaction of parents is not identical with that of children. All the reasoning which has led us to assume that free competition ensures maximum satisfaction was based on the hypothesis that each individual had free choice. But it is not the child who choses to turn egoism into personal capital: it is the parents who decide for him. It is the egoism of parents which is the cause of many of the troubles of humanity. It is absurd to assume that man must be far sighted in all his life's actions except that of giving life to a human being.

In his work on sociology, Pareto suggested that the obstacles encountered gave priority to non-genetic (economic) forces limiting population growth. Such is the child's rationality, in the view of both Pareto and the supporters of some sort of competition between children and consumer or producer goods.

As had already been mentioned, some decisions had a bearing on the meaning one wished to give to life. The starting of a family, the decision to have children, the choice of a career, in the sense of giving significance to life, did not stem from a comparison of value or from an essentially monetary calculation. Financial profit would never give a meaning to life.

Opportunity-cost analysis of the child, in spite of the complexity which it implied over a twenty-year period from the time of conception, certainly did not lack interest. In the same way, the causes of the increase in the cost of children were interesting. But when did this become the main concern?

Professor Ohlin observed that there were unknown economic variables. But were these really a secondary consideration? Farm labour, due to its independent nature and the desire for higher wages, was a modern factor in the decrease in fertility.

However, if the cost of children played an important part in decisions to limit births, the responsibility of the State for the cost of education might tend to increase the birth-rate. When one compared demographic changes in countries whose family pattern evolved differently, one was not entirely convinced that financial support from the State favoured growth.

Did the tax position of bachelors have any bearing on demographic change; and would taxation policy in future change the role of the family?

In 1890, when looking for the connection between mathematical formulae and sociological developments, Alfred Marshall wrote in the preface to his *Principles*: 'The Mecca of the economist is to be found rather in economic biology than in economic mechanics. But biological concepts are more complex than those of mechanics.' This point of view was more valid than ever and the association of several schools of thought after the Coale–Hoover model was a useful contribution. Marshall also wrote that free human ideas did not come to fruition on the lines of a machine. What role, he said, did conventional human necessities play? Comfort, way of living, needs and activities. How delicate and complex were the modifications needed to eliminate causal factors.

In his application of a micro-economic theory of cost-benefit Professor Ohlin was naturally led to refer to the family. Doubtless economists and demographers would feel bound to agree to basing a micro-economic study on the family rather than a larger group. An economist had jokingly said: 'the economic woman'. He should have said 'wife' or 'parent'.

The family was a significant example of a division of the large group, the weakness of which economic semantics had been unable to eliminate. He would here refer to Professor Radley on economic semantics. The dimension of the family varied in space and time. The economic significance of the family varied no less considerably:

according to customary or statutory relationships;
according to social institutions;
according to the degree to which family obligations in their financial connotation were transferred to the State;
according to the level and dispersion of income;
according to demographic waves;
according to stages of medical progress (penicillin, etc.).

The family cell in economics had its effect on spending, employment and saving (theory of optimum saving). Perhaps this was more important than optimum spending, since it served to bolster up the lowest levels of security. This family cell maximised joint family satisfactions, as against rival individual satisfactions.

The family might be motivated towards development and modernisation, or there might be a brake on evolution. Demographic evolution might permit families to move from one condition to another: a conservative absence of change or dynamic population change.

One model integrated the population variant into a scheme of economic growth. Should it not include an adequate variant of a family type? For example, was not the demographic effect more considerable, when viewed through the pressures of children in the family framework, than hypothetical economics suggested?

In a nutshell, today's models in population studies and economic growth turned out to have adopted the assumption implicit in the quantitative and qualitative permanence of the family pattern, both socially and economically.

Professor Bourcier de Carbon thought it evident that the growth of population, both present and future, was not bound to have an immediate effect on total and per capita G.N.P., and this would be more so in the future. (This latter observation pointed to the cause of conflict between the generations, when children made accusations against parents.)

It was also evident that an exponential growth meant a leap in a relatively short space of time. Every balancing curve in such a milieu, although extendable, was cyclic: self-accelerating and self-braking. A century and a half ago Cournot observed that exponentialism without limit was a game for the mathematics class, not a human risk or an experienced truth.

In order to study the growth of $\Delta P/\Delta Y$, it was necessary, thought Professor Ohlin, to know whether economic growth might be broadly explained in terms of conventional inputs. (The accumulation of output was then an alternative to the rearing of children.) Or should technical progress be recognised as having a prior, fundamental, motivating role?

It was wholly a matter of vital impetus as against that of willing scientific determination. Nowadays, one did not readily support Bergson. Science rejected everything which resisted measurement: or rather we did so in the name of science.

This autogenicism was often encountered, for example, when economists tried to discover whether the colonies absorbed more than they yielded. In 1830–1, J. B. Jay had claimed to prove this in regard to the Antilles and the price of sugar, which was twice as dear in France as in Switzerland.

The elementary character of this type of arithmetical calculation, directed towards the past and unaware of the notion of live forces, appeared when one considered a case like the following: was the expense incurred by a student in making a world tour a liability or an asset for him? At his death or the death of his children one might be tempted to reply that at the time the liability was clearly shown as a debit figure. But the asset value was impossible to quantify. One could only criticise our student if he sold his heritage in order to travel!

Professor Ohlin asked us to classify the present fears about the effects of population growth on the economic future:

A.   the catastrophic Malthusian vision updated by the Meadows report;
B.   the more reassuring trends of certain models, e.g. Coale–Hoover and others;
C.   the optimistic outlook for effects of changed cost-benefit on the development of $\Delta P/\Delta Y$.

Here, (B) would particularly detain us. (A) was the opportunity to recall the absence of any scientific importance on certain provisional calculations, when considering the conclusions drawn from these.

One of the difficulties of demographic and economic science was that we were compelled to carry out research only about the past. Hence, models which took account of past experience excluded factors which had played a minor role in the period under consideration. But the result was often that the standardising character of the model, which threw light on the past and was constructed for the past, was of no value for mapping out a suitable policy in the light of developments.

The 'more modest' models than those of M.I.T., aiming at exploring the differential effects of a Δ/P positive (for fertility) on ΔY, were of various types. Of course, they gave a mechanical result, with F the fertility symbol, but without considering the spirit of youth and enterprise which was likely to give an incentive towards decision on the part of the parents. A model could hardly incorporate these. Guyot, who hardly made use of a model, used to speak of acts of saving, not of children. Without denying all its interest and its necessary simplification, the now classic model of Coale and Hoover eliminated some very important, and maybe interesting, assumptions. The proliferation of models was a witness to the ingenuity of demographic economists, dissatisfied with the endeavours of their predecessors.

In any case, a comment on the paper would not stop there. It would criticise some assumptions and the basis and raw materials of the models themselves. Moreover, the report of Professor Guillaumont extended and went more deeply into the criticism of the construction of the models. One did not criticise a model and its applications on the basis of one opinion; only by using it oneself and by trying to improve it, which he himself had not been able to do.

M. Sauvy said that after much research, carried out over thirty years, he did not believe that any conference could look at all the relationships between economics and population within a few pages. He thought that Professor Ohlin was being very bold in trying to do so, and the fact that he did, instead of using several volumes, was simply a mark of his youth. Professor Ohlin's stimulating menu seemed designed merely to make us hungry. He provided an 'inventory' of the problems at issue, but no classification. Many important studies were not quoted, and this should have been done to give the paper a solid basis. In particular, Professor Ohlin had neglected the works of Gini and Mrs Esther Boserup. Nor were relevant factors related to each other; they were looked at 'a little one after the other'. It was astonishing to see the scanty attention given to papers written on the subject, yet accompanied by so many flights of fancy.

From this paper, one would imagine that the conception of economics was that it was easy to explain the past, but it was by no means so easy to predict. The real test of any theory must be its ability to predict, and many wrong forecasts had been made. For example, it had been predicted in 1945–9 that Federal Germany could not give employment to its surplus population without reverting to an agricultural economy. Events had proved these forecasts wrong, and one now spoke of the 'German miracle'. Japan, and other countries, had falsified the predictions about them and contradicted theories and models. The latter were of doubtful value.

M. Sauvy said that he had looked at the 76 less-developed countries and, over a period of ten years, had compared the rate of growth of population and G.N.P. per head. Current models suggested a strong negative correlation. In fact, he found a correlation of $+0.1$, virtually no correlation at all. The implication was that population had had no influence on income per head, and one could not ignore this finding. It showed that current models must have ignored other, presumably human, factors.

Other models had considered France and Western Europe. In France in the nineteenth century there was a low birth rate and an increase in capital. In 1914, French income per head should, according to the models, have been twice that of other countries; but it was not. So one factor at least must have been missing.

M. Sauvy insisted that one could not formulate a theory for all periods and countries. One had to look at each country, in terms of its own particular factors, and try to identify the links between economics and population.

Trying to arrive at a general, universal theory was not likely to lead to useful conclusions. Reading Professor Ohlin's paper, M. Sauvy had been convinced that one could master this subject only after long years of experience.

Professor Schultz wanted to elaborate on this. It had been known for some time that models showing the bad economic consequences of rapid population growth were biased, because they looked only at income per head. The real answer required one to look also at the distribution of income and welfare. The first distribution was between the generations. The reproductive decisions were made now, but the consequences appeared only in the future as subsequent generations grew up. The other dimension was the movement towards the equality of resource endowments between individuals. If it were costless, most societies would agree that greater equality was a good thing. The consequences for distribution of reducing fertility appeared to be a reduction in both inter-personal and inter-generation income inequalities. These two dimensions of income distribution were not sufficiently central to decision making today. The question was how we could go about building them into more of our economic analysis and into our way of thinking about social problems.

Professor Coale did not understand this. If one looked at the normal evolution of fertility trends in less-developed countries, one found that the inevitable sequence was that fertility control first benefited those with higher incomes, thus reinforcing the tendency to income inequality. It was an unfortunate cost in the normal process of reducing fertility.

Professor Schultz said that this was his own characterisation too, though he conceded that during the demographic transition in low income countries the poor did not immediately reduce their fertility, and therefore inequality first increased. Society needed to provide the information and means for reducing fertility to the relatively poor and uneducated. This would aid them to become as innovative as the social élites in terms of understanding, and adopting, family planning as they needed it.

Mr Lengyel believed that the core of Professor Ohlin's paper was on page 11 where he said 'the most serious externality may be found on the time dimension and implies that costs which parents have not taken into account are thrown on children'. Perhaps there was a clash between economic theory and population theory on this point. While there were only local population movements, and few people could hope for more than subsistence incomes, the population problem was very differently conceived. In the nineteenth century maximum migration and the populating of 'empty' countries gave a safety valve which was used by the then relatively developed countries. We were now at the end of this, and the publication of the M.I.T. report had led to a claustrophobic panic. We are now apparently all troubled by the problem of 'space-ship earth'.

This seemed to be largely a historical phenomenon. Malthus was concerned with fixed resources and a growing population. Now we had a race between technological change and increasing population. If the race was lost we were in trouble. If technological progress was fast enough, then there would be not too much risk.

Mr Lengyel therefore thought one had to look at the historical perspective.

The panic was exaggerated but it corresponded to a certain perception and to certain expectations of increasing economic performance. This led us on to the discussion of migration, and to the consequences of moving activity from the periphery of a region to the centre. He was struck by the idea of opposing economic growth to population. In practice, both were always, in a sense, integrally linked; so historical development had a major effect on our perceptions and we were now in a phase which might soon lead to a different view.

Dr Ridker wondered whether Professor Ohlin would comment on what he had said at the point where he argued that the micro-economic approach 'assumes that the motivation behind fertility behaviour has a strong component of economic rationality, it does not imply that people actually get the number of children they want or in retrospect might wish they had had.' Surely when using statistical tests one must assume that people did get more or less the number of children they expected. If not, what did the coefficients of statistical tests show?

Dr Lesthaeghe noted that in the early part of the paper Professor Ohlin concentrated on only one variable – mortality (or, more accurately, infant mortality). Other variables were mentioned, but Professor Ohlin's paper did not offer a theoretical framework to explain their effects on fertility.

He would like to make some more specific points. First, there was little predictive power in saying that there was a time lag between a fall in infant mortality and a fall in marital fertility. In the historical evidence for Europe, all three possible situations occurred: in some areas there was indeed a time lag, as Professor Ohlin suggested; in other areas there was no time lag; and in still other regions there was a reverse lag, i.e. marital fertility fell before infant mortality.

Secondly, in trying to explain the link between infant mortality and marital fertility, Professor Ohlin had said that parents would try to have enough children to make sure that they would be taken care of when they were old. Historical evidence suggested that this was not true. In a Malthusian setting, many old people lived on their own with little or no support from their children. If this was the more common pattern in 1800, in 1900 and in 1960, how could it be responsible for the fertility decline?

The evidence of this pattern could be taken indirectly from average family size. Around 1800, life expectancy was about 35 years, the growth rate 0·5 per cent and the mean age at marriage 26 to 28 years for women. If widows and widowers were cared for by their married children, and single adults also lived with married couples, one would obtain an average family size of six or seven. Taking out single adults and assuming that they lived on their own, even after the age of 30, one would reduce the average family size to about 5·5. Taking out widows and widowers as well, and assuming that they too would live on their own, would give an average family size of 4·5. In many rural areas, the average actual family size varied between 4·5 and 5·0. In all urban areas of Belgium and in several rural districts of the Netherlands, this figure fell to 3·5 or 4·0.

It followed that many unmarried people, single or widowed, must have been living on their own, and that having numerous offspring did not guarantee provision of old-age care. In fact, children were very often waiting for the death of their parents to obtain land, a pre-industrial enterprise, or capital, in order to marry. Moreover, the safest way for a widow to insure her future security was to remarry as soon as possible. The 'classic' idea of a transition from an extended to a nuclear family was often exaggerated; so was the argument that children were a safeguard against poverty in old age.

Dr Lesthaeghe also expressed some doubts about the importance of remittances from children to their parents in the eighteenth century. He noted that, in general, there was very little left over from the family budget of a married child to be passed on to an elderly parent. There were more likely to be remittances from unmarried children to parents, though he thought that this matter was a research topic to be explored, and that the argument on remittances should not be used as an *a priori* one either in favour or disfavour of Professor Ohlin's theory.

Professor Ben Porath wanted to talk about lags in the effects of infant mortality on fertility. The micro-foundations of the idea of a long lag were not convincing because, if it thought of later mortality, then the family would 'stock up' with children. If it was infant mortality, then there need not be so much of a lag. One did not need a comprehensive set of social information, merely one's own experience. Professor Schultz's own study had not found much evidence of a lag and he had reported a strong response, even in a backward part of the population. So one had to invoke more complex arguments for the long lag being a general reaction.

To Dr Ridker, Professor Ben Porath said that of course it was a question of 'more or less'. Any micro-argument here at best gave a general indication of direction, allowing for individual families not achieving what they wanted, and even Dr Ridker had used the phrase 'more or less'. Most studies recognised the importance of random elements.

Dr Ridker said he had phrased the point only in relation to the paper, which emphasised disequilibrium elements. He would have expected the paper to show why this was not a good analysis, and yet he assumed that the testing of the series did not assume such a relationship.

Dr Jones did not want to defend macro-growth models like that of Coale and Hoover, but the criticism that such models ignored the consumption aspect of children was perhaps overdone. If there was any validity in the data, they suggested that there *were* unwanted children. So, the hypothesis that the fertility rate could fall by averting the birth of unwanted children seemed reasonable. Unless one had already done away with all unwanted children, that criticism was not very strong.

Professor Ohlin was grateful to M. Sauvy for assuming that his irresponsible statements were the result of impetuous youth! The truth was they were the result of frustrated middle age, and of the problems of reconciling empirical observations and facts with economic theory. He was struck by what M. Sauvy had said, but found it difficult to accept the idea that there could be no general theory. One must seek to make generalisations, for this was in the nature of all scientific thought. He agreed, however, that there were higher and lower levels of ambition, and perhaps one must settle for something less global.

He was also grateful to Professor Bourcier de Carbon for reminding the conference of Pareto's thinking and putting it in the general framework of sociological thought. He did not disagree with what Professor Bourcier de Carbon had said, and the aim of his paper had been to provoke. He did not feel that the objections made were really serious. Perhaps he had summarised and generalised inadequately a number of applications and his own rather uncertain beliefs. Dr Ridker and others had discussed the implications of the micro-economic approach. Those who felt strongly on this had not argued that this was welfare theory. The aim was just to explain what had happened to fertility. Factors squeezed out of economic tests obviously did affect it.

This way of looking at things could well have implications for welfare. Certainly Professor Schultz took this view, as an argument against undue emphasis on per capita income. Professor Ohlin did not know how far to push the point, but he had mentioned disequilibrium analysis. To claim that people had children that they did not want was surely the argument for family planning. Claiming that people did not know how many children they ought to want was taking the argument one stage further.

What Dr Lesthaeghe had said was in line with his own suggestion that in the real world the family was not a simple social unit, as economic analysis might suggest. This was one field for a good deal of study.

His paper had covered the lag between infant mortality and fertility but, in general, France and a few other countries where fertility had declined very early were major exceptions. In a short paper, it was more reasonable to suggest that a lag was normal. Certainly in underdeveloped countries there *was* such a lag.

Professor Ben Porath agreed that the micro-economic approach did not provide a rationale, but one did have the assumption of rationality in studying various micro-economic problems, and he did not see why people should be less rational in their decisions about family size than about consumption in general. He did not think that it was all a matter of calculation, but that there was obviously trial and error, adjustment, etc. With fertility, there was clearly a social process, including demonstration effects, and economists did not necessarily have the best record of studying such behaviour.

Professor Parikh felt that, on lags, even if Professor Ben Porath argued that the lag could not be less than one year, it must be several years. The ingenious argument of Dr Lesthaeghe on family size showed that support from children did not necessarily come through living with them but could come from giving monetary support or visiting them. Such expectations need not necessarily be refuted by Dr Lesthaeghe's evidence.

Having someone to perform the last rites for one was the reason for insisting on having a surviving male child in many parts of India. So, a change in child mortality made it difficult to predict the size of the family.

Professor Coale also referred to the belief that adverse circumstances were a stimulus to economic growth. He quoted the comment of his colleague Calvin Hoover, twenty years back, that the one thing an Indian peasant did not suffer was inadequate deprivation. He supposed this could now be said of Bangladesh.

On the application of the economic fertility model, he had engaged in many arguments with Professors Schultz, Easterlin and others of its supporters. He wanted now to say that he did not oppose this model, but only its universality. It was important to seek a more balanced view of the factors prevailing when fertility fell. He thought there were three pre-conditions: first, voluntary control over birth which required acceptance of the idea of control – many people did not see this as moral; second, objective conditions making a fall in fertility advantageous to individual couples; third, access to effective methods of birth control. The second condition was the one that economists had concentrated on in the past; the others now needed more consideration.

Professor Schultz agreed that Dr Ben Porath's statement was one of perception. In equilibrium, with given infant mortality, parents could observe what happened to their own children when young and add replacements according to their 'reproductive schedule'. This meant lags of one to five years from the death of a child to replacement. One also found replacement occurring largely among older women. They would normally try to accomplish some regulation where there had been involuntary loss in the early years, but there were always women who did not compensate then, but only started to respond later. In a dynamic world, with falling child mortality, there would not be much effect on fertility in the short run. Older women might respond by not having additional children immediately, but those in their twenties would not do so until their late thirties or forties. Therefore, a ten, twenty, or even twenty-five year distributed lag was explicable simply in terms of this model, where the maximum response might lag a decade or two behind the onset of the decline in child mortality.

As for Professor Coale's three elements, he did not see that we could make much progress until we could isolate the costs of control in different technologies. All three situations needed to be analysed together and economists had concentrated only on the second because it was easier. They now needed to look at the other two. They were beginning to work on the third and would presumably move on to the first.

Mr Black said that Professor Ohlin emphasised the divergence between the economic and the sociological approach. This had been historically true but was no longer so, as he thought the discussions in the conference had shown.

Professor Bourcier de Carbon wanted to ask Professor Ohlin whether, in the social tensions he mentioned, the relation between demographic processes and inflation was important. Professor Kuznets had said that investment in housing and public services was an important element in investment in the U.S.A. The same was true in France and in less-developed countries. Very rapid population growth might therefore be a permanent inflationary factor.

Professor Ohlin was anxious to stress that, in the context of population growth, we knew far too little about economic growth. The same was true of inflation. Sweden had recently had little population growth but much inflation. On a world scale, he would accept the likelihood that commodity shortages, as we now knew them, might aggravate the rate of inflation. However, inflation was mainly a monetary phenomenon.

Mr Black was right that, today, economists were mainly studying fertility and, perhaps, though he disagreed with much of the analysis and found the general understanding of the relationship between economic factors and fertility very obscure, more progress was now being made. There was no question today of the importance of population growth for the less-developed countries of the world. Perhaps these issues should not need discussion but it seemed clear to him, from what had been said, that most participants were at sea. He found this a disturbing state of affairs, especially at a conference where eminent demographers and economists had been brought together to study the problem.

2 The Optimum Rate of Population Growth

Patrick Guillaumont
UNIVERSITÉ DE CLERMONT

I. INTRODUCTORY

In the great theoretical and political discussion of today concerning the economic consequences of population growth, the notion of the optimum rate of population growth should, one might think, have a particularly important place. In fact, it has been strangely ignored. It has certainly been implicit in the formulation of various recent doctrinal issues. The zero rate of population growth proposed more and more often for the United States, as also for the rest of the world, represents one extreme concept of the optimum rate of population growth. But whilst this slogan – decked out with graphs and calculations – has more effect on public opinion than a more elaborate theory, this has not resulted in more light being shed on the discussion. The discussion has merely become more topical, which brings us back to the question: Why has this idea been so little investigated? Are we to think that economists are avoiding the essential or that the idea of an optimum rate of population growth is without foundation? Whilst such a concept seems to be suggested by common sense, in view of the contradictory statements of theory, the latter scarcely appears to support it.

I shall not attempt here to analyse what is in fact an extremely complex question but rather to present a few comments so as to define the elements of the problem. These comments are concerned with three points:

(i) a number of methodological comments on the static optimum of population and the optimum rate of population growth;

(ii) the presentation of an hypothesis regarding the optimum rate of population growth;

(iii) some thoughts on what the concept of an optimum rate of population growth really means having regard to the factors which cause it to vary, to such an extent that it sometimes becomes almost meaningless.

II. THE STATIC OPTIMUM OF POPULATION
AND THE OPTIMUM RATE OF POPULATION GROWTH

While the static theory of an optimum of population has received a great deal of attention in economic literature, though condemned by its static character to remain academic, there appears to have been, with few exceptions, a lack of a dynamic theory on the subject.

Let us provisionally define, in brief and general terms, the static optimum and the dynamic optimum of population:

(i)   *the static optimum:* this is the number (or density) of population which, at a given moment and in the specific conditions of that moment, is the most favourable, having regard to the objectives assumed;

(ii)   *the dynamic optimum:* this is the change in the number (or in the density) of population which, in a given period, is the most favourable, having regard to the objectives assumed.

It is desirable to consider or reconsider:

(i)   why and to what extent the gap between population theory and policy can more easily be filled in by a dynamic theory;

(ii)   what are the stages involved in moving from a static to a dynamic theory in this case;

(iii)   what predecessors or trends are to be found in economic literature concerning the optimum rate of population growth;

(iv)   what conceptual distinctions are necessary to conduct the analysis.

It will be assumed in what follows that changes in the rate of population growth derive exclusively from changes in fertility, from falls in the death-rates resulting either from exogenous factors or from changes in policies corresponding to specific objectives.

A.   *The gap between population theory and policy*

All theories regarding the economic effects of population are inadequate for the formulation of a demographic policy inasmuch as the latter is not aimed merely at achieving economic objectives. We shall come back later to objectives other than economic objectives, or rather, adopting an even more restricted definition, other than those which can be expressed in terms of *products*. For the moment we shall deal exclusively with the latter. And amongst these let us regard product per head as an indicator of welfare and as the objective to be maximised.

The (economic) optimum of population – the static optimum – is generally defined as the size of the population which maximises output per head, all other things being equal. It can be seen at once that the concept is only of limited use since most 'other things' tend to be affected when the size of the population changes. Unless there is an exceptional mobility of all resources, the available capital, techniques, and other factors are significantly changed in the process of the change of the size of the population and, moreover, as a direct consequence of that change. It is for this reason that it is of interest to investigate the optimum changes of population during a period in which all the rest will also change – this will thus represent the change of population for which the rate of growth of output per head is a maximum.

Reference to product per head seems to call for justification of its preference to total product as the objective to be maximised by population change. One cannot forget the fundamental objection made by Sismondi in the King of England's apologia; the mistake, in a word, of disregarding the number of human beings likely to participate in the welfare which it is being attempted to maximise. On the other hand, to consider in some way the total product, in order to calculate an aggregate indicator of collective welfare may well result in vast populations in a state of misery being considered as the optimum. It is perhaps useful to remember here, regarding a dynamic as well as a static theory, Sismondi's criterion, revived by Say but neglected ever since: that the optimum population is the maximum population able to live in 'happiness' or 'plenty' (Sismondi), that is to say enjoying an 'adequate' per capita product.[1] 'Any population which possesses the means of living well is desirable' (Say). Reference to the 'adequate' product per head thus avoids the two pitfalls mentioned and at this point brings political judgement into the picture, without which there can be no optimum.

B. *The various steps from the statics to the dynamics of demo-economics*

To establish the meaning of an optimum rate of population growth, different steps must be distinguished in moving from the statics to the dynamics:

(a) *pure statics:* the economic effects of a demographic change of population are examined, all other things being considered equal. In this way the concepts of overpopulation and underpopulation are defined. They are defined in terms of various criteria, the chief of which are (see Guillaumont 1971*b*, 52–3):

(i) maximum average productivity: this is the static optimum of population;

---

[1] See the description of Sismondi's concept, revived by Say, in Guillaumont, 1969, pp. 80–88, 96–102.

(ii)   zero marginal productivity: this is the point at which concealed unemployment appears;

(iii)   average productivity equal to minimum subsistence: this is the point at which the maximum of population is attained (overpopulation then being only transitory).

(b)   *comparative statics:* a study is made of the extent to which the previous results are modified when one of the other factors is varied (capital, techniques, age structure, etc.). The effects of a change of population are then compared in terms of two different states: the optimum of population, measured by the onset of concealed unemployment or by the point of maximum population may then vary. Sauvy's theory of technological progress, classified in terms of the effect of such progress on the optimum of population, belongs to this type of analysis (Sauvy, 1961).

(c)   *restricted dynamics:* a study is made of the effects on economic growth of a given change of population during a certain period, that is to say at a certain rate, the change in other conditions, in particular of other factors of production, being regarded as exogenous; this framework of hypotheses does not usually make it possible to define an optimum rate of population growth.

(d)   *extended dynamics:* a study is made as before of the effects on economic growth of a change of population during a certain period, but this time taking into account the effects that this change of population exercises on other conditions, in particular on the other factors of production. It now becomes possible to determine an economically optimum rate of population growth. It is thus within this framework that I shall attempt to develop my analysis. It will be seen at once that the abandonment of any *ceteris paribus* clause will make empirical verification much easier.

(e)   *general dynamics:* the change of population ceases to be an exogenous variable and the repercussions on it caused by economic development are brought into consideration; the effects of the change of population are thus studied while taking into account all the repercussions that the various induced changes bring to bear on it. Although it is possible, and over a certain period desirable, to extend the dynamic theory of the optimum population to this framework, I shall confine myself to the previous framework.

C.   *A few predecessors and trends in the economic literature*

As has been indicated above, it is difficult to discover any real trends of thought concerning the optimum rate of population growth. It should however be remembered, even if the list is by no means complete, that there have been a number both of earlier and of more recent contributions to the subject, all of them rather scattered.

(a)   *The shift from static analysis to that of the optimum rate of population growth.* Whilst today the division between static and dynamic analysis is clear, it appears much less so when one studies early authors who examined the problem of the optimum population. Sismondi and Say, for instance, when they considered the desirable trend of population, though their methods were not those of precise analysis, approached the subject from a dynamic rather than a static point of view (Guillaumont, 1969).

In the classical literature as well as in more recent writing on the optimum population, there are unquestionably other 'traces' of dynamic analysis to be found. A particularly noteworthy example is afforded by Meade (1954) in *Trade and Welfare*. Meade, who had presented a theory (1939) of the static optimum of population, defined on the basis of per capita welfare, provides here a twofold static theory of the optimum of population, defined this time both in terms of total welfare and of the optimum of saving – along the lines of Ramsey. He thus poses the problem of the optimum rate of demographic growth and distinguishes it from the static optimum of population which might result from continual achievement of the optimum of saving. The problem has subsequently been studied again in these terms of twofold optimalisation by Morishima (1969).[1]

(b)   *Explicit analyses of the optimum rate of population growth.* There are also to be found several explicit attempts to analyse the problem of the optimum rate of population growth, in particular those by Alfred Sauvy and Goran Ohlin.

It is more than ten years since Sauvy (1961) first demonstrated the underlying reasons for an optimum rate of population growth. The same author has continued to develop his line of thought in other studies (1973, 1972) and in a communication to the present conference to which I take the liberty of drawing attention.

Goran Ohlin's study (1967) advanced a theory of the optimum rate of population growth, on a twofold basis:

(i)   it was based on an examination of the initial demo-economic

---

[1] Another very different example is provided by Kamerschen's attempt to present an operational criterion of the optimum of population and of overpopulation which is at once static and dynamic and which is 'a mixture of both the notion of an economic optimum population at a given moment of time and the optimum population rate of growth over time' (Kamerschen, 1965; 175). In fact this criterion, the coefficient of dependence (the ratio of the population under 20 years old and over 65 to the population aged 20–64), has been rightly criticised as such, whatever its importance may be in other respects for demo-economic analysis.

situation, without treating the optimum change as being a transition from one static optimum of population to another (neither the initial population nor the final population, after the optimum change, is necessarily at the optimum level);

(ii) it was a function of the interactions of the rate of population growth and of the rate of accumulation of capital.

Ohlin's theory has recently been re-examined and developed in certain respects by Susan Hill Cochrane (1973): this author has been particularly concerned with the cost involved in a change of population different from the natural change.

It is similarly in terms of the possibilities of accumulation that in Section III below I shall attempt to develop a theory of the optimum rate of population growth. But I shall attempt to do this firstly while taking account of the effects of population growth on the input of human capital and on technological progress and not merely on the accumulation of material capital, and secondly while assuming that material capital and human skills are complementary as well as capable of substitution for each other, and not merely the latter. Furthermore, in doing so, I shall introduce certain ideas that I have published elsewhere.[1]

(c)   *The optimum rate of population growth and criteria of selection between demographic projects.* Another type of analysis needs to be borne in mind. The analysis of the optimum rate of population growth is by nature macro-economic – whatever in fact the size of the population considered – as is moreover the static theory of the optimum, even if the law of non-proportional returns which is one of its main foundations is of micro-economic origin. But in the past few years proposals regarding population policy have often been made by applying reasoning of a micro-economic type such as the rates of return on measures carried out with a view to birth control (see, for instance, Enke, 1966; Simon, 1969). I have described elsewhere the logical impasses to which calculations of this kind often seem to lead, particularly when they are static (Guillaumont 1971c, 1973). We are still faced with the fact that if we wish to make use of criteria of selection in this field, there must be a logical correspondence between these criteria and the notion of the optimum rate of population growth adopted.

Let us take as an example the cost and benefit criteria of a prevented birth. To any such criterion there must correspond some

---

[1] I advanced the idea of the optimum rate of population growth in terms of the absorption of capital in my thesis of 1964 and subsequently returned to these ideas in my book (1971a, pp. 174, 199–200), but along lines rather different from those that I shall follow here.

optimum rate of population growth, and in practice an optimum fertility rate, if the trend of the death-rate is assumed to be given: the rate of population growth (or the level of fertility) for which the marginal cost and the benefit of the prevented birth would be equal would then represent the optimum. In fact there only exists an optimum rate of population growth in the sense that if the unit cost and the unit benefit of the prevented birth taken independently vary with the number of prevented births (with increase or decrease in the case of the cost, and with an increase in the case of the benefit) in such a way that they reach equality with a positive fertility rate, which is far from certain. Even if this were the case, the resulting 'optimum' rate of population growth would not seem to me capable of being accepted, for two inter-connected reasons: firstly, it is doubtful whether the concept of the benefit of a prevented birth can have an intelligible meaning; secondly, the calculation is carried out in terms of aggregate cost and aggregate product and not in terms of per capita product; it cannot therefore serve to indicate the maximisation of the latter.

In contrast, certain methods of calculation used by the World Bank for the choice of demographic projects take as criterion the discounted change of the product per head in the course of future periods in relation to its discounted cost per head (King, 1970). To this criterion there needs to be a corresponding definition of the optimum rate of population growth: that for which the marginal discounted addition to income per head to be expected in the future from the change in population growth would be equal to the marginal cost per head of achieving this change. Once again, it is necessary here, if there is to be an optimum, for the two elements to reach equality with a positive level of fertility. In any case the criterion is a dynamic one in that it uses a model of growth which makes it possible to analyse the effects of a change in the fertility rate. The whole problem is that of ascertaining the actual values in the model and the real overall relations between population and growth.

In Table 2.1 (on p. 36) a classification has been made of the main types of economic analysis relating to the concept of an optimum in regard to population: the classification has been made in terms of the criteria of optimality adopted and the methods applied (static or dynamic, micro- or macro-economic).

D.   *Certain methodological distinctions relating to the optimum rate of population growth*

In the light of the foregoing survey of the literature in this field it is possible to set out a few essential distinctions necessary for understanding the nature of the optimum rate of population growth.

TABLE 2.1 TYPOLOGY OF ECONOMIC ANALYSES OF THE OPTIMUM WITH REGARD TO POPULATION

Criteria of optimality / Methodology	Welfare or 'total' product		Welfare or 'per capita' product		Welfare or 'adequate' product	Other criteria used
	Cost not taken into account	Cost taken into account	Cost not taken into account[a]	Cost taken into account		
Static						
macro-economic	certain conceptions of the optimum of population (Landry, Meade, 1954)		standard theory of the optimum of population and its extensions in comparative statics		conceptions of Sismondi and Say	criteria of overpopulation: concealed unemployment minimum subsistence other criteria, political, philosophical, aesthetic, etc.
micro-economic		certain calculations of the profitability of birth control (Enke, 1966)				
Dynamic						
macro-economic			optimum rate of population growth (Sauvy, 1961, 1973, Ohlin, 1967)	'optimised' rate of population growth (Cochrane, 1973)	conceptions of Sismondi and Say	limitation of natural resources (Forrester, Meade, 1954)
micro-macro: micro-economic, but using a macro-economic model				relation of the variation in actualised per capita income to the actualised per capita cost of demographic action (I.B.R.D. 1971)		

[a] The cost referred to is the cost of the change in the number or rate by which the population varies in relation to the spontaneous variation

(a)   The optimum rate of population growth must be distinguished from:

(i)   the fastest rate of *transition to the static optimum*, as it has sometimes been defined. This definition is the one adopted by Myrdal (1968, p. 2065) who at once brushes aside the concept, along with that of the static optimum, since they appear to him to be without practical bearing. In point of fact this concept would only have a meaning if it were possible to relate it to a fixed static optimum in the course of the time in which the demographic process is to take place. But this optimum, if it is defined in terms of the criterion of the per capita product, varies with the other conditions. The notion of a maximum rate or an appropriate path of transition to the static optimum could then only have meaning in terms of what we might call a fixed and definitive optimum which would be defined in terms of some criterion other than the economic product (the aesthetics of the environment for instance) so that it would not depend on the movements of other conditions in the economy.

(ii)   the *shift of the static optimum*, itself defined in terms of a constant criterion or combination of criteria. For the two notions of the optimum rate of population growth and of the shift of the static optimum to be identical, it would be necessary for the criteria used to define both the one and the other to be identical (for instance the per capita product) and for the population to be initially at the optimum level. But the shift of the static optimum, once the criteria are the same, no longer has in itself any great significance since it depends on the changes in other conditions and therefore on the real changes affecting the population.

It will be necessary, particularly in Section IV, to come back to the interrelations between these different concepts.

(b)   An *optimum* rate of population growth, defined in terms of the effects of a given demographic change without taking into account the factors which determine it, is to be distinguished from the rate of population growth which will be termed as 'optimised' and which is defined after taking into consideration the cost necessary to modify the spontaneous change of the population.

(c)   The optimum (or 'optimised') rate of population growth may be discovered by making various hypotheses as to the demographic characteristics of the growth:

(i)   a *stable* optimum rate of population growth, whereby one assumes a constant age structure, which also implies a constant rate of growth: the effects of alternative rates of stable growth (with corresponding specific age structures) are then compared;

(ii) a *transitory* optimum rate of population growth, whereby one assumes a variable age structure, such as may arise either if the rate of growth is constant but different from the initial rate, or *a fortiori* if the rate of growth is variable; in the second case a variable optimum rate of population growth is being sought.

III. AN HYPOTHESIS ON THE STABLE OPTIMUM RATE OF POPULATION GROWTH

Is it possible to define a rate of population growth such that the rate of growth of product per head is maximised? I shall attempt here to do this by assuming a stable rate of population growth, that is to say with a constant age structure, and by assuming in addition constant age-specific activity ratios, so that the working population grows at the same rate as the total population. We can thus compare the effects on the growth of product per head of alternative rates of stable population growth, without having to pay attention to the way in which the transition from one to the other is achieved. We are here concerned with the long term.

Generally speaking the reason why an economically optimum rate of population growth may exist is this: the advantages to be expected from population growth are likely to be particularly high for low rates of population growth; and the disadvantages to be feared are likely to be particularly high for high rates of population growth. It is therefore to be expected that the balance of advantages and disadvantages representing an optimum situation will be found at some 'intermediate' rate of population growth.

To summarise these advantages and disadvantages, which cannot be examined here in detail, it is important to distinguish the effects of population growth which will arise with stable growth, as a consequence of the mere growth of the labour factor, the changes of the other factors of production being given induce, from the effects of population growth which induce change in the supplies of the other factors, these effects being both difficult to assess and at the same time important. A synthesis of these different effects involves making a distinction according to the complementarity or substitutability which may exist between labour and the other factors.

1. *Population growth, growth of the labour factor and growth of product per head, when growths of all other factors are given*

Since we are concerned with a dynamic approach, the other things are not given in the sense of being constant, but the rates of growth of factors other than labour (i.e. technological progress, etc.), are here taken as given. I shall refer simply by way of illustration to fixed capital alone and to technological progress, assuming in turn substitutability and complementarity between labour and material capital.

(a)   In the case of substitutability we write

$$\frac{\Delta Y}{Y} = \alpha \frac{\Delta K}{K} + \beta \frac{\Delta L}{L} + \mu \qquad (2.1)$$

$$\frac{\Delta y}{y} = \alpha \frac{\Delta K}{K} + (\beta - 1)\frac{\Delta L}{L} + \mu \qquad (2.2)$$

where Y, y, K, L, represent respectively the total product, the per capita product, capital and the working population.

α, β, μ, represent respectively the elasticity of the product in relation to capital, in relation to labour and the rate of disembodied technological progress.

Since all is given except $\Delta L/L$, the rate of growth of the per capita product is a dependent variable of $\Delta L/L$, a decreasing variable (see Fig. 2.1), unless β is greater than 1: a case in which labour has increasing returns all other things being equal; we may also say that there are large-scale economies due to the dimension $(\alpha + \beta \gg 1)$, that is to say in fact slight density. In any case, if $\beta \neq 1$, population growth goes up or down. $\Delta y/y$: the optimum is shifted to the maximum on the minimum conceivable of $\Delta P/P$.

(b)   In the case of complementarity, growth is expressed in the following way:

$$\frac{\Delta Y}{Y} = \text{Min}\left[\frac{\Delta K}{K}, \left(\frac{\Delta L}{L} + r\right)\right] \qquad (2.3)$$

$$\frac{\Delta y}{y} = \text{Min}\left[\left(\frac{\Delta K}{K} - \frac{\Delta L}{L}\right), r\right] \qquad (2.4)$$

where r represents the rate of technological progress in Harrod's sense (maximum rate of growth of the productivity of labour), and $((\Delta L/L) + r)$ the 'natural' or potential rate of growth.

In this case (see Fig. 2.2) where all is still given except $\Delta L/L$, the growth rate of the per capita product is equal to r so long as $\Delta L/L < (\Delta K/K) - r$ is decreasing with $\Delta L/L$ higher. There is no potential optimum here, but a better or, if one prefers, an optimum zone, that in which $\Delta L/L$ is situated on this side of the point $((\Delta K/K) - r)$. If however we consider – following Sismondi – that with equal growth of the per capita product, the best evolution is that which benefits the largest population, the point where $\Delta L/L = (\Delta K/K) - r$ is the optimum point of population growth (p_0).

Quite clearly, neither $\Delta K/K$, nor μ, nor r, nor doubtless many other factors left out here, are independent on $\Delta L/L$.

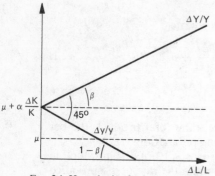

FIG. 2.1 Hypothesis of substitutability (and $\beta < 1$)

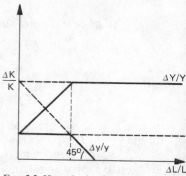

FIG. 2.2 Hypothesis of complementarity

2. Population growth, with consequential changes in factors other than labour and in their productivity

Population growth affects the supplies of the various factors of production other than labour and their productivity and technological progress generally. I shall attempt to summarise these different effects, some of which have been given formal expression in the literature and others of which not, with the result that one side of the picture has come in for more attention in models of demo-economic growth than the other – in this case the negative effects of population growth.

(a) *Effects on the rate of fixed capital formation.* The negative effects of high population growth (high fertility) are in general those associated with the consequential age structure: a very young structure with a high 'dependence ratio' (the ratio of population of non-working age to the population of working age). Since the rate of saving is a decreasing dependent variable of the dependence ratio, high population growth implies a low rate of saving.[1] Whilst such an effect is conceivable, it is perhaps not as obvious as is suggested by a great many demo-economic models of which it is the cornerstone (Coale and Hoover, 1958; Enke, 1971a, b, c; Robinson and Horlacher, 1971). But it is the more likely to arise, the higher is population growth.

[1] The per capita product is dependent on the ratio of dependence and the productivity of the working population. When the rate of saving is a dependent variable of the per capita product, it is then in part dependent on the dependence ratio.

On the other hand it may be noted that in areas of lower population growth, accumulation may depend on the growth of the working population. We have shown elsewhere how, if fixed capital and labour are complementary to each other, an increase in the working population makes it possible for the opportunity to use new capital to grow more than proportionately (Guillaumont, 1971a, 154–9).

In addition to these effects there is the influence exercised on the amount of investment by the reactions on the productivity of the capital that are due to population growth.

(b) *Effects on the productivity of fixed capital and incorporated technological progress.* These effects are generally positive and are particularly noticeable in economies with a low population growth:

(i) the existence of scale economies related to the increase of density (particularly affecting infrastructure) or of number of population (for certain productive investments);

(ii) the opportunity for correcting mistakes in investment;

(iii) a higher average productivity of capital resulting from a younger structure of capital;

(iv) in underdeveloped economies, changes in agrarian techniques when certain thresholds of density are reached (Boserup).

(c) *Effects on investment in human capital and its productivity, and more generally on motivations.* Here again we are faced with contradictory effects. So far as concerns the *amount* of investment in human capital in relation to the number of the population concerned, they are negative: any attempt to maintain or to raise the level of education and health is made more difficult by higher population growth, especially if the latter is very rapid.[1]

When it comes to the *productivity* of the investment it must be borne in mind first that there are particularly marked negative effects of rapid population growth in countries with a very low level of development: the nutritional and sanitary deficiencies consequent on a very high fertility rate have a significant and lasting effect on the productivity of individuals (Guillaumont, 1971c).

On the other hand, the positive effects have been described many times, primarily with regard to industrial economies threatened by stagnation (greater dynamism, greater business initiative bound up with population growth (Sauvy, Dupréel), easier adaptation of the

---

[1] Inversely, without this being a complete offset and though it is inconsistent with the assumption of a constant death-rate, the lowest wastage of human capital in education or health will be found where population growth is balanced by a lower death-rate before the end of the working age.

labour force to a changing structure of production). But this applies also to underdeveloped economies: population growth, by making investment necessary, increases the ability to invest (Hirschman); or, more specifically in the case of rural areas, by making it necessary to abandon extensive agriculture, population growth, as has already been suggested, makes it necessary to change techniques and results in both increased time devoted to work and a greater product per worker (despite a fall in the hourly productivity of labour). Convincing and attractive as these arguments are (Boserup, 1970; Hirschman, 1964), they call for empirical verification and represent a reservation or rather a limit. And this limit may be seen in terms of the challenge required for there to be a creative response. But there is also a limit beyond which no response is possible, creativity is frustrated and innovation is checked. What thus emerges from these theses, as though in echo to the theory of the 'critical minimum effort', is the idea of a 'critical minimum challenge'.

This is another reason, and one of the principal ones, for thinking that population growth may, depending on its rate, exercise sometimes increasing and sometimes decreasing effects on the accumulation of fixed and human capital and on its productivity.

(d)   To summarise these different opposing effects I shall make certain simplifications. Things would be simplified to the greatest possible extent if one could reduce all factors other than labour to a single factor ('the efficient accumulation of fixed and human capital') and assume in a somewhat cavalier fashion that its growth is an alternately rising and falling function of population growth.[1]

Certainly it can be granted that all so-called technological progress must be embodied into investment in fixed capital (K) or in human capital (Q), but it is not possible to consider these two types of capital globally, though they are unquestionably far more complementary than substitutable (Guillaumont, 1971a, 184–91). Logically, the effects of population growth on accumulation regarded in a wide sense should at least be represented by two distinct curves.

To admit complementarity between these two main forms of capital is to admit that for the two curves shown in Fig. 2.3 can be substituted a curve which corresponds to the lowest part of each, which is another way of representing the alternately favourable and unfavourable effects of population growth.

None the less, and still with a view to simplification, we shall attempt to represent these effects differently according to the hypothesis being used as frame of reference: substitutability or

---

[1] A reader concerned only with the general results may go straight to the conclusion of this section and to the following section.

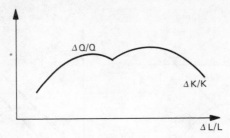

FIG. 2.3 Effects of (stable) population growth on accumulation

complementarity between labour and capital (fixed and human).

3. *The optimum rate of population growth defined according to whether labour and the other factors are substitutable or complementary*

(a) *Substitutability of capital and labour.* Let us first of all disregard the effects of population growth on education and health. Let us consider the effects solely on fixed capital, assuming if need be that a part of technological progress is embodied in it. In the equation (2.2) $\Delta K/K$ rises and then falls in terms of $\Delta L/L$, the maximum being attained at the rate of population growth x:

$$\frac{\Delta K}{K} = f\left(\frac{\Delta L}{L}\right) \quad \text{with} \quad z = \frac{d(\Delta K/K)}{d(\Delta L/L)} > 0 \quad \text{for} \quad \frac{\Delta L}{L} < x$$

and $$z < 0 \quad \text{for} \quad \frac{\Delta L}{L} > x. \tag{2.5}$$

The rate of population growth which maximises $\Delta y/y$ in the equation (2.2) is then that for which:

$$\frac{d(\Delta y/y)}{d(\Delta L/L)} = \alpha\, \frac{d(\Delta K/K)}{d(\Delta L/L)} + \beta - 1 = 0$$

that is $$\frac{d(\Delta K/K)}{d(\Delta L/L)} = \frac{1-\beta}{\alpha}. \tag{2.6}$$

The optimum rate of population growth is thus defined in terms of the differential coefficient of the rate of accumulation in relation to the rate of population growth and of the capital and labour elasticities of the product. However, *if returns are constant in relation to scale* $(\alpha + \beta = 1)$, *the optimum rate p_0 is that for which the differential coefficient of the rate of accumulation is equal to unity* (see Fig. 2.4.i): it is therefore independent of the parameters of the production function.

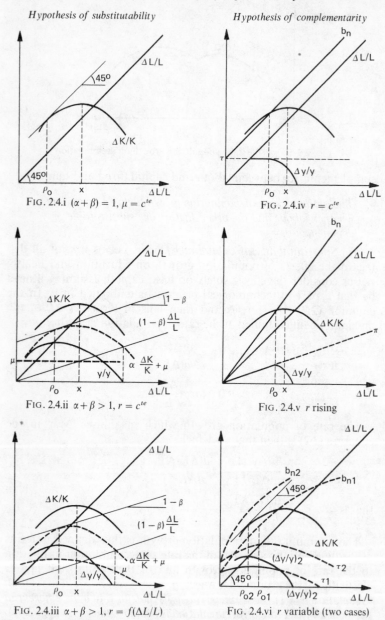

Hypothesis of substitutability

FIG. 2.4.i $(\alpha + \beta) = 1$, $\mu = c^{te}$

FIG. 2.4.ii $\alpha + \beta > 1$, $r = c^{te}$

FIG. 2.4.iii $\alpha + \beta > 1$, $r = f(\Delta L/L)$

Hypothesis of complementarity

FIG. 2.4.iv $r = c^{te}$

FIG. 2.4.v r rising

FIG. 2.4.vi r variable (two cases)

Graphs to determine the optimum rate of growth when accumulation is a dependent variable of population growth

The optimum rate in this case will be determined by the trends of the returns associated with the dimension:

if $\alpha + \beta < 1$, the differential coefficient at the optimum point is > 1, the optimum rate of growth is therefore less;
if $\alpha + \beta > 1$, inversely (see Fig. 2.4.ii);
special case: if $\beta > 1$ (increasing returns to the single factor labour) the differential coefficient is negative: in other words, the optimum rate of population growth is reached on the falling part of the curve of the rate of accumulation.

In all cases *a (constant) rate of exogenous technological progress (μ) exerts no effect on the optimum rate of population growth.*
Several implications may be drawn:

(i)   still within a world of perfect substitutability, assume that technological progress not embodied in fixed capital (in fact chiefly due to education and health) itself rises and then falls in relation to population growth (see Fig. 2.4.iii). A rising element of dis-embodied technological progress tends to raise the level of the optimum rate of population growth (p_0).

(ii)   while assuming that there is complementarity between fixed capital and human capital, consider the function of the minimum of the rates of growth of the fixed capital and the human capital (cf. Fig. 2.3) and use the differential coefficient of this new variable in exactly the same way as was done for the variable of the rate of accumulation in fixed capital.

(b)   *Complementarity of capital and labour.* Apart from these two factors, fixed capital and labour, the concept of the natural rate of growth and of maximum increase of the productivity of labour make it possible to take explicitly into account investment in human capital. We make use here of the hypothesis developed elsewhere by which the natural rate of economic growth depends on the growth of the quantity of human capital (Q), and r on the growth rate of the skill degree ($\rho = Q/L$) one could say more generally on the quality of the population.
Two particular cases need first of all to be considered:

(i)   the case in which r is always higher than $((\Delta K/K) - (\Delta L/L))$ whether r be constant, declining or variable with $\Delta L/L$: in this case the maximum of $\Delta y/y$ is attained when $((\Delta K/K) - (\Delta L/L))$ is a maximum, that is to say when the differential coefficient of the rate of accumulation in relation to $\Delta L/L$ is equal to one: this solution is identical to that in which the factors are substitutable and in which there are no savings on account of the dimension

$(\alpha + \beta = 1)$ (see Fig. 1.4.vi, with r_2 variable, and the comments below).

(ii)   the case in which r is always lower than $((\Delta K/K) - (\Delta L/L))$ and in which its maximum determines the maximum of $(\Delta y/y)$. This is a rather unlikely hypothesis which we may set aside.

Usually r will be in part higher and in part lower than $((\Delta K/K) - (\Delta L/L))$, that is to say that the curves representing G_n and $\Delta K/K$ intersect. We shall take this as our framework.

Let us assume first of all that r is independent of $\Delta L/L$ (see Fig. 2.4.iv). In this case we may adopt the conclusion reached above, p. 45(*b*) (the only difference being that $\Delta K/K$ is variable): there exists an optimum zone – when one keeps within the limits of positive growth[1] – of population growth, that which is situated below the point where $\Delta L/L$ is equal to $((\Delta K/K) - r)$, or, if one prefers, following on from Sismondi, an optimum which is situated at this very point. It is in fact in this zone that the smallest of the two terms $((\Delta K/K) - (\Delta L/L))$ and r of equation (2.4) is highest.

When r increases with the rate of population growth (see Fig. 1.4.v), the zone disappears and is reduced to the single point $((\Delta L/K) - r)$: the optimum rate of population growth is then determined: it is the rate for which the rate of accumulation is equal to the 'natural' or maximum rate of growth of the product $(\rho_0 = (\Delta K/K) - r)$.

When r in turn increases and decreases with the rate of population growth various solutions may appear according to the parameters of the functions. In practice, two solutions are conceivable:

(i)   one, which is not the least plausible, is that of the previous case $(\rho_0 = (\Delta K/K) - r)$: this arises when r increases over a sufficiently long space of time with $\Delta L/L$.

(ii)   the other is that in which the rate of population growth is at the optimum when r is at the maximum: this arises when r decreases as soon as a fairly low level of $\Delta L/L$ is reached (this case is represented in Fig. 2.4.vi with the curves r_1, Gn_1 and $\Delta y_1/y_1$).

Another case is represented in Fig. 2.4.vi (curves r_2, Gn_2, $\Delta y_2/y_2$), mentioned above, that in which r is always higher than $((\Delta K/K) - (\Delta L/L))$. It thus appears that where there is complementarity:

---

[1] In fact, that which is situated between the two points at which $(\Delta L/L) - (\Delta K/K) - r$, inasmuch as the curve of the rate of accumulation cuts the straight line of the natural rate of growth in two points, which is the case for instance if the accumulation function is parabolic. The rate of population growth corresponding to the second point may be negative.

(i) *the optimum rate of population growth is generally situated*[1] *between the point where the differential coefficient of the rate of accumulation in relation to $\Delta L/L$ is equal to one and the point where the rate of accumulation is equal to $\Delta L/L$.*

(ii) *the most likely case is perhaps that in which the optimum rate of population growth is reached when the rate of accumulation is equal to G_n.*

(iii) the optimum rate of population growth in the zone which has just been defined decreases when the level of r and of G_n, if they are constant, rises and even, paradoxically, when r and G_n rise in proportion to $\Delta L/L$. In other words, *the optimum rate of population growth is an inverse function of the maximum rate of growth of the per capita product.*

(c) *Comparison and significance of the results deriving from different hypotheses.* According to which hypothesis is adopted – complementarity or substitutability – the optimum rate of population growth will be determined in different ways:

(i) on the hypothesis of substitutability, the initial demo-economic situation exercises its effects through the returns to scale (sum of $\alpha + \beta$), while this situation has apparently no effect on the hypothesis of complementarity: it is nevertheless possible to take account of this in the definition of the 'natural' rate of economic growth: a limit may be introduced here corresponding to the supply of natural resources – a limit which may of course be just as much political as technical.

(ii) if, on the hypothesis of substitutability, one takes the case where there are decreasing returns to scale, this results in the optimum rate of population growth being situated generally below the point for which the differential coefficient of the rate of accumulation in relation to $\Delta L/L$ is equal to one. Inversely, it appears that, on the hypothesis of complementarity, the optimum rate of population growth is situated at this point or beyond it. There is thus a temptation to conclude that the optimum rate of population growth is higher on the hypothesis of complementarity than on the hypothesis of substitutability. But the validity of such a conclusion would be uncertain, bearing in mind what has been said regarding the phenomena of density (it may be untrue if $\alpha + \beta > 1$), and at the same time bearing in mind that such a conclusion disregards the influence exerted by population growth on non-embodied technological progress – μ on the hypothesis of substitutability.

[1] We have assumed in fact that r does not decrease very quickly with the increase of $\Delta L/L$.

(iii) finally, the existence of exogenous factors affecting the rate of accumulation (for instance, the discovery of exportable minerals, the introduction of external aid, if these are new developments independent of population growth) has different effects on the optimum rate of population growth according to the assumption made: if these effects shift the curve of $\Delta K/k$ uniformly upwards, the optimum rate of population growth is unchanged on the assumption of substitutability and increased on the assumption of complementarity.

All formulations of this type, based, among others, on the hypothesis of stable population growth, represent, it is true, little more than exercises without any real significance and, in any case, scarcely go beyond the simple concept of an optimum rate of population growth, which has been justified above in more literary form. The important thing is to appreciate how various are the influences of population growth, that most of the economic parameters are unquestionably affected by them, and that it is probable that any formulation which only takes a few of these effects into account will give a one-sided picture.

In the absence of an overall, simple theoretical model, one is tempted to go back to the actual trends to see whether the statistics show the results suggested by this line of reasoning. Any restrictive assumption is then set aside, so as to begin with that of stable growth. But even so the problems relating to the very concept of an optimum rate of population growth cannot be eliminated, and it is this concept on which we must now focus.

IV. VARIABILITY OR EVANESCENCE OF THE OPTIMUM RATE OF POPULATION GROWTH

The hypothesis of the optimum rate of population growth which has been presented makes it possible to attempt a general re-examination of the problem as it was defined in the first part of this paper. One is thus brought back to three essential aspects of the optimum rate of population growth in the light of which it can be seen to be extremely relative, variable and, in some senses, evanescent. The optimum rate must in fact be defined in relation:

    (i)   to certain values;
    (ii) to a certain space;
  (iii) to a certain temporal horizon.

Naturally, the demographic policy to which the concept may lead also depends on these various terms of reference.

1. *Values and the formulation of demographic policy*

The meaning of the concept of an optimum rate of population growth naturally depends on the framework of values and criteria adopted. The criterion of the growth rate of the per capita product may be used and interpreted in different ways; in all cases it remains inadequate.

(a) *The growth of per capita product: maximum or adequate?* Let us return to Sismondi's criticism regarding the number of persons whose welfare one is seeking to maximise. It might well turn out in certain conditions that the optimum rate of population growth defined as that which maximises the growth rate of the per capita product is negative (p_0 in Fig. 2.5).

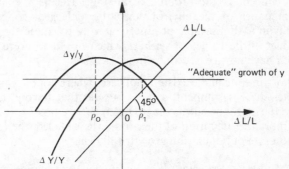

FIG. 2.5 The optimum rate of population growth 'à la Sismondi'

To avoid population decline, one may then adopt a 'Sismondian' definition of the optimum rate of population growth: that which represents the highest rate compatible with a growth rate of per capita product regarded as adequate (point ρ_1 in Fig. 2.5). Is this definition to be regarded as political? All definitions are necessarily so.

(b) *The product: What is its content? – the environmental factor.* This fashionable question is relevant here. According to the exact concept that one adopts of the meaning of product, the optimum rate of population growth, defined in terms of it, may differ. What is involved is the estimation of the costs of population growth, its effects on the environment, on the quality of life, and in similar ways. Such effects are far from being negligible and in some cases it is possible to measure them. These negative effects are to a large extent consequences of population growth, even though the latter is not always responsible for this consequence: a particular example is the deterioration of certain rural landscapes brought about by population decline.

When it comes to determining the optimum rate of population growth, two methods of procedure are possible:

(i)   to retain the criterion of the growth of the per capita product, keeping to the traditional and restrictive concept of the product, and at the same time it is necessary to recognise the existence of other effects on the environment, and to judge these effects by various standards. And in attaching weights to the different considerations, bringing political judgement regarding the optimum to bear.

(ii)   to shift to an 'enlarged' idea of product, taking into account all factors capable of being measured in monetary terms that affect the quality of life, thus making it necessary either to have a 'net' concept of the product of all the costs necessary for the maintenance of the environment (the 'enlarged' concept thus results in a 'diminished' product), or to re-calculate the original product of the values of services which originally were free but which have now ceased to be free.

In short, in spite of the existence of cases where population growth improves the environment, it must be said that beyond a certain density, the more the effects on environment are taken into account or the more the definition of the product is widened, the lower the optimum rate of population growth will be.

(c)   *A different criterion: life expectancy.* One may alternatively reject the per capita product, even thus widened or even in its most complete form, as an indicator of welfare and say that the optimum rate of population growth is that which maximises development, that is to say everything else. But what exactly? Let us say the satisfaction of essential needs: food, health, education, etc. Unquestionably the best indicators of the satisfaction of essential physical needs are expectations of life. On this basis the optimum rate of population growth may be defined as: the rate which maximises expectations of life. What is in fact involved is a definition of the optimum fertility rate, since the optimum rate of population growth is that which corresponds to the fertility rate for which expectations of life are at a maximum. This definition seems at first glance to be purely demographic, but its significance is fundamentally economic, not only because of the intrinsic significance of expectations of life, but also because, so far as a certain level of fertility maximises expectations of life, it does so because of the economic effects of fertility. If, moreover, such a curve could be drawn, it would probably be lower at a lower level of development, for example at a lower per capita product. It might be thought that at most such a definition of the optimum rate of population growth could only serve for under-developed economies. For more advanced economies other criteria are available. One might be tempted to suggest: the quality of life in place of life expectations. But this would be to shift from a perfectly precise concept to a perfectly imprecise one. Moreover, it is possible that in the advanced economies expectations of life are themselves fractions of the quality of life.

(d)   *The formulation of policy: other values.* To take into account the 'economic' effects of population growth on the environment or on life expectations brings the optimum thus determined closer to the objective that policy-makers are seeking to establish, but it does not necessarily make the two identical. Other values are involved, which are frequently introduced in discussions of the static theory of the optimum and which, sometimes in a completely opposite sense, are just as relevant to the optimum of population growth. These values are: aesthetic (those aspects of the environment which cannot be reduced to economic terms), military, philosophical or religious, social (the protection of the health of mother and child), or quite simply political (the strengthening of the national identity, the occupation of virgin territories).

Whilst any overall optimum is related to all the values of the society considered, and whilst the public authorities have the duty of reflecting all of these in its choice of policies, certain specific aspects of the problem are related to population growth. Let me note two of them.

A society's values are not immutable. They not only vary in the course of time – this applies to any policy involving the future, particularly to the choice of a saving rate but also directly as a consequence of population growth. In other words, population growth establishes values in terms of which a different rate of growth may become the optimum. It is probable that in France population growth together with economic growth have, since the war, changed the current ideas with regard, for example, to property or to leisure.

The values with regard to optimum population are reflected in part in the demographic opinions and behaviour of the population. As has often been shown in recent years, there are divergences between opinions (or attitudes) and behaviour (or practice) as far as fertility is concerned. Is the divergence only that in relation to the optimum rate of population growth? In other words, is the optimum rate of growth that which corresponds to the fertility rate desired by households? To take this view would be to neglect all values expressed only at the collective level and all phenomena of inter-dependence between individual decisions. The problem is in some respects the same in the case of the optimum rate of savings, but only in some respects, in that where public savings are concerned there is a possibility of coercion which had no counterpart as far as fertility is concerned.

(e) *The formulation of policy: the cost of optimisation.* The optimum rate of population growth, once determined in itself and as a policy, can only be achieved, if it is different from the actual growth, by the use of certain means. The means involved in achieving the optimum rate of population growth give rise to costs and necessitate a reappraisal of (non-economic) values. These values influence the means adopted to modify the demographic trend and thus the costs involved in achieving it. In this way, which varies from one country to another, the cost of a given change in the fertility rate – allowing for the limitations imposed by the means available in one case or another – may reflect the greater or lesser inclination of the population to approach the rate of growth considered to represent the optimum.

The optimum rate of population growth aimed at must therefore take account of the costs necessary to reach it: this involves moving on from the optimal rate of population growth to the optimised rate of population growth. This adjustment may be made for instance, as has been suggested by Cochrane (1973), by lowering the curve of accumulation drawn in terms of population growth (so that the old and new curves form a tangent at a given point, such that the population growth is 'spontaneous'): the cost of the population policy is then supposed to be subtracted from the accumulation that is probable but not inevitable. There would appear to be grounds, moreover, for raising the question whether population growth has the same effect on accumulation (in a broad sense) and on technological progress whether it is spontaneous or imposed, and in particular what are the induced effects of a policy of control (or of encouragement of births) on a population's receptivity to innovation. I am thinking here particularly of rural areas.

Assuming that an 'optimised' rate of population growth has been determined, is it possible to define corresponding criteria of choice regarding the measures to be implemented at the demographic level? Correspondence implies that the same objectives, reflecting the same values, shall be accepted both for the criteria and for the estimation of optimum growth.[1]

Alternatively, and more simply, knowing the optimised rate of

[1] It is not possible for criteria established in purely economic terms to correspond with an optimised rate of population growth in anything other than purely economic terms. The problem of correspondence was discussed earlier in these terms.

population growth, one can abandon the attempt to reach correspondence with regard to criteria and confine oneself to an analysis of a cost-efficiency type to show, after allowing for limitations of means, the actions necessary to achieve this growth at lowest cost.

2. The area of reference

Naturally, the optimum rate of population growth is not identical for all societies. We have thus far implicitly kept within a national framework but this may be too broad, or too narrow, and in any case, if it is this which is adopted, its significance will vary according to the level of development reached.

(a)   *An optimum of national growth or of local growths?* No matter how attractive it may seem, macro-economic analysis of national development is full of pitfalls. The concept of an optimum rate of population growth applied at a national level, like models of demo-economic growth in the same framework, is an aggregate of very heterogeneous parts. On this account, if on none other, the relationships assumed, particularly between population growth and savings, become very uncertain. One is hesitant at the idea of applying the concept in aggregate terms to a dualistic economy or to an economy with a traditional sector which includes groups which differ in respect of ethnic origin, density, type of agriculture, etc. What is the optimum rate of population growth for Senegal, divided up between Dakar and its suburbs, seemingly overpopulated regions such as the ground-nut area, the new lands of Eastern Senegal, the region of the river, the Casamance? It would seem more sensible, in this case, as when studying the static optimum or the existence of concealed unemployment, to stick to small units.

There are certain effects which unquestionably can only be interpreted at this level (for instance the effect of population growth on agricultural techniques). It is rare to find regional groups, even in non-mixed or dualistic economies, which do not possess numerous relationships with the rest of the national economy: the agricultural credit system, the building of schools and clinics, depend too much on the progress of the national economy for it to be possible to investigate the optimum rate of population growth of an area without considering the effects of national changes, which are themselves linked to the population growth of the whole.

In other words, the existence of demo-economic conditions which differ locally within a country complicates the national problem of the optimum rate of population growth and at the very least makes it necessary to take account of the possibilities of internal migration when assessing it.

(b)   *An optimum of world growth or of national growths?* The same problem arises in rather similar terms regarding the relationships between the optimum rates of population growth of different nations. It is usual for the optimum rate of population growth to be determined independently for and by each country. The arguments advanced in industrialised countries in favour of birth control in Third World countries do not, however, always seem to have the good of the latter exclusively in mind. Inversely, one now hears arguments in favour of curtailing population growth in the industrialised countries because of the effects it has had on the natural resources of the planet, and particularly on those situated in the Third World. Zero growth for everyone would be the world optimum.

This argument and criticisms of it are sufficiently familiar for it to be unnecessary to restate them (see the two points of view in Meadows *et al*, 1972; Sauvy, 1973*a*). There is no contesting the fact that the optimum rate of population growth of each individual nation is affected by the conditions of international exchange; that the exchange of commodities of which there is a limited world supply plays an important role here; that this role is not a one-sided one, and that the demand for such products, in the form of export receipts, represents an essential factor in the capacity for accumulation in the countries supplying these products; that in this way the optimum rate of population growth is just as likely to be increased as decreased in such countries.

This is sufficient to justify our considering the optimum rate of population growth in the national framework, while at the same time recognising that the different national optimum rates of population growth are interdependent and may vary with the level of development reached.

(c)   *The optimum rate of population growth and the level of development: two levels of optimum.* It is easier to agree that the level of development affects the optimum rate of population growth than to define in what direction it does so. It might be thought that the optimum rate of population growth rises with the level of development to the extent that the rate of saving rises in such circumstances. But if we go back to the arguments presented in Section III, an increase of the rate of saving only has this effect on two conditions:

(i)   if there is complementarity of capital and labour;
(ii) if $\Delta K/K$ rises, which assumes, since $\Delta K/K = (1/Y)(K/Y)$, that the increased rate of saving is not offset by an increased rate of replacement investment or by a higher capital/output ratio.

It might also be supposed that the optimum rate of population growth rises with the per capita product because the cost of a given educational activity diminishes with the volume of product, the relative cost of education thus being higher in low-income countries. But there is no question that this is far from the case with regard to achieving a given standard of health.

In fact, there is no question that the main argument is a socio-logical one: if the positive effects of population growth are of this kind, a greater population growth is necessary to maximise the growth of the per capita product in those countries in which the per capita product remains low because the sociological resistance to change is too great.

In support of this argument certain statistical observations can be put forward. A 'factorial analysis of correspondence' by Bara (1973) for the period 1960–70 shows that a first and lower optimum of population growth (measured by the maximum growth of the per capita product) is found for countries with a low rate of population growth (< 2 per cent) and a high rate of growth of per capita product (> 3 per cent) for, roughly speaking, the industrialised countries and that another high optimum can be found for countries with a high rate of population growth (> 2 per cent) (Third World countries). It will be noted however that the rate of population growth which appears to be the 'optimum' for the industrialised countries (from 0·5 to 1 per cent) is in no sense excessive, while that which is found for the countries of the other group (from 2·5 to 3 per cent) represents very rapid growth.

In fact, without adopting this type of analysis, if we represent on a diagram the $\Delta y/y$ function of $\Delta P/P$ for this same period of 1960–70, we can see that the scatter points are roughly divided into two sections, the highest in each of them reaching a peak at an inter-mediate level of demographic growth (see Fig. 2.6). We may make the following interpretation: *the optimum demographic growth found empirically* – and this at two distinct development levels – *is that which maximises the potential growth of production per capita.* In other words, an optimum demographic growth will facilitate the maximum growth of production per capita but will necessarily not entail it. It is a necessary condition for it, but not a sufficient one. In any case the uncertainty of the statistical data and the short period they cover (ten years represents a very short period in this field) make it necessary to be very cautious in any interpretation.

3. *The temporal horizon and the trend of the optimum rate of population growth*

Several of the problems already encountered can be reduced to the

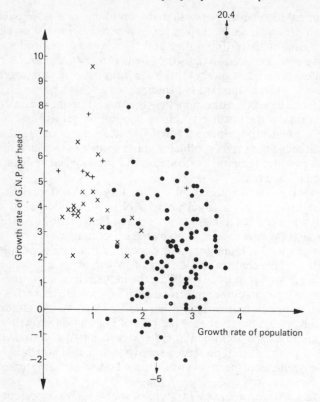

Fig. 2.6 Average annual growth rate of the gross national product per head and growth rate of population 1960–1970: countries of more than 1 million inhabitants (122 countries)

- Countries in Africa, Central America, South America and Asia
× Countries with a market economy in Europe, North America, Japan, Australia and New Zealand
+ European countries with centralised planning

Source: World Bank Atlas, 1972.

question: Over what period of time is the optimum rate of population growth being sought? In our discussion we have implicitly been considering a long period and, in Section III, we have considered a stable rate of population growth. In terms of the short period, that of static equilibrium, the concept of an optimum rate of population growth can hardly have any real meaning except that of the most rapid possible growth or reduction towards the static optimum. But two other cases require examination: that which lies between the short and the long periods; and that which lies beyond the long period. These can be described as the 'medium' period and the 'ultra-long' period respectively.

(a) *Over the medium period: the transitional optimum rate of population growth.* We defined earlier the transitional rate of population growth as that within which age structure could change. In regard to the optimum rate of growth, a particularly important point is involved since any change in the rate of population growth, say in the fertility rate, implies a change in the age structure. Moreover, any change in the fertility rate can only be gradual, so that the hypothesis of a transitional rate of population growth must cover both a change in the rate and a change in the age structure.

One thus comes back to the principles of the demo-economic models conceived over the past fifteen years and deriving from those of Coale and Hoover (1958) and Enke (1971*b*, *c*): a fall in the fertility rate brings about a fall in the ratio of dependence, and with a given productivity or trend of productivity, a corresponding higher per capita product; this results in a higher rate of saving and in turn a higher rise in per capita product. If we keep to the medium period, say less than fifteen years – the period, that is to say in which the growth of the working population cannot be affected – and if we take the assumed saving function as given, the reasoning leads to a low optimum rate of population growth and even, if it is pushed to its logical conclusion, to a negative rate of population growth (the minimum being reached with a zero fertility rate). Most models of demo-economic growth do not concern themselves with the optimum of population growth, but by taking for granted and treating as of major importance the medium-period effects to be expected from a decrease in the fertility rate, implicitly assume that the lowest possible rate of population growth would represent an optimum.

Thus over the medium period – as can be seen in the most common demo-economic models – the optimum rate of population growth is independent of population density. This is the only framework within which this is true, since this is, of course not the case over the short period with the static optimum, nor, as we have seen, over the long period with stable growth, nor, and even less so, as we shall see, over the ultra-long period.

(b) *Over the ultra-long period: return to the static optimum.* The further one extends the period under consideration, and the more, as time passes, the total of the population increases, the more do problems of size and of environment, as affected by density, become important. Population growth over a long period, even at a low rate, cannot go on indefinitely within a limited area. If we are to remain inside the limits of this planet some form of stationary demographic state must be regarded as inescapable.

There is a paradox here in the history of ideas. The concept of the static optimum of population achieved a certain success in the economic literature for more than half a century. Just as it appears to have been dropped – sometimes wrongly, for it could have certain applications in some traditional societies – and is being replaced, not without some difficulties, by a dynamic theory, it suddenly springs up again. It becomes, as a critique of growth, an essential concept, though often defined implicitly or prematurely.

This is unquestionably one of the major problems of the human species. From various points of view one may be convinced of the benefits of a certain population growth and reach the conclusion that the optimum rate of population growth is positive, and then find oneself forced to recognise that, apart from populating other planets, this cannot go on indefinitely.

Thus the static optimum, superseded a thousand times, may ultimately end up by establishing itself as a criterion in a situation in which the environment has the final determining role. The optimum rate of population growth would then again become the most appropriate rate of transition to this quasi-definitive optimum. Definitive, however, it is doubtful whether it could ever be.

(c) *The optimum rate of population growth as a function of the time horizon.* The optimum rate of population growth can thus be seen to vary according to the period under consideration – that is to say according to the period over which we wish to maximise the growth of the per capita product, or any other more complex economic objective (the concept of period covers here both a time dimension and a system of hypotheses):

(i)   in the short period, in conditions of static equilibrium, the optimum rate of population growth can only be defined in relation to the static optimum of population: this would imply the fastest possible movement towards that optimum;

(ii)   in the medium period, the trend of the working population being given, the (transitional) optimum rate of population growth is low, and independent of its density;

(iii)   in the long period (the hypothesis developed in Section III), the optimum rate of population growth is positive: furthermore, it always diminishes with density and perhaps with the level of development;

(iv)   in the ultra-long period, the optimum rate of population growth must tend towards a rate close to zero, the difference from zero simply being enough for a stabilised and quasi-definitive optimum to be reached.

This typology of the optimum rate of population growth in terms of the time horizon under consideration in no sense represents the desirable process of change or of the course of the optimum rate of population growth over a period of time; it indicates the way in which the optimum rate, if it is to be constant, will vary with the length of the period considered; it results from the way in which the effects of population growth are distributed through time. There thus emerges a fundamental conclusion regarding the optimum rate of population growth which may be summarised thus: *it must not grow too quickly to be able to continue to grow over the long period.*

It is obvious that the optimum rate of population growth cannot be reduced to the choice of one constant 'optimum' rate. And this is the more true the longer is the period considered.

(d)   *The optimum population policy.* When we now move on from the optimum rate of population growth according to the time horizon to the optimum course of population, with a growth rate which may, if necessary, be variable – that is to say to the optimum population policy – two additional considerations come in.

Firstly, any optimum population policy must imply an inter-temporal choice. If what was involved was the choosing of one constant rate of population growth, the only way this could be done would be by balancing the effects of this rate in the series of different future periods. A more rapid growth of per capita product over one given period may be preferred, even allowing for a possible reduction of the final objective, or vice versa. When the optimum rate of population growth is variable, such choices present themselves *a fortiori.*

But this rate cannot vary with complete freedom. Since we assume the course of the death-rate to be given, everything depends on the course of the fertility rate: now this cannot change overnight (nor without cost) and has staggered effects on the birth rate through the age structure. We know from the work of Bourgeois-Pichat and Si-Ahmed Taleb (1970), what extraordinary and impossible move-ments in the fertility rate would be implied by a zero rate of popu-lation growth from the year 2000 onwards for such a country as Mexico. There are thus powerful constraints on the optimum rate of population growth, set by the possible rate of change of the fertility rate. Another important conclusion regarding the optimum rate of population growth can therefore be summarised thus: Do not lower the rate of population growth so quickly that you cannot return later to a positive or zero rate.

Obviously, therefore, we cannot propose, even if it were in accordance with inter-temporal preferences, a series of rates of population growth which suddenly become negative, then positive, constant or falling, and finally zero.

We have drawn a graph in Fig. 2.7 of the possible form of an optimum rate of population change, taking account of time preferences and constraints and in terms of two initial situations, one with 'excessive' growth, the other with 'insufficient' growth.

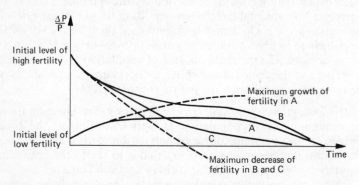

FIG. 2.7 The path through time of the optimum rate of population growth

In the Third World what is generally involved is no more than a problem of optimum demographic brakes. But everywhere what remains to be considered is the shape over several decades of a positive and relatively consistent, though changing, optimum rate of population growth, particularly as it affects densities. Beyond this, the clearly inescapable prospect of a stationary population is not without mystery. Its advent, if it comes, will inevitably be accompanied by unexpected difficulties and reactions.

Apollinaire, at the beginning of the last century, in *Les Mamelles de Tirésias*, a little-known play on population problems, makes a fortune-teller sing:

> Chaste citoyens de Zanzibar
> Qui ne faites plus d'enfants
> Sachez que la fortune et la gloire
> Les forêts d'ananas, les troupeaux d'elephants
> Appartiennent de droit
> Dans un proche avenir
> A ceux qui pour les prendre auront fait des enfants.

There never have been pineapple forests; the herds of elephants are in cemeteries or reserves. But the forests and herds of his imagination, symbols of creation, probably belong to growing populations.

REFERENCES

M. F. Bara, *Liaison entre taux de croissance de population et taux de croissance du PNB par tête*, note non publiée, Clermont, Faculté de Sciences Economiques (July 1973).

E. Boserup, *Evolution agraire et pression démographique*, trad. franç. (Flammarion, 1970).

J. Bourgeois-Pichat et Si-Ahmed Taleb, 'Un taux d'accroissement pour les pays en voie de développement en l'an 2000. Rêve ou réalité', *Population* (Nov–Dec 1970) 957–73.

A. J. Coale and E. M. Hoover, *Population Growth and Economic Development in Low Income Countries. A Case Study in Indian Prospects* (Princeton Univ. Press, 1958).

S. H. Cochrane, 'Population and Development: A More General Model', *Economic Development and Cultural Change*, vol. 21, no. 3 (Apr 1973) 409–22.

S. Enke, 'The Economic Aspects of Slowing Population Growth', *The Economic Journal* (Mar 1966) 44–56.

S. Enke, 'Economic Consequences of Population Growth', *The Economic Journal* (Dec 1971*a*) 800–11.

S. Enke (ed.), *Description of the Economic Demographic Model*, 68 TMP 120, rev. (June 1971*b*) prepared for U.S.A.I.D. by TEMPO, General Electric.

S. Enke (ed.), *Population Growth and Economic Development Background and Guide*, 71 TMP 45 (June 1971*c*), prepared for U.S.A.I.D. by TEMPO, General Electric.

P. Guillaumont, *La pensée démo-économique de J. B. Say et de Sismondi*, ed. Cujas (1969).

P. Guillaumont, *L'absorption du capital*, ed. Cujas (1971*a*).

P. Guillaumont, 'Les principales relations démo-économiques: schéma en vue d'un programme de recherches', *Cahiers de l'ORSTOM*, série Sciences Humaines, 1 (1971*b*) 51–62.

P. Guillaumont, 'Santé et production. Remarques sur quelques aspects de l'économie de la santé en relation avec le développement', *Revue d'Economie Politique* (Jan–Feb 1971*c*) 1–35.

P. Guillaumont, 'Santé, population et planification du développement, communication au Congrès régional africain de population', Accra, (Dec 1971) à paraitre in *Annales Economiques* (1973).

A. O. Hirschman, *La stratégie du développement économique*, trad. franç. (Paris: Ed. Ouvrières, 1964).

D. R. Kamerschen, 'On an Operational Index of Overpopulation', *Economic Development and Cultural Change* (Jan 1965) 169–87.

T. King, *The Measurement of Economic Benefits for Family Planning Projects and Programs*, World Bank, Economics Department Working Paper no. 71 (Mar 1970).

J. E. Meade, *Economie politique et politique économique*, trad. franç. (Paris: Payot, 1939).

J. E. Meade, *The Theory of International Economic Policy*, vol. II, *Trade and Welfare* (Oxford Univ. Press, 1954).

D. Meadows, *et al.*, *Halte à la croissance?* trad. franç. (Paris: Fayard, 1972).

M. Morishima, *Theory of Economic Growth* (Oxford Univ. Press, 1969).

G. Myrdal, *Asian Drama* (New York: Random House, 1968).

G. Ohlin, *Régulation démographique et développement économique*, O.C.D.E., Centre de développement (Paris 1967).

W. C. Robinson and D. Horlacher, 'Accroissement de population et bien-être économique', *Bulletins de démographie et de planning familial*, no. 6 (Sept 1971) 65.

A. Sauvy, *Théorie générale de la population*, 2 vols, P.U.F.

A. Sauvy, Préface à *le Tiers Monde*, 2è éd., Cahier de l'INED (P.U.F., 1961).

A. Sauvy, 'Les charges économiques et les avantages de la croissance de la population', *Population*, no. 1 (1972) 9–26.

A. Sauvy, *Croissance zéro*, (Paris: Calmann Lévy, 1973a).

A. Sauvy, *Le rhythme de variation optimale d'une population*, Comité International de coordination des recherches nationales en démographie, The University of West Indies (Apr 1973b).

A. Sauvy, 'The Optimal Change of a Population', chapter 3 in this volume.

J. L. Simon, 'The Value of Avoided Births to Underdeveloped Countries', *Population Studies* (1969) 61–8.

3 The Optimal Change of a Population

Alfred Sauvy

INSTITUT NATIONAL D'ETUDES DEMOGRAPHIQUES

I. METHOD OF APPROACH AND DEFINITIONS

Since the static concept of an optimal population is in many cases incapable of satisfactory application, one seeks to ascertain the rate of change which is desirable. One is not necessarily concerned with a human population. The problem may arise equally with an animal population (cattle) or with populations of objects (a forest, a collection, financial assets and the like).

The most general form of the problem. Let us take a group made up of *A* units which we wish to increase until it is made up of *B* units. What path should we follow? In order to define an *optimum path* it is necessary to determine what variable is to be *maximised*. One may, for instance, be seeking the most economic result; the rate of change over time may then not necessarily be constant. There is also the question whether one assumes that growth stops or continues once the objective *B* has been attained.

An example. A person who intends to stock his library, which can hold 300 books, over a period of five years, must therefore acquire an average of 60 books a year. If his income is increasing steadily, he may decide to buy an increasing number of books year by year. If on the other hand, he has a strong desire to have them in his possession, he will accept larger financial sacrifices over the initial years so as to obtain maximum satisfaction.

A national population. Let us consider a country in which the public authorities have determined the desirable population. The size of the population *A* must one day be increased to *B*. How should one move from *A* to *B*? If the difference is substantial it is neither desirable nor in some cases possible to make the change in a very short time. Let me take a country with a population of 10 million which sets itself the goal of 15 million. Several years will be necessary for this, even with the help of immigration, since too high a growth rate would involve too great an annual investment. Similarly, if this country with a population of 10 million sets itself the objective of coming down to 7 million, a certain period of time is necessary. The optimal approach does not necessarily entail a constant rate of change as we shall see. If migration is excluded, the desirable rate of change can only be achieved by an increase or decrease in the birth-rate. As a consequence age-distribution is affected and this complicates the problem since this secondary disturbance entails an additional increase or reduction, as the case may be. We shall therefore eliminate the age-distribution effect by studying *stable populations*.[1]

The burdens of growth with a stable population. The growth of a population results in burdens and brings advantages. The burdens are the easier to measure and even to identify. Two stable populations which grow at different rates impose unequal burdens for two reasons:

(i)   they do not involve the same volume of investment required by growth;
(ii) a stable population which grows faster has higher youth-burdens and lower old-age burdens.

The balance depends on:

(i)   the average burden imposed by a young person and an old person;
(ii) the age of entering the working stage and the non-working stage.

In practice, since the balance is almost exact, we may neglect this factor.

II. DEMOGRAPHIC INVESTMENT

In order to ensure for the additional population the same facilities as for the initial population, investment must be made in housing, hospitals, schools, industrial equipment and the like. In other words, simply to maintain the standard of living, the national capital stock must be increased in the same proportion as the population. This may be called *demographic investment*.

If the national capital stock F is equal to α times the national income R and if the population increases by $r/100$ per year, the demographic investment I should, so it seems, be equal to $Fr/100$ per year, that is $R\alpha r/100$. The ratio of the demographic investments to the national income would then be:

$$\frac{I}{R} = \frac{\alpha r}{100}. \tag{3.1}$$

[1] For the definition of a 'stable population', see discussion, p. 77.

This formula, as commonly used, is however not precisely accurate; a growing population has less equipment to amortise than a stationary population.

Total cost of investment. Certain items of equipment relate to specific age-groups (school equipment, industrial equipment, and the like). But once the population is stable, it would needlessly com-

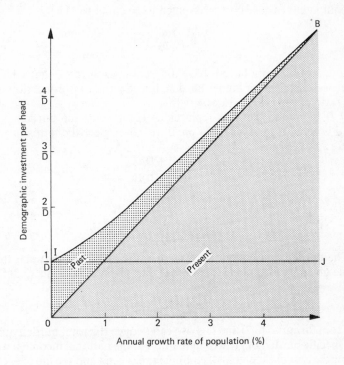

FIG. 3.1 Investment burdens in relation to the growth rate

plicate the problem to take into account these changes in age distribution. We assume that all the investment is necessary from birth.

The total burden is therefore made up of:

(i)   the equipment required by the growth of the population;
(ii) the old equipment that needs to be replaced.

Estimation of demographic investment.[1] Let us consider a demo-graphic investment intended to ensure within a stable[2] population the maintenance of a given level of equipment per head:

let D be the average life in years of this total of equipment, assumed to be fairly long, and $p = r/100$ the geometrical growth rate of the population, assumed to be fairly low.

Estimate (i) shows that the burden per head relating to this total of equipment (whose cost is assumed to be equal to 1) is:

$$Cp = p \frac{e^{Dp}}{e^{Dp-1}}. \tag{3.2}$$

If two stable populations have different growth rates, that which increases faster has a higher burden, but less than in proportion to the ratio of the growth rates.

If D is infinite (i.e. non-replaceable equipment) the burden per head is equal to p. If p is very small we can neglect the terms in p^2, hence:

$$Cp = \frac{2}{D} \frac{1+Dp}{2+Dp}.$$

If the growth is nil ($p = 0$) the burden is:

$$C_0 = \frac{1}{D}. \tag{3.3}$$

The burden consequent on growth is the difference between the value given by formula (3.2) and the value given by formula (3.3),

$$Cp - C_0 = \frac{p}{2+Dp}.$$

From formulas (3.2) and (3.3) we can deduce the total burden and the specific burden of growth in relation to the national income if we know the cost of each item of equipment per head and the life of each item of equipment.

An example from housing. Let R be the national income, P the total population, P_A the working population and $p = r/100$ the growth rate.

We assume the average life of a dwelling to be equal to 100 years and the cost of a dwelling unit to be equal to T years' work (the quotient of the national income by the working population).

---

[1]See 'Les charges économiques et les avantages de la croissance de la population' (Economic burdens and benefits from population growth), *Population* (Jan–Feb 1972) 15–16.

[2]I.e. a steadily growing population (cf. note 1, p. 64).

The proportion of the national income devoted to house building is:

Rate of growth of population	Total burden	Burden due to growth
0%	2·50%	0·0%
1%	3·95%	1·45%
2%	5·78%	3·28%
3%	7·90%	5·40%

To raise the growth rate is costly and to slow it down is beneficial.

III. THE CASE OF A DECLINING POPULATION

This case has hitherto been very little studied and presents different problems. The burden due to the past (the (replacement of life-exhausted equipment) may be hypothetical; for it is not in the interest of the population to replace items of equipment which will not be used. Let us put the question in another way:

If deaths d exceed births n, the volume of items of equipment to be constructed is: $n-(1-m)d$, m being the proportion of all equipment that has become life-exhausted.

If the difference should be negative, the population would have no need to build any equipment for some time ahead. But, after a certain time, the available stock no longer being capable of use, a new period of construction will have to begin. The question arises whether the non-used equipment being assumed to internal migration (see below) may result in equipment still in good condition becoming unusable.

It has been assumed thus far that a new unit of equipment exactly replaces a time-expired unit. But, in periods of technical progress, there is qualitative improvement. For this reason an estimate of demographic investment gives a less favourable result than arises in practice.

Natural resources and their deterioration. The problem of natural resources may be posed in two ways:

(i)   Each member of a population should always have the same supply of natural resources. But this can hardly increase, at least not in some of its forms, in terms of surface area for instance. Land clearance and improvement may, however, offset this. Investment designed to maintain the supply of natural resources per head should be included in the burden of growth.

(ii)   The natural resources may be diminished by man or by the elements; this is the general problem of exhaustible resources as well as pollution and soil-erosion. Exhaustion and damage seems, *a priori*, to be proportional to population. But in practice, this is far from being the case, particularly with regard to the soil.

IV. THE ECONOMIC BENEFITS OF POPULATION GROWTH

The economic benefits of population growth are less apparent than the burdens and more difficult to evaluate. Let us start from the sources from which they may arise:

(i)   *The overheads of the community:* regardless of whether a nation or a region is involved, a certain number of burdens are independent of the population, or increase less quickly than it does. This phenomenon is the counterpart of the equipment which has to be increased in order to give each additional inhabitant the same advantage as others.

(ii)   *General productivity:* whilst agriculture comes up against the law of diminishing returns, industry in contrast benefits greatly from increasing returns with increased output. The productivity of various activities increases (book printing, newspaper production, mechanical engineering, for instance) and new industries may emerge (automobiles, aviation, electronics, and the like). When the size of enterprises is the same, population growth is likely to increase competition and reduce the possibility of monopoly.

(iii)   *Division of labour:* technical progress calls for a more and more elaborate division of labour, which places small populations at a disadvantage; this factor may be linked to the previous one but is not the same.

(iv)   *Increase in population density:* density affects economic standards in various ways (leaving aside the question of diminishing returns in agriculture): *transport* is less costly because the average distance between persons is smaller and the network denser. Benefit is particularly to be felt in two sectors, *education* and *public health.*

(v)   *Pollution and deterioration:* here again, the influence of density is felt in different and sometimes opposite ways; in physical terms pollution and deterioration of natural resources are, *a priori*, proportionate to the population, but we shall see, in connection with sociological and mental factors, that other repercussions may occur.

(vi)   *Structural adjustments:* This little considered factor is perhaps the most important. Numerous maladjustments and distortions occur in a changing economy (occupational, geographical, etc.), either because of errors or because of unforeseen technical innovations. These maladjustments are likely to be corrected more easily in the case of growth; it is always easier to correct a maladjusted structure by additions than by transfers.

Internal migration. Let us take the case of housing with rural-urban migration. Each person must have a dwelling (as was assumed earlier), thus the number of dwellings must correspond to the population. If a village is rapidly depopulated, the migration will leave vacant dwellings still in good condition and create a need for additional buildings elsewhere. Let us suppose migration takes place from area *A* to area *B*. If the population of *A* decreases at a rate superior to $1/D$ (*D* is the life of a unit of equipment), certain dwellings still in good condition can no longer be used, and an equivalent need for additional dwellings will make itself felt. This is more likely to occur with a decreasing or very slowly increasing population.

Mental and sociological factors. Being difficult to measure or even to identify, these are often totally neglected. Various authors (E. Dupreel, E. Boserup, etc.) have pointed out that difficulty often has a creative value. Furthermore, the rise of average age which is a consequence of slow population growth may have adverse economic effects since it is more likely that population of higher average age will be conservative in outlook than a younger one. In a region in the process of becoming depopulated, there is likely to be a lack of initiative and great difficulty in putting new ideas into practice. History does not, on the other hand, provide any example of a decline in population being accompanied by an economic boom. The loss of vitality due to ageing may be offset, to a certain extent, if ageing is recognised and arrangements are made in advance to avert its consequences.

The overall result. The total burdens and benefits of growth together form a complex function. It is to be remembered that we are not discussing the burdens and benefits of a population which is changing over time, but are comparing the fortunes · of stable populations with different steady rates of growth.

V. THE OPTIMAL RATE OF GROWTH

With a fixed rate of growth there are thus burdens and benefits. The curve *C* of burdens is convex downwards (Fig. 3.2). Beyond a certain point, on the other hand, the benefits are unlikely to continue to grow. The principle of response to difficulty always reaches some limit; the curve *A* of benefits is therefore concave downwards. The curve *A* representing the benefits and the curve *C* must necessarily intersect. There exists a rate of growth *OM* such that the tangents in *K* and *L* are parallel and that the difference is the greatest possible.

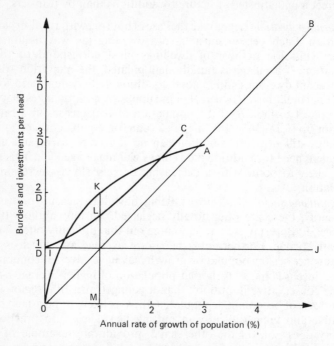

FIG. 3.2 Optimal rate of growth

For the populations of Western Europe it may be reckoned that the annual growth rate of 0·5 to 1 per cent that they have experienced since the war is close to the optimum. Above this, the burdens of demographic investment would have been too heavy; below it, the advantages of growth too slight.

Let us consider the case of a declining population. A very fast rate of decline would present serious disadvantages and is never likely to be desirable. An optimal position of slow decline is conceivable.

Two obstacles. The optimal rate that we thus find is the rate of growth of a stable population – in other words it is for a population which has from the outset a given territory, a given set of techniques, given types of equipment and a given initial population, that we are seeking the most economically advantageous rate of growth.

Even with these somewhat unrealistic hypotheses the optimum would only be a provisional solution. Even supposing that it is possible to establish a population that is completely stable, for instance by appropriate migration, its growth could gradually change the initial conditions, if it is assumed that the territory is limited. For instance, if initially underpopulated, the territory might before the end be less underpopulated or even overpopulated. Technical progress could have an opposite effect.

If a stable population becomes aware that its rate of growth is too fast, it cannot change this rate without changing its age distribution. One can diminish this difficulty by applying the reasoning to sub-populations, for instance a professional population. There is less disruption because the new arrivals start working immediately.

A medical population. Let us consider the number of doctors practising in a country. We shall assume the death-rate to be nil during their working lives (from 25 to 65 years). At the outset, the population is stationary. At some moment it is noticed that the number M_1 of doctors is insufficient and that it should be increased to M_2. The problem is to find the best possible way to move from M_1 to M_2.

Two variables are independent: the economic level and the number of human lives saved. Let us assume that it is possible to reduce everything to economic units. Two objectives are in conflict with each other:

(i) It would be useful to be able to increase immediately the number from M_1 to M_2, since human lives will be saved.

(ii) On the other hand the transition from M_1 to M_2 in a very short time (a year for instance) has various disadvantages as well as being costly; it entails a deterioration in the quality of the medical profession, it imposes heavy burdens on universities and training hospitals and involves certain technological impossibilities. Thus acceleration is costly.

.Moreover 40 years later the retirement of this abnormal number of doctors will make it necessary once again to have recourse to abnormal recruitment. Thus, since it is necessary to take into account the factor of regularity, we shall seek to attain the number M_2 only progressively, over a certain number of years. The solution which is convenient at the administrative level sacrifices human lives.

It may also arise that the goal M_2 is only an intermediate one, a provisional stage, and as a result the assumptions are changed. Without further hypotheses it is not possible to compare the respective costs of the various solutions, nor consequently to define the conditions of optimisation.

A farming population. Let us now take the opposite case: there are, in a country A_1 farmers and calculations have shown that a number A_2 lower than the first would be enough. The problem is to move from A_1 to A_2.

The previous considerations may be reversed: it would be unreasonable (even if it were possible) to stop all recruitment of young people, all entry to the farming profession, for one or more generations. Even if such a policy were feasible, it would result later in new upheavals when these generations went into retirement. The optimal approach leads us to reduce dislocations and to compromise between speed and acceleration. Here again the initial facts must be clearly defined.

VI. THE ACHIEVEMENT OF STABILITY OVER A LONG PERIOD

If a population much higher or much lower than the present number is desired, application of the concept of an optimal rate of change may be made in three stages:

(i)   achievement of a stable state, involving slowing-down or acceleration;

(ii)   a period of stability, for a given time, at a constant rate of change considered optional;

(iii)   achievement of a stationary state, before reaching the desired population.

These operations may be compared to a movement of a space missile which first of all accelerates, then travels at a constant speed, only then to be slowed down before arriving at its destination.

Transition to a stationary population. To bring directly to a stationary state a stable population growing at the rate of 2·5 per cent annually (mortality and fertility rates at each age being constant), a reduction of 2·5 per cent per year in the fertility rates for each will cause births to become constant and the population to become progressively stationary. Moreover, after 15 to 20 years, the decline in fertility rates may be less than 2·5 per cent per year, because the 'stabilised' generation are reaching the age of procreation.

If, however, the death rates of each group decrease, particularly for the younger age groups, constancy of the number of births will not be sufficient to ensure the population attaining a stationary state.

Underpopulation. Certain countries, particularly Africa south of the Sahara, which are very underpopulated, would gain economically by having a much larger population, in some cases ten times larger. One solution for them is to maintain their annual growth and even to increase it by acting on the death-rate. This solution calls for a high rate of demographic investment.

The question of the optimal rate of growth to be attempted depends then on health conditions (possible reduction of the death-rate in the various age groups) and on economic circumstances. The rate attempted should be maintained, whilst reducing so far as possible any disturbances at the beginning and end of the process.

Overpopulation. We are concerned here with the case of absolute overpopulation: that is to say, a highly populated country, which, even using more productive techniques, is likely to remain at subsistence level; in other words, even with a more advanced technology, this population would benefit in terms of its standard of living by being less numerous.

In those countries which seem to be in this position, the objectives pursued have hitherto been seen only in terms of the rate of growth, and the desirability of reducing it, for instance from 3 per cent a year to 2 or 1 per cent.

Making every allowance for the psychological and sociological disadvantages of a reduction in the growth rate, it may be advisable to attempt to reach not the stationary state, which would entail a large increase in the population, but a progressive reduction in the number of births, sufficient to achieve a transition to a state of a stable declining population. Once the country is well into the process of change which, in the first stage, entails a further population increase, it can decide whether to continue it, to slow down or accelerate it.

There is however a difficulty: the drop in the birth-rate temporarily reduces the burden of maintaining the young without increasing to the same extent the burden of providing for old age. If the burden of the young is reduced it is likely that this will give rise to other expenditures or to tax reductions which, once established, may be difficult to alter. This is an additional reason for foreseeing well in advance the implications of an ageing population.

VII. CONCLUSIONS

The notion of an optimal rate of change, which at first sight seems simple, proves more complex than it appears and may even prove meaningless if it is conceived too crudely. Even if the criterion is clearly defined, for instance average income per head, a number of variables are involved which have to be reconciled with each other, particularly the general rate and the regularity. It is only after close examination of a particular case that a specific solution can be suggested.

Discussion of the Papers by Professor Guillaumont and M. Sauvy

Professor Sir John Hicks said Professor Guillaumont's paper fell into three parts. The first was a review of the literature, mainly (but not entirely) devoted to criticism of the conventional (or formerly conventional) idea of an 'optimum population'. It was not entirely devoted to criticism, since there was also an appreciation of the view, attributed to Say and Sismondi, according to which a country was happier the larger its population, provided that product per head was adequate or sufficient (*suffisant* in the French version, which must here be regarded as authoritative). It would have been interesting to contrast this view with that of their great contemporary Ricardo, with whose work Say, at least, had some acquaintance. Ricardo held that mere 'sufficiency' was valueless; and that consequently, if the surplus above sufficiency were the same, 'it is of no importance whether the country has one or ten millions of inhabitants'. This apparently outrageous statement belonged to the same field of discourse as Say's. That the same approach could be taken either way was a matter which Professor Hicks intended to show later to be of some interest.

What was said by Professor Guillaumont on optimum population, he found quite acceptable. Professor Hicks had published his own views[1] and they came to much the same thing as Professor Guillaumont's. The most important part of the point seemed to him to come out sharply in application to terms of trade. Suppose that we could have asserted that the optimum population of Great Britain in 1968 was x millions. Then it was quite probable that we should by the same means have concluded that the optimum population in 1973 was $x - 5$ millions. But what would be the good of that? It might have some bearing on questions of migration, which was the only way in which population could be changed quite rapidly in response to the rapidity with which 'other things' changed. Apart from migration, there was already implied in the age-structure of a particular population a fairly definite prospect of future development. Any possible change in policy (or in practice) could affect that profile only rather slowly; optimum population, in the conventional sense, changed much more rapidly than that.

Professor Hicks said that on all this Professor Guillaumont and he were quite in accord; later on, he was not so sure. For having (rightly) dismissed the conventional optimum as too static, Professor Guillaumont proceeded to replace it by a 'dynamic' optimum which seemed not much better. In doing so, he was following a path which in the field of capital theory was very well trodden. There also economists had discovered that their problem was an inter-temporal problem – a problem which was delimited by constraints in the form of relations between variables that belonged to different dates, or to different periods of time. Their first reaction, once this was grasped, was to try to reduce the problem to one in which this inter-temporality was minimised – the steady state with constant growth rates over time. In the field of steady states, the structure of the economy depended upon its growth rate;

[1] *Social Framework* (Oxford Univ. Press, 1971) Appendix 2.

so if the growth rate was optimised, everything else (or perhaps most other things) would be optimised too.

Professor Hicks said that a great deal of the paper (as its title signified) was concerned with the determination of an optimum growth rate – a problem which, in a world of steady states, was undoubtedly significant, but which, outside that world, did not seem to him to be much more significant than the static problem which it was supposed to replace. He was sorry that he was unable to make much sense of most of the formal part of the paper excepting in a world of steady states, and after the effort which he had made in his latest book to get beyond the steady state in capital theory, he found reverting to the steady state in population theory rather particularly distasteful. He must therefore try M. Guillaumont's patience by skipping over this central part of his work – all that which was in terms of $\Delta K/K$ and $\Delta L/L$ – rather lightly. In its later pages, this paper seemed to Professor Hicks to be going beyond the steady state; Professor Hicks found that part of the paper a good deal more interesting, and would like to devote a good part of the time allotted to him to talking about it.

Even in the central part of his paper, Professor Guillaumont said that he was talking about the population growth rate some time – perhaps fifteen years – ahead. But, excepting in a steady state, one could not regard that – even that – in isolation. What would be the optimum growth rate fifteen years ahead depended on what had happened between now and then, and upon what was expected to happen later on. The problem, in mathematical terms, was a problem of the calculus of variations: the determination of the whole optimum path, from the present (given as initial condition) into some remote future. But even in the calculus of variations, one had to be maximising something; and what was one maximising? One needed an index of economic welfare over time; and how was that to be put together?

The problem, of course, was formally the same as the one treated in quite static welfare economics, where we were baffled by our inability to add up the utility indices of different people. Some of us had tried to short-circuit that trouble by the device of the Pareto optimum, but in view of the close relations between the populations of successive years (apart from migration) it was of little use – because it was so uninformative – here. There was nothing for it but to define an optimum path in terms of some, inevitably arbitrary, weights. (This, he thought, was what was intended by the World Bank economists to whom Professor Guillaumont referred in talking of the introduction of a discount factor. What he wanted to insist on was that there was no discount factor *given by the market*; we had to introduce our own, something which reflected our own preferences, or those which we thought we could 'sell' to other people.)

Professor Hicks wanted to illustrate what happened when the problem was then reformulated in the following way. Suppose we granted to Professor Guillaumont that increasing population, in itself, was a good thing. (There was nothing peculiar about this view; it had excellent authority behind it. Where Adam Smith said that the progressive state was the 'cheerful' state of society – 'the stationary dull, the declining melancholy' – he undoubtedly implied that population, as well as other things, was going up, or down.) But suppose we also held Professor Guillaumont to his admission that increasing population, at however low a growth rate, could not go on indefinitely – apart, Professor Guillaumont said, from the cultivation of other planets; but recent astronomy suggested that we should sooner cultivate the Sahara than Mars, or the depths of the oceans than Venus – then we had a contradiction. The only way in which it could be resolved (in the absence of a discount factor) would be by periodical catastrophe. For $n-1$ periods population would increase at a 'good' rate, then in period n, by Black Death, atom bomb, or some other form of collective suicide, a large proportion would be wiped out, so that the circus could start all over again. He was *not* recommending that solution. If, however, it was to be avoided, there must be some 'trade-off' between the virtues of increasing population and the dangers of excessive population; and one must be given greater weight than the other according to circumstances.

Thus, while he was well prepared to grant Professor Guillaumont that a considerable increase in the population of France might be attended by no serious inconvenience (provided that they did not all want to sun themselves on the Côte d'Azur at the same time) he would beg of him not to preach his philoprogenetive gospel to the people of Bangladesh, of Jamaica, or of Zanzibar, or even to the people of England and Wales.

Professor Coale introduced the paper by M. Sauvy, who had extended the well-known concept of the optimum population from the optimum size to the optimum rate of increase. The concept of optimum size implied that the number of persons in a given territory could be too small or too large for the best advancement of certain social aims (such as maximum per capita income). In between, there was an optimum number neither too small nor too large. The optimum rate of increase was a wholly analogous notion: the growth of population might be too slow or too rapid for the best attainment of stated goals, and there was an optimum rate that was neither too slow nor too fast.

In considering the optimum rate of growth, M. Sauvy balanced the costs and benefits of alternative rates; faster growth entailed higher costs because it required a higher level of investment in housing, hospitals and productive capital to maintain a given per capita endowment of such equipment. However, the level of investment required was not proportional to growth, since investment was needed to replace the stock of capital, as well as to increase it. Current possible investment, as a proportion of the total stock of capital, could be considered as analogous to the birth-rate of a human population. If the stock of capital was to grow as rapidly as the human population, the birth-rate of equipment must equal the death-rate (rate of retirement of old equipment) plus the rate of increase of the population. With no growth, the death-rate equalled the reciprocal of the average lifetime of equipment ($1/D$); but, with a growing stock, the age distribution of equipment had a higher proportion of younger items, and the death-rate was less than $1/D$. Also the productivity of capital was greater when it contained a high proportion of 'young' (generally more technically advanced) items.

In balancing the advantages and disadvantages of growth, M. Sauvy noted the following advantages, among others:

(i)   overheads might be constant, or increase less rapidly than population;

    (ii)   some industries would enjoy economies of scale;

    (iii) with fixed size of firm, a larger population would increase competition;

    (iv) growth would make adjustments to mistaken investments easier.

Optimum growth occurred where the algebraic balance of benefits less costs was the greatest.

Professor Coale said that the classical idea of an optimum size of population seemed to him to be subject to the following objections or qualifications:

1.   It was an exercise in comparative statics, comparing alternative population sizes while holding other factors fixed. And these were factors that would not be fixed if the size of the population were actually different (technology, or the stock of capital, for example); technology and the stock of capital had, in fact, developed to suit the actual size of population, as examples in agriculture showed.

2.   Many of the alleged effects of population size could be offset by trade. Thus, a small population could specialise, and obtain its raw materials as well as its consumption needs on the world market. The theorem of factor-price equalisation suggested that, with unhampered trade, factor prices, including wages, should not be affected by size (for example, Japan and Hong Kong).

3.   A very sparsely settled area, such as Australia, need not spread its population thinly over a large territory, but could choose to settle a limited part densely, since income was not reduced by the existence of the empty space. In fact, Australia was more urbanised than France; thus, Australia might be underpopulated from the point of view of output per unit of territory, but not per head of population. As for the quality of life, and the unpleasant effects of high density, there was a tendency for people to prefer the familiar. With allowance for adjustments, the 'optimum' might be a plateau over a factor of 3 to 10 in population size.

4.   The idea of an optimum rate of increase seemed to suggest a more dynamic point of view, but in some ways it was still an exercise in comparative statics – comparing alternative worlds of constant rates of increase instead of alternative stationary states.

Professor Coale said that demographers employed the concept of a stable population – a population with a fixed schedule of mortality rates by age, and a fixed schedule of fertility rates. If the fertility and mortality rates remained fixed, the population came to have a fixed age distribution and a constant rate of increase. In the special case when the rate of increase was zero, the population was called stationary. M. Sauvy had employed alternative stable populations in analysing the optimum rate of growth, so that his analysis still had a static quality, but he did recognise the alterations in structure that must accompany a change in growth as a complication of, and limitation to, his results.

M. Sauvy did not give much weight to the differences in age distribution between populations with different rates of increase. He asserted that the balance of changes of dependency (more young dependents with faster growth, more old dependents with slower growth) was almost total. In fact, the ratio (persons less than 5 and over 65/persons 15–65) was nearly 1·0 with rapid growth, and only about 0·55 with zero growth. To assert that this difference was unimportant, one must impute much higher costs to the population over 65 than to that under 15. M. Sauvy did note that the older population accompanying slower growth might have adverse economic effects, because it would be more turned toward the past than a younger one. In another context, M. Sauvy once said that a stationary population was a population of old people, ruminating over old ideas, in old houses. The optimum rate of increase, when analysed through a comparison of different stable populations, was appropriate neither to the very long term (of several hundred years) nor to the moderately short term (of 30 to 50 years).

In the long term, the optimum – indeed the only feasible – rate of increase was very close to zero. In a thousand years a growth rate of 0·5 per cent would bring the population of France to over 6 billions; a negative rate of the same magnitude ($-0·5$ per cent) would leave only 400,000 persons.

On the other hand, it took 30 to 50 years for a stable population to establish itself, once fertility and mortality became constant. Population growth showed a property much like inertia. An immediate net reproduction rate of 1·0 in the U.S.A. would lead to levelling off at a total 35 per cent greater; in Mexico or Brazil, immediate replacement from now on would nearly double the population; achieving a net reproduction rate of 1·0 in the year 2000 would provide a population nearly four times as great as the present one.

Dr Ridker was struck by how sensitive to the time horizon the optimum population seemed to be. Could we define the optimum in relation to the very long run? One would then need a new emphasis on the finiteness of the earth. Perhaps an optimum population was that size of population which was sustainable *ad infinitum* at the current quality of life, and without exposing itself to undue risk.

Professor Lajugie believed that, if it was important to take account, as previous speakers had, of the time factor in defining the optimum population, it was equally necessary to bring in the factor of space, and it was on the introduction of this variable into the analysis that he wanted to make some remarks. This brought us back to the problems of disparities in regional development which, stated in general terms of economic development, could only make an abstraction out of demographic facts, and that not only for 'dualist' economies but also for developed ones.

There was a danger in reasoning only in a macro-economic setting. This led to the aggregation of very heterogeneous factors and to the presentation of national averages which were simple abstractions – such as prices, incomes, volume of production, and so on – where concrete realities were localised and very much diversified.

Professor Lajugie agreed that it was necessary to make an effort at abstraction to reach theoretical conclusions which alone could lead to a general science. But when it was a matter of defining the objectives of political economy, it was scarcely less necessary to return to the complexity of reality, and the definition of an optimum population gave us a characteristic example of that necessity.

In fact, the definition of a national optimum remained one of these averages which hid important regional disparities. For example, an optimum defined in terms of the territory of France would conceal situations as different as those in Corsica or Lozère on one hand, and the department of the Nord or the Parisian departments on the other.

To find a concept of the optimum which was truly operational, it would be necessary to take account once more of regional differences in natural and human resources, in productive equipment, and in economic equipment in the broadest sense. In other words, it was necessary to go beyond the definition of an optimum level of population to find an optimum distribution of that population. These preoccupations led one, as he saw it, to the policy of 'aménagement du territoire' in which all countries were engaged, though in differing degrees. This was as true of developed as of developing countries.

If from the level of principles we passed to the level of means, we still found the same problem. To achieve this optimal distribution of population, the choice rested between the play of liberal mechanisms, which translated themselves into inter-regional migration, or the adoption of a voluntary policy for regional development.

Professor Lajugie had no intention, at this point, of treating this problem in depth. He would content himself with recalling that it was certainly not necessary to suppress all labour mobility. Such a solution would be very unsatisfactory from the point of view of changes in productivity. However, it was quite clear that it would become less and less acceptable for such migration to take place on a scale which risked bringing about the desertion of certain regions or certain departments, and that both for economic and social reasons.

In effect, the policy of 'aménagement du territoire' was envisaged, too often, solely from the point of view of the necessary solidarity between members of a national community, which meant that one could not accept excessive differences in the level of income and conditions of life between regions. In fact, it was also an economic basis for this policy to know the burden placed on the national collectivity through the existence of regions which contributed little or nothing to the growth of G.N.P. Moreover, some of these might even be putting a brake on the growth of national product, not only by their insignificant positive contributions but also by the financial charge represented by the necessary budgetary transfers in their favour in the form of state subsidies or other kinds of aid, direct or indirect.

This was another point which could not be satisfactorily developed here. Instead, Professor Lajugie wanted simply to underline the necessity of taking account of this aspect of reality in defining an optimum population which could be one of the foundations of an active policy for bringing about regional equilibrium and a rational regional policy.

Professor Leridon wanted to discuss the relationship between optimal population and optimal growth. Growth from situation A to situation B seemed to imply that in some way B was preferable. One could define the desired rate of growth, but the first effect of population growth was to increase the size of the population. Countries with high birth-rates, for example Brazil, were countries where population growth helped economic growth, but they could well feel that this was leading to overpopulation. So, one had a difference between practice and theory.

Dr Hume wanted to make a plea for a return to Professor Schultz's position, that in measuring optimum population growth in terms of productivity or income, one had to allow for income distribution. For example, Brazil was a country with two populations, one rich and one poor. Population was increasing rapidly among the low-income group, but more slowly among the group with higher incomes. One could not take a homogeneous view of a national population.

Professor Stone wanted to support Dr Ridker. The optimum population must be maintainable. While one could argue in this conference about doing things in time and space, in the not-so-long run one could not do very much. In a homogeneous community, a well-ordered government might bring about changes between regions, the parts of a country with space might not be very attractive, or those who were drawn there might come from other countries.

Professor Stone suggested that what we needed might not be optimum population growth but optimum population decline. The world would be a very uncomfortable place even before we attained the possibility of such a decline. To talk of steady-state growth struck him as absolute nonsense, although he was perhaps still living in the eleventh century. He could not conceive of the horrific numbers that would be implied, nor of the problems resulting from growing population density, and the fact that economies of scale would be overridden by the negative social returns. He did not think that mid-twentieth century arrangements would be with us much longer, and sought support among participants for his idea that most populations in the world become far too big before ultimately reaching a reasonable size.

Professor Robinson wondered if he was the only one mystified by the discussion. Professor Hicks seemed to think that the notion of an optimum population was quite unreasonable, which made Professor Robinson feel a late nineteenth century survival. However, at the bottom of the first page of M. Sauvy's paper, the latter said, 'Let us consider a country where the public authorities have determined a desirable population.' M. Sauvy then discussed how to reach this. Perhaps he was assuming that public authorities were irrational, or maybe they were to ask the views of the Archbishop or some other authority. Was it not possible to think rationally about increasing or decreasing population? Despite what Professor Coale had said, it was not a matter of taking decisions over thousands of years but in the short run. Should a government today support a smaller or a bigger increase in population? There was enough truth in the analysis of comparative statics to show whether growth in a country would increase or decrease welfare. Some African states were manifestly underpopulated, and public services would be better if population were increased. In Asia, it was hard to believe that it was right to be agnostic over whether Bangladesh was better situated fifty years ago with a population of 30 millions than today with 75 millions. The problem was not so incapable of examination by rational thought as to cause us to resort to complete agnosticism.

Professor Robinson conceded that if one decided that the population should preferably fall rather than rise, a lot more sophisticated work needed to be done before one could decide on the desirable rate of change. But there were apparently some high priests sitting at the top table in the conference room, saying that those who took the view that a population should increase or decrease should be expelled from the profession. If so, he felt rather unhappy.

He suspected that much of the world was facing a short period during which serious disaster was quite possible. If one looked ahead only thirty years at a country like India, there could well be a relationship between population and resources that was so far from optimal as to be almost disastrous. Perhaps he had not understood fully what Professor Hicks had said or had misjudged the extent of the agnosticism of him and other participants.

Professor Hicks replied that all he was doing was pleading for a willingness to take into account different situations. He had argued that France could well increase its population, and that the pros were likely to outweigh the cons if it did so. However, he also argued that there were many other countries, of which he had indeed mentioned one or two, where this was not the case.

He wanted to emphasise that these were problems of size versus rates of change. The pros and cons were difficult to analyse and hard to reconcile. He was very much aware of the countries mentioned by Professor Robinson, where any population increase at all would lead to very grave consequences.

Professor Coale also wanted to support what Professor Hicks had said. For each population one knew where one was now, what fertility and mortality rates were, and what were their implications. In Africa, population growth was rapid and increasing. The desired family size appeared to be six to eight children, so that population would increase five or tenfold within a century. It would certainly double within about twenty-five years. These might be underpopulated countries, but 3 per cent population growth there was a social handicap. The six- to eight-child family was a negative benefit. Someone had to look at the full range of cases to see what was the best policy for each.

Professor Robinson asked why Professors Coale and Schultz appeared to assume that the aggregate of individual choices would give the best result for the human race.

Professor Coale denied that this was the case.

Professor Schultz wanted to side with Professor Coale on this issue – for a change! As a first step, one needed to provide subsidies for voluntary birth control to all, but particularly to the poor and disadvantaged. Secondly, one had to search for means of imposing the full costs of having children on parents, as equitably as possible. He believed that the externalities of rapid population growth were often large, and generally negative, but we did not have much empirical evidence about this. What we needed was economic research into how to internalise costs, and into what the magnitudes and personal distribution of those externalities or social costs were in particular countries. One must proceed with great caution before overruling the consumer and producer sovereignty of parents by direct efforts to change their reproductive behaviour.

Professor Létinier believed that this was not a world problem but a national one. The developed countries were experiencing moderate population growth and few economic difficulties. They could increase their overall output without much difficulty. But there were many countries where an increase in population would hold back an increase in the standard of living, and where there was, therefore, a vicious circle. The developed countries could break the vicious circle by helping less-developed countries to reduce their rate of population growth.

At the world level, one had to define the optimal rate of growth for developed countries as one which allowed for the effect on less-developed countries and did not cause them serious problems.

Mr Lengyel noted that everyone seemed to be taking the country as the unit. However, if one federated, surely the optimum would be changed. The country was an artificial unit and, if one increased mobility, one then had new political arrangements, thus changing the optimum. One must take the world perspective or, at any rate, that of a major region.

Professor Létinier argued that one would have to look at sub-areas in the world, in some of which an increase in population would lead to problems, and in others of which it would not.

Professor Parikh was a little surprised that people were not worried about likely technological change in reproduction itself. Any optimum population, even if one could define it, could not be reached for thirty or forty years. By then, perhaps technical change in reproductive techniques would have occurred. Notions of children as 'goods' or even 'bads' would not continue. When asked what he meant, Professor Parikh replied that questioners should go and read Huxley's 'Brave New World'.

He was not worried about the fact that the earth was finite. It was possible to conquer space, and he did not think these problems would worry us in thirty years.

Professor Ohlin noted that in the papers there was a discussion of the optimal rate of growth, but, in the discussion, suggestions had been made that the optimal rate of decline might be more appropriate. Perhaps neither the size nor the rate of growth of population were important. Most empirical evidence pointed to this. He also thought that a discussion of the region was not particularly meaningful. Professor Hicks had pointed out that even if one decided what an optimum was, by the time one had moved towards it the optimum itself would have changed. However, relations between rates of change might be important. Where population was increasing rapidly, technical change and other factors were also changing quickly. Economic growth was dominated by technology. Yet when we thought how fragile were our notions of national boundaries, resources, etc., should we not disregard talk about the optimal size of the national population? It was technology, international trade and mobility which were the main aspects of economic growth. Why should one expect these concepts to be important?

Professor Ben Porath suggested that some of the discussion would never have taken place if participants had thought of its purpose. Most would probably agree that no one expected to have a precise number for the rate of growth, or optimum size, of population for either a country or the world. Even those who plugged an empirical parameter for population growth into a growth model would not do so in this discussion. He agreed that the important thing was not optimal population, but the questions that Professor Robinson had been asking. Which way should a population move? Given how difficult it was to move, and given that adjustment was so slow, the only thing one needed to know was whether the population was bigger or smaller than one wanted, and whether one should, or should not, act on it with gusto. One's judgement on how big a population was, relative to the optimum, would probably be dominated by two or three factors at any moment of time. In the U.S.A. at present, public opinion was against a high rate of population growth, and Professor Coale talked about how long it would be before the American population stabilised. By then, new factors would lead to a desire to increase it. For many reasons, we were mostly interested to know in which direction the rate of increase of population should be changed.

However, unlike decisions on capital formation where one had to play with magnitudes, he saw no need for very complex analysis to answer such questions. One or two considerations would dominate. One had to credit the writers of the papers with being reasonable enough to regard the discussion not as a source of precise numbers, but as a way of dealing with conceptual difficulties.

Professor Robinson was concerned with pages 64–7 of M. Sauvy's paper, where he discussed demographic investment. In planning economic development, demographic investment was the most important result of population growth. Much investment was needed to keep up with population. Looking at the potential results of faster or slower population increase, Professor Robinson was worried about the effect of rapid growth in absorbing investment resources and preventing capital deepening and technological advance, as well as impeding the transfer of population from agriculture to industry. He thought this was very important.

M. Sauvy appeared to say that if the population increased by 30 per cent then one needed 30 per cent more facilities of one sort or another. Scale effects or the present under-utilisation of existing facilities might give some offset. But one had also to consider a diminishing return factor. To rehouse a city for a 30 per cent increase in population was extremely difficult. One was likely to find, as had been done in a study of Detroit in which he had been involved, that a large percentage of the city would require so big a change in population density that it would have to be rebuilt almost entirely, and not just extended by 30 per cent. Had enough account been taken of this kind of issue? He thought that demographic investment was usually underestimated.

Mr Boulier wanted to make a technical point on sustainable populations. He was not clear that the concept was useful. The law of entropy ensured that mankind could last forever. We could have a large population which lasted for a short time, or smaller populations which survived for longer. The optimal pattern presumably depended upon the appropriate discount rate, and it was unclear how that rate should be chosen.

To *Dr Nassef*, the meeting appeared unable to decide on the optimum rate of population growth. In Egypt, which was listed in many of the papers as overpopulated, he thought the rate of population growth should now decrease. But since 96 per cent of the area was uninhabited, he wondered whether this would continue to be true. The time might come when more Egypt could be populated to sustain a higher growth rate.

M. Sauvy began with a general observation. His paper was abstract, and many participants had been speaking of practical applications. There was too little time to look at all the countries one might consider. He had looked at stable populations, and at declining ones. We had to remember that there were different costs for younger and older members of the population, and Professor Coale had looked at these. Professor Coale remembered a sentence of his: that a stationary population was one of old men, in old houses and with old ideas. At least, one had to remember that a stationary population was old. This should not be forgotten.

Professor Coale had talked about underpopulation in Africa and suggested that 3 per cent population growth was too rapid. It was said that a child should not grow too rapidly or it would weaken itself. However, countries were different; there were advantages in growth as well as costs. What one needed was to achieve a reasonable balance between the various factors. He agreed that the results of the correlation stated above, between growth of population and growth of G.N.P. per head, could not hold for the very long run, but one had to remember that if our ancestors in pre-history had found a fruit which rendered them sterile and had never had more than two children, the neolithic revolution would never have happened.

Professor Stone had talked about optimal decline. This had been little studied so far, though there had been examples in history, usually accompanied by catastrophes. But it did seem possible, with much caution, to imagine a decline in population.

M. Sauvy pointed out that today participants were trying to seek positive solutions, but he wanted to introduce a new point of view. One could ask whether an additional member of a population would make it richer or poorer. If he were poorer than us, the average of income would be lower, but we would not be poorer than before. Everything depended on how we made the calculation. For example, in an agricultural population, an immigrant might come to a poor area. If he were poorer than the existing inhabitants, *average* income would fall, but the income of the *original inhabitants* would be as high as before, perhaps higher.

M. Sauvy used an analogy. We were in a railway coach and all the seats were taken. If a man came and slept in the corridor, we would be as well off as before, but the 'average comfort' of the passengers as a whole would have fallen.

Malthus was 'Malthusian' because he saw the poor in the U.K. taking income away from the rich. In France, the higher class was populationist because there was no Poor Law as in Great Britain. These were difficult issues even on the theoretical level. As for the problems of the regions, one should stick to the nation as the basis. In many nations the main task was to reduce the birth-rate. Theories were useless; the real issues were the practical difficulties.

Professor Guillaumont agreed with Professor Hicks in his comments on his paper. But while he would agree that one might not want much population growth in Zanzibar, he still felt that, in general, one ought not to take a definite position but should respect local political choices. After all, trade-off was a political problem.

Technical objections had been made to his comparison of stable rates of population growth, but it was clear that a stable rate could be an optimum. All he had done was to try to compare growth rates, and look at their effect on income per head. The relationship between population growth and the economic optimum seemed important, even if one were uncertain about levels.

In his diagram, he had shown the rates of growth in a number of countries with more than 1 million inhabitants. As with M. Sauvy, he had found very little correlation between population growth and growth of income per head.

However, he observed that the scatter diagram roughly divided itself in two parts, associated with industrialised countries, on one hand, and with under-developed countries, on the other. The upper points of each part of the diagram reached a maximum at a certain intermediate rate of demographic growth: this rate seemed to permit the maximum growth of income per head, but without ensuring it. This was perhaps a necessary, but not a sufficient, condition. He thought there was a need for some concept of optimal population growth, as that which maximised the potential increase in real output per head, even though the increase in real output was not a good measure of welfare.

He agreed that, in the very long run, the optimum rate of population growth would be zero. So, if demographic growth had economic advantages, it would be reasonable to grow, but not too quickly in the short run. Some countries would benefit from growth. What one needed was not a reduction of population but an optimum rate of slowing down population growth. It would be interesting to analyse this type of problem in many different demographic situations. Some choices nevertheless had to be made. Perhaps one should agree with Sismondi, who said that the rate of growth should allow a comfortable standard of living for the whole population. Then one would be interested in the level of income that was compatible with some objective like maximising the rate of population growth.

Here one came back to policy issues and the need for trade-offs between different periods. One needed to define optimal population growth, which was a political notion with different values for each country. The value of children would find a place in this calculation, as would the effect of population growth on income distribution. Everything would depend on the trade-off between the future and the present, and between social groups, but the analysis must be based, in part, on an economic analysis of some of the effects of population growth.

Professor Guillaumont said that participants should remember that his doubts sprang from the fact that some factors were very difficult to evaluate. For example, the effects of growth on accumulation were important, and modified the situation, but he was doing no more than state hypotheses. However, there were historical arguments that needed to be considered, and data of various kinds. Motivations were affected by population growth, as was social capital, and the optimum growth of population depended on the factors underlying the situation. Some variables in the analysis were obviously important, but the problem was how to handle them.

Professor Robinson wished to be allowed to add a frivolous comment. Fifty years back, he had been taught by Professor Pigou, who was a keen mountain climber. On one occasion, Professor Pigou had talked about optimum population, using the then current concepts of comparative statics. Dr Dalton, then at the London School of Economics, had recently written a small book on optimum population. Pigou, lecturing about it, said that an optimum population could perhaps best be understood by thinking of the kind of load that one would take if climbing a mountain. One had to know how much helped and how much hindered. Dr Dalton appeared to have described the optimum population in terms of a mountaineer with a rucksack that was so full that he could just stand still. For every step upwards he slid back one step. Professor Pigou preferred to define optimum population in terms of an almost empty rucksack, containing only a few sandwiches and the minimum amount of equipment which would enable him to climb rapidly. Professor Robinson was worried because the conference gave him the impression that it thought the optimal load was one which allowed the climber to make no progress at all, or just failed to pull him backwards into a crevasse.

Professor Hicks thought that Professor Robinson had misunderstood him. In criticising the concept of an optimum population, he certainly did not intend to suggest that one growth curve might not be preferable to another. He was simply saying that determining a static population, to which one wanted to move, was not very helpful. Progress was bound to be slow; the other things affecting the situation, and so determining the optimum in fifty or a hundred years time, were so difficult to analyse that there was not much point in using it as an objective. He was not in the least denying the need to decide, with current information, that one course of action would be better than another.

He wanted to make another point, and felt that he could do this best in a static context, although he was convinced that it could be generalised. Suppose one looked at the position statically, and one found the hypothetical curve of returns. Technical change would shift this curve upwards. So, at a given population, one would get a higher return. However, there was no necessary reason why the shift should be uniform, moving the curve upwards at all levels of the population. The effect on social product would be different if the population was different. The fact that one got a given change with an existing population of a given size, did not necessarily mean that one could not get a larger improvement with a different population. This was essentially a negative point, but it needed bearing in mind.

Part Two

Fertility as an Exercise in Choice

4 Determinants of Fertility: a Micro-economic Model of Choice[1]

Paul Schultz

UNIVERSITY OF MINNESOTA

I. INTRODUCTION

There are many explanations of why human fertility varies from one society to another and among different groups or individuals within the same society. Attempts to identify and measure the factors that affect fertility and hence to discriminate among current competing causal hypotheses have not been notably successful. This gap in our basic stock of knowledge is both a source of embarrassment to social scientists and an obstacle to the strategic formulation and tactical evaluation of population policies throughout the world.

In this paper I shall stress one framework for interpreting reproductive behaviour, that, in my judgement, holds promise of accounting for certain aspects of fertility and of relating these aspects in a consistent manner to other important forms of household decision-making. Areas of household non-market choice, of which fertility is a complex but readily measured example, have recently drawn increased interest from economists, but the field remains in a state of flux. For this economic approach to yield empirically refutable propositions, broad constraints must be imposed on the more general theory, and at this time it is unclear which set of constraints least impair the model's realism. My objective is to restate the central theoretical elements of this approach to the determinants of fertility, explore briefly unsolved problems with this schema, and speculate on its usefulness.

[1] This paper was written with the support of the Economic Development Center of the University of Minnesota, from a U.S.A.I.D. 211(D) grant for the Conference on Economic Factors in Population Growth of the International Economic Association, September 1973, Valescure, France. It is an elaboration of the paper I presented at the 1972 A.E.A. Meetings in Toronto. I also draw on earlier research supported at the Rand Corporation by a grant from the Rockefeller Foundation; contract NIH 71-2211 from the Center for Population Research, National Institute of Child Health and Human Development, and contracts csd 2151 and 2533 from U.S.A.I.D.

II. TASTES AND BIOLOGICAL DETERMINANTS
OF FERTILITY

If variations in fertility across individuals and groups were a purely random phenomenon, a theory of fertility would have little point. But there is widespread agreement that two sources of systematic variation in fertility warrant a place in any theory of fertility determination – *biological factors* that constrain the reproductive process and determine fecundity or the potential supply of births, and conscious and inadvertent differences in *behavioural factors* that modify the extent to which the biological maximum is realised.

For the policy-maker the more interesting factors affecting fertility are those that can be influenced by administratively and politically feasible policies.[1] Since my continuing objective is to discover promising policy options to facilitate economic and demographic development, I shall emphasise factors that are plausibly linked to policy instruments.

Moreover, numerous factors that might exert some systematic, though presumably minor, effect on fertility are not individually distinguished in the scope of this paper. In formulating a simple statistical model from a conceptual framework, these omitted and frequently unobserved factors are unavoidably relegated to a seemingly random disturbance term. In addition, a substantial fraction of the variability in *individual* reproductive behaviour is in no sense systematic or predictable, resulting from truly stochastic parameters to underlying biological processes.[2] A difficulty with the analytical approach proposed in Section III is that the disturbance term in the resulting statistical model of fertility determination subsumes both true stochastic variability in reproductive behaviour as well as systematic differences in individual fecundity and tastes.

[1] For example, more analytical attention might be given to the relationship between the educational attainment of parents and their fertility than to the relationship between desired family size and fertility. The former relation is subject to obvious policy instruments and can be projected accurately for a cohort as it ages; the latter relation is not yet reliably affected by policy options and has not, to my knowledge, been projected for a cohort with great precision.

[2] It should not be surprising therefore that it is possible to account for a larger fraction of the differences in average reproductive behaviour across groups because these stochastic elements cancel out and the systematic factors appear to 'explain' more of the aggregate variation in fertility. Conversely, it is more difficult to account for the reproductive behaviour of individual families, for a larger share of the variation in fertility will stem from purely random factors and the systematic factors will 'explain' a smaller share of the observed variation in fertility. Appropriate tests of statistical significance, therefore, are *not* explanatory power (i.e., R^2) but the magnitude and sign of estimated coefficients (i.e., effects) relative to their standard errors, or asymptotic standard errors where simultaneous equations or non-linear estimation techniques are required to obtain consistent estimates.

How might this limitation of the current specification of the demand theory of fertility distort or bias subsequent interpretation of empirical evidence on the behavioural responsiveness of fertility to individual and group characteristics?

Biological constraints on fecundity

Expected fecundity of the female varies systematically with age. The proportion of women biologically *incapable* of child-bearing appears to increase gradually with maturity after about the age of 20, and *increase* sharply after 40. By the time women reach the age of 50, virtually all are sterile. In several non-contracepting populations of proven fecundity (i.e., they subsequently had children), intervals between births are also observed to increase gradually from about 24 months for women in the 20–24 age group to about 31 months for the 35–39 age group (Henry, 1966). Thus, both the probability of being incapable of bearing a child and the time required on average for fecund couples to have a child appear to increase with age.

The onset of sterility and the spacing of births may also be influenced somewhat by diet, general health, prevalence of specific diseases, and the prior pattern of child-bearing and breast feeding. It is widely believed that the time between a birth and the reappearance of ovulation is an increasing function of the duration and intensity of the mother's suckling. Since some of these secondary biological effects on fecundity, holding age constant, can be *behaviourally* influenced by social custom or individual choice, observed differences in fecundity might reflect in part differences in desired fertility that could be accounted for within a behavioural framework.[1] The distinction between biological and behavioural determinants of fertility is thus a difficult one to draw, in practice, except where the conditioning factor is clearly exogenous, that is, not subject to individual or even to social choice, such as with age.

Much work is under way characterising the biological determinants of fecundity, but I have not yet found a consensus on how measures of lactation practices, diet, or health status of the mother, for example, affect the duration of postpartum sterility, the rate of conception, or the rate of foetal mortality. Moreover, the values of the essential parameters of these stochastic models of reproduction

---

[1] A mother is free to vary her lactation practices depending upon her desired rate of conception. This decision may also influence the incidence of child mortality among her infants, for mortality is sometimes more frequent among those weaned before the second year of life (Wyon and Gordon, 1971). Also the incidence of pregnancy wastage is clearly affected by a woman's regime of work, diet, etc., and differential spontaneous abortion, miscarriage and stillbirth rates probably reflect more than purely stochastic variability (Freedman and Coombs, 1966; James, 1969).

are generally drawn from casual clinical literature that leaves much to be desired. Only very recently have such parameters as, for example, those linking lactation to intervals between births, been estimated satisfactorily within the context of an explicit stochastic framework. These findings have not yet, to my knowledge, been replicated for different populations.[1] This weak empirical foundation for models of fecundity is undoubtedly related to the complexity of the pertinent biological processes, but it is also a function of the scarcity of longitudinal analyses of individual reproductive histories and the likelihood that these studies are contaminated by induced 'behavioural' variation in reproductive performance.[2]

Finally, in most contemporary societies the biological maximum fecundity is not a binding constraint on the desired reproductive behaviour of a substantial fraction of parents over their entire life cycle. Undoubtedly there have been historical periods when a majority of parents failed to rear to maturity the number of children they wanted, perhaps because of severe child mortality. But in most low-income countries these conditions no longer exist. Child mortality has been falling for three decades or more, and evidence from both anthropology and sociology suggests that a majority of parents in these countries have for some time exercised individual choice or adopted social conventions to limit their reproductive performance. There are also historical instances when the spread or control of specific diseases may have affected fecundity, such as in certain of the Pacific Islands in the nineteenth and twentieth centuries (Pirie, 1972). But such cases are always difficult to document, and are often transparent means for denying the importance of elusive behavioural factors in the control of fertility.[3]

[1] Jain's dissertation (1968) develops a stochastic model of human reproduction and estimates empirically the effect on fecundity of socio-economic factors holding constant (approximately) for duration of lactation across a sample of Taiwanese women. (See also Jain *et al.*, 1970, T. P. Schultz and DaVanzo, 1970.) Studies of child mortality have also begun to use individual survey data and more persuasive methods of multivariate analysis, for example, Shah and Abbey (1971).

[2] Unfortunately, longitudinal histories that include the necessary demographic, economic and biological/nutrition/health information to estimate such a model are still uncommon (Butz, 1972; Butz and T. P. Schultz, 1972; T. P. Schultz and DaVanzo, 1970). Theoretical work in this direction is being undertaken by Robert Michael and Robert Willis at the National Bureau of Economic Research, to gain a better understanding of the determinants of contraceptive behaviour. Their investigation is proceeding in the tradition of Sheps and Perrin (1963), Sheps (1965), Henry (1972), and Mencken and Sheps (1973).

[3] Reynolds Farley's *Growth of the Black Population* (Chicago: Markham Press, 1970) is surely such an instance, where the economic depression is ignored as a possible cause for the drop in U.S. Negro fertility during the 1930s, whereas, on the other hand, the spread of venereal disease is emphasised as a possible explanation (pp. 215–35).

Although the relative importance and range of individual and societal modes of reproduction control are as yet unclear, it is well established that biological constraints on fecundity are today relatively unimportant in accounting for systematic differences in fertility, except perhaps across societies with very different standards of living or endemic disease.

In sum, important differences in biological fecundity are associated with the ageing process.[1] But within age-stratified groups in a given society, differences in a woman's expected fecundity may stem from either exogenous factors, such as perhaps regional health problems, or from endogenous factors, such as prolonged lactation or induced abortion, that may be behaviourally determined with the intention of affecting fertility. Ordinary least-squares estimates of the fertility effects of changes in an exogenous motivating (demand) factor will reflect both the direct effects (via endogenous behavioural channels such as the practice of birth control, etc.) and the indirect effects (via endogenous biological factors).[2] If, as seems intuitively reasonable, exogenous differences in a woman's expected fecundity are not usually correlated with exogenous factors affecting her demand for births, proxies for exogenous biological fecundity may be omitted from the demand model of fertility determination and, if this is true, pose no estimation problems. Moreover, as fecundity becomes a less binding constraint on women having at least the number of children they want, and birth-control technology reduces the cost of curbing excess fecundity, the demand framework should

---

[1] Age in a cross section is also associated with birth cohort effects, and will tend to capture time-variant determinants of fertility that are omitted or measured with systematic error in a predictive model. Willis (1973) for example includes a quadratic in age when he considers in one regression equation the number of children ever born to currently married U.S. white women in 1960 between the ages of 35 and 64 (Table 2, S50). The quadratic in age accounts for part of the cycle in cohort fertility associated with the baby boom. But what is more interesting, the inclusion of three 'economic' determinants of desired fertility (measured contemporaneously) in the regression equation does not modify greatly the explanatory role of the quadratic in age. These results reinforce evidence from other sources that the broad aggregate time-trends in fertility are not yet adequately explained by available evidence assembled in the micro-economic framework.

[2] This net or combined direct and indirect effect of the exogenous variable on fertility is the appropriate estimate for the purposes of policy evaluation unless the structure underlying the relationship can be modified in addition to changing the value of the exogenous variable. Ordinary least squares will provide biased estimates of the causal relationship if either the endogenous direct behavioural (birth control) or indirect biological (lactation) variables are included in the model. Simultaneous equation estimation techniques are then required to obtain unbiased estimates of the structural components underlying the simple correlations among endogenous variables.

account for an increasing share of observed variation in completed fertility.

Demand and the role of tastes

Reproductive behaviour is often associated with the socio-economic characteristics of parents, and these empirical regularities are then attributed to differences among parents in their preferences for offspring. Parents derive intangible rewards and in some cases pecuniary transfers from their children, and differences in their evaluation of these returns are undoubtedly responsible for certain cross-sectional and time-series variations in fertility. The importance of 'tastes' in determining desired fertility is widely emphasised (Easterlin, 1969), but the operational significance of this interpretation is rarely made explicit. To the economist, tastes differ among individuals if they behave differently when confronted by the same prices and endowed with the same resources and productive technology. If tastes are thus defined as the variability in behaviour unexplained by economic constraints, the concept of taste acquires substantive content only when their distribution is related to observable phenomena, or more generally, a model of taste-formation is postulated with refutable empirical implications.[1]

Lacking a psychological theory that specifies relationships between observable characteristics of parents, except perhaps for religion, and their 'tastes' for children, this line of inquiry has not yet been notably productive.[2] Given the non-pecuniary context in

---

[1] Such a model of taste formation is verbally stated by Easterlin (1968) and Fuchs (1956). The hypothesis is essentially that individuals develop their expectation for an acceptable material standard of living on the basis of the economic status of their parents when they are teenagers. If the economic fortunes of the children are better than they anticipated, they feel they can 'afford' somewhat more children than secular trends would predict, and vice versa. Children are essentially supernumerary expenditures that absorb the excess or shortfall of actual to anticipated incomes. The cohort born and raised during the Great Depression, hence, contributed to the postwar baby boom, whereas the offspring of the baby boom are not faring as well as they expected, in part because of their cohort's relatively large size. Consequently, the cohort born in the 1950s is now contributing to the sharp decline in birth-rates in the United States. Though this model may have considerable predictive power to account for cross-sectional and disaggregated time-series variation in fertility in all high-income countries, it has been tested only to a limited extent against U.S. aggregate time series.

[2] To propose that unexplained differences in reproductive behaviour among race or religious groups reflect differences in 'tastes' is, in my judgement, to mask our ignorance. An alternative approach to searching for the sources of ethnic group differences is evident in the observation that Catholic women with a college education have more children than non-Catholics with the same education, but that these

which child satisfactions are obtained by parents,[1] and the highly subjective and intangible nature of certain 'tastes' for parenthood, there is no obvious way presently at hand to integrate and analyse the role of tastes within a theory of fertility.

It is common, therefore, to assume that all individuals share the same utility function embodying their basic preferences. Differences among individuals in appraising specific goods are then attributed to differences in their environmental constraints of which some are assumed to be stochastic.[2] In other words, people are assumed to prefer different amounts of a specific good, even when prices and resources appear to be constant, because of a combination of numerous specific but unobserved 'taste' factors, each independently normally distributed across populations. Pragmatically, the sum of these specific taste-effects on fertility can be represented by a well-behaved disturbance term in a statistical model designed to analyse systematic sources of variation in reproductive behaviour.[3]

---

differences are insignificant between women with lesser education. Implicitly two working hypotheses may be entertained. Is it the Catholic college experience that contributes to 'taste' formation in the United States, or do those with such family-formed tastes elect to enrol in Catholic colleges? Empirical tests can be imagined to refine further one's understanding of the ultimate source of ethnic fertility differentials. It is also obvious, that when one stops with distinguishing differences in behaviour among ethnic groups, one has provided little useful knowledge to the policy-maker which has no leverage on group identification.

[1] In most societies parents are encouraged to satisfy only their own demand for children. With an imperfect market for exchange, children represent a classic example of a non-market commodity that is produced only for the final consumer. Specialisation in child production is uncommon, therefore, except under unusual circumstances (see S. Chueng, 1972).

[2] Alternatively, it may be assumed that parent tastes for children vary and are distributed across populations in a specific fashion. This representation of tastes is in some respects more appealing than the abstraction of a 'representative individual', and in certain circumstances it implies different response estimates from the same empirical evidence. For example, when observations are obtained on only a portion of a population, the distribution of tastes may be estimated by analysing both pieces of evidence: data on the observed population, and the proportion of the population observed with differing characteristics. Gronau (1973*a*, 1973*b*) has used this formulation to study the shadow price of a housewife's time, when market wages are observed for only the portion of the female population that is currently in the labour force.

[3] It is nonetheless important to probe beneath personal values and social norms to determine how they mould individual preferences and the related roles of culture and genetics. But measurable, variable, and potentially policy-manipulatable elements of the individual and his culture are difficult to discern. How important is it to the policy-maker (in contrast with the projector or planner) that Catholics want more children than Protestants? Yet, however conceptualised and quantified, the influence of these 'taste' factors can be properly assessed only after the tangible pecuniary returns have also been isolated and taken into account.

III. THE DEMAND FOR CHILDREN

The family's choice of final consumption activities is constrained by its market income and the time of its members, and typically, exogenous market-wage opportunities provide the rate of exchange between these two scarce inputs in household consumption (Mincer, 1963; Becker, 1965). Since the activity of child-bearing and rearing absorbs a substantial fraction of the family's available time and market income, this general formulation of household demand suggests that one would not expect parents to be indifferent for long to their reproductive behaviour. Can one conclude, therefore, that exogenous differences in market prices, wages and incomes will have a significant bearing on reproductive behaviour? Is the microeconomic framework of choice useful in structuring empirical research on the critical relationships between fertility and the exogenous features of the parents' environment and endowments? These questions have not yet been answered to everyone's satisfaction, but a number of recent empirical studies[1] have interpreted with some success reproductive behaviour as a response to the relative scarcity of resources available to the household and the costs of children. But important unresolved problems remain, as I shall indicate later.

The resource constrained choice framework for understanding the determinants of *demand* for births should eventually incorporate the salient biological, technical and behavioural constraints on the reproductive process that influence the *supply* of births. But as noted above, the biological, psychological and technical factors affecting both the supply and demand of births are not yet adequately identified or conveniently formulated for inclusion in the demand model. Despite these shortcomings, the economic framework of constrained choice appears to provide a general way of approaching the factors dictated exogenously by the environment which presumably motivate parents to want a smaller or larger number of births. Ultimately the test of the usefulness of this simplified approach will be its predictive and integrative power in comparison with alternative frameworks. It would be premature to attempt such an evaluation at this time.[2] In the remainder of this paper I shall

---

[1] The bibliography cites many of these studies. For example, see Becker, 1960; Mincer, 1963; T. P. Schultz, 1969 and a collection of studies in *New Economic Approaches to Fertility*, ed. T. W. Schultz, *Journal of Political Economy*, Supp. 81:2, pt. II, Mar/Apr 1973. A second conference volume will appear in a Mar/Apr 1974 supplement to the *Journal of Political Economy*.

[2] The most obvious reason to postpone such an evaluation is the absence of any comparable alternative structure of logical hypotheses with empirical implications, against which the economic demand model might be judged. Also, the current

consider some of the problems in restricting this formulation of the demand model of fertility to obtain refutable predictions, I shall suggest the difficulty of translating the conceptualised constraints into empirically-observed proxies, and I shall discuss some of the theoretical and econometric problems of identifying and estimating the structure to the household behavioural system, of which fertility is an integral part, when the dynamic life-cycle character of the family unit is explicitly recognised. A mathematical statement of the constrained maximisation approach in the two-good case is presented in the Appendix.

The resources that individuals allocate over their lifetime are ultimately their own time and their initial stock of non-human wealth. It is assumed that time is allocated between two classes of activities: (i) those that yield money, goods or services which can be readily exchanged in a market, and (ii) those that yield goods or services which cannot be exchanged in a market and are therefore valued by the producer solely for their own consumption. Since eating, sleeping and virtually all forms of final consumption require the input of one's own time, all persons engage in the 'production' of some non-market final consumption goods. It is also assumed that all persons allocate some time to the production of goods and services exchanged in the market-place.[1] In this case, if the net disutility associated with the two classes of activity are assumed identical, the net value of time expended at the margin in market and non-market activities would be equalised. The market wage received by an individual then equals the opportunity value of his time in non-market activities (Becker, 1965).

The effect of changes in income on the demand for children depends, within this framework, on the source of income (Schultz, 1969), and hence the price effect embodied in that source. The lack

---

interest of economists in this topic is hardly a decade old, and a consensus among economists would be hard to come by at this time. Moreover, most of the multi-variate empirical testing of the demand model (see Tables 4.A and 4.B) has been prudently focused on cross-sectional differences in fertility that are partially 'explained' by almost any socio-economic variables. The more severe test of the economic approach will be to predict time-series variation in completed reproductive performance. Whether economic theory has any interesting implications for the optimal timing of family formation (birth intervals, etc.) has not yet been established.

[1] It is conceivable that individuals whose spouse was sufficiently productive in the market or who owned sufficient non-human wealth might allocate *none* of their time to market activities. The occurrence of such a 'corner solution' leaves the individual's non-market allocation of time and shadow price of time dependent upon the value of his marginal productivity in each non-market activity, which is ultimately dependent on his spouse's market-determined value of time, non-human wealth, and non-market production possibilities or technology. See Willis (1971, 1973) and Gronau (1971, 1972).

of an invariant positive relationship between income and fertility cannot be interpreted, even loosely, as a challenge to the relevance of economic scarcity and individual choice to the fertility decision. If children require a fixed amount of their parents' time and market resources, it seems only reasonable to anticipate that an exogenous increase in the parents' stock of *non-human* wealth will shift their demand schedule for children unambiguously to the right. But this simplifying assumption that children can be treated as a homogeneous commodity overlooks the essential link between the number of children parents want and the 'endowments' parents want to give each of their offspring. I shall return to this problem and efforts proposed to deal with it.

Exogenous increases in the household's stock of *human* wealth, as reflected by an increase in a parent's permanent (lifetime average discounted) wage-rate, implies both a positive wealth effect and an offsetting increase in the cost of parents' time required in the care and enjoyment of their children.

For linear homogenous separable household production functions (see Appendix), the elasticity of demand for children with respect to either spouse's wage-rate can be decomposed into a weighted combination of the compensated price-elasticity and income-elasticity of demand for children; the price-elasticity is weighted by the value share of the respective spouse's time in the total cost of children minus the value share of the spouse's time in the cost of producing the composite commodity; the income-elasticity is weighted by the value share of the spouse's market earnings in the household's full income (see Appendix). Stronger assumptions are required to prescribe the sign of the wage elasticities, but plausible magnitudes for these weights suggest that the elasticity of fertility with respect to the wife's wage will be *algebraically* smaller than that with respect to the husband's wage, given the time intensity of children and the predominant role of mothers in child-rearing.

Cross-sectional studies of individual countries at all levels of economic development have confirmed the qualitative predictions of this rudimentary demand theory of fertility.[1] In part because of

[1] I have excluded from this survey cross-country comparisons of fertility and its determinants because of my uneasiness with the data. Not only do the usual problems of relative prices and inconvertible exchange rates make international comparisons of income levels treacherous, but also most of the additional data required to test the propositions discussed in this paper are not meaningfully culled from standard international compendiums. For example, no experienced demographer would accept registered birth and death-rates as satisfactory evidence of fertility and mortality levels in most low-income countries, yet official or registered vital rates are the basis for many international cross-sectional regression analyses. Education statistics have their own problems; female labour force participation

the difficulties of measuring a permanent wage-rate, particularly for women not currently in the paid labour force, education has often been assumed to be a satisfactory proxy for lifetime wage-rates. When fertility is then regressed on the educational level of men and women, the women's education coefficient tends to be negative, as anticipated, and several times its standard error, while the men's education coefficient is smaller in absolute magnitude and generally less significant statistically.[1] When regression analysis deals with average earnings for men and women within regional population aggregates, or earnings of individual couples where the husband and wife are currently working, the t values for the women's earnings coefficient tend to be higher than that for the alternative women's education coefficient, and the regression coefficient is more often positive for men's earnings than it is for men's education.[2]

The predicted positive relation between exogenous differences in non-human wealth and fertility is less often tested, because of the scarcity of information on personal non-human wealth and the endogenous nature of related savings behaviour. Although wage and wealth effects on fertility may go far in explaining cross-sectional differences in fertility in high-income countries, the regime of mortality cannot be neglected in low-income countries. How can this 'demographic' variable, whose recent change is the proximate cause for the population explosion in much of the world, be incorporated into the economic demand model of fertility?

IV. CHILD MORTALITY

If we assume that parents are motivated to bear children to accrue

---

rates reflect local conventions; wage-rates for men and women are rarely compiled and when they are available, they tend to represent only a small segment of the labour force, such as that in modern manufacturing. All the criticisms raised later with reference to cross-sectional studies of regional populations within one country, apply with greater force to cross-sectional studies which span the even greater diversity of national institutions, statistical conventions and cultures.

[1] See for example where both male and female education is considered: Ben Porath (1970, 1973) on Israel; DeTray (1973) U.S. counties; Gardner (1972, 1973) rural U.S.; Hashimoto (1973) Japan; Maurer *et al.*, (1973) Thailand; Michael (1971) suburban U.S.; and Schultz (1973) Taiwan (see Appendix Tables 4.A and 4.B).

[2] See for example where income, earnings or wage-rates of males and females considered: Cain and Weiniger (1971) U.S. S.M.S.A.s; DaVanzo (1972) Chile; DeTray (1973) U.S. counties; Gardner (1973) rural N.C.; and Hashimoto (1973) Japan. Male income and female education are analysed for the U.S. by Sanderson and Willis (1971); Simon (1972); and Willis (1971, 1973). (See Appendix Tables 4.A and 4.B.) Because simultaneous equations bias is probably severe when both education and wages are included as explanatory variables in ordinary regressions on fertility, the empirical results of such studies are difficult to interpret and are not reported here.

benefits from their mature surviving offspring, the effects of child mortality on desired fertility can be divided into two partially offsetting effects on (i) the demand for survivors and (ii) the derived demand for births. Child mortality decreases the number of *survivors* demanded by increasing the expected cost per survivor; it increases the derived demand for *births* by increasing the number of births required to obtain a survivor. The final derived demand for births will respond positively to the incidence of child mortality only if the product of the relative change in expected cost per survivor and the price-elasticity of demand for survivors is less than unity (in absolute value). If a given percentage decline in child mortality reduced by the same relative amount the expected cost to parents of rearing a child to maturity, and the decline in child mortality induced a decline in desired completed fertility, then parent demand for additional surviving children must be inelastic (less than one in absolute value). If the family exhibits a tendency to reduce its completed fertility as the incidence of child mortality declines, this would constitute evidence of a tendency toward demographic stability within the family and imply that parents' demand for surviving children is relatively inelastic (Donald J. O'Hara, 1972; Ben Porath and Finis Welch, 1972).[1]

No one can doubt that parenthood is one of the most risky undertakings that economists have proposed to study, and the above formulation implicitly assumes that parents are risk neutral. The potential importance of uncertainty for understanding shifts in fertility has been stressed in the context of low-income countries where child mortality has declined sharply (T. P. Schultz, 1969), but theoretical consideration of this relationship has only recently begun (O'Hara, 1972; Ben Porath and Welch, 1972), and I know of no empirical evidence as yet that separates the effect on fertility of uncertainty (e.g. variance of the incidence of family child-mortality) from that of the expected or average level of child mortality in the family or region.

---

[1] The elasticity of demand for births, B, with respect to the probability of a child's survival to maturity, P, can be expressed as follows:

$$\eta_{BP} = \eta_{SC}\eta_{CP} - 1$$

where S is the number of births that survive from which parents are assumed to derive utility under risk-neutral assumptions, and C is the expected cost of a surviving child which is assumed to depend inversely on P, and be independent of family size. Since it is known that η_{SC} and η_{CP} are both less than zero, if their product is less than unity, the elasticity of demand for births with respect to the probability of survival will be negative. Ben Porath and Welch (1973) illustratively assume that $\eta_{CP} = -1$, whereas O'Hara indicates why it might exceed in absolute value unity. The positive relationship observed between child mortality and fertility is therefore suggestive of an inelastic demand for surviving children, i.e. $|\eta_{SC}| < 1$.

However, individual and aggregate evidence from a variety of low-income countries indicates that the partial relationship between fertility and child mortality is positive and statistically highly significant in such varied environments and time-periods as Bangladesh (1951–61), Puerto Rico (1950–60), Taiwan (1964–9), Chile (1960), and the Philippines (1968). Where fertility is measured as a birth-rate or probability of birth, the multiple correlation is maximised by lagging the incidence of child mortality two to four years. This is, of course, roughly the average time required for a mother to bear another child. There are persuasive reasons to anticipate that older mothers with nearly completed families will weigh heavily the survival or death of earlier children in their decision whether to have an additional (marginal) child. Consistent with this explanation of reproductive behaviour, estimates of the responsiveness of births to child deaths are larger in magnitude and more significant statistically for women over 30 years of age (DaVanzo, 1972; Schultz and DaVanzo, 1970; Schultz, 1971, 1972). Among these older women, the response of birth-rates is also greater to male child deaths than to female child deaths (T. P. Schultz and DaVanzo, 1970; T. P. Schultz, 1972), presumably reflecting preferences for family sex composition.

The death of a young child may also stimulate a *biologically* independent feedback mechanism that will increase the mother's fecundity. If the child was still fed from the breast at the time of his death, the termination of lactation may shorten the mother's period of postpartum sterility and increase her subsequent fecundity and consequent fertility. But the biological mechanism can play only a small role in the widely-noted robust relationship between birth-rates and prior child deaths, for only the *behavioural* factors deter-mining the demand for (and supply of) births can account for the anticipated variation in this relationship according to the mother's age and by the sex of the child that has died.

I am led to conclude that birth-rates of older mothers respond promptly to changes in child mortality, but these short-run adjust-ments are apparently not always sufficient in magnitude to prevent growth in the size of surviving families as the incidence of child mortality declines. Demand for surviving children appears to be price-inelastic, but far from perfectly inelastic. Analysis of cohort data on completed fertility is now needed to determine whether long-run adjustments of fertility to the changing regime of mortality are in fact also taking place. Future rates of population growth in much of the world hinge on the magnitude and the rate at which these adjustments occur.

A reduction in death-rates at all ages also increases the returns to parents of investments in the 'quality' of children relative to the returns from number of children. If child quality and quantity are close substitutes, this shift in the relative returns may motivate parents to seek fewer children, as they augment the resources they invest in each of their offspring (O'Hara, 1972). Increased life expectancy for parents may contribute to their greater valuation of long gestation investments such as child quality, since they have an increasing chance of being alive at any future date to enjoy these distant returns. In sum, the regimen of mortality exerts diverse influences on the family formation process and associated savings and investment behaviour of the household sector. Although the postwar change in mortality may represent a most significant and pervasive shift in the constraints on household behaviour in low-income countries, this phenomenon has received relatively little attention from economists.

The consistent effects on fertility of the shadow price of the husband's and wife's time, and child mortality, account for a statistically significant share of cross-sectional variation in aggregate and individual reproductive behaviour. Encouraging though these empirical results may seem, there still are ambiguities and limitations to this conceptual approach and its current empirical application. In the remaining space allotted to me, I shall comment on a few of the unresolved problems that I find most challenging.

V. THE RESOURCE INTENSITY OF CHILD-REARING

Earlier it was suggested that viewing children as a homogeneous commodity from which parents obtained a uniform flow of 'child services' neglects the qualitative dimensions of child-rearing over which parents exercise some choice. Reproductive motivations are closely related to the amount of time, energy and resources parents want to invest in each of their offspring (Becker, 1960). Widely-observed empirical regularities suggest that parents have a tendency to trade off resource intensity per child for numbers of children (e.g. T. P. Schultz, 1969, 1970, 1971; DaVanzo, 1972).[1] Understanding the

---

[1] Child schooling rates are often more highly (negatively) correlated with fertility than are educational attainments of mothers. Conversely, a positive partial correlation is generally observed between fertility and the rate at which young children enter the labour force in low-income countries. See for example, T. P. Schultz (1969, 1970, 1971); Nerlove and T. P. Schultz (1970); DaVanzo (1972); Maurer *et al.*, (1973). One might conjecture that parents in some poor populations borrow, on balance, from their children over their lifetime rather than invest in them (T. P. Schultz, 1971). Increased attention to the implicitly producer-good (capital) attributes of children may yield additional insights into the determinants of fertility in low-income countries. I have not seen any evidence of a theoretical or empirical nature that might distinguish whether children should be treated as a consumer or producer durable good in the refinement of a demand theory of fertility.

determinants of this trade-off promises to account for much of the systematic variability in fertility in both high- and low-income countries.

Progress in this direction, however, has been slow for at least two reasons. Unrealistic restrictions must be posited, apparently, to obtain refutable predictions from models of family choice in which both parents may contribute through their market earnings and own-time to the production of *three* final consumption commodities, say for example, the number of children, child quality, and other commodities.[1] Second, and more obvious, it is unclear how to quantify the resource cost or consumer value of child quality in focusing empirical research along these lines.

The most interesting theoretical effort to restrict the general three-good model to obtain an analytical reduced-form expression for the derived demand for numbers of children is by Willis (1971). He assumed that the husband does not contribute to household production, holding fixed his full-time labour force participation. With standard assumptions regarding linear homogeneous, separable, production functions and non-reversal of factor intensities, the derived demand for numbers of children is analytically deduced for (i) households in which the wife works in the labour force and (ii) for households in which she does not. Two novel implications follow: an increase in the husband's lifetime wage increases the demand for children by a greater amount if the wife engages in market work; an increase in the wife's education (i.e. market-specific human capital) has a deterrent effect on demand for children *only* if she is engaged in market work. Further extensions of this work (Willis, 1973) treat the wife's labour-force participation decision as endogenous and jointly determined with desired fertility, but this important step toward greater realism is achieved with a serious loss of refutable predictions.

The merit of this model for empirical work rests on the degree to which wives who are out of the labour force are engaged solely in the production of non-market (untradeable) consumption commodities, in Becker's (1965) sense of the word. If instead, non-

---

[1] Without additional restrictions, the only qualitative prediction is the positive sign of the effect of non-human wealth on the demand for both quality and quantity. DeTray (1973) estimated a special form of this model with U.S. county aggregate data and found that the wealth-elasticity of demand for quality per child was not significantly different from zero.

Becker and Gregg Lewis (1973) and Willis (1973) have also explored the implications for demand analysis of the multiplicative interaction between child quality and quantity that enters the household's budget constraint if it is assumed that to change child quality marginally, a parent must also change the quality investments in all intramarginal children.

participant wives are producing at the margin substitutes for market goods and services, as well as final consumption commodities, then the process of factor-price equalisation and the determinants of derived demands are identical for the two classes of households. In high-income societies the analogy between labour-force activity and home production, on the one hand, and Becker's market goods and non-market commodities, on the other, has some appeal. But it is hazardous to extend this formulation to low-income societies where handicrafts, cottage industries, and local barter-markets provide many points of contact between relative market prices and the allocation of a housewife's time. In the low-income environment where market specialisation is less developed, it is hardly surprising that both spouses will typically produce at home some goods that the household will also purchase or sell in the market. The converse might also be a maintained hypothesis in high-income countries, namely, as market specialisation proceeds, husbands will increasingly have a comparative advantage to contribute their time to the production of more non-market consumption commodities, such as children. The realism of Willis's model for high-income countries is, therefore, also conjectural.

If further refinement of the three-good model is not to rely entirely on 'corner solutions', empirical research may have to provide sharper guidance on how theoretical restrictions are to be imposed. What are the economies of scale in the production of numbers of children and child quality; how are these outputs interrelated to other household consumption activities; can production trade-offs be estimated from changes in the relative prices of these other, more nearly marketed, household activities; can one infer, directly or indirectly, more about the manner in which parents assess quality in their offspring, which ultimately must motivate their transmission to children of genetic potential, inherited wealth, education advantage, economic opportunity and culture?

VI. PROBLEMS OF EMPIRICAL INFERENCE AND MODEL SPECIFICATION

As this framework of constrained choice has been adapted to analyse a growing body of data on reproductive behaviour, it is becoming clear that one has difficulty inferring the direction, magnitude and timing of causality from partial correlations among the seemingly relevant variables in a cross-section. Elements of the approach require reformulation, the distinction in each specific context between endogenous and exogenous variables requires more explicit consideration, and finally, improved statistical techniques appear necessary to estimate the underlying structural relations without substantial bias.

Observations on exogenous differences in wage-rates and non-earned income, from which price and income effects might be estimated without simultaneous equations bias, are hard to come by. Virtually all of the decisions parents make over the lifetime affect the subsequent structure of incentives bearing on fertility, and most individuals recognise that their current choices modify these future options. Therefore, many attributes of the household and its members that reflect past or current choices cannot be treated as exogenous to the fertility decision.[1] Proxies that appear initially useful as measures of the opportunity cost of children or of given resource constraints must ultimately be treated as endogenous variables in a broader simultaneous system of behavioural equations.

Mate selection, the life-cycle timing of marriage and the allocation of both spouses' time between market and non-market activities are decisions that are intimately related to similar price and income variables as well as underlying tastes.[2] The extension of fertility models to encompass additional areas of jointly and simultaneously determined household choices has confirmed the importance of interactions among at least these three forms of behaviour: reproduction, the incidence of marriage (legal and consensual, where distinguished) and the sex division of labour-market participation within the family (DaVanzo, 1972; Frieden, 1972; Harman, 1970; Maurer *et al.*, 1973; Nerlove and T. P. Schultz, 1970; T. P. Schultz, 1970). Beyond this core, models of household decision-making might

---

[1] Ordinary least-squares estimates of the structural relationship determining fertility will not have the desirable property of 'consistency' unless all explanatory variables are uncorrelated with the disturbance in the fertility equation. Nor can lagged values of endogenous variables be treated as independent of the disturbance in relationships accounting for the same or related forms of current behaviour, for well-known reasons. For example, the probability that a woman works in the paid labour force will in general not be independent of the disturbance in the relation accounting for her fertility. Labour-force participation patterns earlier in her life-cycle are also influenced by observed and unobserved features of her environment that will be highly serially correlated, and that will continue to affect not only her labour-force participation but also reproductive behaviour. Clearly, individual tastes for children and more generally tastes for a wider array of market and non-market goods may be such an unobserved variable influencing both forms of behaviour. In such a dynamic system of household behavioural relations, simultaneous equations estimators would appear generally appropriate for the study of structural equations determining fertility.

[2] For example, the educational attainment of the wife, which I regarded above as an exogenous determinant of the opportunity cost of her time in child-bearing, is *not* an exogenous variable with respect to her husband's wage-rate, education, or tastes for children. The selection of mates is undoubtedly responsible for the high simple correlation between educational attainments of spouses.

be reasonably extended to incorporate additional allocative choices
that are also probably endogenous to the determination of fertility,
such as savings and non-human capital formation, migration and, as
emphasised in the preceding section, the resource intensity of the
child-rearing process.

But these simultaneous equations models are still formulated in
static terms and tested, most often, against cross-sectional data from
one point in time. Though I would not deny that this abstraction
has proven a powerful generalising device, little attention has as yet
been given to the question of what economic theory and statistical
techniques can say about dynamic models of behaviour. Reproduction occurs sequentially, and the constraints on child-bearing
affect many other areas of economic and demographic decision-
making in the household and are influenced themselves by past
reproductive behaviour.[1]

In cross-sectional studies, explanatory variables are at best
discretely lagged a few years, as noted with regard to child-death
rates, to represent the time required for reproduction to respond and
for birth-control information to take effect (T. P. Schultz, 1971). But
the stochastic biological nature of the reproductive process and the
numerous neglected features of the individual that could affect
reaction times suggest that a distributed lag would be more
appropriate to the study of changes in fertility. Identification and
estimation of these lag structures are, nonetheless, difficult because
of the limited availability of time-series information and the strong
positive serial correlation (over time) of relevant characteristics of
regional populations or individuals, such as wages, non-human
wealth, industrial structure, and schooling.

There is as yet little evidence on the magnitude of parameter bias
introduced by mis-specifying the dynamic process determining
fertility by static approximations estimated from a single cross-
section of observations. In one instance, I report estimates of the
identical demand model for birth-rates from Taiwan first based on
cross-sectional data and then based on combined time-series of
cross-sections, where a dynamic two-component Nerlovian model
of the pooled disturbances is postulated (T. P. Schultz, 1973).
Parameter estimates shift substantially between the traditional
pooled cross-sectional formulation and the dynamic specification
that utilises both dimensions of the time series of cross-sections. The
changes in parameter estimates conform to those predicted by theory
when appropriate weight is ascribed to time-series variation in the

[1] Sanderson and Willis (1971) use numerical simulation and dynamic programming
techniques to explore this sequential family formation process, but unfortunately
there is no empirical foundation for most of their specifications.

estimation procedure. Cross-sectional estimates of the impact on birth-rates of slowly changing environmental constraints, such as child mortality[1] and wage-rates, tend to be biased upward or distorted (see Table 4.A, columns 8a and 8b). Conversely, factors that are less highly serially correlated over time, such as recent family-planning activities, tend to be attributed too small an impact when estimated from a cross-section. Thus, estimates of the parameters to such a dynamic behavioural process may be seriously biased, if they rely only on the information contained in a single cross-section.

Finally, the character of family size suggests that *linear* demand models are too restrictive for the study of fertility. Both theoretical arguments (Willis, 1973) and empirical evidence (Ben Porath, 1973; Hashimoto, 1973; Simon, 1972) have been presented for non-linearity between explanatory variables and fertility. But at a more fundamental level, there is the question of how to specify the utility function with regard to numbers of children, and how the production function for children changes with scale.[2] Linear demand models presuppose that the desirability of *all* increments to family size are affected identically by shifts in economic constraints. It seems reasonable now to study separately the sequential binary choices made in the family-formation process; this approach would in fact determine whether price and income effects differ by birth order.

[1] For example, the systematic portion of the regime of mortality is determined by such slowly changing factors as long-term investments in public health, sanitation, water supplies and transportation, or geography and climate, or socio-economic characteristics of the population, and thus interregional differences in child mortality contain a relatively stable component over time. High positive serial correlation in regional differences in mortality implies that cross-sectional observations on mortality in any single time period contain substantial information about the interregional differences that existed five, ten and perhaps even twenty years earlier. If the factors increasing mortality over the long term were associated with higher levels of fertility in the cross-section, the positive observed relationship between child mortality and fertility would overestimate the direct short-run influence of a change in child mortality on fertility. If the association between the long-term determinants of mortality and fertility were causal, then the observed cross-sectional relationship between child mortality and fertility would also spuriously overstate the long-run influence of mortality on fertility.

[2] Recently Leibenstein (1973) has proposed a new economic framework within which to interpret fertility declines that stress the parity specific benefits and costs of having children. He suggests that the marginal cost declines with additions to the family, and the marginal benefit may increase before it ultimately declines. But the principal thesis of the paper is the importance of 'status goods' which, it is asserted, claim an increasing share of expenditures in a given status group as development compresses the social structure of personal incomes. Until further theoretical elaboration of his approach is set forth, or empirical proxies and methods of application are proposed, I do not see how the framework could be challenged (or illuminated) by obvious sources of data.

VII. EMPIRICAL APPLICATIONS OF THE FRAMEWORK

I have summarised in Appendix Tables A and B some of the salient empirical findings of several recent investigations into the determinants of fertility that have been guided by this model of constrained choice. Great caution should be exercised in interpreting these distilled results, for analytical detail and the questions addressed by the authors differ. Since no consensus has yet emerged on the 'appropriate' specification of the demand model of fertility, investigators have made do with very different sources of data, different proxies for the essential economic variables, and different 'control' variables. None the less, the collected tableau suggests patterns, as mentioned earlier in the paper, and may provide a convenient set of references to a scattered literature.

VIII. IMPLICATIONS FOR PUBLIC POLICY

It is premature to suggest that the demand approach to understanding the determinants of fertility has yet shed much light on the design and evaluation of population policy. The framework, however, challenges the adequacy of current procedures for evaluating the success of family planning, brings into sharper focus a variety of unconventional policy instruments to affect indirectly fertility while advancing other social goals, and raises fundamental questions about the validity of commonly encountered rationales for direct incentive payments to parents in order to slow rapid population growth.

The most common approach to evaluating family-planning programmes is to measure the programme's output of services per unit of input. Information on the age of individuals accepting a method of birth control in the programme and the clinically estimated effectiveness of the method they adopt yields a sophisticated measure of the *potential* number of births averted by the programme's services. But no method has been devised to estimate the extent to which programme-subsidised services replace or substitute for other higher cost and perhaps less reliable sources of birth control available in the private market-place. The more price-inelastic is parent demand for children, the smaller would be the real effect of a family-planning programme on the birth-rate, as a fraction of this potential effect of its services.

If the evaluation of population policies is to be substantially improved, the tenuous link between the distribution of family-planning services and the resultant decline in births must be statistically verified. Indirect inferences cannot be avoided, for there are unobserved links in the complex chain of events that in this case relate policy instruments to ultimate policy objectives. The demand approach to fertility determination stresses the need to identify and to allow for the influence of changing economic and demographic constraints on the household sector that are likely to be changing desired reproductive behaviour. One might anticipate that family-planning activity in many countries would be correlated with these structural changes in the society, giving rise by class and by region to differential rates of birth-control acceptance within the programme. Consequently, all relevant demand constraints must be considered together with family-planning inputs to appraise without bias the *independent* impact of family-planning programmes on fertility (T. P. Schultz, 1972; T. W. Schultz, 1973).

An economist might regard a family-planning programme as an investment augmenting and diffusing a useful stock of knowledge about new techniques of birth control not unlike technical assistance through farm extension agents. By lowering the fixed informational costs and perhaps also subsidising the marginal user costs of modern methods of birth control, this investment should contribute to more efficient patterns of birth-control adoption. Possibly more important than its average effect on the birth-rate might be the personal distribution of programme benefits. Although all classes might benefit from the reduced marginal-user costs, the fixed-informational costs are probably a particularly severe barrier to adoption among segments of the population that reside in remote rural areas and have less sophisticated skills for searching out and evaluating the returns from new products and services. I would hazard to guess that in a dynamic society these informational benefits are likely to be greatest among the lowest classes, and therefore over generations the highest pay-off to family planning will be in slowing or reversing the disconcerting growth of economic disparities among classes in a society.

But few observers anticipate that further improvements in birth-control technology can continue to reduce substantially the cost and increase dramatically the acceptability of newer methods. Given the apparent price-inelasticity of demand for children, one may doubt whether further improvements in birth-control technology will be responsible for a continuing fall in desired or actual fertility. The distinct possibility therefore exists that, as family planning programmes succeed throughout the world during our generation in transmitting their more-or-less *fixed* stock of information and services to all strata in a society, further activity along these lines will have a sharply diminishing pay-off (e.g. T. W. Schultz, 1973).

The past search for policy options to cope with rapid population growth mirrors a natural but none the less one-sided technocratic view of the problem. It seems far simpler to disseminate a better birth-control technology, which is already operational in developed countries, than to modify parent reproductive goals by indigenous processes of social change about which little is known. For example, expenditures on family planning that seek to lower the *supply* price of modern birth-control technology and hence reduce the cost (pecuniary and subjective) of restricting fertility are a widely approved policy response. Alternatively, expenditures on, say, public health that seek to reduce child death-rates, contributing to a downward shift in parent *demand* for numbers of births, is thought to be a counterproductive or at best a controversial policy strategy. Both sets of policy options – the 'supply' and 'demand' sides – need further quantitative study if decision-makers are to be able to select an equitable and efficient mix of family planning and development policies for each social setting.

If, as is often asserted, familial behaviour, involving marriage, reproduction, and women's role in the labour force, is particularly resistant to environmental changes associated with alternative development strategies, then to align development policies to foster the adoption of smaller family-size goals may be ineffectual. Public policy would then wisely emphasise, for the moment, improvements in birth-control technology and the dissemination of these improved techniques to all strata of society. Alternatively, if demand for children is price-inelastic and family-size goals are insensitive to the available mode of birth control, widespread acceptance of better birth-control methods may not independently accomplish substantial reductions in the birth-rate.

A related reaction to the apparent declining efficacy of improved birth-control technology in the aftermath of a successful family-planning programme is to rely on direct economic incentives to change parent reproductive behaviour. The common 'economic welfare' arguments used in this regard to buttress the case for slowing rapid population growth are seriously flawed.[1] In applying economic logic to the evaluation of the consequences of population growth, the unacceptable assumption is implicitly made that children are *nothing more* than a pecuniary investment. Although these average

[1] The micro-economic approach calculates the present value of preventing a birth, as advanced by Stephen Enke, but ignores the non-pecuniary returns from children, and presumes that parent resources expended on their own children are somehow social costs. The second approach constructs a macro-economic growth model and simulates the effect of population growth, as pioneered by Coale and Hoover. Social benefits are essentially measured in terms of per capita income which excludes, conveniently, the non-pecuniary returns parents obtain from their offspring.

productivity or efficiency arguments for slowing population growth by direct incentive payments to parents are conceptually and even empirically inadequate, the consequences of rapid population growth on the personal distribution of income are less ambiguous and these equity effects are possibly more important in the long run.

The attraction of the demand model of fertility is that it identifies environmental conditions that presumably motivate parents to want fewer children and invest more in each child, and moreover, these conditions are generally linked to eminently desirable social-investment programmes that should contribute to a less unequal personal distribution of future income. Support is growing for such programmes as, for example, promoting the health and nutrition of mothers and young children, accelerating the growth of educational opportunities at the elementary and secondary level for women as well as for men, facilitating the entry of women into the labour force, and strengthening the economic and legal status of women and children. These are fundamental changes in any social order that may be resisted by many and could absorb large resources per prevented birth. But the returns to promoting such changes in social organisation and household resource allocation are broader than their effect on birth-rates. To compare the social returns from direct-incentive payments to parents to avert births with indirect investments in social change that promise, among other goals, to reduce desired family size will require two advances in the social sciences. First, agreement must be reached on how to characterise a society's interpersonal and intergenerational goals and their trade-offs. Second, a much improved understanding will be required of how economic and demographic variables influence and are influenced by reproductive behaviour.

Suppose the level and personal distribution of economic resources in a society affect fertility, and the relationship between economic and demographic variables and fertility can be specified and estimated with increasing precision along the lines discussed earlier. It would be surprising indeed if a mix of development policies were not then found that could accomplish nearly all that is currently sought in most parts of the world, but held the added promise of affecting fertility and the *quality* and rate of population growth. The potential of the economic demand theory of fertility outlined in this paper is that it could provide a society, in principle, with a decentralised means of bringing into better balance social and private interests in bearing children. This might be accomplished without sacrificing the important function individuals perform best – evaluating, ordering, and satisfying their own wants.

APPENDIX: AN OUTLINE OF THE HOUSEHOLD PRODUCTION APPROACH TO FERTILITY[1]

This framework is typically stated in terms of a single-period integrated family-utility function, a series of production functions for final untraded consumption commodities, and a budget constraint expressed in terms of both the time of family members and market goods:

$$U = U(Z_1, \ldots, Z_n) \tag{4.1}$$

$$Z_i = f_i(x_i, M_i, F_i), \quad \text{for} \quad i = 1, 2, \ldots, n \tag{4.2}$$

$$Y = \sum_i x_i p_i = W_m N_m + W_f N_f + V \tag{4.3}$$

$$\sum_i M_i + N_m = \sum_i F_i + N_f = T \tag{4.4}$$

where $U(\cdot)$ is the family-utility function; Z represents final consumption commodities; f, production functions using market goods (x); M is husband's time and F, wife's time; Y is money income; p is money prices of market goods; N_m and N_f are husband and wife time allocated to market activities for money wages of W_m and W_f, respectively; V is the return on the family's non-human wealth; and T is the total available time each spouse has to allocate between market and non-market activities.[2]

Assume that there are only two non-market commodities, the number of children, C, and all other commodities, G, and that both production functions are linear homogeneous and independent of each other. The full price of the ith commodity is

$$Z_i \pi_i = M_i W_m + F_i W_f + p_i x_i; \quad i = C, G. \tag{4.5}$$

---

[1] The origins to this approach may be found in Mincer (1963) and Becker (1965), and are stated in the simplified manner presented below by Ben Porath (1973) and elaborated in different directions by Willis (1971, 1973), DeTray (1973), Michael (1971) and Becker and Lewis (1973).

[2] Utility is maximised subject to technology, time, and income constraints when

$$\frac{\partial U}{\partial Z_i} = \lambda \left(\pi_i \cdot \frac{\partial x_i}{\partial Z_i} + \frac{\mu_m}{\lambda} \cdot \frac{\partial M_i}{\partial Z_i} + \frac{\mu_f}{\lambda} \cdot \frac{\partial F_i}{\partial Z_i} \right), \quad \text{for} \quad i = 1, 2, \ldots, n.$$

where λ is the marginal utility of income, and μ is the marginal utility of time. The ratio of marginal products of all inputs in each activity are equal to the ratio of their shadow prices when the optimum allocation conditions are satisfied; for example for the male,

$$\frac{\partial Z_i / \partial M_i}{\partial Z_i / \partial x_i} = \frac{\mu_m / \lambda}{\pi_i} = \frac{W_m}{\pi_i} \quad \text{for} \quad i = 1, 2, \ldots, n.$$

See Gronau (1970) for an empirical application of this simple model to the study of single-person households, or Becker (1965) for further elaborations of the framework.

Full income, I, of the household is then defined as

$$I = \pi_c C + \pi_g G = TW_f + TW_m + V; \qquad (4.6)$$

the full price-elasticity of demand for the jth commodity is

$$\eta_{j\pi_j} = \frac{dZ_j}{d\pi_j} \cdot \frac{\pi_j}{Z_j};$$

and the full income-elasticity of demand for the jth commodity is

$$\eta_{jI} = \frac{dZ_j}{dI} \cdot \frac{I}{Z_j}.$$

The income elasticity is positive if j is not an inferior commodity. The own-price elasticity, holding income constant, must be negative. The elasticity of demand for children with respect to non-human wealth, V, is

$$\eta_{CV} = \frac{V}{C} \cdot \frac{dC}{dV} = \eta_{CI}, \qquad (4.7)$$

and if children are not an inferior commodity, as seems plausible, this expression should be positive in sign.

The shares of the total cost of the ith commodity accounted for by the husband's and wife's time input are

$$S_{mi} = \frac{M_i W_m}{Z_i \pi_i} \quad \text{and} \quad S_{fi} = \frac{F_i W_f}{Z_i \pi_i} \quad \text{respectively.}$$

Following Ben Porath (1973), the elasticity of demand for children with respect to a change in the husband's or wife's wage can be expressed in terms of these value shares, the shares of full income earned in the market by each spouse, and the compensated (holding full income constant) price and income-elasticities of demand for children.[1]

$$\eta_{CW_m} = \frac{W_m}{C} \cdot \frac{\partial C}{\partial W_m} = \eta_{C\pi_c}(S_{mC} - S_{mG}) + \frac{N_m W_m}{I}\eta_{CI} \qquad (4.8)$$

$$\eta_{CW_f} = \frac{W_f}{C} \cdot \frac{\partial C}{\partial W_f} = \eta_{C\pi_c}(S_{fC} - S_{fG}) + \frac{N_f W_f}{I}\eta_{CI}. \qquad (4.9)$$

---

[1] The expression for the derived demand of a factor also includes the possibilities for substitution between husband's and wife's time in production. The above expression for the elasticity of demand for children permits only the substitution in consumption to occur along a given production isoquant. The compensated price-elasticity may be alternatively defined as the product of the share of income spent on other household commodities or the elasticity of substitution between children and other household commodities (but with the opposite sign).

The elasticity of demand for children with respect to a change in the return, r, on the household's non-human wealth, A, where $r = V/A$, is

$$\eta_{Cr} = \frac{r}{C} \cdot \frac{\partial C}{\partial r} = \frac{V}{I} \eta_{CI}. \qquad (4.10)$$

Generally it may be assumed that $N_m W_m > N_f W_f$, since both the wages of males and their market hours worked tend to exceed those of females. The positive income effect associated with a change in male wages will, therefore, usually exceed that associated with a change in female wages, but the price effects are more complex.[1] If it is assumed that the difference between the female time-intensity of children and that of other non-market goods equals or exceeds the difference between the male time intensity of children and that of other non-market goods, or, in other words, that

$$(S_{fC} - S_{fG}) > (S_{mC} - S_{mG}),$$

then the relative magnitude of the income effect prevails and

$$\eta_{CW_m} > \eta_{CW_f}. \qquad (4.11)$$

This formulation of the determinants of consumer demand in terms of price and income-effects yields regrettably few refutable empirical propositions. The effect of an exogenously determined increase in the net price of a child, whether it stems from a shift in anticipated costs or benefits, should decrease demand for children. The effect of an unanticipated permanent increase in income, holding prices constant, should relax the family's resource constraint and stimulate increased demand for children and other non-inferior goods. However, depending upon the ultimate source of the increase in income an offsetting increase in the opportunity cost or time-price of a child may also take place, weakening or even reversing the net effect of the increased income.

Given plausible parameter values for relative wages, market work and time-intensity of non-market goods, one might anticipate that the effect on demand for children of a change in male wages should be more positive than that of a change in female wages. Indeed, even if price and income-elasticities of demand for children were of approximately the same *absolute* magnitude (but of opposite sign), increases in male wages could increase demand for children, and increases in female wages could decrease demand because of the

---

[1] If one assumes that only one spouse, say the wife, allocates time to the production of C and G, stronger conclusions obtain (See Rybczynski, 1955; Gronau, 1970, 1973; Willis, 1971, 1973), notably when the wife ceases to work in market activities altogether.

different value shares attached to each.[1] If the income-elasticity were absolutely smaller than the price-elasticity as seems likely, the relevant wage effects on the demand for children would all be reduced, or more negative.

The only observable source of exogenous variation in the relative price of children is associated with the value of time parents allocate to the care and enjoyment of their children. No progress has been made in measuring the pecuniary or subjective returns derived from children as either producer or consumer goods, respectively. At this point one is again confronted by the jointness of parent choices regarding the number of children they want and the resource intensity of child-rearing they deem optimal. Almost any observable measure of differential costs of child-rearing implicitly reflects some degree of parent choice, and is hence endogenous to the decision-making process that the demand model of fertility seeks to explain.[2]

---

[1] A numerical example may clarify how these relationships might work. Let us assume that men receive a wage 50 per cent greater than women (say \$3 versus \$2); and men work four times as much in market activity as do women (four-fifths as compared with one-fifth of their allocatable time); and women allocate six-tenths of their time to child-rearing and men only one-tenth, with the remainder used in the production of other non-market goods; one-fifth of the household's market income is spent on children; and non-human wealth income (per similar time units as were used to measure wages) amounts to \$0·2, then approximately $S_{fC} = 0·571$, $S_{fG} = 0·129$, $S_{mC} = 0·143$, $S_{mG} = 0·097$, and $I = \$5·20$. Assuming the same absolute magnitude for income and price-compensated elasticities, say $\eta_{CI} = 0·3$ and $\eta_{C\pi_c} = -0·3$, we obtain the results by plugging in the illustrative values:

$$\eta_{CW_f} = (-0·3)(0·442) + (0·077)(-0·3) = -0·110$$
$$\eta_{CW_m} = (-0·3)(0·046) + (0·46)(0·3) = +0·124$$
and
$$\eta_{Cr} = (-0·3)(0·0) + (0·04)(0·3) = +0·012$$

In this example the negative price effect associated with the male wage is less than 3 per cent of the price effect associated with the female wage, whereas the male-wage income effect is more than five times the female-wage income effect. Consequently, the sex specific relative magnitudes of both the price and income effects contribute to the more positive (less negative) effect on the demand for children of a change in men's wages compared with women's wages. Because of the small share of household income that was assumed to flow from non-human assets, the magnitude of a change in the (interest rate) return on these assets elicits a small, but necessarily positive, effect. An unanticipated change in asset level would, of course, affect the demand for children directly via the assumed income-elasticity of $+0·3$.

It might be more realistic to assume that the income-elasticity of demand was much smaller, say $+0·05$. In this case, the elasticity of demand with respect to female wages would be $-0·13$, with respect to male wages $+0·01$, and with respect to a change in interest rates $+0·002$.

[2] One can imagine that regional differences in climate and agricultural conditions might exogenously dictate regional differences in the productivity of child labour with associated effects on desired fertility levels. Analysis of the structure of wages by age, sex and education in low-income countries is an important but neglected field of economic study.

TABLE 4.A SUMMARY OF EMPIRICAL FINDING FOR
(After each regression coefficient the absolute value of the *t* ra

	(1)	(2)	(3)	(4)
Author (year; page)	Schultz (1969; 171)	Schultz (1970; 43)	Nerlove–Schultz (1970; 45)	Harman (1970; 29–30)
Population (time)	Puerto Rico (1951–1957)	Egypt (1960)	Puerto Rico (1950–1960)	Philippines (1968)
Observations (number)	Regions (75*7)	Regions (41)	Regions (78*11)	Individuals (250)
Equation (estimators)[a]	Reduced form (CLS)	Reduced form (OLS)	Structural (TSLS/GLS)	Structural (TSLS)
Dependent variable	Births per 1000 population	Children (0–9) per women (15–49)	Births per 1000 population	Children ever b per women age 35–9
Explanatory variables[b]				
1. Adult education	−1·58 (5·3) [0·15]		−1·95 (3·2) [0·20]	
2. Women's education		−65·2 (4·0) [0·087]		−0·092 (1·6) [0·094]
3. Women's wage				
4. Men's education				
5. Men's wage				
6. Death-rate	1·18 (3·5) [0·27][d]		0·302 (1·6) [0·082][d]	5·76 (3.9) [1·0 [0·048][e]
R^2 (F; df)[c]	0·46	0·537	(27·3)	(3.5)

[a] Form of estimation equation such as reduced-form equations (only exogenous explanatory variables) which r estimated by ordinary least squares (OLS), structural equations (including endogenous explanatory variables) est perhaps by an instrumental variable technique such as two-stage least squares (TSLS), solved reduced-form equ derived from the simultaneous equations estimates of the related structural equations (generally without *t* statistic when a time series of cross-sections are pooled for either a reduced form or a structural equation, estimates r reported using a generalised least-squares procedure (GLS) that assumes a Nerlovian two-component stochastic str to the disturbances. For instrumental variable estimates asymptotic *t* statistics are reported.

[b] For definition of explanatory variables, including those not reported in table, see original studies.

[c] Asymptotic significance of entire equation can be evaluated with the *F* ratio when TSLS estimates are compute Dhrymes (1969). For OLS and GLS of reduced-form equations, R^2 can be used to test the equation's overall sta significance.

ME COUNTRIES ON THE DETERMINANTS OF FERTILITY
rted in parentheses and elasticities at regression means in brackets)

	(6)	(7)	(8a)	(8b)	
z 61)	DaVanzo (1972; 80)	Maurer et al. (1973; 20–9)	Schultz (1972; 36)	Schultz (1972; 38)	
n 1968)	Chile (1960)	Thailand (1960)	Taiwan (1964–1969)	Taiwan (1964–1969)	
ıs	Regions (50)	Regions (71)	Regions (361*7)	Regions (361*7)	
ed form	Structural (TSLS)	Solved reduced form (TSLS)	Reduced form (OLS)	Reduced form (GLS)	
ılised births »0 women 5–9	Children ever born per 1000 women aged 35–9	Children ever born per women aged 35–9	Births per 1000 women aged 35–9	Births per 1000 women aged 35–9	
					1.
$1·8]^f$		$-0·0926 \, [0·13]^h$	98·2 (9·2) [0·37]	$-45·4$ (2·78) [0·17]	2.
	-1589 $(1·84) \, [0·35]^g$	$-22·6 \, [0·16]^h$			3.
		$0·526 \, [0·55]^h$	$-274 \, (16·0) \, [1·4]$	-174 (7·9) [0·98]	4.
	170 (0·33) [0·054]				5.
3) $[5·5]^f$	7·65 (2·72) [0·28]		432 (17·9) [3·9] $[0·28]^e$	172 (8·2) [1·5] $[0·11]^e$	6.
	(14·4; 6, 3)	(13·9; 7, 4)	0·461	0·809	

thmetic sum of lagged coefficients, and averaged t statistics.
ıld death-rate entered regression as the reciprocal of child survival rate. For comparability and ease of inter-
on, the second elasticity estimates are with respect to the child death-rate.
ithmetic average of regression coefficients, t statistics, elasticities and R^2 from five annual cross-sectional regressions.
e women's wage was treated as endogenous to this investigation and is therefore estimated as a linear function of
ıous variables such as women's education, etc.
e solved reduced-form equations are reported without asymptotic standard error estimates. The elasticity estimates
ıucation variables incorporate also the effect of an additional variable that is non-linear in male and female
ion, namely, the relative educational attainment of women to that of men.

TABLE 4.B SUMMARY OF EMPIRICAL FINDING FOR
(After each regression coefficient the absolute value of the *t* r

	(1a)	(1b)	(1c)	(2)
Author (year; page)	Ben Porath (1970 & 1973; S210–S211)	Same	Same	Cain & Weir (1970; Table
Population (time)	Israel (1961)	Same	Same	U.S. urban w census (1960)
Observations (number)	Regions: Jewish towns and Moshavim (429)	Non-Jewish (133)	Kibbutzim (180)	Major cities SMSA (100)
Equation (estimators)[a]	Reduced form (OLS)	Same	Same	Reduced form (OLS)
Dependent variable	Age normalised birth-rate	Same	Same	Children eve per 1000 wo ever married aged 35–44
Explanatory variables[b]				
1. Women's education	−0·132 (10·0) [1·1]	−0·089 (4·2) [0·06]	0·046 (1·5) [0·5]	−53·9[d] (5·4)
2. Women's wage/earnings	—	—	—	−27·2 (3·97) [0·33]
3. Men's education	−0·049 (2·6) [0·4]	0·022 (1·8) [0·11]	0·009 (0·4) [0·1]	—
4. Men's wage/earnings	—	—	—	9·7 (1·84) [0·23]
5. Interaction (1*4)	—	—	—	—
6. Family income/consumption	—	—	—	—
R^2 (F; df)[c]	0·533	0·120	0·017	0·52

	(4a)	(4b)	(4c)	(5)	
61a)	Sanderson & Willis (1971; Table 1)	Same	Same	Michael (1971; 26)	
ensus (1960)	U.S. white married once husband present census (1960)	Same	Same	U.S. suburban survey (1968)	
ated cells	Husband occupation by wife's education categories (101)	Same (98)	Same (98)	Micro households (513)	
d form	Reduced form (OLS)	Same	Same	Reduced form (OLS)	
n ever born men aged 35–44, d 22 years or more	Children ever born per women aged 35–44	Children ever born per women aged 44–54	Children ever born per women aged 55–64	Number of children in household per women aged 35–9	
	−0·175 (4·67)	−0·192 (7·04)	−0·155 (4·43)	−0·0617 (2·18) [0·29]	1.
	—	—	—	—	2.
	—	—	—	−0·0124 (0·47) [0·064]	3.
89[e, f]	−1·77 (2·25)	−0·192 (3·27)	−1·65 (2·47)	—	4.
	0·151 (2·66)	0·150 (3·62)	0·084 (1·58)	—	5.
	—	—	—	0·160 (1·80) [0·086]	6.
	0·253	0·437	0·448	0·018	

	(6a)	(6b)	(7a)	(7b)	(8)
Author (year; page)	Gardner (1972; 522)	Gardner (1972; 522)	Ben Porath (1973; S221)	Same	De Tray (1973; S97)
Population (time)	U.S. urban census (1960)	U.S. rural farm census (1960)	Israel (1963–64)	Same	U.S. census (1960)
Observations (number)	States (48)	Same	Urban families of wage-earners married in Israel (182)	Same	County (516)
Equation (estimators)[a]	Reduced form (OLS)	Same	Reduced form (OLS)	Same	Reduced fo (OLS)
Dependent variable	Children ever born per women aged 40–4	Same	Children ever born per married women aged 40 or over	Same	Children e born per 1 married wo aged 35–44

Explanatory variables[b]

	(6a)	(6b)	(7a)	(7b)	(8)
1. Women's education	−6·5 (0·5)	−17 (2·3)	−47·2[i] (1·44) [17]	−233[i] (1·96) [0·33]	−0·030 (3·19) [0·32]
2. Women's wage/earnings	−40 (5·6)	−39 (4·0)	—	—	−0·30[e] (12·5) [0·30]
3. Men's education	1·6 (0·4)	26 (2·6)	—	—	0·0077 (0·74) [0·08]
4. Men's wage/earnings	—	—	−26·8 (1·38) [11]	−2·44 (0·41) [0·06]	0·074[e] (2·12) [0·07]
5. Interaction (1*4)	—	—	548 (1·28)	2632[j] (1·89)	—
6. Family income/ consumption	3·6 (3·0)	2·5 (1·4)	—	—	0·065[e,h] (2·73) [0·07]
R^2 (F; df)[c]	0·70	0·76	0·306	0·313	0·75

[a,b,c] See Table A.

[d] Women's education variable expressed as percentage of females with *less* than five years of schooling. Variable an inverse measure of educational attainment among the lower tail of the distribution and the regression co has the opposite sign from the other studies that use average or median years of schooling. Its sign has been r here to facilitate comparisons.

[e] Variables expressed in logarithms.

[f] Wife's potential market wage was constructed from 1960 data on the earnings of employed wives adjusted fo worked per week and weeks worked last year to obtain a full-time yearly earnings potential of wives cross-class urban/rural residence, and the education or occupation of the husband (Willis, p. 54).

[g] This coefficient is obtained from a supplemental regression of the occupation/education dummy variable es from the fertility equation against mean income of husbands in these 24 occupation/education categories, w assumed to be a satisfactory proxy for the husband's permanent income.

[h] Median value of owner-occupied housing which is interpreted as a proxy for the wealth or consumption

... (cont.)

	(10a)	(10b)	(10c)	(11)	
en Table 9)	Gardner (1973; S106)	Gardner (1973; S106)	Gardner (1973; S112)	Willis (1973; S50–S52)	
ensus	Rural North Carolina families, where wife reported some labour earnings (1967–70)	Rural N.C. families, (1967–70)	Rural N.C. families, (1967–70)	U.S. census (1960)	
y	Families (240)	Families (511)	Families (511)	Individual urban white, once-married women, living with husband (9169)	
ural)	Reduced form (OLS)	Reduced form (OLS)	Reduced form (OLS)	Reduced form (OLS)	
per 1000 n aged 15–45	Children ever born per currently married women aged 30–49	Children ever born per currently married women aged 30–49	Children ever born per currently married women aged 30–49	Children ever born per currently married women aged 35–64	
[0·19]	−0·15 (2·7) [0·5]	−0·14 (3·7) [0·5]	−0·17 (4·0) [0·6]	−0·176 (14·0) [0·41]	1.
)·26]	−0·43^k (2·0) [0·2]	—	−0·020^k (3·0) [0·6]	—	2.
	−0·05 (0·9)	−0·09 (2·6) [0·3]	−0·09 (2·2) [0·3]	—	3.
	−0·06 (0·6)	—	−0·17 (2·2)	−0·248 (7·35) [0·067]	4.
	—	—	—	0·0202 (7·33)	5.
)·22]	21 (3·2) [0·32]	0·16 (4·1) [0·28]	0·26 (4·8) [0·38]	—	6.
7, 3)	0·23	0·19	0·25	0·047	

s in the county. In Frieden's study (6), housing value also affects (negatively) the proportion married, and ere its net (reduced form) impact on births is about ten per cent less than that reported here.

e schooling variable is transformed according to five steps into an approximation of the monthly full-time wage r women.

e women's schooling (wage rate) variable is squared to capture the non-linearity in the relationship between the n's wage rate and her fertility. The interaction term (variable 5) also approximates this quadratic term since ad and wife educational attainment (and wage rates) are highly correlated.

study (10a) the wife's wage is directly observed for the sample of North Carolina families where the wife reported labour earnings, whereas in (10c) for the entire sample of families the wife's wage is approximated by the county ate for off-farm employment to others than the farm head. The county wage should be a better approximation for genous measure of the value of time that will not be systematically related to the woman's past labour-force nce and consequently jointly determined with her family planning and fertility.

TABLE 4.C RANGE OF ESTIMATES OF THE ELASTICITY OF
FERTILITY WITH RESPECT TO THE CENTRAL VARIABLES
IN DEMAND MODEL[a]

Explanatory variable	Level of per capita income	
	Low (Table 1)	High (Table 2)
Women's education	−0·17 to −0·06	−1·1 to −0·19
Men's education	−0·98 to +0·55	−0·4 to −0·06
Women's wage	−0·16 to −0·35	−0·6 to −0·17
Men's wage	+0·05	−0·11 to +0·23
Family income	—	+0·09 to +0·38
Mortality	+0·05 to +0·28	—

[a] Certain of the estimates appears not to be comparable because of functional form of model estimated or nature of proxy variables analysed. The studies of Willis (1971) and DeTray (1972) fit a model partially in logarithms. Willis obtained an unusually large elasticity of fertility with respect to his proxy for female full-time potential market earnings of −1·99. DeTray obtained elasticity estimates that are within the ranges reported. The interaction model estimated by Sanderson and Willis (1971) are reported without elasticities or variable means, and are hence not represented in the table. Cain and Weininger (1970) female education variable is not comparable with the other average or median years of schooling variables (see note *d*, Table 4.B). The Kibbutzim case (Ben Porath, case 1c) is excluded as non-comparable. The non-Jewish communities in Israel are classified with the studies of low-income countries although they are reported in Table 4.B. Median years of schooling in these communities is 4·9 for males and 0·7 for females, contrasted with between 8 and 10 for both sexes in the Jewish settlements of Israel.

REFERENCES

G. S. Becker, 'An Economic Analysis of Fertility', *Demographic and Economic Change in Developed Countries*, Universities-National Bureau Conference Series 11 (Princeton, N.J., 1960) 209–31.

—— 'A Theory of the Allocation of Time', *Economic Journal*, 75:299 (Sep 1965) 493–517.

G. S. Becker and H. G. Lewis, 'On the Interaction between the Quantity and Quality of Children', *Journal of Political Economy*, suppl. *81*:2, II (Mar/Apr 1973) S279–88.

Y. Ben Porath, *Fertility in Israel, an Economist's Interpretation: Differentials and Trends, 1950–1970*, RM-5981-FF (Santa Monica, Calif.: The Rand Corporation, Aug 1970). (Repr. in *Economic Development and Population Growth in the Middle East*, ed. Charles A. Cooper and Sidney S. Alexander (New York: American Elsevier, 1972) pp. 503–39.)

—— 'Economic Analysis of Fertility in Israel: Point and Counterpoint', *Journal of Political Economy*, suppl. *81*:2, II (Mar/Apr 1973) S202–33.

Y. Ben Porath and F. Welch, *Chance, Child Traits, and the Choice of Family Size*, R-1117-NIH/RF (Santa Monica, Calif.: The Rand Corporation, 1972).

W. P. Butz, *Research and Information Strategies to Improve Population Policy in Less Developed Countries*, R-952-AID (Santa Monica, Calif.: The Rand Corporation, Feb 1972).

W. P. Butz and T. P. Schultz, 'An Information Strategy for Improving Population Policy in Low Income Countries', P-4802 (Santa Monica, Calif.: The Rand Corporation, Apr 1972).

G. G. Cain and A. Weininger, 'Economic Determinants of Fertility: Results Using Cross-Sectional Aggregate Data', mimeo (Madison: Univ. of Wisconsin, 1971).

S. N. S. Cheung, 'Enforcement of Property Rights in Children and the Marriage Contract', *Economic Journal, 82*:326 (June 1972) 641–57.

J. DaVanzo, *The Determinants of Family Formation in Chile, 1960*, R-830-AID (Santa Monica, Calif.: The Rand Corporation, Aug 1972).

D. N. DeTray, 'Child Quality and the Demand for Children', *Journal of Political Economy*, suppl. *81*:2, ii (Mar/Apr 1973) S70–95.

P. J. Dhrymes, 'Alternative Asymptotic Tests of Significance and Related Aspects of 2SLS and 3SLS Estimated Parameters', *Review of Economic Studies, 36*:2 (Apr 1969) 213–26.

R. Farley, *Growth of the Black Population* (Chicago: Markham Publishing Co., 1970).

R. Freedman, L. Coombs and J. Friedman, 'Social Correlates of Foetal Mortality', *Milbank Memorial Fund Quarterly, 44* (1966) 327–44.

A. Frieden, 'A Model of Marriage and Fertility', Ph.D. dissertation (Univ. of Chicago, 1972).

B. Gardner, 'Aspects of the Fertility of Rural-Farm and Urban Women', *Southern Economic Journal, 38* (Apr 1972) 518–24.

—— 'Economics of the Size of Rural Families: U.S. Population', *Journal of Political Economy*, suppl. *81*:2, ii (Mar/Apr 1973) S99–122.

R. Gronau, 'The Value of Time in Passenger Transportation: The Demand for Air Travel', Occasional paper no. 109, National Bureau of Economic Research (New York, 1970).

—— 'The Effect of Children on the Housewife's Value of Time', *Journal of Political Economy*, suppl. *81*:2, ii (Mar/Apr 1973*a*) S168–99.

—— 'The Intra-Family Allocation of Time: The Value of the Housewives' Time', (*American Economic Review*, Sep 1973*b*).

A. J. Harman, *Fertility and Economic Behavior of Families in the Philippines*, RM-6385-AID (Santa Monica, Calif.: The Rand Corporation, Sep 1970).

M. Hashimoto, 'Economics of Postwar Fertility in Japan', *Journal of Political Economy* (Mar/Apr 1974).

L. Henry, *Selected Writings*, trans. M. Sheps (New York: American Elsevier, 1972).

—— 'Some Data on Natural Fertility', *Eugenics Quarterly, 8*:2 (June 1961) 81–91.

A. K. Jain, 'Fecundity Components in Taiwan: Applications of a Stochastic Model of Human Reproduction', unpub. dissertation (Univ. of Michigan, 1968).

A. K. Jain, T. C. Hsu, R. Freedman and M. C. Chang, 'Demographic Aspects of Lactation and Postpartum Amenorrhea', *Demography, 7*:2 (May 1970) 255–71.

W. H. James, 'The Effects of Maternal Psychological Stress on the Foetus', *British Journal of Psychiatry, 115* (1969) 811–25.

H. Leibenstein, 'An Economic Theory of Fertility Decline', Harvard Economic Research Discussion paper (Apr 1973).

K. M. Maurer, R. Ratajczak and T. P. Schultz, *Marriage, Fertility, and Labor Force Participation of Thai Women: An Econometric Study*, R-829-AID (Santa Monica, Calif.: The Rand Corporation, Aug 1972).

J. Menchen and M. Sheps, *Models of Human Reproduction* (Univ. of Chicago Press, forthcoming).

R. T. Michael, 'Education and the Derived Demand for Children' (Univ. of Chicago Workshop mimeo, 1971).

J. Mincer, 'Market Prices, Opportunity Costs, and Income Effects', *Measurement in Economics: Studies in Mathematical Economics in Memory of Yehuda Grunfeld*, ed. C. Christ *et al.* (Stanford Univ. Press, 1963) pp. 67–82.

M. Nerlove and T. P. Schultz, *Love and Life between the Censuses: A Model of Family Decision-Making in Puerto Rico, 1950–1960*, RM-6322-AID (Santa

Monica, Calif.: The Rand Corporation, Sep 1970). (See also P-4573-1, May 1971.)

D. J. O'Hara, *Changes in Mortality Levels and Family Decisions Regarding Children*, R-914-RF (Santa Monica, Calif.: The Rand Corporation, Feb 1972).

P. Pirie, 'The Effects of Treponematois and Gonorrhea on the Populations of the Pacific Islands', *Human Biology in Oceania*, *1*:3 (Feb 1972) 187–206.

W. Sanderson and R. J. Willis, 'Economic Models of Fertility: Some Examples and Implications', *New Directions in Economic Research*, *51st Annual Report* (New York: National Bureau of Economic Research, Sep 1971) 32–42.

T. P. Schultz, 'An Economic Model of Family Planning and Fertility', *Journal of Political Economy*, 77:2 (Mar/Apr 1969) 153–80.

—— *Fertility Patterns and Their Determinants in the Arab Middle East*, RM-5978-FF (Santa Monica, Calif.: The Rand Corporation, May 1970). (Repr. in *Economic Development and Population Growth in the Middle East*, ed. Charles A. Cooper and Sidney S. Alexander (New York: American Elsevier, 1972) pp. 401–500.

—— 'An Economic Perspective on Population Growth', in *Rapid Population Growth* (Baltimore, Maryland, and London: Johns Hopkins Univ. Press for National Academy of Sciences, 1971) pp. 148–74.

—— 'Explanations of Birth Rate Changes over Space and Time: A Study of Taiwan', *Journal of Political Economy*, supp., *81*:2, ii (Mar/Apr 1973) 238–74. (See also, for more extensive study, RM-1079-RF, Nov 1972, The Rand Corporation.)

T. P. Schultz and J. DaVanzo, *Analysis of Demographic Change in East Pakistan: Retrospective Survey Data*, R-564-AID (Santa Monica, Calif.: The Rand Corporation, Sep 1970).

T. W. Schultz (ed.), *New Economic Approaches to Fertility*, *Journal of Political Economy*, supp., *81*:2, ii (Mar/Apr 1973).

F. K. Shah and H. Abbey, 'Effects of Some Factors on Neonatal and Post-neonatal Mortality', *Milbank Memorial Fund Quarterly*, *49*:1 (Jan 1971) 33–57.

M. C. Sheps, 'Application of Probability Models to the Study of Patterns of Human Reproduction', *Public Health and Population Change*, ed. Sheps and J. C. Ridley (Univ. of Pittsburgh Press, 1965) 307–32.

M. C. Sheps and E. B. Perrin, 'Some Changes in Birth Rates as a Function of Contraceptive Effectiveness: Some Applications of a Stochastic Model', *American Journal of Public Health*, *53* (1963) 1031–46.

J. L. Simon, 'The Effect of Husband's Income and Wife's Education upon Various Birth Orders', mimeo (Sep 1972).

R. J. Willis, 'The Economic Determinants of Fertility Behavior', Ph.D. dissertation (Univ. of Washington, 1971).

—— 'A New Approach to the Economic Theory of Fertility Behavior', *Journal of Political Economy*, suppl., *81*:2, ii (Mar/Apr 1973) S14–64.

J. B. Wyon and J. E. Gordon, *The Khanna Study* (Cambridge, Mass.: Harvard Univ. Press, 1971).

Discussion of the Paper by Professor Schultz

Professor Demeny, opening the discussion, said that the extension of the theory of household choice to non-market goods, and in particular to child services and consequently to fertility, was a development in economic theory that was still in its infancy. However, the infant had now lived long enough to demonstrate its capacity to survive beyond a shadow of doubt. While excessively rapid gain in weight, as measured by the volume of published papers, might be a cause of some bewilderment for the outsider who took only an occasional peek into the crib, it was obviously a source of pride and joy for those who played, and continued to play, the assorted roles of parent, midwife, nurse and pediatrician around the promising baby. If the metaphor was perhaps pardonable, given the subject matter of the conference, it should be stopped short of assigning to Paul Schultz the role that he occupied in that company. Suffice it to say that the role was an illustrious one, and that there were no economists today better qualified to issue the succinct health report and medical history that his paper represented. It was an authoritative and lucid exposition that, beyond reflecting the major strengths and weaknesses of the existing state of the theory and its empirical applications, also offered a number of novel formulations and insights. In keeping with the nature of its subject, it was rich in technical detail that did not lend itself easily to verbal discussion. But the methodological minutiae were balanced by uncharacteristically brave examinations of larger issues, including that of the implications of the theory for the formulation of population policy. Claims of relevance on that score offered a convenient focal point for his necessarily brief and inadequate introduction to the discussion of the paper.

Since on numerous past occasions, mostly in informal and generally less than successful debates with sociologist colleagues, Professor Demeny had done his best to defend and advocate the conceptual framework underlying the economic theory of fertility discussed in the paper, he felt that it would be proper to limit himself to comments that were of a critical nature when speaking in a company that was bound to be intellectually well-attuned to the fundamental ideas in the theory. Concerning those ideas, there was probably little scope for disagreement among economists, provided that one disclaimed any narrowly defined notion of what economics was about.

Economics was the study of choices; it concerned the allocation of scarce resources, including time, for achieving desirable ends. No restriction was imposed by the discipline as to the nature of those desirable ends so long as it could realistically be assumed that the ends were convertible to each other – in other words, so long as prices could be assigned to them, even if in concept only. This property attached fairly to most things human beings desired – refrigerators and children, lamb chops and Beethoven's music, nuclear submarines and giraffes undisturbed in their natural habitat. The proposition that a scientific analysis of the demand for babies and bicycles had significant elements of commonality would always have been accepted by economists, well before bicycles were invented. Numerous important practical applications of the insight were, indeed, always part of the complex social arrangements, intended or unintended, regulating human fertility.

Why then, were the attempts to develop a formal theory, elegantly stated in the Appendix of Professor Schultz's paper, of so recent a vintage? The answer must be that the potential practical applications not already available from commonsense economics did not until recently appear sufficiently great to make the effort worth while. The intrinsic intellectual appeal of the exercise was, of course, there, but alone it was not enough, since there were countless equally satisfying intellectual pursuits that did not elicit the apparently pervasive distaste most people felt, in varying degrees, for thinking about topics like sex and children in overtly prosaic terms. Under the influence of increasing, although typically vaguely specified, concern about what was called the population problem, and under the influence of the increasing attempts to modify demographic behaviour through explicit public policy, the situation had now changed. The justification for the efforts discussed by Professor Schultz, as in most other fields of economic theorising, must be found in the application of the acquired knowledge. Professor Demeny had the impression that, if the interpretations offered by the paper were correct, the case thus far was less persuasive as to the productivity of the new theory in producing useful policy advice extending beyond the large chunk of solid common sense that was always available for practical men from the basic grasp of the quite obvious economic elements determining fertility.

Classifying one's own thinking had its obvious advantages, of course, and the sharpened analytical insights from theory should perform the same useful, if not indispensible, function that, say, the theory of tariffs performed in helping to set better tariffs. Efforts to develop and embellish the theory of household choice applied to fertility should continue with vigour. There was at least one pitfall on the way, however, that, judging from the paper, had not entirely been avoided. In order to breathe life into theoretical constructs, econometric modelling nowadays inevitably accompanied theory. By definition, this required reliance on the available empirical data base. Since this was restricted and lopsided, so were the specifications of the models. In drawing conclusions from them, the temptation was very strong to forget about their unhappy parentage and to see the world, and the available policy instruments for changing it, through the distorting glass of feasible models.

The commonsense economics of fertility suggested a wide range of potential policy choices that could be experimented with, given the blessing of the political process. Econometric modelling from a restricted data base tended to limit the options submitted for testing to the political process to begin with. The dangers were obvious.

The conceptual framework of the micro-economic theory of fertility rested on two pillars. There were on the one hand, tastes and on the other, prices and incomes. The natural, though not exclusive, preoccupation of the economist was with the latter. Professor Demeny said that his comments would reflect this preoccupation. He asked what we were offered by tested theory thus far. The Appendix to Professor Schultz's paper provided a synoptic guide to nineteen studies. The key explanatory variables employed in them amounted to barely half a dozen items; education (men's, women's, adults'); wages (men's and women's); the death-rate (or the rate of infant mortality); and family income (or consumption). If interpreted as instrumental variables in a policy model, this offered an almost grotesquely thin menu of choice for collective action. Not that the potentially affecting significance of reducing infant mortality or of increasing female employment or adult education in influencing fertility was to be disputed. But to think that the manipulation of such variables added significant new weaponry to population policy was almost certainly an exaggeration and often amounted to wishful thinking. More or less explicitly, lowering infant mortality, raising employment opportunities, and increasing education had been, and were now, present among the objectives pursued by governments and, commonly and at least significantly, among the objectives pursued by individuals.

That population policy considerations could somehow speed up the overall level of developmental effort on the governmental level seemed to him an extremely far-fetched idea. The population problem, if there were such a problem, manifested itself, among other things, in keeping the resources available for such efforts lower than would be desirable. The crux of the matter, then, was the particular *mix* of the developmental policies. But the framework in which the discussion of the economics of fertility was cast did not present us with meaningful trade-offs. How much women's education were we to give up for how much gain in infant mortality? The question was meaningful (as were many other questions of a similar nature) but, unfortunately, the demographic yield of investing programmes that helped to achieve either of these objectives was not known with sufficient precision to permit a sound answer. Thus we were likely to be left with the platitudinous proposition that economic and social development would be helpful in solving the population problem – the more development, the better – but the structure of development measures, the real policy issue, remained determined without reference to demographic considerations.

Naturally, the normal process of development might, in due course, generate demographic behaviour that would remove the concern with socially excessive fertility. In retrospect, then, a well-specified model might help to clarify why demographic transition occurred, but that was a contribution to historical analysis rather than to policy decisions. It would seem that the simple-minded interpretation of price and income effects on fertility would typically focus attention on policies that were far more specifically and directly linked with the behaviour of which modification was sought than the opaque variables discussed in the econometric, and for that matter, sociological literature. First, they would naturally focus (in situations of excessive demographic growth) on policies that directly affected decision-making with respect to birth control, and did so at relatively moderate economic and at minimal political cost. This meant, for practical purposes, that the earliest priority should go for the so-called family planning approach. This called, not for adult education *qua* population policy, but for provision of information on birth control; not for increasing female wage rates, again, *qua* population policy, but for lowering the price of means of fertility limitation, or even for making them available free.

Professor Schultz was critical of such policies on two grounds. One was that they were often, he would himself say always, justified on the basis of faulty economic reasoning. The two cornerstones of the standard argument, indeed, made little sense, at least on the basis of commonly-accepted political assumptions. To say that fertility reduction was desirable because lower fertility would bring higher income per head was, of course, obviously a *non sequitor*. An excellent and time-honoured use of income was precisely to have children and enjoy them. To declare that people should have lower fertility because it was good for *them* was crass paternalism. But the correct conclusion from this was not necessarily to abandon the policy line pushed for the wrong reasons, at least not before checking if perhaps there existed better reasons to support it. The better reasons were not hard to find in most situations: they rested in pervasive net negative externalities attached to individual aspects of individual demographic behaviour. When just about any head of a family had cause to be sorry (if well-informed) about his neighbours' fertility behaviour (not because of the harm to the neighbours and their children, but because of the harm to him and his children) the stage was set for collective action to change the terms of the social bargain under which demographic acts took place; that was to say, for a modification of the signals that controlled individual fertility behaviour in everyone's best interest. If such simple steps as providing subsidised birth-control information and devices could accomplish part or all of the task needed to generate the desired change, family planning was obviously a most attractive policy. Needless to say, these comments, *mutatis mutandis*, were easily rephrased to take care of situations when individual fertility behaviour fell short of what was socially desirable, hence need be stimulated.

The second reason for Professor Schultz's pessimism about family planning as a policy was far more cogent. If fertility was excessive because parents wanted more children than society wanted them to want, offering birth control know-how alone was no solution. Or, at any rate, what little good a straight family-planning policy would accomplish was likely to be costlier than standard estimating methods would suggest, either because of the operation of a substitution effect (public expenditures replacing private efforts) or because diminishing returns to programme expenditures set in early and rendered the benefit/cost ratios unattractive. Apart from the apparently all-too-rare instances when this description did not apply, we were then back to the thorny problem of how to modify prices and incomes effectively, beyond and perhaps instead of family-planning programmes. Unless his earlier comments were far off the mark, Professor Demeny felt that remedies that worked would tend to be a good deal more unpleasant than operating on the familiar variables, better values for which everyone was in favour of, that figured in econometric analyses of the determinants of fertility. When some European countries made the granting of marriage licences dependent on the demonstration that the new husband-to-be had sufficient sources of income to support his future wife and their children-to-come, that is, attached an often prohibitive price to marrying, while also attaching a variety of all-too-palpable penalties on having illegitimate children, they of course practised the Beckerian logic well over a century before Becker.

The list of similarly rigged social arrangements that went a long way to explain historically low fertility in the West was quite impressive. There was no reason to assume why the examination of the logic of the economic theory of fertility, in combination with the examination of the externalities attached to fertility behaviour, should not lead, in the conditions of contemporary societies, to an equally impressive, if perhaps quite different, list. The necessary common element in such a list of policy measures was that they put an increasing portion, and in the limit the full share, of the social costs of demographic behaviour on the social unit responsible for generating it, or – what amounted to the same policy but might carry different political costs – rewarding positive behaviour up to the full amount of the social benefit it generated. This, of course, tended to be an unpopular prescription, happily lacking in discussions of higher wages, better education, liberation of women and low death-rates – discussion that in fact assumed away, perhaps correctly, but perhaps not so, that a problem did exist.

Whether price and income policies that might be suggested by a hard-headed analysis based on the economic theory of household choice could bring closer a solution of the population problem was a question that obviously exceeded the limits of this discussion. Since internationalisation of the externalities of household demographic behaviour involved political and organisational costs that might be deemed high by most contemporary developing societies, given their existing perceptions of the problem, and given their existing political mechanisms, it might well be that no new social contract concerning these matters was possible and one had to fall back on a combination of ineffective policies and of hoping for the best. It was indeed hard not to be philosophical in contemplating the most likely course of demographic-economic development in the coming decades. It held out the promise of a sustained sense of *déjà vu*, continuing a developmental line that rapidly increased the gap between what man could be, were he able to control his affairs, and what he, in fact, was.

The prospect of those nations where a brighter future was still feasible for joining the ranks of those where perhaps it no longer was, appeared all too clear. The latter were said to have a population problem, the former were said to lack it. The implicit logic was that the remaining Brazils of the developing world should permit themselves to become like Bangladesh, by which time it would be demonstrated to everybody's satisfaction that they indeed had a problem so that some kind of meaningful action could begin.

In the meantime, lack of effective policy action on influencing fertility certified this state of affairs as by definition optimal, in the sense that it was the best of the possible worlds under the given circumstances. The tempting Panglossian interpretation, however, should be avoided. The overwhelming impression that human societies somehow lived below their true potential could hardly be avoided even by the most casual observer. Analysis of the structure of human choices, in particular of the decision-making process with respect to fertility, might clarify the central issues of population policy and hence open up new potentials hitherto unaccessible to society. The economic theory of fertility presented by Professor Schultz had a potentially important role to play in this task, even though the crux of the problem lay in the field of politics rather than in the field of pure theory or of econometrics.

Professor Schultz wished to thank Professor Demeny for his thoughtful summary and critique of the final section of the paper, devoted to the possible policy implications of the 'demand' approach to fertility determinants. While he agreed with some, he could not accept all of the remarks that had been made.

Professor Létinier made two points. First, was the theory of choice applicable to underdeveloped populations? Professor Schultz's theory seemed to apply to developed countries, but he was not sure whether one could get valid conclusions for less-developed countries where populations were beginning to grow. He did not want to condemn the theory because it was capable only of solving the problems of developed countries.

He thought that the theory could be useful to underdeveloped countries that were trying to reduce the rate of demographic expansion. However, in developed countries also one could try to restrain demographic progress. He thought that the theoretical variables, and quantitative measures of them, in models like those of Professor Schultz, could be used to intervene demographically in underdeveloped countries, though he wanted to make it clear that he was looking at population growth rates in the range of 6 to 8 per cent. However, he believed that it was important to prevent a population explosion in developed countries because their rate of population increase limited the aid they could give to less-developed countries. How much was available depended on world population and this in turn depended on the active population. In developed countries, the potential contribution depended on a dichotomy: one was looking at two types of country, and the ability of developed countries to help less-developed ones was limited.

Professor Ohlin wanted to raise a question. Perhaps both on the policy implications and on the working of explanatory theory one had to be concerned about market failure. Government intervention was often justified by pointing to such failure. Professor Demeny had already pointed to one source of failure, namely, considerable externalities. The reason why he was worried was that the working of private choice also differed because of ignorance, uncertainty and risk.

To understand how fertility decisions were taken, it was not enough to study price and income effects in markets, using econometric methods. Perhaps one needed to look also at the whole process of search and information gathering, and this could be as useful as other questions relating to markets. Fertility decisions were both few and irrevocable in the life of the normal human being, and the pressures that came from social and institutional forces were perhaps different for bicycles or gramophone records.

Dr Gavin Jones wanted to point to the application of Professor Schultz's theory to underdeveloped countries. He thought the theory was basically just as applicable as to the developed countries. If not, the present theoretical developments were less interesting to him. One was looking at people's ability to control their situations, and one could perhaps look at a spectrum. One began with the assumption that people did find ways and means to control fertility and family size. This was done in developed countries more easily than in underdeveloped countries, but the theoretical underpinning applied to both.

Professor Schultz's paper could perhaps focus more on underdeveloped countries and their characteristics. The demand from children on a mother's time was affected by family structure, the availability of servants, and differences in the relative earning potential of women, and therefore the opportunity-cost of having children.

Professor Bourcier de Carbon wanted to reflect on the degree of specificity of an economic good and of a demand function. Could a child be regarded as a good which had a price and a cost in the market? The position of any economic good on a scale of value was perhaps subject to variation. If one were considering a child, that position would probably depend on whether one was looking at a man or a woman. For example, a woman's desire to have children was not the same at all ages. Similarly, the amount of time available for looking after other children depended on how many children the family already had. He also believed that the problem was somewhat linked with risk. Did this discourage fertility? Purity and the family situation were important. To make a family life, all elements had to come in. Thus the idea of the child as an economic good was not useful in looking at a growth process where one attached a different value to each element; for example, to the eldest child; to a son rather than a daughter because he allowed one to achieve one's own ambition, and so on.

Professor Perlman felt that two points had been largely ignored in the historical literature on population. First, there was the role of disease as against mortality. In the nineteenth century economic advances in countries that industrialised led to reductions in mortality. They were achieved simultaneously with advances which led to a reduction in contagious diseases. Therefore people not only lived longer, but were healthier too. In the twentieth century we had eliminated death among the young, but had not been so successful in reducing the diseases which remained, especially diseases like chronic gastro-enteritis, which created unemployment. So, perhaps the theory of fertility choice had to look at the problem of getting a satisfactory family labour force. In many underdeveloped countries, two or three workers could keep a family at a satisfactory standard of living. But to have an average of two or three at work perhaps required a total adult family of three times that size. He thought that this was a rational explanation, and if one discussed the problem with people in South East Asia or Latin America they would agree. There was little data on this but he was sure that the problem was a relevant one.

Professor Perlman thought that the essence of the issues we were discussing related to the timing of two choices. Easterlin of the University of Pennsylvania had worked on the perceptions of economic well-being, and Alan Sweezey, in a paper, had shown more cultural dependence on tastes than Easterlin had suggested. Perhaps such ideas should be incorporated into Schultz's theory of choice.

Professor Perlman referred also to results of the work of Dr Pinchas Schwinger, a student of his at the University of Pittsburgh. This showed that if one considered the age of a mother, one got a high negative correlation coefficient between national economic activity, particularly disposable national income, and the age of the mother at the time of the birth of the second child, with a one-year lag. The relationship for the first child was less. The relationship for the third, fourth and fifth child was very low. He assumed this meant either that the family by then was committed to having more children, or else that by that time the father had reached a position of job security and seniority etc., and so was less worried about basic conditions in the family. One element in the theory of choice must therefore be that one should not treat all children as equal. The timing of the birth of the second child, in particular, reflects the degree of economic prosperity. As for later parities, other (non-economic) considerations seemed dominant.

Professor Ben Porath referred to what Professor Demeny had said about the need to consider population policies. The excess demand for policy recommendations resulted from the current concern with underdeveloped areas, which meant that money was provided for research because people wanted answers to important questions. The kinds of study that Professor Schultz had surveyed were far from able to supply this excess demand. In more conventional situations, excess demand led to an increase in price or deterioration of quality. There was a similar danger here, and one should not press the theory too soon to lead to policy recommendations.

Professor Ben Porath said that when travelling in Europe, with its current inflation, he rarely admitted to being a professional economist, and there was a far longer tradition of policy recommendations covering inflation. It was difficult to reproduce economic behaviour, and the present paper was only a tentative effort to see whether one could do so in a particular field. Professor Ohlin had spoken about the problem of searching out and transferring information; Professor Ben Porath felt that one needed to transfer knowledge from other branches of economics into the field of population. He recalled that, before the Second World War, economists, when using mathematical or statistical equations, sometimes referred to them as laws. We now had a more modest view of our quantitative and formal work. We were simply concerned with a tentative search; with trial and error; with insights; with eliminating false arguments. For policy conclusions one needed common sense and intelligence. It was too early to ask for the kind of weaponry that Professor Demeny sought.

Professor Urquidi pointed out that in the discussion of the factors affecting fertility in underdeveloped countries, one tended to forget the very high rate of population growth in many parts of the world. He wanted to say this because when countries were in this sort of situation, where children were abundant, he wondered if it made any sense to talk about choice at all. It had been asked whether the theory applied at all to underdeveloped countries. One had to remember that underdeveloped countries had at least two main sectors, including a large rural population. Perhaps, in these situations, procreation rarely resulted from deliberate choice. There were no economic values involved, but families unthinkingly had one child after another. This was also becoming true in many urban areas in less-developed countries because of migration to the towns, and what was now called 'marginality'.

Those one was talking about were poor, and rarely regularly employed. Perhaps the urban middle class in underdeveloped countries, and increasingly regular wage earners, did take care of the future and did consider economic aspirations as well as the housing they had, in deciding whether to have more children. He wanted to emphasise that the fertility problem still remained outside the growing middle-class groups. Inter-disciplinary work was needed. He did not see how economists could discuss population and leave out sociologists and anthropologists. Integration was needed, and the area to be integrated went far beyond economics.

Professor Coale said that Professor Urquidi had expressed his own feelings. Professor Urquidi would perhaps be surprised to know that he himself also felt that one should seek a sociological view. Professor Coale's sociological friends would be even more surprised! He was reminded of the reactions of Duesenberry to a paper by Gary Becker which argued that fertility could be treated as an exercise in the economic theory of consumers' choice. Professor Duesenberry had explained the difference between economics and sociology as follows: economics was concerned with the choices people made, while sociology taught that people had no choice.

One body of evidence was on unwanted fertility in the U.S.A. This was defined as happening when a pregnancy, not the result of an interruption of contraception, resulted in a birth. To parents who did not want more children, about 20 per cent of the offsprings born in the early 1960s were a result of such unwanted pregnancies. It was found that for women in poor families with more than five children, the majority of pregnancies were unwanted. To a large extent, the problem was psychological, or otherwise, inaccessible birth control. Similarly, unsuccessful abortions in some Latin American cities led to more hospital treatment than was required for live births. There was too little access to fertility control. In Africa, if one asked people how many children they wanted, the response was that they wanted seven or eight. However, the same respondents said that they wanted these children at four-year intervals. They did not think about the relationship between their two answers; they thought of spacing children in order to protect the mother but did not convert this into the number of children that would be born during a lifetime. They were not looking at lifetime income or at children as consumer goods.

Professor Hermalin observed that Professor Coale had just made the point that Professor Schultz noted the biological components of fertility but did not give them much emphasis. Perhaps more work needed to be done on this because there were views on the rate at which children should be borne as well as on their numbers. In Taiwan, there was evidence that families where the mother experienced rapid child-bearing took action to acquire contraceptives quite independently of family numbers. In reply to Professor Perlman, Professor Hermalin said that Professor Schultz noted what happened if one had increased life expectancy, or if there was more investment in children. He would just like to say that, in Taiwan, families who viewed children as 'factors of production' for their old age were less educated and perhaps had lower life expectancy. The families which were less concerned with such issues tended to live longer and to be less concerned with the return to themselves.

Professor Parikh replied to Professor Urquidi's comment on urbanisation and industrialisation. He agreed that the implied savings rate was greater than observed in India, and therefore perhaps not realisable. If even the likely growth rates were optimistic, then the prospects for meeting agricultural demands were even better. If economic growth did not take place, meeting demand (backed by purchasing power) for food would be no problem. However, there would be an urban problem which could not be tackled without resources. As a prognosis for the American situation, he suggested that since the U.S.A. had now withdrawn from Vietnam, money previously going into the war effort could go into building urban infrastructure.

Professor Demeny replied to Professor Ben Porath. He thought that basically they agreed. Professor Demeny had asked for healthy common sense and for proceeding through debate. His particular approach would be a Pavlowian one, with a mixture of reward and punishment. However, economic theory was influential and did seep through to politicians, and there was therefore a danger that they would formulate the problem in an economic way. Perhaps this constrained the set of choices they regarded as feasible. This linked to what Professor Perlman said about direct interference with taste. Just as, for example, with criminals one tended to use education rather than imposing heavy penalties, so with consumer sovereignty one could have suitable social action on tastes. Perhaps economists *had* set the process back.

Professor Schultz replied to the discussion. He insisted that his was only a rudimentary analysis which he labelled 'the demand theory of fertility'. While it might not be still-born, it was still in its infancy and one could not yet judge what it might provide in the way of policy conclusions. Five or six years' study of data might well bring forth important insights. He certainly believed that Professor Demeny had been too dismal in his forecast about the small pay-off that was likely to come if this approach was used in underdeveloped countries.

Professor Schultz wondered whether the crude variables used in exploratory econometric studies were relevant to underdeveloped countries, and agreed that the specification and measurement of these variables should now be refined. The next round of research would try to incorporate the kind of concept mentioned by Professor Ohlin and Dr Jones. It would have to isolate the real variables and rework and refashion data to check out these subtler implications of the theory.

However, if crude variables were used, they were at least consistent with common sense, and were nonetheless able to account for much of the differences between fertility in low-income and high-income countries and differences within those countries. If these were crude variables they, at least, should be examined along with direct population-policy variables. In Taiwan, for example, one had better results in estimating the pay-off to family-planning activities when one held even these crude price and income variables constant than without such controls.

What about other criteria by which we judged the value of methodology in economics? One common criterion was the ability to account for variation in behaviour. For example, Professor Coale had talked to him when he had begun working in this field, and explained that the micro-economic approach would not be very beneficial because in underdeveloped countries fertility was not obviously related to 'demand' factors. However, looking at econometric work from twelve countries did suggest that economic variables were important, though variables like education could fit into the framework of other disciplines as well.

With the intellectual challenges in the population area, research economists were moving into the field. An agenda for research was needed. He would like more discussion of the complex technical issues which his paper had tried to pose.

To broaden the analysis, one should perhaps deal with taste formation in relation to price and income effects. Very few people had tried to study the evolution of taste. Easterlin had speculated about it, but few others in quantitative fields had done so. Perhaps biological constraints were not very important. Sex preference appeared to be important at the micro-level, but it was not clear that it made much difference for the whole society or the whole population.

Professor Schultz wanted to applaud what Professor Perlman had said about disease and would like to see more study of morbidity and how it affected resource and expenditure patterns in less-developed countries.

All the issues raised here could be studied within the demand framework, but he admitted that there was much more unexplained variation in fertility, however defined, in less-developed than in more-developed countries.

5 Fertility in Israel: a Mini-survey and some New Findings*

Yoram Ben Porath
MAURICE FALK INSTITUTE, JERUSALEM

I. INTRODUCTION

The demographic scene in Israel is characterised by a wide range of variation in fertility rarely observed in a country with a similar per capita income (1784 dollars in 1972), and by a variety of experiences over time. Much of the richness of the data is associated with the ethnic-religious heterogeneity of the population: in addition to Jews who constitute approximately 85 per cent of the population, there are Moslems and Druze with significantly higher levels of fertility than the Jews; Christian Arabs occupy a middle position. Within the Jewish population there is unusual variety emanating from the simple fact that about 60 per cent of the population age 15+ is foreign born and another 36 per cent of the population are first generation Israelis.

In 1948 there were only 672 thousand Jews in Israel; Jewish population in 1972 was 3·194 millions.[1] A huge wave of immigration came in the period 1948–52 when the population doubled. Since then there were ups and downs in the immigration flow. While the pre-1948 population was mostly of Eastern and Central European origin, the post-1948 immigration included Jews both from mostly Arab countries in Asia and Africa and from Europe and America. The resulting fertility in Israel and completed family size were influenced by the diversity of fertility experienced in the Jewish communities of origin, by the special conditions prior to immigration (particularly in Europe during and after the Second World War), and by the experience of immigration. Movement in fertility over time in Israel is thus not just a response to changing conditions in Israel,

* This paper is partly a summary of past work and partly a report on some ongoing research. I wish to acknowledge the programming and research assistance of Y. Melnick, E. Livne and E. Hakak, and to thank the staff of the Israel Central Bureau of Statistics for their cooperation. The research was partly financed by the Ford Rockefeller Program in support of Social Science Research on Population Policy and by the Israel Foundations Trustees.

[1] I shall refer here to Israel in its official borders which do not include the territories administered by Israel since June 1967. Some of the data after 1967 refer also to the population of East Jerusalem.

but most likely a gradual adjustment of behaviour from levels shaped by the determining variables elsewhere to new and different conditions in Israel.

For an economist it is natural to theorise within a framework that emphasises maximisation of utility subject to resource constraints. Like many other students of fertility behaviour today I find in the household production model offered by Becker (1965) and in the demand theory suggested by Lancaster (1966) a useful framework for the study of fertility, because of the explicit role they give to the activities and constraints within the household and their interactions with market phenomena. The problems analysed are familiar: the relation between family size and the value of time of parents, particularly mothers; children's traits and expenditure on children; the cost of contraception; the role of difference in various abilities ('productivity') of parents; the role of child mortality. The new framework facilitates the analysis of interrelationships among variables that are often unobserved directly. A terse way of describing one common aspect of the new treatment of most of these problems is a general disenchantment with the income effect and a reliance on a variety of substitution effects, i.e. a judgement that with more resources there are important changes in the implicit prices attached to various activities and that observed associations with income are 'contaminated' by various price effects on which one is able to say something based on economic considerations. We are more at a loss in tackling changes or differences in tastes (emphasised in the studies of Richard A. Easterlin, 1968, 1969) and in information. This may be a particularly important handicap in the analysis of the Israeli situation.

I shall not present this framework here. It is laid out in detail in some of the papers that I cite (the Supplement to *The Journal of Political Economy* (March–April 1973) includes several papers using a similar framework. See also recent surveys by Schultz, 1973 and Nerlove, 1973). It is however clear that the new home economics, to use Marc Nerlove's language, just provides a framework that has to be filled up with content; i.e. further restrictions have to be put either on the structure of preferences or on the nature of the technology or the specification of resources if meaningful statements are to be made. The sources of these restrictions can be one's own hunches, the ideas coming from general demographic research (even when they are not formulated in an economist's jargon), or more important, the interaction with the data. The state of the art seems to recommend an agnostic or at least a flexible approach in which specific ideas are confronted with the data, thus opening a dialogue between the theory and the data, in which one learns what to discard and what to focus attention on. The research reported here is part of an incomplete participation in such a dialogue.

The second section of this paper is a very brief summary of some of the major developments in fertility in Israel. The third is a cursory report on some past research. The fourth part of the paper reports on current work on fertility, education and child mortality.

II. *MAJOR TRENDS IN FERTILITY IN ISRAEL*

A rough idea of some of the major 'facts' can be derived from Table 5.1, where total fertility is the measure of fertility. These

TABLE 5.1 TOTAL FERTILITY,[a] 1951–1971

	Jews				$\frac{AA}{EA}$	Non-Jews			
	Total	Born in Israel	Asia and Africa	Europe and America		Total	Moslems	Christians	Druze and others
	(1)	(2)	(3)	(4)	(5)	(6)	(7)	(8)	(9)
1951	4·0	3·5	6·3	3·1	2·03	—	—	—	—
1956	3·7	2·7	5·6	2·6	2·15	7·3	7·6	4·7	6·9
1961–2	3·4	2·7	5·0	2·3	2·11	7·8	9·1	4·7	7·5
1966	3·4	2·8	4·5	2·5	1·80	8·2	9·7	4·3	7·4
1971	3·5	3·2	4·1	3·1	1·32	7·4	8·7	3·4	7·1
	Composition of population age 15 + (per cent)								
1971	100·0	25·1	30·5	33·3		11·1	7·8	2·4	0·9

[a] Sum of age-specific birth ratios for all women aged 15–49.
Source: Central Bureau of Statistics, *Statistical Abstract of Israel, 1972*, Table II/24, p. 84.

figures (and the complete time series) show the following picture.

Total fertility of the total Jewish population declined during the first decade and then stabilised at approximately 3·4. This is a net outcome of partly opposing trends within the population. Jews born in Asia-Africa (henceforth AA), the group with highest Jewish fertility, experienced a decline in fertility of more than a third over twenty years. The two other Jewish groups, those born in Israel (Is) and those born in Europe and America (EA) experienced what may be described as a swing: a decline in fertility in the first decade, stabilisation in 1958 to 1963 and an increase since. As a result, relative differentials between AA and EA started to narrow only in the last decade (Table 5.1, column 5).

In the non-Jewish population there is a clear trend of decline in total fertility among the Christians starting from 1966; among

Moslems there is some increase toward the early 1960s, and since then some decline. This is the group with highest fertility in Israel and probably one of the highest in the world.

One might add that short-term fluctuations around those trends tended to conform to the level of economic activity among all groups including non-Jews and AA Jews (this is reported in my 1973*b* and in Schwinger 1969).

We know that 'total fertility' has some severe limitations as an indicator of changes in completed fertility. Total fertility may be an even poorer indicator when one considers migrant populations with some of the children acquired abroad. What seems to require further checks is the recent increase in fertility among EA and Israeli born Jews. There is no doubt however about the decline in fertility among AA Jews. This can be contrasted with the persistently high Moslem fertility, which may be showing just the first signs of decline.

The decline in fertility among the AA Jews is clearly just one aspect of what sociologists would term modernisation and is associated with a rapid rise in incomes and many other changes in education and other economic and cultural characteristics that have occurred during the process of adjustment of this group in Israel. It is also quite clear that the Moslem (and mostly rural) population was exposed to a narrower range of influences. Rapid rise in income based largely on employment in the Jewish sector (see my 1966) is being followed by a lagged, and still modest, transformation in other variables that are usually considered fertility depressing. The trends in the level of schooling of women (as revealed in the differentials by age in the 1961 census of population) indicate a later turning point in the schooling of Arab women compared to AA women (see Fig. 5.1).

The aggregate figures do not however give firm answers to the mechanisms involved. A primitive standardisation by education leaves a lot that is unexplained in the changes over time (my 1970*a*). Labour-force participation of women (which should be regarded as jointly determined with fertility rather than determining) has increased over time, but not very sharply and not much differentially among groups (see Table 5.2).

Schooling of children and young adults has also increased markedly over time, but it seems that the increase was greater among the children of EA parents than among the children of AA parents.

The subsequent discussion I regret to say will not explain the trends over time. I have referred to it here both as a background and as the eventual challenge. A study of the 1961 census which is now under way and comparisons with the recent data will, it is hoped, shed some light on the broader issues.

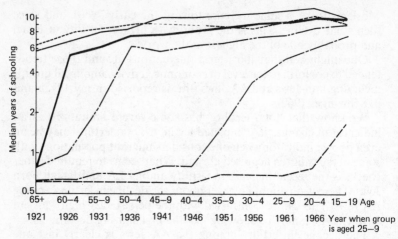

Fig. 5.1 Age profiles of women's education, by population group: 1961 – median years of schooling (semi-log scale).

Jews
Israel-born
  Israel-born father
  AA father
  EA father
Asia-Africa born
Europe-America born
Non-Jews

Source: Central Bureau of Statistics, Languages, Literacy and Educational Attainment, pt I, Census publication no. 15 (Jerusalem, 1963) Tables 28–34. Reproduced from Ben Porath (1972).

III. *SOME ISSUES IN PAST CROSS-SECTION RESEARCH*[1]

Cross-section data are a natural arena for trying things out, and maybe even getting some quantitative notions about the underlying structure.

Two points have to be remembered, however: (a) cross-section parameters of the major variables may be affected by processes of adjustment over time, because diffusion, or speed of adjustment, is likely to be related to the same variables that affect long-term behaviour. (b) There is a basic econometric difficulty in most cross-section studies: when the object of inquiry is family size, treated as an

---

[1] This section is mostly a summary of some past work. Those who read my 1970*a*, 1973*a* papers can omit this section without missing much. I refer here generously to some of my earlier papers identified only by the year of publication.

endogenous variable, there are not many exogenous variables around. Variables traditionally considered, such as the labour-force participation of women or the length of marriage, are clearly determined to some extent jointly with family size, partly by left-out, unobserved, taste and price variables. This may be true also of education, the central variable in the subsequent discussion. Another way of saying more or less the same thing is that we do not have direct observations on the pure taste variation across individuals nor of the 'true' implicit or explicit prices that shape individual behaviour, but only on imperfect proxies correlated with both. At present the choice is between daring experiments in simultaneous estimation (e.g. Nerlove and T. P. Schultz, 1970) and careful consideration of simple relationships where it is not uncommon to see dependent and independent variables changing places.

Even before education was appropriated by economists, its relation to fertility and family size was widely observed. There are many reasons why education could affect family size and in one form or another we are familiar with them all (I have listed some in sketchy models of utility maximisation in my 1970*b* paper). My present concern is with the question whether the specific forms in which education and fertility are associated can tell us something about the relative importance of the various mechanisms.

The simple hypothesis with which the trip through the data began was based on Becker's theory of the allocation of time (1965). Goods purchased in the market and time enter into the production of final commodities. Raising children uses more of the mother's time relative to other goods than do other final commodities. In a context of linear homogeneous and separable production functions for child services and other goods, with no reversal of factor intensity, the relative price of children *vis-à-vis* other goods moves directly with the value of time. Education is, *inter alia*, one of the important determinants of the value of time. Thus, the implication for empirical research is a negative association between fertility and the education of women. Where men are concerned, their lesser role in child-rearing makes the substitution effect less important (but there is a larger income effect).[1]

---

[1] The elasticity of the number of children (n) with respect to the value of time of a husband or wife (w) is:

$$\eta_{nw} = \eta^*_{n\pi_n}(\alpha_n - \alpha_s) + \gamma\eta_{nI}$$

where $\eta^*_{n\pi_n}$ is the Hicks compensated price-elasticity for children. α_n, α_s are the share of the value of time in the full prices π_n, π_s of n and s, respectively. γ is the share of the value of the wife's (or husband's) time in the full income of the family, η_{nI} is the income-elasticity of children, and s is composite consumption (see my 1973*a*).

The main findings concerning the role of education in explaining fertility differentials in Israel are the following:

1. Education of women explains part of the differences between ethnic groups in the Israeli population but leaves much that is unexplained. This comes out in standardisations of aggregate data of the number of children ever born (1972) and in regressions of individual data (1973a, Table 4) where dummy variables for continent of birth and period of immigration are significant and account for much of the individual variance.

2. Where average birth rates of communities (standardised for women's age composition; 1973a, Table 2) are regressed against median schooling of men and women, fertility is more consistently and sharply associated with women's than men's education. (A notable exception is the regression for kibbutzim, where the economic argument is weaker.) Here too there is a significant effect of the composition by origin.

TABLE 5.2   RATES OF LABOUR-FORCE PARTICIPATION OF
JEWISH WOMEN AGED 14+

	1956	1960	1971
All Jewish women	26·5	27·3	29·8
Born in Israel	27·4	36·8	38·8
Born in Asia and Africa	20·2	21·8	25·1
Immigrated:			
1947	21·8	19·2	22·0
1948–54	⎱ 19·9	⎱ 22·2	25·5
1954–60	⎰	⎰	27·7
1961+			23·1
Born in Europe and America	29·8	32·5	34·1
Immigrated:			
1947	31·2	34·1	34·2
1948–54	⎱ 28·3	⎱ 31·3	31·7
1955–60	⎰	⎰	39·0
1961+			35·7

Source: Central Bureau of Statistics, *Statistical Abstract of Israel* (1972).

3. In data for individual households where the number of children ever born is the dependent variable there was a clearer relation with women's than with men's schooling. The education effect differs between origin groups.

4. However, the relationship between the number of children ever born and women's education (as observed in the Family Expenditure Survey (F.E.S.) sample) has an interesting shape: the number of children declines very sharply from women with no education to women with 1–4 years schooling, and then declines

much more mildly. In the samples I examined it was not clear whether women with 13+ years of schooling had more or fewer children than women with 9–12 years of schooling.

Similar non-linearities were observed by Willis (1973) in U.S. data. His argument is that at higher levels of education, because of the correlated higher income of husbands, the value of time is shaped less by education and more by husband's income. However, Gronau (1973) reports tentatively a relatively small effect of husband's income on wife's value of time. Willis offers an 'interaction model' that allows a decline of the (absolute) slope of the fertility-education relation as husband's income (or education) increases. This proved to be a reasonable summary of U.S. data and also of the Israeli data, giving an alternative expression to the non-linear relationship observed (see Tables 7 and 8 in my 1973*a*).

There are many issues here. The intensity of child-rearing in terms of mother's time relative to other goods is a matter that requires some elaboration. The role of the mother in pregnancy and the delivery of the baby is unquestionable, but the decision to have babies is taken as a commitment for a longer period. It has been established both in Israeli data and elsewhere that as far as the influence of the presence of children on women's labour-force participation is concerned, the effect is strong in the very first years of life and then it declines (see Gronau, 1973; Landsberger, 1973; Leibowitz, 1972; Smith, 1972; Hill and Stafford, 1971; and my 1973*a*). On the other hand, as the children grow up they exert stronger pressures on the money budget of the family (those who have not been exposed to this directly can find some evidence in Landsberger, 1973).

We know that there are within-country and between-country differences in the care of young children. There are differences in the institutions used, in the age at which children leave home, the hours they spend out of home, the use of baby-sitters, maids, house-keepers, governesses, etc. This may be an indication of some substitution in production (between mother's time and other arrangements) and/or substitution in consumption between the quality that parents think is associated with mother's care and other goods, or there may be income or education effects on the demand for quality in children (see Leibowitz, 1973). Some of these questions cannot be resolved, but looking at women's time allocation would help. Several studies of U.S. data suggest that small children are associated with a greater withdrawal from the labour force of college-educated women than less educated ones, and that educated women devoted more time to children than less educated ones (Leibowitz, 1972; Hill and Stafford, 1971; Gronau, 1973). In the Israeli data it seems to me that as far as

TABLE 5.3 LABOUR-FORCE PARTICIPATION RATE OF JEWISH WOMEN,[a]
BY NUMBER OF CHILDREN AGED 0–17, CONTINENT OF BIRTH,
AND YEARS OF SCHOOLING, 1971

Number of children	Years of schooling		
	0–8	9–12	13+
Israel born			
0	21·0	51·4	79·5
1	20·2	38·7	75·7
2	19·2	32·6	63·6
3	9·7	21·1	60·9
Asia-Africa born			
0	15·8	35·6	62·4
1	18·9	29·3	51·5
2	20·7	41·4	48·0
3	14·6	18·0	45·4
Europe-America born			
0	19·3	35·1	56·5
1	28·7	57·9	62·5
2	13·7	24·1	62·4
3	1·3	17·1	67·0
Difference between women with 2 children and 1 child (2–1):			
Israel born	−1·0	−6·1	−12·1
Asia-Africa born	1·8	12·1	−3·5
Europe-America born	−15·0	−33·8	−0·1
Difference between women with 3 and 2 children (3–2):			
Israel born	−9·5	−11·5	−2·7
Asia-Africa born	−6·1	−23·4	−2·6
Europe-America born	−12·4	−7·0	4·6
Difference between women with 3 children and 1 child (3–1):			
Israel born	−10·5	−16·7	−14·8
Asia-Africa born	−4·3	−11·3	−6·1
Europe-America born	−27·4	−40·8	4·5

[a] Married, divorced and widowed.
Source: Central Bureau of Statistics, unpublished data.

labour-force participation is concerned the reverse is true, at least
for part of the population. In my 1973*a* (Table 11) I have shown that
the presence of children below five hardly affects labour-force
participation of EA women with nine or more years of schooling,
and that in the whole population this effect declines as educational
level rises. In the 1968 and 1971 labour force surveys one can see that
an increase in number of children (under 17) from one to two or to
three has a very modest effect on the labour-force participation rates
of EA women with 13+ years of schooling, while there is a greater
(and not monotonic) effect on women with less education (the data

TABLE 5.4 MEAN WEEKLY HOURS OF HIRED DOMESTIC HELP BY NUMBER OF CHILDREN AGED 0–17, CONTINENT OF BIRTH, AND YEARS OF SCHOOLING: 1971[a]

Number of children	Years of schooling		
	0–8	9–12	13+
Israel born			
0	0·90	1·65	2·88
1	0·60	2·34	6·31
2	0·48	3·26	10·13
3	0·18	1·96	11·32
Asia-Africa born			
0	0·08	0·50	1·50
1	0·17	1·30	6·28
2	0·11	1·59	4·54
3	0·06	1·21	6·39
Europe-America born			
0	0·49	1·90	2·76
1	0·49	4·32	5·90
2	0·27	3·07	7·20
3	0·31	2·31	9·14
Difference between women with 2 children and 1 child (2–1):			
Israel born	−0·12	0·92	3·82
Asia-Africa born	−0·06	0·29	−1·74
Europe-America born	−0·22	−1·25	1·30
Difference between women with 3 and 2 children (3–2):			
Israel born	−0·30	−1·30	1·19
Asia-Africa born	−0·05	−0·38	−1·85
Europe-America born	0·04	−0·76	1·94
Difference between women with 3 children and 1 child (3–1):			
Israel born	−0·42	−0·38	5·01
Asia-Africa born	−0·11	−0·09	0·11
Europe-America born	−0·18	−2·01	3·24

[a] The population is the same as that of Table 5.3.
Source: Central Bureau of Statistics, unpublished data.

for 1968 are presented in my 1970*a* paper; the data for 1971 in Table 5.3). For AA women the different sources are not consistent. An interesting piece of evidence in this connection is the data on the employment of housemaids (who very often baby-sit in addition to doing housework). Women with less than 13 years of schooling tend to use fewer hours of help per week with increased family size while women with 13 + years of schooling employ an *increasing* amount of domestic help as the number of children increases (Table 5.4). This supports evidence that I used before (1973*a*, Table 13) on expenditures on maids, and provides some direct indication of the use of substitutes in home duties of women with high opportunity costs. It leaves unresolved the question of whether this substitution affects the time input into child care or into other home chores. Leibowitz (1972) inferred from U.S. and French data that there is more time input into child care by more educated women so that substitution occurs in home duties *other* than child care. (We shall know more about the Israeli case once my colleague Reuben Gronau completes his current work on the subject.)

Education plays a central role both in the theory and the empirical work in this discussion. Even if it were a perfect indicator of years spent in school (which we know it is not) the measured education variable is an imperfect and non-linear proxy to several 'true' variables and at various locations along the education scale a different true variable may be more potent. That there is a need for a refinement in the theory and measurement, is a general, and trivial, proposition. In the Israeli case there is a concrete need not to depend on a single small sample, but to explore more and larger bodies of data, so that the heterogeneity of the population becomes an asset rather than a constraint. In the next section there are some preliminary results in this vein.

IV. *CURRENT RESEARCH: MIGRATING PARENTS, EDUCATION AND CHILD MORTALITY*

In this section I discuss some work still in its preliminary stages. I shall pursue one issue suggested by the earlier work, i.e. the nature of the fertility-education relationship, and discuss another issue – the role of child mortality.

As indicated, a large fraction of the adult population is foreign born. Particularly interesting is, I think, the population of couples who got married abroad and possibly started to have children abroad and when they immigrated to Israel were still young enough to have the option of more children. (Matras, 1973, has already discussed the importance of the distinction by place of marriage.)

The Israeli 1961 census of population includes an unusual piece of information: couples married abroad were asked about the number of children born abroad and of those the number who died under the age of five. This allows us to examine surviving children rather than all children born and, more important, to analyse the effect of child mortality on fertility.

An idea of the magnitude of the child mortality rates involved is given by Table 5.5 (a more extensive survey of Jewish child mortality is given by Schmeltz, 1971). Behind the means there is a wide variation over countries, over time, and over individuals. For example, immigrants from the Yemen report a loss of close to 50 per cent of their children born abroad compared with around 14 per cent for immigrants from Syria and Lebanon. Likewise, the decline in child mortality abroad can be traced in the data by age at immigration and date of immigration.

Child mortality is a problematic variable to analyse: even in a very poor environment parents have a certain amount of discretion in the attention, care and resources that they devote to keeping their children alive and healthy, so that child mortality is probably not a

TABLE 5.5 CHILDREN OF JEWISH FOREIGN-BORN WOMEN MARRIED ONCE: PERCENTAGE WHO DIED ABROAD UNDER THE AGE OF FIVE (BY MOTHER'S CONTINENT-OF-BIRTH AND YEARS OF SCHOOLING)

Years of schooling	Asia-Africa born	Europe-America born
Total	23·5	11·2
0	27·4	19·6
1–4	18·1	12·6
5–8	14·2	10·7
9–10	11·3	8·0
11–12		8·3
13+		7·5

Source: Central Bureau of Statistics, *Marriage and Fertility*, pt II, Population and Housing Census 1961, publication no. 32 (Jerusalem, 1966), Table 27.

perfectly exogenous variable. The same variables that make some people have many children may make them careless (or careful) in keeping them alive. In the following I shall ignore this and regard mortality as exogenous.

In analysing the effects of child mortality on fertility I shall use a framework designed to deal with exogenous traits of children (Ben Porath and Welch, 1973; Ben Porath, 1973c), which generated the following implications:

1. Holding *expectations* concerning child mortality constant, those who, out of a given number of births, lost more children will be inclined to have more children, but probably not enough to compensate fully for those that died. The logic is simple: those who have, out of a given number of births, lost more children have, *ceteris paribus*, a lower real income; they will revise downwards their consumption plans for all normal goods; that is why if surviving children were a normal good there would be no *complete* replacement of deceased children. However, there is no reason to think that people would want to absorb the *whole* loss in terms of surviving children. They are likely to want to distribute the loss over all normal

goods (in other words the marginal propensity to consume surviving children is not unity). That is why there will be *some* replacement of deceased children. Full replacement is consistent with zero income-elasticity for surviving children.

2.   Expecting lower mortality of children can either raise or lower the number of births depending on the price-elasticity of children. A useful analogy is to think of the effect of technical progress on the derived demand for a factor of production. It is the same here: a decline in child mortality reduces the cost of a surviving child and thus raises the desired number of surviving children, depending on the demand-elasticity of children and on the share of costs incurred before death out of the total cost of raising a surviving child (see my 1973c). Given that the demand for children is not likely to be very elastic and that only a fraction of costs is being saved by increased survival, the implied encouragement to births is likely to be more than offset by the fact that fewer births are now needed for one survivor (see T. P. Schultz, 1973a,b).

3.   As noted by O'Hara (1972), the demand for surviving children may in fact decline if one expects lower mortality because of the increased rate of return in investment in child's quality. This can be looked at in terms of the quantity-quality formulation of Lewis and Becker (1973), or my more specialised formulation (1973c).

4.   There are no clear implications about the *pure* uncertainty aspects which depend on a stronger specification of the form of the utility function. (See Rothschild and Stiglitz, 1971, 1972. O'Hara, 1972, worked on the uncertainty aspects.)

All this is one way of saying something about what lies behind the usual expectation of finding reduced child mortality associated with reduced fertility.

There are two separate phases in the family formation process that I want to discuss – births abroad and births in Israel. There are three types of independent variables here: child mortality, schooling of husband and wife, and time variables – age, length of stay in Israel.

V. *BIRTHS AND SURVIVAL BEFORE IMMIGRATION*

As Table 5.6 indicates, we are dealing with two very different populations as far as the level of fertility abroad is concerned. There are differences here of between 3·7 to 1·8 in the number of births abroad and narrower differences of 2·3 to 1·2 in the number of survivors from abroad.

Let me first consider the role of education in the two origin groups. There are marked differences in the distribution of women by education (Table 5.7). Most of the AA women are bunched in

TABLE 5.6 MEAN BIRTHS ABROAD AND SURVIVORS[b] ABROAD TO JEWISH WOMEN[a]

| Age in '1961 | Immigrants from Asia and Africa | | Immigrants from Europe and America | | AA less EA | |
	Births (1)	Survivors (2)	Births (3)	Survivors (4)	Births (5)	Survivors (6)
	Immigrated before 1948					
16–34	0·3	0·3	0·4	0·4	−0·1	−0·2
35–54	2·4	1·7	0·6	0·5	1·8	1·2
55+	3·8	2·8	1·8	1·6	2·0	1·2
	Immigrated 1948+					
35–44	3·6	2·8	1·2	1·1	2·8	1·7
44–54	5·3	4·0	1·6	1·4	3·7	2·3
55+	5·6	4·0	1·9	1·7	3·7	2·3

[a] Married Jewish women (married once), married abroad, who immigrated to Israel before the age of 50.
[b] Births *less* deaths below age 5.
Source: Central Bureau of Statistics, based on data from the 1961 census of population.

the zero schooling category, with less than 1 per cent at the top (13+ years), while more than half of the EA group have from five to ten years of school with 3–9 per cent at the very bottom (0 years) and 4–10 per cent at the top (13+ years). In the regressions based on

TABLE 5.7 EDUCATIONAL LEVEL OF JEWISH WOMEN 1948+ IMMIGRANTS[a] AGED 35–44 IN 1961, BY CONTINENT OF BIRTH

Years of schooling	Asia-Africa %	Europe-America %
0	54·7	1·2
1–4	10·3	7·2
5–8	23·7	52·4
9–10	5·8	18·7
11–12	4·0	13·6
13+	1·5	6·9
Total	100·0	100·0

[a] See note *a* in Table 5.6.
Source: Table 5.A.

data for individual couples (Table 5.8) the coefficients of education represented by dummy variables have a very different pattern in the two groups: among EA the largest difference in the number of births is between women without schooling and those with 1–4 years. In the other educational categories the differences tend to be systematic but quite small in absolute terms. When we look at the differences per year of schooling we see that among women of all age-groups below 55 an additional year of school at the bottom is associated with a difference of a quarter to almost one half a child while in the highest categories it is more like one-twentieth of a child. The range

TABLE 5.8 REGRESSION OF BIRTHS ABROAD (BAB) TO JEWISH WOMEN 1948+ IMMIGRANTS[a] AGED 35–44 IN 1961, BY CONTINENT OF BIRTH

	Asia-Africa		Europe-America	
	Regression coefficient	t	Regression coefficient	t
Constant	−1·339	1·9	0·490	0·2
Death-rate abroad	1·932	10·2	1·186	11·6
Wife's age: in 1961	−0·088	3·7	−0·040	5·2
at immigration	0·259	16·0	0·076	17·4
Wife's years of schooling[b]				
0	0·858	6·2	1·163	6·7
1–4	0·745	3·8	0·070	0·9
9–10	−0·687	2·8	−0·144	2·9
11–12	−1·064	3·7	−0·157	2·7
13+	−1·930	4·2	−0·243	3·0
Husband's years of schooling[b]				
0	−0·142	1·0	0·279	1·7
1–4	−0·181	1·1	−0·064	1·0
9–10	0·097	0·5	−0·011	0·2
11–12	−0·024	0·1	−0·166	3·0
13+	0·224	0·8	−0·181	2·9
R^{-2c}	0·241		0·181	
Standard error of estimate	2·190		0·914	
Number of observations	1834		2627	

[a] See note *a* in Table 5.6.
[b] The base for the groups of dummy variables is wives with 5–8 years schooling and husbands with 5–8 years schooling.
[c] The coefficient of determination (R^2) adjusted for degrees of freedom.
Source: Table 5.B.

of years of schooling over which large declines of fertility are associated with schooling is somewhat broader among older women (55+). The pattern is quite different among AA women, where the stronger educational effects are at the (relative) top, among the relatively small number of women with 5–8 or more years of schooling (Fig. 5.2).

In examining 'surviving' children (i.e. births abroad minus deaths abroad of children under 5) the difference is even more marked (when the child death-rate is excluded as an *explanatory* variable) because more often than not AA women with 1–4 years of schooling have

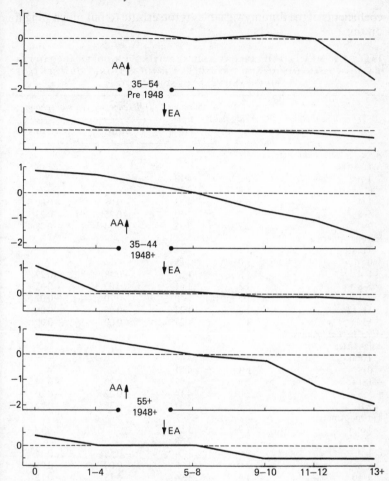

FIG. 5.2 Regression coefficients of births abroad to Jewish women[a] who immigrated before the age of 50, by age in 1961, date of immigration, and years of schooling.

[a] See note *a* to Table 5.6.
Source: Table 5.B.

slightly more children than women with no schooling (Table 5.9). In general the differentials by education are narrower for surviving children than for births, because of the inverse association between death-rates and education of women. (The coefficients of husband's education are somewhat erratic. In linear equations they tend to be positive for AA and negative for EA but the pattern of the coefficients of the dummy variables is too erratic to put much weight on this.)

TABLE 5.9 MEAN BIRTHS ABROAD AND 'SURVIVING' CHILDREN ABROAD PER JEWISH WOMAN IMMIGRANT,[a] BY AGE AT IMMIGRATION, CONTINENT OF BIRTH, AND YEARS OF SCHOOLING

Years of schooling	Births abroad	Survivors from abroad	Difference per years of schooling	
			Births	Survivors
Aged 35–9 at immigration				
Asia-Africa				
Total	5·3	4·12		
0	5·8	4·30	—	—
1–4	5·6	4·53	−0·08	+0·09
5–8	4·2	3·62	−0·35	−0·23
9+	3·7	3·35	−0·14	−0·08
Europe-America				
Total	1·7	1·51		
0	3·0	2·25	—	—
1–4	1·8	1·53	−0·48	−0·29
5–8	1·8	1·61	0·00	+0·02
9–10	1·5	1·40	−0·10	−0·07
11–12	1·4	1·28	−0·05	−0·06
13+	1·4	1·27	0·00	−0·00
Aged 40–4 at immigration				
Asia-Africa				
Total	5·9	4·44		
0	6·4	4·61	—	—
1–14	5·9	4·97	−0·20	+0·14
5–8	5·0	4·14	−0·22	−0·20
9+	3·9	3·37	−0·31	−0·22
Europe-America				
Total	1·9	1·68		
0	3·3	2·58	—	—
1–4	2·0	1·74	−0·52	−0·34
5–8	2·0	1·78	0·00	+0·01
9–10	1·6	1·44	−0·13	−0·12
11–12	1·4	1·28	0·10	−0·08
13+	1·4	1·33	0·00	+0·02

[a] See note *a* to Table 5.6.
Source: Central Bureau of Statistics, *Marriage and Fertility*, pt II, Population and Housing Census 1961, publication no. 32 (Jerusalem, 1966), Tables 23, 27.

These patterns could give an impression of a process of diffusion of decline in fertility that started early in EA communities and later in AA communities and that has spread along the education scale starting from the top. This process has already covered most of the EA community except the very bottom, but older cohorts still exhibit the effects of its earlier phases. The current AA generations are in the

midst of the process; the differentials by education are more pronounced at the top but have not gone all the way down.

This is not a substantive statement. It does not put a finger on
the things that control this process of decline in number of children.
The point just made is that the different patterns may suggest that the
cross-section relation between births and education reflect also
dynamic factors and not only, or mainly, the effects of static
differences associated with education.

TABLE 5.10 THE DERIVATIVES AT THE MEANS OF BIRTHS ABROAD[a] WITH
RESPECT TO THE NUMBER OF CHILD DEATHS ABROAD[b]
(Per cent)

Years of schooling	Age in 1961 and date of immigration					
	16–34	35–54 before 1948	35–44 1948 +	45–54 1948 +	55+	
					before 1948	1948 +
Asia-Africa						
I[b]	1·111	0·889	0·950	0·787	1·010	0·768
	(32·2)	(14·2)	(28·4)	(21·0)	(12·7)	(16·0)
II[c]	0·683	0·533	0·488	0·607	0·967	0·705
Europe-America						
I[b]	0·904	1·074	1·028	1·013	1·172	1·014
	(6·3)	(19·1)	(21·3)	(22·7)	(24·0)	(17·8)
II[c]	1·000	1·825	0·982	0·882	1·083	1·067

[a] See note *a* to Table 5.6.
[b] The coefficient of deaths abroad (DAB) in a regression where the dependent variable is births abroad (BAB) and the other independent variables are age, age at immigration, and schooling of wife and husband (the full regression is not shown).
[c] Based on the coefficient of the child death-rate ($\hat{\gamma}$) in Table 5.B, the average child death-rate $\overline{(CDR)}$, and average births abroad $\overline{(BAB)}$, as follows:

$$\frac{\partial BAB}{\partial DAB} = \frac{\hat{\gamma}}{\overline{BAB} + \hat{\gamma}\overline{CDR}}$$

Source: Data from the 1961 census of population.

The other central variable in the equation for fertility abroad is
the child death-rate experienced by the couple. I have already
indicated the misgivings that arise about putting the number of
deaths as an independent variable in a fertility equation. To the
extent that there are errors common to deaths abroad and births
abroad, using their ratio as an independent variable will partly
correct for the upward bias of the coefficients of deaths abroad.
On the other hand the random element in births abroad introduces
a downward bias into the coefficients of the ratio of deaths to births
abroad. In Table 5.10 the derivative of births abroad with respect
to child deaths abroad implied by the two formulations are

presented. 'Replacement' is stronger among EA than AA women, but is quite high for both groups.

The regression coefficients of the death-rate abroad are no greater for EA than for AA women; the smaller derivatives for AA are a consequence of the larger number of births among AA (if $\hat{\gamma}$ is the estimated regression coefficient of CDR, child death-rate, on BAB births abroad, the effect of an additional child death on births is $\partial(BAB)/\partial(DAB) = \hat{\gamma}/[(BAB)+\hat{\gamma}(CDR)]$. In the discussion below of the effect of child mortality abroad on births in Israel I speculate about this difference. In terms of the theoretical framework presented earlier full replacement is associated with zero price-elasticity for surviving children if experience of child mortality affects expectation, and it implies zero income-elasticity for children if expectations are independent of experience. More than full replacement is consistent with inelastic demand in the former (or with substitution with 'quality') and is not expected to occur in the latter case.

VI. *BIRTHS IN ISRAEL*

This second phase in family formation is of course much more complex. Given both the complexity and the opportunity that the data afford, I hope eventually to do a better job here, and must stress the preliminary nature of what is being presented at the moment. For some migrants the act of migration may have been a planned phase of the life cycle. For others, probably for a majority of immigrants to Israel, the span of time in which immigration was expected was relatively short so that rather than making a joint decision on the number of children to be born abroad and in Israel, the number of 'imported' children was a datum on arrival in Israel which should have affected behaviour in the second phase of family formation. Conditions in Israel would lead a couple with given characteristics to desire a different family size in Israel from what they would under some other conditions. But couples transplanted in the middle of family life are likely to adjust their desired family size differentially, depending presumably on the magnitude of the required adjustment, the size of family they already have, the flow of information and so on. Here again, variables that are postulated to affect the desired family size are likely to be relevant in the adjustment process, and this of course includes education. Even when the desired family size is not revised there may be changes in the achieved family size depending on the degree to which the new levels of child mortality are taken into account.

As Table 5.11 indicates, AA women have much higher fertility compared to EA women in Israel as well. It is interesting to note that among AA women over 35 there is not much difference in the total number of births between those who immigrated before 1948 and those who immigrated from 1948 on. The younger AA women (16–34) who immigrated earlier did have fewer children than those of the same cohorts who immigrated later. EA women of *all* ages show the reverse: those who immigrated earlier to Israel had on the whole more births than those who stayed abroad. The young ones at least are likely to end up with more surviving children than those of the same age who immigrated later.

TABLE 5.11 BIRTHS IN ISRAEL AND TOTAL BIRTHS TO JEWISH WOMEN[a] WHO IMMIGRATED BEFORE THE AGE OF 50

	Asia-Africa		Europe-America	
	Immigrated		Immigrated	
	before 1948	1948+	before 1948	1948+
Births in Israel				
16–34	3·4	2·7	1·9	1·1
35–44		2·0	1·7	0·9
45–54	3·5	0·6		0·3
55+	2·0	0·3	0·7	0·1
Total births				
16–34	3·7	4·6	2·4	1·9
35–44		5·6	2·3	2·1
45–54	5·9	6·0		1·9
55+	5·8	5·9	2·5	2·0
Total 'survivors'[b]				
16–34	3·7	4·3	2·2	1·9
35–44		4·8	2·8	3·1
45–54	5·2	4·7		3·3
55+	4·8	4·4	4·2	3·7

[a] See note *a* in Table 5.6.
[b] Births *less* deaths abroad below age 5. This overstates the true number of survivors because no account is taken of deaths in Israel.
Source: Based on data of the 1961 census of population.

In the relation between fertility and education something similar to what has been observed about births abroad is repeated here (Tables 5.12 and 5.C): among EA there is a sharp jump in births going from 0 to 1–4 years of schooling (a difference of about one child in the younger and longer-resident groups), with other changes being much milder. Among AA the change in fertility with education tends to be less concentrated at the bottom of the education ladder; what is not repeated is the sharp decline at the top – the few women with 13+ years of schooling do not differ significantly from those with 11–12 years of schooling. The similarity between the patterns abroad and in Israel suggests that in spite of the changing condi-

TABLE 5.12 TWO REGRESSIONS OF BIRTHS IN ISRAEL (BIS) FOR TWO
SELECTED GROUPS OF JEWISH WOMEN 1948+ IMMIGRANTS[a] AGED 35–44 IN
1961, BY CONTINENT OF BIRTH

	Asia-Africa		Europe-America	
	Regression coefficient	t	Regression coefficient	t
Number of observations	1837		2627	
Regression I				
Constant	4·990	9·8	2·624	11·8
Births abroad	−0·175	8·7	−0·274	14·7
Deaths abroad	0·087	2·5	0·457	9·2
Wife's age at immigration	−0·115	8·7	−0·057	10·2
Wife's length of residence in Israel	0·083	9·8	0·025	3·7
Wife's years of schooling[b]				
0	0·565	5·5	0·553	3·5
1–4	0·369	2·6	−0·106	1·5
9–10	−0·206	1·1	−0·051	1·1
11–12	−0·377	1·8	−1·530	2·9
13+	0·015	0·0	−0·072	1·0
Husband's years of schooling[b]				
0	0·056	0·6	0·166	1·1
1–4	0·093	0·2	−0·020	0·3
9–10	−0·472	3·6	0·029	0·6
11–12	−0·473	3·0	0·014	0·3
13+	−0·668	3·4	−0·028	0·5
$\bar{R}^2$	0·286		0·285	
Standard error of estimate	1·602		0·823	
Partial derivative of births in Israel with respect to:				
Survivors from abroad	−0·175		−0·274	
Deaths abroad	−0·088		0·183	

tions people behave as if the same 'true' variables that operated
behind education abroad continued to be relevant in Israel.

Let me now turn to the other major issue here – the effect of child
mortality abroad on fertility in Israel. I have already noted the fairly
wide differences in the incidence of child mortality abroad, across
countries of origin, education, and individuals. There is no exact
record of the time-path of child mortality by origin of parents in
Israel; it is quite clear however that a steep decline to negligible
levels has occurred in all groups. A study from the vital statistics for
1960–3 estimated the infant mortality rate at 24·8 per thousand
births: 26·4 for AA women, 23·9 for EA, and 20·5 for the Israel-born
(see Schmelz, 1971; Peritz and Bialik, 1968). Data for the early
1950s suggest that the rate for EA was not much different and the
rate for AA was closer to 50 per thousand and declining fast
(Kallner, 1958; see also Halevi, 1973). Infant mortality is 80–90 per

TABLE 5.12 (cont.)

	Asia-Africa		Europe-America	
	Regression coefficient	t	Regression coefficient	t
Regression II				
Constant	4·912	9·9	2·582	11·6
Births abroad	−0·182	10·8	−0·241	13·6
Deaths abroad	1·269	9·1	0·796	8·4
Wife's age at immigration	−0·113	8·8	−0·057	10·0
Wife's length of residence in Israel	0·076	4·5	0·026	3·8
Wife's years of schooling[b]				
0	0·509	5·1	0·664	4·2
1–4	0·347	2·5	−0·102	1·5
9–10	−0·203	1·2	−0·052	1·1
11–12	−0·368	1·8	−0·149	2·8
13+	−0·071	0·2	−0·068	0·9
Husband's years of schooling[b]				
0	0·006	0·1	1·332	0·9
1–4	0·065	0·5	−0·010	0·2
9–10	−0·467	3·6	0·024	0·5
11–12	−0·457	3·0	0·015	0·3
13+	−0·645	3·4	−0·021	0·4
$\bar{R}^2$ (adjusted)	0·315		0·285	
Standard error of estimate	1·569		0·825	
Partial derivative of births in Israel with respect to:				
Survivors from abroad	−0·182		−0·241	
Deaths abroad	0·169		0·447	

[a] See note *a* in Table 5.6.
[b] See note *b* in Table 5.8.
Source: Table 5.C.

cent of deaths below 5 so we can safely assume that in Israel immigrants experienced a very low rate of child mortality, much lower than most of them had experienced abroad.

How did the experience of child mortality abroad (or to be exact, deaths below age 5 of children *born* abroad) affect subsequent fertility?

Births in Israel (*BIS*) are expressed in absolute numbers and rates per year spent in Israel. The experience with children born abroad is expressed in two forms (regressions I and II in Tables 5.12 and 5.13). Ignoring now the other variables we note the following:

$$BIS = \alpha_1 BAB + \alpha_2 DAB$$
$$= \alpha_1 SAB + (\alpha_1 + \alpha_2)DAB \tag{5.1}$$

$$BIS = \beta_1 BAB + \beta_2(DAB/BAB)$$
$$= \beta_1 SAB + (\beta_1 + \beta_2/BAB)DAB \tag{5.2}$$

where *BIS* is births in Israel, *BAB* is births abroad, *DAB* is deaths abroad, and *SAB* is survivors abroad ($= BAB - DAB$).

The first line in each case is the equation as estimated. The second line is a different way of looking at the coefficients; for a given set of exogenous variables we expect those with a larger imported number of surviving children (*SAB*) to want to add to it less

TABLE 5.13　DERIVATIVES OF BIRTHS IN ISRAEL[a] WITH RESPECT TO SURVIVORS ABROAD AND DEATHS ABROAD: ALTERNATIVE FORMULATIONS

		Age in 1961 and date of immigration				
	16–34[b]	35–54 before 1948	35–44 1948+	45–54 1948+	55+ before 1948	55+ 1948+
Asia-Africa						
Derivative with respect to survivors from abroad[c]						
I	−0·294	−0·400	−0·175	−0·164	−0·269	−0·132
II	−0·271	−0·394	−0·182	−0·173	−0·298	−0·131
Deaths abroad[d]						
I	0	−0·258	−0·088	−0·166	−0·249	−0·107
II	0·424	0·103	0·170	−0·008	−0·178	−0·069
β_2[e]	1·323	1·175	1·269	0·881	0·460	0·378
	(11·5)	(4·2)	(9·1)	(5·9)	(0·9)	(2·1)
Europe-America						
Derivative with respect to survivors from abroad[c]						
I	−0·428	−0·393	−0·274	−0·101	−0·186	−0·086
II	−0·416	−0·335	−0·241	−0·085	−0·160	−0·077
Deaths abroad[d]						
I	0·349	0·270	0·183	0·053	0·005	−0·024
II	1·212	1·525	0·448	0·204	0·242	−0·012
β_2[e]	1·358	1·112	0·796	0·473	0·718	0·124
	(5·4)	(1·2)	(8·5)	(6·1)	(5·3)	(1·5)

[a] See note *a* to Table 5.6.
[b] Both length-of-residence groups.
[c] I: The coefficient of births abroad in the regressions of Table 5.B ($\hat{\alpha}_1$ in equation 5.1); II: The coefficients of births abroad in type II regressions which include child death-rate instead of deaths abroad (β_1 in equation 5.2).
[d] I: The sum of coefficients of births and deaths abroad in the regressions of Table 5.B ($\hat{\alpha}_1 + \hat{\alpha}_2$ in equation 5.1); II: $\beta_1 + \beta_2/BAB$ (see equation 5.2 in text).
[e] Coefficient of child death-rate in II. Figures in parentheses are *t* ratios.

than others. On the other hand, omitted variables are likely to affect both *SAB* and *BIS* in the same direction, i.e. those who had children abroad beyond what is expected on the basis of their education, age, etc., are likely to want more children than others. We therefore expect both α_1 and β_1 to be negative and to lie between zero and -1. The theory suggests that α_2 and β_2 should be positive – those who for a given number of births lost more children will be more inclined than others to have more births, i.e. replacement. If expectations with respect to child mortality are independent of experience and the demand for children is to some extent income-elastic we expect $(\alpha_1 + \alpha_2)$ and $(\beta_1 + \beta_2/BAB)$ to be negative, so that those who achieved a certain number of survivors with more births and deaths would revise down their desired family size. If however expectations with respect to child mortality are affected by experience so that those who have lost more children expect to lose more children in the future, it may lead them to have more births than others who expect all their children to survive (unless demand is very elastic). If mortality of children is largely infant mortality this matter of expectations cannot be a very important factor except for women close to the end of the child-bearing period, because the family can still replace children if they are lost. If, however, there are fears of later mortality (because of war for example) then even younger women will 'stock up' and those who have already lost more children more than others.

Note however that the reaction of births in Israel to child mortality abroad is just part of the total reaction. Births abroad already include part of the response to deaths abroad. In the extreme case, if people responded quickly to child mortality abroad, they will exhibit no response in Israel.

The findings from the regressions are the following (see Tables 5.12, 5.13, and 5.C):

1.   Of the two formulations, the one that uses BAB and the child death-rate as independent variables (regression II in Tables 5.12 and 5.13) is somewhat superior to that using BAB and DAB (the absolute numbers). Note that II allows for a smaller effect of a death when the number of births is larger

$$\left[\frac{\partial(BIS)}{\partial(DAB)} = \beta_1 + \frac{\beta_2}{BAB}, \frac{\partial^2(BIS)}{\partial DAB \, \partial BAB} = \frac{-\beta_2}{(BAB)^2} < 0 \right].$$

This would be one way of taking account of the fact that given a certain number deaths more births may already include some response to these deaths.

2.   The derivatives of births in Israel with respect to survivors abroad (SAB) come out more or less equal in the two formulations. The derivatives with respect to death abroad are much larger in regression II than in regression I.

3.   For all groups the coefficient of births abroad is negative and significant, while the coefficient of deaths abroad is positive and mostly significant.

4.   There is quite a difference between AA and EA in the magnitudes of the coefficients: among AA the positive derivative with respect to DAB is quite small, smaller than the negative derivative with respect to survivors abroad. There is thus only moderate replacement in Israel of children who died abroad among AA women. On the other hand the EA derivatives with respect to death abroad

are large, larger in absolute terms than the derivatives with respect to survivors abroad.

5. The derivatives with respect to DAB decline with age and rise with the length of residence in Israel. The old and the more recent immigrants presumably have already compensated for some of the deaths abroad.

6. The combined effect of an additional child-death abroad on births both abroad and in Israel leaves AA women with fewer surviving children than they would otherwise have (about a quarter to one-third on the average), i.e. replacement is not full. EA women end up with more children than they would otherwise have (about one-sixth to a quarter on the average). This can be inferred from Tables 5.10 and 5.13 and from regressions of total births and survivors on deaths abroad (Table 5.14).

Similar results are obtained when the dependent variable is births per year of residence in Israel (Table 5.15).

The difference between AA and EA can arise from several sources: it is not unreasonable to find more response to child mortality among families with small completed family size than among large families. This may have to do with how definite is the desired family size. It seems intuitively plausible that there is a higher probability for an only child, or one of two children, to be replaced than a child who is one of seven or eight children. If a larger fraction of the AA women do not practise family planning or are less efficient at it this would also provide an explanation, although to my mind not entirely independent of what has just been said.

It is also possible that, given a smaller desired family size and a shorter period of child-bearing among EA, these will be more prone to stock up with children on the basis of expectation rather than to react to child deaths as they occur. This could lead to a greater-than-unity effect of deaths on birth if the demand for surviving children is inelastic. It could also lead to larger numbers of surviving children if the expected death-rate was larger than the objective death-rate, i.e. if couples lag in the perception of the decline in child mortality. It is also reasonable to find more replacement in a group that because of immigration seems to revise its desired family size upwards than in a group that may be revising it downwards, but this would not explain why the response to child deaths among EA has also been greater in terms of BAB.

An even more speculative, but perhaps more valid, reason is the different source of child mortality for Jews immigrating from Europe and those immigrating from Asia and Africa. We are dealing with a population that was very much affected by the Second World War.

TABLE 5.14 THE EFFECT OF CHILD DEATHS ABROAD ON THE TOTAL NUMBER OF SURVIVING CHILDREN[a]

	Age and date of immigration					
	16–34	35–54 before 1948	35–44 1948+	45–54 1948+	55+ before 1948	55+ 1948+
Asia-Africa	0·074 (1·6)	−0·326 (4·1)	−0·130 (3·3)	−0·283 (7·7)	−0·282 (2·9)	−0·308 (6·6)
Europe-America	·0·294 (1·7)	0·314 (3·7)	0·203 (3·5)	0·066 (1·4)	0·145 (2·7)	−0·011 (0·2)

[a] These are regression coefficients of *DAB* on total survivors

$$STOT = BIS + BAB - DAB$$

in regression equations that include in addition to deaths abroad (*DAB*) dummy variables for education of husband's and wife's age and age at immigration. The population here is identical to that of the other regressions reported here (see note *a* to Table 5.6). Figures in parentheses are *t* ratios.
Source: Based on data of the 1961 census of population.

TABLE 5.15 TWO REGRESSIONS OF THE RATIO OF BIRTHS IN ISRAEL TO LENGTH OF RESIDENCE IN ISRAEL FOR JEWISH WOMEN 1948+, IMMIGRANTS[a] AGED 35–44 IN 1961, BY CONTINENT OF BIRTH

	Asia-Africa		Europe-America	
	Regression coefficient	t	Regression coefficient	t
Number of observations	1837		2627	
Regression I				
Constant	0·835	14·2	0·450	6·9
Births abroad	−0·019	−8·6	−0·043	8·8
Deaths abroad	−0·007	1·7	0·063	4·7
Wife's age in 1961	−0·013	8·8	−0·007	4·3
Wife's years of schooling	−0·013	4·0	−0·010	1·7
Wife's years of schooling squared	0·0001	0·4	0·0004	1·2
$\bar{R}^2$	0·130		0·037	
Standard error of estimate	0·189		0·228	
Regression II				
Constant	0·829	14·4	0·432	7·0
Births abroad	−0·020	10·8	−0·037	8·2
Death rate abroad	0·123	7·5	0·090	3·5
Wife's age in 1961	−0·013	8·9	−0·007	4·4
Wife's years of schooling	−0·008	6·5	−0·001	0·5
Husband's years of schooling	−0·004	3·6	−0·003	2·0
$\bar{R}^2$	0·162		0·035	
Standard error of estimate	0·185		0·2	

[a] See note *a* in Table 5.6.
Source: Table 5.D.

Those who lost children under the age of 5 in Europe very often also lost older children, or all their children, and their fertility behaviour after the war abroad and in Israel was a basic re-formation of families, rather than the replacement of infants that died in a backward environment.

Do we learn anything from the cross-sections analysis of infant mortality that may help to understand the time series? As noted, child mortality was very high in the Jewish communities of Asia and Africa. If it is indeed true that there has been considerable replace-ment of deceased children among Jewish AA women (although less than among the EA) then this constituted an important element in their high level of fertility. If most of the reaction to child mortality (particularly for women who have anyhow a long period over which they will have children) takes the form of (not necessarily full) replacement of deceased children rather than 'laying in stocks' of children on the basis of expectations, then the objective fact of the much lower infant mortality in Israel should have affected births in Israel. This would provide one explanation for the decline in fertility in Israel of AA women and maybe even of the decline in fertility of EA women in the fifties (where the early fifties high in fertility may have been partly associated with replacement). Friedlander (1973), who reported a fairly similar decline in fertility among immigrants from three countries in Asia and Africa in spite of diverse experience in Israel in terms of urbanisation and labour-force participation, has already conjectured that child mortality may be an explanation. It is however clear that if this were the major source of decline in fertility it could not persist very long, and could not account for a decline in more than about one-fifth to a quarter in births. It may be an unappealing but still valid description of reality to argue that the weights of different factors behind the fertility change over time have altered.

Data that are now available will allow a much more thorough analysis of such other factors. Because what has been presented here is just a first crack at the child mortality problem, this is presented as a rather tentative conclusion.

VII. *CONCLUSION*

I have presented here some material on at least two levels. What I sought to achieve is to convey an idea of the type of questions or puzzles posed by the demographic scene in Israel. Some of these are standard in the economic research of fertility. For example, the relation between family size and the time allocation of women has been treated by Israeli economists in more or less the same manner as the problem was treated in the U.S.

The particularly Israeli puzzles have to do with immigration and with the rapid change to which a large part of the population has been exposed in its total economic and social life. Here the Israeli experience may be more relevant to countries in the midst of a demographic transition rather than to the developed countries of Europe and America.

Work on the dynamic aspects is barely starting, as is well reflected in the discontinuity between the second and third parts of the paper. In two or three years we shall be at least much more familiar with facts, thanks to work under way by several Israeli demographers; regrettably one cannot sell theoretical developments in the future's market.

Economics as a discipline dealing with certain 'economic variables' or exploring economic motives has not yet proved very important here. Underlying the research reported here is however a view of economics as a method of studying social phenomena as if they were generated by the behaviour of utility-maximising families or individuals. While I am convinced that this approach has already yielded many insights into demographic research, it remains to be seen how far we can go in explaining dynamic situations of the sort described here. Commenting on a study by T. P. Schultz, James Tobin said recently that 'An alternative hypothesis would be that individual fertility responds to changing national, even international, cultural norms, which are not to be understood by studying individual or regional differences' (1973, p. S276). If he is right the kind of economics practised here would not suffice.

APPENDIX

TABLE 5.A EDUCATIONAL LEVEL OF JEWISH WOMEN[a] WHO IMMIGRATED
BEFORE AGE 50
(Per cent)

Years of schooling	Age in 1961 and date of immigration					
	16–34	35–54 before 1948	35–44 1948+	45–54 1948+	55+	
					before 1948	1948+
Asia-Africa						
0	52·9	62·6	54·7	64·6	74·8	72·5
1–4	11·2	8·3	10·3	7·3	5·2	7·2
5–8	28·1	20·2	23·7	21·6	14·0	14·2
9–10	4·1	5·0	5·8	4·1	4·0	2·6
11–12	2·7	3·1	4·0	1·8	2·0	2·1
13+	1·0	0·8	1·5	0·6	0·0	1·4
Total	100·0	100·0	100·0	100·0	100·0	100·0
Europe-America						
0	2·1	2·9	1·2	3·7	8·3	9·4
1–4	12·6	3·8	7·2	12·6	5·1	19·6
5–8	44·6	39·0	52·4	50·2	40·7	42·8
9–10	14·8	22·2	18·7	13·4	21·3	12·9
11–12	14·6	21·0	13·6	14·1	15·6	11·2
13+	11·3	11·1	6·9	6·0	9·0	4·1
Total	100·0	100·0	100·0	100·0	100·0	100·0

[a] See note *a* in Table 5.6.
[b] Both length-of-residence groups.
Source: Data of the 1961 census of population.

TABLE 5.B   REGRESSION OF BIRTHS ABROAD (BAB) TO JEWISH WOMEN[a] WHO
IMMIGRATED BEFORE AGE 50

		Age in 1961 and date of immigration				
	16–34[b]	35–54 before 1948	35–44 1948 +	45–54 1948 +	55 + before 1948	55 + 1948 +
Asia-Africa						
Constant	−2·431	−1·339	−1·339	1·861	1·579	13·232
	(7·7)	(1·9)	(1·9)	(1·3)	(0·8)	(3·9)
Death-rate abroad	1·422	1·414	1·932	3·677	4·540	4·594
	(11·9)	(5·0)	(10·2)	(12·2)	(7·8)	(11·2)
Wife's age in 1961	−0·033	0·006	−0·088	−0·060	−0·072	−0·458
	(2·7)	(0·3)	(3·7)	(1·5)	(2·3)	(4·5)
Wife's age at immigration	0·239	0·177	0·259	0·139	0·165	0·378
	(24·2)	(10·0)	(16·0)	(5·1)	(8·2)	(3·6)
Wife's years of schooling[c]						
0	0·189	1·040	0·858	0·585	0·606	0·818
	(2·3)	(4·1)	(6·2)	(2·7)	(1·2)	(2·3)
1–4	0·164	0·475	0·745	0·859	−0·429	0·593
	(1·4)	(1·2)	(3·8)	(2·5)	(1·1)	(1·1)
9–10	−0·295	0·134	−0·687	−0·546	−0·004	−0·210
	(1·7)	(0·3)	(2·8)	(1·3)	(0·005)	(0·3)
11–12	−0·703	−0·005	−1·064	−1·138	−0·897	−1·209
	(3·3)	(0·1)	(3·7)	(2·1)	(0·7)	(1·4)
13 +	−1·454	−1·620	−1·930	−1·553	—	−2·002
	(4·3)	(1·5)	(4·2)	(1·5)	(—)	(1·9)
Husband's years of schooling[c]						
0	0·027	0·128	−0·142	−0·186	−0·402	−0·828
	(0·3)	(0·5)	(1·0)	(0·9)	(1·0)	(2·8)
1–4	−0·086	−0·141	−0·181	−0·754	0·568	−0·794
	(0·8)	(0·4)	(1·1)	(2·8)	(1·0)	(2·1)
9–10	−0·129	−0·019	0·097	0·014	0·292	−0·493
	(1·1)	(0·06)	(0·5)	(0·05)	(0·5)	(1·0)
11–12	−0·311	0·174	−0·024	−0·618	−0·671	−0·228
	(2·2)	(0·5)	(0·1)	(1·6)	(0·8)	(0·3)
13 +	−0·195	0·005	0·224	−0·050	−1·526	0·164
	(1·1)	(0·01)	(0·8)	(0·1)	(1·8)	(0·3)
$\bar{R}^2$	0·264	0·277	0·241	0·169	0·330	0·224
Standard error of estimate	1·616	2·004	2·190	2·616	2·497	2·667
Number of observations	2498	484	1837	1109	250	571

For notes see p. 166.

TABLE 5.B (cont.)

	16–34[b]	35–54 before 1948	35–44 1948 +	45–54 1948 +	55+ before 1948	55+ 1948 +
Europe-America						
Constant	0·325	−0·818	0·490	0·617	−2·667	−0·879
	(1·1)	(4·4)	(0·2)	(1·1)	(6·4)	(1·2)
Death-rate abroad	0·849	1·192	1·186	1·560	2·077	2·208
	(3·6)	(10·4)	(11·6)	(11·0)	(10·9)	(9·9)
Wife's age in 1961	−0·034	0·007	−0·040	0·002	0·035	0·160
	(3·5)	(1·6)	(5·2)	(0·1)	(4·5)	(4·6)
Wife's age at immigration	0·069	0·045	0·076	0·022	0·068	−0·140
	(11·9)	(8·6)	(17·4)	(2·5)	(10·4)	(3·6)
Wife's years of schooling[c]						
0	0·633	0·740	1·163	1·114	0·833	0·416
	(3·1)	(5·2)	(6·7)	(6·0)	(5·5)	(2·3)
1–4	−0·103	0·085	0·070	0·180	0·094	−0·004
	(1·1)	(0·7)	(0·9)	(1·6)	(0·5)	(0·03)
9–10	−0·065	−0·089	−0·144	−0·061	−0·471	−0·563
	(0·8)	(1·5)	(2·9)	(0·6)	(4·6)	(3·8)
11–12	−0·265	−0·153	−0·157	−0·313	−0·453	−0·592
	(2·8)	(2·4)	(2·7)	(3·0)	(3·9)	(3·6)
13 +	−0·395	−0·324	−0·243	−0·358	−0·659	−0·507
	(3·5)	(3·8)	(3·0)	(2·4)	(4·4)	(2·0)
Husband's years of schooling[c]						
0	0·722	0·868	0·279	−0·091	−0·314	0·442
	(3·4)	(4·4)	(1·7)	(0·4)	(1·2)	(2·0)
1–4	0·197	0·065	−0·064	−0·035	−0·072	−0·094
	(1·8)	(0·5)	(1·0)	(0·3)	(0·4)	(0·7)
9–10	−0·023	−0·160	−0·011	−0·150	−0·031	−0·132
	(0·3)	(2·5)	(0·2)	(1·5)	(0·3)	(0·9)
11–12	−0·005	−0·112	−0·166	−0·116	−0·124	−0·330
	(0·1)	(1·7)	(3·0)	(1·1)	(1·1)	(2·0)
13 +	0·111	−0·011	−0·181	−0·146	0·064	−0·129
	(1·1)	(0·2)	(2·9)	(1·27)	(0·6)	(0·7)
R^2	0·175	0·208	0·181	0·128	0·242	0·164
Standard error of estimate	0·852	0·847	0·914	0·127	1·501	1·497
Number of observations	988	1511	2627	1632	1704	1106

Age in 1961 and date of immigration

[a] See note a in Table 5.6. Figures in parentheses are t values.

[b] Both length-of-residence groups.

[c] See note b in Table 5.8.

Source: Data of the 1961 census of population.

TABLE 5.C   REGRESSION OF BIRTHS IN ISRAEL **(BIS)** OF JEWISH WOMEN[a] BY AGE IN 1961 AND CONTINENT OF BIRTH

	Age in 1961 and date of immigration					
	16–34	35–54 before 1948	35–44 1948+	45–54 1948+	55+	
					before 1948	1948+
Asia-Africa						
Number of observations	2498	489	1837	1109	250	571
Constant	−0·398	5·273	4·990	3·150	4·894	2·544
	(1·3)	(6·8)	(9·8)	(4·5)	(3·1)	(1·8)
Births abroad	−0·294	−0·400	−0·175	−0·167	−0·269	−0·132
	(13·5)	(7·8)	(8·7)	(10·5)	(4·3)	(7·1)
Deaths abroad	0·296	0·142	0·087	0·061	−0·020	0·025
	(6·5)	(1·7)	(2·5)	(2·6)	(0·2)	(1·0)
Wife's age at immigration	0·054	−0·100	−0·115	−0·049	−0·092	−0·011
	(4·8)	(5·0)	(8·7)	(3·5)	(3·4)	(0·4)
Wife's length of residence in Israel	0·232	0·029	0·083	0·002	0·032	−0·097
	(20·0)	(1·5)	(4·8)	(0·09)	(1·2)	(2·3)
Wife's years of schooling[b]						
0	0·923	1·468	0·566	0·288	0·535	0·205
	(11·6)	(5·9)	(5·5)	(2·8)	(1·3)	(1·4)
1–4	0·401	0·966	0·369	0·268	1·326	−0·170
	(3·6)	(2·6)	(1·7)	(1·7)	(1·9)	(0·8)
9–10	−0·104	−0·480	−0·206	−0·078	−0·755	−0·075
	(0·6)	(1·1)	(1·7)	(0·4)	(1·0)	(0·2)
11–12	−0·560	−0·139	−0·377	−0·496	−1·862	−0·349
	(2·8)	(0·3)	(1·8)	(1·7)	(1·7)	(1·0)
13+	−0·417	−0·244	0·015	0·329	—	−0·579
	(1·3)	(0·2)	(0·0)	(0·7)	(−)	(1·4)
Husband's years of schooling[b]						
0	0·182	−0·035	0·058	0·072	−0·155	−0·143
	(2·2)	(0·2)	(0·6)	(0·7)	(0·5)	(1·2)
1–4	2·669	−0·214	0·093	0·248	−0·680	−0·132
	(2·7)	(0·7)	(0·18)	(1·9)	(1·4)	(0·9)
9–10	−0·052	0·087	−0·166	−0·166	0·180	−0·256
	(0·5)	(0·3)	(3·6)	(1·2)	(0·4)	(1·3)
11–12	−0·310	−0·820	−0·473	−0·172	−0·443	−0·077
	(2·3)	(2·2)	(3·0)	(0·4)	(0·7)	(0·3)
13+	0·031	0·370	−0·668	−0·235	0·748	−0·052
	(0·2)	(0·7)	(3·4)	(1·1)	(1·0)	(0·2)
R^2	0·345	0·374	0·286	0·142	0·355	0·091
Standard error of estimate	1·540	1·940	1·602	1·235	2·080	1·073

For notes see p. 168.

TABLE 5.C (cont.)

	Age in 1961 and date of immigration					
	16–34	35–54 before 1948	35–44 1948+	45–54 1948+	55+ before 1948	55+ 1948+
Europe-America						
Number of observations	988	1511	2627	1632	1704	1106
Constant	1·124	3·812	2·624	1·915	1·775	0·272
	(3·9)	(15·8)	(11·8)	(6·4)	(6·2)	(1·0)
Births abroad	−0·428	−0·393	−0·274	−0·101	−0·186	−0·086
	(13·2)	(11·0)	(14·7)	(6·9)	(10·0)	(7·2)
Deaths abroad	0·777	0·663	0·457	0·154	0·191	0·062
	(5·2)	(7·6)	(9·2)	(5·1)	(4·4)	(2·4)
Wife's age at immigration	−0·012	−0·079	−0·057	−0·037	−0·043	−0·004
	(1·2)	(11·7)	(10·0)	(6·1)	(8·4)	(0·8)
Wife's length of residence in Israel	0·082	0·005	0·025	−0·007	0·031	0·016
	(8·4)	(0·9)	(3·7)	(1·0)	(5·9)	(1·2)
Wife's years of schooling[b]						
0	1·068	1·154	0·555	0·189	0·620	0·069
	(5·2)	(6·2)	(3·5)	(1·9)	(5·9)	(1·0)
1–4	−0·039	0·124	−0·106	0·007	0·133	0·072
	(0·4)	(0·8)	(1·5)	(0·1)	(1·1)	(1·4)
9–10	−0·084	−0·088	−0·051	−0·027	−0·215	0·042
	(1·0)	(1·1)	(1·1)	(0·5)	(3·0)	(0·8)
11–12	−0·164	−0·081	−1·530	0·021	−0·365	−0·025
	(1·7)	(1·0)	(2·9)	(0·4)	(4·6)	(0·4)
13+	−0·192	−0·179	−0·072	−0·066	−0·224	0·197
	(1·7)	(1·6)	(1·0)	(0·8)	(2·2)	(2·0)
Husband's years of schooling[b]						
0	0·615	0·494	0·166	0·205	0·675	0·099
	(2·8)	(1·9)	(1·1)	(1·7)	(3·8)	(1·2)
1–4	−0·034	0·146	−0·020	0·084	−0·356	−0·028
	(0·3)	(0·9)	(0·3)	(1·5)	(2·5)	(0·6)
9–10	−0·012	0·095	0·029	0·037	−0·038	0·060
	(0·1)	(1·1)	(0·6)	(0·7)	(0·5)	(1·1)
11–12	−0·054	0·009	0·014	−0·054	−0·048	0·007
	(0·6)	(0·1)	(0·3)	(1·0)	(0·6)	(0·1)
13+	0·038	0·033	−0·028	0·063	−0·094	−0·133
	(0·4)	(0·4)	(0·5)	(1·0)	(1·2)	(2·0)
$\bar{R}^2$	0·411	0·223	0·285	0·074	0·272	0·048
Standard error of estimate	0·853	1·092	0·823	0·678	1·031	0·547

[a] See note *a* in Table 5.6.
[b] See note *b* in Table 5.8.
Source: Data of the 1961 census of population.

TABLE 5.D REGRESSION OF THE RATIO OF BIRTHS IN ISRAEL TO LENGTH
OF RESIDENCE IN ISRAEL FOR JEWISH WOMEN[a] BY CONTINENT OF BIRTH

	Age in 1961 and date of immigration					
	16-34[b]	35-54 before 1948	35-44 1948+	45-54 1948+	55+	
					before 1948	1948+
Asia-Africa						
Number of observations	2498	484	1837	1109	250	571
Regression I						
Constant	0·666	0·521	0·835	0·341	0·222	0·294
	(12·9)	(14·5)	(14·2)	(3·8)	(1·3)	(2·2)
Births abroad	−0·022	−0·018	−0·019	−0·020	−0·014	−0·012
	(6·2)	(7·6)	(8·6)	(9·7)	(7·5)	(6·5)
Deaths abroad	0·032	0·006	0·007	0·008	0·004	0·002
	(4·0)	(1·4)	(1·7)	(2·6)	(1·4)	(0·6)
Wife's age in 1961	−0·008	−0·006	−0·013	−0·003	−0·002	−0·003
	(4·5)	(8·0)	(8·8)	(1·8)	(2·0)	(1·4)
Wife's years of schooling	−0·021	−0·012	−0·013	−0·006	0·002	−0·003
	(5·0)	(3·13)	(4·0)	(1·4)	(0·5)	(1·0)
Wife's years of schooling squared	0·001	0·003	0·001	−0·000	−0·001	−0·000
	(1·9)	(0·9)	(0·4)	(0·02)	(1·3)	(0·1)
R^2	0·061	0·318	0·130	0·092	0·238	0·086
Standard error of estimate	0·272	0·094	0·189	0·162	0·070	0·105
Regression II						
Constant	0·678	0·510	0·829	0·320	0·219	0·302
	(13·2)	(14·3)	(14·4)	(0·1)	(4·3)	(2·2)
Births abroad	−0·020	−0·018	−0·020	−0·020	−0·013	−0·012
	(6·9)	(9·2)	(10·8)	(11·0)	(8·3)	(7·3)
Deaths abroad	0·178	0·058	0·123	0·091	0·036	0·026
	(8·8)	(4·4)	(7·5)	(4·6)	(2·1)	(1·5)
Wife's age in 1961	−0·009	−0·006	−0·013	−0·003	−0·002	−0·004
	(5·0)	(8·2)	(8·9)	(1·6)	(2·1)	(1·5)
Wife's years of schooling	−0·007	−0·002	−0·001	−0·001	−0·003	−0·002
	(1·9)	(4·3)	(0·5)	(0·7)	(8·3)	(0·3)
Husband's years of schooling	−0·007	−0·001	−0·003	0·001	−0·002	−0·001
	(0·3)	(0·3)	(2·0)	(0·8)	(0·8)	(1·2)
R^2	0·085	0·340	0·162	0·108	0·240	0·089
Standard error of estimate	0·268	0·092	0·185	0·161	0·070	0·104

For notes see p. 170.

TABLE 5.D. (cont.)

	16–34[b]	35–54 before 1948	35–44 1948+	45–54 1948+	55+	
					before 1948	1948+
Europe-America						
Number of observations	988	1511	2627	1632	1704	1106
Regression I						
Constant	1·008	0·353	0·450	0·215	0·103	0·033
	(10·2)	(25·6)	(6·4)	(4·3)	(9·3)	(1·4)
Births abroad	−0·083	−0·020	−0·043	−0·014	−0·009	−0·007
	(8·5)	(11·2)	(8·8)	(5·8)	(13·2)	(6·6)
Deaths abroad	0·221	0·033	0·063	0·019	0·009	0·006
	(4·7)	(7·5)	(4·7)	(3·9)	(5·6)	(2·6)
Wife's age in 1961	−0·019	−0·004	−0·007	−0·003	−0·001	0·000
	(6·6)	(17·8)	(4·3)	(3·3)	(3·2)	(0·03)
Wife's years of schooling	−0·046	−0·009	−0·010	−0·003	−0·006	−0·003
	(4·9)	(6·0)	(1·7)	(1·1)	(7·9)	(2·7)
Wife's years of schooling squared	0·002	0·004	0·004	0·002	0·002	0·002
	(4·3)	(4·6)	(1·2)	(1·1)	(4·5)	(2·4)
$\bar{R}^2$	0·122	0·264	0·037	0·026	0·146	0·040
Standard error of estimate	0·277	0·055	0·288	0·109	0·038	0·049
Regression II						
Constant	0·873	0·321	0·432	0·202	0·093	0·031
	(9·1)	(26·0)	(7·0)	(4·2)	(8·5)	(1·3)
Births abroad	−0·079	−0·016	−0·037	−0·011	−0·008	−0·006
	(7·7)	(9·8)	(8·2)	(5·3)	(12·8)	(6·3)
Deaths abroad	0·340	0·056	0·090	0·053	0·030	0·011
	(4·4)	(7·1)	(3·5)	(4·2)	(5·9)	(1·5)
Wife's age in 1961	−0·020	−0·004	−0·007	0·003	−0·001	−0·000
	(6·7)	(17·3)	(4·4)	(3·3)	(3·1)	(0·2)
Wife's years of schooling	−0·010	−0·009	−0·008	−0·004	−0·004	−0·004
	(5·9)	(7·2)	(6·5)	(2·3)	(2·7)	(2·8)
Husband's years of schooling	−0·003	0·002	−0·004	−0·003	0·004	0·005
	(2·6)	(0·2)	(3·6)	(2·0)	(0·3)	(0·5)
$\bar{R}^2$	0·102	0·249	0·035	0·026	0·136	0·031
Standard error of estimate	0·280	0·056	0·228	0·109	0·039	0·048

[a] See note *a* in Table 5.6.
[b] Both length-of-residence groups.
Source: Data of the 1961 census of statistics.

REFERENCES

G. S. Becker, 'A Theory of the Allocation of Time', *Economic Journal*, LXXV (Sep 1965) 493–517.

—— and H. G. Lewis, 'On the Interaction between the Quantity and Quality of Children', *Journal of Political Economy*, LXXXI, no. 2, pt II (Mar/Apr 1973) S279–88.

Y. Ben Porath, *The Arab Labor Force in Israel* (Jerusalem: Falk Institute, 1966).

——, *Fertility in Israel, an Economist's Interpretation: Differentials and Trends, 1950–1970*, RM-5981-FF (Santa Monica, Calif.: Rand Corporation, Aug 1970a). Repr. in *Economic Development and Population Growth in the Middle East*, ed. Charles A. Cooper and Sidney S. Alexander (New York: Elsevier, 1972) pp. 501–39.

——, *On the Association between Fertility and Education*, Department of Economics Research Report no. 20 (Jerusalem: Hebrew Univ., 1970b).

—— and F. Welch, *Chance, Child Traits, and Choice of Family Size*, report prepared for National Institutes of Health and the Rockefeller Foundation, R-1117-NIH/RF (Santa Monica, Calif.: Rand Corporation, Dec 1972).

——, 'Economic Analysis of Fertility in Israel: Point and Counterpoint', *Journal of Political Economy*, LXXXI, no. 2, pt II (Mar/Apr 1973*d*) S202–33.

——, 'Short Term Fluctuations in Fertility and Economic Activity in Israel: 1951–1969', *Demography* (May 1973*b*).

——, *On Child Traits and the Choice of Family Size*, Discussion paper 731 (Jerusalem: Falk Institute, June 1973*c*).

Central Bureau of Statistics, *Marriage and Fertility*, pt II, 1961 census publication no. 32 (Jerusalem: 1966).

——, *Statistical Abstract of Israel 1972*, no. 23 (Jerusalem: 1972).

R. A. Easterlin, *Population, Labor Force, and Long Swings in Economic Growth – The American Experience*, National Bureau of Economic Research: general ser. no. 86 (New York and London: Columbia Univ. Press, 1968).

——, 'Towards a Socio-Economic Theory of Fertility: A Survey of Recent Research on Economic Factors in American Fertility', *Fertility and Family Planning: A World View*, ed. S. J. Behrman, Leslie Corsa Jr and Ronald Freedman (Ann Arbor: Univ. of Michigan Press, 1969).

D. Friedlander, 'The Fertility of Three Oriental Migration Groups in Israel: Stability and Change', *Papers in Jewish Demography 1969*, ed. U. O. Schmelz, P. Glikson and S. Della Pergola (Jerusalem: Institute of Contemporary Jewry, Hebrew Univ., 1973) pp. 131–42.

R. Gronau, 'The Effect of Children on the Housewife's Value of Time', *Journal of Political Economy*, LXXXI, no. 2, pt II (Mar/Apr 1973) S168–99.

H. S. Halevi, 'Fifty Years of Jewish Infant Mortality in Eretz Israel', *Papers in Jewish Demography 1969*, ed. U. O. Schmelz, P. Glikson and S. Della Pergola (Jerusalem: Institute of Contemporary Jewry, Hebrew Univ., 1973) pp. 179–90.

C. R. Hill and F. P. Stafford, 'The Allocation of Time to Children and Educational Opportunity', Discussion paper, Institute of Public Policy Studies, Univ. of Michigan, presented at the Econometric Society meetings, New Orleans (Dec 1971).

G. Kallner, *Perinatal and Maternal Mortality in Israel (1950–1954)*, Central Bureau of Statistics: special ser. no. 75 (Jerusalem: 1958).

K. J. Lancaster, 'A New Approach to Consumer Theory', *Journal of Political Economy*, LXXIV (Apr 1966) 132–57.

M. Landsberger, 'Children's Age as a Factor Affecting the Simultaneous Determination of Consumption and Labor Supply', *Southern Economic Journal* (Oct 1973).

A. S. Leibowitz, 'Education and the Allocation of Women's Time', mimeo (New York: National Bureau of Economic Research, 1972).

J. Matras, 'On Changing Marriage and Family Formation Among Jewish Immigrants Communities in Israel: Some Findings and Some Further Problems', *Papers in Jewish Demography 1969*, ed. U. O. Schmelz, P. Glikson and S. Della Pergola (Jerusalem: Institute of Contemporary Jewry, Hebrew Univ., 1973) pp. 265–76.

M. Nerlove, 1973.

M. Nerlove and T. P. Schultz, *Love and Life Between the Censuses: A Model of Family Decision Making in Puerto Rico, 1950–1960*, RM-6322-AID (Santa Monica, Calif.: Rand Corporation, Sep 1970).

D. J. O'Hara, *Changes in Mortality Levels and Family Decisions Regarding Children*, R-914-RF (Santa Monica, Calif.: Rand Corporation, Feb 1972).

E. Peritz and O. Bialik, 'Infant Mortality in the Jewish Population of Israel', *Israel Journal of Medical Sciences*, vol. IV, no. 5 (1968).

M. Rothschild and J. Stiglitz, 'Increasing Risk I and II', *Journal of Economic Theory*, II (1970) 225–43 and III (1971) 66–84.

U. O. Schmelz, *Infant and Early Childhood Mortality Among the Jews of the Diaspora* (Jerusalem: Institute of Contemporary Jewry, Hebrew Univ., 1971).

T. P. Schultz, 'Explanation of Birth Rate Changes over Space and Time: A Study of Taiwan', *Journal of Political Economy*, LXXXI, no. 2, pt II (Mar/Apr 1973*a*) S238–74.

——, 'A Preliminary Survey of Economic Analyses of Fertility', *The American Economic Review: Papers and Proceedings*, LXIII, no. 2 (May 1973*b*) 71–8.

P. Schwinger, 'The Business Cycle and Fertility', Hewbrew mimeo (Leon Recanati School for Business Administration, Tel-Aviv Univ., May 1969).

J. P. Smith, 'The Life Cycle Allocation of Time in a Family Context', Ph.D. dissertation (Univ. of Chicago, 1972).

J. Tobin, 'Comment on T. Paul Schultz, "Explanation of Birth Rate Changes over Space and Time: A Study of Taiwan"', *Journal of Political Economy*, LXXXI, no. 2, pt II (Mar/Apr 1973) S275–8.

R. J. Willis, 'A New Approach to the Economic Theory of Fertility Behavior', *Journal of Political Economy*, LXXXI, no. 2, pt II (Mar/Apr 1973) S14–64.

Discussion of the Paper by Professor Ben Porath

Dr Tabah, introducing the paper, said that it represented the application of ideas covered in the first discussion, and he had enjoyed reading it very much. It was a study of fertility in Israel. Israel should not be seen simply as two sectors, but as a laboratory where one could find a population with great cultural diversity. The original Jewish immigrations had been from Central and Eastern Europe. More recently, they had been from Western Europe, and were now increasingly from Africa and Latin America.

The first major characteristic was the existence of a varied ethnic and cultural situation. 60 per cent of the population were immigrants. The family cycle in Israel represented an interesting adaptation process. It was an extraordinary country because of rapid growth. Population had doubled over four years. There was constant transformation, both because of immigration and because of social and cultural factors. Education was significant, but income per head was relatively low.

In Table 5.1, Professor Ben Porath showed the overall fertility of women in Israel. Dr Tabah was surprised that it was not higher. There seemed to be a difference in fertility between the population from Europe and from elsewhere. Professor Ben Porath's analysis was 'transversal', and based on family-income surveys. It attempted to determine whether fertility was a function of education, of the work a woman did, or of length of life.

On the theoretical plane, the choice was about the rationality of what happened. The variables were exogenous, as in Becker's well-known theory. One found contradictions between the social activity of the woman and fertility. Education did not explain differences between social groups; the characteristics of the woman were more important than those of the man. The correlation was negative, but it was interesting to see what happened with different ethnic groups. One did not get the same result in the U.S.A., where women seemed more likely to work the more they were educated. The situation in Israel before immigration was important. One found that women who had lost children tended to compensate in other ways. The analysis seemed to contradict the hypotheses of demographers. A fall in infant mortality was associated with a disposition to reduce fertility. However, in Israel, society was not the same as in most underdeveloped countries. For example, he saw a big difference in the situation in Egypt.

Dr Tabah thought it hard to analyse the problems of fertility and employment with existing methods. Scientific analysis of the type of data we had, for example from censuses, did not easily provide the kind of variables we needed. Census data was poor in backward countries. Nevertheless, we needed information about them urgently.

We therefore had to base ourselves on the studies which it was possible to make, for example fertility surveys. It was extremely difficult to get information about contraception, and while much work had been done in the last ten years, it was necessary to increase the size of samples. Usually the problem was that one could only look at perhaps 2000 women, and this did not give enough data to throw light on the large number of variables one was trying to consider, though work done in collaboration with the United Nations had been valuable. One needed to introduce a larger number of variables, for example education and employment. If we could only do this, we should get more valuable results. Most existing studies were unsatisfactory, with the exception of the very good one by Freedman on Taiwan. What one needed were such studies of fertility which were repeated every five years, considered 2000 families, and looked at fertility as related to the income of both the man and the woman. A strong relation was found at both low and high levels of income. It appeared that the activity of the woman was different at different stages in the building of the family. It was necessary to make theoretical studies too. For example, studies carried out in the 1940s had no satisfactory foundation. Those concerned should have realised that the influence of the outside environment was very important. These were methodological points, but they were what interested him.

Professor Ben Porath said that his paper was concerned with two major issues. First, many studies suggested an inverse association between fertility and education; the question was what explanation, or mechanism, dominated this relationship. Several studies had examined the hypothesis that the relationship reflected the effect of the value of the time of women (which rose with education) on the price, and thus on the demand, for children within a framework of household choice. This was one type of a static hypothesis. An alternative view would be that if there were a process of diffusion in which the population shifted from one level of fertility to a lower one, and if those with more education shifted earlier, this also would generate an inverse relationship between education and fertility, but one which would disappear once the shift had ended. Although the research surveyed indicated some support for the value-of-time hypothesis, it could be observed in Fig. 5.2 that the relationship tended to become flat when one considered more 'advanced' groups in the population, which could be presumed to have largely completed the 'diffusion' process. Steep declines of fertility with education could be observed among Jews who came from Arab countries in North Africa and the Middle East, where the decline in family size was still going on.

The second major issue was the effect of child mortality on fertility. This was one way of learning something about the nature of the demand for children. Participants here described the decision on children as 'irrational'. Were they referring to births or to surviving children? If, on the average, people tended to have more children once they had lost some, this might indicate that they had some notion of the number of (surviving) children they wanted, which would reject one sense of the word 'irrationality'.

The data for Israel were particularly suitable for study because immigrants had experienced very high levels of child mortality abroad, and also high variances. The findings in Table 5.14 were that, on average, families from Asia and Africa reacted to the death of a child by an additional three-quarters of a birth, while families from Europe and America reacted by slightly more than a full birth. This suggested a high degree of insistence on a particular number of children. The use of a decision framework did not, however, imply that each individual literally went through an explicit calculation.

Dr Ridker agreed that the relationship between education and fertility could be looked at only in terms of diffusion or the value of time; but did not the two explanations turn out to be very similar?

Professor Ben Porath thought if one found a negative relationship between education and fertility, one could say that a situation had been reached where information was not important. He pointed out that in Israel there was a big difference in fertility according to whether women had been to college or not.

Professor Létinier wanted to discuss the definition and measurement of the family production function for the household. The availability of housing must be an important influence on the number of children. How was it effected? To have one more child required more accommodation, so that one had to add the cost of housing to the cost of the incremental child. This must go into the production function.

There were then two possible situations; that with no extra child, or that with one extra child and the necessary accommodation. However, there was a third possibility; having another child and yet using the same house. In this third case there was no production cost, because there was no extra cost of housing. The child would then compete with housing as a kind of commodity. One could look either at the cost of extra housing, or at the relationship between the child and the existing housing.

Mr Conde noted the comments in the paper on the great diversity of fertility in Israel. Was this true? Did there seem to be a strong correlation between fertility and income-distribution? Tables 5.1 and 5.2 suggested that the most fully-occupied women had fewest children. One wondered whether non-Jews were less fully assimilated. Were there similar differences for them? And had Jews from Africa become more similar to Jews from Europe?

Dr Nassef said that interest had increased recently in fertility differences between religious groups, and in many cases these seemed to show general similarity when differences in socio-economic variables were controlled. In other words, differences between groups seemed to arise more from social and cultural differences between those groups. Perhaps Professor Ben Porath could have looked more usefully at levels of fertility between religious groups, after taking socio-economic differences into account.

Professor Ben Porath agreed with Professor Létinier on housing. A more detailed model, which differentiated between complements and substitutes for children, might be better. One supposed that if there were high substitutability between children and the standard of living, people would take the extra child without taking more housing, but this need not be the case. Observation suggested a close link between the size of house and the number of children. In a situation where one could choose the size of house and prices were the same for everybody, then, in cross-section data, there would be no need to put in the housing variable. But if housing did not adjust well, then, even in a cross-section study, one would have to take account of the facts that Professor Létinier had mentioned.

On fertility and income distribution, he thought he had been misinterpreted. He would like to say that he thought that countries with similar levels of income showed less variability in fertility than Israel, because their populations were more homogeneous. He had not mentioned income differences in his paper, but wanted to point out that the relationship between education and fertility seemed to be stronger than that between income and fertility.

As for non-Jews in Israel, most of these were Arabs, and they were mostly Moslems. The percentage of Jews in Israel was given on page 136; the rest of the population was made up of non-Jews. Studies he was engaged on would soon be completed, and these would enable him to say more about the fertility of non-Jews in Israel.

On time trends, he did dwell on the difference between non-Jews and immigrants. The decline in fertility for Jews from Arab countries had been quite large since 1948. One reason could be seen from Fig. 5.1. If one looked at this as a time series, one saw a sharp increase in the amount of schooling of Jewish women. The table showed turning points for the various groups. The increase in schooling of Arab women was very recent and still not very important. Also the non-Jews experienced a very high increase in income, so perhaps the turning point in fertility for non-Jews was only now occurring. He agreed that this was important, but had not yet completed his work on it.

As for religion, the main omission was that he had not controlled his data for differences in religiosity *within* the Jewish population.

Dr Tabah thought Mr Conde was right; one must distinguish between numbers of children and type of population. Again, on whether education was more important than income in leading to differences in fertility, we simply did not know. The correct thing would be to carry out a multi-variant analysis to discover this.

Part Three

Economic Factors in the Decline of Fertility in Europe

6   The Role of Economic Factors in Birth-rate Trends and Fluctuations*

H. Leridon†

INSTITUT NATIONAL D'ETUDES DEMOGRAPHIQUES, PARIS

'The idea that changes in fertility are a positive function of
economic conditions has such innate appeal that it is probably
futile to pile up against it.' (Alan Sweezy, 1971)

I. INTRODUCTION

We all think we know something about that mysterious creature we
call *homo oeconomicus*, but is he also ἄνθρωπος δημογράφικος? This
certainly is the assumption implicit in any economic analysis of a
series of demographic variables. *Homo oeconomicus*, no doubt, owes
his success to the qualities we attribute to him: he is a rational man,
well informed, forward-looking, and he is, to boot, in some way
quantifiable. He has a holding and husbands it, he earns an income,
he saves, he consumes – all of which can be expressed in monetary
terms. Even his time can be measured, his time of work, of rest, of
leisure, his years of education, his working life, his retirement. Time
and money can be related in many ways (cf. Guitton, 1970).

There has always been a strong temptation to deal preferably with
things quantifiable, and it is hardly surprising that economic theory
should so long have concentrated on wealth rather than on well-
being. The concept of utility of economic goods opened the first
breach in this system and let in the whole theory of consumer choices.
'Satisfaction' is now one of the few not directly measurable concepts
used by economists. More generally speaking, the psychological
dimension of economic behaviour is gaining more and more recognition. When economists speak of the propensities to consume, to
save and to invest, or of the expectations of the economic subject,
they are in the realm of psychology. But they regard psychology
rather as a back-cloth, or sometimes as an ultimate explanation, and
most often do not build it into their models as they do utility and
satisfaction.

But while economists, as a first approximation, can manage with

* Translated by Elisabeth Henderson.

† *Author's note*. The study resulting in the first part of this paper is fully described
elsewhere (Leridon, 1973). The author is conscious that the present summary has
proved too compressed to avoid certain methodological misunderstandings, which
were revealed by the subsequent discussion.

this kind of *homo*, the demographer feels that his ἄνθρωπος is a much more complex creature. To make matters worse, the demographer has far more reasons than the economist to think in terms of married couples. Whether it is the husband or the wife who decides that a television set is to be bought, is of no interest to anyone other than sales managers or advertising agents; it is a very different matter whether it is the husband or the wife who 'decides' that there is to be another baby. Clearly, one has to explore many avenues to find an explanation of the reproductive behaviour of couples; economic interpretation certainly is one of them, but there is little chance of its leading straight to the point.

The purpose of this paper is to examine to what extent it is possible to detect an influence of economic variables on the birth-rate, or more precisely, whether the trends of the former can explain those of the latter.

At this level of analysis we can do without an explicit and complete behavioural model. Economic theories of reproductive behaviour have developed along three main lines, as follows:

1. *Investment models*, where the output expected from an addi-tional child (during its working life) is compared with the cost of its upbringing, education, etc.[1]

2. The inclusion of children as 'durable goods' *in the theory of utility and choices*: this somewhat odd category of durable goods is expected to yield immediate and long-term satisfactions, but the cost of their 'acquisition' and upkeep are conditioned by the expected satisfactions (especially via education) and the parents' income.[2]

3. Most recently, this analysis has been extended by taking account of '*time allocation*', that is, by the simultaneous study of family budgets in terms of money and of time (cf. T. P. Schultz, 1969; Willis, 1973).

In principle, time changes in the fertility of marriages can be studied with the help of these models, since they can be compared with the time series of costs and income. But there may, in addition,

---

[1] Cf. e.g. S. Enke, 'The Economic Aspects of Slowing Population Growth', *The Economic Journal*, 76, no. 301 (Mar 1966); 'The Economics of Government Payments to Limit Population', *Economic Development and Cultural Change*, 8, 2 (July 1960). This approach was severely criticised by H. Liebenstein, who called it an intellectual gadget: 'Pitfalls in Benefit-cost Analysis of Birth Prevention', *Population Studies*, 23, 2 (July 1969).

[2] See H. Liebenstein, *Economic Backwardness and Economic Growth* (New York: J. Wiley and Sons, 1967) ch. 10; and especially, G. Becker, 'An Economic Analysis of Fertility', *Demographic and Economic Change in Developed Countries* (Princeton Univ. Press, 1960). More recently see R. Easterlin, 'Toward a Socio-Economic Theory of Fertility: a Survey of Recent Research on Economic Factors on American Fertility', *Fertility and Family Planning: a World View* (Ann Arbor: Univ. of Michigan Press, 1969).

be changes in preferences (the authors of these models always insist on the fact that the 'quality' of desired children may change, especially with income), and these variables do not lend themselves to measurement. There is a great risk, therefore, that observed movements may be explained by a change in preferences, in order to preserve the consistency of the model, but without being able to prove anything about such a change.

The aim of this paper is much less ambitious. We know that any change in an index like the birth-rate always leaves one fundamental question open: is the observed variation temporary (e.g. does it correspond to a postponement of births to be made good later), or is it going to create a definite plus or minus? No attempt will be made, for the time being, to answer that question. Instead, we shall try to find out whether any given factor is operative at all, regardless of whether its influence on the behaviour of couples is temporary or durable.

This explains our choice of a rather short time-horizon. Over the centuries, fertility changes clearly cannot be explained in economic terms alone; since the seventeenth century, not only our economic system has changed, but our society as well.

II. METHODS OF ANALYSIS AND PREVIOUS STUDIES

Reference to business cycles proved a good starting point for the kind of study we are concerned with here. Clement Juglar was led by his description of recurrent trade crises to ask himself whether there were not periods for marriages and births just as there were for trade crises, and he looked for a coincidence of the extremes of the various series. Many theorists of the business cycle since then have at some time or other asked themselves a similar question, but without pushing the analysis very far.

This 'pioneering' work was taken up again more systematically in the years 1935 to 1940. The first approach was to look for a correlation between the deviation of a fertility index from the trend, and the deviation from the trend of one or several economic indices (plus, possibly, the marriage rate); the time unit is generally the calendar year. Galbraith and Thomas (1941) compared employment and birth-rates in the United States, 1919–37 (correlation 0·80); Kirk (1960) carried on with the addition of the marriage rate on the one hand, and of per capita income and industrial production on the other, and, for the period 1920–41, managed to explain 60 per cent of the fertility variance, 30 per cent of it by the intermediary of the marriage rate; Basavarajappa (1971), working with Australian data for the period 1920–37, similarly obtained very high correlations between fertility and employment production per head. Other, less systematic, studies dealt with the periods of the great economic depression.

Two important conclusions may be drawn from this whole body of work:

1. *The 1939–45 war was a turning point:* very satisfactory correlations up to 1940 or so weaken or disappear after the war.

2. *Marriage rates and fertility rates often vary at the same time,* because both are influenced by the same factors; but it does not follow that fertility rates vary because of marriage rates (cf. the interpretation of Kirk, 1960), for fertility variations generally affect all birth ranks, whereas the effect of the marriage rate is restricted to the first only.

A second analytical method was worked out by the National Bureau of Economic Research in the U.S.A. This is known as the *reference cycle method* and involves the prior precise determination of business cycles on the basis of all available indicators; the high and low points are dated, and their succession then serves as the 'time base'. Year-by-year comparison of changes in some index (e.g. the birth-rate) with those in the economic indicators is then replaced by a study of the behaviour of that index during successive cyclical upswings and downswings. Provided the hypothesis of co-variation is correct, one thus gets maximum coincidence of movements in the two series under comparison.

G. Becker (1960) applied this principle to the U.S.A. for the period 1920–56, and A. Santini (1970) covered a whole century of Italian history (1863–1965) in the same manner. Since the Second World War, the method has proved much less effective because business cycles are damped.

Finally, research is in hand on a third method, though to my knowledge nothing has been published about the subject under discussion. This is known as *spectral analysis*, or more correctly cross-spectrum analysis of several series taken two by two. In addition to its technical difficulties, this method has the drawback of being very demanding on one point: it needs long uninterrupted series.

III. THE CASE OF FRANCE, 1949–1970

In a study of French data we introduced the novel feature of using monthly series instead of annual ones, as was done in all the work so far quoted. We did this for two reasons. First, since the amplitude of economic fluctuations is diminishing, they ought to be followed more closely, that is, on a more detailed time scale; and secondly, the transition from an annual to a monthly scale means passing from a 'short' series (twenty years) to a 'long' series (240 months), which allows of more sensitive significance tests, by whatever method they are conducted. Our choice also had a number of consequences worth mentioning. It required great confidence in the quality of monthly statistics, it restricted the number of explanatory series, and, most important, it made prior seasonal adjustment of the series imperative.

Our study is fully described elsewhere (Leridon, 1973); here we shall merely sketch its broad lines. We looked for a correlation between the *residuals after elimination of the trend and of the seasonal component*. The residuals were calculated by two methods; under the first, we defined the shape of the trend *a priori* (in the event, a straight line), and under the second we made no assumption at all about the trend, but determined it simultaneously with the seasonal component and the residual, as is done by the *Institut National de la Statistique et des Etudes Economiques* (Meraud and Tymen, 1960).

Our choice of economic series was guided by the requirement that they must be representative of variables which can be taken as *indicators of the economic climate* such as it is experienced by couples at any one moment. None of these indicators, therefore, must be limited to a restricted sector of the economy, and changes in each of them must be directly perceptible to people who, after all, do not read monthly business reports, or indeed be directly *induced* by the couples themselves.

As suitable indicators for our purpose we chose *industrial production*, because of its effect on the level of activity and earnings; the *number of job seekers unable to find work*, because it is subject to considerable psychological amplification; and the increase in *savings bank deposits*, restricted to the French system of 'Caisses d'Epargne', a widespread and popular system of deposit available to private persons and limited to small amounts (total at present 20,000 F) because it may be taken as a sign of greater financial ease and a certain confidence in the future.

As regards demographic variables, we considered not only the *monthly birth-rate*, but also the *marriage rate* and, for reasons to be explained presently, even the *death-rate*. All these figures are put together in Table 6.1 and Fig. 6.1, which show, in addition, also the sum of annual age-specific fertility rates and percentage increases in the purchasing power of disposable income per head of population (for which only annual figures are available).

Table 6.1 yields no conclusions for our purposes. The economic recessions of 1952–3 and 1959 do not seem to have had any effect

TABLE 6.1 ANNUAL DATA FOR FRANCE, 1949–1970

Year	Birth-rate per 10,000	Sum of age-specific fertility rates ×100	Marriage rate per 10,000	Job seekers (000)	Saving (increase in deposits m.F)	Industrial production 1959 = 100	Increase in industrial production (%)	Increase in purchasing power per head (%)
1949	209	299	163	131	67	56		
1950	204	293	157	153	97	59	5.4	
1951	195	279	151	120	48	65	10.2	
1952	192	276	148	132	87	66	1.5	
1953	188	269	145	180	132	67	1.5	6.1
1954	187	270	146	183	142	73	9.0	5.7
1955	185	267	144	160	206	81	11.0	3.2
1956	183	266	135	110	154	87	7.4	1.5
1957	184	268	140	80	104	95	9.2	6.7
1958	181	268	139	95	201	99	4.2	7.5
1959	183	274	142	141	334	100	1.0	4.0
1960	179	273	140	130	206	108	8.0	4.7
1961	181	281	136	111	232	114	5.6	−2.1
1962	176	278	135	101–127[a]	321	121	6.1	1.6
1963	181	286	142	97–140[a]	350	127	5.0	6.4
1964	181	290	144	98–114[a]	593	138	8.7	5.2
1965	176	283	142	142	442	142	2.9	6.8
1966	174	277	138	148	512	151	6.3	4.0
1967	168	264	139	196	533	156	3.3	3.1
1968	167	256	143	254	595	161	3.2	2.4
1969	167	252	151	223	779	178	10.6	3.2
1970	167		154	262	779	188	5.6	4.0
							Average 6.0	Average 4.1

[a] Including repatriates from Algeria.

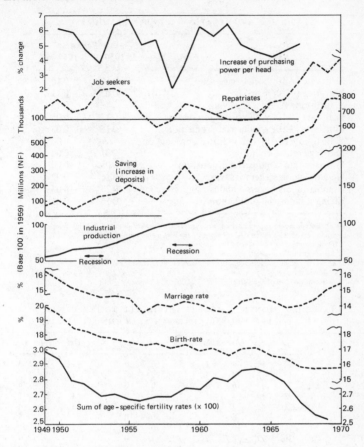

FIG. 6.1 Annual data, France, 1949–70.

on the birth-rate, which was falling anyway, and the down-turn of fertility in 1964 does not follow an economic recession.

The *natality trend*, therefore, seems to be entirely autonomous in origin. What about fluctuations around the trend? We correlated the residuals of different economic series (and of the marriage rate) with the series of residuals of the birth-rate for different lags of the latter. The strongest correlations were nearly always obtained with a ten-month lag, as we had reason to expect on the basis of a prior study of the lag problem.

The *coefficients of correlation* (see Table 6.2) are nearly all close to zero, and have *no significance*. This negative result led us to query the validity of our method of eliminating the seasonal component,

TABLE 6.2 CORRELATION BETWEEN RESIDUALS

	Period	
	1950–9	1959–69
Birth-rate (-10)[a] × marriage rate	0·10	0·10
Birth-rate (-10) × saving	0·02	$-0·11$
△ Birth-rate (-10) × △ saving		0·23
Birth-rate (-10) × number of job seekers	$-0·12$	0·05
Birth-rate (-10) × industrial production	$-0·15$	0·03
△ Birth-rate (-10) × △ industrial production		0·00
Marriage rate × saving	$-0·01$	0·02
Marriage rate × industrial production	0·03	0·00
Number of job seekers × saving	0·16	0·02
Number of job seekers × industrial production	$-0·27$[b]	$-0·05$
Saving × industrial production	0·16	0·01

Note. Except where otherwise indicated, the residuals were obtained by the complete (second) method. The 'deviations' obtained by the first method are preceded by the sign △.

[a] i.e. birth-rate after a time lag of 10 months.

[b] Significant at the level of 1 per cent.

The levels of significance for each series ($N = 120$) are as follows:

$R_1 = 0·24$ at the level of 1 per cent

$R_5 = 0·18$ at the level of 5 per cent

TABLE 6.3 MONTHLY DEATHS ATTRIBUTED TO INFLUENZA
(DEATH-RATE PER 100,000 INHABITANTS, IN ANNUAL TERMS)

Year	Jan	Feb	Mar	Apr	May	June	July	Aug	Sep	Oct	Nov	Dec
1949	229	92	19	4	1	1	0	0	0	1	2	3
1950	8	13	12	8	4	1	0	0	0	1	3	5
1951	68	91	49	16	4	2	0	0	0	2	2	4
1952	9	12	10	4	1	1	0	0	0	1	2	5
1953	98	221	42	7	2	0	0	0	0	1	3	4
1954	11	19	16	8	3	1	0	0	0	1	3	5
1955	13	18	28	10	3	1	0	0	0	1	3	7
1956	21	39	29	8	2	1	1	0	0	2	5	9
1957	40	35	9	3	2	1	0	0	2	50	110	73
1958	29	19	14	7	2	1	0	0	0	3	5	8
1959	13	27	30	63	30	5	1	0	1	3	5	6
1960	105	154	40	8	2	1	0	0	1	5	4	9
1961	18	13	7	5	2	1	0	0	0	7	7	8
1962	17	28	62	43	7	2	0	0	0	2	6	12
1963	17	44	108	26	4	1	1	0	0	3	3	7

Source: Aubenque, Damiani and Deruffe, 'Essai d'appréciation de l'incidence de la grippe sur les fluctuations de la mortalité', *Etudes et Conjoncture* (Sep 1965) 121–7.

or better, to reconsider the nature of the ensuing residual. We used fluctuations in the *death-rate* as a suitable check, for it has often been observed that a fall in the number of conceptions coincided with major influenza epidemics, which in turn are responsible for the main sudden spurts in the death-rate of developed countries. As a temporary phenomenon whose effects last only a few months,

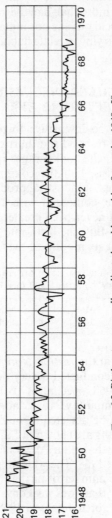

FIG. 6.2 Birth-rate, seasonally adjusted and lagged by 9 months, 1949–58.

influenza is an excellent example of the kind of 'short-term' events of which we wanted to know the repercussions on the birth-rate.

For the whole of the period 1949–63, the correlation between the rate of influenza deaths (Table 6.3) and the deviation of the birth-rate from its trend (nine months later) works out at −0·34 (which is significant at the level of 1 per cent). If one takes only the winter months (November to April) the coefficient of correlation rises to −0·44, and for the months of January and February, it reaches −0·73, and thus explains more than half the variance of fluctuations.

This incursion into a field outside our initial limits has confirmed, *a contrario*, the pitfalls of trying to relate fluctuations in the birth-rate and in the economy.

IV. MORE DETAILED DISCUSSION OF SOME EXCEPTIONAL EVENTS

If the birth-rate, then, is so insensitive to the short waves of the economy, does it at least respond to a hurricane? We have a good example in the events which shook France in May and June 1968. At the height of the crisis, half the country was on strike; the (seasonally adjusted) index of industrial production stood at 113 in May and at 130 in June, compared with 163 in April and July; political uncertainty had never been greater, at any rate not since May 1958. In spite of all this, the birth-rate placidly remained the same throughout the first six months of the following year:

SEASONALLY ADJUSTED BIRTH-RATE,
JANUARY TO JUNE 1969 (per 1000)

Jan	Feb	Mar	Apr	May	June
16·6	16·9	16·9	16·6	16·8	16·8

G. Calot and S. Hemery at the *Institut National de la Statistique et des Etudes Economiques* conducted a very detailed comparison of births in 1969 and in 1968, specific as to legitimacy, age of the mother and size of the community. No variation beyond the habitual limits of fluctuations can be detected throughout the early months of 1969. Day-by-day results are shown in Fig. 6.4 in the form of the ratio of the number of births on any day of 1969 to the number of births on the same day of 1968. The wide amplitude of fluctuations is due to the fact that the number of births is appreciably lower on Sundays (and holidays) than on weekdays;[1] each marked high corresponds to a Sunday (or holiday) in 1968, each marked low to a Sunday in 1969. In order to eliminate these fluctuations, the series was smoothed by means of a moving 7-day average.

On the horizontal scale we marked also the approximate date of *conception* (in 1968) for any birth in 1969, so as to locate the 'critical'

[1] See the Note by J. Vallin and H. Le Bras in *Population*, 1970, no. 6, p. 1268–73. This note, however, contains an error in the estimate of the Sunday shortfall, which is 7 per cent compared with other days, not 15 per cent.

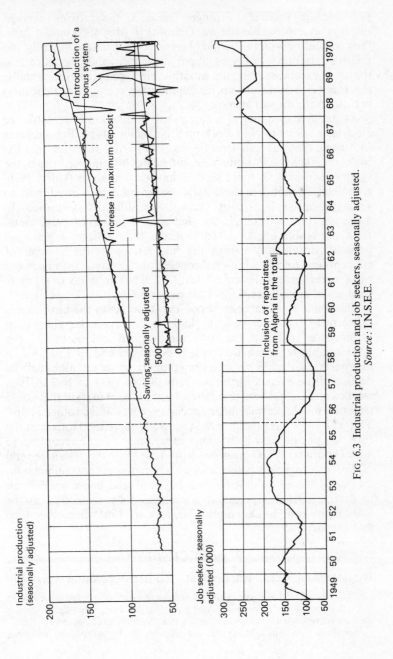

FIG. 6.3 Industrial production and job seekers, seasonally adjusted.
Source: I.N.S.E.E.

period more precisely. Strangely enough, the moving average displays an appreciable rise from (about) 16 May 1968 until 1 June, thus coinciding with the period of greatest uncertainty. Actually, the relative variation is not great (about 10 per cent) and it is not certain that it is exceptional. In the monthly birth statistics, incidentally, this result does not show up, for the monthly average (for February) is close to the annual average.

As another example of a somewhat similar kind, we took the electricity failure in New York on 9 November 1965. Press reports in August 1966 suggested, on the basis of partial statistics, that the big blackout was followed nine months later by a marked rise in the number of births. A more serious statistical analysis (Udry, 1970) completely demolished these initial assertions, which owed more to sensation-hungry journalists than to scientific demonstration. In any case, there is little chance that such a pin-point event could have detectable effects, given that the distribution of gestation periods considerably damps the fluctuations in the number of conceptions: for 100 additional conceptions on day J, the maximum birth increment occurs around day $J + 270$ but amounts to no more than seven or eight additional births per day.[1]

After these two examples of non-events so far as the birth-rate is concerned, it is interesting to look at a spectacular short-term disturbance. In Japan, the birth-rate dropped in 1966 to 13·7 per 1000 inhabitants, compared with 18·6 in 1965 and 19·3 in 1967 – a (temporary) fall of 28 per cent (for comparison we mention that the decline of the French birth-rate from 18·1 in 1964 to 16·7 in 1968 worked out at 2 per cent annually). The only explanation that could be found for this extraordinary occurrence was an astrological one. The year 1966 was placed under the two signs of the Horse and the Fire, a coincidence which recurs every sixty years; according to ancient popular beliefs given much prominence in the press at the end of 1965, this spelt very bad luck for girls born under that conjunction: they are destined to 'destroy their husband' and hence are difficult to marry. This interpretation is confirmed by anomalies in the masculinity ratio in December 1965, January 1966, December 1966 and January 1967.[2]

V. CONCLUSION

The last example demonstrates that a modern population is perfectly

[1] The *New York Times* journalists actually gave proof of glaring ignorance in focusing attention on the births of 8 and 9 August, that is nine months on the dot after the famous evening; the peak should instead have occurred around 5 August.

[2] See the two notes by J. N. Biraben in *Population*, no. 1 (1968) 154–62, and no. 1 (1969) 119–23.

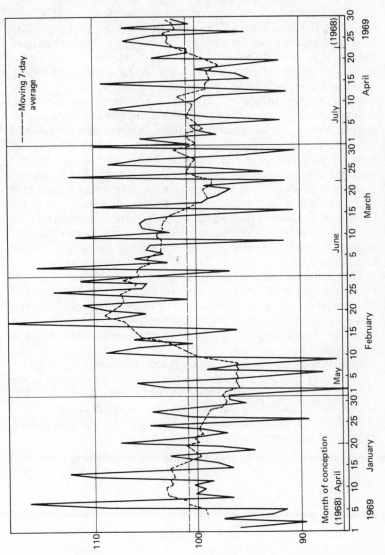

FIG. 6.4 Day-to-day ratio of 1969 to 1968 births (per 100).

capable of altering its birth-rate considerably and temporarily, if only it has strong enough reasons to do so; but these reasons, to judge by the previous examples and by our own analysis, have little or nothing to do with economic fluctuations. This is a disappointing conclusion. Even without being inclined to regard economic variables as preponderant among the determinants of fertility, it is, after all, reasonable to expect couples to react to the conditions of the moment and hence to make some slight adjustments in the timing of additions to their family.

Reproduction, to the extent that it is suitably controlled, is something that looks to the future. What matters is the image that couples have of the world in which their children are to live and of those children's chances of finding their place and getting on in that world. This image is not affected by a mere hiccup of the economy (even if it entails some loss of income), but it might be changed by a severe economic crisis. The reason why the events of May 1968 had no influence on the birth-rate in France may well be that the French never believed they would generate profound upheavals; on the other hand the Japanese, in 1966, took a much more serious view of the risk of having a daughter marred by an astrological blemish.

This brings us back to one of the aspects of behavioural models mentioned earlier. By their insistence on the notion of the 'quality of children' and on 'changing tastes' in this matter, the model-builders make it clear that the most important variable in their models is at once the most abstract, the most autonomous and the most exogenous.

Commenting on the article by G. Becker (see note 2, p. 180) J. S. Duesenberry quipped: 'Economics is all about how people make choices. Sociology is all about they don't have any choices to make'.

Perhaps we should say, rather, that the choices made by couples are not always what the economist believes – nor, for that matter, necessarily what they themselves believe.

APPENDIX

TABLE 6.A MONTHLY RESIDUAL OF BIRTH-RATE: DEVIATION OF THE SEASONALLY ADJUSTED RATE FROM THE TREND, PER 100,000

Year	Jan	Feb	Mar	Apr	May	June	July	Aug	Sep	Oct	Nov	Dec
1950	44	2	3	46	-49	13	44	-76	-20	76	4	-50
1951	30	13	-72	34	-4	-12	111	-45	-39	25	-51	4
1952	12	-2	6	24	-9	3	-22	10	11	-1	15	-27
1953	-10	26	8	-33	-14	12	30	23	2	-39	-40	17
1954	26	22	-37	9	12	-21	10	22	-6	9	-5	-25
1955	4	-11	5	21	-11	11	17	0	-29	4	-4	11
1956	-24	19	9	-23	17	-16	23	10	-9	-16	-15	0
1957	22	26	1	-15	-10	3	-50	11	29	12	5	8
1958	-21	12	7	-43	24	62	-57	-87	5	46	34	21
1959	-20	-6	-17	21	0	-18	-5	8	2	14	19	6
1960	-46	1	-5	-23	8	19	4	4	26	-12	-32	8
1961	9	-3	-25	23	18	2	-9	-10	-14	9	28	30
1962	-20	5	-5	-19	-14	-32	-22	45	-16	-1	17	-21
1963	-16	19	37	-26	-36	44	5	-14	12	3	-11	-21
1964	10	32	-13	3	-21	8	21	-41	24	11	-15	-2
1965	39	-9	-24	5	-10	-6	-1	18	3	3	1	-33
1966	18	3	-3	1	8	13	-9	14	-20	-7	9	17
1967	-9	-11	-36	28	32	-13	-9	-1	-1	4	-18	7
1968	20	-13	5	-2	2	-5	-3	-3	14	0	-8	-7
1969	-8	22	14	-20	10	5	11	-40	-4	14	3	40

TABLE 6.B MONTHLY RESIDUAL OF JOB SEEKING: DEVIATION OF THE SEASONALLY ADJUSTED NUMBER FROM TREND ($\times 100$)

Year	Jan	Feb	Mar	Apr	May	June	July	Aug	Sep	Oct	Nov	Dec
1950	-72	-10	15	27	68	4	-10	-11	2	8	0	26
1951	1	-36	-42	48	22	-7	-29	2	-15	-13	23	-12
1952	-39	6	11	-13	-6	-6	-3	-13	-33	16	-14	54
1953	29	-2	8	16	3	-5	10	-3	0	-8	-5	-12
1954	-13	19	-3	1	27	13	22	12	5	-41	-27	-8
1955	-16	17	46	-2	-10	9	-3	5	2	9	1	-20
1956	-6	44	14	-8	-27	-15	-4	19	4	-27	-10	22
1957	12	9	-13	-30	-9	6	-13	-6	1	10	2	2
1958	3	-3	2	9	3	8	-17	-19	-26	-16	-26	-27
1959	67	104	7	13	-28	-8	-22	-16	-26	0	5	26
1960	31	12	-6	13	3	-15	-3	8	-14	-29	6	6
1961	18	43	-5	-17	-10	3	-6	7	-7	-4	1	10
1962	-4	-11	17	-7	-35	-70	3	229	-90	-80	0	-11
1963	-12	57	23	-20	-4	2	-10	-3	13	-6	-7	3
1964	3	-12	-8	21	-6	-17	-14	-9	-11	12	-14	-37
1965	45	20	26	-13	2	10	-10	-2	34	9	7	17
1966	-23	-28	-6	-6	-10	-3	1	-6	5	9	5	5
1967	-25	-60	-27	22	3	11	9	-2	-6	3	40	27
1968	-59	-50	-11	-89	-7	122	28	48	71	13	-17	-21
1969	-78	-58	2	-27	-19	8	23	30	23	-1	-20	-12

TABLE 6.C MONTHLY RESIDUAL OF SAVINGS: DEVIATION OF SEASONALLY ADJUSTED FIGURE AND TREND, IN MILLIONS OF FRANCS

Year	Jan	Feb	Mar	Apr	May	June	July	Aug	Sep	Oct	Nov	Dec
1950	−9	11	−15	−36	38	21	−66	−46	3	11	6	−11
1951	24	13	−30	−11	−1	7	−2	32	3	−32	0	26
1952	88	−4	−82	−6	13	−15	14	−3	5	27	−2	−30
1953	20	17	−1	9	5	5	−16	−117	21	28	0	3
1954	−33	−19	57	−11	−3	−11	−16	−43	17	35	−5	2
1955	−77	−13	1	−11	33	−1	−48	−60	−4	20	19	46
1956	−57	−42	47	−33	−5	20	−12	43	−31	−5	−46	32
1957	89	30	13	40	−11	−60	29	113	−18	−47	61	−91
1958	18	43	142	118	−158	1	134	38	−33	27	19	12
1959	−209	−12	85	92	−9	1	−41	−34	11	−87	−46	227
1960	−168	−55	−12	11	6	−17	11	19	39	14	−68	−15
1961	119	16	−39	−10	0	20	−27	−22	55	−60	−20	39
1962	8	−22	37	−18	−5	−17	8	41	12	−60	21	59
1963	−104	19	−9	−28	25	4	−25	83	−100	19	−5	−181
1964	476	202	−192	−20	112	−1	−202	−15	−29	57	45	−107
1965	50	32	4	−10	4	−19	100	27	−108	90	1	−76
1966	99	65	−2	51	−81	89	14	−64	−48	25	−11	74
1967	91	−81	−52	138	−68	−7	27	−55	88	140	22	−251
1968	−257	−101	422	−202	6	102	−240	−65	−22	283	−202	−99
1969	526	56	−115	58	−216	86	−163	−561	596	309	13	−156

TABLE 6.D MONTHLY RESIDUAL OF INDUSTRIAL PRODUCTION: DEVIATION OF SEASONALLY ADJUSTED INDEX FROM TREND (1959 = 1000)

Year	Jan	Feb	Mar	Apr	May	June	July	Aug	Sep	Oct	Nov	Dec
1950	17	20	-44	5	11	-22	5	32	-17	-6	18	-33
1951	2	21	-10	-4	4	-13	1	20	-2	-3	-4	-19
1952	11	12	3	-2	-18	-7	3	20	-10	5	15	-26
1953	-13	8	-4	-6	12	18	-8	-16	9	-5	12	9
1954	-4	-15	-4	-4	15	9	-4	-10	12	-1	-2	3
1955	-7	-6	-7	7	2	-5	5	18	-22	6	11	12
1956	9	-77	11	25	-1	7	23	-24	-4	25	-5	-16
1957	-6	9	7	-7	-7	10	18	-27	7	9	1	-10
1958	2	10	2	-7	-18	26	45	34	-16	-5	-2	11
1959	0	-14	-10	1	-3	-7	10	11	-19	-8	14	25
1960	-21	6	-1	-12	-3	-21	10	24	-11	-18	6	10
1961	-5	13	4	-24	-4	-17	-18	52	-18	-24	-6	7
1962	15	7	-13	-19	19	-24	-20	42	-14	-8	25	22
1963	-14	-30	-70	14	45	13	1	-17	5	15	-5	-14
1964	12	25	-25	0	7	25	12	-67	29	34	20	-9
1965	-12	5	-11	-16	6	37	-21	-34	24	12	6	34
1966	-49	20	18	-24	-13	33	12	-54	39	9	4	16
1967	-12	4	15	-25	-15	42	-15	-46	33	7	2	9
1968	-3	22	92	130	-303	-115	88	29	-10	26	12	35
1969	21	-35	-31	13	27	1	16	-66	33	49	-23	-55

REFERENCES

K. G. Basavarajappa, 'The Influence of Fluctuations in Economic Conditions on Fertility and Marriage Rates, Australia, 1920 to 1938 and 1946 to 1947', *Population Studies*, vol. 25, no. 1 (1971).

V. Galbraith and D. Thomas, 'Birth Rates and the Interwar Business Cycles', *Journal of the American Statistical Association*, XXXVI (Dec 1941).

H. Guitton, *A la Recherche du Temps Economique* (Paris: Fayard, 1970).

D. Kirk, 'The Influence of Business Cycles on Marriage and Birth Rates', *Demographic and Economic Change in Developed Countries* (Princeton Univ. Press, 1960).

H. Leridon, *Natalité, saison et conjoncture économique*, I.N.E.D.-P.U.F. (Paris, 1973).

J. Meraud and A. Tymen, 'Les variations saisonnières de l'activité économique', *Etudes et Conjonctures* (Apr 1960).

A. Santini, *Nuzialità, Natalità e cicli brevi dell'economia. L'esperenzia Italiana tra il 1863 a il 1965*, Dipart. Statist. Matam. (Univ. di Firenzi, 1970). Résumé in *Quaderni Storici*, Ancona, no. 17 (May 1971).

T. Paul Schultz, 'An Economic Model of Family Planning and Fertility', *Journal of Political Economy*, 77, 2, pt II (Mar–Apr 1969).

A. Sweezy, 'The Economic Explanation of Fertility Changes in the United States', *Population Studies*, vol. 25, no. 2 (July 1971).

J. R. Udry, 'The Effect of the Great Blackout of 1965 on Births in New York City', *Demography*, vol. 7, no. 3 (Aug 1970). See note in *Economie et Statistiques* (Dec 1970).

R. J. Willis, 'A New Approach to the Economic Theory of Fertility Behaviour', *Journal of Political Economy*, 81, 2, pt II (Mar–Apr 1973).

Discussion of the Paper by
M. Leridon

Professor Rasmussen opened the discussion by saying that he had had some difficulties in commenting on this paper, and not only because he was far from being a demographer. He was also far from clear what the author wanted to say. He started by arguing that the motives behind the behaviour of human beings was much more complex than economists assumed. Professor Rasmussen thought that, as professional economists, we should agree on this, though we might add a 'So what?' to the statement. The consequence, of course, need not be that the approach of the economists was bound to fail in the attempt to present a (partial) picture of human behaviour. It was, in fact, easy to demonstrate that economists had been relatively successful, in many ways, by working on the assumption of a *homo oeconomicus*, including the assumption of profit maximisation in market economies.

This also seemed to be M. Leridon's viewpoint. He stated that the purpose of his paper was to try 'to detect an influence of economic variables on the birth-rate', but, on the whole, the conclusions of the paper seemed to be that such an influence could not be detected on the basis of data for France from the post-war period.

It was trivial, but necessary, to note that, taking these negative conclusions into account, these findings could not and would not be generalised too far. There was ample evidence of changes in birth-rates which could be explained by economic variables. The obvious facts that mattered, however, were complicated in a modern, industrialised country like France, where full employment and growth had prevailed over virtually the whole post-war period. This was extremely important.

Professor Rasmussen went on to consider the methods applied by M. Leridon. The data used were monthly, as against the usual annual series. The arguments for this were, first, that the changes in economic indicators were relatively small for the years considered (1949–70) and, second, that instead of 20, one got 240 observations.

As to the first point, one might question the net gain, because the author cleared all the data for seasonal variations. This, of course, meant that changes in the variables considered remained small, and the argument referred to was weakened. In fact, one might ask why the author could withstand the temptation to shift the emphasis of the paper, and, if not concentrating on the seasonal fluctuations, at least include them into the model. This might prove a fruitful excercise, because month to month fluctuations were significant in all countries.

M. Leridon had used three explanatory variables: industrial production, the number of job seekers unable to find work, and the increase in savings bank deposits. It was very surprising to see the last variable appearing. It was a general and well-known fact that changes in savings bank deposits were very hard to interpret, not only because of the difficult problem of how to deflate the time series, but also because so many factors lay behind them.

Was the situation in France different, in this respect, from that in other industrialised countries?

The endogenous variable was the birth-rate, but the marriage rate and even the death-rate were also used. The reason for considering the death-rate was that 'it has often been observed that a fall in the number of conceptions coincided with major influenza epidemics, which in turn are responsible for the main sudden spurts in the death-rate of developed countries'. In other words, the death-rate was used as a proxy for the number of conceptions. This pointed towards an interesting study of the seasonal fluctuations. Was influenza so important, or was 'influenza' in the statistics a proxy for many things? On the whole, as already stated, the results were not promising.

Perhaps in a desperate mood, the author looked for any influence of unique events. He reported on three cases. First, the crisis in France in May–June 1968. Nothing came out. Second, the blackout in New York on 9 November 1965. Again nothing came out, and perhaps that case should be counted only as a joke. It reminded one of the popular explanation of the rapid increase in the birth-rate in Denmark during the war – the curtain (blackout). Of course, it turned out that the explanation was that births had been postponed during the crisis of the 1930s but were resumed under the full employment situation created during the war. Third, the fall in the birth rate in Japan from 1965–6 was considered to be explained by an astrological phenomenon, 1966 being under the sign of the Horn and the Fire, which, according to popular belief, would spell bad luck for girls born in that year. Again, this sounded like a joke, though the author seemed inclined to accept it. He might even be right! If it were true, the story would entertain many a classroom in the years to come. It was a pity that there were sixty years between these interesting configurations – and in the meantime we should all be dead!

The author had tried several hypotheses in vain. He could rightly claim to have put forward some fresh ideas. The notorious fact was a decline of 20 to 25 per cent in the birth-rate over the 20 years considered. It might be assumed that the author – although he did not say so – had tried to wipe out the effects of changes in the age distribution. But had he tried the simple theory of the effects of 'urbanisation'? Any attempt in this field would run into difficulties because modern communications, in a broad sense, tended to spread the way of life of the metropolis into smaller towns and rural areas. If this were true, we were confronting a very difficult problem: how to measure 'urbanisation'. Even so, one might guess that the word 'urbanisation', as a proxy for modern life, might turn out to be a key word. To put it another way: France might be beyond the stage where crude and simple economic variables were able to explain changes in the birth-rate. This suggestion admittedly did not go very deep. What kind of mechanisms were, in fact, working behind that curtain? The author himself raised that question in his last paragraph but two, which could be endorsed.

Many of the papers presented to this conference proved the usefulness of using socio-economic indicators beyond those considered in the paper, for example, the comparison of Flemish and Walloon villages presented by Dr Lesthaeghe and Professor van de Walle. It would have been surprising if M. Leridon's attempts to use very rough economic indicators had proved successful.

M. *Leridon* said that the conference was devoted to 'economic aspects of population growth' and his own paper was concerned with trends and *fluctuations* in the birth-rate, although the effect of the trade cycle in a country like France meant that it was hard to formulate a hypothesis, let alone to test it. Professor Rasmussen had said he was not surprised by the lack of result, but M. Leridon thought that the results were significant for a number of countries between the First and Second World Wars. He wanted to explain that his conclusions were derived from a large study where he had explained why he had chosen a particular series, and what technique he used to get monthly figures.

Professor Rasmussen had treated what had happened to the Japanese birth-rate in 1966 as a joke, but there had been a significant decrease in fertility then not found at any time except during wars, and this needed study. Within developed countries he did think that it was worth looking at these problems. The choice of explanation was not easy and we must look further than from economic variables to social ones. He did not believe that the reduction of fertility in developed countries was simply a question of fashion.

Professor Coale agreed that what had happened in Japan was not a joke, but a very interesting phenomenon. This happened every 60 years, but obviously there was much less voluntary control of births in 1906, and no effect of this phenomenon was visible in the time series of births at that time. However, the relationship between male and female births, which varied very little in any population, did rise by more than any other hypothesis could explain. It rose from 105 male births per 100 female births to somewhere around 108 or 109. There was a corresponding increase in 1905 and 1907. What happened was that it was possible for a few parents, who did not want girls to be registered in that year, to have them registered as having been born in 1905 or 1907. As for 1966, the Japanese denied that they were superstitious about these things, but nevertheless they seemed to have made certain by not taking chances.

Mr Boulier said that on theoretical grounds one should not expect temporary fluctuations in economic activity in developed countries to affect fertility rates, since child bearing and marriage were long-term commitments which were influenced by such things as permanent income and long-term employment prospects. And on empirical grounds, the use of deviations from trends in fertility and economic activity was subject to three shortcomings. First, it was sensitive to the techniques chosen to measure the trends. In Basavarajappa's work on Australia, the magnitudes, and even signs, of the correlations between deviations from trends in age-specific fertility rates and in gross domestic product depended upon whether first or second degree polynomials were used to fit the trends. Second, the method was sensitive to the lag chosen for fertility. Silver's work for the U.S.A. provided examples. Third, the method missed major changes in fertility of long duration. M. Leridon's technique would miss the American baby boom, because it lasted ten years.

Professor Ben Porath said that while he agreed with Professor Rasmussen, one ought to distinguish two matters. If this was a first study on the topic, one might argue that there was no hope of learning very much. However, there were a number of other studies, especially in the U.S.A., relating short-term fluctuations in economic activity to short-run fluctuations in the birth-rate. So the fact that one did not find any correlation in France was interesting in itself. One could not drop the issue simply by saying that, *a priori*, any relationship was unlikely. The question was why there was some relationship in other countries, and what it meant where that relationship existed. He agreed with the spirit of the criticisms. The short-run link was not with family size. There was no evidence that short-run fluctuations led parents to change the number of births. Perhaps there were minor adjustments in timing, but no long-run consequences. However, the theory behind all this was unclear, so perhaps there was a need for a theory like that advocated by Professor Guitton in the previous session, with stochastic elements and life-time considerations.

Thus one was likely to get a very different result if there were a major recession than if there were a short-term slump which was expected to end quickly.

Professor Rasmussen thought that the hypothesis in the paper might well work in some countries at some times. All he was saying was that it did not hold in post-war France, where employment was continually full or nearly full.

Professor Robinson was more interested in the link between demographic research and development economics. He wondered whether research was being done on what he saw as the policy variables. Should we be able to give an idea to those engaged in economic development as to what the best strategies were? For example, he had been particularly concerned with Bangladesh, where the central problem was whether one could raise the standard of living in a Malthusian country, with a 3 per cent population growth per annum. He had been fascinated by the various studies of what had happened in Europe in the nineteenth century, and was interested to see what emerged from these. But he wondered whether what happened there applied to a world of mass media, population ministries, and public discussion of contraception. For, today, one policy variable was publicity. He wondered what the results of publicity were where it had been tried. Had attempts been made to find them? For example, in advertising, a company which wanted to see what was the result of an advertising campaign would look at the change in sales due to this campaign in one city in which there had been advertisement as compared with another in which there had not. He wondered whether there were similar studies in the field of population. In this respect, countries with population problems might be guided on how to handle such an experiment. For example, could one have an intensive birth-control drive in Bombay and contrast the results with Calcutta where no similar drive was taking place?

Again, he wondered whether there had been sufficient study of the effects of housing. For example, the British census provided information about a number of elements like whether a house had water inside or outside, whether it had outside or inside sanitation, and so on. This seemed to him a useful set of data; perhaps work correlating this with size of family was being done. However, if there was such research, then there was a lack of communication between those carrying it out and others in the field, including economic planners.

Another variable was that in some countries parents had to pay for education. In the U.K. only the snobs did; the others did not. There seemed to be no question that in the U.K. educational expenditure was taken into account in planning the size of families.

In the 1930s, he had been concerned with discussions on what effect there might be on the population if the welfare state were introduced, and again in similar discussions in the 1940s when certain services were being started. He wondered whether more recent studies had been carried out. There also seemed to be no adequate analysis of the effects of female employment. There was a difference between employment in an office and employment of the cottage type where the woman worked amid the family. Much of the effects of child-bearing were concentrated in the years that the wife had to devote to protecting the children. How far was this consistent with various forms of employment? These were questions he would like to see answered. He knew that he was ill-informed; perhaps people had looked at these issues and found them to be dead ends. However, these were things that a general working economist would like to know. He would like a closer relationship between the working theories and research topics of both economists and demographers.

Professor Coale said that it would take a long time to answer the questions Professor Robinson had asked, and maybe some of them would be answered in later sessions. However, he did agree with the need for more research.

Professor Guitton noted that M. Leridon's report was full of hope and encouragement, but he felt some despair. The paper seemed to be poised mid-way between the joy of discovery and the pain of failure. Perhaps, with modern growth theory, one might expect that we should be looking more at steady growth than at fluctuations. However, Professor Hicks had told him that the trade cycle had not disappeared in the world of growth models. He wondered whether the demographic cycles were linked to physical and political factors. M. Leridon had reminded us of Juglar, who was preoccupied much earlier than anyone else with whether fertility and nuptiality were linked to the cycle.

M. Leridon's method might provide one way of describing whether there was a demographic cycle linked to the general economic cycle. Professor Guitton did not think there was a demographic cycle. The average indices were too gross to show it in any case. But the paper did talk of spectral analysis – of moving from a more gross to a more detailed correlation, as Professor Schultz had explained in a previous session. So he thought that M. Leridon pinned his hopes still to spectral analysis, and multi-variant methods. Professor Guitton doubted whether this was likely to be successful. Using monthly data was interesting, but one needed a long series for spectral analysis and one might then possibly discover whether or not there was a cycle.

Perhaps Professor Robinson's remarks about publicity were important here. Gabriel Tarde had built a philosophy in which he imagined that the cause of the unhappy world in which we live was imitation. Was this the important thing in demography? We should perhaps remember this.

Professor Guitton ended by saying that he had talked of the 'quality' of the child; he would put this point again. Perhaps there was a distinction between the economics and the sociology of people like Duesenberry.

Professor Schultz wanted to return to what Professor Robinson had said. Traditional demographic research had not been inclined to develop causal models, but others could speak about the variety of techniques that had been used. He was concerned with housing problems and thought that this was relevant in Eastern and Western Europe, especially in 1945 when conditions were regionally so varied. But, in less-developed countries, there were often questions in the census asking about housing, but they seemed to have been of little value in accounting for fertility differences.

Dr Ridker did not think that this was the point of what Professor Robinson had said about housing. Professor Robinson was asking what difference it made if there was, or was not, a correlation between the indices in the paper and economic variations. What was the implication for policy, for example? This had been troubling him throughout the session, and Professor Robinson had put his worries in another way. Why should one not look at the other variables? And what difference would it make whether spectral analysis worked or not?

Professor Robinson argued that one needed to distinguish pre-conditions from causes. He thought that housing conditions were a pre-condition of effective contraceptive policies.

Professor Létinier believed that one of the most important conclusions in the paper was that there were no correlations now, but that there had been correlation before the war. Economic crises might be an explanation. Before the war, fluctuations had been larger. Since the war, the only significant fluctuation had been in 1952. He agreed that statistical analysis of the problem was difficult, but why should one not try? If conditions similar to those now had existed in some of the smaller pre-war cycles, this should show something.

Professor Guillaumont pointed out that the paper looked at short-run factors influencing fertility. It did not look at the political implications, though these were intellectually interesting and might help in long-run studies.

He wondered which economic variations, in the short run, could affect fertility, why and when? Was the state of employment important? An important factor could be price changes.

He also wondered what was the lag between economic variations and their impact on fertility. Whatever the variables, there was the problem of this lag in its effect on fertility. This kind of analysis might be very good, but it was also very hazardous. The family did not take its decisions about how many children it was going to have from month to month, reacting to current economic conditions. Perhaps one could deal more usefully with annual data.

M. Leridon replied to the discussion. To Mr Boulier, he said that the method was different from that in the quoted study. The method was intended to calculate trends, seasonal components and residuals.

To Professor Rasmussen, he said that when he was talking about savings bank deposits, he was concerned with the French 'Caisses d'Epargnes'. These were concerned only with small depositors, and their deposits appeared to be a useful indicator of how households reacted to the cycle in terms of their savings.

To Professor Guillaumont, he would say that lags *were* important. One had to choose the biological lag of ten months, and this did give the best correlation. As for the choice of variables, he was limited by his use of monthly statistics, but had also used quarterly figures, and still found no sign of periodicity.

To Professor Guitton, the point of principle was that seasonal factors led to much of the variation; so it was necessary to limit their effects, and various methods of spectral analysis could do this.

To Dr Ridker, M. Leridon said that there had been many references to policy issues in earlier sessions. He would just say that there were some influences which affected fertility, and others which did not. So, if, for example, we found a positive correlation between industrial production and fertility, were we going to reduce industrial production in order to reduce fertility? Similarly, did an increase in female employment increase or decrease the number of births? Professor Robinson had suggested experimenting with the use of publicity, but he would like to suggest that there were dangers in making inferences from this. For example, one could not be sure that all other elements remained constant in the two cities while the propaganda campaign was carried out in one of them.

7 Economic Factors and Fertility Decline in France and Belgium

R. Lesthaeghe and E. van de Walle

OFFICE OF POPULATION RESEARCH, PRINCETON

I. INTRODUCTION

If the populations of the developing world were perceiving their best economic interest with the same logic as members of the academic profession, the birth-rate would be low where income per head is low and fertility control would be an accepted method of influencing the well-being of individuals. Logically, large families would prevail in rich countries and among rich people, and the poor would get no children. Unfortunately this kind of reasoning is of little help. The etymology of proletarian is *proles*, progeny. Even two hundred years ago, Jacques the Fatalist was granting to his master: 'Nothing populates like the rabble.'

Authors of the time offered several explanations of the paradox of an association between prolificacy and want. According to Diderot,

> One more child is nothing for them, charity feeds them. And then, too, it's the only pleasure that costs nothing; they console them-
> selves at night, at no expenses, for the calamities of the day...[1]

Maurice de Saxe, Field Marshal of France, had an economic explanation:

> ...it has always been observed that a craftman's or peasant's business improves with the more children he gets, because he puts them to some work as soon as they are six or seven years old.[2]

These rationalisations, with their curiously familiar ring, may well refer to a transitional stage where the upper classes were already limiting their fertility, whereas the lower classes ignored birth control. The direction of class or income fertility differentials before the wide-scale introduction of contraception is still a matter of dispute. The few available series suggest that the fertility of well-to-do couples may well have been highest (e.g. Charbonneau, 1970). It is

---

[1] Denis Diderot, *Jacques le Fataliste et son Maître*, Editeurs des Portes de France (Porrentruy, 1946), p. 41.
[2] Maréchal de Saxe, 'Réflexions sur la propagation de l'espèce humaine', *La curiosité littéraire et bibliographique*, vol. 2 (Paris, 1881) p. 63.

difficult, however, to accept uncritically the generalisation of Chaunu (1966):

> The birthrate of the rich and mighty is more generous than that of the poor: under the old Regime, this is the first rule... The very high birthrates of the elite in the 17th century (8 children on the average) can be explained by the female age at marriage (18 years) and by lactation assistance from wet nurses coming from the lower strata of the population.

The contrast between élite and lower classes may well have been less marked than that between scores of little-known social groups with customs and mores susceptible of influencing reproduction. Moreover, two essential distinctions are in order: (a) between overall fertility and marital fertility, (b) between levels of fertility, in the absence of long-term trend, and the stage reached in the control of fertility during the historical transition from high to low rates. These distinctions must be reviewed before we turn to the subject of relations between economic factors and fertility in nineteenth-century France and Belgium.

II. ADJUSTMENT MECHANISMS OF FERTILITY

Although stable fertility *levels* may well be subject to one kind of influence from socio-economic status and income, differential fertility *trends* present a different problem altogether. It may be that reproduction in a distant past was more abundant, and families larger among rich couples than among poor ones, for a number of reasons. The former may have had better health and less miscarriages, non-nursing mothers had shorter birth intervals, and infant deaths were probably less frequent in wealthier households. These factors, and possibly others, did not imply any conscious decisions by the couples. On the other hand, controlled fertility today tends to be increasingly associated with income, either because parents have the children they can afford, or because they treat them as consumer goods, competing with other items for a limited income. A positive relation between reproductive performance and income has often been postulated, both at high and low levels of fertility. We are dealing with a different issue when we are discussing long-term trends in fertility rather than static levels. The transition between high and low fertility follows other rules, and among Western populations, the decline has historically started among the upper classes. The process was a transitional phenomenon, and its particular relation to economic determinants has sometimes been accounted for by introducing a variable associated with income, necessary to trigger the decline of fertility: e.g. the access to contraceptive methods, education, or even a secular outlook.

What follows is mainly concerned with the fertility decline; we are dealing with trends, not primarily with levels. But we must say a few words about pre-malthusian adjustment mechanisms of fertility. This is where the other distinction mentioned above becomes crucial: the distinction between overall fertility and legitimate fertility. Economic factors may condition the decision to marry or, after marriage, they may determine the number of offspring. (There may be a subsidiary influence of the economy on illegitimate fertility.)

Most of the classical treatises of political economy start with a section on population. Not only is labour a factor of production, directly proportional to population size; but also, Ricardo surmises (1817), labour itself is produced in response to market forces, as any other commodity:

> It is when the market price of labour exceeds its natural price that the condition of the labourer is flourishing and happy, that he has it in his power to command a greater proportion of the necessaries and enjoyments of life, and therefore to rear a healthy and numerous family...

This interpretation of the relation between reproduction and demand for labour has now been stored in the museum of irrelevant theoretical insights. The time-horizon required for the mechanism to apply is simply too long, and the intervening steps between the market stimulus favouring a marriage (or even birth) and the subsequent entry of offspring in the labour force are fraught with too many uncertainties. Furthermore, once concluded, the marriage unleashes a potential of fertility during a period of fifteen or twenty years which could be entirely unrelated to the future needs of the market-place. In Dupâquier's words (1972), the mechanism may be a good accelerator of population, but it is a poor brake.

Nevertheless, marriage has played an important role in adapting the population of Western societies to their resources in the long run. Rural population sizes and densities were often remarkably stable over time, and this feature was related to marital customs, which subjected the creation of any independent household to the condition of a roof and a bread-winning occupation. Whether this was an implicit adaptation to economic necessities, or the accidental consequence of customs regulating the transmission of property, is largely irrelevant here. It is possible to construct an elementary demographic model where a new marriage would be permitted only when a dwelling is vacated by a death. Within a reasonable range of mortality, the system can be kept in equilibrium by varying ages at marriage or the proportions marrying, and by accounting for the remarriage of widows. (For a description of such a model, see Dupaquier and Demonet, 1972.)

Contemporary authors had recognised the existence of such a system. Cantillon, for one, described it in detail (1755), and the census takers in Switzerland thought, as late as 1888, that marital status data were the best available indicators of the social and economic development of a people.

> At the conclusion of a marriage, one of the most serious considerations taken into account, except in relatively few instances, is undoubtedly the question whether the spouses are able to provide, not only for their own sustenance, but also for the children to be born from their union. It can therefore be recognized that the number of marriages, as well as the succession of its increases and decreases, is closely correlated to the opinions held within the population concerning economic conditions of the time and related expectations for the future.[1]

If such a system was functioning in many rural communities of Europe, who then was setting the rules of the game? In other terms, what form of social constraint was powerful enough to prevent young people from simply building a shack and trusting God's providence, as they seem inclined to do in many parts of the world? Was it parental authority, public opinions, or building codes and land-use customs? Dupâquier suggests (1972) that 'building a new house was above the means of even a very thrifty former servant.' Such a statement would be incomprehensible in countries of Africa where a hut can be assembled at the expense of a few days' work. Was the cost prohibitive in Europe, or was there a shortage of free land? Were there rules against squatting? Braun notes (1972) the existence of a *numerus clausus* of chimneys per community in the Zürich lowlands, when a new house could only be built after another had been brought down.

If a piece of land was needed as a rule to establish a household, it is conceivable that inheritance or the prospect of inheritance could influence nuptiality and the birth-rate. But inheritance customs were by no means uniform in Europe. Habakkuk has argued (1955) that, other things being equal, there should be fewer marriages in single-heir regions, while marital fertility should be higher in regions of partible inheritance. It is plausible that primogeniture was not favourable to the marriage of cadets, while the subdivision of

---

[1] Statistique de la Suisse, *Les résultats du recensement fédéral du 1er décembre 1888*, 88 (Berne, 1893) p. 8*.

patrimonies encouraged marriage by those who gained title even to a fraction of land. Habakkuk's hypothesis that the latter use contraception routinely to curb the level of their fertility, is more controversial, but it can be modified to say that the decline of marital fertility can be expected to start in partible inheritance regions.

The former inheritance rule encouraged the departure of landless children to other regions or to cities where they would earn enough money to settle on their own; the latter system tended to maintain the heir on the land, where they combined agriculture with complementary activities such as seasonal migration and cottage industry. Braun has shown (1972) how cotton weaving and spinning favoured the settlement of highlands around Zürich in the eighteenth century by early marrying populations despite the poor quality of the land which had prevented until then the establishment of traditional communities with indivisible land rights. But whatever the inheritance system, a rapid expansion of the industrial and service sectors of the economy could result in substantial population increases by decreasing the importance of a link to the land. E. W. Hofstee has argued (1954) in the instance of Holland that the development of a salaried class in the cities as well as in the countryside led to an upheaval of marital behaviour. This he calls the 'proletarian transitional phase'. When the wage-earner's lot ceased to be subordinated to family agriculture, the precariousness of their sustenance began to be unrelated to their age, and they had no more grounds for postponing their marriages.

What precedes can now be summarised as a series of hypotheses, under four headings from A to D, to which we shall refer when we discuss the cases of France and Belgium. These hypotheses concern the link between marital fertility and nuptiality.

A. Fertility came down first in regions characterised by an intensive nuptiality. The reader may recognise the modified Habakkuk hypothesis that we mentioned earlier.

B. External factors of an economic or legal nature were first operative to change nuptiality. The subsequent decline of fertility is at least in part the result of population pressure resulting from earlier and more universal marriage. This mechanism has been postulated by Hofstee (1954) and Petersen (1960) in the Netherlands.

C. In the classical statement of demographic transition theory, married couples start to control their fertility under the pressure of economic and social incentives. As nuptiality ceases to function as the traditional balancing mechanism, the proportion married is free to rise. Spengler (1938) has interpreted the French data pertaining to the latter part of the nineteenth century in this way.

D. Finally, it is possible to argue that legitimate fertility and nuptiality have yielded to common influence, without being directly linked to one another.

A. J. Coale (1969) has described a series of indices that will be used here to test these hypotheses. The indices include standardised measures of legitimate fertility (I_g) and of the proportion married (I_m) that are defined as:

$$I_g = \frac{BL}{\sum F_i m_i} \tag{7.1}$$

$$I_m = \frac{\sum F_i m_i}{\sum F_i w_i} \tag{7.2}$$

The meaning of the symbols in equations (7.1) and (7.2) is as follows: BL is the number of legitimate births during the period of five years centred on the date of estimation; m_i and w_i are respectively the married women and the total number of women in age group i at the date of estimation; and F_i is the marital fertility of a high-fertility standard population, the Hutterites, in the five-year age group i. We might as well define here our measures of overall fertility (I_f) and of illegitimate fertility (I_h); they involve in addition to already cited variables: BI, the number of illegitimate births, and B, the total number of births of the five-year period; and u_i, the non-married women by age group:

$$I_f = \frac{B}{\sum F_i w_i} \tag{7.3}$$

$$I_h = \frac{BI}{\sum F_i u_i} \tag{7.4}$$

Note that

$$I_f \simeq I_g \cdot I_m \tag{7.5}$$

for low values of I_h, the illegitimate fertility index.

III. FRANCE IN THE NINETEENTH CENTURY

The proper study of the relation between fertility and nuptiality, and of their interaction under the influence of socio-economic variables, would require time series on population and the economy extending far back into the past. But statistics become available in France only at half course of the great transformation of the institutions and the economy. There had been already in the eighteenth century a large expansion of cottage industry that broadened the basis of rural life and paved the way for the coming development of manufacture. There can be no question of massive industrialisation on the English or Walloon pattern; nevertheless the French economy of the first part of the nineteenth century had benefited from the overthrow of the Old Regime. Modernisation and social progress were making great strides. The French Revolution had abolished the land privileges of the nobility and the clergy, and property was trickling slowly down to the land users. The civil code had imposed a uniform and equalitarian treatment of inheritance. It is true that the institutions and customs of the Old Regime persisted for a long time – witness the survival of primogeniture and the stem family in regions such as Bearn (Bourdieu, 1962). Nevertheless, the existence of the traditional mechanism linking fertility and marriage to the economy can no longer be postulated. And finally, on the demographic side, the progressive diffusion of a new strategy of fertility control by individual couples became obvious even before the Revolution.

The reorganisation of the State had important statistical fallouts: the beginning of the official vital statistics, periodic censuses, and an overwhelming volume of administrative statistics on a wide variety of topics. At least shreds of information exist for the whole century on the basis of an almost invariant geographical unit, the *département*. The data are less and less detailed and more and more unreliable as we go back in time. At any rate, the analysis of the relationship among variables must be restricted to ecological correlations from which it is unsafe to draw inferences about individuals. At the very least we can say whether there exists in space a link between the measured phenomena, for example, between the wealth of the regions and their legitimate fertility or their nuptiality.

The demographic indices used here were computed from the result of a detailed reconstruction by *département* of the female population of France (van de Walle, 1973). The standardised measures I_g and I_m, described above, could only be computed from 1831 on.

Thus our analysis starts very late, when the decline of fertility is well under way in most *départements*, and almost over in a few. We shall also restrict ourselves to a short period between 1831 and 1866. It is among the least well-known periods of the demographic history of France, and one where the range of values of both I_g and I_m is the widest. As such, it lends itself well to the study of the relation between marital fertility and marriage during the demographic transition. It is immediately obvious that the correlation coefficients exceed -0.75 for the whole period under review. How is this relationship explained in our previous framework of hypothesis from A to D?

The sequence of changes provides a first clue towards an interpretation. If it could be shown that the decline of I_g precedes the rise of

I_m, this would go a long way toward supporting hypothesis C against hypothesis B. But we are limited by the lateness of our data. Since marital fertility starts going down before the Revolution, how can we hope to check on the priority of nuptiality changes? (A new source of data may yet bring a partial solution to the problem. The deaths were registered by age and marital status from the beginning of the century, well before the corresponding information is provided for the living-in censuses. We are now studying these data extracted from the National Archives and trying to push the estimation of age at marriage back to the Napoleonic period. It will be possible to go back even more for the proportions never marrying. Since there are practically no marriages after age fifty for women, the proportions single above fifty at the beginning of the century preserve the evidence of non-marriage in successive generations of the past. It is too early to describe any results, but it appears possible to go back much further in time than we do in the present paper.)

The data from 1831 on can be used to show that I_g correlates better with future I_m's than with contemporary ones, while the opposite is true for I_m (Table 7.1). On the whole, this finding confirms hypothesis C. But the *r*'s remain high, even with a lag of twenty years.

TABLE 7.1   CORRELATION COEFFICIENTS
BETWEEN I_g AND I_m.
FRENCH *DEPARTEMENTS*, 1831–1851

	r between 1831 I_g and I_m at various dates	r between 1831 I_m and I_g at various dates
1831	−0·778	−0·778
1836	−0·774	−0·762
1841	−0·788	−0·740
1846	−0·789	−0·711
1851	−0·804	−0·681

Another way of checking the hypotheses can be used. We introduce an economic indicator which is clearly related to the demographic indices, and we try to fit the variables into a simple causal model. We are attempting to answer the following question: Are economic variables influencing marital fertility through the proportion married, the proportion married through marital fertility, or the two jointly? Our economic indices are not ideal, but they reflect landed income per head in the *départements*, a factor that must affect the decision to marry and have children. The estimates of landed income were the outcome of administrative surveys taken in 1821 and 1851 for the purpose of fiscal reform. They are based on records of leases and sales during a long period, and on the results of the *cadastre*. The estimates of income per person employed in agriculture, and of disposable income per head about 1864, are borrowed from a study by Delefortrie and Morice.[1]

There is little doubt that the indices used reflect the economic position of the *départements*. Since they are strongly inter-correlated, and refer to an ill-defined period, they may be assumed to reflect lasting characteristics, and there can be no major objection to exploring the relationship between pre-1821 regional incomes and I_g's or I_m's in 1831; pre-1851 income and I_g's or I_m's in 1851; and between the Delefortrie-Morice estimates for 1864 and the demographic indices for 1866. The correlations between each triad of variables are presented in Table 7.2. The diagrams give zero order correlation coefficients and (between brackets) the partial correlations. The latter coefficients indicate what is left of the association between two variables when the influence of a third one is eliminated by statistical means. If 'holding constant' a variable reduces the correlation coefficient drastically, it may be inferred that the variables were not related directly, but only through a common influence.

Here, too, the results tend to confirm the hypothesis of a direct influence of economic factors on marital fertility, and of an indirect one only on the proportions married. The hypothesis D that fertility and nuptiality were related because of the common influence of income can be rejected, since a very high correlation subsists after the economic variable is accounted for. The causal links seem to be those implied in hypothesis C: the marital fertility of *départements* is a function of their economic welfare, and nuptiality is most intensive where fertility is low. In other terms, it would seem that traditional checks to marriage were relaxed where marital fertility was being controlled.

The economic indicators used, landed revenue in particular, reflect the nature of private wealth at a time when France had not begun the industrial revolution. Indices of the geographical distribution of industry and trade, or even of urbanisation, result in non-significant correlations. The only clear association is the high positive correlation between industrialisation or urbanisation and illegitimate fertility (I_h). As for marital fertility, it is obvious that it was

---

[1] The results for 1821 and 1851 are taken from 'L'enquête de 1851 sur les revenus territoriaux de la France continentale', *Bulletin de statistique et de législation comparée du Ministère des Finances*, vi (July–Dec 1879) 110–29 and 185–99. For 1864, see Nicole Delefortrie and Janine Morice, *Les revenus départementaux en 1864 et 1954* (Colin, 1959).

TABLE 7.2 ZERO ORDER AND PARTIAL CORRELATION COEFFICIENTS
BETWEEN A PER CAPITA INCOME VARIABLE AND I_g (LEGITIMATE FERTILITY)
OR I_m (PROPORTION MARRIED)

French départements at selected dates

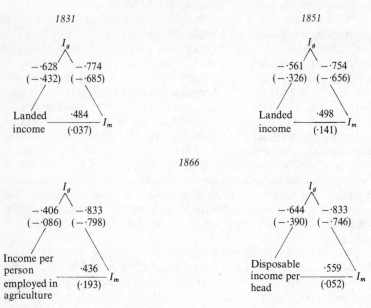

	1831		1851

1831

I_g

$-\cdot628$ $-\cdot774$
$(-\cdot432)$ $(-\cdot685)$

Landed $\cdot484$
income $(\cdot037)$ I_m

1851

I_g

$-\cdot561$ $-\cdot754$
$(-\cdot326)$ $(-\cdot656)$

Landed $\cdot498$
income $(\cdot141)$ I_m

1866

I_g

$-\cdot406$ $-\cdot833$
$(-\cdot086)$ $(-\cdot798)$

Income per
person $\cdot436$
employed in $(\cdot193)$ I_m
agriculture

I_g

$-\cdot644$ $-\cdot833$
$(-\cdot390)$ $(-\cdot746)$

Disposable
income per $\cdot559$
head $(\cdot052)$ I_m

Note: Partial correlation coefficients are between brackets.

controlled before the industrial take-off, and that birth control had
allowed the shedding of traditional marriage restrictions by 1831.

It is interesting to confront the French case with an instance of
early industrialisation and late fertility decline. In Belgium, fertility
does not start to decline before the second part of the nineteenth
century. *A priori*, this is a place where one would expect marriage
to play its traditional role of malthusian check in full view of
statistical records.

IV. THE ECONOMIC DEVELOPMENT OF BELGIUM
IN THE NINETEENTH CENTURY

The fertility and nuptiality transitions in Belgium started in the
second half of the nineteenth century, at a time when the country was
already characterised by considerable industrialisation in comparison to the rest of Continental Europe. Not only was there heavy

industry in certain areas, but even the rural parts had large populations employed outside of agriculture.

Consequently the demographic transformations occurred under entirely different conditions from those in France. The adoption of the Napoleonic Code and the redistribution of land after the French Revolution had had hardly any effect on agriculture and land tenure sixty years later. Other branches of economic activity had become important and played a more considerable role. The first wave of industrialisation spread over Wallonia between 1800 and 1820. From 1830 on, the Walloon textile industry became totally independent of local agriculture as raw materials were imported and processing with modern machinery left no place for a cottage industry. In 1850, the coal fields of Hainaut and Liège produced more than northern France and the Ruhr together, and Walloon metallurgy had shifted completely from charcoal to coke. The zinc, glass and chemical industries were growing apace. As early as 1846, more than 20 per cent of the active population of Hainaut and Liège was employed in heavy industry. This percentage grew almost linearly to 50 per cent in 1910.

Predominantly agricultural regions could also be found in Wallonia, adjacent to these centres of early industrialisation. But, nowhere was there a close association between agriculture and rural textile industry. This combination was typical for Flanders. From the middle of the eighteenth century on, rural Flemish society was characterised by a symbiosis of textile industry and subsistence agriculture. The textile raw material, flax, was produced locally and was spun and woven by cottage workers. A substantial proportion of those engaged in agriculture were tenants and they worked only very small and fragmented plots. In many cases, this rural proletariat was dependent on both sectors, cottage industry and intensive agriculture. The census of 1846 revealed, for instance, that a quarter of the active male population of east and west Flanders was employed in the linen industry or in related artisanal activities, whereas agriculture accounted for 30 to 45 per cent of employment.

The potato blight and the competition of cotton caused severe crises in the middle of the nineteenth century and the men gradually left the linen sector. Between 1846 and 1856, figures for employment in agriculture rose substantially, which, no doubt, hints at a rise in concealed structural unemployment. After that period, the number of men in cottage industry declined. The women took over with lace making and embroidery.

The urban population increased little during the first half of the century. The combination of agriculture and rural industry, together with high employment rates for women, secured a basic income which, although very low, kept the dense rural population on the land. Moreover, the growth of Flemish urban textile enterprises was severely hampered by unstable market conditions, the competition of English cotton fabrics, and insufficient investment. A gradual drift of the marginal rural population to the cities started only during the second half of the century. This process was accelerated by the agricultural crisis of the 1880s, when the import of American wheat caused the collapse of prices and land values. At this time, poles of labour demand like the cities of Antwerp and Brussels developed more fully, together with the industrial areas of Wallonia and Northern France. From then on, temporary migration movements, daily or weekly commuting, and seasonal migration tapped the Flemish labour reserves. At the end of the century, Flanders had become largely a dormitory area, with a population still living in semi-urbanised countryside or in medium size towns, but employed in other sectors than cottage industry or agriculture. The large employment of women in lace and embroidery, one of the most striking characteristics of the nineteenth century, disappeared only with the First World War, and the disparity between the income levels of Flanders and Wallonia lasted until the middle of the twentieth century.

Consequently, the decline of marital fertility in Belgium, affecting Wallonia since 1865, and Flanders since 1885, has a totally different economic background from the demographic changes in France.

V. MARITAL FERTILITY AND NUPTIALITY IN BELGIUM

In 1846, when the first census was taken, the Belgian demographic situation was still highly typical of a Malthusian type of population control. Marital fertility levels were relatively homogeneous and high and population growth was restricted by high mortality and very late marriage. The index of marital fertility (I_g) varies in the 42 *arrondissements* from 0·700 to 0·890, and the index of nuptiality (I_m) from 0·350 to 0·425. In the first half of the century the mean age at marriage for women was probably about 27 years and reached 29 years in certain areas. Between 15 and 20 per cent of the women were still single at the age of 50 years. There is a possibility, however, that these nuptiality characteristics were typical of the nineteenth century rather than a left-over from the eighteenth, but data for the period 1740 to 1810 are insufficient to establish a trend.

We must refer the reader to earlier work (Lesthaeghe, 1972) for a detailed description of the demographic transition of the Belgian *arrondissements.* Only limited traits of the evolution will be discussed here.

The first important element is the fact that the nuptiality transition starts first, followed some ten years later by the decrease in marital fertility. The industrial *arrondissements* of Hainaut and the *arrondissement* of Philippeville lead the way: I_m increases clearly after 1856 and I_g decreases from 1866 on. Between 1866 and 1880, I_m increases everywhere, in Flanders as in Wallonia. In the former region, however, there is not yet any sign of a decline in marital fertility. Hence, the sequence is undeniable: nowhere does a reduction of marital fertility occur without a preceding decrease in the mean age at marriage. Hypothesis C, mentioned p. 209 above, seems therefore inapplicable to the Belgian case.

The degree of association between I_g and I_m differs between Flanders and Wallonia. In the latter case, one finds, as in France, a high correlation coefficient, varying between -0.69 and -0.84; in Flanders this coefficient is between -0.29 and -0.63. These coefficients are presented in Table 7.3 for the period 1880–1910. We have, however, replaced I_m by a slightly different measure: the proportion of ever-married women in the age group 20 to 24 years (abbreviated as EM). This measure reflects cohort behaviour better, and it is independent of nuptiality schedules existing earlier. At any rate, the correlation between EM and I_m is always above 0.95.

The relationship between EM and I_g can be analysed by introducing an economic variable that will bring forth the nature of this relationship. This is done in a similar way as for France (Table 7.2), except that the economic variable here is the degree of industrialisation measured as the ratio of the numbers employed in modern industrial sectors to the numbers of those employed in the traditional branches: agriculture, cottage industry, rural artisanal activities and domestic service. The logarithm of this ratio yields a linear relationship to both EM and I_g, and this variable is referred to in the table as 'Log. occup. str.'

The three variables are interpreted in a set of elementary causal models. In the first model, the correlation between EM and I_g is supposed to be spurious and reflects only their respective relationship with a common causal factor, industrialisation (hypothesis D). The second model reflects hypothesis B: industrialisation influenced nuptiality, which in its turn caused a shift in marital fertility. This sequence is inversed in model 3, conforming to hypothesis C. If a specified causal model is appropriate, the observed correlation r should equal the theoretical correlation r', obtained by multiplying the other two correlations in the triad.

In Flanders, 1880, model 2 (hypothesis B) seems to be most

TABLE 7.3   ZERO-ORDER CORRELATION COEFFICIENTS BETWEEN I_g AND EM, BY LANGUAGE REGION, BELGIUM, 1880–1910

1880	1890	1900	1910

Wallonia (N = 19)

I_g ——— ·970 ——— I_g ——— ·934 ——— I_g ——— ·955 ——— I_g

            −·692   −·764   −·752

−·715   −·728   −·822   −·755

            −·689   −·787   −·836

EM ——— ·926 ——— EM ——— ·976 ——— EM ——— ·984 ——— EM

·926   ·938   ·934

I_g ——— I_g ——— I_g ——— I_g

            −·587   −·582   −·629

−·558   −·360   −·595   −·586

            −·294   −·382   −·575

EM ——— EM ——— EM ——— EM

     ·799   ·912   ·949

Flanders (N = 22)

appropriate: EM is the intermediate variable. This is in line with the fact that I_g follows the evolution in I_m with a certain time lag. But model 1 best reflects the situation once the decline in I_g becomes more substantial. There is no longer any relationship between the nuptiality and marital fertility transitions. The original correlation between them was merely the result of the direct effect of industrialisation on each of them separately. In Wallonia, however, the correlation between EM and I_g is far too high to be explained by the effect of the occupational structure, and model 2 seems most appropriate. In 1910, the transition had already entered such an advanced stage that none of the models seems to be applicable. Model 3, implying that the restrictions on nuptiality are relaxed only in as much as marital fertility is brought under control, seemed to be a realistic assumption in France. Here, it is inapplicable to both the Walloon and Flemish cases.

Thus, the difference between the demographic transition in Flanders and Wallonia is not limited to the fact that the decline occurs earlier in the former region. The mechanism of relations between industrialisation, fertility and nuptiality are different as well. So far, we have no ready interpretation for the persistence of the correlation between EM and I_g in Wallonia, and its disappearance in Flanders.

TABLE 7.4 TEST OF THREE ELEMENTARY CAUSAL MODELS LINKING MARITAL FERTILITY (I_g), THE PROPORTION EVER-MARRIED WOMEN AGED 20–24 (EM) AND THE OCCUPATIONAL STRUCTURE (LOG OCC. STR.) BY LANGUAGE REGION, BELGIUM, 1880–1910

	Model 1 (hyp. D) $x_3 \searrow x_1 (I_g)$ (Log occ. str.) $\nearrow x_2$ (EM)			Model 2 (hyp. B) $x_3 \rightarrow x_2 \rightarrow x_1$ (Log (EM) (I_g) occ. str.)			Model 3 (hyp. C) $x_3 \rightarrow x_1 \rightarrow x_2$ (Log (I_g) (EM) occ. str.)		
	r_{12}	r'_{12}	diff.	r_{13}	r'_{13}	diff.	r_{23}	r'_{23}	diff.
Flanders (N = 22)									
1880	−0·558	−0·329	0·229	−0·519	−0·354	0·165	0·634	0·290	0·344
1890	−0·369	−0·225	0·144	−0·447	−0·257	0·190	0·653	0·169	0·484
1900	−0·595	−0·560	0·035	−0·714	−0·466	0·248	0·784	0·425	0·359
1910	−0·586	−0·511	0·075	−0·644	−0·465	0·179	0·794	0·377	0·417
Wallonia (N = 19)									
1880	−0·714	−0·354	0·460	−0·537	−0·471	0·066	0·660	0·383	0·277
1890	−0·728	−0·454	0·274	−0·619	−0·534	0·085	0·734	0·451	0·283
1900	−0·822	−0·617	0·205	−0·704	−0·663	0·046	0·804	0·583	0·224
1910	−0·755	−0·587	0·168	−0·768	−0·577	0·191	0·764	0·580	0·184

—— causal relation assumed
---- spurious relation assumed

VI. ECONOMIC DEVELOPMENT AND DEMOGRAPHIC TRANSITION IN BELGIUM

A widespread theory among Belgian geographers, sociologists, economists and demographers explains the time gap in the fertility decline of the language regions as a direct result of the differences in industrialisation between Flanders and Wallonia. According to this view, the later decline in Flanders is consistent with the persistence of cottage industry, the dominance of agriculture, and with economic backwardness. In contrast, the traditional cultural traits were more quickly overrun in the more modern, highly industrialised Walloon society: the decline of religious authority, the strength of political engagement, the development of the nuclear family and birth control would all be consistent with a new set of values originating in industrialisation.

We have tried to verify these hypotheses empirically, by introducing a second index of occupational structure in addition to the one already defined: the proportion of the male labour force in agriculture. In the first part of the analysis both language regions will be treated separately. Later on, we will explore the possibility that the demographic divergence between Flanders and Wallonia might be caused by the economic disparities.

By means of multiple correlation analysis, first of all the *levels* of economic variables are related to the *levels* of demographic variables. The values of R^2, the proportion of the variance of EM or I_g explained by the independent economic variables, are presented in the left-hand columns of Tables 7.5 and 7.6. (See pp. 222–3.) It is clear from these results that the importance of the economic differentiation should not be underestimated. The differences in occupational structure explain between 40 and 65 per cent of the regional variations in EM and I_g, in Wallonia as well as in Flanders.

The next step consists of predicting the *relative change* in marital fertility (ΔI_g) for the period between t and $t+x$, on the basis of the *level* of industrialisation at time t. The value of ΔI_g is measured as

$$\Delta I_g = \frac{I_g^t - I_g^{t+x}}{I_g^t - 0 \cdot 200}.$$

Our index of change in marital fertility is the ratio between the observed drop in I_g after time t and the total potential drop (setting the lower boundary of I_g arbitrarily at $0 \cdot 200$). The values of R^2 appear in the upper right corner of Tables 7.5 and 7.6. Once more it is clear that the degree of industrialisation conditioned the proportion of the fertility decline realised between time t and $t+x$. In both linguistic regions 50 to 70 per cent of the variance of ΔI_g was explained by the indices of occupational structure.

The analysis can be pushed one step further: *relative changes* in I_g (ΔI_g) can be related to *relative changes* in industrialisation. This is done in the bottom corner of Tables 7.5 and 7.6. The values of R^2 decrease but they explain still 30 to 50 per cent of the variance of ΔI_g

in Wallonia. Consequently, in each of the language regions, the economic characteristics and changes had an obvious effect on the levels of control of marital fertility and on the pace of the fertility decline.

A similar strategy can also be adopted for the analysis of EM. In this case,

$$\Delta EM = \frac{EM^{t+x} - EM^t}{0.800 - EM^t}.$$

The values of R^2 with ΔEM as criterion appear in the lower sections of Tables 7.5 and 7.6. Except for the last period, 1900–10, the influence of the levels of industrialisation is again clear and R^2 varies between 0.30 and 0.50 in Wallonia; in Flanders, however, these coefficients are insignificant. The evolution in nuptiality was the most advanced in the regions with the most developed economic structure, but the transformation in nuptiality behaviour between 1880 and 1910 is not linked to the economic change in that period. The reason for this phenomenon is to be sought primarily in the agricultural crisis of the 1880s. A number of Flemish *arrondissements* were affected in such a way that I_m or EM decreased considerably between 1880 and 1890. After 1890, the value of ΔEM reached high levels because nuptiality in these areas was making up for the setback. One might conclude from the low correlation between the occupational structure and ΔEM that the relationship between nuptiality and economic structure does not hold in Flanders. But quite the contrary is true, especially for the rural areas. On the basis of the census of 1900 it is possible to calculate values of I_m solely for the rural parts of the *arrondissements* (cities of 10,000 or more inhabitants being eliminated). From the special census of occupations and industries of 1896, we can also calculate several indices reflecting the presence of cottage industry, agricultural and other day labourers and persons in domestic service (variables x_1 and x_3 of Table 7.7). In Flanders, there is a very strong negative correlation between EM (x_4) and these two variables; but the relation with overall employment in agriculture and EM is the weakest of the three there, whereas this relationship is the most pronounced in Wallonia.

The high correlation between the proportion of day labourers, cottage workers and servants on the one hand and nuptiality on the other in Flanders does not conform entirely with the thesis of Hofstee on the 'proletarian phase'. In Belgium—in Flanders and in Wallonia —industrialisation certainly led to a lowering of the mean age at marriage among the working classes. The rural proletariat, with its nucleus of day labourers and cottage workers, was certainly not characterised by early nuptiality or by a high fertility. The urban

TABLE 7.5 PROPORTION OF THE VARIANCE OF I_g, ΔI_g, EM AND ΔEM EXPLAINED (R^2) BY THE CHARACTERISTICS OF THE OCCUPATIONAL STRUCTURE, TWENTY-TWO FLEMISH ARRONDISSEMENTS, 1880–1910

	I_g 1890	I_g 1900	I_g 1910	ΔI_g 1880–1910	ΔI_g 1880–1900	ΔI_g 1890–1910	ΔI_g 1890–1900	ΔI_g 1900–1910
Proportion males in agriculture + log occ. str.								
1890	0·362	—	—	0·535	0·605	—	—	—
1900	—	0·516	—	—	—	0·571	0·699	—
1910	—	—	0·532	—	—	—	—	0·521
Δ Proportion males in agriculture + log occ. str.								
1890–1910	—	—	—	0·342	0·150	—	—	—
1890–1900	—	—	—	—	—	0·428	0·282	—
1900–1910	—	—	—	—	—	—	—	0·477

	EM 1890	EM 1900	EM 1910	ΔEM 1880–1910	ΔEM 1880–1900	ΔEM 1890–1910	ΔEM 1890–1900	ΔEM 1900–1910
Proportion males in agriculture + log occ. str.								
1890	0·472	—	—	0·040	0·001	—	—	—
1900	—	0·641	—	—	—	0·077	0·102	—
1910	—	—	0·653	—	—	—	—	0·208
Δ Proportion males in agriculture + Δ log occ. str.								
1890–1910	—	—	—	0·005	0·042	—	—	—
1890–1900	—	—	—	—	—	0·232	0·366	—
1900–1910	—	—	—	—	—	—	—	0·007

TABLE 7.6 PROPORTION OF THE VARIANCE OF I_g, ΔI_g, EM, AND ΔEM EXPLAINED (R^2) BY THE CHARACTERISTICS OF THE OCCUPATIONAL STRUCTURE, NINETEEN WALLOON *ARRONDISSEMENTS*, 1880–1910

		I_g 1890	I_g 1900	I_g 1910	ΔI_g 1880–1910	ΔI_g 1880–1900	ΔI_g 1890–1910	ΔI_g 1890–1900	ΔI_g 1900–1910
Proportion males in agriculture + log occ. str.	1890	0·450	—	—	0·701	0·662	0·660	0·452	—
	1900	—	0·527	—	—	—	—	—	0·600
	1910	—	—	0·663	—	—	—	—	—
Δ Proportion males in agriculture +Δ log occ. str.	1890–1910	—	—	—	0·484	—	0·413	—	—
	1890–1900	—	—	—	—	0·319	—	0·307	—
	1900–1910	—	—	—	—	—	—	—	0·422

		EM 1890	EM 1900	EM 1910	ΔEM 1880–1910	ΔEM 1880–1900	ΔEM 1890–1910	ΔEM 1890–1900	ΔEM 1900–1910
Proportion males in agriculture + log occ. str.	1890	0·567	—	—	0·400	0·455	0·321	0·382	—
	1900	—	0·553	—	—	—	—	—	0·202
	1910	—	—	0·525	—	—	—	—	—
Δ Proportion males in agriculture +Δ log occ. str.	1890–1910	—	—	—	0·588	—	0·396	—	—
	1890–1900	—	—	—	—	0·489	—	0·315	—
	1900–1910	—	—	—	—	—	—	—	0·208

TABLE 7.7 ZERO-ORDER CORRELATION COEFFICIENTS BETWEEN CHARACTERISTICS OF THE OCCUPATIONAL STRUCTURE AND THE PROPORTION WOMEN EVER-MARRIED AGED 20–24, RURAL PARTS OF *ARRONDISSEMENTS*, BY LANGUAGE REGION, BELGIUM, 1900

		Flanders (N = 19)[a]			Wallonia (N = 19)		
		x_2	x_3	x_4	x_2	x_3	x_4
Farm labourers and cottage weavers / Non-agricultural male population, 15–54	x_1	0·47	0·79	−0·91	0·92	0·64	−0·43
Male population active in agriculture / Male population, 15–54	x_2		0·39	−0·35		0·59	−0·63
Female farm labourers, servants, lace makers and other female cottage workers / Non-agricultural female population, 15–54	x_3			−0·76			−0·39
Proportion women ever-married in age group 20–24	x_4						
Proportion of variance of x_4 explained by x_1, x_2 and x_3 ($R^2_{4·123}$)[b]				0·84			0·57

[a] The three *arrondissements* of the province of Limburg are omitted.
[b] The value of R^2 is corrected for the effects of the number of independent variables ($n = 3$) approaching the number of observations ($N = 19$).

workers, and especially the workers of the modern industrial settings, have set the pace for the nuptiality transition, whereas the behaviour of the rural proletariat is strongly discordant. In contrast to what Hofstee claims to hold for the Netherlands, one cannot speak in Belgium of a homogeneous behaviour of the salaried sections of the population.

VII. SOME LIMITS OF THE ECONOMIC EXPLANATION

In the previous section we have clarified the extent to which marital fertility and nuptiality were influenced by the degree of industrialisation. Some important traits of the Belgian transition still defy an explanation on economic grounds. It is indeed difficult to explain the important differences between the values of I_g in Flanders and those in Wallonia on the basis of difference in industrialisation. An analysis of covariance executed for the 1900 and 1910 data shows that the differences in I_g continue to exist despite the elimination of the differences in economic development. Even after the introduction of other covariates, such as literacy, infant mortality or even nuptiality, the average level of marital fertility in Flanders stays well above the average in Wallonia.

The contrast between both demographic regions stands out very clearly when one follows the line that separates the regions of early and late fertility decline. This line coincides with the language border. To show this feature more clearly, 43 pairs of communities were selected randomly. Each pair consists of a Flemish and a Walloon village located on opposite sides of the border, but no more than 10 kilometres apart from one another. In terms of economic development and characteristics the pairs are not necessarily homogeneous, but, on the whole, there is no difference between the aggregate of Flemish and of Walloon villages. Table 7.8 describes the development of a demographic contrast along this language border: in the middle of the nineteenth century there was practically no difference between the birth-rates in the Flemish and in the Walloon sets; in 1909–11 the Flemish birth-rates were on the average 7 per thousand points higher than the Walloon ones.

The role of the linguistic factor stands out even further when the pattern of geographical diffusion of the marital fertility decline is followed. The rural Walloon *arrondissements* just south of the language border adopt marital fertility control immediately after the industrial regions of Hainaut, even before there is a start of decline in I_g in the industrial basins of Liège and Verviers. The rural *arrondissements* on the Ardennes plateau lag behind within Wallonia,

TABLE 7.8 DISTRIBUTION OF FORTY-THREE PAIRS OF COMMUNITIES
ACCORDING TO THE DIFFERENCES IN BIRTH-RATES (FLEMISH AND
WALLOON COMMUNITIES LOCATED ON THE LANGUAGE BORDER),
1845–1969

Birth-rate in Flemish community minus birth-rate of Walloon community	1845 1847	1875 1881	1909 1911	1935 1937	1965 1969
			Number of pairs		
−8·0% and more	4	0	0	0	0
−7·9/−4·0	4	3	1	2	1
−3·9/0·0	19	6	1	4	10
0·1/3·9	11	13	8	14	25
4·0/7·9	3	11	18	17	6
8·0/11·9	2	9	8	5	1
12·0 and more	0	1	7	1	0
Total number of pairs	43	43	43	43	43
Average difference between birth-rates of Flemish and Walloon communities	−1·16	+3·76	+7·13	+4·45	+1·73

Note: Calculations based on unpublished data collected by H. Damas, Centre d'Etudes de la Population et de la Famille, Brussels.

but precede the most industrialised Flemish *arrondissements*, located in the vicinity of the leading area of Hainaut.

In the case of Brussels with a linguistically mixed population, there is again a striking inverse correlation between I_g and the proportion of French speakers. In 1910 the correlation coefficient reached -0.880 between these two variables in the twelve communities making up the Brussels conurbation. No similar correlation coefficient between I_g and any other social or economic variable could be found.

VIII. CONCLUSION

Most European countries have undergone two parallel mutations between 1850 and 1930: the industrial revolution and the demographic transition. There were many different social and cultural settings, and many economic situations in Europe at the time; but the mutations occurred in a relatively short time. The diversity is brought out by the examples of France and Belgium. France was a forerunner in adopting a neo-malthusian pattern of reproduction even before the industrial revolution had started. Belgium industrialised first, and adapted its nuptiality and its legitimate fertility after. These national contrasts should not distract from the fact that the two countries had themselves heterogeneous component regions, both economically and demographically. Outward-lying provinces of France, such as Brittany or Alsace, delayed the fertility decline until the end of the nineteenth century. In Belgium, the Flemish districts extricated themselves from a pre-industrial stage of the economy with great difficulty. Moreover, we find a multiplicity of different mechanisms behind the apparent simplicity of the inverse relation between nuptiality and marital fertility. The fact that the explanations seem to be different from country to country and region to region must inspire caution when we attempt to draw general conclusions. A more thorough investigation of the facts draws us further and further away from the simple script that was once attributed to the demographic transition.

What part did industrialisation on the one hand, social and cultural modernisation on the other hand, play in the fertility decline? Different viewpoints have resulted in laying the stress either on the role of economic transformations, or on cultural particularisms. But a detailed study of the demographic history of regions must shift the emphasis continuously from one of those poles to the other. Furthermore, it is fairly easy to find statistical indicators of economic variables (e.g. income, occupational distribution) but difficult to measure important cultural factors, such as the laws and the mores, inheritance systems, religion and the secularisation of attitudes, or even geographical isolation.

To compound the pitfalls, moreover, there is constant interaction between cultural and socio-economic characteristics. Their joint influence can be found in France and Belgium. In France, there is glaring evidence of a correlation between fertility and wealth; but low income regions such as Brittany are also characterised by linguistic particularism, illiteracy and the intensity of religious belief. Similar mixtures can be found in Belgium, where legitimate fertility levels and speed of their decline conform overall to economic development in each language region, but where the border between the regions cleaves the country into two different demographic worlds.

The relationship between marital fertility and nuptiality takes different forms according to the regions. In France, the fertility decline appears to precede the nuptiality changes, whereas the opposite is true in Wallonia, and there is no direct relation in Flanders. This raises the question as to whether these relations are a function of the stage reached by the economy at the time when fertility declines, or whether they are the result of the cultural uniqueness of each situation.

REFERENCES

P. Bourdieu, 'Célibat et condition paysanne', *Etudes Rurales*, 5–6 (1962) 32–135.
R. Braun, 'Early Industrialization and Demographic Changes in the Canton of Zürich (Switzerland)', mimeographed paper given at Princeton Seminar (1972).
R. Cantillon, *Essai sur la nature du commerce en général*, first published 1755, I.N.E.D. (1952).
H. Charbonneau, *Tourouvre-au-Perche aux xviie et xviiie siècles*, I.N.E.D., Travaux et Documents, cahier no. 55 (Presses Univ. de France, 1970) pp. 107–11.
P. Chaunu, *La civilisation de l'Europe classique*, Les Grandes Civilisations (Arthaud, 1966) p. 190.
A. J. Coale, 'The Decline of Fertility in Europe from the French Revolution to World War II', *Fertility and Family Planning: A World View*, ed. S. J. Behrman, Leslie Corsa and Ronald Freedman (Ann Arbor, 1969) pp. 3–24.
J. Dupâquier, 'De l'animal à l'homme: le mécanisme auto-régulateur des populations traditionnelles', *Revue de l'Institut de sociologie*, 2 (1972) 177–211.
J. Dupâquier and M. Demonet, 'Ce qui fait les familles nombreuses', *Annales E.S.C.* (July–Oct 1972) 1025–45.
H. J. Habakkuk, 'Family Structure and Economic Change in Nineteenth-Century Europe', *Journal of Economic History*, xv, 1 (1955) 1–12.
E. W. Hofstee, 'Regionale verscheidenheid in de ontwikkeling van het aantal geboorten in Nederland in de 2e helft van de 19e eeuw', *Koninklijke Nederlandse Akademie van Wetenschappen, Akademiedagen*, vol. 7 (1954).
R. Lesthaeghe, "Vruchtbaarheidscontrole, nuptialiteit en sociaaleconomische ver-anderingen in België, 1846–1910', *Bevolking en Gezin*, 2 (1972) 251–99.
W. Petersen, 'The Demographic Transition in the Netherlands', *American Sociological Review*, 25, 3 (1960) 334–47.
D. Ricardo, *The Principles of Political Economy and Taxation*, first published 1817, (Everyman's Library, 1911) p. 53.
J. J. Spengler, *France Faces Depopulation* (Durham, 1938), p. 73.
E. van de Walle, *The Female Population of France in the Nineteenth Century* (Princeton, 1973).

Discussion of the Paper by
Professor van de Walle and Dr Lesthaeghe

Professor Coale made some remarks by way of general introduction. For about ten years there had been collaboration between Princeton and a number of European demographers in an ambitious study of the decline in birth-rates throughout Europe since about 1800. Demographers had long been aware that changes in fertility and mortality accompanied industrialisation and had named this process the 'demographic transition'. However, their ideas were based on impressionistic study of data in a few countries. The present study was carrying out a further analysis, province by province: there were about 700 provinces in Europe. Livi Bacci had published a study on Portugal and was about to publish one on Italy. Van de Walle himself had published a study on France, and another volume on France would follow. Similarly, Lesthaeghe had studied Belgium. The paper for discussion originated from these studies of France and Belgium.

Professor Schultz introduced the paper itself. Researchers who wanted to learn about the 'demographic transition' had generally been frustrated in their study of contemporary low-income countries by the fact that time-series were regrettably short and/or fragmentary. They could compile data on cohort fertility, and other variables, but lacked other data. Consequently, a good deal of work had proceeded to interpret cross-section variations in past or current reproductive behaviour, as a function of the current characteristics of the relevant population. It was obvious, however, that prior conditions were relevant to an understanding of why reproductive performance differed at any point in time. Alternatively, to examine variations in current fertility rates was to compromise the relevance of economic theory in choosing possible determinants of desired fertility. For current-period fertility rates might be substantially affected by changes in the timing of births within an individual's lifetime; existing, static, choice theory had regrettably little to say about this.

The challenging promise of historical analyses of the demographic transitions in the West was that they would provide long enough time-series on fertility. With appropriate economic and social indicators, one would be able to explore, with statistical rigour, different causal models or hypotheses about economic and demographic change. In particular, one could analyse the time ordering of changes occurring across individual, or small, regional populations. Differences in these correlations over time could be used to help improve the specification of the causal model. This might provide prima facie evidence about the time dimensions of individual, and social, adjustment lags, *if* the explanatory variables really were exogenous to fertility, or for that matter, to nuptiality. That was, *if* they were not subject to the control of parents, or subsequently affected by the individual or collective behaviour of parents.

This goal of historical demography was an exacting one. The paper for discussion aspired to that very difficult task which few, if any, investigations he had seen had previously attempted. It was therefore an exciting, thoughtful and methodologically important paper that he hoped would establish a pattern which would be followed in subsequent innovative work. However, he would like to add, not as a criticism of the paper but as a statement of his own shortcomings, that he was not well-versed in the relevant underlying literature in historical demography, or indeed in economic history, either in English or in French. Some of his difficulties in understanding the aim and interpretation of the paper might reflect his own lack of fundamental knowledge in the field.

The authors proposed four, possibly incompatible, hypotheses to explain the change in: (1) an index of current marital fertility rates, I_m, and (2) an index of age-specific marriage rates, I_g. These were as follows: a) marital fertility appeared to fall first in the regions where marriage was early and prevalent; b) exogenous economic and legal changes increased the number of marriages and this depressed economic resources per head and caused marital fertility to fall; c) exogenous factors induced couples to control fertility within marriage, which subsequently permitted earlier marriage; d) nuptiality and marital fertility appeared to be subject to similar unobserved factors, without being causally linked to each other. Perhaps this last hypothesis represented something of a straw man for the authors to knock down, or perhaps he will not understand their point.

The time-lags implicit in these hypotheses were not made explicit; nor was it clear whether it was changes over time, or levels, that were causally linked. But, clearly, the feedback effect in hypothesis b) could not be less than Malthusian (i.e. measured in generations), whereas the lags in c) and a) might be shorter.

Professor Schultz said he could not do justice to the array of correlations and partial correlations reported by the authors. These looked at levels and rates of change in the two demographic indices and at individually-fashioned measures of economic development. For France, industrialisation was measured by income; for Belgium, by the composition of employment.

Professor Schultz wanted to try to summarise the conclusions of the paper and to take issue with some of these, as he reviewed them.

In France, there was a negative relationship between marital fertility and nuptiality. Marital fertility fell first and nuptiality rose afterwards. The evidence cited was the negative correlation of I_g in 1831 and I_m in 1851. Hypothesis c) was supported by Table 7.1. However, Professor Schultz was puzzled over the methodology by which the authors rejected hypothesis d) in Table 7.2. To test how exogenous changes in economic conditions worked their way through to I_g and I_m, simultaneous equations would have to be specified in identified form and estimated. This must be so unless it could be argued that the change in I_g, in earlier periods was pre-determined from the point of view of those adapting their marriage pattern twenty years later. If this was what the model postulated, then this should be stated and the estimation carried out appropriately.

In Belgium, Wallonia appeared to have been industrialised independently of agricultural change. This had happened early, and fertility fell from 1865. Flanders was tied to linen and flax and suffered a depression which meant that it did not benefit significantly from industrialisation until 1900. Even then it did not approach the position in Wallonia until the middle of the twentieth century.

The text suggested that the evidence for Belgium indicated that when nuptiality increased, then ten or more years later marital fertility fell. However, Table 7.3 was used to support this statement, and his understanding of the hypothesis was that the simple correlation should be higher between current nuptiality and lagged marital fertility than between the concurrent indices. This pattern prevailed in only one of three cases in Wallonia, but did appear to fit the hypothesis in all three cases in Flanders. The statistical significance of these differences in the correlations was not reported. Moreover, should not the test be formulated in terms of lagged differences rather than levels of the indices?

The evidence assembled in Tables 7.5 and 7.6 did not allow the strong statements in the text (page 221) that industrialisation and changes in marriage rates were insignificant from about 1890–1900. Differences in fertility across regions persisted and, by 1900–1910, they were attributed by the authors only to cultural and linguistic factors. However, the authors had earlier stated that Flanders did not catch up economically until the middle of the twentieth century. The interesting evidence presented for the border regions of Wallonia and Flanders was, nevertheless, very striking. There was much data in this paper, but he could not see how some of it related to the major conclusions. A broader monograph, with more closely reasoned logic, was undoubtedly in the back of the authors' minds. The careful comparison of a few models, and variations in their lagged structure, should be highlighted more clearly. Changes in the conception and measurement of variables for the comparative analysis of France and Belgium might also be avoided, for this shift in analytical framework weakened the otherwise strong contrasts.

The analysis might also consider the product of the two indices, I_g and I_m, which defined the total reproductive outcome for the population. Unless a compelling case could be made for one index being exogenous, it could not be causally used to explain the other, unless other statistical techniques were used and the statistical system explicitly identified. Moreover, in order to identify the model, additional exogenous factors that might have contributed to the demographic transition should be specified and measured, including the variables briefly mentioned on page 225, i.e. literacy, better schooling and infant mortality.

Professor Schultz was pleased that the authors were now apparently going to test the working hypotheses derived from these regional correlations, by using longitudinal reconstructions of economic and demographic events from individual life-cycles from their village populations. To extend the frontiers of historical demography in this difficult direction would be an enormous contribution.

Professor van de Walle said he was pleased with Professor Schultz's comments. Perhaps he should have explained in the paper more of what was being done, but he was grateful to Professor Schultz for explaining this. He should explain that it was difficult to lag phenomena in France because one picked up the story when the decline in fertility had almost come to an end. The decline began in the eighteenth century, and when one found statistics at departmental level it was too late to explain it. With these difficulties, the data perhaps did not give a good indication of what was happening.

Dr Lesthaeghe said that his thinking had been evolving in a similar way for some time. He was now building a more elaborate causal model.

Responding to Professor Schultz's remark that general fertility was the most appropriate variable, he claimed that general fertility was essentially a construct of two totally different variables – nuptiality and marital fertility. He would hold to what he had done, and would especially stress the value of the split for Western European experience.

With regard to the study of the time-lag between changes in nuptiality and in marital fertility, he agreed with Professor Schultz that the study could be expanded, using more elaborate methods. The crude model suggested that the change in nuptiality preceded that in marital fertility.

In an earlier paper (in Dutch), other variables than those referred to in this text have been included. There, it seemed that infant mortality was of very little significance in explaining variations in marital fertility within each region of Belgium: the coefficient of determination (r^2) was only 1 per cent for Flanders and 2 per cent for Wallonia. Taking the country as a whole, the coefficient was 27 per cent. The sign of the correlation coefficient was then positive instead of negative. These small correlation coefficients could not be accounted for by a lack of variation in infant mortality: in 1900, for instance, the coastal area had an infant mortality rate of well above 300 per thousand, whereas in the Ardennes it was about 100 per thousand.

In the earlier paper, he had also looked at a measure of urbanisation and at an index of occupational structure. In both cases, he had observed that the regression lines with marital fertility for the two language areas were almost perfectly parallel. The regression line for Flanders always had the higher intercept. If the data were pooled together for the whole of Belgium, the new regression line cut obliquely across the regression lines for the two individual language areas. This showed that the fertility transitions for the two regions were dissimilar, and that their transitions should be analysed separately.

One exception to this finding was the relation between marital fertility and secularisation. To measure the latter variable he had used a proxy – the percentage of votes for the Socialist and Liberal parties. Areas with a high percentage of such votes (i.e. with a low percentage of votes for the Christian Democratic Party) were traditionally characterised by a high degree of secularisation. From 1919 until 1950, the correlation between Sunday Mass attendance and the percentage of the non-Catholic vote varied from 0·85 to 0·90. Since there were very few Protestants in Belgium (about 1 per cent) the proxy could be assumed to measure secularisation adequately.

Of all the explanatory variables used, secularisation was the only one to yield similar regression lines with marital fertility both for each region and for the whole of the country. It was worth noting that the economic background variables always yielded separate regression lines and that the only variable for which this was not the case was a typical sociological one. Furthermore, the explanatory power of the secularisation variable was the highest of all, even within regions.

Professor Ohlin said that he was excited by the paper, and indeed by all the findings of the Princeton project. Professor Schultz had talked from an econometric and rigorously methodological point of view, so he would now like to turn to the more traditional prejudices of a demographic historian.

He missed some things in the paper. First, France was put into one box; Belgium into another. There had been suggestions in recent years that the industrial belt in Europe (concentrated especially on coal) showed similar tendencies everywhere. It was suggested that the determining factors were not national, but social and economic. From what had been said on the importance of the socialist vote, it was perhaps less a matter of secularisation than of picking up the regions most characterised by their industrial pattern.

Professor Ohlin wondered whether the economic factors referred to in the paper were sufficiently represented by the variables considered. For example, they must do poorly in representing the complexity of the industrial revolution, and the modernisation that occurred in the nineteenth century.

As for mortality, so far infant mortality had been considered; but overall mortality was highly relevant, too, since our ultimate interest was in economic growth.

Dr Lesthaeghe thought that Professor Ohlin's remarks needed to be amended. The coal belt was indeed an important economic phenomenon and did cut straight through Belgium. However, miners in the French and German parts of the coal belt were characterised by much higher marital fertility than the remainder of the non-agricultural population. In Belgium, coal miners had the lowest marital fertility in the whole of the country, and the coal-mining regions were the first to adopt a neo-Malthusian pattern of reproduction. Dr Hays of Cornell University was also studying fertility of miners and had noted this anomaly. Like Dr Lesthaeghe, he had been unable to give an accpetable explanation for the discordant behaviour of miners in Belgium.

In response to Professor Ohlin's reference to the correlation between the Socialist vote and the level of industrialisation, Dr Lesthaeghe said that his correlation was indeed present, but was by no means as strong as was often believed. Even in the Ardennes, with very little industry, there were *arrondissements* where the non-Catholic vote represented about 60 per cent of the total. Also, in Catholic Flanders, there were several semi-rural pockets characterised by a high socialist vote.

Another problem concerned the interpretation of the substantial correlation between I_m and I_g in Wallonia. Normally, one would expect I_m to be a causal antecedent to I_g, but it was somewhat difficult to explain the large variations in I_g by the much smaller variations in I_m.

Professor Khachaturov thought that while the paper was mainly historical and methodological, one must try to apply historical conditions to the present day. One ought to compare the historical situation in France with that since 1945, where there had been big changes since the Second World War. Several factors were important; for example, the rate of growth of productivity, demographic policy and change in the structure of population. His question might be outside the subject, but he wondered what kind of comparison one got between the present French and Belgian situation and the situation in the past.

Professor van de Walle replied that there was a discontinuity between past and present in France. Fertility had declined everywhere, but fertility was higher in the north and lower in the south today. In Belgium, too, the old differentials did not apply to the present.

Dr Lesthaeghe explained that the traditionally high marital fertility in Limburg had been reduced drastically between 1960 and 1970. As a result, marital fertility was now slightly lower in Flanders than in Wallonia and the variance of fertility according to social status, religion, income, degree of urbanisation or education was drastically reduced.

He had also looked back at the evolution of Limburg. Coal was mined there from the 1920s on, and as a result the province became rapidly industrialised. However, a large portion of the industrially active population was made up of immigrants (Italians, Slavs), and the local population was only partially affected. Since the Second World War, Limburg had become a real boom area with the development of very modern sectors of industry. Despite this rapid industrialisation, the largest drop in marital fertility had occurred only after that date; it coincided with a sudden acceleration of the secularisation trend. This indicated that fertility in Limburg did not respond so well to a large change in economic variables, such as industrialisation or occupational structure, but reacted rather to a change in cultural dimensions.

M. Leridon wanted to ask two questions. First, he wondered whether one could draw links between fertility and various other factors in the region. Even with a fall in the variance of the permanence of behaviour, the phenomenon only began about 1931. So he wondered how much permanence there was.

Professor van de Walle agreed about nuptiality, but was not sure about marital fertility. However, there were changes in the relative positions of the *départements*. For example, Normandy had once had the lowest fertility but had been overtaken later by other *départements*.

M. Leridon then came to his second question, about methodology. There were references to a theoretical correspondence with the maximum possible fertility; but possible fertility could vary. A study for Germany showed considerable differences in lactation habits. He wondered whether the result was altered by having one figure for marital fertility.

Professor van de Walle said that the index used was Professor Coale's, but his own opinion was that all the indices used in the paper were much too aggregated.

Professor Coale pointed out that, so far as the index was concerned, he had chosen the highest fertility on record as the standard. He was choosing a standard that reliably listed fertility by age in a very high-fertility population.

Professor Schultz wanted to follow up what Professor Ohlin had said. In his introduction to the discussion, he had not stressed his concern over the choice of variables to be linked with I_g and I_m. He was disturbed to find the belief among economists that, with rising incomes, nuptiality or fertility would naturally go down. Choice theory had looked at this problem and he wanted to emphasise the lack of any necessary relation. To seek the economic determinants of fertility, one had to go beyond indices of overall economic well-being and consider the distribution of income-earning opportunities between the sexes. One could look at the roles of the sexes; at the relationship between male and female incomes; between male and female education, etc. We could then, perhaps, link fertility declines with advances in female education, income, etc.

As for the different effect of 'income' between the two parts of Belgium, the conclusions drawn by the authors from their regression analysis did seem to be significant, and should be tested with other data that were not in the paper. However, when it was done, it would not be surprising if the regressions gave different results for the two parts of the country. Perhaps one should also combine all information about Belgium for infant mortality or other characteristics of industrialisation, on the lines suggested in Professor Ohlin's remarks. What was not significant in each region might be important across regions.

Mr Black noted that Professor van de Walle had explained that the data for France came late in the process of demographic decline resulting from industrialisation. He wondered what were the prospects of getting data for earlier periods in the demographic process. Could one find data which would parallel that which had regularly been obtained for English parishes? Could we get a real insight into the origins of the process, and so into the real origins of the transition?

Professor Bourcier de Carbon was interested in the significance of the historical references and of those of the present day. He noted the reservations of the authors on global statistics. However, even a study of heterogeneous situations needed to look at a number of causal phenomena. Did the expression 'the world has changed' have significance for economists at all, given their claims to generality?

In eighteenth-century France, there had been great variety of activity. There had then been a change, because of the development of roads and railways, the latter coming in the 1840s. Many areas lost a high proportion of their population, but improved transport meant that small industries developed. He did not know how these affected fertility and nuptiality. With continuing industrial development in the last quarter of the century there were major changes. The working population increased considerably and there was a growing distinction between urban and rural populations, especially in the first half of the twentieth century. Textile firms in the north-east lost half their establishment. Similarly, foundries grew rapidly. There were no figures, but the correlation should be sufficient to show the complexity of the situation. It would be very difficult to carry out research on such a large and varied area in the way that the authors had done.

Dr Lesthaeghe replied to Mr Black that nobody had carried out in Belgium any work of the type done by Professor L. Henry. Much seventeenth and eighteenth century material still needed collecting. Some historians had looked at a few villages in Flanders for the period 1740 to 1780, when there was a movement towards more substantial pre-industrial activity. A section of the marginal rural population had moved into the production of linen, as a result of improved conditions for exporting linen to Latin America. This had perhaps led to a reduction in the mean age at marriage. Combined with short birth intervals, a lower mean-age at marriage meant a higher birth-rate and, despite the very high mortality, a substantial population increase resulted. Population growth rates of between 0·5 and 1·0 per cent continued to exist for nearly a century. Economically, the situation was characterised by unemployment, or disguised unemployment, and resulted in several crises. In France, from 1790 it was likely that the mean age at marriage had gone up again and that excessive population growth was prevented in the typical Malthusian way. However, much of the material on this experience was still unexplored in the archives.

Professor van de Walle said that he was happy to have the last word in the discussion, since no one would refute him! The criticisms of the paper made by participants tended to cancel each other out. Some said there was a lack of universality; others regretted the level of aggregation of the indices used in the paper and suggested a need to look at local areas. He did agree about the need to look at various levels of explanation. However, all Western countries had finally reduced fertility in much the same way, despite different economic and social conditions.

Professor Ohlin had said that the national unit was perhaps not significant, but he would himself stand by the importance of national boundaries. Linguistic borders were certainly important. In each national unit, one had a combination of factors. In some countries, for example Belgium, infant mortality was unimportant. In France it was very high and was correlated to total fertility. Combining rural incomes and mortality, one could explain a large part of the variance.

Professor Coale said he had hoped to have a paper on Hungary but this had not been possible. However, he did have a brief account of the work that had been done from Dr Egon Szabady (see Chapter 8, p. 238). The Hungarian research was being carried out by the Demographic Research Institute in the Central Statistical Office in Budapest, which had said that it would participate in the study by looking at provinces where fertility had fallen. Unfortunately, many of the researchers had left the project, and it had not yet been completed.

The Hungarian study had calculated marital fertility, overall fertility and nuptiality in the period 1880–1910, for four decennial censuses. At that time Hungary was an area where national fertility was low even before 1900. Yet Hungary was predominantly agricultural and the reduction in fertility was not linked to an advance in literacy, as elsewhere. Hungary was an anomaly within the classic idea. To put the point more sharply, the decline in mortality and fertility occurred at the same time, and at about the same pace, as in the U.K., but the U.K. was the locus of the first step in the industrial revolution, and industrialisation in Hungary was much later.

If we looked at marital fertility by province in Europe in 1900 (the mid-point of the process of transition) we could see the importance of national boundaries. The level of fertility in France was low, although there were differences by region within France. Outside France, the lowest marital fertility in 1900 for any one province was in Hungary. This was in a small, illiterate province on the Rumanian border.

Dr Szabady's report said that the Hungarian research team had looked at the data, and carried out simple correlations between marital fertility and other relevant variables. A simple correlation between infant mortality and marital fertility showed no significant result. Nor did a correlation between female literacy and marital fertility. It was thought that marital fertility in 1911 might be related to agricultural income, or net income by county, the latter being used to estimate agricultural production. Neither variable gave any significant result.

The study also looked at the social and occupational distribution of the population, and at the relation of this to fertility. It had looked at both peasants and landowners, and had found no correlation here either. So the net effect was at the county level (the sub-national unit in Hungary); there was no significant relationship. It was now proposed to follow a study carried out earlier by Professor Demeny and to go to units smaller than the county. The reason was that, in Hungary, differences seemed to be linked to such special groups as the Magyar Protestant population. Wherever they lived, there was a lower birth-rate than in Catholic or non-Magyar areas.

Professor Demeny said it was a long time since he had looked at this data. But perhaps the Hungarian situation was linked to the rural land-tenure system, which led to situations where peasants might feel it necessary to keep down the size of their families in order to prevent the division of land. It had not been possible to produce a labour surplus until emigration became possible, at the end of the century. These were small peasants who discovered that a reduction in the number of children increased the standard of living to the 'appropriate' level. In most places, the reduction of fertility was an outcome of the judgement that keeping up fertility would reduce the standard of living. Indeed, the stage seemed to be reached where it was discovered that limiting the family to even less than two children per farm meant that the peasant could actually become rich. By the end of the nineteenth century, there were a number of villages where it was common for families to have one child, and for sons and daughters to intermarry. The explanation of the Hungarian situation therefore lay in the cultural pattern. Peasants developed a taste for good houses, good furniture and good utensils.

8 Economic Factors in the Decline of Fertility in Hungary in the Nineteenth and Early Twentieth Century

E. Szabady

DEMOGRAPHIC RESEARCH INSTITUTE, BUDAPEST

As it is known, several studies have dealt with the surprising fact that on the easily delimitable areas of Hungary in the period of industrialisation and maybe even in the epoch of pre-industrialisation, a significant birth control developed similar to that of Western Europe. This fact was stated, with Coale's method, as the basis of the calculation of indices I_m, I_g, I_h by counties for the years 1880, 1890, 1900 and 1910. The indices delimitable by smaller or larger regions (several counties) behave in a similar way. We have shown that in the era when marital fertility shows a linear decrease in the southern regions of Hungary, it increases in the eastern part of the country. In other regions of the country a fluctuation–decreasing or increasing trend–can be observed as compared to 1880 or 1890.

The typifying of line diagrams of marital fertility stimulated us to typify in a similar way also the index of marriage rate I_m. Again delimitable regions developed. The intensity of marriage decreased to a minimum extent in the whole country in the years 1880–1910. In certain regions, however, it showed a linear increase, in other regions it corresponded to the average of the country, then in the third type–divided into several sub-types–it fluctuated.

On a national scale I_m and I_g do not show any relation–indicating that in this epoch in Hungary there was no unambiguous inter-relation between the intensity of marriage and fertility. It was stated that the counties (parts of regions) where birth control became wide-spread, can be divided into two groups. In one of the groups the ratio of married couples grows, in the other group it declines. In a similar way also those counties can be included in several groups where marital fertility increases.

Naturally the regional typifying of the area of Hungary by Coale's indices stimulated us to explain the differences between regions. Using a correlation method we sought the interdependence between infant mortality and marital fertility, supposing that the substitution was to a certain extent the determinant of the change in fertility. Unfortunately, the result $r = 0.26$ cannot be considered as significant.

In a similar way we studied the interrelation between literacy of women aged 15–49 and I_g on county level, for 63 counties in all the four decades. This did not show a significant correlation either.

We thought that the development of fertility was connected with agricultural production, giving the greater part of the national income of the Hungarian national economy or with the county cadastral net incomes available in 1911, and serving as a basis for the estimation of agricultural production. Neither the comparison of the data of the county marital fertility nor the theoretical value of agricultural production gave a result.

We sought an interrelation between the social or occupational distribution and fertility. We developed two occupational categories: one contained the agricultural proletarians (navvies, agricultural servants, owners of land under 0.5 hectare), the other smallholders with up to 25 hectares. The study started from the idea that these two strata formed the overwhelming majority of the Hungarian agricultural population. We had to state that there was no correlation between the socio-occupational structure or its change and the development of fertility. Also in counties where the majority of the population is Roumanian, Slovakian or Greek Orthodox the decrease and increase of I_g can be observed. Therefore it became evident that the factors investigated did not themselves change fertility in a measurable way.

Not only the method of simple linear correlation raised difficulties in the statement of interrelations, for it is known also that the history of Hungarian national economy in the nineteenth century forms a specific background. In Hungary the industrial revolution came later; after the elimination of feudalism in 1850 it was not the industrial production but the agricultural production which increased faster (probably in Hungary, too, the derived increase developed), until in 1880 – using Rostow's nomenclature – we lived in the preparatory, grounding stage of the take-off era. It is also known that immediately before the First World War agriculture produced 62 per cent of the Hungarian national income. Also, in the epoch of industrialisation Hungary remained an agricultural country – and an agricultural country in which both the capitalist large estates and the strengthening peasant medium estates could be found at the same time, with small peasant farms hardly producing for the market and with about 3 million agricultural proletarians, the family members included. In Hungary, due to the poor internal consumers' market, shortage of capital and the survival of the feudal infrastructure even in the epoch of industrialisation, those industrial branches developed which obtained their raw materials from agriculture, that is the food industry and the primary extractive industries. The Hungarian industrialisation did not begin with the textile industry; female labour was employed to a minimum extent; channels of communication were built before the development of industry; the working class and factory workers were not recruited from manufacturers and artisans but from agricultural proletarians. And finally in the economic growth before the First World War the labour force played a much smaller part than in Western countries.

As our analyses, conducted until now on county level with simple linear correlation, do not explain the interrelations between fertility and economic development, in the future we have to try to analyse more homogeneous demographic-economic units instead of the administrative units investigated, taking into consideration that in Hungary regions and micro-regions accumulate side by side with a great difference in history, economic development, culture and language. There is no doubt that our methods have to be replaced by finer methods – those of multivariate analysis.[1]

[1] For some comments on this chapter, see pp. 236–7 above.

Part Four

Economic Factors in the Decline of Fertility in the Third World

9 Empirical Research in Taiwan on Factors Underlying Differences in Fertility*

Albert I. Hermalin
POPULATION STUDIES CENTER, UNIVERSITY OF MICHIGAN

I. INTRODUCTION

The attention given to fertility levels, trends and differentials in recent years has resulted in an increase both in empirical research, designed to establish facts and relationships, and in theory development, which has sought to synthesise this rapidly expanding body of knowledge. Conceptual models of a social, psychological, and economic nature have been advanced (see as examples Freedman, 1967; Fawcett, 1970; T. W. Schultz, 1973).

The fruitfulness of these theories rests eventually on their ability to account for established relationships and to expand knowledge systematically. The objective of this paper is to present some of the empirical findings concerning fertility in a developing country, Taiwan, with which any comprehensive theory must deal. Taiwan appears to be midway through a demographic transition from high to low fertility, and thus presents interesting challenges to theory development.

Of course, theory and observation can never be entirely divorced, and in selecting the empirical research to be reviewed, some structure is necessary. In keeping with the auspices of this conference, we will focus on variables related to economic models of fertility, and which bear relevance, therefore, to such concepts as demand for children, costs and quality of children, and resources. We do not attempt, however, to apply any particular economic model to the data, nor will we dwell unduly on whether an observed relationship tends to confirm or reject theoretically derived propositions.

* Research for this paper was supported in part by a grant from the National Institute of Child Health and Human Development. Dr Eva Mueller made a number of helpful suggestions. Jacqueline Lelong was of valuable assistance in carrying out tabulations and bibliographic research.

A review paper of this type owes much to the many investigators whose works have been cited. They are not, of course, responsible for the manner in which their findings have been employed. Many other important aspects of Taiwanese fertility patterns, which could not be included here, may be found in the works cited.

Our data are drawn from a number of investigators who are often pursuing different objectives. We will utilise results based on both micro and macro data. This eclectic and empirical approach will entail, therefore, some sacrifice in coherence and uniformity.

II. DEMOGRAPHIC AND SOCIO-ECONOMIC SETTING

Our concern centres on the period since 1950, with particular emphasis on the 1960–70 decade. A brief excursion back, however, helps set the stage and is not without interest in appraising the determinants of fertility. (Much of the discussion of this early period draws heavily from Liu, 1972, and Barclay, 1954.)

During the period of Japanese rule, 1895–1945, Taiwan was regarded mainly as a supplier of agricultural products. Industrial development to any appreciable extent did not take place until the mid-1930s. The system of agriculture at the start of the period was one of traditional, subsistence, small-scale cultivation; a high proportion of the farms were operated on rental land and cultivated by a closely-knit household. Birth-rates and death-rates were both high, in the neighbourhood of 40 per 1000.[1]

The Japanese approach to increasing agricultural production was to keep the social organisation intact and to take steps to increase production per farm, along with some expansion in the number of farms. To this end, they introduced a number of innovations into Taiwanese agricultural practice, among them: irrigation, chemical fertilisers, crop rotation and new rice strains. The scale factors in terms of per farm averages in number of workers, cultivated land, or fixed capital did not change significantly over the colonial period (Liu, 1972, p. 4 and Tables 3 and 4). This system was eminently successful and agricultural production in total and per farm increased markedly. The gains from these increases were mainly captured by the Japanese through their control of the commercial and processing enterprises, and through taxation and their charges for the innovations. As a result, income per family was relatively static throughout the period (Liu, 1972, Table 5).

Since agriculture remained labour intensive, the Japanese took steps to increase population growth by decreasing mortality, there being little room for achieving higher fertility. With judicious expenditures on public health and high administrative skill, they made great strides in reducing mortality from plague, cholera and

[1] Statistics are not available until after 10 years of Japanese rule. The data for 1906–9 show crude birth-rates and death-rates of 40·3 and 33·3 per 1000 respectively (Liu, 1972, Table 7). Barclay (1954, p. 145) conjectures that, as of 1895, the death-rate may have been over 40.

malaria (Barclay, 1954, pp. 133–9). The effects were dramatic, and by 1930 the crude death-rate was about 20 per 1000. Birth-rates rose slightly in response to better health conditions, so that the rate of natural increase ranged from 23 to 25 per 1000 during the decade of the 1930s. The rise in growth rates did not, of course, have any immediate impact on the labour force. During the 1920s, most of the net increase in the labour force entered agriculture, while during the 1930s, a high proportion of the net gain was absorbed by the rapidly growing industrial sector. This latter development averted undue pressure on agricultural production (Liu, 1972, p. 12 and Table 11). Liu further notes that most of the Taiwanese in the industrial sector were confined to manual or semi-skilled workers, that their income was not very different from those of farm workers, and that they 'were generally kept away from modern contacts ... As a result, industrialisation brought neither improvement in standard and style of living nor modern attitudes to the population at large' (Liu, 1972, p. 13). He suggests that these factors help explain the lack of significant difference in fertility between cities and rural areas in the 1930–45 period.[1]

In addition to reducing the death rate, the activities of the Japanese led to an increase in educational levels. Liu reports that enrolment rates in primary school increased from 21 per cent for boys and 4 per cent for girls in 1917 to 81 and 61 per cent respectively in 1943 (Liu, 1972, p. 11). Education was fostered as a means of facilitating the adoption of agricultural innovations and health and sanitation measures. Opportunities beyond the primary level were severely limited, however, and few Taiwanese attained a university education.

Taiwan prior to 1945 thus seems to accord well with what Easterlin (1973, p. 26) has described as a pre-modern fertility situation. The circumscribed nature of the gains in education and urbanisation did not serve to increase the price of children nor shift tastes to goods and away from children. There were few new consumer goods available, and little change in income. Improvements in public health and medical care increased the supply of children, slightly through higher fertility and largely through lowered mortality. Social and family structure were basically unaltered, and any motivation for fertility regulation seemed insufficient to overcome the costs, largely psychic at this point. In Easterlin's phrase (1973, p. 16), 'The "threshold" of fertility regulation has not yet been reached'.

[1] Barclay (1954, p. 251, Table 78) compares the gross reproduction rates of cities with the non-urban portions of their prefectures, for 1930 and 1935. Cities generally showed lower rates, but this was not universally so, and the variation across cities was as large as the variation in areas outside of cities.

Following the restoration of Taiwan to China in 1945, there was a seven year period of post-war dislocation occasioned by this change-over, war-related damage to physical equipment, and problems attendant to the absorption of a large number of migrants from the mainland. Since about 1952, however, Taiwan has ex-

TABLE 9.1 INDICATORS OF ECONOMIC AND SOCIAL DEVELOPMENT FOR TAIWAN AREA, REPUBLIC OF CHINA, 1952–1969

	1952	1956	1960	1964	1969
Economic indicators					
Gross National Product (GNP) Index[a]	100	133	172	254	401
Per Capita Real National Income Index[b]	100	111	125	168	217
Savings as percentage of national income	4·8	4·9	6·9	15·6	20·9[b]
Agricultural Production Index	100	121	143	178	224
Total Industrial Production Index[c]	100	155	245	410	940
Electric Power Production Index	100	158	255	419	783
Percentage of net domestic product from industry	18	22	25	28	32
Percentage of male labour force over 11 in non-agricultural occupation	42	45	49	50	60[d]
Education indicators					
Percentage of population 6 and over who are illiterate	42	37	27	22	15
Percentage of primary-school graduates enrolled in junior high school	34	47	51	55	75
Communication and transportation indicators					
Daily newspaper circulation per 1000	28	40	55	70	
Radios per 1000 families	34	105	350	555	621
Posting of domestic letters per capita	8	17	33	32	34
Long distance calls per capita	0·6	1·0	1·4	1·8	2·2
Health indicators					
Death-rate per 1000	10	8	7	6	5
Life expectancy for males	51	59	61	64	66
Population per doctor	1,610	1,537	1,553	1,520	1,412

Source: Council for International Economic Cooperation and Development, *Taiwan Statistical Data Book, 1970.* (This is taken from Freedman *et al.,* 1972a, Table 3.)

[a] At constant price of 1964, and adjusted for gain or loss due to changed terms of trade.
[b] 1968 data.
[c] Includes manufacturing, mining, electricity, gas and water.
[d] For male labour force over 14 years of age.

perienced rapid social and economic development, which may be gauged in part from the indicators presented in Table 9.1. Noteworthy in this development is the increasing importance of industrial production, both in terms of labour force and as a share of net domestic product, the rising educational attainment of the population, the growth in mass media, and a continuing favourable trend in health and mortality indicators. An extensive land-reform programme carried out from 1949–53 greatly reduced the proportion of farmers who were tenants, increased the number of farms, and reduced the average size of holdings. The terms of the land programme encouraged intensive cultivation, so that the average number of workers per farm did not fall as fast as the size of holdings (Liu, 1972, Table 3). The net effect of these changes was to reduce the employment demands on the industrial sector and the volume of migration to the cities. The latter factor was also aided by a tendency to locate new industry outside the cities, both as a matter of policy and as a reflection of relative land availability and costs. This enabled a significant proportion of the industrial labour force to remain in their semi-urban or rural locales, and also became an important source of farm family income. Mueller (1973, p. 29) reports data which show approximately 40 per cent of farm family income arising from non-farm earnings.[1]

Notwithstanding these considerations, a migration trend toward the cities is clearly evident. From 1961–6, the net in-migration rate to the five largest cities was at an annual average of 15·9 per 1000 persons. There was also in-migration to the middle-size cities (above 50,000) and out-migration from the smaller cities (less than 50,000) and rural areas (Speare, 1969, p. 34). During the decade of the 1930s, the ten largest cities grew at an average annual rate of 5·1 per cent, compared to 3·1 per cent for the remaining areas.[2] As a result, 22·4 per cent of the Taiwanese (excluding the mainland Chinese immigrants and other non-Taiwanese) resided in these cities in 1960, compared to 15·2 per cent in 1940 (Speare, 1969, pp. 20–1). Liu (1972, p. 24) suggests that these developments in agriculture on one hand and industry and urbanisation on the other, often led to the following familial arrangement: the eldest son took over the farm and helped finance the education of the younger sons. They in turn, once they were established in the cities, turned over their shares of the farm (to which they were entitled under Chinese inheritance patterns) to the oldest son at little or no cost, and helped provide support for the parents. Thus, the small farm holdings were not further sub-divided and the entire household could benefit from the rising industrial opportunities.

This period also witnessed the development of organised family-planning programme activities. A voluntary agency programme started in 1954; in 1959, a more intensive effort was carried out as part of a maternal and child-health programme; a large-scale

[1] Though not restricted to farm families, note also that 44 per cent of males employed in manufacturing in 1965 lived outside the 10 largest cities (Speare, 1969, p. 22). This includes commuters to the city.

[2] The difference is somewhat exaggerated by the immigrants from the mainland, who settled primarily in the cities.

experimental programme was carried out in the city of Taichung during 1963, which made use of the new intra-uterine contraceptive device; and from 1964 on, there has been a rapidly expanding, intensive, island-wide programme (Freedman and Takeshita, 1969, pp. 12–15, 313–21).

Fertility in the early 1950s remained at the high pre-war levels and with declining mortality, the annual rate of natural increase was in excess of 35 per 1000 throughout most of the 1950–60 decade.

In contrast to the pre-war situation, there appears to be a number of factors emerging in the 1950s conducive to fertility regulation. Even without a change in the desired number of children, the number of surviving children would be in excess of their desires for more and more families because of the favourable trends in mortality. The increasing educational opportunities and the attendant costs initiate considerations of child quality and the price of children, while developing tastes for alternative life-styles among the parents. The increased flow of consumer goods might further shift tastes away from children. The small land area of Taiwan, its good transportation system and growing mass media, together with close-knit familial arrangements, would serve to diffuse new ideas quite rapidly. The organised family-planning efforts helped at first to legitimate the adoption of contraception and, with time, also to reduce the market costs of such behaviour for increasing numbers of families. Rising per capita income, in Easterlin's accounting (1973, p. 18), which we are largely following here, is seen as having both a positive effect on number of children desired as well as a negative effect through increasing consumption aspirations. Davis (1963, p. 352) has pointed out that many of the currently industrialised countries reduced their fertility during a period of rising incomes and has suggested that the desire to take advantage of emerging opportunities acts as a deterrent to fertility.

Whether or not we have identified the salient factors and their direction of influence, fertility clearly did begin to decline during the 1950s and has continued a steady downward trend up to the present. Table 9.2 shows the elements of this change. Total fertility which was at a high point of 7051 in 1951 declined to 4000 in 1970. Most of this decline is accounted for by the decreasing age-specific fertility rates at the older ages, notable above age 40 in the 1950–60 decade and above age 30 in the 1960–70 decade. This age pattern suggests that the early efforts at fertility regulation have been directed toward keeping actual fertility in line with desired fertility, and matches closely the fertility experiences of European and other countries which have substantially lowered their fertility (Coale, 1969).

The survey data to be presented in the following sections tend to confirm this observation and serve to amplify the sense in which Taiwan was earlier characterised as midway through a demographic transition. There has been relatively little change in desired number of children but sharp increases in the proportion of couples using contraception. Differentials in desired number of children by socio-economic characteristics, though in predictable directions, are stable. Differentials in contraceptive use are more apparent at the earliest

TABLE 9.2 TAIWAN: FERTILITY RATES AND PERCENTAGE CHANGE, SELECTED YEARS, 1951–1970

	1951	1956	1960	1965	1970	1951–1960	1960–1970	1960–1965	1965–1970
						Percentage of change			
de birth-rate	50·0	44·8	39·5	32·1	27·2	−21·0	−31·1	−18·7	−15·3
l fertility rate	7,051	6,528	5,772	4,825	4,000	−18·1	−30·7	−16·4	−17·1
specific fertility rates:									
15–19	68	51	49	36	40	−27·9	−18·4	−26·5	+11·1
20–24	288	265	254	261	238	−11·8	−6·3	+2·8	−8·8
25–29	350	341	334	326	293	−4·6	−12·3	−2·4	−10·1
30–34	312	297	256	195	147	−17·9	−42·6	−23·8	−24·6
35–39	226	223	170	100	59	−24·8	−65·3	−41·2	−41·0
40–44	132	105	79	41	20	−40·2	−74·7	−48·1	−51·2
45–49	35	23	13	6	3	−62·9	−76·9	−53·8	−50·0

Sources: Demographic Reference: Taiwan Republic of China, vol. II, (1965) Table 14–1, pp. 5–7 and Table 12, pp. 2–3.
1965 Taiwan Demographic Fact Book, Republic of China, Table 10, pp. 256–7.
1970 Taiwan Demographic Fact Book, Republic of China, Table 10, pp. 20–1 and Table 12, p. 286.

date of observation but diminish rapidly within a relatively short space of time.

In the next section, we present in some detail the pattern of differentials on fertility-related variables in terms of many of the socio-economic characteristics discussed above. Subsequent sections will investigate the role of women's labour-force participation and variables bearing on child quality.

III. SOCIO-ECONOMIC CHARACTERISTICS AND DIFFERENTIAL FERTILITY

In this section we will examine the relation of education, urbanisation, mass media exposure, and ownership of modern goods to fertility-related variables, including age at marriage. The desirability of including women who have not yet completed their child-bearing in this type of analysis presents a problem in choosing an appropriate fertility characteristic. Variables such as number of living children are strongly influenced by marriage durations; and since the socio-economic characteristics are also related to age at marriage, there is a confounding effect.

Table 9.3 presents three fertility measures for women characterised by education and urbanisation levels, within two broad age groups. These data come from three surveys based on probability samples of all married women in the child-bearing years in Taiwan, with the exclusion from the sampling frame of a small number of townships in which most of Taiwan's small aborigine population lives. The third survey conducted in 1970 involved a re-interview of 50 per cent of the 1967 sample, supplemented by an appropriate sampling of marriages which occurred between 1967 and 1970. The samples are strictly comparable only for women in the 22–39 age range and comparisons across surveys will use only this age grouping. (For additional details on the surveys and trend analysis across them see Freedman *et al.*, 1972*a*.)

The data for educational level indicate a steady gradation toward lower fertility levels with increasing education. This is true of all three fertility measures. For the younger women there is little difference between number of children expected and the number reported as ideal.[1] The older women generally already have more children than they desire. The educational differentials for this age group are greater for number of children expected than number considered ideal, since the former reflects differential success at fertility regulation as well as differences in the number desired (or ideal). In 1967, for example, older women with no education expect 0·6 more children than they consider ideal, while senior high women expect 0·3 children in excess of their desired number. For both age groups and all time periods, the difference in ideal number of children between the highest and lowest educational categories is about one child.

The trends by level of urbanisation are similar to those for education, but they are not as distinct nor as large. City women generally expect and desire smaller numbers of children than rural women. The differences between the number expected and ideal for older women do not vary greatly across urbanisation levels,

---

[1] Expected children are the number of living children plus the number of additional children, if any, the wife reports as wanting. Ideal number (also referred to as desired number) is the number given in answer to the question 'If you were just getting married and could have the number of children you want, how many would you like to have when you are through having children?'

TABLE 9.3 DIFFERENTIALS BY EDUCATION AND URBANISATION FOR THREE FERTILITY MEASURES, BY AGE: 1965, 1967 AND 1970

	1965			1967			1970		
	No. of living children	Total no. expected children	Ideal no. of children	No. of living children	Total no. expected children	Ideal no. of children	No. of living children	Total no. expected children	Ideal no. of children
AGE AND EDUCATION									
Age 22–9									
None	2·4	4·1	3·9	2·5	3·9	3·8	2·7	3·9	3·8
Primary	2·3	3·8	3·7	2·2	3·6	3·6	2·4	3·7	3·6
Junior high	2·0	3·5	3·4	1·9	3·3	3·2	2·1	3·4	3·2
Senior high	1·8	3·0	3·0	1·4	2·9	2·9	1·5	2·8	2·9
Age 30–9									
None	4·7	5·0	4·3	4·4	4·8	4·2	4·4	4·9	4·1
Primary	4·4	4·7	4·2	4·2	4·5	4·0	4·2	4·6	3·9
Junior high	4·1	4·3	3·7	3·6	3·9	3·5	3·6	4·0	3·5
Senior high	3·4	3·7	3·3	3·1	3·5	3·2	3·0	3·3	3·2
AGE AND URBANISATION									
Age 22–9									
Rural	2·3	4·1	4·0	2·2	3·9	3·8	2·4	3·8	3·8
Urban township	2·3	3·8	3·6	2·3	3·6	3·5	2·4	3·8	3·6
Small city	2·4	3·7	3·6	2·2	3·5	3·5	2·3	3·6	3·3
Large city	2·4	3·7	3·6	2·2	3·4	3·2	2·3	3·5	3·3
Age 30–9									
Rural	4·6	5·0	4·4	4·4	4·8	4·3	4·4	4·8	4·1
Urban township	4·6	4·9	4·1	4·2	4·6	4·0	4·1	4·5	3·9
Small city	4·0	4·2	4·0	4·0	4·3	3·9	4·0	4·5	3·8
Large city	4·3	4·6	3·9	3·8	4·0	3·7	3·9	4·3	3·7

Note: The number of cases in each educational and urbanisation category, for both age groups combined, are shown in Table 9.4.

suggesting that differential success in regulating fertility was relatively small.

In order to disaggregate, in a rough way at least, the differentials in desired number of children from the degree of success in fertility

TABLE 9.4 IDEAL NUMBER OF CHILDREN AND EVER-USE OF CONTRACEPTION BY SELECTED MODERNISATION MEASURES FOR MARRIED WOMEN AGED 22–39 TAIWAN: 1965–1970

Modernisation measures[a]	Ideal number of children			Percentage ever-used contraception[b]			Number of cases		
	1965	1967	1970	1965	1967	1970	1965	1967	1970
Education									
None	4·1	4·1	4·0	19·4	32·9	50·9	1449	1525	839
Primary	3·9	3·8	3·8	31·9	42·3	53·7	1311	2135	1325
Junior high	3·6	3·3	3·3	51·4	58·3	71·4	181	289	194
Senior high or more	3·2	3·0	3·0	60·2	65·5	79·2	108	196	133
Urbanisation									
Rural township	4·2	4·1	3·9	21·4	32·9	48·2	1227	1628	1004
Urban township	3·9	3·8	3·8	25·7	40·1	53·8	902	1240	753
Small city	3·8	3·7	3·6	31·7	44·0	62·2	303	333	199
Large city	3·7	3·5	3·5	43·3	55·4	69·1	617	944	535
Newspaper reading									
Daily	3·4	3·2	3·2	58·4	61·4	73·5	305	593	356
Frequently	3·6	3·5	3·3	40·9	49·2	61·0	132	333	95
Seldom	3·8	3·8	3·6	34·6	40·5	57·7	434	596	278
Never/can't read	4·1	4·0	3·9	21·9	35·6	52·0	2178	2623	1762
Mass media exposure									
Low		4·1	4·0		30·0	47·0		1254	943
Medium		3·9	3·7		40·9	58·1		1862	1126
High		3·4	3·3		55·0	71·8		1029	422
Number of modern objects owned									
0–3 objects	4·2	4·1		19·4	35·4		1245	1207	
4–5	4·0	4·0		27·3	35·6		770	939	
6–7	3·9	3·8		28·5	39·2		548	812	
8 or more	3·6	3·5		51·4	52·5		486	1187	
Total	4·0	3·8	3·8	28·1	41·1	55·5	3049	4145	2491

[a] Data not available on all measures for each time period.
[b] Includes sterilisation.
Note: This is taken from Freedman *et al.*, 1972a, Table 7.

regulation toward that goal, we focus in Table 9.4 on ideal number of children and the proportion of women using contraception, for a number of socio-economic characteristics.

Before turning to these data some evidence concerning their validity may be in order, since questions are often raised about the meaningfulness of interview reports on behaviour and attitudes concerning fertility and contraception. Freedman *et al.* (1972*a*, p. 291) show that the reported increase in levels of contraceptive use are in close accord with independent estimates from the service statistics of the family-planning programme. From the longitudinal feature of the 1967 survey, it was determined that 74 per cent of those who said they wanted more children had a birth between 1967 and 1970, while only 13 per cent who reported wanting no more children in 1967 had a birth in the following three-year period (Freedman *et al.*, 1972*b*, p. 159). This indicates substantial consistency between expressed preferences and subsequent behaviour. Further evidence of consistency is seen from : (1) The fact that approximately 80 per cent of the women above the age of 30 report wanting no more children, which accords with the data in Table 9.3 indicating that actual fertility on the average has exceeded the desired number, and (2) a substantial increase over the three surveys in the proportion of women wanting no more children who are using contraception (Freedman *et al.*, 1972*a*, p. 292). The foregoing relationships indicate that the pattern of responses in the interview surveys is meaningful and point up as well the increasing rationalisation of the fertility process in Taiwan.

The data in Table 9.4 show that between 1965 and 1970, the ideal number of children declined slightly from 4·0 to 3·8.[1] There were small declines of roughly equal magnitude for each category of the modernisation variables, so that differentials by characteristic were basically the same at the beginning and end of the period. Comparable data for a longer time-span are unavailable, but the 1962 study in the city of Taichung revealed an average ideal number of 3·8, which is little different than the average of large city residents in 1965 (Freedman and Takeshita, 1969, p. 40). This evidence thus suggests that during the 1960s there were only small changes in desired number of children, based on the particular operational definition utilised. This measure, it should be noted, might be rather slow to change, since women would be influenced by their current fertility in reporting on the idealised situation.

All the differentials in ideal number shown in Table 9.4 show that women who could be characterised as more modern, desire smaller numbers of children than those who are less so. The socio-economic characteristics are highly correlated with one another, but multivariate analysis indicates that each has some independent effect. To gauge the magnitude of the differentials, we can roughly compare the pattern in the United States: the educational differential of one child in Taiwan in 1970 between the highest and lowest strata

[1] This change is statistically significant at the 5 per cent level (Freedman *et al.*, 1972*a*, Appendix, p. 296).

appears to be about twice as large as that among white women in the United States and slightly less than the educational differential among Negro women (Ryder and Westoff, 1971, Table IV-1, p. 54, using 'total desired' as the closest measure to the Taiwanese measure of ideal number); the differential of 1·6 children in total expected by education in 1970 for women aged 30–39, in Table 9.3, is about 60 per cent larger than a comparable measure for the same age group in the United States in 1972 (U.S. Bureau of The Census, 1973, Table 9.9; the educational categories for the U.S. data are less detailed than for Taiwan).

In contrast to the stability of differentials in ideal number of children, Table 9.4 shows that there have been sharp changes in the patterns of contraceptive use. From 1965 to 1970 there were substantial increases in the proportion of women who ever used contraception overall and within each of the categories. Contraceptive use increased fastest, however, for the less modern components of the population. As a result, the differentials between the highest and lowest strata of each characteristic narrowed both in absolute percentage points and proportionately from 1965 to 1970. Among the educational categories, for example, contraceptive use for those with no formal education rose from 19 to 51 per cent between 1965 and 1970, while it increased from 60 to 79 per cent for the highest educational category. A sizeable differential still existed in 1970 but it was considerably reduced over the five-year period.

The patterns described are consonant with the earlier discussion of the factors making for fertility change. Those who are more modern, in terms of the variables examined, have adopted smaller family-size norms in response to changing opportunities and demands. Though the actual fertility of older women at all levels of modernisation is likely to exceed their desired size (see Table 9.3), the more modern will come closer to achieving their goal. This is so because of earlier and more widespread adoption of contraceptive practices. With respect to such practices, those who are more educated, urban and informed through mass media can be expected to have displayed greater knowledge, access, resources and willingness to innovate than their less modern counterparts. Over a relatively short span of time, the market and subjective costs of fertility regulation were apparently reduced for the less modern sector and led to a rapid rise there in the adoption of contraception. In this regard the organised family-planning programme may have played a significant role. Areal multivariate analysis of programme effectiveness by Hermalin (1971) and T. P. Schultz (1973) indicate that the programme had a stronger impact on fertility in the less modern areas, with high pre-programme fertility. Also, the Taichung city experiment in 1963 found little correlation between acceptance from the programme and socio-economic status (Freedman and Takeshita, 1969, Ch. VII).

To this point we have, in the main, inferred the nature of economic behaviour and attitudes from the social and economic position of Taiwanese couples. A number of studies, however, have treated these variables explicitly and analysed their interrelationships as well as their relevance for fertility and family planning. D. Freedman (1972) showed that couples who had just the number of children desired and were using contraception were more likely than other couples to be savers and to own a larger number of modern objects, even after controlling for family income, wife's education, and demographic characteristics. Though the direction of causality cannot be established from these data, 'they do support the hypothesis that the planning-motivation syndrome which enables a couple to successfully plan their family size also enables them to accumulate savings, even while they purchase more of the goods which provide some of the immediate material gratification of modernisation' (D. Freedman, 1972, p. 504). Other analysis of the correlates of modern consumption patterns show that many aspects of modern behaviour and attitudes tend to cohere. Ownership of modern objects was found to be related to family income (as expected), the couple's education and the husband's occupation, with the educational characteristics somewhat more important than income (D. Freedman, 1970, p. 30, note 15). In addition, the level of ownership was found to relate to innovative practices by the self-employed and to modern beliefs about factors affecting advancement, after controlling for income.

A study by Mueller (1972) focused on the relationships between the economic utility of children, aspirations for children's education, sensitivity to the cost of raising children, consumption aspirations, and fertility and family planning. A few salient findings from the study are as follows:

1. There is a very high level of aspiration for children's education in Taiwan. About two-thirds of the husbands interviewed in 1969 expected to send one of their children to college. Aspirations for children's higher education did rise with the educational level of the father and ability to estimate the costs involved was closely related to educational level.

2. A scale measuring the perceived utility of children (with higher scores representing greater expected benefits from children) was inversely related to husband and wife's education and family income.

3. Sensitivity to the cost of raising children was directly related to husband's education and the level of consumption aspirations,

even after controlling for income and parity. It was negatively related to the perceived utility of children.

· 4.   Perceived utility was positively related to the ideal number of children and negatively related to contraceptive use; sensitivity to the cost of raising children was negatively associated with ideal number of children and positively related to contraceptive behaviour. These relations held after adjustments for the husband's and wife's education and income.

Mueller sums up by suggesting 'that rising income fosters a sense of economic independence from children and raises the consumption and educational aspirations of parents, as well as the perceived cost of raising children' (1972, pp. 395–6). The fact that couples with higher education and income desire both more modern goods and services as well as higher quality children (in terms of higher education) suggests that these factors operate together to reduce the number of children desired. This accords with the discussion of Willis (1973, p. 28) that child quality and non-child satisfactions may be complements rather than substitutes.

These studies indicate that economic motives have come to play a part in fertility behaviour in Taiwan. They have an effect which is independent of socio-economic or demographic status and in some cases are equally important as explanatory variables. The case must not be overstated, however. Multivariate analyses employing economic attitudes, socio-economic statuses, and demographic characteristics as explanatory variables explain little of the variance in fertility-related attitudes and behaviours. Though this is typical of survey data, Mueller (1972, pp. 385, 402) also shows that many Taiwanese husbands had ambivalent attitudes toward family size, often citing economic reasons for smaller numbers of children as well as non-economic and traditional advantages from larger family size.

In addition to the degree of utilisation of contraception and abortion, age at marriage and the proportion of the population marrying are important determinants of the level of fertility. The decline in age-specific fertility between 1960 and 1970 at the two youngest ages, shown in Table 9.2, is the result of declining proportions married, rather than a change in age-specific marital fertility. The marital fertility rates for these two age groups actually increased throughout the decade. The changing proportions married by age are shown in the top panel of Table 9.5. The data show a steadily decreasing proportion married at the two youngest ages, pointing toward a later age at marriage.[1]

---

[1] A separate analysis reveals that the proportion married at 20–24 is correlated (-0.90) with the singulate mean age at marriage, so that this age group provides a good indicator of age at marriage.

TABLE 9.5 TAIWAN: PERCENTAGE OF WOMEN
CURRENTLY MARRIED, BY AGE

Age of women	Per cent currently married						
	1961	1965	1966	1967	1968	1969	1970
15–19	12·5	9·2	8·7	8·9	8·5	8·1	8·0
20–24	60·9	58·3	57·7	56·4	54·2	51·8	50·3
25–29	89·3	88·8	88·7	88·4	88·3	88·2	88·1
30–34	91·6	92·8	93·0	93·1	93·5	93·3	93·0
35–39	89·8	91·5	92·1	92·5	93·0	93·2	93·2

Source: *1970 Taiwan Demographic Fact Book*, Part A, Table 8.

PERCENTAGE OF WOMEN 20–24 CURRENTLY MARRIED,
BY EDUCATION AND RESIDENCE, 1966 AND 1971

Educational attainment	Per cent currently married					
	1966			1971		
	City resi- dence	Outside of cities	Total	City resi- dence	Outside of cities	Total
Senior high and over	24·5	24·6	24·5	22·8	13·7	17·1
Junior high	38·9	40·6	40·0	40·9	29·9	33·8
Primary	59·0	59·4	59·3	55·5	54·2	54·5
Literate	67·5	71·7	70·9	73·8	69·4	70·4
Illiterate	74·5	74·0	74·1	81·4	72·5	73·8
Total	51·9	59·0	57·4	46·7	48·4	48·0

Source: Unpublished tabulations from the Ministry of Interior, Republic of China, Taiwan, China.

There are sharp differentials in age at marriage by educational attainment of females, as shown in the lower panel of Table 9.5. (The data for 1966 are from a complete enumeration of birth records and the household register, and for 1971 from a sampling of records for approximately 500,000 women.) In 1966 and 1971, the more educated marry later than the less educated. This is true for both city and non-city dwellers, but the trend over the five years is quite different by residence. For the city women, there are indications that age at marriage has started to decrease, since the proportions married have moved upward for a number of educational categories. In the non-city areas, age at marriage has continued to increase, so that by 1971 the proportions married were lower there at each educational level than in the cities. This is a sharp change from the pattern in 1966, when, within educational levels, there appeared to be a slight tendency for non-city women to marry earlier. (We note parenthetically that the apparent trend toward later age at marriage in Taiwan shown in the top part of Table 9.5 is due, in part at least, to the increasing educational attainment of women and the strong relationship between education and age at marriage. A more detailed examination of this point is given in Anderson, 1973.)

The unavailability of data for other years and the apparent recency of the changes noted, make it difficult to gauge whether a new

TABLE 9.6 TAIWAN: MEAN IDEAL NUMBER OF CHILDREN BY AGE AT
FIRST MARRIAGE, DATE OF MARRIAGE AND EDUCATION, 1967

Date of marriage and wife's education	Total	Age at marriage				N
		18 or less	19–20	21–22	23 or over	
1964–1967						
Less than primary	3·4	3·4	3·7	3·4	3·3	245
Primary or more	3·3	3·6	3·4	3·2	3·2	476
1961–1963						
Less than primary	3·7	3·8	3·7	3·7	3·5	315
Primary or more	3·3	3·6	3·4	3·2	3·2	377
1956–1960						
Less than primary	3·9	3·9	3·9	3·9	3·8	681
Primary or more	3·7	3·7	3·8	3·6	3·6	468
1948–1955						
Less than primary	4·3	4·3	4·2	4·4	4·0	923
Primary or more	4·0	4·1	4·1	3·8	3·6	667
1947 or earlier						
Less than primary	4·4	4·5	4·5	4·0	3·7	509
Primary or more	4·0	4·1	4·0	3·9	3·8	268
Total	3·9	4·1	3·9	3·7	3·5	4929

Source: Island-wide Survey of Knowledge, Attitude and Practice of Family Planning, Taiwan, 1967.

age-at-marriage pattern is evolving. One can speculate that the rising income levels in the cities are facilitating earlier age at marriage. In addition, increasing knowledge about contraception may be contributing to a change in marriage and reproductive patterns. It is known, for example, that city women are more likely to adopt contraception from the programme for spacing purposes and to adopt it at earlier ages than non-city dwellers.

Age at marriage can affect fertility by altering the period of exposure to child-bearing. It is also possible that women who marry at different ages differ in the number of children they desire. This appears to be the case in Taiwan, as shown in Table 9.6. For each calendar period of marriage, which serves to control duration of marriage, women who married at a later age tended to desire, on average, a smaller number of children than those who married at younger ages. This was true for both educational levels. At each age at marriage, educational differentials persisted, but their magnitudes were smaller than those shown in Table 9.3. Since we have just noted that education is strongly related to age at marriage, it is possible that the educational differentials previously observed operate partly through age at marriage.[1] The degree to which age at marriage influences fertility is of some relevance to economic, household decision-making theories of fertility, since assumptions must be made about the extent to which decisions concerning numbers of children are made prior to marriage, at the outset of marriage and during the course of marriage.

IV. FEMALE LABOUR FORCE AND FERTILITY

Economic models of fertility often give salience to the role of female labour-force participation because the opportunity cost of children is increased when a woman is able to work. This factor, however, does not appear to be an important determinant of fertility behaviour in Taiwan at its current stage of development. Some of the evidence and implications are reviewed below.

1. From the surveys described in the previous section, and an interim interview with husbands in 1969, 47 per cent of wives aged 22–39 could be classified as currently working. This includes part-time employment and work at home as well as away from home. Of working wives, 84 per cent were working at home, full or part-time, and the at-home employment of farm wives accounted for 44 per cent of all working wives. Thus, labour-force participation for females is mainly connected with agriculture and small, family-owned businesses (Mueller *et al.*, n.d., p. 27).

2. There was no difference in ideal number of children desired between working wives and non-working wives, either before or after applying appropriate socio-economic and demographic control variables. Contraceptive use was somewhat higher among working wives, particularly among wives of farmers who work at least 20 hours per week during the year (Mueller *et al.*, n.d., Tables 3, 4, 5). The authors suggest, therefore (p. 27), that while labour-force participation does not serve to modify ideal family size, working

[1] The use of only two educational categories in Table 9.6 compared with four in Table 9.3 may serve to truncate differences.

wives may be 'more motivated than others not to exceed their ideal family size'.

3.   Additional analyses show that wives usually can obtain only limited types of work which pay poorly. Hence, the opportunity cost of an additional child is low. Also, the fact that such a high proportion of the work is done at home allows women to combine more easily economic and maternal roles. Investigation of the attitudes toward working wives and the reasons for employment lead the authors to conclude: 'It appears reasonable to attribute this finding (the lack of effect of female labour-force participation on family-size goals) to widespread negative attitudes toward a working role for married women. Apparently, women who work derive little social esteem or self-esteem from their work role. The motivation to work seems to be predominantly economic. To earn esteem as wives and mothers, working women conform to social norms regarding family size. Even educated women who have white-collar jobs observe the family-size norms which prevail in their own social groups ...' (Mueller *et al.*, n.d., p. 27).

Although labour-force participation of married women in Taiwan does not demonstrate the strong effect on fertility exhibited in some of the more industrialised countries, the labour-force activities of single women may be of some importance. Speare *et al.* (1972, p. 4) from a 1971 survey of women, married and unmarried, aged 18–29, found that 70 per cent of the single women who were not in school had worked away from home. In addition, the range of employment opportunities appears greater for single than for married women. Mueller *et al.* (n.d., p. 18) found that nearly 80 per cent of husbands and 90 per cent of wives wanted their daughters to work before marriage. Employment of young single women may be a factor leading to later age at marriage. Mueller (1973, p. 45) suggests that the pressure among rural families to marry off their daughters early may be reduced when they are employed and can accumulate money for a dowry. In addition, work in a modern setting may expose the young women to alternative life-styles, raise consumption aspirations, and thereby reduce the desired number of children. Speare *et al.* (1972, Table 1) found that within the 18–29 age span, single women had a smaller ideal family size than the married, within three age categories. The size of the differential increased with age, perhaps reflecting the effect of length of experience in the work force, but there was no explicit control for labour-force participation. Though the work experience now being accumulated by single women may affect their future fertility, the analysis by Mueller *et al.* (n.d., p. 18) of those now married did not reveal that previous work experience had any impact on marital fertility.

V. OTHER FACTORS RELATED TO CHILD QUALITY

In the economic theory of fertility behaviour advanced by Willis and others, the concept of child quality plays a central role. Child quality considers 'those characteristics of children that provide satisfaction (or dissatisfaction) to their parents as commodities produced with time and goods according to household production functions' (Willis, 1973, p. 19). In the general formulation of the model the production function for child quality can vary across birth orders, but the simpler specification necessitated for testing the model with available data requires the additional assumptions that the production functions for child quality are equal for each child and that 'parents choose an equal level of child quality for each child born' (Willis, 1973, p. 21). We call attention below to certain features of Taiwanese society that may make these assumptions less tenable there than in other settings. Whether the model still proves useful under these circumstances must await an appropriate test.

The first feature we note in this respect is the importance of sex preference in fertility decisions and behaviours. Though the sex of a child would not be viewed as 'produced' by inputs of time and commodities, the sex composition of children does seem to relate to satisfactions and, more importantly perhaps, to fertility decisions. It would thus be a factor that a model of fertility behaviour might well take account of.

Chinese tradition and family structure emphasise the importance of sons and this is still evident in Taiwan in 1970. Women of reproductive age reported 2·1 sons as the ideal number and this was little changed from 1965 (Freedman *et al.* 1972*a*, pp. 287–8). These authors also show that the number of living sons is strongly related to fertility. Their findings are shown in Table 9.7. These data show that controlling for number of living children, those with sons are more likely to: have a smaller ideal family size; want no more children; be using contraception; expect that their actual fertility will not exceed their ideal number.

Another aspect of sex preference and one which bears more closely on the assumption of equal household production functions, is the level of education that parents want their sons and daughters to attain. Aspirations to send daughters to college are high in Taiwan. Nearly half the fathers plan to send their daughters to college, which compares with two-thirds who plan to send sons. About one-third of the fathers in Taiwan plans to give their sons more education than their daughters. Fathers with a high school or more education were much more likely than others to plan equal educational attainment. (These relationships are from Arnold, 1972, pp. 233–7.)

TABLE 9.7 FERTILITY VARIABLES BY NUMBER OF LIVING CHILDREN AND LIVING SONS FOR WIVES AGED 22–39
TAIWAN: 1965, 1967, 1970

No. of living children, no. of living sons	Mean ideal no. of children			Mean additional no. of children wanted			Percentage wanting no more children			Percentage currently using contraception[a]			Percentage who expect more children than their ideal			No. of cases		
	1965	1967	1970	1965	1967	1970	1965	1967	1970	1965	1967	1970	1965	1967	1970	1965	1967	1970
0 children	3·5	3·2	3·2	3·3	3·0	2·9	6·3	3·4	6·3	0	5·2	6·2	0·8	0·0	3·7	127	175	73
1 child																		
0 sons	3·5	3·4	3·4	2·5	2·3	2·3	3·3	1·6	1·0	3·9	2·8	6·5	2·0	0·6	2·1	153	246	96
1 son	3·5	3·2	3·2	2·3	2·1	2·1	5·2	6·6	6·4	5·9	6·5	8·8	1·5	0·8	2·2	136	249	126
2 children																		
0 sons	3·8	3·8	3·7	1·8	1·8	1·6	8·6	8·0	5·4	10·9	6·9	20·3	4·7	6·2	11·6	128	125	93
1 son	3·4	3·3	3·2	1·4	1·2	1·1	19·0	26·5	31·3	11·5	23·0	28·9	1·6	1·8	4·7	252	380	244
2 sons	3·3	3·2	3·1	1·1	1·0	0·8	21·6	30·6	37·3	13·4	26·9	34·4	3·0	0·5	3·5	134	196	133
3 children																		
0 sons	4·1	4·0	4·1	1·6	1·6	1·4	14·3	8·3	12·0	8·6	8·5	10·2	48·6	53·9	47·1	70	60	56
1 son	3·9	3·8	3·8	0·9	0·8	0·6	28·6	37·7	50·7	16·8	27·5	40·5	6·5	7·7	9·2	185	295	179
2 or more sons	3·5	3·5	3·4	0·5	0·4	0·4	69·4	69·1	79·1	31·4	43·8	54·7	2·7	4·1	7·4	337	570	356
4 children																		
0 sons	4·1	4·1	4·2	0·9	1·2	1·7	41·9	30·3	19·3	12·9	15·2	30·8	54·8	66·7	51·9	31	33	17
1 son	4·2	4·1	4·0	0·5	0·5	0·5	53·8	56·9	54·3	19·7	44·0	43·1	37·1	42·9	41·0	132	183	121
2 or more sons	4·0	4·0	4·0	0·1	0·1	0·1	91·3	90·0	93·3	40·3	51·4	62·8	11·1	14·0	13·1	469	654	418
5 or more children																		
0 sons	4·5	4·0	3·7	0·7	0·6	0·7	60·6	57·7	58·2	21·2	34·6	35·8	78·8	92·3	91·1	33	26	22
1 son	4·2	4·2	4·2	0·2	0·3	0·3	77·6	75·6	76·8	27·1	33·3	42·9	85·0	76·8	67·4	107	135	75
2 or more sons	4·6	4·6	4·4	0·1	0·1	0·1	96·2	94·9	97·2	35·9	47·9	63·4	62·4	57·4	52·4	755	818	482
Total	4·0	3·8	3·8	0·8	0·8	0·7	57·3	55·6	61·1	24·4	34·1	44·0	25·6	21·4	21·7	3049	4145	2491

[a]Includes sterilisation.
Note: This is taken from Freedman *et al.*, 1972*a*, Table 11.

This finding suggests another reason why the more educated couples may prefer smaller families. Not only do they have high consumption aspirations and educational aspirations in general, as previously noted, but their desire for equally high educational attainment of their children may place an additional constraint on their resources.

This conjecture gains more salience from consideration of the relation of educational attainment to number of siblings. A number of studies in the United States and Great Britain have shown that children from large families tend to achieve less education than those from small families. This relationship does not appear to hold in Taiwan at present. Arnold (1972, pp. 135–48) shows that the number of siblings or brothers does not have any effect on the educational attainment of male respondents. If anything, there is some indication of less education for those with fewer siblings. He suggests that this may arise because in a country with many small businesses and farms, 'children from small families would be recruited for full-time work and could not attend school, whereas children from larger families could share the work part-time and attend school as well' (Arnold, 1972, p. 140). A related possibility was outlined earlier, in which older brothers in farm families helped finance the higher education of younger brothers. In traditional Chinese society, status was enhanced by having a son attain scholastic success, and extensive family and clan support for a promising student was not uncommon (Yang, 1945, pp. 50–1, 139–41). Though these traits do not fully explain why *average* educational attainment should be similar across sibship sizes or document that differential allocation of resources across sons does take place, they do point up the possibility of unequal production functions.[1]

A third feature of Taiwanese society which bears relevance to the question of child quality is the importance of the perception of economic benefits from children. Such benefits are not inconsistent with the formulation of child quality given at the outset of this section, but they often receive less emphasis than the subjective satisfactions from and the expenditures for children. Table 9.8 shows a fairly strong relation between ideal number of children and the level of assistance expected from married sons. Wives who expect both to live with their married sons and to get financial assistance from them, report a larger ideal family size than those who expect neither type of assistance. It should also be noted that 67 per cent of the wives expect both kinds of help when they are older and only 10 per cent expect neither. (These data are from Freedman *et al.*, 1972a, pp. 289–90.) This widespread sentiment would appear to be

---

[1] Data on the distribution of educational attainment of brothers would be helpful on this point but are not now available.

a major impediment in achieving substantially lower fertility levels. As Mueller (1972, p. 403) points out, policies such as the promotion of pension programmes and assisted housing for the elderly, which enhance economic self-reliance, might accelerate the lowering of family size norms.

TABLE 9.8   WIFE'S[a] IDEAL NUMBER OF CHILDREN, BY HER EXPECTATIONS FOR FUTURE HELP FROM SONS, TAIWAN: 1970

Wife's expectation of future help from married sons:	Wife's ideal number of children				Per cent	No. of cases
	1 or 2	3	4	5 or more		
Expects both to live with them and to get financial help from them	3·1	23·8	51·6	21·5	100·0	1564
Expects only one kind of help	5·4	33·1	49·6	11·9	100·0	520
Expects neither kind of help	15·1	44·3	34·3	6·3	100·0	239
Total	4·8	28·0	49·4	17·8	100·0	2323[a]

[a] These data were tabulated for those wives whose husbands also were interviewed in 1969 in the E.C.F. study (wives aged 20–42 in 1970).
Note: This is taken from Freedman *et al.*, 1972a, Table 12.

VI. CONCLUSION

This paper has reviewed some of the salient trends and patterns in Taiwanese fertility, with particular attention to their connection with economic behaviour and attitudes. We have attempted to show that the relation to such variables, which seems to emerge from a historical perspective, is also mirrored in cross-sectional studies conducted in the 1960s. Economic considerations and substantial control over fertility are clearly evident in the Taiwan of 1970. Most of the fertility decline to that date must be attributed to the growing ability to avert births in excess of the number desired.

Many of the investigators have gone beyond socio-economic statuses to study explicitly the role of various economic behaviours and attitudes. They find that consumption patterns and aspirations, educational aspirations and concerns about the costs of children are significantly related to fertility behaviour. This is in general agreement with the thrust of many current economic models. On the other hand, female labour-force participation, which plays a central role in many of these models, has not yet emerged as an important factor in Taiwan. In addition, awareness of the economic benefits from children, which receives less attention in many of the frameworks, plays a substantial role in fertility behaviour.

The focus in this paper on the relevance of economic variables is not meant to suggest that an economic framework necessarily provides the best approach for explaining fertility in a country like Taiwan. As Ryder (1973, p. 66) has stated, normative patterns play an important role, though they may be difficult to identify and measure. We have shown that one such pattern, the importance of sons in Taiwanese society, has strong effects on fertility behaviour. Other indicators of normative patterns not explored in this paper, are fertility differentials among ethnic groups (see Freedman *et al.*, 1972), and the persistence of relative fertility differentials of areas over time, which are not fully explainable by socio-economic variables.

Another possible indication of the importance of non-economic factors is in the rate of change of fertility attitudes and behaviour since 1970. As is well known, starting in April 1971, there was a rapid series of developments which brought about a closer relation between the United States and the government of mainland China, and between that government and many other countries. These developments are likely to have aroused concern in the Taiwanese population about their continued economic development and future status. A survey of wives under the age of 30 conducted in the fall of 1971 shows sharp declines in ideal family size in each educational category between 1970 and 1971 (these surveys were 18 months apart) and substantial increases in contraceptive use (for details, see Freedman *et al.*, 1971). In addition, the total fertility rate decreased 9 per cent in 1972, the largest proportionate decline on record (earliest available date is 1949). Rather than uncertainty, these changes may reflect, of course, the start of a new phase of Taiwan's demographic transition, in which the cumulative effects of the rapid social and economic development and an aggressive family-planning programme lead to significant reductions in family-size norms. Probably both factors were at work, and a longer time perspective and additional research will be needed to sort out their relative importance.

REFERENCES

J. E. Anderson, 'The Effect of Changing Educational Attainment Distributions on Fertility, 1966–1971', *Taiwan Population Studies Working Paper*, mimeograph, Population Studies Center, Univ. of Michigan, 1973.

F. S. Arnold, *A Model Relating Education to Fertility in Taiwan*, unpub. Ph.D. dissertation, Department of Economics, Univ. of Michigan, 1972.

G. W. Barclay, *Colonial Development and Population in Taiwan* (Princeton Univ. Press, 1954).

266   *The Decline of Fertility in the Third World*

A. J. Coale, 'The Decline of Fertility in Europe from the French Revolution to World War II', *Fertility and Family Planning*, ed. S. Behrman, L. Corsa, Jr and R. Freedman (Ann Arbor: Univ. of Michigan Press, 1969) pp. 3–24.

K. Davis, 'The Theory of Change and Response in Modern Demographic History', *Population Index*, 29, 4 (1963) 345–66.

R. A. Easterlin, 'The Modernization of Family Reproductive Behavior', paper prepared for U.N. Symposium on Population and the Family (August 1973).

J. T. Fawcett, *Psychology and Population: Behavioral Research Issues in Fertility and Family Planning* (New York: The Population Council, 1970).

D. S. Freedman, 'The Role of the Consumption of Modern Durables in Economic Development', *Economic Development and Cultural Change*, 19, 1 (1970) 25–48.

—— 'The Relationship of Family Planning to Savings and Consumption in Taiwan', *Demography*, 9, 3 (1972) 499–505.

R. Freedman, 'Applications of the Behavioral Sciences to Family Planning Programs', *Studies in Family Planning*, 23 (Oct 1967) 5–9.

—— and J. Y. Takeshita, *Family Planning in Taiwan* (Princeton Univ. Press, 1969).

——, L. C. Coombs and M.-C. Chang, 'Trends in Family Size Preferences and Practice of Family Planning: Taiwan, 1965–1970', *Studies in Family Planning*, 3, 12 (1972a) 281–308.

——, A. I. Hermalin and T. H. Sun, 'Fertility Trends in Taiwan: 1961–1970', *Population Index*, 38, 2 (1972b) 141–66.

A. I. Hermalin, 'Taiwan: Appraising the Effect of A Family Planning Program Through An Areal Analysis', *Taiwan Population Studies Working Paper*, no. 14, mimeograph, Population Studies Center, Univ. of Michigan, 1971.

P. K. C. Liu, 'Economic Development and Population in Taiwan Since 1895: An Overview', *Population Papers*, no. 1, Institute of Economics, Academica Sinica, Taipei (June 1972).

E. Mueller, 'Economic Motives for Family Limitation', *Population Studies*, 27, 3 (1972) 383–403.

—— 'The Impact of Agricultural Change on Demographic Development in the Third World', *Demographic Growth and Development in the Third World* (to be published by IUSSP).

——, R. Cohn and S. Reineck, 'Female Labor Force Participation and Fertility in Taipei', unpub. working manuscript, n.d.

N. B. Ryder, 'Comment', *Journal of Political Economy*, LXXXI, no. 2, pt. II (1973) 65–9.

—— and C. F. Westoff, *Reproduction in the United States 1965* (Princeton Univ. Press, 1971).

T. P. Schultz, 'Explanation of Birth Rate Changes Over Space and Time: A Study of Taiwan', *Journal of Political Economy*, LXXXI, no. 2, pt. II (1973) 238–74.

T. W. Schultz (ed.), 'New Economic Approaches to Fertility', proceedings of conference 8–9 June 1972, *Journal of Political Economy*, LXXXI, no. 2, pt. II.

A. Speare, Jr, *The Determinants of Rural to Urban Migration in Taiwan*, unpub. Ph.D. dissertation (Ann Arbor: Univ. of Michigan, 1969).

——, M. C. Speare and H.-S. Lin, 'Urbanization, Non-Familial Work, and Fertility in Taiwan', paper prepared for the Population Association of America annual meeting (Apr 1972).

U.S. Bureau of the Census, 'Birth Expectations and Fertility: June 1972', *Current Population Reports*, ser. P-20 (248).

R. J. Willis, 'A New Approach to the Economic Theory of Fertility Behavior', *Journal of Political Economy*, LXXXI, no. 2, pt. II (1973) 14–64.

M. C. Yang, *A Chinese Village: Taitou, Shantung Province* (New York: Columbia Univ. Press, 1945).

Discussion of the Paper by
Professor Hermalin

Dr Lesthaeghe introduced the paper and said that, in constructing a theory on marital fertility, there seemed to be two types of approach, basically describing the poles of a continuum. The first was what we would call a minimum theory, where only a small fraction of the variance of the dependent variable was explained, but where this was done on the basis of a sophisticated model explicitly stating the nature of the relationships. The second was a 'less minimal' approach. This included many more relevant variables and explained more of the variance but at the cost of considerably less sophistication as far as the understanding of the underlying mechanisms were concerned.

Professor Hermalin's paper lay much closer to the second pole than to the first. He was aware of the complex nature of the phenomenon of fertility, and was not trapped in a too-narrow framework, typical of the type of analysis described as 'minimum theory'. The author clearly felt that he should present a summary report of the findings of other authors and of himself. Hence, the paper was essentially a review of the current state of the art. Consequently, a technical discussion focusing on methodological aspects was not in order.

However, it was fortunate that Professor Hermalin's paper gave such a cohesive and clear literary discussion, since this allowed one to see the forest rather than the individual trees. In this more general context, it was striking that several demographic, social and economic changes now observed in Taiwan were occurring according to a scenario that resembled European experiences in more than one aspect. First, it seemed that the modernisation of nuptiality and marital fertility in Taiwan occurred simultaneously. This was equally the case in several Western European areas. There, those who broke away from the Malthusian marriage-patterns also tended to be more modern in their fertility behaviour.

Second, a high female participation in the labour force in Taiwan was not *ipso facto* an incentive to fertility reduction, as long as the majority of these women were employed in agriculture and/or cottage industries. The same observation was also made in nineteenth century Europe.

Third, the section of the population in Taiwan that started relatively late to control its fertility was now progressing at a considerably higher tempo than earlier starters. This led to a drastic reduction in the variance of the fertility variables. The process was found equally in many European settings, where those populations with a late start in the decline in marital fertility tended to engineer a substantial decline in a much shorter period.

Dr Lesthaeghe said these similarities indicated that the presumed gap between the fertility transition in Western Europe a century ago, and the present changes in several Asian countries, was not as wide as was often believed. Several findings from historical research in Western Europe might be retested in current 'laboratory' situations, among which Taiwan had been the most prominent.

Professor Coale said that he would like to come to his own defence, since his works had been quoted in the paper. He had found a correlation between the proportion in Russia of the population married and distance from the Baltic. An explanation was that in the late nineteenth century there were changes in nuptiality taking place in Russia and the 1897 censuses caught the population at a time when it could reflect these differences.

Professor Åkerman pointed out that if one compared northern Europe and Taiwan, it must be possible for a historically trained person to explain more than had been explained so far. Deep studies could add to what demographers, economists and sociologists had done so far. He thought there was more data from the late seventeenth century in Scandinavia than there was today for Taiwan.

This was a big challenge because we did not know much, for example, on literacy, and he thought this was a much more interesting topic than had been suggested. One aspect of the modernisation process of great interest was whether increasing literacy made the behaviour pattern change. In Sweden by around the middle of the seventeenth century, most people could read. The fertility pattern was unchanged, but there was a fall in child mortality in the eighteenth century, and in some places this had occurred as early as 1740. So, he thought one should be looking for links between what had happened in Western Europe, Taiwan, Asia in general or Latin America. On what Professor Coale had said, it would be interesting to see the diffusion pattern of mass emigration compared to the same pattern of fertility decline.

Dr Lesthaeghe defined his variable called 'literacy'. It indicated the percentage of the population aged over fifteen that was able to read and write. He agreed that one might obtain different results if one could specify educational level rather than making the simple dichotomy: literacy versus illiteracy. For Switzerland, Mrs F. van de Walle had found a non-negligible correlation between marital fertility and the proportion of the population that had gone further than primary education. Unfortunately, such detailed data on educational levels were not available for Belgium for the period studied.

Professor Schultz said that he also had looked at Taiwan, and tried to analyse the relationship between female participation in the labour force and fertility. Even if one looked at narrower sectors, for example, the non-agricultural labour force, there was still no clear relation between the role of women in the labour force and the birth rate. Household participation was high in *all* sectors.

In Thailand, if one separated the agricultural and non-agricultural sectors, one then found that participation in non-agricultural activities was inversely related to fertility. In each country, one had to define one's sectors very carefully for the concept of labour-force participation to be inversely related to fertility, as in high-income countries.

Professor Hermalin had described the choice framework as defective because it neglected sex preference among parents. Professor Schultz said that the strong preference for sons was not unique to Taiwan. This deserved study in order to distinguish between the Malthusian notion of reproduction and that which stressed behavioural choice. However, sex preference need not always be a significant factor for aggregate behaviour.

He noted the extraordinarily high educational expectations that parents had for their offspring in Taiwan. This was interesting, but did not conflict with the theory of choice.

Professor Parikh was a little at a loss. Professor Schultz had claimed that cross-section data substantiated his hypothesis. Professor Ben Porath said that in Israel the dynamics of modernisation were perhaps more important than education. Professor Hermalin also suggested this. Where were we left? If we wanted to reduce fertility, did we press for the education of women, or for modernisation?

Professor Guitton wanted to make a general remark. There had been a great deal of discussion on the opposition between rational economic variables (choice) that were perfectly formed and necessary to legitimise the theory. Against this, there were also exogenous variables that were psychological or social, and outside the system. This implied that they were different things; choice, and the absence of choice, as Professor Coale had put it in an earlier discussion. We were constantly pulled between the rational and the irrational. Our difficulties stemmed from this insistence on the dichotomy.

What was the 'quality' of a child? Could it be measured? There was also a distinction between education and instruction. The French minister of education had tried to introduce sex education into schools and had distinguished between education and instruction. Where information was given, that was instruction; education was something quite different. We were concerned, perhaps, with doctrinal or religious preferences. He would like to pose the question: did one speak of education or instruction over contraception? Was it a question of literacy as such, added to education?

When it was suggested that, as in monetary terms, one could talk about the desired demand for children, or the ideal size of the family, one was leaving to parents decisions about the correct number of children. Was this a macro- or micro-economic decision? Was it macro-economic, with the parents looking at all factors? Or was it a narrow decision? Whatever it was, he doubted whether one could say that anyone knew how many children they wanted. If one had an illiterate woman, what were the rational elements of choice? The idea of an optimum was not a valid notion. He simply did not understand the idea of children being wanted by the wife alone. And was there no room for stochastic variables, for risk, for uncertainty; for a decision made one way, and regretted ten or fifteen years later?

Professor Guitton said he was simply expressing a worry, though it would, perhaps, be resolved during the next few days.

Professor Coale, replying to Professor Schultz, said it seemed to him that preference about the sex of children *did* make a difference to the size of the family. If one had a family where all the conceptions were intended, and if one wanted two boys, this was likely to give one four children. If one simply wanted two children, then the family would be only half as big. Sex preference *did* help to form tastes. It was an example of the cultural determination of tastes. It would affect the reaction to a fall in infant mortality, etc.

Professor Létinier recalled that in an earlier discussion he had been critical about the application of the theory to the number of children born in less-developed countries. Professor Guitton now said there was no choice in developed countries. He did not think that this was true. One did have choice, in the sense of deciding not to have children. He thought there was some meaning to the idea of the optimum family, though the husband and wife would have to agree about it, though the facts were imprecise, and there was a link between such decisions and economic and other factors. All one needed was to say there was a link between several variables and fertility. One then had a basis for policy conclusions.

Professor Guitton replied that he had not said there was no choice but that a theory of choice must also allow for non-rational elements. He did not see a dichotomy between rational choice and absence of choice, but a convergence of the two.

Professor Bauchet also wondered why Professor Coale thought sex preference important. He could not see how it altered the demographic attitude of the population. Was the balance between the sexes really significantly different in different populations?

Professor Coale thought that two propositions were being confused. Given most hypotheses, sex preference made no difference to the sex composition of the population. But if the number of male offspring was important, then the size of the family would be altered.

Professor Schultz explained that the income-elasticity of demand for children and the strength of sex-compositional preferences for children were important in determining the size of particular families. He agreed that this was an interesting issue, but mainly at the micro-economic level; he was not yet clear how significant a factor it was at the macro-economic level.

Professor Ben Porath was not sure how far he disagreed with what had been said. If there were no difference in the parameter determining the sex ratio in the population, and all the variations in sex ratio were random, then preferences could not alter the aggregate ratio in the total population. As for sex parameters and their effects on the size and sex composition of the population, there was not much evidence that they varied significantly.

Professor Coale said that there was one empirical finding on this. Questions had been asked in a study in the U.S.A. in the 1970s. When aggregated, these showed that people wanted 1·06 boys for every girl. This was the ratio that already prevailed. Why that should be was a mystery. Moreover, if one asked what ratio of boys and girls people wanted if they had two, three, etc. children, one found that of those wanting two children, 90 per cent wanted a boy and a girl, whereas the actual ratio was about 50–50.

Professor Ben Porath said he had found that if a family already had two children of the same sex, then 61 per cent wanted a third, whereas where there was already a boy and a girl in the family, only 57 per cent did. (This was in a joint paper with Finis Welch.)

Professor Hicks recalled that his own work had had a good deal to do with the theory of choice. He had therefore spent much of the session wondering whether that theory could be applied to some similar problem to that of the size of family. The only example he could think of was contributions to religious organisations. He wondered how much one would learn in that case from applying income-elasticities, etc. His guess was that one would learn only a little. Variables which operated in other ways would be important, and he thought that the situation there was the same as in the case now being considered.

Professor Åkerman pointed out that in the papers both by Professor Hermalin and Professor Ben Porath, one found a concept of 'modernisation'. Using this old concept in a new way, we could avoid methodological confusion. Up to now, we had put too much emphasis on economic variables. These were important, but they had to be combined with psychological and socio-psychological indicators into a more complex concept of change. For example, historians found no correlation between the onset of the demographic transition and industrialisation. The whole process of transition seemed to have started a hundred years before industrial take-off in certain countries. We therefore also had to focus our interest on the highly dynamic agricultural sector of these countries.

Professor Hermalin replied to the debate. As a sociologist, he had been afraid of alienating both economists and sociologists in the conference. That he had not done so gave him some relief.

To Professor Åkerman, he said that he also had been struck by the similarities between historical work and what was happening in Taiwan. He agreed that more data and analysis was needed, but what there was should be quickly followed up. However, the work in Taiwan emphasised that demographic transition could be studied in the West only through documents, while one could make more intensive, contemporary studies in Taiwan. Although what was happening in Taiwan might seem similar to what was happening in older countries, the pattern in Hong Kong was different. There, there were still some puzzles to solve. Professor Hermalin said he had not written the paper in order to apply the choice model, or any other. However, a lot of the variables met with in Taiwan were the same as in the choice model, so that it seemed interesting to go beyond the status variables.

There were some problems in deciding the kind of theory that was relevant. One should not criticise the conceptual framework of the choice model simply because one did not like it. At the moment, there were several competing models, and one needed to see which gave the best results. At least the choice theory was there on the table, and that was healthy. The discussion had illuminated aggregate and individual effects. However, this was a household model, and sex preference might have more effect than Professor Ben Porath thought.

There was a problem of strategy. If one observed a difference in fertility related to religion or language, this difference might simply be a cover for our ignorance. It was often just a name for some other process. If the formulation overlooked the important control variables, that was serious.

To Professor Schultz, Professor Hermalin said that he agreed that the paper by Eva Müller supported what Professor Schultz had said about the fact that dividing up the female labour force by sectors made no difference. This central variable in many studies was not important in Taiwan. He said that he did not say that educational aspects contradicted the choice model.

But he had found that some of the simplifications in the model did not hold in Taiwan. Perhaps males were given more education, or perhaps the family decided in advance which children it would support strongly in order to help the whole family. If so, this would seriously affect the choice model.

On policy issues, the family-planning movement had enabled the less-educated to catch up in contraceptive methods, and this had led to a rapid decline in differences in the use of contraceptives. The programme probably did reduce the market cost of fertility regulation, and gave contraceptive knowledge that probably speeded up the process of fertility decline.

Professor Hermalin replied to Professor Guitton that he did not come down on the side either of rationality or non-rationality. He agreed that both elements were there, if by non-rational one meant normative considerations. Certainly, it was not true that there was no choice in underdeveloped countries. In Taiwan, the correlation between demographic and socio-economic data collected in the period before 1940, and what had happened in the 1950s and especially the 1960s, pointed to increasing rationalisation of the fertility process. Professor Hermalin agreed that how to separate education from instruction was important. He wondered whether a child with a middle-class background was more successful because its family helped it more. This was an important question, to which there was no explicit answer, but he had cited the studies by Arnold which tried to tease out the implications.

As for what Professor Guitton had said about desired family size, he could see why Professor Guitton was unhappy; indeed, no one was happy with our ability to measure such concepts. The data reported in the paper on desired family size were obtained from women at different ages and did not represent a longitudinal study. A long-term follow-up study in the U.S.A., covering twenty years, showed that preferences about family size expressed at marriage did not correlate well with eventual fertility. On the other hand, though the concepts were difficult to make operational, this did not mean that the data simply represented meaningless responses. In the Taiwan studies, what women said about desired family size and about wanting more children showed a strong relationship with their behaviour over the next three years.

10 A Comparative Study of Population and Agricultural Change in Some Countries of the ECAFE Region*

N. V. Sovani

GOKHALE INSTITUTE OF POLITICS AND ECONOMICS, POONA

I. INTRODUCTORY

In countries where in recent decades populations have been increasing rapidly and where the extent and rate of industrialisation have not been notable, the interrelations between population change and agricultural change assume enormous importance. Is there, in such countries, any systematic association between changes in demographic variables such as fertility, mortality (or the resulting natural rate of population change) and migration on the one hand and changes in total and per capita agricultural output on the other? Beyond this, can the causal relations, if any, between these be identified? These crucial questions were the focus of the comparative study of population and agricultural change carried out in three countries of Asia – Japan, India and Sri Lanka – by the Population Division of ECAFE. The study was with reference to subnational area units, such as districts or prefectures, in order to bring in the variegated patterns of change in this field that were usually smothered in national aggregates. In Japan the 46 prefectures were studied for the period 1900–40. In India only two provinces were covered; 12 districts in the Punjab were studied over the period 1911–71 and 13 in Orissa during 1951–71. The 22 districts of Sri Lanka were studied over the period 1946–71. Taiwan, not included in the ECAFE study, is included here. As the presentation of data occupies a large part of the available space I shall allow the data to speak for itself regarding the pattern of changes in population and

---

* This paper is mainly based on a study carried out at the Population Division of ECAFE during 1970–3. The data and analyses regarding Japan, India and Sri Lanka presented in this paper are from the report of this study. Until the report has been released to the public by the ECAFE, the data and the analyses should be regarded as confidential and should not be quoted.

agriculture and concentrate on their interrelationships in the relevant periods in these countries before attempting to bring the findings together.

II. JAPAN

Table 10.1 presents the natural rate of population change and the rate of net migration for each prefecture in Japan during 1900–40. Table 10.2 gives an index of agricultural production in each prefecture for selected years during 1890–1940. Table 10.3 presents the per capita income relatives in each prefecture for selected years during 1905–40.

In the context of the type of countries mentioned at the beginning of the paper Japan is not a representative case. Even at the beginning of the period under study industrialisation was well underway, with only half the national income arising in agriculture and the proportion of labour force engaged in agriculture declining to 58 per cent from 75 per cent in 1880. Industrial development continued to be rapid in the following period and it dominated population movements during the period rather than agriculture (which was also expanding). Bearing this in mind, the interrelations between demographic and economic data presented in the three tables showed consistent patterns throughout the period.

Per capita income relatives (total goods production) were positively correlated[1] with the degree of industrialisation in the prefectures and negatively with the proportion of agricultural production in the total goods production. The rank correlations between prefectural per capita income relatives, the degree of industrialisation in the prefectures and the rate of increase of agricultural production in the prefectures on the one hand, and the natural rate of increase of population in the prefectures were statistically not significant throughout the period. And yet the declines in fertility which began in all prefectures around 1925 were correlated positively with the degree of industrialisation in them. The absence of correlation between the degree of industrialisation and the natural rate of population increase in the prefectures is explained by the fact that changes in mortality were not correlated with industrialisation.

Inter-prefectural migration was more intimately related to industrialisation than to changes in agriculture. The rate of increase of agricultural production in the prefectures was not significantly correlated with inter-prefectural migrations throughout the period. The rank correlations between per capita income relatives and migration were positive and significant throughout.

[1] 'Correlation' everywhere in this paper stands for 'rank correlation'.

Name of prefecture	1900–1905		1905–1910		1910–1915		1915–1920		1920–1925		1925–1930		1930–1935		1935–1940	
	N	M	N	M	N	M	N	M	N	M	N	M	N	M	N	M
Hokkaido	18·1	38·0	21·4	41·9	22·7	20·1	19·7	39·2	23·9	-9·3	22·1	3·9	20·7	-1·7	17·1	-3·7
Aomori	24·5	-2·9	18·3	-3·4	19·5	-6·8	15·7	-18·9	18·6	-4·5	20·1	-5·4	20·5	-3·4	15·7	-11·1
Iwate	20·2	-5·4	13·2	-6·4	15·2	6·0	11·5	-14·0	17·2	-3·4	18·7	-3·0	17·7	-4·5	15·4	-7·4
Miyagi	27·5	-9·3	14·0	-8·1	17·2	4·0	14·3	-10·0	19·1	-2·0	20·0	-1·9	19·5	-4·7	16·8	-12·0
Akita	20·5	-2·0	15·0	-3·1	15·6	-5·2	13·2	-22·0	17·7	-8·5	19·6	-8·9	19·4	-10·6	15·3	-14·2
Yamagata	19·2	-12·7	13·9	-7·1	15·4	-0·2	12·2	-13·8	17·1	-5·8	17·4	-8·1	16·3	-10·9	14·0	-14·7
Fukushima	18·9	-2·7	13·1	-5·0	15·2	-0·8	12·4	-2·1	18·4	-5·3	19·1	-8·6	17·9	-8·4	15·3	-10·3
Ibaraki	17·5	-2·2	11·1	-2·1	13·6	-0·8	12·7	-7·0	15·6	-4·9	16·7	-4·8	15·8	-7·0	13·1	-4·4
Tochigi	19·4	1·2	13·9	-1·3	16·7	-1·6	11·4	-10·7	19·7	-9·0	19·2	-9·0	17·5	-7·8	14·3	-12·6
Gumma	13·7	-0·8	13·2	-1·4	15·5	3·1	14·7	-5·9	16·3	-2·5	16·5	-4·7	15·7	-6·8	13·3	-5·2
Saitama	16·8	-4·6	11·6	-5·5	14·7	-0·6	11·6	-14·2	14·5	-2·2	14·6	-5·7	13·7	-4·8	11·8	-2·1
Chiba	13·9	-4·0	9·3	-4·4	11·5	-3·4	8·9	-16·7	10·2	-0·8	12·5	-2·9	12·9	-2·9	10·3	-5·5
Tokyo	10·2	31·6	7·0	30·5	10·2	-2·6	10·5	50·3	13·4	32·3	17·2	26·2	16·5	21·2	14·0	18·3
Kanagawa	14·1	1·2	14·5	12·3	13·2	-5·6	10·1	15·8	13·5	4·3	17·7	17·9	16·3	12·5	14·4	24·5
Niigata	16·1	-8·3	12·9	-9·2	14·9	1·0	9·5	-25·4	13·8	-5·8	14·8	-6·9	14·4	-9·5	12·7	-7·1
Toyama	18·0	-15·8	14·1	-10·6	16·6	-2·2	7·0	-28·2	11·9	-5·6	12·4	-5·8	10·7	-7·7	7·5	-3·8
Ishikawa	13·8	-9·9	11·8	-9·9	13·1	-4·0	7·0	-17·8	7·7	-6·8	7·6	-6·9	6·4	-5·0	3·3	-7·7
Fukui	14·9	-9·5	9·7	-7·1	12·3	0	6·8	-21·2	10·0	-10·1	9·1	-3·3	7·5	0·5	5·8	-7·3
Yamanashi	18·8	-2·6	12·6	-2·3	15·1	-1·6	13·0	-18·6	16·6	-9·0	17·0	-6·7	16·9	-11·0	15·0	-9·8
Nagano	13·4	-2·0	11·0	-3·3	13·5	2·8	10·4	-0·3	14·6	-4·9	15·5	-4·9	14·1	-14·7	11·7	-14·9
Gifu	16·5	-7·2	11·6	-1·1	15·4	3·4	12·6	-14·8	14·8	-3·2	15·0	-7·6	13·5	-6·5	11·6	-6·0
Shizuoka	17·9	-1·4	14·4	-2·8	17·1	6·9	14·4	-8·3	18·1	-1·9	18·6	-3·8	17·1	-1·9	13·5	-6·4
Aichi	13·2	1·6	16·8	2·7	15·8	5·0	9·0	-5·7	13·9	8·6	15·1	6·6	14·9	8·0	13·6	8·3
Mie	15·2	-4·6	11·1	-6·5	13·8	-3·4	7·3	-14·1	12·9	5·1	14·0	-5·3	11·8	-9·6	9·0	-6·1
Shiga	11·3	-9·6	8·9	-0·3	12·0	-3·2	4·4	-14·8	9·4	-5·8	10·4	-2·2	8·8	-4·1	6·8	-10·0
Kyoto	12·6	5·5	8·0	8·6	10·0	14·1	4·4	-2·7	9·7	10·3	10·7	11·1	10·8	9·7	9·0	-4·1

TABLE 10.1 (cont.)

Name of prefecture	1900–1905 N	1900–1905 M	1905–1910 N	1905–1910 M	1910–1915 N	1910–1915 M	1915–1920 N	1915–1920 M	1920–1925 N	1920–1925 M	1925–1930 N	1925–1930 M	1930–1935 N	1930–1935 M	1935–1940 N	1935–1940 M
Osaka	7.4	20.6	6.3	25.9	8.4	11.2	3.4	24.4	11.9	28.3	13.7	20.7	13.7	32.8	12.7	14.7
Hyogo	11.7	1.2	10.9	3.4	12.8	4.3	7.4	10.1	13.1	2.1	13.2	3.2	12.5	9.3	10.2	11.7
Nara	13.3	-7.3	13.0	-10.5	15.6	-1.1	9.7	-19.2	13.1	-5.5	12.1	-8.0	10.0	-2.1	7.1	-7.4
Wakayama	12.1	-5.6	12.0	-6.1	14.4	5.5	9.4	-17.6	13.7	-2.8	13.5	-2.6	11.9	-3.6	8.8	-8.4
Tottori	9.7	-5.1	9.5	-7.8	11.8	6.3	10.5	-15.2	13.0	-4.9	13.5	-5.1	10.6	-16.9	7.7	-11.3
Shimane	6.3	-3.7	6.3	-4.9	8.6	1.9	5.0	-17.6	8.5	-5.8	7.9	-3.9	8.5	-7.6	6.1	-8.8
Okayama	8.8	-1.8	8.1	-3.1	10.3	1.5	6.3	-12.9	9.5	-5.9	10.0	-3.5	9.9	-3.4	6.6	-7.9
Hiroshima	10.2	-0.3	9.8	0.3	12.2	0.2	8.2	-22.7	12.1	-2.2	12.4	-3.8	11.6	0.9	8.2	-1.2
Yamaguchi	8.1	-1.9	7.3	-2.2	9.5	1.8	6.3	-13.7	10.4	1.1	10.5	-2.8	10.7	-0.7	6.4	10.6
Tokushima	11.7	-7.5	9.8	-6.8	11.0	-2.1	7.6	-25.8	11.1	-5.9	12.8	-6.6	11.7	-9.9	9.2	-13.5
Kagawa	8.8	-8.4	11.2	-6.9	14.9	-1.4	12.5	-32.1	13.5	-7.2	13.4	-5.9	12.5	-10.0	8.7	-15.1
Ehima	11.8	-6.4	11.6	-7.4	13.5	3.2	9.3	-23.8	13.9	-5.0	14.5	-7.0	13.7	-11.1	11.1	-10.1
Kochi	10.4	-3.6	9.6	-2.7	10.6	4.6	7.6	-17.2	11.7	-5.9	11.7	-2.8	10.4	-11.8	6.8	-9.1
Fukuoka	13.9	4.7	10.6	6.0	12.3	2.8	7.9	24.3	15.2	-0.9	14.5	7.1	14.9	5.2	12.4	14.2
Saga	13.3	-6.0	13.1	-8.9	14.3	-4.3	10.7	-15.2	14.2	-10.0	13.5	-11.9	13.2	-15.0	10.5	-6.6
Nagasaki	8.8	11.4	9.5	7.2	10.8	-8.5	9.6	-2.6	15.8	-8.5	15.3	-2.3	14.9	-3.8	12.5	-0.7
Kumamoto	9.3	-2.8	9.2	-3.7	10.0	4.9	9.0	-20.8	13.9	-2.2	14.7	-5.0	14.1	-8.7	10.8	-13.8
Oita	8.8	-4.0	8.4	-3.4	10.8	1.0	7.5	-20.1	12.5	0.6	12.4	-6.0	11.4	-5.4	8.6	-11.2
Miyazaki	11.7	3.6	11.8	3.2	14.1	9.4	12.1	1.0	18.0	-3.2	18.6	2.3	18.6	-0.9	14.7	-10.9
Kagoshima	12.6	1.7	13.2	0.6	14.2	7.1	13.0	-13.9	18.3	-7.3	15.8	-4.7	17.9	-11.4	13.3	-13.6
Okinawa	5.4	3.0	6.5	3.7	7.5	7.9	6.5	2.6	17.6	-3.4	17.0	-2.2	16.9	-4.1	14.2	-4.6
Total	11.7		11.1		13.3		9.9		14.5		15.2		14.6		12.0	

N = Natural rate of population change per 1000.

M = Net migration rate.

Source: Derived from *Jinko Tokai Soran* (Demographic Statistics), Institute of Population Problems, Tokyo, 1943.

TABLE 10.2   INDEX OF AGRICULTURAL PRODUCTION IN THE
PREFECTURES OF JAPAN FOR SELECTED YEARS DURING 1890–1940
(1930 = 100)

Prefecture	1890	1905	1920	1930	1935	1940
Hokkaido	4·20	30·12	53·38	100·00	84·02	148·49
Aomori	36·06	42·01	62·76	100·00	69·59	161·86
Iwate	44·32	51·09	80·95	100·00	86·80	117·57
Miyagi	45·05.	43·12	73·67	100·00	81·42	130·52
Akita	31·22	44·48	69·77	100·00	80·37	92·70
Yamagata	42·14	59·13	79·75	100·00	102·37	121·97
Fukushima	61·05	62·97	75·55	100·00	94·58	152·50
Ibaraki	47·37	62·12	89·03	100·00	103·66	146·38
Tochigi	43·01	53·54	78·05	100·00	97·23	131·62
Gumma	58·35	63·41	82·82	100·00	105·10	178·33
Saitama	58·59	69·58	81·23	100·00	110·41	154·56
Chiba	49·43	64·97	80·47	100·00	110·54	132·01
Tokyo	29·15	89·59	106·71	100·00	118·30	193·39
Kanagawa	75·45	67·09	83·10	100·00	98·67	149·93
Niigata	48·57	62·25	74·19	100·00	119·92	135·90
Toyama	55·96	68·32	82·21	100·00	109·36	116·55
Ishikawa	56·91	67·54	82·37	100·00	115·36	115·38
Fukui	52·06	73·35	81·80	100·00	115·20	118·88
Yamanashi	60·51	80·45	83·82	100·00	116·16	207·81
Nagano	69·92	92·00	103·87	100·00	113·73	163·50
Gifu	50·00	61·66	80·12	100·00	106·33	128·47
Shizuoka	39·86	59·54	71·40	100·00	108·30	164·87
Aichi	37·87	60·51	72·37	100·00	110·09	129·46
Mie	48·70	59·47	73·17	100·00	105·03	122·27
Shiga	61·47	72·71	82·18	100·00	105·71	110·57
Kyoto	53·84	69·37	81·03	100·00	103·34	113·68
Osaka	59·10	66·16	76·10	100·00	88·72	91·18
Hyogo	45·52	72·55	76·51	100·00	103·44	111·29
Nara	48·10	62·29	78·09	100·00	101·86	103·45
Wakayama	40·71	59·32	71·93	100·00	100·63	128·41
Tottori	43·43	61·52	79·11	100·00	104·65	125·96
Shimane	43·90	69·84	86·59	100·00	104·32	119·23
Okayama	43·96	67·24	81·36	100·00	115·77	128·88
Hiroshima	45·69	66·10	79·46	100·00	109·29	128·41
Yamaguchi	58·16	77·62	81·41	100·00	103·51	118·20
Tokushima	46·59	70·59	78·44	100·00	106·62	136·15
Kagawa	35·51	56·15	71·04	100·00	109·21	129·76
Ehime	42·28	61·35	84·26	100·00	110·59	144·70
Kochi	45·15	75·30	81·24	100·00	97·65	125·13
Fukuoka	41·57	64·83	77·68	100·00	104·17	112·15
Saga	43·90	63·84	75·59	100·00	116·19	114·19
Nagasaki	52·75	67·43	85·34	100·00	119·02	136·15
Kumamoto	53·54	72·35	89·37	100·00	115·74	133·04
Oita	42·25	67·24	76·75	100·00	107·67	119·12
Miyazaki	32·35	53·47	73·23	100·00	97·94	119·27
Kagoshima	36·47	67·31	75·22	100·00	110·91	117·97
Japan	45·52	62·81	78·05	100·00	103·97	131·99

Note: Agricultural production estimates at current prices from Dr Thomas Cleaver's 'Regional Income Differentials in Japanese Economic Growth', unpublished Ph.D. dissertation (Harvard University, 1971). These have been deflated for calculating the index by price deflators for the relevant years developed in K. Okhawa *et al.*, *Growth Rate of Japanese Economy Since 1878*, Economic Research Series I, Institute of Economic Research, Hitotsubashi University (Tokyo, 1957) p. 130. As the production estimates are averages for three years centred at the particular year in the table, the price deflators have also been averaged over the relevant three years.

TABLE 10.3 PER CAPITA INCOME RELATIVES FOR PREFECTURES IN JAPAN
IN SELECTED YEARS DURING 1890–1940

Prefecture	1890	1905	1920	1930	1935	1940
Hokkaido	256·74	104·52	106·11	107·31	101·05	100·86
Aomori	72·76	43·70	51·56	56·75	39·70	58·30
Iwate	89·96	58·31	69·25	65·97	64·08	65·72
Miyagi	93·10	62·83	66·80	61·32	49·03	49·66
Akita	84·59	77·77	89·31	79·43	68·52	61·68
Yamagata	123·38	67·76	68·26	60·08	55·13	50·75
Fukushima	114·61	68·75	64·07	55·27	55·86	62·61
Ibaragi	120·80	79·21	80·30	69·59	79·43	83·83
Tochigi	133·93	121·69	102·60	90·88	79·14	70·17
Gumma	127·47	89·81	79·64	75·98	71·86	88·33
Saitama	98·72	79·49	67·20	66·52	67·13	78·03
Chiba	102·31	96·70	81·35	76·59	71·23	63·20
Tokyo	53·28	143·08	131·88	117·90	107·01	144·74
Kanagawa	95·28	115·16	169·96	165·81	178·66	211·13
Niigata	67·00	60·07	66·24	67·53	75·95	70·73
Toyama	106·04	59·83	70·13	82·05	96·31	97·62
Ishikawa	75·85	81·39	87·95	92·83	95·71	79·21
Fukui	88·17	124·81	95·69	105·89	106·69	78·94
Yamanashi	96·69	77·65	62·72	57·09	55·84	65·97
Nagano	112·87	87·15	81·70	75·30	64·86	68·87
Gifu	83·10	72·85	68·74	77·29	83·15	73·80
Shizuoka	83·96	71·95	89·71	95·63	94·09	93·89
Aichi	85·47	112·93	117·24	139·08	138·25	142·57
Mie	104·49	89·95	96·93	93·76	98·19	83·85
Shiga	111·76	96·44	75·42	94·64	107·82	73·20
Kyoto	143·72	118·69	97·53	100·25	83·75	76·98
Osaka	279·07	249·50	202·77	210·18	184·58	157·09
Hyogo	121·26	254·10	215·32	184·84	159·20	148·46
Nara	129·17	74·07	79·07	68·49	72·87	63·63
Wakayama	91·94	107·09	90·02	102·69	94·83	81·07
Tottori	82·70	66·81	64·87	63·32	60·22	58·23
Shimane	73·36	53·12	58·53	65·37	65·99	61·21
Okayama	96·20	104·86	91·66	92·34	98·40	85·27
Hiroshima	82·13	64·49	83·11	70·10	66·87	72·10
Yamagushi	80·70	70·98	81·23	97·08	109·68	103·20
Tokushima	69·16	64·42	62·31	65·69	66·76	61·76
Kagawa	62·18	67·14	70·70	78·20	87·17	65·74
Ehime	61·82	74·86	80·19	84·84	99·88	91·38
Kochi	80·44	81·87	68·14	66·55	59·27	63·80
Fukuoka	88·13	148·97	136·98	122·59	192·70	146·54
Saga	89·33	98·91	101·20	80·15	80·08	64·32
Nagasaki	93·52	81·30	84·87	89·85	71·89	66·91
Kumamoto	89·30	74·30	77·32	62·17	62·23	55·14
Oita	84·05	77·44	79·02	82·31	74·49	65·32
Miyazaki	97·37	73·53	71·44	80·94	76·92	69·86
Kagoshima	74·93	62·25	49·98	51·99	53·22	45·14

Note: Per capita income relative means the prefectural per capita income expressed as proportion of the per capita national income. The latter in each case is 100.

The income concept used by Dr Cleaver is that of net income produced in goods-producing sectors. It does not include tertiary income or that arising in construction. The national income figures are three-year averages overlapping the benchmark years, e.g. the 1920 estimate is really an average of 1919, 1920 and 1921. None of the estimates includes Okinawa.

Source: Cleaver, op. cit.

III. INDIA

TABLE 10.4 PERCENTAGE RATES OF CHANGE OF TOTAL AND RURAL
POPULATION AND OF NET MIGRATION BALANCE IN THE TWELVE DISTRICTS
OF THE PUNJAB (INDIA) DURING THE DECADES 1911–1971

District		1911–21	1921–31	1931–41	1941–51	1951–61	1961–71
Hissar	1	1·58	9·97	1·93	3·58	47·33	37·5
	2	0·5	8·4	10·2	0·4	48·0	36·8
	3	−4·2	−1·3	−2·5	−11·0	+14·1	+7·5
Rohtak	1	7·81	4·48	18·38	13·63	26·59	24·8
	2	5·8	3·1	17·0	12·0	26·3	21·7
	3	−1·4	−1·7	−3·4	+5·8	−5·6	−5·8
Gurgaon	1	−6·85	9·31	14·96	8·01	28·22	37·0
	2	−7·0	8·6	13·7	4·1	25·1	33·6
	3	−4·0	−0·6	−3·1	+6·6	−3·6	+5·4
Karnal	1	3·52	2·79	16·71	10·06	38·34	32·5
	2	3·3	0·3	15·7	2·5	41·3	32·7
	3	−0·9	+2·2	−1·3	+5·0	+4·7	−0·3
Ambala	1	−1·61	9·11	14·13	7·50	35·02	18·6
	2	−1·7	8·5	10·4	−0·3	21·8	19·5
	3	−3·3	+1·3	−0·5	+6·5	+3·2	−7·5
Kangra	1	−0·54	4·56	12·35	4·05	15·33	
	2	−0·3	4·4	12·0	0·3	16·0	
	3	−3·5	+1·2	+2·8	+5·0	−6·7	
Hoshiarpur	1	1·00	11·30	13·46	−7·47	12·75	21·6
	2	2·5	9·2	11·7	−10·1	9·9	21·0
	3	−7·8	+2·2	−2·5	−23·9	−11·0	−4·6
Jullundur	1	2·58	14·76	19·43	−6·50	16·27	17·8
	2	2·7	13·9	15·0	−17·8	15·3	15·0
	3	−5·1	+3·0	−2·2	−24·7	−9·0	−4·9
Ludhiana	1	9·80	18·70	22·0	0·79	26·64	37·9
	2	9·5	14·2	18·1	−6·2	17·7	29·4
	3	+1·5	+2·9	+2·2	+19·1	0·0	+13·8
Ferozepur	1	14·9	5·22	23·03	−7·27	26·97	17·4
	2	13·3	1·8	20·9	−9·7	23·0	17·6
	3	+1·8	+6·3	+2·8	−24·0	−3·1	−9·2
Amritsar	1	5·52	20·20	25·16	−15·67	12·28	18·7
	2	4·5	11·8	17·3	−16·5	11·7	20·6
	3	+2·2	+5·7	+3·7	−34·9	−15·4	−4·8
Gurdaspur	1	2·08	13·17	19·14	−1·24	16·06	23·5
	2	2·8	12·4	17·4	−9·4	14·6	23·2
	3	+5·2	+1·3	−3·0	−16·9	−10·6	−4·1
Punjab	1	3·28	10·23	17·87	−0·57	25·0	
	2	3·0	7·0	14·0	−5·0		

1 = Percentage rate of change of total population.
2 = Percentage rate of change of rural population.
3 = Percentage rate of change of net migration balance.

TABLE 10.5 PERCENTAGE RATES OF CHANGE (ANNUAL COMPOUND) OF
OUTPUT, CULTIVATED AREA AND PRODUCTIVITY IN THE TWELVE DISTRICTS
OF THE PUNJAB (INDIA) DURING THE DECADES 1911–1971

District		1911–21	1921–31	1931–41	1941–51	1951–61	1961–71
Hissar	1	−5·1	1·20	−5·10	11·4	10·9	3·8
	2	0·7	0·95	−1·94	1·3	5·6	−0·4
	3	−5·8	0·25	−3·23	9·9	5·0	4·2
Rohtak	1	0·9	−5·40	2·62	5·7	4·6	4·4
	2	2·2	−0·84	−0·82	0·6	2·1	0·2
	3	−1·3	−4·61	3·47	5·2	2·5	4·2
Gurgaon	1	−3·4	1·12	−0·57	3·1	5·6	5·6
	2	−0·2	0·80	0·20	−0·1	2·7	−0·1
	3	−3·3	0·30	−0·78	3·2	2·8	5·7
Karnal	1	2·5	−4·01	1·54	6·3	7·5	7·5
	2	−0·1	−0·56	−0·57	1·9	5·1	1·8
	3	2·5	−3·47	2·13	4·3	2·3	5·6
Ambala	1	−5·1	0·09	0·32	4·9	4·6	3·2
	2	−1·1	0·46	−0·05	−0·5	1·7	2·2
	3	−3·9	−0·37	0·37	5·3	2·9	1·0
Kangra	1	−2·6	1·40	−0·12	4·0	2·5	
	2	−0·4	−0·53	0·45	−1·1	0·2	
	3	−2·2	1·93	−0·57	5·2	2·3	
Hoshiarpur	1	0·9	1·42	−0·53	0·9	3·8	6·4
	2	−0·2	−0·15	0·14	−0·3	0·8	3·0
	3	1·1	1·58	−0·67	1·3	3·0	3·2
Jullundur	1	−1·1	0·25	0·03	0·4	4·2	7·7
	2	−1·6	0·74	−0·28	−1·2	2·8	3·1
	3	0·5	−0·49	0·31	1·6	1·3	4·5
Ludhiana	1	1·3	0·70	1·60	0·9	4·3	12·3
	2	−1·4	0·68	−0·29	−1·15	1·8	5·7
	3	2·7	0·02	1·90	2·00	2·4	6·2
Ferozepur	1	−3·6	0·58	1·02	1·9	3·5	6·2
	2	−1·5	0·95	−1·12	0·2	1·5	1·4
	3	−2·1	−0·37	2·16	1·6	1·9	4·8
Amritsar	1	−1·8	0·15	0·03	1·9	1·8	9·5
	2	−1·6	0·44	−0·21	1·3	0·9	2·3
	3	−0·2	−0·29	0·24	0·5	0·9	7·1
Gurdaspur	1	−0·9	−0·04	0·84	−2·1	2·2	8·5
	2	−0·7	0·72	0·68	−3·2	0·7	3·0
	3	−0·2	−0·72	0·17	1·2	1·5	5·4
Punjab	1	−1·7	−0·41	0·40	3·1		
	2	−0·4	0·32	−0·51	0·2		
	3	−1·3	−0·72	0·90	3·0		

1 = Percentage rate of change of (annual compound) output.
2 = Percentage rate of change of (annual compound) area.
3 = Percentage rate of change of (annual compound) productivity.

TABLE 10.6 PERCENTAGE RATES OF CHANGE OF TOTAL AND RURAL
POPULATION AND OF NET MIGRATION PER DECADE IN THE THIRTEEN
DISTRICTS OF ORISSA (INDIA) DURING THE DECADES 1951–1971

		1951–61	1961–71			1951–61	1961–71
Orissa	1	19·8	25·0	Keonjhar	1	26·3	28·5
	2	17·6	22·4		2	23·8	24·8
	3	−0·1			3	+1·5	−2·7
Balasore	1	28·0	29·4	Koraput	1	18·0	36·9
	2	25·1	30·9		2	18·0	31·9
	3	+6·1	−0·7		3	+4·4	+9·0
Bolangir	1	16·4	18·2	Mayurbhanj	1	17·0	18·7
	2	16·4	15·6		2	15·2	18·2
	3	−1·4	−3·8		3	−4·6	−6·6
Cuttack	1	21·6	25·1	Boudh Khandmals	1	12·6	20·5
	2	18·7	24·0		2	12·6	18·1
	3	+4·0	+2·3		3	−3·6	−3·8
Dhenkanal	1	22·6	25·8	Puri	1	18·7	25·4
	2	22·6	26·5		2	16·4	22·1
	3	−0·1	−1·6		3	+2·5	−3·1
Ganjam	1	15·2	22·4	Sambalpur	1	15·9	22·2
	2	13·9	18·4		2	11·6	17·1
	3	−3·4	−0·1		3	+1·8	+2·2
Kalahandi	1	17·6	15·2	Sundergarh	1	37·4	35·9
	2	16·4	12·9		2	16·4	27·0
	3	−4·6	−11·1		3	+12·5	+7·6

1 = Percentage rate of change of total population.
2 = Percentage rate of change of rural population.
3 = Percentage rate of change of net migration balance.

Punjab: Table 10.4 presents the rates of change of total and rural
population and migration in twelve districts of the Punjab during
1911–71. Table 10.5 gives rates of change of output, cultivated area
and productivity per acre in the twelve districts during 1911–71.

Migration between districts in the Punjab was not significantly
correlated with the rate of change of agricultural production, except
in two decades, 1941–51 and 1951–61. Even among these two the
correlation during 1941–51 must be treated as spurious because the
migration was known to be due to the partition of the Punjab in
1947. On the whole therefore there was not significant correlation
between migration and the rate of change of agricultural output.
But it may be noted in this connection that during the first three
decades (1911–1941) there was a positive correlation between output
per acre and migration. Districts with higher outputs per acre gained
by net in-migration. In the last three decades, however, there was no

TABLE 10.7 PERCENTAGE RATES OF CHANGE (ANNUAL COMPOUND) OF
OUTPUT, CULTIVATED AREA AND PRODUCTIVITY IN THIRTEEN DISTRICTS
OF ORISSA (INDIA) DURING 1951–1971

		1951–61	1961–71			1951–61	1961–71
Orissa	1	4·9	3·2	Keonjhar	1	3·6	0·9
	2	1·0	1·8		2	−1·5	0·5
	3	3·9	1·4		3	5·1	0·4
Balasore	1	3·9	4·0	Koraput	1	3·3	2·2
	2	−0·5	1·9		2	0·9	2·6
	3	4·5	2·1		3	2·3	−0·4
Bolangir	1	7·6	0·8	Mayurbhanj	1	3·5	2·6
	2	2·5	0·4		2	−1·0	1·8
	3	5·0	0·4		3	4·5	0·8
Cuttack	1	4·7	5·7	Boudh Khandmals	1	−3·4	6·2
	2	0·3	2·6		2	−4·1	0·9
	3	4·4	3·1		3	0·7	5·1
Dhenkanal	1	7·7	3·5	Puri	1	4·9	3·1
	2	2·0	1·1		2	1·1	0·5
	3	5·6	2·4		3	3·8	2·6
Ganjam	1	9·0	7·1	Sambalpur	1	4·1	3·7
	2	1·6	6·9		2	0·9	0·9
	3	7·3	0·1		3	3·2	2·7
Kalahandi	1	9·9	−1·1	Sundergarh	1	4·0	−4·3
	2	4·2	0·5		2	1·3	−2·5
	3	5·4	−1·6		3	2·6	−1·9

1 = Percentage rate of change (annual compound) of output.
2 = Percentage rate of change (annual compound) of area.
3 = Percentage rate of change (annual compound) of productivity.

such correlation. In the last two decades also there was no correlation
between migration and urbanisation in the Punjab.

The association between the changes in agriculture and the natural
rate of population change has to be studied indirectly in the Punjab
because it is not possible to calculate the natural rate of population
change during the different decades. The migration rates calculated
by reverse survival and such other methods assume uniform
mortality in the districts and make nonsense of calculating natural
rates of population change by utilising them. There was no correlation between the rates of change of total population and of
agricultural output during the first two decades (1911–21 and
1921–31). In all the subsequent decades they were positively and
significantly correlated, even in the decade 1941–51 where the
correlation has to be treated as spurious. If this is considered
together with the lack of correlation between migration and agricultural change noted above, it is highly unlikely that the natural rate

of change of population and agricultural output could have been very significantly correlated with one another.

Orissa: Table 10.6 gives the rates of change of total and rural population and that of migration for the thirteen districts of Orissa during 1951–71. Table 10.7 presents rates of change (annual compound) of agricultural output, cultivated area and productivity in the same thirteen districts during 1951–71.

No correlation was found between the rates of change of total agricultural output, area under crops and productivity per acre on the one hand and the rate of change of total or rural population on the other, in both the decades. So too migration was not correlated with the rate of change of output, area or productivity. Migration, however, was significantly correlated with urbanisation in both the decades.

IV. SRI LANKA

Table 10.8 presents the rates of change of total and rural population and migration in the 22 districts of Sri Lanka during the period 1946–71. Table 10.9 presents the rates of change of agricultural area and production of principal crops in the districts of Sri Lanka during 1952–70.

TABLE 10.8 RATES OF CHANGE OF TOTAL AND
RURAL POPULATION AND NET MIGRATION RATES
FOR THE DIFFERENT DISTRICTS OF SRI LANKA
DURING 1946–1971

District		1946–53	1953–63	1963–71
Colombo	A	2·69	2·60	2·55
	B	1·62	2·46	1·43
	C	2·94	3·05	2·80
Kalutara	A	1·98	1·90	1·84
	B	1·92	1·78	1·70
	C	−2·85	−0·87	−1·45
Kandy	A	2·40	2·18	1·72
	B	2·40	2·22	1·68
	C	−3·55	−2·56	−5·31
Matale	A	3·60	2·44	2·90
	B	3·75	2·28	3·25
	C	−2·76	−0·76	0·47
Nuwara Eliya	A	2·79	2·00	1·73
	B	2·70	2·10	2·38
	C	−1·41	−5·38	−3·91
Galle	A	1·90	2·01	1·70
	B	1·79	1·90	1·55
	C	−3·43	−0·34	−3·12

TABLE 10.8 (cont.)

District		1946–53	1953–63	1963–71
Matara	A	2·33	2·20	1·62
	B	2·30	2·26	2·02
	C	−3·77	−9·67	−8·25
Hambantola	A	3·58	3·68	2·80
	B	3·60	3·68	3·15
	C	1·15	−1·44	−0·06
Jaffna	A	2·00	1·80	1·72
	B	1·94	1·98	1·36
	C	−0·54	−1·26	−6·38
Mannar	A	4·77	3·25	3·18
	B	5·00	3·10	3·48
	C	15·28	5·06	2·00
Vavuniya	A	6·10	6·92	4·19
	B	4·72	8·88	3·30
	C	17·50	22·94	6·93
Batticaloa	A	4·20	4·19	3·55
	B	4·68	4·45	3·26
	C	9·74	8·18	1·94
Amparai	A			3·43
	B	3·9	4·10	2·78
	C			
Trincomalee	A	1·45	5·14	3·90
	B	5·3	7·35	3·70
	C	−6·41	14·95	3·97
Kurunegala	A	3·73	3·13	2·40
	B	3·72	3·15	2·60
	C	3·85	−3·17	−2·09
Puttalam	A	4·54	2·84	3·01
	B	3·18	2·74	2·19
	C	3·01	4·43	2·29
Anuradhapura	A	7·34	5·56	4·18
	B	7·62	5·67	5·30
	C	25·08	14·52	7·48
Polonnaruva	A			4·50
	B	7·4	5·72	5·09
	C			1·68
Badulla	A	3·30	3·50	2·15
	B	3·0	3·39	2·10
	C	1·32	0·15	−4·93
Monoregala	A			4·70
	B	3·12	3·42	2·18
	C			8·89
Ratnapura	A	2·98	2·50	2·46
	B	2·88	2·62	2·02
	C	−0·70	−1·55	—

TABLE 10.8 (cont.)

District		1946–53	1953–63	1963–71
Kegalle	A	2·32	2·00	1·60
	B	2·3	1·80	1·58
	C	−4·15	−4·78	−3·56

A = Rate of total population increase (annual compound).
B = Rate of rural population increase (annual compound).
C = Rate of migration.

TABLE 10.9 PERCENTAGE RATES (ANNUAL COMPOUND) OF CHANGE OF
AREA UNDER, AND OUTPUT OF, PRINCIPAL CROPS TOGETHER WITH
PER CAPITA (RURAL) AGRICULTURAL OUTPUT IN THE DISTRICTS OF
SRI LANKA DURING 1952–1971

District	Rate of change of area under principal crops[a] (annual compound)		Rate of change of production of principal crops[a] (annual compound)		Agricultural output (principal crops)[a] per capita (rural)		
	1952–62 %	1962–70 %	1951–62 %	1962–70 %	1951 Rs.	1962 Rs.	1970 Rs.
Colombo	0·1	0·2	1·89	1·25	123	122	111
Kalutara	0·3	0·2	3·79	0·94	155	202	194
Kandy	−0·96	−0·12	1·87	0·6	270	271	252
Matale	−0·76	0·1	3·12	−0·18	251	288	223
Newara Eliya	−0·03	0·6	2·1	0·7	423	442	410
Galle	−0·28	0·8	3·0	1·2	135	161	156
Matara	0·3	0·3	3·4	−0·23	154	185	160
Hambantola	0·7	0·2	3·3	2·6	174	183	181
Jaffna	1·4	2·9	8·2	1·0	35	77	76
Mannar	1·6	2·4	4·6	3·0	289	372	379
Vavunia	3·9	2·2	15·9	1·26	153	386	267
Batticaloa Amparai	1·6	0·3	7·1	3·6	170	254	267
Trincomalee	3·1	1·6	10·9	1·0	179	304	228
Kurunegala	0·3	0·1	3·5	0·5	249	275	248
Puttalam	0·7	0·2	3·3	−0·18	191	215	166
Anuradhapura Polonnaruva	3·2	1·3	12·7	−1·87	124	294	180
Badulla Monoregala	0·7	0·0	2·8	0·2	245	246	203
Ratnapura	0·3	0·3	1·9	3·0	226	220	241
Kagalle	−0·39	0·0	2·8	1·6	209	241	245

[a] Principal crops include tea, rubber, coconut and paddy.

As the agriculture data for 1946 are defective, comments on
changes in agriculture and population are confined to the period
1952–70 only. During both the periods the natural rate of change of
population and those of the change of agricultural output were not
correlated. The rates of migration also were not correlated with the
rates of change of agricultural output in the districts.

V. TAIWAN

Information readily available in regard to Taiwan is for the island as a whole and not for sub-national areas. Yet the experience in Taiwan is too precious to be bypassed on that account and an attempt is made here to deal with the data for the country as a whole.

The vital rates of natural increase in Taiwan during 1915–56 were as follows:

TABLE 10.10   VITAL RATES OF INCREASE OF
CHINESE[a] IN TAIWAN 1915–1956

Year	Birth-rate	Death-rate	Rate of natural increase
1915	40·9	30·5	10·4
1920	41·7	28·9	12·8
1925	43·6	24·8	18·8
1930	46·1	21·4	24·7
1935	45·7	20·9	24·8
1940	44·4	19·4	25·0
1956[a]	43·4	8·3	35·1

[a] All Chinese in the civil registers of Taiwan Province.
Source: Irene B. Taeuber, 'Population growth in a Chinese microcosm: Taiwan', *Population Index*, vol. 27, no. 2 (Apr 1961) 120–1.

In Table 10.11 are presented relevant data regarding the changes in agriculture in Taiwan during 1911–60.

TABLE 10.11   GROWTH OF AGRICULTURAL OUTPUT IN TAIWAN,
1911/15–1956/60

Period	Agricultural output in T$ millions (constant prices) (1935–7 = 100)	Cropped area hectares (000)	Agricultural labour force (000)	Worker days per hectare cropped	Agricultural output per cropped hectare T$ (1935–7 = 100)
1911–15	162	806	1155	135	172
1916–20	204	865	1124	179	194
1921–25	238	920	1126	175	202
1926–30	288	982	1188	173	221
1931–35	364	1079	1286	168	251
1936–40	423	1138	1374	171	286
1951–55	515	1502	1742	160	256
1956–60	645	1576	1725	163	300

Sources: T. H. Lee, *Intersectoral Capital Flows in the economic development of Taiwan, 1895–1960*, Cornell University Press, Ithaca, 1971; T. H. Lee, *Process and Pattern of Growth in Agricultural Production of Taiwan*, Economic Essays, vol. I, Graduate Institute of Economics, National Taiwan University (Nov 1970).

VI. POPULATION GROWTH AND
AGRICULTURAL CHANGE

Against the background of the data and analyses of interrelations between demographic and agricultural variables presented thus far the patterns of relationships common to the countries can be discussed. With advantage these can be discussed in terms of two problems bearing on the population aspects of economic development. Do changes in agricultural output affect population changes, directly or indirectly? Do they do so contemporaneously or with a lag between one and the other? I will discuss the two questions in that order.

The main common finding in regard to Japan, India and Sri Lanka seems to be the absence of any significant statistical correlation between the rate of change of agricultural output on the one hand and the natural rate of change of population and migration on the other. This finding is limited to contemporaneous and direct correlations and not to indirect or lagged ones. The data are not adequate to test the latter. In regard to Taiwan Dr Lee has argued that there seems to be a negative association between the crude death-rate and the standard or per capita real income of labour in agriculture during 1895–1960. As the birth-rate was near constant throughout the period and as per capita real income of labour in agriculture generally varied as the total agricultural output, the natural rate of population change and that of agricultural output seemed to be positively related to one another.[1] Dr Lee is referring to an indirect relationship mediated through the per capita real income of labour in agriculture through time and his finding in no way contradicts the finding in regard to Japan, India and Sri Lanka. In fact it underlines the necessity of probing more deeply the indirect and through-time relationships.

Unfortunately, the inadequacy of available data prevents the examination of such relationships. Even the relationship between changes in the components of the natural rate of population change and agricultural output cannot be examined because of the lack of reliable vital statistics in India and the limitations of agricultural data in Sri Lanka. However, the relationship may be probed a little further by studying the declines in fertility and agricultural change in more recent times in these countries as relatively more data are available regarding them.

Japanese experience is not very relevant in this connection,

[1] T. H. Lee, *Process and Pattern of Growth in Agricultural Production of Taiwan*, Economic Essays, vol. I, Graduate Institute of Economics, National Taiwan University (Nov 1970) 20–1.

because it is known that industrial rather than agricultural development was associated with fertility declines in the prefectures. For examining the relationship between fertility and agricultural change, Taiwan's experience is more relevant, but not complete. In Taiwan the rate and extent of industrial development was not rapid before 1960, but even so the proportion of the total labour force engaged in agriculture had declined from 72 per cent in 1911–15 to 58 per cent in 1951–5 and further to 54 per cent during 1956–60. The changes in the structure of employment, together with the agricultural development sketched earlier, did not affect fertility till 1960. The decline in fertility began in 1959 and has continued at accelerating rates since, mainly due to increasing practice of contraception. Between 1959 and 1965 birth-rate fell from 41·2 to 32·1. Nearly 93 per cent of the decline in fertility was due to a fall in the age specific fertility of women over 30 years of age.[1] Though the fertility decline began in big cities around 1957, it spread to all areas and the differentials between urban and rural fertility have tended to narrow with the passage of time.

In contrast with this, the fertility decline in Sri Lanka since 1953 was preceded and accompanied by a sizeable increase in agricultural output but unaccompanied by industrial development or rapid urbanisation. The rate of decline of birth-rates averaged 1·2 per cent per year between 1953 and 1963 and accelerated to 1·7 per cent during 1965–8.[2] The fall was largely attributable to the rise in the age at marriage and only to a small extent to increasing practice of contraception. In India (i.e. Punjab and Orissa) fertility was unchanged in Orissa but there were indications that it had declined in some districts of the Punjab during 1961–71. A two time-point survey carried out in Khanna in Ludhiana district in 1954–9 and again in 1969, confirmed the fall in fertility and found that it was mostly attributable to rise in the age at marriage and little to increased contraceptive practice.[3] In the Punjab also the indicated fall in fertility had been preceded and accompanied by a rapid rise in agricultural output and industrial and urban development was relatively small as compared to Taiwan during recent decades.

Sri Lanka and these areas of the Punjab furnish almost pure cases to study the relationship between agricultural change and fertility decline. The fact of a decline in fertility associated with agricultural

[1] R. Freedman and V. Muller, 'The Continuing Fertility Decline in Taiwan, 1965', *Population Index*, vol. 33, no. 1 (Jan–Mar 1967) 6, 15.

[2] N. H. Wright, 'Recent fertility change in Ceylon and prospects for a national family planning programme', in *Demography*, vol. 5, no. 2 (1968).

[3] John Wyon et al., *The Khanna Study: Population Problem in the Rural Punjab* (Cambridge, Mass.: Harvard University Press, 1971) p. 312.

development is rather unexpected in received theory on the subject. The current position is embodied in these words:[1] 'Historically in Asia and elsewhere, increases in productivity and expanded areas of cultivation have led to increased populations living in traditional ways. The impact on fertility was likely to be a temporary increase in fertility.' Demographic transitions have been generally associated with development but not of the agricultural type only. The recent experience in Sri Lanka and the Punjab directs attention to the new possibility of agricultural development in itself leading to such a transition, maybe by a different path or paths, in a given social milieu. Further discussion of this phenomenon may be useful.

Now to the inverse problem. Is an increase in population, directly and contemporaneously, indirectly or through time, favourable or unfavourable to agricultural development? It is patent that population change affects production mainly through changes in the labour force and in savings through its effect on consumption. The relationship between population and labour force is a lagged one – the other relationship is possibly more direct and quick. It is not possible to examine the latter in regard to the countries covered here because of lack of adequate data. Only the relationship between agricultural production and labour engaged in agriculture can be studied here.

So far as Japan is concerned, as the absolute number of labour force engaged in agriculture remained almost constant during 1900–40, the problem of change in labour force affecting agricultural production does not signify.

Agricultural labour force increased by more than 50 per cent in Taiwan during 1911/15–1956/60 and the total labour input measured by working days nearly doubled during the same period. Working days per worker in agriculture increased from 116 in 1911–15 to 141 in 1921–5 and remained around that level up to 1955. They increased to 155 in 1956–60. Worker days per cropped hectare increased from 135 in 1911–15 to 163 in 1956–60. They peaked at 179 in 1916–20 and fluctuated between this and 168 up to 1940. In the 1950s they dropped to 160–3. The relationship between land productivity, cultivated area and income per worker is shown in Fig. 10.1. The production elasticity of labour during the period before 1926–30 has been estimated at 0·27 by Dr Lee. It declined slightly to 0·25 during 1926–40 and again increased to 0·28 in the period after 1950.[2] It would seem from this that increased labour inputs was a factor of considerable importance in increasing agricultural output

[1] Report of the Proceedings of the Second Asian Population Conference, Tokyo (1972) chap. IV, para. 17.

[2] T. H. Lee, *Process and Pattern of Growth*, op. cit.

and that the increase in agricultural labour force did not hamper the growth of agricultural output throughout the period.

In the Punjab a cross-sectional regression analysis with output as the dependent variable and the proportion of cropped area under

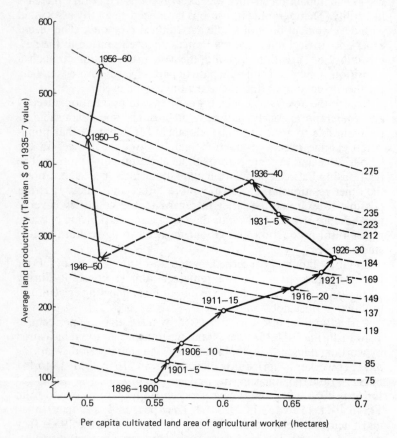

FIG. 10.1 Historical growth path of labour productivity in Taiwan's agriculture, 1895–1960.

Source: T. H. Lee, *Process and Pattern of Growth*, op. cit., p. 31.

irrigation and labour input per acre as the independent variables for the years 1911, 1921, 1931 and 1941 showed that while irrigation had a positive and significant effect on the output, input of labour per acre had a weak and insignificant effect on the output in all the years. A more detailed multivariate regression analysis was done for the

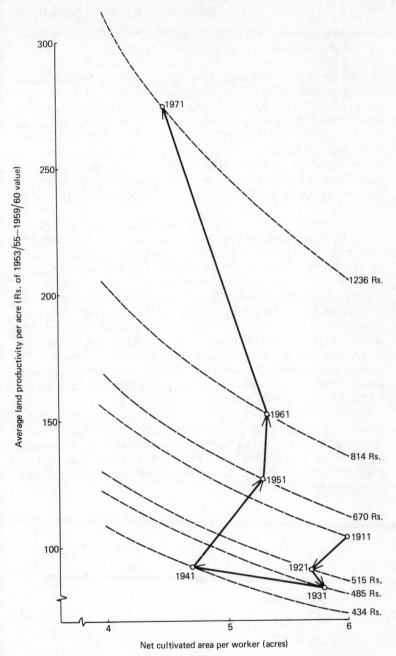

FIG. 10.2 Historical growth path of labour productivity in Punjab's agriculture, 1911–1971

years 1951, 1961 and 1971. For overcoming the difficulties of non-comparable categories from one census to another, only male labour in agriculture has been taken into account. These analyses showed that labour input was a factor of the greatest consequence to output in whatever combination of inputs it was considered, in all the three years. In 1971, however, irrigation inputs took precedence over labour inputs. Marginal product of labour inputs seemed to rise all along. In 1951 it was Rs. 285; it rose to Rs. 555 in 1961 and further to Rs. 899 in 1971 in one set of equations and a similar trend was shown by other sets. The relationship between male labour in agriculture, the cultivated area per male worker and the output per male worker in the Punjab through the six decades is portrayed in Fig. 10.2.

In Orissa a cross-district multivariate regression analysis regarding agricultural output and inputs such as land, water, fertilisers and labour for 1971 showed that land was the factor of greatest consequence. The regression coefficient of labour input became significant only when land input was eliminated.

It seems reasonable to infer that the change in the labour force in the Punjab before 1941 and in Orissa in 1971 did not help agricultural production. In later years in the Punjab, however, the increase in the labour force was of help in increasing agricultural production. The historical growth paths of labour productivity in Taiwan and the Punjab portrayed in the two charts also indicate a similar conclusion. An analysis on similar lines cannot be done for Sri Lanka because of lack of relevant data.

Is it reasonable to conclude from this that an increase in population (and its lagged effect on labour force) is not a hindrance to agricultural development under all circumstances? If agricultural development is sufficiently buoyant and sustained, increase in population can be a help rather than a hindrance to agricultural development.

Discussion of the Paper by
Professor Sovani

Professor Eastman said that Professor Sovani's paper presented extensive data on rates of change in population, migration, agricultural output and output per capita for sub-national or sub-regional units in Japan, the Punjab, Orissa and Sri Lanka, and also for Taiwan as a whole. The data, which covered several decades, were used to analyse the relationship between agricultural and population change in a set of case studies rather than on a comparative basis. The general results of some regression analysis, using supplementary information on irrigation and fertiliser use, were also indicated, but the actual equations were not given.

The paper contained three sections: one on the relationship of population change to change in agricultural output; another on the relationship between agricultural change and fertility; and a third on the relation of change in population to agricultural development.

Professor Sovani wrote, in relation to the wealth of information he presented, 'I will allow the data to speak for itself'. Professor Eastman unfortunately found himself hard of hearing and was unsure of the answers the data gave him. Indeed, he was unsure of the questions that were being asked in the formulation of the research project. He therefore welcomed the opportunity for a discussion.

The main conclusion of the first part of the study was that there was no significant correlation between the rate of change of agricultural output and either the natural rate of population change or migration. The significance of this result was difficult to grasp in the absence of a theoretical context which would specify or test what was the source of the increase in agricultural production and the type of micro-economic response that might exist. For instance, if we were dealing with an increase in output owing to technical change, but this change was labour saving to the extent that the marginal product of labour did not rise, no response in population to an increase in output would be consistent with an assumption that labour was an investment good. (Such might be the case in rice growing in Indonesia.)

On the other hand, if children were a consumption good, the type of technical change might not matter, as a temporary rise in the average product of labour would be expended on more children. However, if the increase in total product was owing to returns to higher labour skills, and was not available to unskilled labour, progress would be associated with groups that grew in human capital, not in labour.

Obviously, one could ring the changes on different models. The data collected determined, in part, what theories could be tested, and the theories affected what data was collected. The point was that the conciseness of the paper obscured the significance of the work, because the questions that could be handled were not specified.

Professor Sovani went on to some results, from parts of the sample periods and countries, which revealed some reduction in fertility during agricultural growth. This he regarded as contrary to 'received theory', which Professor Eastman supposed to be some sort of Malthusian theory of perfectly elastic labour supply. Here again, it would be useful to probe the micro-economic basis of the problem and see what more could be said about the phenomena that were observed.

Professor Eastman said we had begun the conference feeling critical of the usefulness of applying the theory of individual choice to population change; that we had nevertheless been doing mostly that; and that we should apply more of it to the data being examined here to try to grasp its significance better.

The last part of the paper containing the vice versa problem, seemed much more straightforward. It asked whether an increase in population was favourable to agricultural development, or what was the production function? It turned out that the marginal productivity of labour in agriculture was positive, but the way the results of regressions run on various data were presented would not permit any more exact conclusion. In any event, the production function itself would have changed over the decades considered.

Professor Sovani thought that it was clear from Professor Eastman's introductory statement that most of the questions the latter raised had arisen from the fact that the paper was an attempt to condense a one-thousand page report into twenty pages. As a result, he was afraid that he would not be able to give detailed answers to all the questions raised by Professor Eastman.

The study on which the paper was based arose from an ECAFE resolution asking for an inquiry into how far population pressure in the ECAFE countries was hindering the attainment of economic and social objectives. In response, the Population Division of the ECAFE had evolved, in consultation with Professor Richard Easterlin, this project of a comparative study of population and agricultural change in some countries of the ECAFE region. The analyses were made with reference to smaller areas, like districts or prefectures, in order to identify relationships that might be obscured in national or regional aggregates. The study was based on the available data and covered periods of more than two decades in each case. Because the changes to be studied were rather long-term ones, they could not be studied over shorter periods without the results being misleading. In this context, the central objective of the inquiry was to find out whether there was any systematic relationship between changes in the demographic variables like fertility, mortality and migration, on the one hand, and changes in agricultural output on the other.

The study covered three countries, Japan, India and Sri Lanka. Taiwan was originally included, but had to be dropped midstream because it was suddenly declared a 'non-country' for U.N. purposes. Among the three countries included, Japan was not a very happy choice for studying comparative changes in agriculture and population but was chosen nevertheless.

The study found very little or no relationship between changes in agricultural production and changes in the natural rate of population change and migration. The relationships tested were contemporary and direct. There was not sufficient data to test lagged relationships between the two, and the data were also inadequate for testing direct relationships. As such, the findings were bald and simple.

The other objective of the study was to look at the phenomenon of population pressure. He had not touched that aspect in the paper but it had been dealt with in the fuller report. It was found that population pressure was one of the most nebulous concepts. After going through the gamut of ten definitions of population pressure, he found it hard to say conclusively whether, in any given region, population pressure existed at a point of time and/or whether it was increasing or decreasing through time. It seemed that most definitions of population pressure were formulated in aggregate terms and the pressure they depicted was felt more by the demographers, economists and population conferences than by the people themselves who were supposed to be groaning under it. He was convinced that 'felt' population pressure had to be studied at the micro-level, for evolving operative population policies.

The regressions for Punjab and Orissa had been carried out for the census years only. Though agricultural data were available from year to year, population data were available only for the census years. That was the reason for confining the regressions to census years only. Within the limitations imposed by this, the regressions showed that the marginal productivity of male labour in agriculture in the Punjab had gone on increasing in the successive census years of 1951, 1961 and 1971 and that increase in the labour force was an important factor in the increase of agricultural output in those years.

Professor Ohlin wondered whether conclusions about changes in land tenure were included. When studying such long-run changes, some alterations of this kind must have occurred.

Professor Hermalin recalled that Professor Sovani had noted that there were problems in obtaining data for such a study. The fact that Taiwan had been mentioned led him to give a word of caution. In the pre-Second World War situation, an increase in agricultural production per head, or per household, did not necessarily mean an increase in income per head, or per household. In Taiwan, a lot of the increased income had gone to Japanese entrepreneurs who supplied new strains of seed, ran milling operations, etc. In linking macro and micro theory, one therefore had to be careful to check on one's inferences.

Replying to Professor Ohlin's query, *Professor Sovani* said he would have liked to include changes in land tenure in the analysis, but there was not sufficient information on that point either in the Punjab or in Japan.

As for Taiwan, he was aware that most of the gains in agricultural production in that country during Japanese rule probably went to Japanese and not to Taiwanese. However, he did not wish to pronounce on this. Professor Lee had suggested that the general standard of living in Taiwan had risen during this period and he was simply relying on Professor Lee's opinion.

Mr Boulier wondered what Professor Sovani's opinion was on, for example, Esther Boserup's findings on the relation between agricultural population and output.

Professor Sovani replied that his study did not find any such relationship.

Professor Coale thought Mrs Boserup's thesis was clearest in its application when the initial population density was low, agriculture primitive and the slash-and-burn method was used. Progress to more settled cultivation could result from increasing population density. With settled agriculture already there was no similar adaptation. Perhaps the right conditions were not found in Sri Lanka, the Punjab or Japan.

Professor Schultz wanted to learn more about the link between falling fertility and the marriage rate. He wanted to hear of any leads on how economic theory might explain cultural variations in the responsiveness of nuptiality. He would like to note that in Taiwan, in contrast to Sri Lanka and the Punjab, the age at marriage was apparently not an important vehicle for the fall in the birth-rate. He wondered whether there were any clues from Professor Sovani's work on the factors underlying the pattern of fertility adaptation through changes in the age at marriage.

Professor Sovani replied that though the study had looked at smaller areas, the data were still aggregative at that level, and so also were the findings.

Professor Rasmussen thought that Mrs Boserup would want to generalise her theory.

Professor Sovani's view was that, even so, most of Mrs Boserup's cases were those of primitive agriculture, and only a few of settled agricultural conditions. He did not think that the analogy was the same here. All his studies were concerned with long-settled agriculture and not with new frontiers.

Professor Ohlin wanted assistance in interpreting the two attempts to portray historical growth paths. He was not sure what was the hypothesis at issue.

Professor Sovani said that the figures showing the historical movement of agricultural production per male labour in agriculture in the Punjab and agricultural labour in Taiwan were intended to show nothing more. They were not intended to test any hypotheses. It was easy to understand these figures. One knew total cultivated area per agricultural labourer as well as the average productivity per acre or hectare for different years. It was easy to plot the last two and to calculate from them the income isoquants.

M. Leridon wondered how Professor Sovani defined the equal revenue curve.

Professor Sovani said that this was easy. One knew income per head, and one had to calculate what combination of land and labour gave the required curve. It was a kind of isoquant. Agricultural production was divided by an amount of labour on the assumption that the entire product went to labour.

Professor Parikh was not sure about the tests that Professor Sovani used on his second hypothesis. He understood that the aim was to see whether an increase in the labour supply affected the marginal productivity of labour. Surely one then needed to go to micro-economics and to estimate the production function.

Professor Schultz wondered whether, when Professor Sovani analysed cross-section data in Section VI of his paper, he estimated marginal, or only average, productivity of labour. If so, did he actually need any micro-economic data? Could Professor Sovani summarise the results for marginal productivity of the productive factors?

Professor Sovani said that these were given in detail in the full report.

Professor Schultz believed that the growth path for the Punjab showed average productivity falling from 1911 to 1931. If one took the regional production functions, did these also show a fall in marginal productivity? If so, that would be very interesting. What had happened in the period 1951–71 was not surprising; one would expect marginal productivity to increase. But he would very much like to know what happened earlier.

Professor Sovani was not sure whether marginal productivity fell during the period 1911–31, but was sure that any change was insignificant.

Professor Schultz replied that there were two meanings of 'insignificant'. One was that only a small correlation was found when one used some classical statistical test, or a relatively large standard error for a parameter estimate. The other meaning was that one was confident that there was such an effect, but that when one estimated its magnitude, this was found to be small.

Professor Parikh said that if the hypothesis to be tested was the result of an increase in population per unit area, he wondered how one distinguished this from cross-section data, ignoring changes in technology. And if this was not the hypothesis being tested, then what did Professor Sovani really expect?

Professor Sovani said that Professor Parikh was reading too much into his analysis. Its aim had been simply to discover whether the production function would show the separate contributions of labour, fertilisers, etc. to increased agricultural production. No other hypothesis was being tested.

Professor Guitton suggested that the information in the diagrams was very rich and should be developed; but he would like to be more certain of its implications. When the curve fell, as it occasionally did, what did this tell us? Could we infer that the growth path exibited a kind of cycle? In other words, was the fall a decrease or simply slower growth?

Professor Guitton had been struck by the results of these international discussions. Population pressure appeared to be a fundamental concept, but when one asked what it was, one almost reached a stage of despair. Professor Sovani admitted that he did not know what it meant, but economists would be unhappy if what seemed to be the underlying motive force could not even be understood. Malthus's problem was surely that of studying various aspects of demographic pressure; birth-rates, death-rates, marriage rates, and so on. Were not demographic variables the motive force? Or was some other influence the basic one?

There appeared to be no feedback in physical factors, but one would surely have great difficulty in formulating any theory if one could not define population pressure. If one could not, how could one hope to understand the behaviour of the rest of the system? Could Professor Sovani put these worries to rest?

Professor Sovani replied that when the curve of agricultural production per labourer in the charts declined, this did not necessarily show that income per head of total population had fallen. He was as worried as Professor

Guitton about the difficulty of defining population pressure, but thought that and attack at the micro-level might offer more hope.

Professor Parikh said that when the curve fell, this meant a fall in income per head, but what was the effect of the monsoon? Why did one not have fluctuations in income per head from year to year according to whether the monsoon was good or bad? He was surprised that there seemed to be a long period in which income per head fell, and then another long period in which it rose. Surely there ought to be more random movement; or did prices more than adjust?

Professor Sovani emphasised that these were the results of observations in the census years and did not show a time path.

Professor Parikh accepted this but was still surprised at how little variation there was. Was this a result of the concept or coincidence?

Professor Sovani said one should not read too much into the analysis.

Professor Ohlin said that, looking more closely at the figures, he found that the measure of labour productivity was output per head. One then had the equal income curves and this provided a simple diagram. However, he wondered where the marginal data came from to allow Professor Sovani to work on the production function.

Professor Sovani said that the data did not come from the figure. Two or three types of regression had been fitted, and all these would be given in detail in the full report.

Professor Schultz wondered whether the reason for the stability in the diagram was that only the census years had been examined, or whether there was some other stabilising factor? If one took data for the regions, these could presumably be split up into twenty or thirty smaller regions. If one then found them all following the same pattern, something interesting really had been happening in Punjabi agriculture until about 1941. Could the calculations be done for each region, and could the distortion induced by a good or bad monsoon be avoided?

Professor Sovani said that the data had not been averaged over the years, so that the vagaries in any year were reflected in the analysis. The historical movement of agricultural production, per head of male agricultural labour, had been analysed for each district in the Punjab and many districts had shown the same pattern as that for the total area. Some districts did show a different pattern. However, he was not sure whether these district patterns would be fully displayed in the final report.

Professor Rasmussen wondered whether there was consistency.

Professor Sovani said there was not. Some districts showed a different pattern.

Mr Black wanted to take the conference back to the wider question of employment. The O.E.C.D. had looked at employment creation. While he could not offer Professor Guitton information about the turning point in Malthusian analysis, it did seem that productivity was often increased by new technologies. However, one found that restructuring fiscal and trade policies, as well as carrying out public works schemes, did not increase rural employment very much. So there was a question whether over-population was a problem, however one might define it.

Professor Parikh pointed out that there was some evidence that new agricultural techniques did increase the demand for labour, and that the average wage had increased, for example, in the Punjab. The need now seemed to be to spread the new agricultural techniques and hope that this would increase the income of the agricultural population. He was quite optimistic about what might happen in India.

Mr Black agreed that there were certainly areas where this was true, but he did not think there were any in Black Africa.

Professor Schultz said that, for demographers and economists, the Green Revolution raised more issues than a discussion of the marginal product of labour. He was suggesting that in the long run the Green Revolution might increase the amount of capital, and might lead to an increase in wages. However, the balance was not predictable even in India. There was little evidence for other countries.

The techniques of the Green Revolution were most successful where other facilities were ample, such as water supply, fertilisers, credit, etc., but in other, less well-endowed parts of India, it seemed likely that incomes would fall. It might well be that economic conditions would develop which would induce massive migration, resulting from economic and technical change not previously seen in Asia. He worried about this problem, if only for the twenty-first century.

Dr Ridker agreed that this was very important, but did not think one had to look so far into the future to become worried. In 1947, India had consumed 15 ounces of food grain per head per day. The figure was the same in 1972. This was not explicable in terms of variations from year to year, because the range seemed to be from about 14 to about 16. So, one could say if one wished that there was no increase in population pressure, but it did mean that a great deal of effort had gone into increasing aggregate output to no good effect in terms of welfare.

Part Five

Population, Resources and Environment

11   India in 2001 *

Kirit S. Parikh
INDIAN STATISTICAL INSTITUTE, NEW DELHI

I. CAN INDIA SURVIVE THE FUTURE?

Will India's economic development be able to catch up with the population growth? What prospects are there for her to meet the challenge of growing population? Would she be overwhelmed by the burden of nearly a billion people? Or would she be able to feed, house and clothe this billion in comfort?

In this paper I propose to look at these problems. I shall confine myself (at least here) to identifying the problems in a quantitative manner and to suggesting solutions which are technologically feasible. I shall not go into the question of the political implications of suggested solutions, nor shall I speculate on the likelihood of such solutions being achieved in practice. I shall also assume that institutional changes, wherever necessary, will take place over the long period considered.

To begin with I shall identify the likely growth of population and income till 2001 and estimate the demand for various resources. In particular I shall be concerned to estimate the demand for agricultural products, for energy and for urban facilities. I shall concentrate on these sectors, as being those which affect the quality of life of the vast majority of the population. I shall then examine the prospect of meeting these demands with the currently known technology. Finally I shall attempt to identify the need for technological change in these sectors. Though this is the objective of my research, I shall confine myself here primarily to looking at the agricultural sector.

II. POPULATION PROJECTIONS FOR A.D. 2001

India's population in A.D. 2001 will crucially depend upon the success of the effort being made towards family planning. The extent to which the present and future generations adopt the philosophy 'a small family is a happy family' will determine the size of India in A.D. 2001. For the purpose of this article, however, there is no need

* I wish to thank Suresh Tendulkar for his valuable contribution to this paper.

to make an exact projection; it will be sufficient to make estimates of upper and lower bounds on the population projections for 2001.

Though no official projection is available for the demographic characteristics of India in A.D. 2001, a number of private projections are available. For example, the National Commission on Agriculture has made some projections which are given in Table 11.1.

TABLE 11.1 PROJECTIONS OF INDIAN
POPULATION: RURAL AND URBAN[a] (MILLIONS)

Year	Rural	Urban[b]	Total
1961	362·60	79·61	442·21
1971	440·17	110·07	550·24
1980	490·61	160·02	650·63
1985	505·70	196·98	702·68
2000	454·76	409·23	863·99

[a] As on 1 July. The actual compound rate of growth of total population during 1961–71 was observed to be 2·21 per cent per annum. For the period 1971–81 a rate of growth of 1·85 per cent, as assumed by the office of the Registrar General, has been used. For the decades 1981–91 and 1991–2001 population is assumed to grow at the rates of 1·55 per cent and 1·30 per cent per annum respectively.
[b] Assumed to grow at 4·25 per cent per annum during 1971–85, at 5 per cent per annum thereafter.
Source: National Commission on Agriculture, *Projections of Demand for Selected Agricultural Commodities in India 1975–2000 A.D.* (Mar 1973) Table 7, p. 34.

These projections, as can be seen from the footnotes to Table 11.1, are based on fairly optimistic projection of the success of the family-planning effort and consequent reduction in growth rates. The total population of 864 million in 2000 can be considered to be a *lower bound* on the expected population.

There is evidence that education is a very important item in the success of family-planning drives. Table 11.2 shows the results of a survey carried out in 1960–1. This finding is also consistent with some later surveys (Sarkar, 1973). A recent finding of K. N. Raj and associates that the birth-rate in Kerala has declined substantially during the latter half of the 1960s lends additional support to this, as Kerala is the state in India with the highest literacy among men and women. In fact Sarkar (1973) estimates that for Calcutta the gross marital fertility rate decreases from 177 for illiterate women to 98 for women with education above class 8. Considering all this evidence and also the fact that education has been expanding rapidly over the last 20 years, the above projections seem to be reasonable.

However, to obtain an *upper bound* on the projection we assume that the same growth rate in population as was observed between

TABLE 11.2 EDUCATION AND FAMILY PLANNING: URBAN
INDIA PERCENTAGE AT EACH EDUCATIONAL LEVEL WHO
HAVE EVER PRACTISED FAMILY PLANNING
(OTHER THAN ABSTINENCE)

Educational level	Husband	Wife
Illiterate	0·75 (4599)	1·75 (9460)
Literate but below primary	2·20 (2888)	7·30 (2384)
Primary	3·45 (2327)	11·85 (1865)
Middle English	7·60 (2075)	20·30 (1052)
Matriculation	16·75 (2339)	36·00 (994)
Intermediate	24·10 (696)	28·45 (184)
Graduate and above	32·75 (1235)	40·70 (220)

Note: Numbers in brackets refer to number in that class of educational level in the sample.
Source: Tables with Notes on Family Planning, 1960–61, National Sample Survey, Cabinet Secretariat, Government of India.

1961 to 1971 will prevail till 2001. This assumes no significant success in the family-planning effort. Moreover we will assume that the census estimate of population of 548 million in 1971 was an under-estimate, as is believed by some demographers, and we will take it to be 555 million. The projection made on this basis gives a population of 1127 million in A.D. 2001 which can be taken to be an upper bound.

III. PROJECTION OF URBAN POPULATION

In order to project the urban population in 2001, we need to understand what are the causes behind rural urban migration. That people migrate to urban areas in the expectation of a higher standard of living seems to be self evident. Yet it is important to study the dynamics of urbanisation if one is to control it. We have constructed a model (Parikh, n.d.) to predict the growth of the city of Bombay so as to understand the dynamics of its growth.

The basic hypotheses are as follows:

(i) The number of jobs in the manufacturing sector in a given time period is a function of the number of jobs in the manufacturing activity in the proceeding time period.

(ii) The total number of jobs in the economy at a given point of time is a function of the number of jobs in the manufacturing sector at that point of time.

(iii) The number of migrants into the metropolis during a given period of time is a function of the net increment in jobs during that period of time.

(iv)   The population at the end of time period equals the sum of:
   (a) the population at the start of the time period;
   (b) the net natural growth of the initial population; and
   (c) the net migration into the city.
(v)   The number of jobs in each of the following sectors at any given point of time is a function of the population in the metropolis at that time:
   (a) commerce (wholesale and retail trade, financial services);
   (b) transport services;
   (c) power and gas supply services;
   (d) sanitary services;
   (e) educational and scientific services;
   (f) health and medical services.
(vi)   The construction activity in the metropolis depends on all other economic activity and the number of jobs in construction at any given time is a function of total number of jobs in the economy.
(vii)   The number of jobs in public administration at any given time period is a function of time. The definition of activities, e.g. manufacture, commerce, transport and communications, etc. is the same as used in the census of 1961.

The hypotheses formulated above are summarised mathematically in Table 11.3.

Using the decennial census data from 1911 to 1971 we test these hypotheses through regression analysis. We find all of them to be significant (Table 11.4) at 5 per cent level and most of them to be significant at 1 per cent level (t tests for coefficients and F test for the equations). When time is introduced as an independent variable, there is no significant change in the coefficients. Similar results were obtained when differences were used.

The set of equations is used to project Bombay's population in 2001. We assume that no active policy will be pursued to discourage migrants into Bombay (e.g. by restricting creation of new jobs in the city). The population in 2001 is estimated to be between 12·6 to 15·2 million. With the 1971 population of 6 million, this implies a growth rate of 2·55 to 3·18 per cent per annum.

However to get an upper bound we will assume that the total urban population will grow at the rate of 3·25 per cent per annum. The total urban population in 1971 was 110 million. Thus we project the urban population to be 310 million in A.D. 2001. We shall use this figure with both the projections of population to arrive at estimates of rural populations. These are summarised in Table 11.5, and we use these for projecting demands for various goods.

The model suggests that to restrict the growth of Bombay one

TABLE 11.3 URBAN GROWTH MODEL OF BOMBAY

1.	$MFG_t = f(MFG_{t-1})$	where	MFG_t = no. of jobs in manufacturing sector at time t.
2.	$TOT_t = f(MFG_{t-1})$	where	TOT_t = total no. of jobs in the economy at time t.
3.	$MIG_t = f(TOT_t - TOT_{t-1})$	where	MIG_t = net migration into the metropolis between $t-1$ and t.
4.	$P_t = P_{t-1} + MIG_t + NET_t$	where	NET_t = natural addition to the population between $t-1$ and t, and P_t and P_{t-1} are populations at time 't' and '$t-1$' respectively.
5.	$COM_t = f(P_t)$	where	COM_t = no. of jobs in the commercial sector at time t.
6.	$TRAN_t = f(P_t)$	where	$TRAN_t$ = no. of jobs in the transport sector at time t.
7.	$GAS_t = f(P_t)$	where	GAS_t = no. of jobs in the power and gas supply services at time t.
8.	$EDU_t = f(P_t)$	where	EDU_t = no. of jobs in the educational and scientific services at time t.
9.	$SAN_t = f(P_t)$	where	SAN_t = no. of jobs in the sanitary service at time t.
10.	$HEL_t = f(P_t)$	where	HEL_t = no. of jobs in the health and medical services at time t.
11.	$CON_t = f(TOT_t)$	where	CON_t = no. of jobs in construction sector at time t.
12.	$PUB_t = f(t)$	where	PUB_t = no. of jobs in public administration (at all levels) at time t.

and lastly the number of remaining jobs is expressed as an accounting identity in

13. $SERV_t = TOT_t - (MFG_t + TRAN_t + COM_t + GAS_t + EDU_t + SAN_t + HEL_t + CON_t + PUB_t)$

Note: The time interval at which data are available is 10 years and the period $(t-1, t)$ therefore represents the decade between $t-1$ and t.

has to restrict the growth of employment opportunities in it. The fact that new industries still want to come to Bombay implies that Bombay provides economies of agglomeration, and that dispersal of employment opportunities may slow down economic growth. Yet a very careful recent study of optimum industrial location in the state of Maharashtra (of which Bombay is the capital) indicates that economies of agglomeration manifest themselves in cities of 250,000 to 300,000, and that, for Maharashtra at least, dispersal of industries would also be economically advantageous. Though diverting future migrants to such smaller cities would not reduce 'urban' population

TABLE 11.4 RESULTS OF URBAN GROWTH MODEL

Serial no.	Dependent variable	Regression coefficient (b) attached with variables				Constant of the equation (a)	Coefficient of determination	F-ratio
		MFG_{t-1}	P_t	TOT	MFG_t			
1.	MFG_t	1·67^b (0·18) 9·15				−163·56	0·98	83·82^b
2.	TOT_t				2·06^b (0·12) 16·23	299·17	0·98	263·42^b
3.	$MIG_{t-1,t}$			1·0961 (0·1818) 6·0279		239·5184	0·9478	36·3365^b
4.	COM_t				0·3700^b (0·0512) 7·2187	72·1940	0·9455	52·1104^a
5.	$TRAN_t$				0·2457^b (0·0387) 6·3376	15·2230	0·9305	40·1661^b
6.	CON_t	0·01039^a (0·0021) 4·8924				−0·6246	0·8886	23·9356^a
7.	CAS_t	0·0024^b (0·0003) 8·0000				−2·2048	0·9619	75·9099^a
8.	SAN_t	0·0044^b (0·0006) 7·1420				1·1015	0·9444	51·0082^b
9.	HEL_t	0·0067^b (0·0002) 25·9273				−4·8344	0·9955	672·22^b
10.	EDU_t	0·0096^b (0·0009) 10·3031				−9·1267	0·9725	106·1543^b
11.	PUB_t	0·0191^a (0·0043) 4·4299				4·4903	0·8674	19·6244^a
12.	$RETAIL_t$	0·0418^a (0·0081) 5·1462				50·4951	0·8982	26·4841^a
13.	$WHOLE_t$				0·06899 (0·02323) 2·9667	39·1173	0·7458	8·8018
14.	$ROAD_t$	0·0172^a (0·0034) 4·9341				−2·6224	0·8902	24·3463^a
15.	$RAIL_t$	0·0045 (0·0018) 2·5493				17·4963	0·6841	6·4990
16.	FIN_t				0·0469^a (0·0083) 5·5855	5·4628	0·9122	31·1979^a

Note: All the equations are linear, i.e. of the form $Y = a + bx$. The numbers below the coefficient are standard error and *t*-value.
  ^{a} Indicates significance at 5 per cent level.
  ^{b} Indicates significance at 1 per cent level.

as defined by census, it would reduce problems of urbanisation considerably. However, many small-scale industries can be located in rural areas if they are not too far away from an urban centre. Thus such dispersal should lead to reduction in urban population.

A deliberate policy to disperse industries to rural areas has not been actively pursued over the past decade. If such a policy were pursued, the rate of increase of urban population should come down.

TABLE 11.5   RANGE OF PROJECTIONS OF POPULATION IN 2001
(millions)

	Rural	Urban	Total	Urban population as per cent of the total
Low aggregate population with high proportionate urbanisation	554	310	864	35·88
High aggregate population with low proportionate urbanisation	817	310	1127	27·51

Compared to this 310 million the urban population projected by the Agricultural Commission is 409 million. This assumes that the influx into urban areas not only cannot be contained by a sensible policy of industrial dispersal but that it will accelerate. The estimate of 409 million of urban population seems too high and we reject it.

IV. PROJECTIONS OF CONSUMER DEMAND

We propose to use the Engel curves based on the National Sample Survey data on consumer expenditure for projecting the consumer demand. The implicit assumption is that the Engel curves would remain unchanged over the next 30 to 35 years. Since the cross-section data are expected to yield long-run Engel curves and we confine our analysis to broad groups of commodities, this may not be an unreasonable procedure for getting the orders of magnitude for the range of likely demand for various agricultural commodities.

The Engel curves have been worked out separately for rural and urban areas and their use for projection purposes requires the following information for A.D. 2001:

(a) the rural and urban breakdown of the total population;
(b) the overall per capita expenditure;
(c) the rural–urban differential in per capita expenditure.

We have already specified the assumptions regarding the rural urban breakdown of the total population in Table 11.5.

The overall level of per capita expenditure in A.D. 2001 depends on the rate at which the per capita expenditure may be expected to grow over the rest of the century. This in turn depends crucially on the rate of growth of population (specified already) as well as the rate at which the aggregate national income is expected to grow as determined by the rates of investment and savings. As far as technological prospects are concerned, the growth rate of national income can possibly exceed 10 per cent per annum. The implied policies may, however, be hard to implement in the real world with its political and institutional constraints. It seems reasonable to expect a gradual stepping up of rates of investment and other efforts that would result in a gradual increase in the rate of growth of aggregate consumer expenditure. The assumed alternative sets of growth rates are shown in Table 11.6.

TABLE 11.6 ALTERNATIVE ASSUMPTIONS
REGARDING THE GROWTH RATES OF AGGREGATE
PRIVATE CONSUMPTION EXPENDITURE

	(*per cent per annum*)		
	1971–81	1981–91	1991–2001
'Likely' alternative	4·5	5·0	5·5
'Optimistic' alternative	5·5	6·5	7·5

Combining the assumptions of Table 11.6 with the assumptions relating to the growth rate of population, the resulting rates of growth of per capita consumer expenditure are given in Table 11.7.

TABLE 11.7 IMPLIED GROWTH RATES OF PER CAPITA
EXPENDITURE (PER CENT PER ANNUM)

	1971–81	1981–91	1991–2001
PG: High population, high growth	3·30	4·30	5·30
Pg: High population, low growth	2·30	2·80	3·30
pG: Low population, high growth	3·65	4·95	6·20
pg: Low population, low growth	2·65	3·45	4·20

Notes:
High population refers to high aggregate population with low proportionate urbanisation (Table 11.5).
  Low population refers to low aggregate population with high proportionate urbanisation (Table 11.5).
  High growth refers to 'optimistic' growth alternative (Table 11.6).
  Low growth refers to 'likely' growth alternative (Table 11.6).

As regards the rural–urban differential in per capita total expenditure, it may be observed that some differential is inevitable because of the processing-transportation-distribution component added to whatever is imported into the urban sector from the rural areas, as also the imposed needs (like intra-city transportation) and induced needs (such as going to movies) in the urban surroundings. The current ratio between urban and rural per capita total expenditure has been observed to be around 1·5. This may be taken to be an upper limit when urbanisation cannot be checked. As a result we use this ratio for working out rural and urban per capita expenditure for the case with low aggregate population with high proportionate urbanisation. On equity grounds an argument can indeed be made to reduce the urban–rural differential. This, however, may reasonably be associated with the low proportionate urbanisation because through the same set of policies adopted to restrict the expansion of urbanisation, the reduction of urban–rural differential may be expected. We assume this differential to be reduced to 1·25 for the high aggregate population with low proportionate urbanisation. The resulting rural and urban levels of per capita total expenditure are presented in Table 11.8.

TABLE 11.8 PER CAPITA MONTHLY EXPENDITURE,
RURAL AND URBAN IN A.D. 2001
(RS AT PRICES OF 1971)

	Rural	Urban
PG: High population, high growth, low urban–rural differential	92·38	115·48
Pg: High population, low growth, low urban–rural differential	59·86	74·83
pG: Low population, high growth, high urban–rural differential	106·07	159·10
pg: Low population, low growth high urban–rural differential	68·92	103·39

It is clear that the projections corresponding to pG (low population, high growth and high urban–rural differential) provide an upper limit on the per capita expenditure whereas those corresponding to Pg indicate a possible lower limit. Lack of family planning coupled with indifferent effort towards economic development result in a per capita monthly expenditure of less than Rs 60 for rural population. Success in both these directions leads to Rs 106 which is more than 1·75 times that level.

The latest available report of the National Sample Survey on household consumer expenditure is for the nineteenth round covering the period July 1964 to June 1965 (N.S.S., 1971).

The Engel curves have been estimated by Jain and Tendulkar (1973) on the basis of the data available for the nineteenth round for rural and urban areas separately. It may be noted that for all the items considered here, the best forms of Engel curves (in terms of goodness of fit) turned out to be linear, semi-log, and hyperbolic – all with *variable* elasticities with respect to total per capita expenditure. We summarise below the prediction formulae as also the point elasticity formulae for these forms of Engel curves:

Type of Engel curve	Prediction formula	Point elasticity formula
1. Linear (L)	$y_p = y_0 + \beta(x_p - x_0)$	$\beta \dfrac{x_p}{y_p}$
2. Semi-log (SL)	$y_p = y_0 + \beta \log_e \dfrac{x_p}{x_0}$	$\beta \dfrac{1}{y_p}$
3. Hyperbola (H)	$y_p = y_0 + \beta \left[\dfrac{1}{x_p} - \dfrac{1}{x_0} \right]$	$\beta \dfrac{i}{x_p \cdot y_p}$

Notes:

y_0 and y_p = base year actual and forecast for the prediction year of the per capita monthly expenditure on a particular commodity;

x_0 and x_p = base year actual and forecast for the prediction year of the per capita monthly total expenditure;

β = slope parameter of the Engel curve.

Using these formula and the estimated coefficients presented in Tables 11.A and 11.B in the appendix, we estimate per capita monthly expenditure on each commodity for the rural and the urban areas separately. The next problem relates to translating these expenditures into quantities. For this purpose we require the retail prices of various commodities in 1964–5. In the absence of any data on retail prices we adopt the following procedure:

Firstly, for foodgrains as a group the rural and urban retail prices are derived from the National Sample Survey report by dividing the value of expenditure on foodgrains by the quantities consumed.

Secondly, the ex-factory prices for various commodities are taken from those reported for the year 1961–2 by Saluja (1972).

Thirdly, we assume that the *relative* retail price structure for various commodities in 1964–5 was the same as the relative price structure of ex-factory prices for the same commodities in 1961–2. The validity of this assumption depends on the unchanged commodity specific proportionate importance of indirect taxes (that were practically negligible on agricultural commodities) and margin between the two years. This procedure is adopted for all the commodities except cotton clothing for which we work out the per capita availability of cotton clothing for 1964–5 and use the growth rates of per capita expenditure on clothing from our projection

TABLE 11.9 PROJECTIONS OF DEMAND FOR AGRICULTURAL
OUTPUT (MILLION TONNES UNLESS OTHERWISE INDICATED)

		pG	pg	PG	Pg
1.	Cereals	266	244	398	351
2.	Rice	137	121	197	174
3.	Wheat	56	51	77	68
4.	Other cereals	73	72	124	109
	of which: bajra	11	11	19	17
	jowar	28	28	49	43
	maize	17	16	28	25
5.	Pulses	53	44	76	64
	of which: gram	22	18	31	26
6.	Oilseeds	14	10	21	15
	of which: groundnut	9	7	13	10
7.	Sugar-cane	352	231	575	376
8.	Fruit and vegetables	100	66	150	99
9.	Milk and milk products	116	73	182	116
10.	Meat and fish	6	5	9	7
11.	Eggs (billions)	50	39	57	54
12.	Bidi and cigarettes (billions)	644	500	919	725
13.	Other tobacco	131	103	190	152
14.	Cotton (billion bales)	190	97	328	178

Notes:

12·5 per cent allowance for seed, feed and wastage is made in terms of gross production for items 1 to 6.

The demand for rice, wheat and other cereals for human consumption has been derived on the basis of the observed percentage of per capita expenditure on cereals in 1961–2. These percentages are as follows:

	Rural	*Urban*
Rice	54%	57%
Wheat	14%	29%
Other cereals	32%	14%

Other cereals are broken down into bajra, jowar and maize, pulses into grams, and oilseeds into groundnut on the basis of recently observed percentages.

For sugar and gur, the ratio of sugar and gur to sugar-cane has been assumed to be 10 per cent which has been observed in the past.

The demand for meat and fish separately from eggs has been derived on the basis of the observed percentage of per capita expenditure on meat, fish and eggs together in 1961–2. The percentages are:

	Rural	*Urban*
Meat and fish	54%	61%
Eggs	46%	39%

The demand for bidi and cigarettes as distinct from other tobacco has been obtained on the basis of the observed percentage of per capita expenditure on bidi, cigarettes and other tobacco in 1961–2. The percentages are:

	Rural	*Urban*
Bidi and cigarettes	47%	63%
Other tobacco	53%	37%

The demand for clothing (in terms of million metres) has been converted into demand for raw cotton using the conversion ratio of 0·0066 standard bales of 180 kg per metre of cloth.

exercise to arrive at the per capita demand for clothing. With these assumptions we project the demand for the various agricultural output for 2001, and these are given in Table 11.9.

As would be expected, the demand for all agricultural products is higher for the cases with high population than the cases with smaller population. However, though the difference in population is only 30 per cent, the demand for agricultural produce is more by 50 per cent. This is because in the high population cases, rural population, which devotes a larger proportion of its expenditure on food, is larger.

Compared to our minimum estimate of the requirement of food-grains (cereals + pulses) of 268 million tonnes, the Agricultural Commission's estimate based on nutritional targets for the same population is between 155 to 172 million tonnes. 172 million tonnes are enough only if foodgrains can be distributed equitably to all. If the implied political and institutional changes are to be ruled out, the estimates of Table 11.9 are reasonable if food shortages are to be avoided.

V. PROSPECT FOR AGRICULTURAL PRODUCTION IN 2001[1]

Can India, with its given land resource, produce this much output? I will now attempt to answer this question.

Figure 11.1 shows how India is divided into different agro-climatic zones. These divisions are based on the need and availability of moisture, and on the type of soil. Agricultural activity in these zones can be further divided into irrigated or rain-fed and dry on the basis of whether irrigation is available or not. Unirrigated land is divided into rain-fed and dry based on whether the annual assured rainfall exceeds 90 cm or not.

Based on a large number of experiments (about 40,000) carried out on farmers' fields over 1968–9, 1969–70 and 1970–1 we have estimated the yield response of different crops and their varieties to different levels of fertilisers in the different sub-divisions of these zones. Figures 11.2 and 11.3 show these estimated fertiliser response curves for wheat and paddy for one of these zones. The curves for nitrogen (N), potash (K) and phosphorus (P) are given separately as we find no significant interaction effect when two or more fertilisers are applied together, and the increases in yield are found to be additive.

It is clear in Fig. 11.2 that wheat variety 5 is dominant, in the sense that the yield is higher for that variety at all levels of fertiliser

---

[1] Most of this section is based on the work being done currently at the Indian Statistical Institute on 'Optimum Demand for Fertilizers', financed by the Fertilizer Association of India.

applications. In comparing yields we restrict ourselves to the maximum fertiliser dosage tried out in the experiments. In other words we only permit interpolations and not extra-polations.

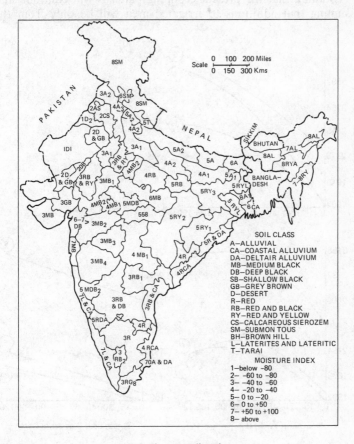

FIG. 11.1 India, agro-climatic zones.

Notes:
1. Zone name consists of moisture index soil class.
2. Subscript refers to subdivision of a zone.

Similarly in Fig. 11.3, rice variety 3 is dominant. We identify dominant varieties for all zones for which data are available and these are shown for wheat in Fig. 11.4. We have estimated similar response functions for jowar, bajra, maize, gram, groundnut and cotton. Unfortunately the data do not cover all the zones. We will assume that for a given crop the uncovered area gives the same response as the average of the covered areas.

Assuming that the present cropping patterns will continue and assuming that additions to irrigated area will be only from the

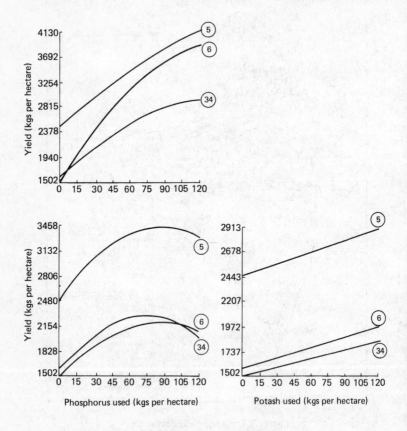

FIG. 11.2 Yields of different varieties of wheat (Zone–$4A_1$).

schemes for irrigation which are at present proposed to be implemented by 1980, we estimate the area under various crops in each of our sub-divisions of the agro-climatic zones.

We can now pose the problem: given these data on area, irrigation and crop-yield response to fertilisers, what are the minimum amounts of fertilisers (N, P and K) required to produce the outputs desired?

The formal model is described in the appendix. The above problem is solved for the extreme case PG and for comparison the case pG, and the results obtained are given in Table 11.10.

It should be emphasised that these results are based on current technology in terms of available strains etc. and it is reasonable to

TABLE 11.10 PROSPECTS FOR AGRICULTURAL OUTPUT IN 2001
(IN MILLION TONNES)

CASE **PG** HIGH POPULATION–HIGH GROWTH

Crop	Projected demand	Production	Nitrogen	Phosphorus	Potash
Rice	197	168	5·05	2·47	2·43
Jowar	49	38	1·00	0·60	0·50
Bajra	19	24	1·00	0·19	0·47
Maize	28	22	0·61	0·28	0·32
Wheat	77	73	1·88	0·88	0·82
Cotton	59	11	0·67	0·29	0·42
Groundnut	13	12	0·24	0·33	0·27
Gram	31	12	0·26	0·50	0·33
Total			9·71	5·54	5·56

CASE **pG** LOW POPULATION–HIGH GROWTH

Crop	Projected demand	Production	Nitrogen	Phosphorus	Potash
Rice	137	137	0·15	0·88	0·52
Jowar	28	28	0·10	0·20	0·14
Bajra	11	11	0	0	0
Maize	17	17	0·06	0·09	0·22
Wheat	56	56	0·50	0·30	0·34
Cotton	34	11	0·67	0·29	0·42
Groundnut	9	9	0·18	0·22	0·22
Gram	22	12	0·26	0·50	0·33
Total			1·92	2·48	2·20

assume that many newer strains will be available by 2001. Even with existing strains, it is clear that for the case pg there is no difficulty in meeting the demand for foodgrains. There is a shortfall in cotton and gram, but there should be no difficulty in attaining the required output by shifting acreage from other crops to these two crops.

However, for case PG, there are shortfalls in almost all the crops. However, it should be emphasised that we have assumed irrigated area not to increase beyond what is projected for 1980. Clearly this is an underestimate, as by 1980 not more than 50 per cent of potential irrigable land will be brought under irrigation. Moreover we have restricted fertiliser applications at or below the dosages tried in the

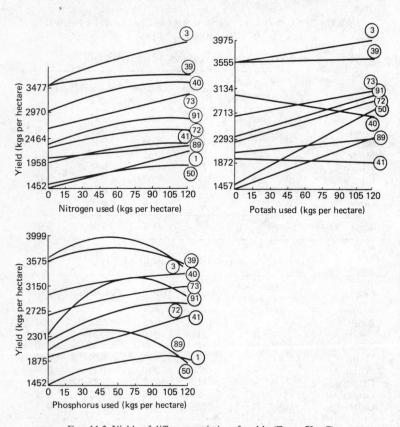

FIG. 11.3 Yields of different varieties of paddy (Zone–7I + C).

fertiliser trials. These dosages are also less than those applied in many countries. There is no HYV available for gram today as not much effort has been directed so far towards evolving HYV's of pulses. Similarly for cotton, some HYV's have just been evolved but have been only meagrely covered by our data. One could expect that it would be possible to produce much more food than is shown by the calculations.

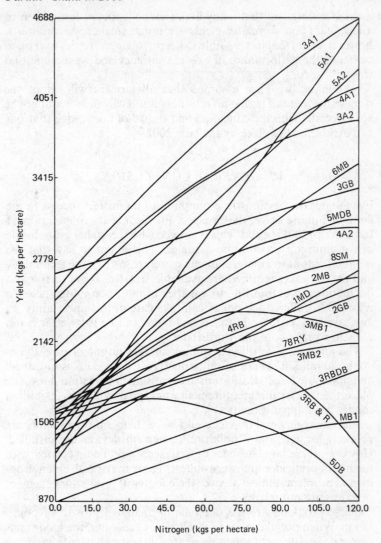

FIG. 11.4 Wheat (irrigated) yield response to fertiliser, dominant varieties in different zones.

There is however, need for some qualifications to all these:

(a) The results are based on the average response over a period of only three years. Though these were not exceptional years, one should not expect that the average of these years provides an expected value estimate.

(b) It is observed that many high yielding varieties lose vigour in a few years and thereafter yields are much smaller. Agronomists, however, claim that it is possible to keep evolving varieties to replace or better the performance of existing varieties and we assume that this will be so.

(c) Finally, we have assumed that all farmers will adopt the dominant variety. There is no rational reason why this should not be so, especially with the education and spread of knowledge that one can expect to take place by the year 2001.

VI. GENERAL CONCLUSIONS

Even under the pessimistic assumption of no further success in the family-planning drive, the prospect for feeding the population of India in A.D. 2001 is good. This is so even with the higher growth-rate of consumption expenditure assumed. This is not to say that the required output will materialise but merely to say that the technology and the resources required are available. Yet, this is not to rule out fluctuations in output due to vagaries of monsoon. Nonetheless a reasonable buffer-stock policy can take care of this uncertainty. In any case, the yet-to-be-born 'second India' can be fed, and it is too early to worry about the 'third India'.

The amount of fertiliser required for the output of case PG is about 20 million tonnes of nutrients $(N + P + K)$. This is not at all an impossible target. If substantial expansion of irrigation does take place, then the fertiliser requirement would go down. Thus 20 million tonnes is an upper estimate.

The environmental impact could be negligible if these plants are properly located, and if pollution abatement devices are installed. However, these large dosages of fertiliser would be associated with the use of pesticides and weed-killers. These may result in environmental problems almost all over the country, if proper management practices are not introduced.

These problems are the outcome of unabated growth of population. When population is controlled as in case pG, the foodgrains demand is easily met though there are still some shortfalls in cotton and gram. Moreover the fertiliser requirement goes down to no more than 6·60 million tonnes, and the pollution problem is substantially controlled.

Thus reduction of population not only improves the per capita consumption, it also substantially reduces environmental problems. The quality of life improves in many ways with a smaller family. A small India is a happy India.

APPENDIX

TABLE 11.A BASE YEAR CONSUMPTION EXPENDITURE PER CAPITA
PER MONTH AND SLOPE COEFFICIENTS OF ENGEL CURVES (RURAL)

Serial no.	Commodity	Form of Engel curve	1964–5	β
1.	Food grains	Semi-log	11·14	6·4155
2.	Pulses	Semi-log	1·12	1·0510
3.	Milk and milk products	Linear	1·44	0·0761
4.	Oil, oilseeds and products	Linear	0·76	0·0243
5.	Meat, fish, eggs, etc.	Semi-log	0·54	0·5535
6.	Sugar, sugar candy, gur, etc.	Linear	0·74	0·0355
7.	Fuel and light	Semi-log	1·20	0·8264
8.	Tobacco and products	Semi-log		
9.	Beverages and refreshments	Linear	0·28	0·0118
10.	Vegetables, fruit, nuts, etc.	Linear	0·95	0·0293
11.	Clothing	Linear	2·03	0·1422

Notes:

$Xo = Rs. 24.93$ (1964–5) for the rural areas.

We have assumed that the per capita overall monthly total expenditure (for both the sectors together) increased by 5 per cent over the period 1964/5–1970/1. Thereafter the growth rates specified in Table 11.6 apply.

TABLE 11.B BASE YEAR CONSUMPTION EXPENDITURE PER CAPITA
PER MONTH AND SLOPE COEFFICIENTS OF ENGEL CURVES (URBAN)

Serial no.	Commodity	Form of Engel curve	1964–5	β
1.	Food grains	Hyperbola	8·44	− 56·1666
2.	Pulses	Semi-log	1·21	0·6696
3.	Milk and milk products	Linear	2·81	0·0814
4.	Oil, oilseeds and products	Semi-log	1·29	1·0266
5.	Meat, fish, eggs, etc.	Linear	1·09	0·0275
6.	Sugar, sugar candy, gur, etc.	Semi-log	1·04	0·6353
7.	Fuel and light	Semi-log	1·80	1·3301
8.	Tobacco and products	Log-linear	0·57	0·7939
9.	Beverages and refreshments	Linear	1·27	0·0499
10.	Vegetables, fruit, nuts, etc.	Linear	2·34	0·0623
11.	Clothing	Linear	2·32	0·1242

Notes:

$Xo = Rs. 36.55$ (1964–5) for the urban areas.

For note on total expenditure, see Table 11.A.

OPTIMUM REQUIREMENT OF FERTILISERS

Symbols used:

N, P and K = dosages of fertiliser (kg per hectare) applied.

p_n, p_p, p_k = prices of fertiliser (*Rs* per kg).

A_i^z = area in zone z devoted to crop i.

Z = number of zones.

C = number of different crops considered.

$\bar{Y}_i$ = required output of crop i.

$Y_i^z(N_i^z, P_i^z, K_i^z)$ = yield (kg per hectare) of ith crop in z^{th} zone as a function of fertiliser dosages.

$\alpha, \beta, \sqrt{\delta}$ = coefficients of yield response functions.

Minimise cost of fertiliser

$$F = \sum_{z=1}^{Z} \sum_{i=1}^{C} (p_n N_i^z A_i^z + p_p p_i^z A_i^z + p_k K_i^z A_i^z)$$

to produce the required quantities of agricultural produce

$$\sum_{z=1}^{Z} Y_i^z(N_i^z, P_i^z, K_i^z) \quad A_i^z \geqslant \bar{Y}_i \quad i = 1, \ldots, C$$

within available area in each zone;

$$\sum_{i=1}^{C} A_i^z \leqslant \bar{A}^z \quad z = 1, \ldots, Z$$

Given the yield response functions of the dominant variety in the zone

$$Y_i^z = \alpha_i^z + \beta_{1i}^z N_i^z - \beta_{2i}^z (N_i^z)^2 + \gamma_{1i}^z P_i^z - \gamma_{2i}^z (P_i^z)^2 + \delta_{1i}^z K_i^z - \delta_{2i}^z (K_i^z)^2$$
$$i = 1, \ldots, C \quad z = 1, \ldots, Z$$

It is obvious that if any fertiliser at all is to be required all constraints are binding.

We want to minimise the Lagrangian

$$L = F + \sum_{i=1}^{C} \lambda_i \left(\bar{Y}_i - \sum_{z=1}^{z} Y_i^z A_i^z \right) + \sum_{z=1}^{z} \lambda^z \left(\sum_{i=1}^{C} A_i^z - \bar{A}^z \right)$$

The first order condition for an extremum are

$$\frac{\partial L}{\partial N_i^z} = 0 = p_n . A_i^z - \lambda_i \frac{\partial Y_i^z}{\partial N_i^z} A_i^z$$

which gives

$$\frac{p_n}{\lambda_i} = \frac{\partial Y_i^z}{\partial N_i^z} = \frac{\partial Y_i^x}{\partial N_i^x} = \frac{\partial Y_i^y}{\partial Y_i^y} \quad i = 1, \ldots, C$$

$$\frac{p_p}{\lambda_i} = \frac{\partial Y_i^z}{\partial P_i^z} = \frac{\partial Y_i^x}{\partial P_i^x} = \frac{\partial Y_i^y}{\partial P_i^y}$$

and

$$\frac{p_k}{\lambda_i} = \frac{\partial Y_i^z}{\partial K_i^z} = \frac{\partial Y_i^x}{\partial K_i^x} = \frac{\partial Y_i^y}{\partial K_i^y}$$

and

$$\frac{\partial L}{\partial A_i^z} = 0 = p_n N_i^z + p_p P_i^z + p_k K_i^z + \lambda^z - \lambda_i Y_i^z.$$

which gives

$$\lambda^z = \lambda_i Y_i^z - p_n N_i^z - p_p P_i^z - p_k K_i^z$$
$$= \lambda_i Y_j^z - p_n N_j^z - p_p P_j^z - p_k K_i^z \quad z = 1, \ldots, Z$$

REFERENCES

L. R. Jain and S. D. Tendulkar, 'Analysis of Occupational Differences in Consumer Expenditure Pattern', *Sankhya*, ser. B, quantitative economics (1973).

National Sample Survey, *Tables with Notes on Household Consumer Expenditure and Enterprise for Rural and Urban Areas of India*, no. 189, Cabinet Secretariat, Government of India (1971).

A. K. and K. S. Parikh, *A Model of Metropolitan Growth: A Case Study of Bombay*, forthcoming technical report, City and Industrial Development Corporation of Maharashtra, Bombay.

M. R. Saluja, 'Structure of the Indian Economy: 1964–65 Input-Output Relations Among 144 Sectors', *Sankhya*, ser. B, vol. 34, pt 4 (1972) 433–62, plus Table.

B. N. Sarkar, *Some Results in Family Planning Surveys*, technical report, Indian Statistical Institute (May 1973).

12 Population Growth, Economic Growth and the Environment in the United States

Ronald G. Ridker
RESOURCES FOR THE FUTURE, WASHINGTON, D.C.

I. INTRODUCTION

The most recent spate of intellectual and scholarly interest in the resource and environmental consequences of population and economic growth arises from two main sources. The first has to do with predictions of growing scarcity of natural resources and environmental carrying capacity. The most extreme version is to be found in the doomsday literature of the last two or three years which in one way or another argues that population and economic growth are pressing against the finite limits of the earth and soon must stop if catastrophe in the form of dramatically increased death-rates throughout the world is to be avoided. In less extreme form this theme can be found in worries over the increasing dependence of major consumers of natural resources on foreign sources of supply and over the growing economic costs of correcting local environmental problems. The second source of recent interest is with the effects, particularly the economic and social effects, of the declining rates of growth of population currently being experienced in most developed countries, a concern that is characterised by the question 'will ZPG lead to ZEG', that is, 'will zero population growth eventually result in a stagnant economy and society?'

This paper speaks to these concerns by reviewing what is known about the resource and environmental effects of the growth in population and the economy that are likely to occur in the United States during the next quarter to half century. In doing so it will summarise the principal findings of a study developed by Resources for the Future for the U.S. Commission on Population Growth and the American Future (1972); but since these findings are now in print, emphasis will be placed on the rationale for the assumptions that went into this analysis and on the policy conclusions that can be drawn from them.

II. DETERMINANTS OF RESOURCE AND ENVIRONMENTAL PRESSURES

Whatever the relationships are between resource use and environmental pressures on the one side and population and economic growth on the other, one thing is clear: these relationships are strongly influenced by a host of intervening variables such as tastes, institutions, technology and trade relations, changes which cannot be ignored in any long-run analysis. The situation is further complicated by the fact that many of these variables are poorly defined and measured. As a consequence, there is no simple, direct way to trace out the relationships involved. The best that can be done is to list the principal determinants of resource and environmental pressures and to consider what the most reasonable and useful assumptions are to make about them over time.

These determinants are usefully grouped under seven headings. First, of course, are *demographic variables*: the size of the population, its rate of growth, its age, sex and racial structure, the number and size of the households involved, and labour-force participation rates. All these factors influence the amount and composition of consumption goods purchased as well as the level of economic activity. The latter, of course, are important determinants of the throughput of materials and hence the resource and environmental pressures experienced. Second, the *standard of living*, measured by per capita G.N.P. or income, plus the distribution of this standard of living among various groups within the population, plays a similarly important role in determining the throughput of materials. A third factor is what we shall call the *style of living*, in particular, preferences for various kinds of goods and ways of using them. Certainly, a style of life that includes throw-away bottles, suburban living and high compression automobiles places vastly more pressure on the environment than does one that involves less emphasis on packaging and advertising, apartment living, and mass transit. Fourth, the *geographic distribution* of both population and economic activities can have a significant impact. The more concentrated such activities are the more difficult it is for pollution to be absorbed and assimilated through natural environmental processes; on the other hand, a more dispersed economy requires more resources for transport, recycling and treatment of residuals. Fifth, the *technological methods* used at each stage of economic activity, from mining and energy conversion through transport and production to emission and treatment of effluents, can make a great difference in both the character and magnitude of the problems arising as a consequence of population and economic growth. A sixth set of factors, often overlooked but likely to play an increasingly important role in the future, involves *international relations*, in particular, the terms at which the United States can acquire resources and finished commodities from abroad. Finally, all these factors are influenced by *institutions and policies*: by the way markets work, by rules and regulations governing the management of effluents and land use, by import policies with respect to fuels and minerals, by decisions made with respect to location of public investments, and so on.

Obviously, each of the determinants does not operate completely independently of the others. In particular, the movement towards ZPG which seems to be under way in the United States can have significant effects on all the other determinants, especially on those associated with the level of economic activity. In what follows, therefore, we begin by discussing the demographic variables, move on to discuss the effect of these variables on the rate of economic growth, and then return to discuss likely changes in the other determinants, especially those changes which are more or less independent of the demographic changes.

Population

At the outset let us make perfectly clear that under any reasonable assumption about births per woman during the next few decades, the population of the United States will grow quite substantially during the next quarter to half century. If ZPG is taken literally to mean a cessation of population growth, we are still a good way from achieving it. There are three reasons for this. First, the United States has a relatively young population, with a large fraction of women just entering child-bearing years. Even if these women decide to have no more than the 2·1 children necessary for replacement, this age structure will result in population growth of nearly 50 per cent before stability is reached. Second, to achieve ZPG immediately, U.S. women would have to have an average of only slightly more than one child for some decades into the future, at least until the age distribution stabilises itself. While it is true that fertility and expectations about completed fertility among young women have fallen sharply in the last five years (U.S. Bureau of the Census, 1972), the most recent survey on birth expectations reports that women aged 18–24 expect to complete their child-bearing years with an average of 2·1 children, a far cry from the 1·2 or so necessary to achieve immediate ZPG (Frejka, 1970). Put in terms of birth-rates, to achieve ZPG and sustain it over time the crude birth-rate would have to fall from 16 to less than 10 per thousand and remain there for some decades, an event that appears highly unlikely in the near future. Third, all the above ignores net immigration which has been averaging 400,000 per year. This figure is more than 20 per cent of the natural increase in population in recent years. There is no reason to believe that it will decline in the near future.

What has happened in recent years is a decline in fertility and fertility expectations that sets the stage for the ultimate achievement of ZPG, or something very near it. Between 1957 and 1969 the total fertility rate (TFR) has steadily fallen, the five-year averages from 1955–9 through 1965–9 being 3·69, 3·46 and 2·63. Today, this figure probably stands at around 2·05. Will Women's Lib and the easing of abortion laws cause this figure to fall still further? Before we conclude that it will, it is wise to remember the history of the past 50 years. Between 1920–4 and 1935–9, the TFR fell from 3·25 to 2·24 and most analysts at that time predicted that it would continue falling or stabilise near that level. Instead, it steadily rose until it reached a peak of 3·69 during the 1955–9 period.

Perhaps the best we can do is to assume that young women will do more or less what they say they intend to do as stated in fertility expectation surveys. This assumption yields a projection similar to the Census Bureau's Series E, which assumes an average of 2·1 children per woman entering marriage age. It places us on a trajectory which in the absence of immigration would lead to zero population growth by about 2030. But as can be seen from Fig. 12.1, considerable population growth is in store before that point is reached.

Much of the work we undertook for the Population Commission was based on this Series E projection, which includes a constant net immigration of 400,000 per year. To indicate the difference that would be involved if some other projection were to occur, we used Series B, a projection that assumes an average of 3·1 children per woman and the same immigration figure. While this latter projection now appears unrealistically high, it is still useful as a contrast to see what would happen if we were wrong about Series E.

In the process of moving towards ZPG, the population will become significantly older, the average age rising from 32 in 1970 to 37 in 2020. Some commentators have suggested that this will mean a significantly older and less progressive labour force. In fact, however, the average age of those who comprise the bulk of the labour force, that is, those between the ages of 25 and 64, would increase from only 39·3 to 39·9. The principal changes are to be found in the dependent portions of the population, those less than age 16 decreasing from 31 to 25 per cent, and those over age 64 increasing from 10 to 13 per cent. In absolute numbers, these figures mean a slight increase in the younger age group but a near doubling in the size of the older group, and as a consequence a significant shift in the composition of goods and services, public as well as private, demanded by this population.

The labour force, both in terms of size and as a percentage of total population, should become much larger. For the most part, this will result from an increase in the percentage of the population in the

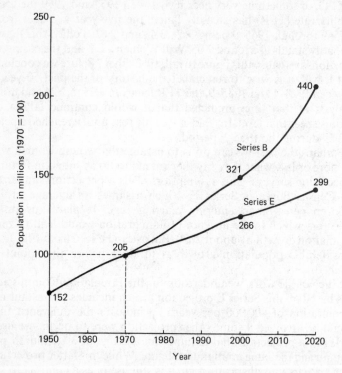

FIG. 12.1 U.S. population with projections, 1950–2020*

* These projections come from U.S. Bureau of the Census, *Current Population Reports*, ser. P-25, no. 470. They have now been superseded by the projections presented in ser. P-25, no. 498 which shifts the base from 1970 to 1972. This shift in base explains the minor differences between the numbers presented in this figure and the new Series E projections.

age group 16 to 64 from 59·6 in 1970 to 64·1 per cent in 2020; but an additional factor is likely to be increased female participation rates resulting from fewer children to take care of at home. If we assume no break from trends in age of retirement and hours of work, these changes could result in the labour force increasing from 85 million in 1970 to 146 million in 2020, an increase of 72 per cent compared to a population increase of 46 per cent. The labour force would then comprise 49 per cent of the population compared to 41 per cent today. The possibility that the age of retirement and hours of work might fall more rapidly than trend was taken into account by special runs of the model, as discussed below.

All these consequences are based on projections of the population as a whole, very little work having been done on the likelihood and effects of different fertility patterns among different segments of the population. One simulation study of the racial implications of ZPG indicates that if a net reproduction rate (NRR) of 1 had been reached during the period 1965–70 for both segments of the population, the percentage non-white would change very little, increasing from 12·2 in the 1965–70 period to 13·7 by 2015–20; whereas if the NRR of the non-white population decreased slowly, not reaching unity until 2040, the percentage non-white would reach 22 by 2015–20 (Attah, 1973). Given the fact that fertility patterns appear to be converging, not just among racial groups but also among educational and income classes, the change in the percentage non-white is likely to be closer to the lower end of this range (Ryder, 1973). Since casual observation also suggests that expenditure patterns for persons in the same income class are also converging, we are probably justified in ignoring the effects on consumption patterns and styles of living of changes in fertility patterns among different groups.

Population effects on the economy

Historically, periods of rapid population growth have been associated with rapid economic growth in the United States. Is this association likely to hold in the future? Will ZPG mean ZEG?

Much of the rapid population growth experienced by the United States was the result of immigration, which, because of the human capital typically embodied in that movement, is far more favourable for economic growth than is natural increase. No one expects the massive immigration of the eighteenth and nineteenth centuries to recur in the future. Moreover, this increase occurred during a period in U.S. history when there were abundant open lands, untapped minerals and timber, and non-divisible investments in transport and communications that could be exploited more fully with additional labour. But this easily tapped frontier has all but disappeared. Of more importance in the future will be the magnitude of effective demand, which in addition to sheer numbers, depends upon income levels, internationally as well as domestically, the degree to which tastes are homogeneous, and the extent to which firms are able to take advantage of specialisation through horizontal integration, vertical disintegration and international trade. With respect to massive immigration and economies of scale requiring increased population to exploit, therefore, history is unlikely to repeat itself. If the slow-down in population growth results in a slow-down of economic growth, it will result from other effects of the projected population changes.

Effects on inventiveness. Theories linking technological change to population growth tend to be either demand- or supply-oriented. Both suggest technological growth is positively related to population growth. Demand-based theories argue that increased population growth generates problems calling for solutions which stimulate inventive activity at a faster rate than does a stable population (Schmookler, 1966). Supply-oriented theories are generally related to the law of large numbers: the larger the population, the larger the number of people with inventive and innovative skills.

As might be expected, empirical tests of these hypotheses are not very convincing: 'inventiveness' is not well defined and measured and there are too many intervening variables that cannot be held constant.[1] But of more importance is the fact that both these theories ignore the role of government and the extent to which research has been institutionalised. Demand for the services of knowledge creators and the direction of their efforts is strongly affected by the financial support made available to them. Moreover, through its support for education, the government has the power to alter the proportion of scientists and innovators in the society. Surely these influences are more important than the effects of population growth, size, or density at this stage in U.S. history.[2] It seems safest to

[1] In a recent paper, Allen C. Kelley reviews this evidence and carries out several statistical tests of his own: 'Demographic Changes and American Economic Development: Past, Present and Future', U.S. Commission on Population Growth and the American Future, *Economic Aspects of Population Change*, vol. II of Commission research reports (Washington, D.C.: U.S. Government Printing Office, 1973). While the evidence tends to support the contention that inventiveness (typically measured by the number of patents per thousand population) increases with population size and density, at least up to a point, none of the tests are able to hold constant such obviously important factors as the type and quantity of education, the financial support provided to inventors and innovators, and the possibilities of international division of labour in knowledge creation and its dissemination, to mention just a few.

[2] An additional problem with these theories, especially those on the demand side, is the optimistic bias implicit in them: population growth is assumed to throw up challenges that are not just met, but 'over-responded to' so that the per capita growth rate does more than just hold its own. If population growth forces the use of less productive land, whatever new seeds come along must do more than offset the decline in yield if the net result is a rise in per capita growth rates. While the presence of new knowledge often does open up new vistas resulting in a cumulative impact on discoveries, it is just as likely that beyond a certain point increased population could lead to an overload of problems, the response of the innovator or scientist being less than equal to the challenge. This would appear to be the case with many of our social problems which, magnified by increasing numbers and densities, generate increased effort at solutions but little concrete progress.

conclude that the rate of innovation, at least during the next half century or so, is not likely to be affected by the demographic changes envisioned during this period.

Effects on labour productivity. Quite independently of population effects on inventiveness and innovation, it is sometimes argued that a decrease in population growth will slow down the advance of labour productivity. Two reasons can be cited for this argument. First, the decreased growth rate increases the average age of the labour force and reduces its rate of turnover, thereby reducing the rate at which new knowledge is introduced. Second, because smaller families are under less economic pressure, members of the labour force may be inclined to expend less effort and hours at work.

We have already indicated that the average age of the bulk of the labour force would not in fact increase by very much. But even if it did, one must remember that the fraction of the population in the labour force would also increase quite significantly, yielding a social dividend that could be used to offset these negative effects. It is quite likely, for example, that a significant portion of this dividend would be devoted to improving the quality of the education system, including greater efforts at adult education and retraining. The second argument, that parents with fewer children expend less effort or hours at work, is difficult to test since available evidence is typically related to family income rather than to work effort. One recent study (Simon, 1971) that takes into account the possible trade-off between work on the part of the wife and the husband found no effect. In a modern setting where children do not supplement family income to any appreciable extent, where there are opportunities and pressures for the woman with no children to work outside the home, and where few individuals – really only the self-employed – have significant opportunities for varying work effort or hours, this finding seems quite reasonable.

There is little reason to believe, therefore, that the rate of growth in man-hour productivity is likely to be very strongly associated with population growth rates during the next half century. In any long-run study it is probably best to assume no association but at the same time to increase the fraction of output devoted to the education sector over what it might otherwise be (or at least not permit it to fall as rapidly as it might solely as a consequence of the decline in the fraction of school-age children in the population). Such assumptions were incorporated into our study.

Effects on savings rates. The evidence linking family size and savings is ambiguous. Some studies have indicated a negative relationship after controlling for income, while others suggest that family savings rates increase with the first and second child and drop thereafter. This latter result could be due to a substitution of children for other consumer durables, at least up to the point where size of family makes further substitutions too difficult. Whatever the relationship, household savings represent a small, and probably increasingly small, fraction of total savings in the United States. Over 80 per cent of the private sector's new capital comes from sources internal to the investing sector; over 60 per cent of private capital formation comes from the corporate sector; in the period 1930–55 over 95 per cent of the sector's invested resources came from internal sources; and all these ratios have been rising over time.[1] Moreover, if it chooses, the government can play an independent role in affecting aggregate savings rates through its fiscal policy.

An important qualification may be that population growth influences business savings rates through its effect on aggregate demand and profit rates. While far from certain, it is possible that a slow-down in population growth would adversely affect profit rates (or expected profit rates) and hence business savings rates. Whether or not this will occur depends largely on the government's ability to maintain full employment through its monetary and fiscal policy, the next subject on our list.

Effects of government responses. While there may be reasons to believe that the government will find it increasingly difficult to respond appropriately when unemployment threatens, it is hard to believe that such increasing difficulty could be due to a decline in population growth. Of course, a slow-down in the growth rate of aggregate demand due to a decline in population growth could add to these difficulties, at least for a time before the labour force begins to grow at a slower rate. But this problem should not be particularly difficult to resolve.

However, the attempt to maintain employment and profit margins for special groups in the face of declining population growth could lead to a decline in the ability of the economy to adjust to changes. When aggregate demand is increasing rapidly, declining industries are permitted to die a slower, more graceful death. If their more rapid decline in a ZPG economy led to preferential government treatment – typically easier to introduce than to eliminate – rigidities could be built into the economy with detrimental impacts on overall productivity. But this is only one of many possibilities. Another is that improved social security systems and increasing per capita incomes could make the death of old industries less painful. It is difficult to know how seriously to take any of these possibilities.

[1] See Allen C. Kelley, op. cit., for a review of studies related to the points made in this paragraph.

Everything considered, therefore, the principal effect of ZPG on the economy is likely to be the increase in the fraction of the population in the labour force, which, at least during the next fifty years or so, could significantly increase the growth rate of per capita income. Some significant changes in the composition of final demands for private and public goods could occur; but population-induced changes in inventiveness, in man-hour productivity, in aggregate savings rates and in government responsiveness are not likely to be important. During a time horizon relevant for current attitudes and ways of doing business, at least, ZPG need not and probably will not lead to ZEG or anything approaching it.

Standards and styles of living

Rapid growth in the economy and hence in the standard of living in the United States has been sustained in large part by a favourable set of preferences, for savings over consumption, for private goods and services over public goods and services, and for work over leisure. While it is difficult to say much about how such preferences might change in the future, and even more difficult to predict changes in life styles, we can at least say that, *in the absence of policy changes*, we see no reason to believe such changes will be in the direction of conserving on resources or environmental carrying capacity.

Consider the preferences for savings over consumption. The personal savings rate might rise if with growing opulence and fewer children we become sated with goods and services, or if we channel increasing portions of our incomes into housing (for example, second homes). But the expectation of routine prosperity and economic security guaranteed through extensions of unemployment, health, and old age and survivors insurance is likely to dampen individual incentives to save. So too would be the persistence of secular price inflation. Increased leisure would also operate in the same direction, increasing consumption especially of recreational goods and services. On net these trends may mean less personal savings. But this is a trend that can be offset by business and government savings behaviour. Provided we are willing to let businesses and government save for us, long-term growth prospects need not be seriously affected by this shift in preferences.

So far as shifts in preferences amongst types of goods are concerned, there seems to be some evidence to indicate a shift from private to public goods and services, and within each category from goods to services. Since cross-section consumption data indicate that the income elasticities of demand for services and many types of public expenditures tend to be higher than for other kinds of goods, there is some reason to believe that such shifts will continue in the future as incomes rise. But a large fraction of public goods involve construction and a significant component of what are called consumer services involves transportation, both heavy users of resources, especially of energy.

A significant shift in preference for leisure over work could have a major impact on resource requirements, at least so long as this shift is not offset by increased automation that results in more goods to be enjoyed during the increased leisure hours. In recent years, work hours per year have ceased their slow, long-term decline. In addition, increasing numbers of women have been entering the labour market. One possible explanation is the need for additional income in the face of the price inflation of recent years. But these changes seem to be independent of family income. Indeed, often it is the wives of well-off husbands who appear most eager to give up leisure for work. An alternative explanation may be that for many in our society work has ceased to be considered a 'bad' to be avoided to the extent one's income permits. That is, perhaps over time the work-place is offering increasing numbers of non-monetary as well as monetary benefits: a pleasant, physical environment, interesting, 'meaningful' things to do, friends, status, respect – and sufficient on-the-job leisure to take advantage of these opportunities. As machine-paced labour is replaced by more automated processes, and as jobs of more intrinsic interest increase in number, this phenomenon is likely to become more and more important. So far as the economy and resource needs are concerned, the result is almost the same as if off-the-job leisure increased, except that it shows up as a decline in man-hour productivity rather than as a decline in work hours or labour-force participation rates.

To account for these possible changes in preferences and styles of living, we assumed no change in the overall propensity to consume and save, a continuation in the trend towards services and public goods, and shifts in the composition of consumer purchases that arise from changes in the numbers of families in different age, income, and family size classes, using data derived from the latest available (1960–1) Survey of Consumer Expenditures.[1] We then considered two alternative assumptions about labour productivity and work hours. First, we permitted man-hour productivity to continue growing at 2·5 per cent per year and annual work hours to decline by 0·25 per cent per year, more or less on trend. As a second alternative we considered the effect of a decline in work hours by 1·0 per cent per year. While still far from a zero economic growth case, the shift towards leisure implied by this second, low economic growth

---

[1] The distribution of household income was assumed to remain constant, a deficiency which we shall attempt to correct in future work.

case is fairly dramatic: instead of weekly work hours falling over a thirty-year period from 40 to 37 in the high growth case, they would fall to 29 in the low growth scenario.

It should be noted that the equivalent low growth case can be generated by assuming a fall in the growth of man-hour productivity to 1·5 per cent per year while holding to the first assumption about annual work hours. Considering the possibility of on-the-job rather than off-the-job leisure increasing, this may be more realistic; but in no way does it change our analysis.

Technological changes

For our purposes five types of technological changes should be distinguished. The first, overall changes in labour productivity, has already been considered. The others involve changes in materials used per unit of output, changes in the generation of residuals per unit of output (or per unit of materials input), changes in the emission of these residuals per unit of residuals generated, and changes in character of these emissions, that is, the extent to which these wastes are emitted in the form of pollutants rather than in some form that is not harmful to the environment or man.

So far as materials other than energy used per unit of output are concerned, the trend has been distinctly downward. Twenty years ago a ton of peaches would produce 40 cases of canned fruit; today 55 cases can be produced from one ton. In addition, the composition of materials has changed dramatically, energy and capital substituting for labour, cheaper materials substituting for higher cost minerals, chemical fertilisers and pesticides substituting for land and natural manures. There is no reason to believe that such changes will not continue in the future, although the particular direction they will take is difficult to predict.

In general the amount of wastes generated per unit of materials input has also been improving. For example, in 1943, the production of container board generated 0·45 tons of waste per ton of final product, whereas by 1963 this figure had dropped to 0·21. For the economy as a whole it is difficult to generalise because of the introduction of new processes, products, and materials over time.

The third type of technological change, changes in the emission of wastes per unit of residuals, has to do with the extent of recovery and recycling. Here the picture is mixed, the trend since the Second World War involving less recycling of waste paper and more recycling of a number of metals. The principal factors influencing these trends are changes in the geographic distribution of the sources of wastes – for example, suburbanisation trends that make collection of waste paper more costly – and the relevant prices which are, of course, subject to influence by government policy. Considering the fact that the incentives for recycling and recovery have been few in the past, it seems quite likely that there is considerable scope for improvement in these directions.

The last category of technological change involves the form in which the wastes are emitted. In large part, this has to do with pollution treatment technology, but change in production processes can also have a significant effect on the toxicity of the wastes. Over time, as the chemical industry has learned to synthesise compounds not found in nature, and hence in general not readily assimilated by plants and animals, the situation has worsened. Treatment technology, however, has been improving and with the proper incentives can be expected to continue improving.

The projection of this mixed bag of effects is, of course, very difficult. To do so without introducing technological fixes that may never happen, we have played it very conservatively, permitting ongoing changes to work their way out but not introducing much that is new. Ongoing shifts from one material to another in particular uses – e.g., plastic for metal pipe production – are permitted to continue up to some specified maximum; and today's best practice is assumed to become the average practice in each industry by the year 2000. But new processes, substitutions and products, with both their good and bad effects, have for the most part been left out.

Geographic distribution

By now the principal trends in distribution of population and economic activities are well known and documented: the emptying out of the countryside, the rapid territorial spread of metropolitan areas, and the reduction in population densities in many central cities. A continuation of these trends is likely to result in an increase in the percentage of the population living in metropolitan areas from 71 in 1970 to 85 in the year 2000 and an increase in the geographic area classified as urban from 200 thousand square miles in 1960 to 500 thousand square miles by 2000. By the latter date, this would mean that one-sixth of the land area of the United States (exclusive of Alaska and Hawaii) would be devoted to urban settlement (U.S. Commission on Population Growth, 1972, ch. 3).

While it is reasonable to assume a continuation of the trend towards urban living, continued reductions in population densities within metropolitan areas are far less certain. A reduction in the size, and an increase in the age, of household units, increasing costs of owning and operating automobiles (because of rising costs of fuel and efforts to cope with pollution and congestion during commuting hours) and investment in mass transit all work in the opposite direction. To account for such possibilities we considered the consequences for air quality of several alternatives with respect to urban densities, one requiring that 10 per cent of the additional economic activity that might otherwise locate in metropolitan regions be located outside these areas, another restricting the geographic spread of current metropolitan areas, and so on. Several of the results are presented below.

Other factors

International developments and changes in institutions and policies with respect to resource use and pollution control could all have significant impacts on the relationships between population, the economy, resources and the environment. Consider the long-run ramifications of increasing difficulties in assuring access to petroleum at reasonable cost, or the introduction of mechanisms to effectively manage the allocation of common property resources such as air, water and land. While short-run response elasticities may be low, there is little doubt that such changes could profoundly alter the impact of population growth on resources and the environment during the time horizon considered here.

Since the purpose of our study was to ask whether the United States could continue along the same general path it has been on, and in the process to highlight the effects of changes in population and the economy, we assumed few changes in these general factors. For example, while we assumed a high rate of consumption of minerals and energy by the rest of the world we also assumed that a relatively free trade regime would prevail. Moreover, in most of the basic scenarios studied the institutional and policy regime was assumed to be constant as of about 1967–70. But to indicate the effect that a change in this regime could have, a few variations in environmental policy were also explored and are reported on below.

III. THE CONSEQUENCES

The consequences of the assumed changes in these determinants were examined in two ways: first using a dynamic input-output model of the economy designed to highlight the resource and environmental elements under study,[1] and second comparing these

---

[1] The core model was developed by Clopper Almon at the University of Maryland. We added resource, pollution and treatment cost coefficients to its 185 sectors, made the consumption and government expenditure functions more sensitive to demographic changes and introduced technological changes in the I/O matrix. In addition, several subsidiary models were developed, for example, one to estimate regional air pollution problems and another to assess demand and supply for water regionally.

results with those obtained from more detailed and conventional studies of specific sectors such as energy and agriculture. Those results that are most salient for the discussion of policy and research implications are presented below.

The economy

To simplify the task, four basic scenarios were developed from the set of alternative assumptions with which we worked: a high population – high economic growth case (B–H), a low population – low economic growth case (E–L), and the two intermediate cases (B–L and E–H). In all four cases, we started by assuming no change in resource or environmental policy from the base period. Table 12.1 presents the results.

As can be seen, by the year 2000 the U.S. economy will be somewhere between double and triple its current size, with all that that entails for resource and environmental pressures. A slowdown in population growth will help, of course: it results in a higher per capita income and a smaller GNP, that is, greater per capita material welfare with a smaller throughput of materials. But even with a significant shift towards leisure – and despite the shift towards services built into these projections – it is clear that we shall face much greater resource and environmental pressures in the future than we have so far.

Resource adequacy

Fig. 12.2 (p. 340) presents a picture of the total amounts of 5 of the 19 minerals studied that are needed to achieve these basic scenarios between now and the year 2000. The bars representing an 'active recycling policy' reflect our judgement about the additional amount of recycling (over and above what was already present in the base period) that should be feasible given current technology and proper incentives. For these minerals, as well as for the others studied, the slow-down in population growth is not as effective in saving on resources as is a reduction in economic growth; but the combination of both plus an active recycling policy can achieve a considerable saving. Unfortunately, at this juncture we do not have a good idea about the cost in economic or environmental terms involved in this much recycling.

Fig. 12.3 presents a picture of annual energy requirements. Because it assumes only modest changes in energy technology from the base period – an assumption that is rapidly becoming outdated – the breakdown by fuels is probably not very significant. For example, gasification of coal will probably be necessary before the turn of the century to meet some of the natural gas requirements. But the

TABLE 12.1 DEMOGRAPHIC AND ECONOMIC INDICATORS FOR ALTERNATIVE
POPULATION AND ECONOMIC ASSUMPTIONS, NO POLICY CHANGE

| | | *Absolute figures* | | | | | | | |
| | | 2000 | | | | 2020 | | | |
Indicator	1970	B–H	E–H	B–L	E–L	B–H	E–H	B–L	E–L
Population (millions)	205	321	266	321	266	440	299	440	299
Labour force (millions)	85	136	127	136	127	186	146	186	146
Households (millions)	62	106	101	106	101	145	113	145	113
GNP per capita ('67$)	3937	8125	9098	6452	7218	12661	14625	8632	9946
Disposable income per capita ('58$)	2595	5399	6018	4241	4721	8650	9848	5804	6558
GNP (bil. '67$)	807	2608	2420	2071	1920	5571	4373	3798	2974
Consumption (bil. '67$)	524	1704	1577	1339	1237	3747	2899	2514	1930
Investment (bil. '67$)	99	341	309	278	252	688	551	492	400
Government (bil. '67$)	186	579	548	468	442	1170	948	813	659
Defence (bil. '67$)	62	97	102	88	92	149	158	128	133
Non-defence (bil. '67$)	124	482	446	380	350	1021	790	685	526
Net exports (bil. '67$)	−3	−17	−15	−13	−11	−33	−25	−22	−16
Total output (bil. '67$)	1326	4174	3843	3334	3064	8900	6933	6124	4747
Primary (bil. '67$)	84	207	192	174	161	406	318	297	231
Mining (bil. '67$)	22	59	57	49	47	119	100	87	72
Construction (bil. '67$)	57	181	164	148	133	382	296	274	209
Manufacturing (bil. '67$)	585	1776	1628	1437	1316	3689	2877	2587	2012
Food (bil. '67$)	93	214	198	184	170	405	312	306	234
Paper (bil. '67$)	22	73	66	58	53	155	119	107	82
Petroleum (bil. '67$)	26	60	62	51	52	115	105	87	76
Chemicals (bil. '67$)	45	152	142	120	112	321	254	218	173
Primary metals (bil. '67$)	44	122	111	100	90	251	197	180	140
Rubber and plastics (bil. '67$)	14	54	48	43	38	117	88	80	60
Stone and clay (bil. '67$)	14	48	43	39	35	101	79	74	56
Textiles (bil. '67$)	25	69	60	52	46	140	102	89	65
Lumber and wood (bil. '67$)	12	43	39	34	31	92	71	63	49
Leather (bil. '67$)	4	14	10	11	7	31	20	20	12
Services (bil. '67$)	600	2009	1858	1575	1454	4424	3442	2966	2295
Electricity (bil. '67$)	19	72	66	58	53	163	127	114	88
Consumption purchases (bil. '67$)	524	1704	1577	1339	1237	3747	2899	2514	1930
Durables (bil. '67$)	52	207	188	159	144	478	362	314	236
Non-durables (bil. '67$)	128	333	313	278	261	667	525	482	377
Services (bil. '67$)	344	1164	1076	902	832	2602	2012	1718	1317

[a] % increase from B–H.
Source: U.S. Commission on Population Growth (1972) adapted from Table 2, p. 41.

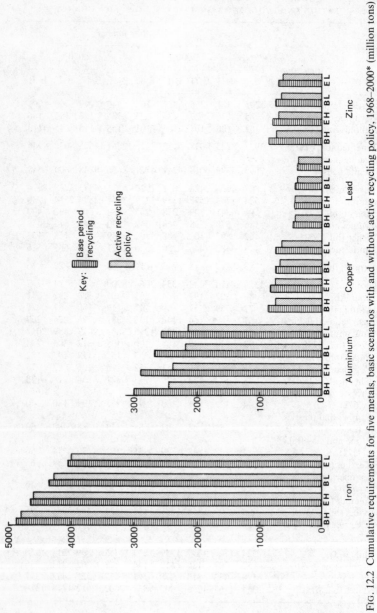

FIG. 12.2 Cumulative requirements for five metals, basic scenarios with and without active recycling policy, 1968–2000* (million tons)

*From U.S. Commission on Population Growth (1972) p. 97.

breakdown does indicate in general terms the extent to which we shall continue to be dependent on petroleum.

When these requirements projections are matched against supply projections for the United States and against demand and supply projections for the rest of the world, the principal conclusion that emerges is that the United States is not likely to experience any

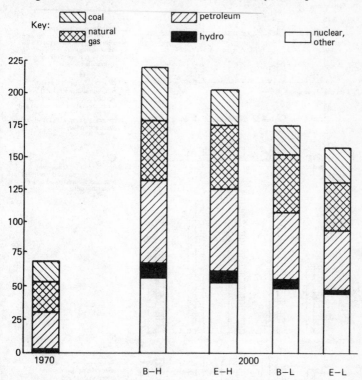

FIG. 12.3 Annual requirements for energy, basic scenarios* (quadrillion Btu)

* Derived from U.S. Commission on Population Growth (1972) p. 43.

truly serious shortages during the next quarter to half century solely as a consequence of population and economic growth. By serious shortages we mean shortages that would cause the relative price of a significant number of these minerals and fuels to increase by more than 50 per cent or so. Other factors may of course come into the picture to upset this conclusion, a point we must return to before concluding this essay. Environmental groups may refuse to permit the construction of a sufficient number of nuclear or other electric power plants or the Organization of Petroleum Exporting Countries may successfully impose monopolistic control over a large fraction of the world's petroleum supplies. But strictly as a consequence of population and economic growth in this country and perhaps also in

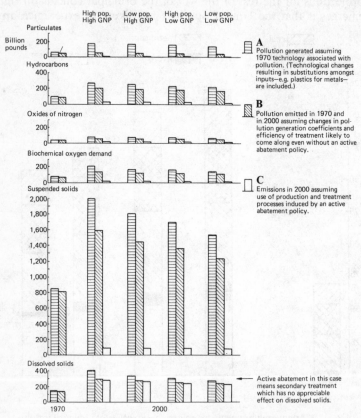

FIG. 12.4 Pollution generated and emitted under alternative assumptions

the rest of the world, the United States is likely to be able to find the necessary supplies to meet rising demands without price increases of such a magnitude that the general welfare is endangered.

Pollution

Fig. 12.4 illustrates our findings with respect to a number of different pollutants. The bars labelled A represent the amount of various pollutants generated in 1970 and likely to be generated in the year 2000 under alternative assumptions about population and economic growth. The bars labelled B in 1970 indicate the amount of these pollutants emitted, the difference between A and B indicating the small amount of treatment present in that year. The bars labelled B in the year 2000 indicate the amount of various pollutants likely to be emitted in that year assuming the same level of treatment as in 1970 but taking into account the changes in technology that are likely to come along even in the absence of an active abatement policy. In principle, such technological changes could result in either a higher or a lower level of residuals per unit of output; in fact, however, most of the changes we investigated reduce residuals. To a large extent, this result arises from the assumption that best practice in 1970 becomes average practice by the year 2000. While this assumption by itself is very conservative, we have left out new processes and products that might come along to raise new problems.

To arrive at the bars labelled C, representing an active abatement policy, we applied the U.S. Environmental Protection Agency's (E.P.A.) recommended emission standards for 1975. While it appears likely that the technology will exist by 1975 to meet these standards, we have applied them in the year 2000, by which time, at least from a technological point of view, it should be possible to surpass them.

As far as we can judge, the cost of meeting these standards does not appear excessively expensive. In 1970, the annualised costs of pollution abatement were estimated by E.P.A. to be $8·45 billion (1967 dollars), about 1 per cent of G.N.P. To meet the emission standards implied by this active abatement policy, we estimate that these costs will have to rise to between $34 billion (for the case of E–H) and $47 billion (for the case of B–H) by the year 2000 (all figures in 1967 dollars). Although very large numbers, they still amount to less than 2 per cent of G.N.P. in the year 2000. To make room for such expenditures we would have to give up less than one-tenth of one percentage point in annual growth of G.N.P. Once again, however, there are some qualifications to which we must return in discussing policy implications.

It should be noted, however, that the pollutants we have studied for the most part have relatively short half-lives. Because of data and other analytical problems, radiation, heavy metals, persistent pesticides, and similar pollutants that can accumulate in the environment over time were not studied in as much depth.

Regional problems

A second qualification to our analysis of pollution problems arises from regional concerns: some regions could face serious problems even though they achieve the 1975 emission standards. To determine whether this is the case, we developed regional projections for three air pollutants in 47 cities and applied them to a general air diffusion model.

Table 12.2 summarises the results for a special case in which the land area of each city expands in proportion to its population increase, thereby keeping density constant. As can be seen, a growing number of cities will not be able to meet the ambient standards without the active abatement policy. But even with it, Los Angeles

TABLE 12.2 NUMBER OF CITIES AMONG FORTY-SEVEN STUDIED NOT MEETING SPECIFIED AMBIENT STANDARDS

| | | 2000 | | | | | | | |
| | 1970 | No policy change | | | | Abatement policy | | | |
		B–H	E–H	B–L	E–L	B–H	E–H	B–L	E–L
SO_2 (80 micrograms)[a]	2	2	3	1	1	0	0	0	0
SO_2 (60 micrograms)[a]	4	6	6	4	5	0	0	0	0
NO_2 (100 micrograms)[a]	36	41	43	41	42	2	3	2	2
Particulates (75 micrograms)[a]	36	27	32	15	19	0	0	0	0
Particulates (60 micrograms)[a]	44	42	43	32	37	0	0	0	0

[a] Annual arithmetic mean in micrograms per cubic metre.
Source: U.S. Commission on Population Growth (1972) Tables 10, 11, 12, pp. 52–6.

and San Diego will not be able to meet the NO_2 standard.[1] For these two areas, both of which are already above the NO_2 standard, something must give: the use of the internal combustion engine, immigration of people and activities, or the standard itself. More detailed studies of metropolitan areas not included in our sample of 47 are uncovering additional cases of this sort.

If we assume that urban land area expands less rapidly than population, the situation worsens rapidly. On the other hand, when in one run of this model we assumed that 10 per cent of the additional economic activities that would otherwise have located in these urban areas were instead required to locate in non-urban areas, the situation improved only marginally, reducing the number of cities not meeting the sulphate standards from two to one and the number not meeting particulate standards from 27 to 17, while those not meeting the *nitrate* standard remained the same.

A final point of interest about these regional projections is their

---

[1] In the E–H case, Philadelphia will also be above the standard in 2000. The fact that the E–H case presents more regional environmental difficulties than do the other cases results from a combination of factors, the most important of which is the assumption that land area expands in proportion to population. See U.S. Commission on Population Growth (1972) p. 51.

great diversity. Population density is increasing in some, while it is decreasing in others. For sulphates in 1970, the highest average concentration level for any city is six times that of the lowest. Even with an active abatement policy, some areas will grow worse over time, while others improve. Moreover, the trend is not the same for all three pollutants: particulate levels are likely to fall in a number of cities even without an active abatement policy, while nitrate levels are likely to worsen in some even with such a policy.

Other consequences

A number of other resource and environmental problems were studied in this same context: the pressure on outdoor recreation land, on agricultural land and on water resources; several environmental problem clusters related to city size and density; and some institutional problems that are likely to arise from the attempt to solve resource and environmental problems. While space does not permit review of these findings, it is of interest to point out that while a change in per capita G.N.P. appears to be more important than a change in population in causing resource and environmental problems associated with the industrial and transport sectors, the opposite is true for those activities that are heavy users of land and water such as outdoor recreation and agriculture. It is also of interest to note that the need for public intervention to regulate and control the external costs of population and economic growth will grow significantly in *all* the cases studied, and that while such interventions can accomplish a great deal to relieve the resource and environmental pressures of growth they will further alter the relatively unfettered way of life that was considered characteristic of America a few years back.

IV. SOME POLICY IMPLICATIONS

Some of the policy implications stemming from this analysis are fairly obvious. For example, since a steady, controlled movement towards a ZPG appears to be socially beneficial at this stage in U.S. history, and since such a movement is now occurring, the principal goals of policy affecting fertility should be to encourage and strengthen the trend, to monitor developments, and to be ready with policies to keep the United States on this trend should signs of significant changes in fertility patterns begin to appear. Similarly, it should be clear that attempts to monitor long-term developments in the resource and environmental areas, such as this one, need to be remade periodically. Such periodic monitoring is probably the only way to obtain sufficiently early warnings about resource and environmental problems that require long lead times to resolve.

Instead of listing all such implications, this section will concentrate on two which warrant a bit more discussion and which at the same time may serve to emphasise some of the qualifications that need to be attached to the above analysis.

Direct versus indirect approaches

It has become commonplace in the last few years to hear calls for ZPG and ZEG as ways to contain the encroachment of man on the earth's limited supplies of raw materials and environmental carrying capacity. In contrast to measures like zoning, effluent charges, and mass transit, such policies would operate indirectly on our resource and environmental problems. They are said to be necessary because the direct measures are only palliatives, attempting to correct the symptoms rather than attacking the main causes.

So far as population growth is concerned there is little argument. Even if there were no necessity for such growth to cease, its continuance provides no social advantages and a number of costs at this stage in U.S. history. But the same cannot be said about economic growth which, with appropriate changes in composition, can be utilised to solve many of the problems it creates. The question of whether it must also cease is of more interest.

There can be no doubt that all population and economic growth must someday cease. Exponential growth in a limited space cannot continue forever. Technological advance can postpone that ultimate day, but it cannot repeal the laws of nature. But this fact by itself is of little relevance. Far more important is the question, when? Must it cease within our lifetime, that of our grandchildren, or some far-off distant generation? It makes an enormous difference for policy today how we answer this question.

Unfortunately, the information does not exist with which to answer it, except to say that we see no reason why growth must cease within the next 50 years or so. Beyond that point, we must admit our ignorance. We do not know what kind of disasters we may be letting ourselves in for by permitting economic growth to continue; but we are also ignorant of possible technological and institutional breakthroughs that may come along not just to save future generations from disaster but perhaps to make them substantially better off than the current generation. For the time being, therefore, we can still choose whether to slow growth down as a way of coping with our problems or to rely on more direct attacks on the problems that face us.

Within this fifty-year time frame, our analysis strongly suggests that as policy instruments for dealing with raw materials, shortages and pollution, direct measures are far superior to across-the-board restrictions on population and economic growth. The clearest indication of this is found in Fig. 12.4 which compares the reductions in pollution that might be achieved using direct and indirect approaches. Other examples can be found by comparing the amount of reduction in G.N.P. per capita that would be necessary to curtail the emission of a given pollutant, say sulphur oxides, by a given amount, with the extent of the reduction in G.N.P. per capita that would occur as a consequence of a more selective approach. Our analysis indicates that a one percentage point reduction in G.N.P. per capita would reduce this pollutant by 0·87 per cent, but that if the output of the five sectors with the highest emission coefficients were reduced by 2·5 per cent this same 0·87 per cent reduction in sulphur oxides could be achieved with only a third of a percentage point reduction in G.N.P. per capita. An even more dramatic example would involve a direct attack on the automobile, which by itself accounts for 12 per cent of hydro-carbon emissions, 60 per cent of carbon monoxide emissions and 25 per cent of nitrogen oxide emissions from all man-made sources. The same argument applies to resources, at least to resources in general: given the substitution possibilities that are present, why reduce the consumption of all resources because a few are in short supply?

Of course, such direct approaches will result in some slow-down in economic growth. But with the exception of a few especially vulnerable regions, the extent of this slow-down is not likely to be great during the next quarter to half century. Beyond this period, it is possible that measures which bite more heavily into aggregate economic growth will prove necessary. But that is as it should be. So long as other options are available, including the option of changing the composition of growth, there is no sense in limiting aggregate economic growth until we have to.

Piecemeal, restrictive measures versus structural changes

A more difficult issue involves the question of which direct measures to use. All that Fig. 12.4 suggests is that we have the technological know-how to reduce future emission levels at a reasonable cost, despite the population and economic growth that will occur in the interim; it does not say that policies can or will be devised to accomplish such reductions. This would not be the first time that we accomplished far less than we know how to do.

Most of the measures in use today, especially in the environmental field, can be characterised as restrictive. The imposition of standards that must be met by a certain date is perhaps the best example. Even effluent charges, or full-cost pricing, which for good reasons most economists favour, are restrictive in the sense that the person faced with the charge is induced to restrict his own behaviour to reduce the burden of these additional costs. While it is somewhat more difficult to characterise resource policy in this same way since subsidies for research and exploration are also part of the scene, it is certainly the case in both the resource and environmental fields that most of our policies are not integrated into any overall framework that considers all the ways of skinning the cat and all the consequences of doing so by different methods. To illustrate the kinds of problems that can arise from such piecemeal, restrictive approaches, we take an example from the energy and urban transport fields, first considering the resource and then the environmental sides of these interrelated problems.

On the basis of the assumptions incorporated into our study, there appear to be adequate supplies of petroleum to meet the world's needs during the next half century or so, if not considerably beyond. One might be inclined to predict from this that our current energy system based on liquid petroleum fuels can continue for some time to come.

But it is not difficult to make a case to the contrary. Consider a few of the problems the United States will face in the energy field during the next 10 to 15 years. Suppose that the OPEC cartel becomes stronger and decides to set its long-term price on the basis of the costs of producing alternative sources of petroleum in the United States, rather than in relation to its much lower costs of production. The choices for the United States would involve reliance on imports – with all the attendant balance of payments, political, and military risks which that would entail – attempts to break the cartel through the application of colonial policies – which the United States as well as the Europeans may have lost the will if not also the capacity to adopt – or efforts to reduce our long-run dependence on foreign oil. Most likely the United States would try to opt for this latter course.

But the production of oil from offshore sources, tar sands and shale will involve serious environmental problems, problems that will not be resolved cheaply, quickly, or to the satisfaction of many local groups with the power to hold up developments. On the basis of this scenario, either environmental concerns will be subverted or the life-span of our liquid energy system will be short, despite the existence of adequate worldwide supplies.

The alternatives on the supply side are to develop coal gasification, and nuclear, solar, and geothermal sources of electricity. Some of these alternatives raise new kinds of environmental concerns, perhaps the most serious being the need to store highly lethal, radioactive wastes from breeders in ever-increasing amounts for literally thousands of years. But in any event, unless significant changes occur in our transport system, the extent to which gas and electricity can be substituted for liquid fuels will be quite limited. Sooner or later we shall have to look for alternatives on the demand side, that is, alternatives which reduce our need for liquid fuels. If we do so by restrictive means, for example, by permitting the price of fuel oil and petrol to rise significantly, considerable hardships will result for an extended period of time, until structural changes in our transport system, commuting patterns, and the layout of cities are forced to occur. If we anticipate these structural changes, at least by building them into new urban developments, many of these hardships can be avoided.

A similar conclusion emerges when regional problems are considered. As we have seen, at least two urban areas in our sample of 47 will not be able to achieve the ambient standards set by EPA, solely through the use of emission controls on internal combustion engines; and more detailed studies of other cities and pollutants will undoubtedly provide additional examples. Now it may be that the standards are too stringent and should be relaxed. But when we add in the problems of motor congestion consequent to the growth of populations in urban areas during the next half century, it seems highly probable that restrictions on the use of the private car in many central cities will be necessary in any event. Once again, planned structural changes in city form, commuting patterns, and mass transit systems will be required to achieve an orderly and timely transition.

The principal purposes in presenting these examples are to demonstrate the need for more comprehensive approaches to the problems we face and to suggest a situation in which more resource conservation and environmental improvement may be possible at less economic and social cost through planned technological, institutional, and urban design changes than by the application of the more traditional approaches of regulatory agencies. The latter may ultimately induce the same changes, but the social cost of doing so is likely to be much higher.

V. SUMMARY AND CONCLUDING QUALIFICATIONS

This paper began by discussing the principal determinants of resource and environmental pressures, making clear that population growth is only one and that the nature of the relationships with demographic variables depends very significantly on the other determinants. It then discussed what was most reasonable to assume about changes in each of the determinants for the United States during the next quarter to half century, with special attention to the likely effects of demographic changes on the rate and character of economic growth.

The assumptions about future changes in these determinants were then utilised to derive economic, resource and environmental consequences. The following conclusions, among others, emerge from this analysis:

(i) no *serious, long-term* shortages of resources are likely to arise *solely as a result* of expected population and economic growth during the next quarter to half century;

(ii) with proper changes in policy, pollution emissions can be contained at reasonable cost for the nation as a whole, although this is probably not true for some important regions;

(iii) economic growth appears to be more important than population growth in causing resource and environmental problems associated with the industrial sector, but these roles are reversed when considering problems associated with activities that are heavy users of land and water;

(iv) in general, direct attacks on specific resource shortages or pollutants are more effective than across-the-board restrictions on population and/or economic growth within the limited time frame considered; and

(v) among the direct attacks possible, structural changes (e.g. planned changes in urban design, institutions and technology) are likely to be less costly than restrictive measures (like taxes and emission standards).

A number of important qualifications to this analysis were also discussed, in particular the fact that this picture for the United States could be changed quite significantly by international developments different from the relatively sanguine assumptions used in this analysis about the rest of the world. One final, related qualification should be added. These results apply to the United States, a capital- and land-rich country. The resource and environmental consequences of population and economic growth in poor, densely populated countries are certain to be far more serious and difficult to cope with.

REFERENCES

E. B. Attah, 'Racial Aspects of Zero Population Growth', *Science*, vol. 180, no. 4091 (15 June 1973) pp. 1143–51.

T. Frejka, 'United States: The Implications of Zero Population Growth', *Studies in Family Planning*, no. 60 (Dec 1970).

S. Kuznets, 'Population Change and Aggregate Output', *Demographic and Economic Change in Developed Countries* (Princeton Univ. Press for the N.B.E.R., 1960).

N. B. Ryder, 'Recent Trends and Group Differences in Fertility', *Toward the End of Growth*, Charles F. Westoff *et al.* (Englewood Cliffs, N.J.: Prentice Hall, 1973) pp. 57–68.

J. Schmookler, *Invention and Economic Growth* (Cambridge, Mass.: Harvard Univ. Press, 1966).

J. Simon, 'The Influence of Population Growth on Per Worker Income in Developed Countries', mimeo (1971).

U.S. Bureau of the Census, *Current Population Reports*, ser. P-25, no. 498 (Dec 1972).

U.S. Commission on Population Growth and the American Future, *Population, Resources, and the Environment*, ed. Ronald G. Ridker, vol. III of Commission research reports (Washington, D.C.: U.S. Government Printing Office, 1972).

Discussion of the Papers by
Dr Ridker and Professor Parikh

Professor Létinier said that Dr Ridker had tried to find the answer to the question put to the public a few years ago on the use of resources and the environment. Where we confined to zero growth because of the fear of environmental self-destruction? Dr Ridker had looked at the availability of raw materials to the U.S.A. over the next fifty years. Professor Létinier said he would try to summarise the question, the methods and the results; he would see what reservations he had about Dr Ridker's proposals, and what points there were for discussion.

On page 315, Dr Ridker mentioned seven factors acting on the consumption of raw material. Two of these related to the demographic situation, i.e. rate of growth of population, standard of living, etc. Technology was important, in that it represented the consumer of raw materials. Dr Ridker went on to study the action of these factors. He first took a set of hypotheses and looked at the effect on them of demographic growth and economic expansion, but holding other factors constant, i.e. he had looked at the projected status quo without any active modifying policy. Secondly, he went on to look at the effect of active policy measures on these secondary factors. In the first stage, Dr Ridker looked at the effects of demographic growth. His first hypothesis was based on weak growth; it took the population projection of the American Census Bureau based on 2·1 children per woman, which was the renewal rate. Secondly, he looked at a high fertility rate of 3·1 children per woman. He went on to look at the consequences of these growth rates for the total population and for the labour force. With the weak rate of demographic growth, there would be a steady increase in the population which, from 1970 up to the year 2020, meant a tremendous increase to a total of 291 million inhabitants. Professor Létinier thought the age structure of the population was favourable, but others would call it unfavourable. Taking the 3·1 rate of births, the total would be 440 millions by the year 2020. In both cases the labour force would increase, but in the case of the high fertility assumption, the ratio of the labour force to the total population was lower. Dr Ridker went on to examine the possible favourable effects under the two assumptions, comparing the two rates of fertility. He examined the implications of economic growth as measured by GNP per capita of the active population, and then made use of two assumptions, one for a high and the other for a low growth rate. These were combined to give a model with four basic alternatives, having different population growth rate and economic growth rate assumptions. Maximum GNP occurred for the high economic growth and low demographic growth assumption. Using classic methods, Dr Ridker's team had taken up these projections and looked at their consequences for raw material usage, consumption, pollution, etc.

Looking at the conclusions in terms of the effect on the availability of raw materials and on pollution, Professor Létinier thought them optimistic. There were some reservations about energy supplies, mainly because of the uncertainty about the pricing policies of the oil-exporting countries.

On the question of pollution, the story was rather more worrying, with the possibility that a number of towns would not apply the pollution rules which were expected to increase costs: so pollution could be a problem. There was also some concern about regional differences, and Professor Létinier wondered whether this was a question of the distribution of industry.

In the second part of the paper, Dr Ridker looked at the factors which had been treated more conservatively in the basic study. Professor Létinier had only a few points to make on this section. If one pursued a policy of active reduction of pollution, in order to satisfy U.S. standards a large absolute expenditure was required, but this was small relative to GNP, say 2 per cent for the worst assumption, which led to a lower level of pollution than existed in 1970. Obviously if there were a reduction in economic or demographic growth, there would be a reduction of the expenditure required below this level. It seemed that direct intervention was more effective than the indirect results of suppressed growth, so that direct action seemed better.

Professor Létinier thought the study very competent, and approved the methods used. He also approved the results, but with one important reservation on a demographic point. He wanted to know the meaning of the figures given in relation to the economic figures in general. One reached GNP figures which were weaker depending on whether one was dealing with high or low growth rates. He noted the comparison of figures on Table 12.1, page 339, and said that an examination showed that they corresponded to the different hypotheses in the study. He wanted to know why the lower income per capita was the result only of higher demographic growth rate which gave a lower ratio of active labour force to the total population. Dr Ridker had taken account of the higher contribution of women through reduced fertility, but thought it might be different if women used nurses instead of rearing children themselves. The age-group structure of the population seemed to be important in that if there was an increase in fertility, the number of children would increase but not the active population. After 16 years, the active population would increase and the disequilibrium would correct itself. If Dr Ridker had taken the results for 70 years instead of 50, Professor Létinier thought the picture would have been different and he was curious to know what the difference would have been.

Professor Robinson, opening discussion of Professor Parikh's paper, said that he found it very interesting but would fasten on only some aspects of it. He started with Professor Parikh's conclusion at the end of the paper that 'the prospect for feeding the population of India in A.D. 2001 is good'. Professor Parikh was asking, and attempting to answer, the very important question familiar to all readers of Malthus. In the period 1971–2001, was population likely to be growing faster than the food supply could be made to grow— even under favourable conditions? If so, the decline of food standards, malnutrition, and their repercussions on the mortality rates, would be the inevitable equilibrating factor. Professor Parikh was not asking what was the optimum population or the optimum rate of population change. He reached the conclusion that, until 2001, it might be possible to make the food supply grow with population, despite an increase of not less than 60 per cent in population on his low assumption, and possibly a doubling of population on his higher assumption.

For estimating purposes, it was necessary to separate urban and rural demands, and for this purpose Parikh attempted a very interesting estimate of the potential growth of Bombay. Professor Robinson did not propose to pursue this because he was anxious to look principally at what Professor Parikh had to say on the supply side.

First, Professor Robinson looked at Professor Parikh's estimates on the demand for food. Professor Parikh began with population estimates, rural and urban. He had then taken alternative assumptions about the growth of aggregate private consumption, with a lower 'likely' alternative (4·5 per cent) annual growth 1971–81, rising to 5·5 per cent) and a higher 'optimistic' alternative (5·5 per cent annual growth 1971–81, rising to 7·5 per cent at the end of the century). Professor Robinson thought these figures represented legitimate working hypotheses rather than actual attempts to forecast. It was to be remembered that they were hypotheses about consumption rates and not about growth of GDP. Currently, the gross investment ratio in India was (speaking from memory) about 14 to 15 per cent. This rate of growth of consumption could be achieved only by raising the investment ratio to 20 per cent or more. Thus, with consumption representing a declining portion of GDP, its growth would imply appreciably higher rates of growth of GDP (about 1 per cent higher). They were very much higher rates of growth of consumption than had been achieved in recent years. They were the rates of growth that all were anxious to see achieved, but had hitherto been unsuccessful in achieving. From these alternative hypotheses about aggregate consumption, Professor Parikh had reached his assumed rates of growth of consumption per head.

At first, Professor Robinson had thought this a curiously paradoxical way of proceeding. Professor Parikh had assumed, in effect, that the potential GDP in India was independent of its population – that the marginal 263 millions in the higher estimate of population made no net addition to GDP. But the more Professor Robinson thought about it, the less implausible the assumption seemed. With the smaller population there was much less investment in demographic social capital (about 45 per cent less), more investment in industrial development, more chance of absorbing under-employed rural manpower, and more deepening of investment. As a working hypothesis, it did not seem to him obviously untenable.

Professor Parikh had asked what were the implications for the demand for food. Taking cereals as the central problem, present consumption was about 105 million tons. Professor Parikh's calculations, made in the usual way, suggested the need to increase cereal production by from 2·5 to 3·3 times, depending on the assumptions about the rates of population growth and of economic growth. Professor Robinson regarded 3·3 as the most likely estimate. Was it possible to increase cereal output 3·3 times before 2001?

Professor Parikh tackled this question in terms of what were the responses of different soils in different agro-climatic zones of India to attempts to increase output. These were: (i) by adopting the most suitable already-existing new varieties, (ii) applying to them amounts of fertiliser that had actually been shown by experiments to yield certain given results. Thus there was no extrapolation of known effects. Professor Robinson emphasised that these were experimental farm data under optimum conditions regarding other inputs and regarding timing of cultivation, which were not always achieved on the farm. Professor Parikh had calculated the intensity of farming procedures necessary to meet his given demands, in terms of required fertiliser inputs. His figures showed that the amount of nitrogen required varied from 2·3 million tons for the 3·3 estimate to 9·7 million tons, which represented the most difficult case; 8·0 million tons were required for the most probable population growth estimate. India at present had low yields and low nitrogen use. What was involved was a closer approximation to what was being done in Taiwan, South Korea and other Asian countries. The problems of producing the necessary nitrogen and other fertilisers were not obviously unsurmountable.

Professor Parikh had made similar calculations for all other essential foodstuffs, and the conclusion he reached was in terms of the whole body of foodstuffs. Professor Robinson asked how far one should be satisfied with Professor Parikh's verdict. If he remained, for the moment, only partially satisfied, it was because he found some difficulty, despite the paper, in interpreting Professor Parikh's full procedures.

Cereal output required a group of inputs. (1) Land: in recent years, if Professor Robinson remembered correctly, about half the increase in cereal output had come from increased yields per acre; about half had come from increased acreage, including increased double cropping. Was he right in supposing that a constant cropped acreage was implicitly assumed? If so, there was a hidden reserve of resources there which over the years might add 10–20 per cent or more to the cropped acreage. This was, of course, an exhaustible reserve.

(2) Fertiliser – this had been studied in depth. (3) Cultivation. (4) Water supply, at the times required by the improved varieties. The new varieties were usually described as 'input-responsive', but they could not respond without their inputs. What was assumed about water? Did the sentence that referred to this mean that irrigation was assumed not to be extended, or did it mean that it was assumed that irrigation would be extended to match the proposed uses of fertiliser? If there was any assumption of increase in multi-cropping, one had to ask where the water would come from, for irrigation outside the monsoon season. In Pakistan and Bangladesh, this was one of the major constraints.

Professor Robinson thought that if he had been trying to do a similar piece of work he would have been anxious to satisfy himself about the water constraint. Much too little was known about the availability of sub-soil water, the rate at which it was replenished, the maximum possible density of tube wells drawing on it and the sources from which it was replenished – seepage from the Himalayas and other mountain areas, seepage from rivers, seepage from irrigation canals. It was, for example, known that in Pakistan, of 100 units of water taken out of rivers, something like 60 were lost by seepage out of irrigation canals and about 20 by evaporation, so that only about 20 got to the plants irrigated. Could seepage out of the irrigation canals be recovered by pumps?

Professor Robinson asked this because he had been seeing something of a very different study of the Indian food problems in the twenty-first century. The Minister of Irrigation and Power and his staff had been looking into the feasibility of a scheme to dam the Ganges/Jumna where it started to become brackish (near Patna) and, copying Soviety techniques, to reverse the flow of one of the Ganges tributaries. The scheme would use off-peak nuclear power, at low opportunity cost, to pump water over the Central Indian watershed, recovering as much hydro power as possible from the subsequent downward flow, and irrigating a large proportion of the arid areas shown on Professor Parikh's map.

This was only one of various schemes that might be examined. The River Brahmaputra and its annual flood created one of the great hazards of Bangladesh agriculture. Could it be impounded, or part of the flood water diverted round the Himalayan foothills to feed into the Minister's south-flowing irrigation feeder? These were the vast, and vastly expensive, projects that were likely to be the price of demographic *laissez-faire*.

Professor Robinson did not despair of feeding the Indian population even beyond 2001 – even to 2051 with a possible population of some 2000 millions. But what a formidable opportunity cost the feeding of this population would have in terms of other developments foregone and the reduced chances of raising Indian standards of life.

Professor Parikh said that Professor Robinson had given an admirable and very complimentary presentation, but there was one point he wished to clarify. The yield response curves were based on simple fertiliser trials carried out in farmers' fields, in which farmers had been selected randomly. Excepting the fertilisers applied, all the practices were those followed by the farmers. The data therefore did not suffer from the usual problems of experimental maximisation of yield, achieved irrespective of the costs of obtaining such record yield.

Professor Robinson said that surely the demonstrator was in control, not the farmer, and this made a big difference.

Professor Parikh disagreed. The demonstrator simply supervised the application of specified amounts of fertiliser on different plots. As for the irrigation assumption, this was that no further land would be brought under cultivation other than that planned during the fifth Five Year Plan, i.e. the next six or seven years.

Professor Coale made a brief comment on Professor Létinier's point about the favourable ratio of the labour force to the total population. There were two estimates of fertility in Dr Ridker's paper, and part of the advantage attached to the greater labour-force participation of women with lower fertility. It was partly misleading to say that the age-composition advantage was transitory: the advantage remained, in that higher fertility meant a permanently higher dependency burden.

Dr Ridker thought that Professor Létinier might have compared two equilibrium points and it was possible that this did not give a comparable advantage. But comparing 1970 with an equilibrium situation did give an advantage.

Professor Létinier replied that he had said that an advantage in per capita production would result from a better ratio of the total to the active population because of lower fertility. He had not said that both elements were transitional. One was permanent, i.e. the higher female participation resulting from lower fertility, but Dr Ridker had overestimated its effect on the GNP. The second factor was transitory, and this related to the age structure of the population. This gave lower productivity if we started with a given population and then increased the number of children, but not the number in the labour force. This situation did, of course, correct itself as children moved into the labour force. What Dr Ridker had said was correct for a stable population, but Professor Létinier was concerned about the year 2000 and the year 2020. What happened then was of great interest.

The advantage from the higher GNP per capita with a lower fertility rate was overestimated, because GNP per capita was a bad indicator if one compared two populations with different age structures. Consumption per unit would be better and this would result in Dr Ridker's scales being different. He did give his figures with reservations, and Professor Létinier could not quibble about that. It was with Dr Ridker's interpretations that Professor Létinier differed.

Professor Schultz agreed with the main thrust of Dr Ridker's argument. It was when it moved on to policy choices that he was not sure what Dr Ridker was advocating, when he suggested that the piecemeal application of effluent charges was less preferable than broader 'structural changes'. This phrase should be defined more precisely. Professor Schultz was afraid of the view of planned cities, and the engineered evolution of society, that had been propounded in the United States for a number of years. For example, Dr Ridker said that it was cheaper in the long run to have planned 'structural changes' relating to city transport, etc. in order to accomplish an orderly and timely transition. How were we to accomplish far-sighted planning of this sort? Did we have the ability to foresee the needs of the future better than others?

Mr Black agreed with those who attacked the imposition of our concepts and definitions on less-developed countries. He agreed that a new measure of personal satisfaction was needed because existing national income statistics were not very useful. He thought the piecemeal approach seemed more relevant to the U.S.A. and to other defenders of the existing system. Abandoning growth rate criteria would mean structural changes. We needed a new definition and a new model, and since the less-developed countries were unfortunately developing on the pattern of the developed countries, such a new model would not gain acceptance in a country like India. Could we not suggest Sweden, or possibly Switzerland, as a model economy, since there were signs in those countries of dissatisfaction with the current deterioration in the way of life. Perhaps there could be an investigation into some moral concept of economic growth; otherwise we should remain prisoners of the GNP growth model.

Mr Boulier suggested that, if there were proper pricing of social resources, this might lead to structural planning as recommended by Dr Ridker. It might be better to plan now, rather than run into the need for greater and more comprehensive planning later.

Professor Coale pointed out that underdeveloped countries were not, at present, preoccupied with environmental damage. We would hate to see a regard for the environment reduce the concern in the wealthier countries for the problems of inadequate diet and general poverty in lower-income countries. Imposing environmental improvement was interpreted by some countries as condemning them to poverty, as appeared from the recent Stockholm conference. Whereas developed countries were taking measures to prevent smoke, effluents, etc., in developing countries dirty smoke was what they were aiming for, because this meant the production of manufactured goods. Western countries must not try to impose environmental standards prematurely, before the less-developed countries had achieved higher standards of living.

Professor Hicks believed that the distinction between less-developed and developed countries was inadequate; for example, Japan had witnessed a very rapid increase in the standard of living, as commonly measured, of a kind that was highly desirable. Yet already, at a very early stage, there was congestion. It was a question of the density of population and many other factors. He agreed with Professor Coale's general point that it was a matter of ordering priorities, and that some of the most obvious needs, for example food, had an absolute priority, whereas other things rose in relative importance later.

Professor Parikh, quoting Mrs Ghandi at the Stockholm conference, said that poverty was the greatest pollutant. Where 50 per cent of people were below the poverty line and, as some had estimated, 70 per cent suffered malnutrition, environmental concern was rather too ethereal for most Indians. It was perhaps not realised that measures could be taken at a lower cost, at this stage, to avoid the environmental mess that the developed countries had got themselves into. It was possible to locate the polluting industries away from population centres. It was also possible, at the design stage, to make provision for the installation of anti-pollution measures later on, when they became necessary.

Dr Ridker asked Professor Parikh about yields on experimental farms, and suggested that there might be other inputs, such as the standard of farm management, which could have increased yields. If Professor Parikh's study had been completed thirty years earlier, would it not have indicated that India would be self-sufficient today, and with a higher standard of living? And, if the developments of the Green Revolution could have been allowed for, would Professor Parikh not have forecast that India would today be exporting large amounts of food? Since the farmers chosen for the experiment must be above average, because they had enough intelligence to use fertiliser properly, were not marginal or subsistence farmers, and were willing to divide their land into a number of parcels for the experiment, the results must be on the optimistic side.

Professor Robinson referred to the previous year's I.E.A. conference on agricultural policies in the underdeveloped countries at which many of these points were discussed. Agreement had been reached there that many things had to be right – markets, transport facilities, credit facilities and so on – for the Green Revolution to succeed. There were fundamental constraints but they could be overcome. Professor Robinson was not 100 per cent satisfied with Professor Parikh's explanation, since the latter distinguished between cultivation decisions made by autonomous farmers and those made by experimenters. The experimenters insisted that optimisation should be achieved, so that they got their scientific results. One could not assume that farmers optimised in the same way.

Dr Jones, referring to Professor Hicks's point about the Japanese experiment, said that Japanese success was rapidly leading to environmental problems. As for poverty being the great pollutant, one needed to look at power politics, which provided the framework for economic development and environmental preservation. Broadly speaking, it was the dirty industries that the wealthy countries were prepared to see the poorer countries develop. The latter would be playing into the hands of the developed countries if they accepted this and did not fight for change in the policies of the developed countries which hindered their balanced industrial development. Java already had pollution problems, for example, sewage in the rivers, but this was nothing compared with the pollution problems that could occur with the growth of dirty industries.

Dr Nassef noted that Professor Parikh's paper had concentrated on the agricultural sector, but one could infer from the projections of urban population, in Tables 11.1 and 11.5, that there would be a considerable increase in the non-agricultural labour force. Nothing was said about the possibility of such a change.

Professor Eastman wanted to talk about the control of externalities and about the different tastes in different countries, with respect to the standard of living. Individual countries could usually plan and control the legislation they wanted according to their individual priorities. If a country had higher standards on environmental conservation, this meant an increase in costs which made the country less competitive in export markets. There was a different kind of problem where common resources were involved, specially at frontiers. For example, the Great Lakes were common to the U.S.A. and Canada. Other problems were more serious, even if they would not have much effect by the year 2000. For example, there was the pollution of the stratosphere and the decrease in oxygen through deforestation. He therefore saw a need for a general agreement between countries, which could possibly form the subject of a future conference.

Professor Parikh again commented on the nature of the farm trials. In theory, the country was first divided into districts, a number of which were chosen completely at random; then individual villages were chosen in each district; then individual farms within each village. He agreed that at this last level there was a considerable likelihood that choice was not random because it was easier to contact and to get co-operation from the more advanced farmers. Secondly, even though the trials were supposedly under the normal conditions of farming, except for fertiliser application, psychological distortions were possible. The experimenter might insist on more weeding labour, more insecticides etc., but he was a poor man. He did not have his own resources and no extra fertiliser was available. It was more likely that extra inputs would come from the farmer himself, or in the form of organisational input such as better timing, proper spacing, etc. Professor Parikh concluded that the data might not match exactly what the farmer could achieve in normal conditions, but they were an indication of what might be possible with increasing education.

Wide acceptance of the high-yielding varieties was likely in thirty years, even though progress at present was still limited. The Green Revolution in India was still mainly a wheat revolution, and area increases were far more important than yield increases. Data indicated that higher yields were possible in all areas and, where the water supply was assured, the higher yielding varieties of wheat had been widely accepted. This was not the case with rice, where there was a strong preference for the traditional varieties, but Professor Parikh thought that in thirty years there might be serious shortages, and prices would break this preference.

On Dr Ridker's point, if he had done his calculations thirty years ago, he would not have known about the higher-yield varieties. Also, India had not expanded the amount of irrigation, or produced fertiliser, to the extent that she might have done if planning had been done thirty years ago. Part of his exercise, therefore, was to help planning for the future.

On water, Professor Parikh said experiments had been done in farmers' fields for rain-fed and irrigation areas separately. Different varieties had been tried in most regions and some varieties proved to be dominant at all levels of fertiliser use. One footnote to his study was that when the results were presented to Indian agricultural scientists, many did not believe that in the next five years India would not need extra fertiliser if everyone switched to the new varieties.

Professor Ohlin asked whether a higher price for the traditional varieties of rice was offset by the disadvantage of lower yields.

Professor Robinson replied that while the earlier of the new varieties of rice, such as IR8, were unpopular because of their taste or other qualities, the new generations, the IR20s, were preferred for both their quality and taste. Some of the newest hybrids were indistinguishable in taste from the traditional varieties. But he was still very dubious how far it was possible to turn over completely to the new varieties without improving the water supply.

Dr Lesthaeghe made a demographic point. The projections on p. 304 showed a population growth rate of 1·8 per cent between 1971 and 1981, and subsequently one of 1·5 and 1·3 per cent. He stressed that these growth rates could not be reached if the pattern of nuptiality currently existing in India remained unchanged. Under a hypothesis of constant nuptiality, marital fertility would have to go down as far as the level recently observed in Bulgaria, i.e. to one of the lowest levels on record, in order to achieve the growth rates used in this paper. It was, therefore, very important to state explicitly what demographic hypotheses were being used when a certain population growth rate was accepted for economic projections.

Professor Létinier noted that Professor Parikh's demographic projections had been based on the extrapolation of rates but with no examination of the components. Dr Lesthaeghe had mentioned two components but there was also mortality, and India had a very high mortality rate. If a restriction of births were not achieved, and if, as was very likely, there was a sizeable reduction in mortality, the population figure was likely to be higher than the highest in Professor Parikh's hypotheses.

Professor Parikh agreed with Dr Lesthaeghe that changes in the nuptiality rate were implied if the figures in Table 11.2 were to be realised. Such lower rates were being achieved in rural areas of India, and he expected them to spread with education. If there were no further success in reducing the birth-rate, and if there were a decrease in death-rates, then the population would be higher than projected. This was plausible, but he thought it likely that there would be enough success in family planning to offset the fall in the death-rate. He had been told on the previous day that death-rates in India were low and not expected by demographers to reduce further. The figures for mortality were 62 per 1000 for those in the age group 0–4 years, and 5 per 1000 for those in the age group 5–14 years. Life expectancy was 49 years for males and 44 years for females.

Professor Coale pointed out that research was needed in India because the register of deaths was very poor, and a reliable mortality rate therefore not available. Methods had been devised before the last census in 1971 to get information on child mortality, by asking questions about the number of children born and the number who had survived to mothers. Unfortunately the new methods had not been used. The figures quoted by Professor Parikh were not fully reliable.

On the reliability of projections of the technical progress on agricultural output, he had himself been involved eighteen years ago with Calvin Hoover in such estimates for India. These had been accurate for the output of foods. Technical prospects were now better, and he therefore supported Professor Parikh's conclusions.

Professor Robinson said that to any working economist the data revealed great differences between India, Taiwan, Japan and Singapore in the adjustment of fertility rates to mortality rates. He did not like to be told that things could not happen in India that did happen elsewhere – were there sociological or religious assumptions that economists were not aware of ?

Professor Coale replied that the differences were not fully understood, but that one could expect a slower decline in India than in Singapore. This was not because of physiological reasons, but because of lower literacy, more-slowly declining infant mortality, and traditional attitudes to the family, etc. From the European decline to the Asian decline, it was known that factors relating to the social transformation, i.e. the modernisation process, had proceeded more rapidly elsewhere than in India. The decline in fertility was associated with these changes. There were areas in India, where illiteracy was highest and the culture generally receptive to change, where the process could probably be accelerated, with a concentrated programme. But the greatest resistance was to the factors influencing decline in the rate of infant mortality.

Professor Robinson noted that Singapore had experienced a very rapid change in a relatively short period, thanks to a concentrated effort.

Professor Hermalin agreed with Professor Coale that there were some pointers, but there were many mysteries. There were considerable differences in the size and scope of social organisation between Singapore, Taiwan and Korea. Also, a change in thinking was representative of the factors Professor

Coale had mentioned. He thought a lot more could be done in countries that had been less successful to date, in that once the policy started to be implemented, his experience showed that important outcomes could come from specific decisions along the way. One example was the very different experiences of Taiwan and India in the introduction of the intra-uterine device. He agreed that this was perhaps not the best possible contraceptive but, in Taiwan, doctors had been called in to help women with discomfort in the early stages. In India, where there had been no such sustained effort, disappointment had filtered down via the field workers and the I.U.D. programme had failed in the main.

Professor Åkerman asked why there was no mention of mainland China. He thought that a lot must be known about it and, since there had been a great transition there, it would be very useful to compare it with India.

Professor Coale said a distinguished colleague of his was devoting her full time to the demography of China but the findings were as yet unpublished. No data were available since the 1953 registration of population, so that demographers were dependent on the casual observations of visitors. But the picture from these was quite uniform and showed a very sharp reduction in fertility. There was now strong propaganda in favour of small families – not just for the good of women's health, but now for the economic development of China. There were indications that this decline in fertility was linked to birth control, abortion, the manufacture of pills, late marriages and a shorter child-bearing period associated with women working. Since the Chinese population throughout South-East Asia seemed to have low fertility rates, associated with the adoption of birth control and a higher age of marriage, this picture for mainland China was convincing and plausible.

Professor Parikh wondered whether there were great differences in access to medical practice between Thailand and India, not just in the number of doctors per 1000 of population but also in the cost in time of seeing a doctor. In India, the position was still not very good, so that one could be sceptical about the introduction of the intra-uterine device.

Professor Hermalin replied that there were great differences in the infra-structure. Taiwan had very good public health and a high ratio of doctors to population for a country at its level of development. One reason was that the medical profession had been the one open to Taiwanese under the Japanese. Access to a doctor was therefore fairly easy. However, he felt that the difference between the two countries was more a matter of the response to discomfort rather than a purely medical question.

Professor Coale explained that he had not been trying to get at basic causes but had made a statement of fact, i.e. that educational and health changes were slower in India and that fertility reduction was similar.

Dr Ridker replied to Mr Boulier and Professor Schultz. On the question of piecemeal *versus* structural changes to cope with externalities, he shared their fears about turning over the planning process to professional planners rather than accepting the market mechanism. But he did not see how one could excape from doing this to some extent in order to correct for the operation of the private market. On Mr Boulier's advocacy of proper pricing now to create a better situation in the future, he pointed out that at present there were enormous benefits from sunk capital, and that until this capital was used up, the prices needed to induce new behaviour would be so high that many problems of income distribution and equity would arise. This was why he had looked at structural change, for example the introduction of a mass transit system to give a more acceptable situation from the equity point of view.

Professor Létinier had said that GNP was not a good measure of welfare. Dr Ridker agreed, but he was concerned only with whether it was an adequate index for measuring economic growth, since he did not intend it as a welfare measure. The dependent population was on average less than the working population, and he should have taken this into account more fully.

On an earlier day, Professor Ohlin had said that we knew even less about the consequences of population growth than we did about the determinants of population growth. The papers by himself and by Professor Parikh were about consequences, but Dr Ridker did not know how one compared relative ignorance! On the consequences side, there were more policy levers, for example, the rate of savings and technical progress via research investment. Therefore, it was very difficult to project, in the abstract, what would happen as a result of population growth. Assumptions about policy variables had to be made. On the determinants side, very little could be controlled.

Professor Létinier still thought that GNP was a bad index for comparisons between different situations with different age structures. It took no account of the higher activity rate of females, and there *ipso facto* underestimated production where fertility was higher. GNP was a bad measure of welfare, because children needed to consume less than adults.

Professor Parikh said that several points needed to be made for an underdeveloped country like India. First, among the rural poor, families might simply grow, as people might not know about relevant birth control techniques; the spread of education would make a difference. If the family wanted to plan, its ability to do so depended on acquiring a knowledge of relevant techniques. On the other hand, if the demand for children was quite inelastic, then one should not over-emphasise the role of education. We would go instead for a spread of knowledge of contraceptive techniques, as well as for women's education. Women's education was important both for welfare reasons and because the adoption of contraceptive techniques was related to the level of education.

Professor Robinson felt that not enough research had been done on the consequences of continued population growth; for example, the effect of the very high Asian population growth rates on the world. Professor Coale's point that only a half per cent growth rate of population was possible if we were not to have a nonsense situation in the near future was very salutary, in the light of the growth rates of 3 per cent that were quite common in Asia. The dialogue between economists and demographers had been fruitful, but there was a need to look more at the economic consequences of demography, since planners had different problems. The International Economic Association obviously had a field for work in the not-too-distant future.

Part Six

Population Growth and Employment

13 Rural – Urban Migration, Unemployment and Job Probabilities: Recent Theoretical and Empirical Research

Michael P. Todaro
THE ROCKEFELLER FOUNDATION

I. THE PROBLEMS

Until recently, research on rural–urban migration in less developed countries has been largely dominated by the work of geographers, demographers and sociologists. For the most part, economists have preferred to ignore migration while operating within the confines of their traditional 'two-sector' models. In the case of a 'closed' economy these sectors usually consisted of the agricultural and the industrial with the implicit understanding that one could substitute 'rural' for 'agricultural' and 'urban' for 'industrial'. Emphasis has been placed on traditional economic variables such as output growth rates, terms of trade, savings and investment, and relative efficiency. The efficient allocation of human resources between sectors, if discussed at all, has been assumed to be a natural out-growth of a self-adjusting mechanism which functioned to equate sectoral marginal productivities. Rural–urban migration was portrayed as a manifestation of this self-adjusting mechanism (with its implicit full-employment assumptions) and, as such, was not deemed to be of sufficient intrinsic importance to warrant detailed theoretical and empirical investigation.

The discouraging record of the 1960s in relation to rapid urbanisation and growing levels of urban unemployment in developing nations, however, has underlined the inadequacy of treating migration as a phenomenon of secondary importance. If nothing else, it has shaken development economists out of their complacency and faith in the 'long-run' allocative efficiency of the market mechanism and has forced them to question the applicability of their traditional economic models to the realities of the social, economic, and institutional environments of contemporary less-developed nations. The evidence is clear. Urban areas have grown extremely rapidly and, in many cases, at unprecedented historical rates. Between 1960 and 1970, for example, the population of urban areas is estimated to have grown by 60 per cent in Africa, 52 per cent in Latin America, and 51 per cent in South Asia, while rural areas grew by only 16 per cent in the same decade (Stolnitz, 1973, Tables 36–7). Simultaneously, urban unemployment and underemployment emerged as a problem of utmost importance and concern to politicians, planners and researchers alike. Without question, the phenomenon of accelerated rural–urban labour migration has been the principal cause of both the high rates of urban population growth and the rising levels of urban unemployment. In many African cities in particular, urban growth rates of 7 to 10 per cent per annum are not uncommon and are not likely to diminish in the coming decade.

Thus, the study of the causes and determinants of rural–urban migration and the relationship between migration and relative economic opportunities in urban and rural areas is now of utmost importance. Since migrants comprise the majority of the urban labour force in developing nations, the level of rural–urban migration has been and will continue to be the principal determinant of the supply of new job seekers. And, if migration is the key determinant of the urban labour supply, then it stands to reason that in order to understand the nature and causes of urban unemployment (which in essence represents an excess of job seekers over job opportunities), it is necessary to better understand the process of rural–urban migration. Government policies to ameliorate the urban unemployment problem must be based, in the first instance, on knowledge of who comes to town and why.

In this paper, we shall attempt to review some recent literature on the economics of rural–urban migration with special emphasis on what appears to be a growing theoretical consensus. We shall then summarise the emerging quantitative data on migration from selected country studies in Africa, Asia and Latin America. Our overall intention is to indicate where we now seem to stand on this crucial issue both in terms of completed and ongoing theoretical research and its policy implications.

II. THE MIGRATION PROCESS AND THE CHARACTERISTICS OF MIGRANTS

The factors influencing the decision to migrate are varied and complex. Since migration is a selective process affecting individuals with certain economic, social, educational, and demographic characteristics, the relative influence of economic and non-economic factors may vary not only between nations and regions but also within defined geographic areas and populations. As pointed out above, much of the early research on migration tended to focus on social, cultural, and psychological factors while recognising but not carefully evaluating the importance of economic variables. Emphasis has variously been placed, for example, on (i) *social factors* including the desire of migrants to break away from traditional constraints of social organisations, (ii) *physical factors* including climate and meteorological disasters, (iii) *demographic factors* including the reduction in mortality rates and the concomitant high rates of rural population growth, (iv) *cultural factors* including the impact of 'extended family' relationships and the so-called 'bright lights of the city' theories, and (v) *communication factors* resulting from improved transportation and the introduction of radio, television and the cinema.

Needless to say, all of the above 'non-economic' factors are relevant. However there now seems to be widespread agreement among economists (e.g. Frank, 1971; Stiglitz, 1969; Byerlee, 1972; Fields, 1972*b*; Harris and Todaro, 1970) and non-economists (e.g. Gugler, 1968; Mortara, 1965; Prothero, 1965; Thomas, 1970; Hutton, 1969, etc.) that rural–urban migration can be explained to a great extent by the influence of economic factors. These economic factors include not only the standard 'push' from subsistence agriculture and 'pull' of relatively high urban wages, but also the potential 'push-back' of high urban unemployment. However, we shall reserve discussion of the economic components of the 'push', 'pull', and 'push-back' phenomena to the next section.

Migrant characteristics

It is convenient to divide the main characteristics of migrants into three broad categories – demographic, educational, and economic:

1. *Demographic characteristics.* The principal demographic characteristic of urban migrants, at least in Africa, is that they tend to be young males between the ages of 15 and 25. Various studies in Africa have provided quantitative evidence of this phenomenon in Kenya (Remple, 1970), Nigeria (Callaway, 1967), Tanzania (Sabot, 1972), and Uganda (Elkan, 1960). However, the proportion of migrating women seems to be on the increase as evidenced by Caldwell's study (1969) of Ghana. In Latin America a recent review of rural–urban migration by Thomas (1970) indicates that women apparently are now in the majority of the migration stream, probably as a result of Latin America's relatively advanced state of urbanisation as compared to other developing continents.

2. *Educational characteristics.* One of the most consistent

findings of rural–urban migration studies is the positive correlation between educational selectivity and migration. There
seems to be a clear association between the level of completed
education and the propensity to migrate (Caldwell, 1969; Remple,
1970; Todaro, 1971a; Sabot, 1972). In Sabot's recent study of
Tanzania, the relationship between education and migration is
very clearly documented especially in terms of the impact of urban
employment opportunities on educational selectivity. Sabot finds
a rising proportion of secondary-school leavers in the migration
stream. He attributes this phenomenon to the fact that limited
urban employment opportunities are becoming increasingly
available only to workers with some secondary education. Thus,
the devaluation of primary-school education as a requirement for
employment acceptability is now apparently having repercussions
on the decision to migrate among those with limited primary
education.

3. *Economic characteristics.* It is very difficult to make any valid
generalisations about the economic characteristics of migrants.
For many years the largest percentage of urban migrants were
those poor, landless, unskilled individuals whose rural opportunities were for the most part non-existent. In colonial Africa,
seasonal migration was a dominant factor with migrants from
various income levels seeking short-term urban jobs. Recently,
however, with the emergence of a stabilised, modern industrial
sector in most urban areas of the less-developed countries, the
financial assets of migrants from rural areas become important
only to the extent that individuals with larger financial resources
can survive longer while searching for the elusive urban job. Since
educational attainment is an important basis for the rationing of
limited employment opportunities and since there typically is a
strong correlation between educational attainment and family
status, it is safe to assume that with rising unemployment the
sons and daughters of the better-off rural families will constitute
a rising proportion of future migrant streams.

III. TOWARD A GENERALISED THEORY OF THE ECONOMICS OF RURAL–URBAN MIGRATION

Historically, the economic development of Western Europe and the
United States was closely associated with and, in fact, often defined
in terms of the movement of labour from rural to urban areas. For
the most part, with a rural sector dominated by agricultural activities
and an urban sector focusing on industrialisation, overall economic

development was characterised by the gradual reallocation of labour out of agriculture and into industry through rural–urban migration, both internal and international. Urbanisation and industrialisation, therefore, became synonomous, and this historical model which lay behind the concept of 'development planning' as a blueprint for the emerging nations became widely recognised and accepted by development economists.

In the 1950s and early 1960s leading development theorists led by Arthur Lewis (1954) and Ranis and Fei (1961) depicted the process of economic development largely in terms of the reallocation of 'surplus' rural labour through intersectoral population flows from low productivity agricultural activities to more productive urban employment opportunities. The actual phenomenon of rural–urban migration was implicit in their two-sector models, but little direct attention was devoted to the economic determinants of this migration. As in the case of most general neoclassical equilibrium models, intersectoral migration was conceived of as a process that would eventually equalise relative marginal products in a full-employment economy.

The overwhelming evidence of the 1960s in which developing nations witnessed a massive migration of their rural populations into urban areas in spite of rising levels of urban unemployment and underemployment has led economists to question the validity of the Lewis–Fei–Ranis models of development. In a series of articles, I and a number of my colleagues (see, for example, Todaro, 1968, 1969, 1971*b*; Harris and Todaro, 1970; Johnson, 1971; and Fields, 1972*b*) have attempted to develop a theory of rural–urban migration which can explain the apparently paradoxical relationship (at least to economists) of accelerated rural–urban migration in the context of rising urban unemployment. I would like to devote the remainder of this section to a summary of this basic model and its various extensions and then in the next section review some of the emerging evidence which provides preliminary empirical support for the general validity of this theory in Latin America, Africa and Asia.

The basic nature of the migration model

Starting from the assumption that migration is primarily an economic phenomenon which for the individual migrant can be a quite rational decision despite the existence of urban unemployment, the model postulates that 'migration proceeds in response to urban–rural differences in *expected earnings* with the urban employment rate acting as an equilibrating force on such migration' (Harris and Todaro, 1970). Our fundamental premise is that migrants as decision makers consider the various labour-market opportunities available to them as between the rural and urban sectors and choose the one which maximises their 'expected' future income.

In essence, the theory assumes that members of the labour force, both actual and potential, compare their 'expected' incomes for a given time horizon in the urban sector with prevailing average agricultural incomes and migrate if the former exceeds the latter. Rather than equilibrating marginal productivities (and, therefore, in a competitive model, actual real wage-rates), rural–urban migration in this model acts as an equilibrating force which equates rural and urban 'expected' incomes. Since expected incomes are defined in terms of *both* wages and employment opportunities or probabilities (see below), the ultimate intersectoral equilibrium situation permits the existence of sizeable rates of urban unemployment. Rates of rural–urban migration in excess of the rate of growth of urban employment opportunities can therefore be characterised as a disequilibrium phenomenon.

In short, there are three characteristics of the basic model:[1]

(i) migration is stimulated primarily by rational economic considerations;

(ii) the decision to migrate depends on 'expected' rather than nominal wage differentials where the 'expected' differential is determined by the interaction of two variables, the nominal wage and the probability of successfully obtaining employment in the urban sector; and

(iii) migration rates in excess of urban job-opportunity growth rates reflect a disequilibrium situation.

Policy implications

While such a theory might at first glance seem to devalue the critical importance of the phenomenon of rural–urban migration by portraying it as an adjustment mechanism by which workers allocate themselves between rural and urban labour markets, it does lead to a series of very important policy implications for development strategy with regard to wages and incomes, rural development and industrialisation. Among the more important of these policy implications are the following:

1. *Reducing imbalances in urban–rural employment opportunities.* Since migrants are assumed to respond to differentials in expected incomes it is vitally important that imbalances between economic opportunities in rural and urban sectors be minimised. Specifically, if we define the urban 'expected' wage as the nominal wage,

[1] For a more detailed description and mathematical statement of the overall model see Harris and Todaro (1970) and the Appendix to Todaro (1971*b*).

W_u, multiplied by the probability of obtaining an urban job, P_u (where P_u is defined as the number of urban jobs, E_u, divided by the urban labour force L_u), so that the urban–rural 'expected' income differential is $W_u . E_u/L_u - W_r$, then the *larger* the differential between nominal urban and rural wages, $W_u - W_r$, the *lower* must be the urban employment rate, E_u/L_u, to equilibrate 'expected' incomes. Alternatively, this specification indicates that the larger the gap between urban and rural nominal wages, the higher must be the urban *unemployment* rate, $1 - E_u/L_u$, before migration in excess of job opportunities ceases. It follows that permitting urban wage rates to grow at a greater pace than average rural incomes will stimulate further rural–urban migration in spite of rising levels of urban *unemployment*. This heavy influx of people into urban areas gives rise not only to socio-economic problems in the cities, but it may also eventually create problems of labour shortages in rural areas, especially during the busy seasons.

2. *Urban job creation is an insufficient solution for the urban unemployment problem.* The traditional economic solution to urban unemployment, i.e. the creation of more urban jobs, can in the absence of simultaneous attempts to improve rural incomes and employment opportunities lead to the paradoxical situation where more urban *employment* leads to higher levels of urban *unemployment*! Once again, the imbalance in 'expected' income-earning opportunities is the crucial concept. Since migration rates are assumed to respond positively to *both* higher urban wages and higher urban employment opportunities (or probabilities), it follows that for any given positive urban–rural wage differential, $W_u . W_r$ (in most L.D.C.s W_u is typically three to four times as large as W_r), higher urban employment rates, E_u/L_u, will widen the expected differential and induce higher rates of rural–urban migration.

Elsewhere, I have attempted to demonstrate theoretically the conditions under which an increase in urban employment opportunities can, through the induced migration that follows, lead to higher levels of urban unemployment (Todaro, 1971*b*). The important concept here is what I have called the 'elasticity of migration' or the 'migration response parameters'. This elasticity may be defined as the percentage change in the size of the urban labour force resulting from a percentage change in the urban–rural expected income differential, or $(\delta L_u/L_u)/(\delta d/d)$, where $d = P_u . W_u - W_r$. In the appendix to the above cited paper, I have demonstrated that the absolute level of urban unemployment will rise if the elasticity of migration exceeds the urban–rural expected differential as a proportion of the urban wage multiplied by the unemployment rate, i.e. if

$$\frac{\delta L_u/L_u}{\delta d/d} \frac{P_u W_u - W_r}{W_u} \cdot \frac{(L_u - E_u)}{L_u}.$$

The empirical value of this elasticity is important for policy decisions in order to predict what the impact of a policy designed to generate more urban *employment* will be on the overall level of urban *unemployment*. As we shall see below, in a recent empirical study of Brazilian wages and unemployment, Whitaker and Schuh have computed an elasticity of 2·32 indicating a sizeable migration response parameter.

3. *Indiscriminate educational expansion will lead to further migration and unemployment.* The basic model and especially its extension by Fields (1972a) and Edwards and Todaro (1973) also has important policy implications for investment in post-literacy educational expansion. The heavy influx of rural migrants into urban areas at rates much in excess of new employment opportunities has necessitated a rationing device in the selection of new employees. Although within each educational group such selection may be largely random, many observers have noted that employers tend to use educational attainment as a criterion for hiring, selecting those with more education in preference to those with less. (See, for example, Blaug, Layard and Woodhall, 1969; Krueger, 1971; Rado, 1972; and Fields, 1972a.) Jobs which could formerly be filled by those with primary education now require secondary training; those formerly requiring a secondary certificate now necessitate a B.A., and so on. (See Sabot, 1972, for evidence from Tanzania.) It follows that for any given urban wage, if the probability of success in securing a modern sector job is higher for those with more education so too will be their expected income differential and the more likely they will be to migrate to the cities. Our basic model can easily be specified to deal with migrants of varying educational attainment.

The point is that as job opportunities become more scarce in terms of the number of job applicants, increasing pressure will be placed on students to proceed further along the educational ladder. The private demand for education, which in many ways is a 'derived demand' for urban jobs, will continue to exert tremendous pressure on governments to invest in post-primary school facilities. But for many of these students, the spectre of joining the ranks of the 'educated unemployed' becomes more of a reality with each passing year. Government overinvestment in post-primary educational facilities often then turns out to be an investment in idle human resources which is not only bad economics but, in the long run, is likely to be bad politics if recent events in Ceylon (Sri Lanka) and East Pakistan (Bangladesh) are at all instructive.[1]

4. *Wage subsidies and traditional shadow pricing can be counter-productive.* A standard policy prescription of economists for generating urban employment opportunities is to eliminate factor-price distortions through the use of 'shadow prices' implemented by means of wage subsidies or direct government hiring. Since, in general, actual urban wages exceed the market or 'shadow' wage as a result of a variety of institutional factors including minimum wage legislation, it is often correctly argued that the elimination of wage distortions through a subsidy system will encourage more labour-intensive modes of production. While such policies can be effective measures for generating more urban *employment* opportunities, they can also lead to higher levels of *unemployment* in accordance with our argument above about induced migration. The overall welfare impact of a wage-subsidy policy when both the rural and urban sectors are taken into account is not *a priori* clear. Much will depend on the level of urban unemployment, the magnitude of the urban–rural expected income differential, and the parametric value of the elasticity of migration.[2]

5. *Programmes of integrated rural development should be encouraged.* Policies which operate only on the demand side of the urban employment picture such as wage subsidies, direct government hiring, elimination of factor-price distortions, and employer tax incentives are probably considerably less effective in the long run in alleviating the *unemployment* problem than are policies designed directly to regulate the supply of labour to urban areas. Policies of rural development are crucial in this regard. Close and informed observers of the African scene such as Lewis, Harbison, Eicher, Frank and Hunter all agree on the central importance of rural and agricultural development if the urban unemployment problem is to be effectively solved. The ultimate objective of almost all proposals for rural development as a means of improving the unemployment situation is the restoration of a proper balance between rural and urban incomes and the elimination of ill-conceived government policies which greatly bias development programmes toward the urban industrial sector.

[1] For a more detailed explication of this argument see Edwards and Todaro (1973).
[2] For a further treatment of the wage subsidy-welfare issue, see Harris and Todaro (1970) pp. 132–5.

Given the political difficulties of reducing urban wage rates, the need continuously to expand urban employment opportunities through judicious investments in small- and medium-scale labour-intensive industries, and the inevitable growth of the urban industrial sector, every effort must be made to broaden simultaneously the economic base of the rural economy. The unnecessary incentives for rural–urban migration which now exist need to be minimised through creative and well-designed programmes of integrated rural development. Such programmes would focus on income generation, both farm and non-farm, employment growth, health delivery, educational improvement, infrastructure development and other social service improvements. Successful rural development programmes adapted to the socio-economic and environmental needs of particular countries and regions, are, in our opinion, the only viable long-run solution to the problem of excessive rural–urban migration. To assert, however, that there is an urgent need for policies designed to curb the excessive influx of rural migrants is not intended to signal an effort to reserve what some have called 'inevitable historical trends'. Rather, the implication of the migration model presented above is that there is a growing need for a 'policy package' that does not *exacerbate* these historical trends towards urbanisation by artificially creating serious imbalances in economic opportunities between urban and rural areas.

IV. RECENT EMPIRICAL STUDIES OF MIGRATION, WAGES AND EMPLOYMENT OPPORTUNITIES

In this section we shall attempt to review some recent empirical research, much of it still unpublished, on the relationship between rural–urban migration and employment opportunities. The relative paucity of research by economists on the migration phenomenon is a result of the normal lag between analytical problem identification and empirical testing of new hypotheses and theories. The scattered research on migration and employment in Latin America, Asia and Africa reported below represents only the tip of an emerging iceberg of widespread quantitative migration research currently being undertaken or initiated. Finally, it should be pointed out that although many of the following studies were not conceived as precise empirical tests of the Todaro migration theory *per se*, they all represent indirect, and in some cases, direct tests of the conclusions and policy implications of this theory.

LATIN AMERICA AND THE CARIBBEAN

1. *Brazil*

In an attempt to analyse the impact of development policy on labour absorption in Brazil, Whitaker and Schuh (1971) have developed an econometric model of the industrial labour market using cross-sectional data. Their purpose was to estimate the demand and supply equations for labour employed in the manufacturing sector of Brazil. One of the further objectives of Whitaker and Schuh's research was to test two of the major implications emerging from the Todaro model, namely (i) that the rural–urban expected wage differential must be decreased primarily through a more rational policy directed towards agriculture in order to resolve urban employment problems, and (ii) that attempts to resolve unemployment in urban areas via wage subsidies to urban workers are self-defeating.

In the course of their econometric analysis, Whitaker and Schuh have estimated a parameter for the elasticity of labour supply to urban industry, similar in concept to our elasticity of migration. The estimated value of this parameter turned out to be quite elastic, namely, 2·32. On the basis of their analysis, Whitaker and Schuh conclude that the 'implications of Todaro's model on rural–urban migration are supported by the structural coefficients in the estimated supply equation' (op. cit., p. 31). Specifically, they find that a wage increase of 10 per cent in the farm sector would reduce the quantity of labour supplied to the industrial sector by more than 10 per cent. Given an imperfect labour market, such a policy would appear to have potential for reducing rural–urban migration.

Whitaker and Schuh then proceed to test the argument that wage subsidies in urban areas might exacerbate the problem of urban unemployment. They show that 'if the subsidy is paid to the worker, the econometric results support Todaro's proposition. The supply function for total industry is quite elastic (2·32). If the wage subsidy were only 10 per cent of the market wage, the increase in the quantity of labour supplied to the industrial sector would be in excess of 23 per cent. Presumably, employment would remain the same since nothing has changed on the demand side. The result, of course, would be an increase in urban unemployment.' (op. cit., p. 32)

The evidence of a rather high elasticity of Brazilian urban labour supply reported by Whitaker and Schuh is one of only two pieces of hard empirical evidence that I am aware of about this important employment policy parameter for developing countries.[1] However, strong indirect evidence in the African context is reported by

---

[1] See discussion of T. H. Lee's research on Taiwan in the section on Asia below for a description of a similar finding in the Asian context.

Professor Dharam Ghai (1970) of the Institute of Development
Studies in Kenya in his analysis of the 1964 Kenya Tripartite
Agreement in which the Government and private employers agreed
to automatically increase their total employment by 15 and 10 per
cent respectively, while the trade unions, for their part, agreed to hold
the line on wage demands for a twelve-month period. In his paper
Ghai observes that:

> Owing to financial stringency, the Government found itself unable
> to carry out its pledge. In all, 34,000 jobs were found for persons
> who were either landless or previously unemployed. But it is
> doubtful whether these represented a net increase in employment;
> for while many of the private firms adhered to the letter of the
> agreement by taking on more employees, they violated its intent
> by not hiring new employees to make good the loss caused by
> normal attrition of the labour force. Furthermore, even if the
> agreement was successful in creating some new jobs, it did not
> make any particular impact on the level of urban unemployment,
> for prospects of wage employment stimulated an additional flow
> of migrants from the rural areas. It is clear that policies of this
> nature can create additional employment only in the very short-
> run period.

2. *Jamaica*

Another recently completed study conducted by Professor Gene M.
Tidrick (1972) of Williams College focuses on the determinants of
the level of unemployment and the relationship between employment
growth, migration and unemployment in Jamaica. Tidrick argues
that 'whereas the rate of modern sector employment growth is
largely a function of wage *trends*, the level of unemployment is a
function of the wage structure' (op. cit., p. 2). He goes on to argue
that given the sizeable gap between wages in the urban and rural
sectors of Jamaica, increases in employment opportunities in the
high-wage urban sector make unemployment more attractive for
rural migrants (i.e. they are willing to migrate to the city knowing
that they are likely to be unemployed for a certain period of time
but prepared to tolerate this situation in the expectation of eventually
securing a lucrative urban job).

Analysing trends in Jamaican wages, employment and unemployment since 1950, Tidrick concludes that:

1. In spite of relatively satisfactory rates of urban employment
growth and heavy migration abroad, Jamaica failed to reduce its
urban unemployment 'because any reduction in the number of
unemployed or increase in the rate of hiring raises the probability

of obtaining a high-wage job and induces further supply-withdrawal from the low-wage sector' – i.e. through rural–urban migration (op. cit., p. 35).

2.   The long standing shortage of labour in agriculture can coexist with high levels of open urban unemployment and continuous rural–urban migration 'because the unemployed prefer unemployment and the uncertain prospect of a high-wage job to the certain prospect of low-wage, steady employment. Why do they prefer unemployment? Because their *expected* [italics my own] lifetime earnings are greater if they remain temporarily unemployed.' (op. cit., pp. 35–6)

3.   Given the expected income differential between urban and rural areas, 'every job created in the high-wage sector will tend to wipe out more than one job in the low-wage sector' (op. cit., p. 26). Although Tidrick does not estimate precisely how many individuals will move from the low- to the high-wage sector for every additional new job created in the latter, his above assertion provides further support for our argument that, *ceteris paribus*, more urban employment will lead to more urban unemployment.

ASIA

1. *India*

In an unpublished paper, C. J. Haulk (1970) has attempted to test our principal hypothesis that 'as long as the expected urban wage is greater than the rural wage, then rural to urban migration will take place' against longitudinal data from India over the period 1900–60. To test the hypothesis, data for migration rates, rural wages, expected urban wages, and urban unemployment rates were collected. Since much of the data was not available in a usable form, it was necessary for Haulk to rework a lot of the information gathered from numerous published sources.

The procedure used was to ascertain whether there was any correlation between the differential between expected urban wages and average agricultural incomes and the percentage redistribution of the population from rural to urban areas over the sixty-year period of study. Using a five-year lag for population movements, Haulk found a very close correspondence between changes in expected income differentials and changes in population distributions. Furthermore, these movements operated in both directions. For example, whenever the urban–rural expected differential widened, there was a significant rural–urban movement of people, whereas when the income differential narrowed, net migration was very much lower. On the basis of his estimates Haulk concludes that 'the Harris–Todaro hypothesis is confirmed by Indian experience' (op. cit., p. 10).

2. *Taiwan*

There has also been a recent study of migration in Taiwan which seems to confirm our hypotheses about the relationship between rural–urban migration, wage differentials and employment opportunities. At a Sino-American Conference on Manpower held in Taiwan in June 1972, T. H. Lee of that country's Joint Commission on Rural Reconstruction presented a paper on 'Wage Differentials, Labour Mobility and Employment in Taiwan's Agriculture' (1972). Lee first reviewed trends in farm employment and the out-migration of agricultural labourers in Taiwan in the period 1952–70 and then tried to identify the principal factors influencing the mobility of Taiwanese agricultural workers. He documents how the rate of outflow of rural labour rose from less than one per cent in the early 1950s to over six per cent by 1970. Lee then attempts to discover whether nominal wages differentials or urban job opportunities had more of a decisive influence on the decision to migrate (note that our theory argues that it is a combination of both). He finds that 'labour mobility is determined by *both* employment opportunity and relative income or wage differentials depending on the change in economic situations'.

Using multiple regression analysis, Lee then demonstrates that for Taiwan there is (i) a strong negative relationship between real farm family income and the net outflow rate and (ii) a strong positive relationship between urban wages and employment opportunities and net outflow rates (op. cit., p. 19). Finally, he estimates first the elasticity of migration with respect to employment opportunities and second, the same elasticity with respect to urban wages and finds both to be high and statistically significant. While these elasticities are not the same as our elasticity of migration which relates migration to changes in expected differentials, it is clear from the data that an estimate of this elasticity would also yield a coefficient greater than one.

AFRICA

Although our expected income differential theory of migration was developed within an African context and, in many ways, is probably more applicable there than perhaps in some Asian and Latin American countries, still there remains today very little solid quantitative and econometric research on migration in Africa. Admittedly, there are a number of scattered case studies for various countries and one major undertaking now in the process of completion in Tanzania (Bienefeld and Sabot, forthcoming). However, for the most part, these studies were designed more to quantify and describe the characteristics of migrants than to analyse carefully the precise economic determinants of rural–urban migration. Nevertheless it is useful to review briefly those studies which seem to be shedding some new light on the relationship between migration and employment opportunities in Africa.[1]

1. *Tanzania*

Perhaps the most extensive and carefully designed economic research on migration in Africa is that of Bienefeld and Sabot (op. cit.) for Tanzania. Their project formed the basis of a National Urban Mobility Employment and Income Survey of Tanzania prepared for the Ministry of Economic Affairs and Development Planning. The report which at present is still in draft form and not yet released for public consumption presents the results of a detailed analysis of more than 5000 survey questionnaires administered to migrants in seven Tanzania towns. The survey was designed to yield answers to the general questions of (i) what has been happening to urban migration, (ii) why has it been happening, (iii) what are the consequences, and (iv) what are the policy implications of urban migration. Although it is not possible at this time to detail many of the preliminary findings of the survey, we can point out that these findings seem to confirm the importance of both wage differentials *and* employment probabilities in the decision to migrate.

However, in a recent paper which has been distributed and is based on the data compiled by the Tanzania survey, Sabot (1972) investigates the relationship between education, income distribution and rates of rural–urban migration in Tanzania. With regard to the determinants of migration, Sabot summarises his findings with the following statement:

> Economic factors clearly play a highly significant role. The differentials in the rates of migration by educational level, by sex, by receiving town, and over time are all consistent with differentials in the money returns to migration. Money returns consist mainly of two factors, *relative wages and relative employment opportunities* [italics my own] ... a relatively lower net rate of return in strictly economic terms to migration for subgroups is associated with a relatively lower rate of migration and when the rate of return falls

[1] For the most recent review of migration research in Africa, see Byerlee (1972).

over time for a certain sub-group, so does the rate of migration (op. cit., p. 48).

With regard to the specific relationship between migration and education, Sabot finds that the educational composition of the rural–urban migration stream has adjusted to changes in employment opportunities (probabilities) in urban areas. For example, as jobs have become more scarce, employers have tended to fill new openings with the more educated secondary-school leavers rather than with primary leavers who may have obtained equivalent jobs in the recent past. With the lowered probability of primary-school leavers securing an urban job, the proportion of primary leavers in the migration stream has declined and the proportion of secondary-school leavers has increased.

2. *Other African migration studies: Kenya and Sierra Leone*

There have been a number of other migration studies of African countries over the past few years. However, as Byerlee correctly points out in his survey of migration research in Africa, 'although the essential elements of the Todaro model of migration have been empirically tested in the U.S. and other developed countries, no rigorous test of the model has been undertaken in Africa' (Byerlee, 1972, p. 9). He notes that although Remple (1970) conducted an extensive survey of urban migrants in the major towns of Kenya as a specific test of the Todaro model, the study suffered from serious conceptual, methodological and measurement weaknesses which precluded it from being a valid scientific experiment. However, in a more recent study of migration in Kenya, Johnson (1971) finds that the rate of growth of urban jobs and the rate of unemployment are significant determinants of out-migration from the rural sector.

An attempt to test the Todaro model in Sierra Leone was also undertaken recently by Levi (1971). Using multiple regression analysis with registered unemployment as the dependent variable and measures of urban and rural incomes and employment opportunities as independent variables, Levi found that average rural income (as measured by the proxy of per capita food production) 'has a strong influence on the rate of migration from the land, with the obvious policy implication that if it can be increased, unemployment in the towns can be reduced' (op. cit., p. 24). This result is similar to those reported above by Schuh for Brazil and Lee for Taiwan. Levi also finds that the effect of employment opportunities on the decision to migrate seems to be relatively more important than real wages, although his regression results are not particularly conclusive on this point. We would agree with Byerlee that Levi's study, while a useful first step, does not represent (nor, for that matter, was it intended to represent) a thorough test of the expected income migration model.

V. SUMMARY AND CONCLUSIONS

Rural–urban migration is the key determinant of urban labour supplies in most developing nations. Urban labour forces, swelled by this influx of rural migrants, have been growing at rates considerably in excess of rates of urban employment growth causing widespread and worrying problems of urban unemployment. An understanding of the nature and determinants of rural–urban migration is, therefore, of primary importance if L.D.C. governments are to formulate policies to control successfully the proliferation of urban unemployment problems.

We have attempted in this paper to summarise the theoretical policy and empirical aspects of one particular economic model of the process of rural–urban migration. On the theoretical side, this model characterises migration as a phenomenon that is (i) stimulated primarily by rational economic considerations, (ii) motivated at the individual decision-making level by considerations of 'expected' rather than nominal urban–rural wage differentials, and (iii) manifested as a disequilibrium situation in which urban unemployment rates rather than wages or prices function as the equilibrating variable.

Included among the policy implications of the model are the following:

1. The importance of reducing the present imbalance between urban and rural expected incomes primarily through policies which simultaneously hold the line on urban expected income growth while stimulating the growth of rural agricultural and non-agricultural economic opportunities.

2. The recognition that urban *employment* creation *per se* is an insufficient solution, and, in fact, may exacerbate the urban *unemployment* problem.

3. The possibility that unbridled post-literacy educational expansion without sufficient attention to rural and urban job creation will merely represent an investment in *idle* human resources concentrated in an explosive urban environment.

4. The realisation that traditional instruments of economic policy to stimulate urban employment such as wage subsidies and 'shadow' pricing may, in fact, be counter-productive.

Finally, we reviewed recent empirical country studies of rural–urban migration as it relates to wage differentials, job probabilities and employment opportunities. Evidence from Brazil, Jamaica, India, Taiwan, Tanzania, Kenya and Sierra Leone seems to support (with varying degrees of scientific validity) the proposition that rural–urban migration should be viewed within an 'expected' income context that emphasises the interactive effects of wage differentials and urban unemployment rates on intersectoral labour mobility. Clearly, the research results reported in this paper represent at most very preliminary and not too rigorous tests of our migration theory. However, they do represent an important first step and, with the growing interest and active research on this subject among development economists, it should not be long before more definitive studies begin to appear.

REFERENCES

M. A. Bienefeld and R. H. Sabot, *The National Urban Mobility Employment and Income Survey of Tanzania* (Dar es Salaam, forthcoming).

M. Blaug, R. Layard and M. Woodhall, *The Causes of Graduate Unemployment in India* (Harmondsworth: Penguin, 1969).

D. Byerlee, 'Research on Migration in Africa: Past, Present, and Future', African Rural Employment paper no. 2 (East Lansing: Department of Agricultural Economics, Michigan State Univ., 1972).

J. C. Caldwell, *African Rural–Urban Migration* (Canberra: Australian National Univ. Press, 1969).

A. Callaway, 'Education Expansion and the Rise of Youth Unemployment', *The City of Ibadan*, ed. P. C. Lloyd, A. L. Mabogunje and B. Awe (London: C.U.P., 1967).

E. O. Edwards and M. P. Todaro, 'Educational Demand and Supply in the Context of Growing Unemployment in Less Developed Countries', *World Development*, I, 3–4 (1973) 107–17.

W. Elkan, *Migrants and Proletarians* (London and New York: O.U.P., 1960).

G. S. Fields, 'The Private Demand for Education in Relation to Labor Market Conditions in Less Developed Countries', discussion paper no. 160, Economic Growth Center, Yale University (1972a).

G. S. Fields, 'Rural–Urban Migration, Urban Unemployment and Underemployment, and Job Search Activity in LDC's', discussion paper no. 168, Economic Growth Center, Yale University (1972b).

C. R. Frank, 'Urban Unemployment and Economic Growth in Africa', *Oxford Economic Papers*, XX, 2 (1968) 250–74.

D. P. Ghai, 'Employment Performance, Prospects and Policies in Kenya', *East Africa Journal*, VII, 11 (1970) 4–11.

J. Gugler, 'The Impact of Labor Migration on Society and Economy in Sub-Saharan Africa: Empirical Findings and Theoretical Considerations', *African Social Research*, no. 6 (1968) 463–86.

J. R. Harris and M. P. Todaro, 'Migration, Unemployment and Development: A Two Sector Analysis', *The American Economic Review*, LX, 1 (1970) 126–42.

C. J. Haulk, 'Rural–Urban Migration in Low Income Countries', mimeo (1971).

C. R. Hutton, 'The Causes of Labour Migration', *Urbanization in Sub-Saharan Africa*, ed. Gugler (Kampala: 1971).

G. E. Johnson, 'The Structure of Rural–Urban Migration Models', *Eastern Africa Economic Review*, I, 1 (1971) 29–46.

A. Krueger, 'Turkish Education and Manpower Development: Some Impressions', *Essays on Labor Force and Employment in Turkey*, ed. D. R. Miller (1971) pp. 225–6.

T. H. Lee, 'Wage Differential, Labor Mobility and Employment in Taiwan Agriculture', paper presented to the Sino-American Conference on Manpower in Taiwan, Taipei (1972).

J. F. S. Levi, 'Migration and Unemployment in Sierra Leone', *Manpower and Unemployment Research in Africa: A Newsletter*, Center for Developing Area Studies, McGill Univ., Montreal, IV, 2 (1971) 20–5.

W. A. Lewis, 'Economic Development with Unlimited Supplies of Labour', *Manchester School of Economic and Social Studies*, XXII (1954) 139–91.

G. Mortara, 'Factors Affecting Rural–Urban Migration in Latin America', paper presented at World Population Conference, Belgrade, Yugoslavia (1965).

R. M. Prothero, 'Characteristics of Rural–Urban Migration and the Effects of their Movements upon the Composition of Population in Rural and Urban Areas in Sub-Saharan Africa', paper presented at World Population Conference, Belgrade, Yugoslavia (1965).

E. R. Rado, 'The Relevance of Education for Employment', *The Journal of Modern African Studies*, X, 3 (1972) 459–75.

G. Ranis and J. C. H. Fei, 'A Theory of Economic Development', *The American Economic Review*, LI, 3 (1961) 533–56.

H. Remple, 'Labor Migration into Urban Centers and Urban Unemployment in Kenya', unpublished Ph.D. dissertation, Madison: Univ. of Wisconsin (1970).

R. H. Sabot, 'Education, Income Distribution and Urban Migration in Tanzania; unpublished paper, Economic Research Bureau, Univ. of Dar es Salaam (1972).

J. E. Stiglitz, 'Rural–Urban Migration, Surplus Labour, and the Relationship Between Urban and Rural Wages', *Eastern Africa Economic Review*, I, 2 (1969) 1–27.

G. J. Stolnitz, 'Population and Labor Force in Less Developed Regions: Some Main Facts, Theory and Research Needs', paper presented at Ford Foundation Seminar on the Employment Process, Bogota, mimeo (1973).

R. N. Thomas, 'Internal Migration in Latin America: Analysis of Recent Literature', paper presented to the National Conference for Latin Americanist Geographers, Ball State Univ., Muncie, Indiana (1970).

G. M. Tidrick, 'Wage Spillover and Unemployment in a Wage Gap Economy: The Jamaican Case', Williams College, Massachusetts, mimeo (1972).

M. P. Todaro, 'An Analysis of Industrialization, Employment and Unemployment in LDC's', *Yale Economy Essays*, VIII, 2 (1968) 329–402.

M. P. Todaro, 'A Model of Labor Migration and Urban Unemployment in Less Developed Countries', *The American Economic Review*, LIX, 1 (1969) 138–48.

M. P. Todaro, 'Education and Rural–Urban Migration: Theoretical Constructs and Empirical Evidence from Kenya', paper presented at a Conference on Urban Unemployment in Africa, Institute for Development Studies, Univ. of Sussex (1971*a*).

M. P. Todaro, 'Income Expectations, Rural–Urban Migration and Employment in Africa', *International Labour Review*, CIV, 5 (1971*b*) 387–414.

M. D. Whitaker and G. E. Schuh, 'Labor Absorption and Development Policy: An Analysis of the Brazil Case', Rio de Janeiro, mimeo (1971).

Discussion of the Paper by Dr Todaro

Dr Shorter opened the discussion.[1] The Todaro model of rural to urban migration is rich with implications, he said, for empirical examination. It is dissappointing, however, to read in the paper before this conference that little solid research based on the model has so far been done. I am personally reluctant to comment on the policy implications of the model without first being fairly certain of the theoretical reasoning, and having some assurance that the world really looks as the model says it does.

The 'new' variable, added by Todaro to the wage-differential model, is a migrant's probability of obtaining an urban job. The variable is denoted by π, and is defined as follows:[2]

$$\pi = \frac{\gamma N}{S-N}, \qquad (13.1)$$

where γ is the rate of increase in urban employment, N. S is the urban labour force inclusive of the employed and unemployed. The numerator measures the number of jobs that become available during a period of time, and the denominator represents the pool of unemployed persons available for selection into these jobs. Migrants join the pool upon arrival in the city.

The probability variable is one in which new migrants and members of the pool are all alike, so that everyone, irrespective of his date of entry, or personal characteristics, has an equal chance of selection for new jobs. It simplifies the formulation of a model to assume that there is no planning beyond one time period. In that event, an immigration rate, m, is determined by the differential between expected urban earnings, πW_u, and rural wages, W_r. We choose the following form of the relationship which is convenient for certain types of estimation:

$$m(t) = f[\pi(t) . W_u(t)/W_r(t)]. \qquad (13.2)$$

The immigration rate is defined with reference to the urban area as the rate of increase in the urban labour force, S, due to immigration. From the standpoint of rural origins, a proper definition of m would be out-migrants divided by the population at risk at the origin. However, I shall keep to the convenience of m defined in relation to the size of the urban labour force for the moment, and justify this decision in terms of a destination model to be presented below. The relative sizes of labour forces in different cities are indicative of differences in the factors that facilitate migration, such as communication networks, friends and relatives, and diversity of job possibilities. These have a positive influence on migration apart from π and W_u, and one way of holding them constant is to specify the immigration rate.

[1] Dr Todaro was unfortunately unable to be present at the conference for the discussion of his paper.

[2] Michael P. Todaro, 'Income Expectations, Rural–Urban Migration and Employment in Africa', *International Labour Review*, CIV, 5 (Nov 1971) 387–413.

The whole increase in the labour force is the sum of two components, within-city growth of the labour force, g, and additions from outside m. Thus,

$$\dot{S}(t)/S(t) = g + m(t). \tag{13.3}$$

Within-city growth, g, is shown without a date because it is defined, like γ, as an exogenous variable that is held constant over time. In reality, the determinants of g include the age and sex structure of the urban population, its fertility and mortality, and labour-force participation rates. These factors which change with time, would need to be considered in a full treatment of this variable.

If there is to be no change over time in the proportion of the labour force employed, i.e. $d[N(t)/S(t)]/dt = 0$, then the equilibrium condition is:

$$\frac{\dot{N}}{N}(t) = \frac{\dot{S}}{S}(t). \tag{13.4}$$

The equilibrium condition can also be expressed as follows by substituting definitions for the left and right sides of the equation:

$$\gamma = g + m(t). \tag{13.5}$$

The values of γ and g are given exogenously, and m is assumed to be an increasing function of expected urban earnings. It follows that an immigration rate in excess of the equilibrium rate cannot be sustained. The pool of unemployed will rise faster than the number employed, π will decrease, and the inducement for immigration will decline. Proof of stability is more complex. I only want to give a sketch of the Todaro model as a basis for discussion.

The probability of obtaining an urban job refers to employment in the modern sector. Groups of immigrants can expect, on average per person, to obtain the expected earnings, πW_u, although individuals cannot. Therefore, a footnote to the theory is to mention that any inclination to avoid risks would militate against migration. In fact, the situation is not as risky as the model says it is. There are marginal jobs available as well as modern ones. In addition, there are urban subsidies in the form of social services, so the factors encouraging migration are not limited to expected urban earnings.

The late Alvaro Lopez Toro[1] extended the Todaro model by supposing that immigrants are allocated according to three exhaustive probabilities which they evaluate in reaching migration decisions. In addition to the probability of obtaining an urban job, he defines a secondary probability of finding marginal employment, and finally a residual probability of remaining wholly unemployed. The secondary probability of marginal employment raises the attractiveness of immigration and leads to higher equilibrium values of m and lower ratios of N to S. Explosive urbanisation occurs so long as expected marginal earnings fail to decline below the rural wage. A fixed cost

---

[1] Alvaro Lopez Toro, 'Migracion y Marginalidad Urbana en Paises Susdesarollados (Migration and Urban Marginality in Underdeveloped Countries), *Demografia y Economia*, IV, 2 (1970) 192–209.

of migration may be added to the rural wage in this model to make the comparison of expected rural and urban earnings more realistic.

Research on the range of urban employment opportunities would help to clarify the quantitative dimensions of the problem we are discussing. It cannot be assumed that urban enterprise is modern enterprise. Although the organisation of production in urban areas undoubtedly differs from its organisation in rural areas, a broad range exists in the urban areas from small to large scale, and from 'low' to 'high' technology. For immigrants there are many alternative points of entry. We need to know more about sequences of jobs that migrants hold after arrival and about the incomes associated with those sequences.

The probability concept, as used in the Todaro model, is defined in two radically different ways which may be explained. As presented above, the net number of new jobs appears in the numerator. Members of the pool of unemployed have a chance only to obtain jobs to that extent. Apparently, employed persons have a type of tenure. If there is any job turnover, it is of a special kind, because the employed do not revolve back into the pool of unemployed and share chances with immigrants.

If the quantity of jobs happens to decline over a period of time, the value of π will actually be negative. In fact, π is not a probability at all, but rather an index that indicates prospects for employment, and it should be evaluated on that basis. The negative sign merely shows that overall employment is shrinking. In a true probability, the denominator would measure the number of persons at risk of an event, and the events would be counted in the numerator. Both numerator and denominator would be expressed in time units because the risk of occurrence is related to time. For example, jobs obtained per annum would be placed in the numerator, and man-years of availability to be selected would appear in the denominator. Neither numerator nor denominator would be 'net'.

The implications of assuming no job turnover can be compared with the conclusions that follow from an assumption of continuous turnover. Suppose that everyone is terminated once each time period and that hiring is not preferential in terms of previous service. As the time unit $\rightarrow 0$, turnover would $\rightarrow \infty$. The probability of obtaining a job would be:

$$\pi' = \frac{N(t)}{S(t)}. \tag{13.6}$$

Both the first and second definitions (13.1 and 13.6), give a probability of 1·0 if there is full employment: $S(t) = N(t)$. The reason this is so in the first formulation is that $(S - N)$ may be interpreted as consisting entirely of new entrants, all of whom would be employed during the period. A more precise way to formulate the first probability, π, would be the following:

$$\pi = \frac{\gamma N(t)}{S(t) - N(t) + (g + m)S(t)} = \frac{\gamma N(t)}{(1 + s)S(t) - N(t)} \quad \text{(where } g + m = s\text{)}. \tag{13.7}$$

Note that the denominator now shows clearly that the pool in any period consists of the stock plus the increment added by g and m. Comparison shows that $\pi' = \pi$ only if $N(t) = S(t)$ and the system is in equilibrium with $\gamma = g + m$. If there is unemployment, then $N(t) < S(t)$, and we would have the following inequality:

$$\frac{N(t)}{S(t)} = \pi' > \pi = \frac{\gamma N(t)}{S(t) - N(t) + (g + m) S(t)}. \tag{13.8}$$

In statistical work, the first concept, π, as clarified in (13.7), is conveniently estimated from urban data that provide estimates of N and S at successive dates. The definitions of labour force and of the division between employed and unemployed are left open.

For reasons unclear to me, Todaro shifted from the first definition of the probability given in (13.1) to the second one given in (13.6) in his second *AER* article[1], and again in the paper before this conference (p. 5). Several other writers have also used the second formulation (Fields,[2] Haulk,[3] Lee[4]). If a choice is to be made, it seems to me that the advantages of retaining the original concept are the following:

1. The first concept places migrants in a pool of job seekers more like themselves than does the second concept which groups them with the entire labour force.

2. The numerator of the first concept refers to a rate of change which will vary sensitively among cities and over time with changes in employment prospects. In the second concept, the comparable numerator is a stock, and the properties of stock variables make them less powerful for the explanation of differences in flows. Neither concept is a true probability, but rather an index of employment prospects. As such, the first formulation would appear to be more sensitive, and therefore superior to the second one.

3. Finally, the second formulation leads easily, although not necessarily, to the classical wage-differential model we want to replace. For example, in the conference paper, the second concept, π', is denoted by P_u, so that expected earnings become $P_u W_u$. This is nothing more than a form of the classic variable, average earnings per person in the labour force. In the notation of this comment, $P_u = \pi' = N(t)/S(t)$. Hence, $P_u W_u = W_u N(t)/S(t)$, which is average urban earnings over the entire labour force. If expected urban earnings are specified in this way, one cannot learn by statistical analysis whether the probability of obtaining an urban job has an influence on migration flows independently of sector differentials in earnings (cf. Haulk, n.d.). The use of the first concept, π, encourages, although it does not guarantee, specification of the probability variable separately from the wage variable.

[1] John R. Harris and Michael P. Todaro, 'Migration, Unemployment and Development: A Two-Sector Analysis', *American Economic Review* LX, 1 (Mar 1970) 126–42.

[2] Gary S. Fields, 'Rural–Urban Migration, Urban Unemployment and Under-employment, and Job Search Activity in LDCs', discussion paper no 168, Economic Growth Center, Yale University (1972).

[3] C. J. Haulk, 'Rural–Urban Migration in Low Income Countries', mimeo (n.d.).

[4] T. H. Lee, 'Wage Differential, Labor Mobility and Employment in Taiwan's Agriculture', Sino-American Conference on Manpower in Taiwan, Taipei (25 June–2 July 1972).

I come next to the problem of empirical research based on a Todaro model. The formulation of migration models for statistical estimation needs to take account of three separate, but interrelated aspects of the labour-allocation mechanism. These can be described by considering three partial models, each designed to explore the determinants of an aspect of the migration matrix that describes the net flows of migrants from origins, j, to destinations, i. If the demographic information is more limited, only one of the models may be capable of estimation.

Destination model. In a destination model, the problem is to explain the allocation of net migrants among cities. Migration data are frequently available only in this form, and this type of model is often used. Rural wages are assumed to be the same everywhere and fixed costs of moving are also assumed to be the same from all locations. π is defined as in (13.7) above. We then have for the destination model the following relationship:

$$m_i^d(t) = f[\pi_i(t) . W_{u,i}(t)/k] = \frac{1}{k} . f[\pi_i(t) . W_{u,i}(t)] \qquad (13.9)$$

The resulting model is a multiplicative one in which k has no effect on standardised coefficients of the regression.

Origin model. When data on origins of the migrant streams are available, the distribution of out-migrants among origins can be studied. In this instance m should be redefined as a probability of out-migration in which the denominator is the size of the population at risk at the place of origin. In this instance, we treat the attraction of urban areas as everywhere the same, so that the numerator becomes a constant that does not affect the standardised coefficient of regression:

$$m_j^0(t) = f[k/W_{r,j}] = k . f[1/W_{r,j}]. \qquad (13.10)$$

Interaction model. Data on net migration streams from places j to places i permit the use of an interaction model. Instead of putting all the determinative variables in a single equation, it is suggested that interaction variables alone be used to explain that part of the variation in m_{ij} not already predicted by the distribution of migrants among destinations (13.9) and origins (13.10). I shall not try to anticipate here the best form of such an interaction equation, since it will need to be evaluated by empirical work with that aim. One possible formulation is the following:

$$M_{ij}^r(t) = f[(\pi_i(t) . W_{u,i}(t)/W_{r,j}) - D_{ij} + (S_i(t) . S_j(t))]. \qquad (13.11)$$

In this expression the dependent variable is the net quantity of migration to i from j. The influence of the size of the labour force at risk of migration at the origin and of the size of the labour force at destination (see remarks above about information networks, etc.) is entered as a single variable, $(S_i(t) . S_j(t))$. The effect of fixed costs is represented by distance, D_{ij}, and of the expected relationship of earnings, by $(\pi_i(t) . W_{u,i}(t)/W_{r,j})$, also entered as a single inter-action variable.

I have tried to show that the concerns of demographers with particular kinds of quantities and rates of migration have application in economic models for migration, and that it may be instructive to recognise the allocative and interactive aspects of migration decisions separately. A single equation combining (13.9), (13.10), and (13.11) to explain M_{ij} would yield spurious results because observations that pertain to i or j alone would enter as values of a variable repetitively.

Todaro's work has shown that exogenous changes in γ, W_u, and W_r may have important effects on rural to urban migration and employment rates in the urban areas. The value of g is also determinative, and should not be neglected, because the results of actions to reduce within-city population growth come only after a time. The weak spot in the whole discussion is that the actual strength of the relationship among variables in the Todaro model is not known. He has mentioned a number of empirical studies that show an interest in the problem, but of those I was able to consult, none was convincing, owing either to specification of a different problem than the one at issue here, or lack of statistical significance in the results. We must agree with Todaro that new empirical work is the next order of business.

Professor Parikh said he had tried to apply a similar model for the city of Bombay. With reference to equation (13.2), he said that the probability of finding a job in the rural area had not been included, but that it should be included in the denominator to avoid incorrect results. Using agricultural production as a proxy for the probability of finding a rural job, he found that its inclusion changed the sign of the coefficient in his model of Bombay.

A major limitation of this and other papers before the conference was that they used data about the labour force originally collected for sociological purposes. Coale and Clark had used similar data to show relationships at the level of the primary, secondary and tertiary sectors. They seemed to have taken most of the cream from the statistics, and the remaining milk was not very good! The data were too unreliable to tell one much about the labour force. Professor Hicks's comments had represented only one step in a long history of rather transient analysis aimed at disaggregating such phenomena. One could look at the problem from the viewpoint of production or consumption. The production approach took actual or potential hours of work and disaggregated them by occupation. This approach had been well illustrated in a paper by Mrs Esther Boserup. However, in order to make headway in economic analysis, it was necessary to look at the consumption side and to measure household wellbeing, if only by using proxy measures, such as life expectancy or educational and cultural opportunities. Professor Parikh thought economists were reaching the limit of analyses with the data they had.

Professor Ben Porath pointed out that Dr Todaro's paper showed no interaction with the literature on the search for jobs, on information, and on the micro-theory of unemployment. He thought this was relevant here, even though the literature was mainly concerned with developed countries. There might be a need to enrich the empirical content of the study, distinguishing between net and gross migration and allowing for a difference between the rate of unemployment for the educated and for the uneducated. The urban wage that migrants expected was only half the picture. They were also concerned with the risks relating to their old and new jobs. There was no mention in the theoretical part of the paper of the employers' side. Employers were surely as important as employees, if we were considering the whole question of employment. One needed to look at both supply and demand. Professor Robert Hall of M.I.T., and others, had established a correlation between wage rates and unemployment in major cities in the U.S.A. This was consistent over time, so they were not concerned with a disequilibrium situation. Paul David, at Stanford, had written a very interesting paper which tried to combine migration studies with job search and many other considerations.

Mr Black and *Professor Sovani* stressed the inappropriateness of definitions used by international agencies for situations in developing countries. The agencies were forced into using common data for international comparisons. A meeting of West African planners on the use of human resources had agreed unanimously that there was no problem of unemployment in Africa. As a result of this, there was no serious discussion about definitions and data. The economists of developing countries had great difficulties in liaison with their policy makers.

Professor Ohlin thought the situation was appalling. Whatever one's theoretical viewpoint, it was monstrous that the problem should be discussed with no conception of how people worked, how wages were obtained, what assets were possessed, etc. A dynamic concept of unemployment was badly needed. If our concepts of unemployment were good enough in developed countries, that did not necessarily mean that they were applicable to less-developed countries.

As for the Todaro model, it did not bring out sufficiently the gambling aspects of job search. If the expected wage in the urban labour market was much higher than in the rural one, the migration decision might well be affected by such prizes in the lottery of the urban job market.

Professor Hermalin's experience of the introduction of family planning had shown him that small differences in the way it was done could be very important for results. This was a crucial issue if we were considering going on to policy implications. The backgrounds could be very different, and it was not uncommon for an unsuccessful effort to condemn the theory, when often the real reason was a difference in the 'fine tuning' of the programme to the specific needs of the area. The whole process of implementation gave one new ideas about the data and a new understanding of things which could not have been foreseen at the start. In this way, administration interacted with theory to complicate the whole process and to make it difficult to isolate a small set of key variables.

Dr Hume said that the present lack of empirical evidence to support Dr Todaro's model raised the question of its relevance for policy at this time. Essentially, Dr Todaro was saying that for given urban/rural wage differentials, there was a level of urban unemployment which would stem the drift of migrants into the cities. The difficulty was that this 'equilibrium' rate was probably often much higher than any 'social optimum' rate; hence the condition given by a migration elasticity greater than unity. The policy authority was therefore forced into employing arbitrary measures to intervene in the free migration process to secure an optimum, rather than an 'equilibrium', rate of rural/urban labour transfer.

Professor Schultz felt that, in the absence of Dr Todaro, he should assume the duties of attorney and reply to some of the comments. The first thing that needed emphasising in Dr Todaro's framework was his concern with the possible divergence of wages from shadow prices in both the urban and the rural sector. If one were looking at expected earnings, then the classic equilibrium system, based on the typical classical assumptions, did not work out neatly. The policy implications here were important because frequently-endorsed policies could be self-defeating, and might even decrease per capita product. If empirical data verified the model at the micro level, then the policy implication was that investment was needed to increase rural income and employment opportunities rather than to try to add urban jobs. This policy implication was difficult to find in any other literature, and this was a significant new point in Dr Todaro's paper.

Second, one needed to build in dynamic job-search processes, including uncertainty. The choice between equation (13.1) and equation (13.6) was not very important, although it was an empirical issue that deserved more study. Whether the exponents in the expected income function were one or not was also an empirical question. Expected utility was not generally equal to the utility of expected income, unless the income elasticity of utility was one. Risk aversion, particularly at low income and wealth levels, was a reasonable hypothesis that could be tested empirically, using data on migration, wage rates and employment probabilities. Unfortunately, to his knowledge, it had not been done.

Professor Schultz agreed with Dr Shorter that the empirical work on migration had thus far been disappointing, but this was not a criticism of the assumptions underlying the model. We needed to establish the elasticity of response of the migration function, and he thought that data were increasingly available from surveys at the local and national level. The Todaro framework was a starting point from which more complex theoretical analysis and better focused empirical research would follow. If wages were not equal to shadow prices, policy-makers should be concerned with this form of dualism. Whether a society could accomplish a social optimum in this case was doubtful.

Dr Hume disagreed with Dr Todaro's assertion that shadow pricing could be counter-productive. In principle, and if properly done, shadow pricing should precisely take account of secondary responses to investment decisions. If the migration elasticity was greater than one, shadow wages should take this migration into account by giving greater emphasis to projects in the rural areas.

Professor Schultz replied that this was true only if one defined shadow prices to include rural as well as urban wages, but this constituted a revised definition.

Professor Giersch wondered whether, if urban life had so much attraction to the rural population, there was enough research into institutional structures, such as trade unions. He asked how far migrants' job expectations were based on correct information. How many returned because of disappointed hopes?

14 Problems of Maintaining Employment in Developing Countries in the Face of Rapid Population Growth

Abdel-Fattah Nassef
INSTITUTE OF NATIONAL PLANNING, CAIRO

I. INTRODUCTION

There is a growing concern over the serious impact of population growth on the prospects of socio-economic development. Although such an impact may be felt in the developed countries, it is a critical issue in the developing countries. Thus, a better understanding of the complex interrelationships between population changes and socio-economic development is essential for the appropriate formulation, implementation and evaluation of plans and programmes for social and economic progress.

Demographic developments affect many of the social and economic variables influencing the welfare of the people. Among the implications of population trends, the employment aspects occupy a prominent place. The analysis of manpower consequences, therefore, is a fundamental requisite to the selection of a proper employment policy which, in turn, is an integral part of the overall development plan.

The purpose of the present paper is to examine the broad consequences of the anticipated demographic trends on both the size and structure of the economically active population in the last thirty years of the twentieth century, with particular emphasis on the case of the less-developed regions of the world. The data used are those available in the recent projections prepared by the International Labour Office, the Food and Agriculture Organisation, and the Population Division of the United Nations.

II. POPULATION GROWTH AND THE SIZE OF THE LABOUR FORCE

The economically active population is determined by a host of demographic, social and economic factors, the most important of which are those associated with the size and structure of the population. Thus, the simplest indicator of the potential labour force, which can be obtained from the age and sex distribution of the population, is the total number of persons who are within the working age limits. According to the United Nations 'medium' variant projections, the working-age population (15–64 years old) in the less-developed regions (L.D.R.s) is expected to increase by 116 per cent between the years 1970 and 2000.[1] Such an increase, which amounts to 1·6 billion persons, results in a substantial rise in the demand for new job opportunities, a problem which should be given a careful attention, along with the appropriate efforts required for eliminating or at least minimising the extent of unemployment and underemployment of the existing labour force. In comparison, it is to be noted that the projected increase of the working-age population in the more developed regions (M.D.R.s) is only 33 per cent during the same period.[2]

The projections show considerable variation in the relative growth in the size of the population in the working age range between the major areas of the world. Four of the major areas show an increase higher than the world average (89 per cent), while the other four areas may have lower percentage increase. The major areas expected to have higher relative increase in the working-age population, during the 1970–2000 period, are Latin America (142 per cent), Africa (138 per cent), South Asia (135 per cent), and Oceania (100 per cent); whereas those which may experience lower relative increase are Europe (22 per cent), U.S.S.R. (34 per cent), Northern America (52 per cent) and East Asia (68 per cent).[3]

Since not all persons 15–64 years of age are economically active and not all persons below age 15 or above age 65 are inactive, such a crude indicator is quite insensitive to the various socio-economic factors affecting the propensity of different population groups to participate in economic activities. A better assessment of the economically active population, therefore, may incorporate information on activity rates. The labour force in the L.D.R.s, projected in this way, shows an increase of about 91 per cent between 1970 and the year 2000, implying an average exponential annual rate of

[1] Unless otherwise stated, the discussion is based on the United Nations 'medium' variant of population projections, and the other projections of the labour force and urban population corresponding to the 'medium' variant.

[2] The less-developed regions consist of Africa, Asia except Japan, Latin America except Temperate South America, and the Pacific Islands of Melanasia, Polynesia, Micronesia.

[3] The rates of growth in this and the preceding paragraph are derived from the data given in United Nations, 'World and Regional Population Prospects', and 'Demographic Trends in the World and its Major Regions, 1950–1970', *Symposium on Population and Development*, Cairo, 4–14 June 1973.

growth of 2·2 per cent; as compared to a growth of 33 per cent, or annual rate of 1·0 per cent, in the M.D.R.s (Table 14.1 pp. 398–9). During the thirty-year period, it is expected that the growth of the economically active population will vary significantly among the major areas. The anticipated growth rate is highest in Latin America (2·6% per year) and lowest in Europe (0·7% per year). Other areas of high annual rates of growth are Africa (2·5%), South Asia (2·4%) and Oceania (2·1%). The labour force of the U.S.S.R. is expected to experience a relatively low annual rate of 0·9 per cent, while the corresponding rates for Northern America and East Asia are of intermediate magnitude (1·5% each).

The size of economically active population is simply the product of the total population and the crude activity rate (i.e. $LF = P \cdot W$, where P is the total population, LF is the size of the economically active population, and W is the crude activity rate). Therefore, the variation in the growth rates of the labour force in the L.D.R.s and M.D.R.s as well as in the major areas referred to above is a function of the anticipated differences in the rates of population growth and changes in the levels of activity rates. For instance, the anticipated average annual rate of population growth is 2·3 per cent in the L.D.R.s between the years 1970 and 2000; while the corresponding rate in the M.D.R.s is only one per cent. Among the major areas, relatively high rates are expected to prevail in Africa (2·9%), Latin America (2·8%), South Asia (2·5%) and Oceania (2·0%), whereas lower rates are projected for Europe (0·7%), the U.S.S.R. (1·0%), Northern America (1·3%) and East Asia (1·4%) during the 1970–2000 period (Table 14.1).

The estimated crude activity rate, on the other hand, is 39·8 per cent in the L.D.R.s in 1970, 4·9 percentage points below that of the M.D.R.s. By the year 2000, it is projected that the crude activity rate will decline by 1·4 percentage points in the L.D.R.s, and by 0·2 percentage points in the M.D.R.s. Similar differences may be found among males and females in the two groups of regions, where the estimated activity rate for 1970 is 52·9 per cent for males and 26·4 per cent for females in the L.D.R.s, 4·2 and 6·7 percentage points below the corresponding rates for the M.D.R.s.

The crude activity rate is a weighted average of age-specific activity rates, w_x, where the proportions of the total population in the different age groups, c_x, are used as weights (i.e. $W = \sum c_x \cdot w_x$). Consequently, the differential in the level of the crude activity rate between the L.D.R.s and the M.D.R.s may be explained by the differences in the age structure of the population and the age pattern of activity rates. For instance, one finds that age-specific activity rates for males in the L.D.R.s are higher than those of the M.D.R.s for all age groups, even though the crude male activity rate is lower in the former than in the latter, as mentioned above. The explanation of such an apparent contradiction lies in the differences in the age structure of the male population between the two categories of regions. Thus, if the male population of the L.D.R.s had the same age structure as that of the M.D.R.s, its crude activity rate would have been 63·3 per cent: 6·2 percentage points higher than the estimated rate for the M.D.R.s. When the same procedure is applied in the case of females, the differential between the L.D.R.s and M.D.R.s is reduced from 6·7 to 2·5 percentage points. On the whole, if the population of the L.D.R.s in 1970 had the same age and sex structure as that of the M.D.R.s, its overall crude activity rate would have been 46·4 per cent, 1·7 percentage points higher than the estimated rate for the M.D.R.s.

The striking contrast between the age structure in the L.D.R.s and the M.D.R.s may be illustrated by the differences in the relative shares of the broad age groups in the total population. Thus, the children below age 15 represent 41·4 per cent of the total population in the L.D.R.s in 1970, while the corresponding proportion in the M.D.R.s is 26·8 per cent. On the other hand, the age structure of the population in the L.D.R.s is characterised by a relative deficiency of adults in the working age, 15–64, as compared to that of the M.D.R.s: 55·3 and 63·6 per cent in 1970, respectively. Finally, the proportionate share of old persons, 65 years of age and over, is significantly lower in the L.D.R.s (3·3%) than in the M.D.R.s (9·6%). It is to be noted that the broadly based and sharply tapering age distribution of the population in the L.D.R.s is primarily a result of the high fertility rates in these regions; the effect of mortality on the age structure is, in general, of a little magnitude.[1]

One of the important implications of the type of age structure prevailing in the L.D.R.s is the existence of a heavy load of dependency. A crude index of dependency is the number of persons below age 15 and those aged 65 and over per 100 of persons in the working age, 15–64. Whereas this ratio is estimated as 57 in the M.D.R.s in 1970, its value is as high as 81 in the L.D.R.s for the same year. Among the major areas, Africa has the highest ratio (87), while Europe and the U.S.S.R. have the lowest ratio (57 each). It is anticipated that the ratio will remain almost constant (around 57–8) in the M.D.R.s up to the year 2000. In the L.D.R.s no significant change in the level of dependency is expected to occur during the 1970–80 decade, after which an important decline may take place in

[1] On the relative effect of the levels of fertility and mortality on the age structure, see A. J. Coale, 'How the Age Distribution of Human Population is Determined', *Cold Spring Harbor Symposia on Quantitative Biology*, vol. XXII (1957) pp. 83–9.

TABLE 14.1 ABSOLUTE SIZE AND ANNUAL RATE OF GROWTH OF URBAN, RURAL AND TOTAL POPULATION, AND AGRICULTURAL, NON-AGRICULTURAL AND TOTAL LABOUR FORCE FOR MAJOR AREAS OF THE WORLD, 1970–2000

Major area	1970	1980	1990	2000	1970/ 80	1980/ 90	1990/ 2000	1970/ 2000
	Absolute numbers (millions)[a]				Annual rate of growth (per cent)			
WORLD TOTAL								
Total population	3632	4457	5438	6494	2·0	2·0	1·8	1·9
Total labour force	1499	1781	2140	2582	1·7	1·8	1·9	1·8
Agricultural labour force	770	801	835	864	0·4	0·4	0·4	0·4
Non-agricultural labour force	729	980	1305	1718	3·0	2·9	2·7	2·9
Urban population	1352	1854	2517	3329	3·1	3·1	2·8	3·0
Rural population	2280	2603	2921	3165	1·3	1·2	0·8	1·1
MORE DEVELOPED REGIONS								
Total population	1090	1210	1336	1454	1·0	1·0	0·8	1·0
Total labour force	488	542	592	649	1·1	0·9	0·9	1·0
Agricultural labour force	101	75	49	22	−2·9	−4·2	−7·5	−5·1
Non-agricultural labour force	387	467	543	627	1·9	1·5	1·4	1·6
Urban population	716	864	1021	1173	1·9	1·7	1·4	1·6
Rural population	374	346	315	281	−0·8	−0·9	−1·1	−1·0
LESS DEVELOPED REGIONS								
Total population	2542	3247	4102	5040	2·5	2·4	2·1	2·3
Total labour force	1011	1239	1547	1933	2·0	2·2	2·2	2·2
Agricultural labour force	669	725	786	842	0·8	0·8	0·7	0·8
Non-agricultural labour force	342	514	761	1091	4·1	3·9	3·6	3·9
Urban population	635	990	1496	2155	4·4	4·1	3·7	4·1
Rural population	1907	2257	2606	2885	1·7	1·4	1·0	1·4
EAST ASIA								
Total population	930	1095	1265	1424	1·6	1·4	1·2	1·4
Total labour force	427	497	578	663	1·5	1·5	1·4	1·5
Agricultural labour force	258	262	266	264	0·2	0·2	−0·1	0·1
Non-agricultural labour force	169	235	312	399	3·2	2·8	2·5	2·9
Urban population	266	387	541	722	3·7	3·3	2·9	3·3
Rural population	664	708	725	703	0·6	0·2	−0·3	0·2
SOUTH ASIA								
Total population	1126	1486	1912	2354	2·8	2·5	2·1	2·5
Total labour force	429	535	688	884	2·2	2·5	2·5	2·4
Agricultural labour force	293	325	363	409	1·0	1·1	1·2	1·1
Non-agricultural labour force	136	210	325	475	4·3	4·4	3·8	4·2
Urban population	238	370	556	793	4·4	4·1	3·6	4·0
Rural population	888	1116	1355	1561	2·3	1·9	1·4	1·9
EUROPE								
Total population	462	497	533	568	0·7	0·7	0·6	0·7
Total labour force	203	214	230	249	0·5	0·7	0·8	0·7
Agricultural labour force	44	32	22	11	−3·2	−3·7	−7·0	−4·6
Non-agricultural labour force	159	182	208	238	1·4	1·3	1·3	1·3
Urban population	292	339	388	438	1·5	1·3	1·2	1·4
Rural population	170	158	145	131	−0·7	−0·9	−1·0	−0·9

TABLE 14.1 (continued)

Major area	1970	1980	1990	2000	1970/ 80	1980/ 90	1990/ 2000	1970/ 2000
	Absolute numbers (millions)[a]				*Annual rate of growth (per cent)*			
U.S.S.R.								
Total population	243	271	302	330	1·1	1·1	0·9	1·0
Total labour force	123	141	152	161	1·4	0·8	0·6	0·9
Agricultural labour force	39	30	18	4	−2·6	−5·2	−15·0	−7·6
Non-agricultural labour force	84	111	134	157	2·8	1·9	1·6	2·1
Urban population	139	174	214	252	2·3	2·1	1·6	2·0
Rural population	104	94	89	77	−1·0	−0·5	−1·4	1·0
AFRICA								
Total population	344	457	616	818	2·8	3·0	2·8	2·9
Total labour force	132	165	211	276	2·2	2·5	2·7	2·5
Agricultural labour force	95	109	124	132	1·4	1·3	0·6	1·1
Non-agricultural labour force	37	56	87	144	4·1	4·4	5·0	4·5
Urban population	77	125	203	320	4·8	4·8	4·6	4·7
Rural population	268	332	413	498	2·1	2·2	1·9	2·1
NORTHERN AMERICA								
Total population	228	261	299	333	1·3	1·4	1·1	1·3
Total labour force	88	106	122	140	1·9	1·4	1·4	1·5
Agricultural labour force	4	3	2	2	−2·9	−4·1	—	−2·3
Non-agricultural labour force	84	103	120	138	2·0	1·5	1·4	1·7
Urban population	169	204	245	284	1·9	1·8	1·5	1·7
Rural population	59	56	54	50	−0·5	−0·4	−0·8	−0·6
LATIN AMERICA								
Total population	283	377	500	652	2·9	2·8	2·7	2·8
Total labour force	88	113	147	194	2·5	2·6	2·8	2·6
Agricultural labour force	37	39	41	42	0·5	0·5	0·2	0·4
Non-agricultural labour force	51	74	106	152	3·7	3·6	3·6	3·6
Urban population	158	238	350	495	4·1	3·9	3·5	3·8
Rural population	125	139	150	157	1·1	0·8	0·5	0·8
OCEANIA								
Total population	19	24	30	35	2·3	2·2	1·5	2·0
Total labour force	8	10	12	15	2·2	1·8	2·2	2·1
Agricultural labour force	2	2	2	2	—	—	—	—
Non-agricultural labour force	6	8	10	13	2·9	2·2	2·6	2·6
Urban population	13	17	21	25	2·7	2·1	1·7	2·2
Rural population	6	7	9	10	1·5	2·5	1·1	1·7

[a] The projected numbers of urban, rural and total population are taken from United Nations, 'World and Regional Population Prospects', *Symposium on Population and Development*, Cairo, 4–14 June 1973. Rural population for the world, more developed and less developed regions, has been slightly adjusted to take account of the discrepancies between international immigration and emigration assumptions referred to in that reference. Agricultural and total labour force figures are those furnished by the Food and Agriculture Organization of the United Nations, in 'Projections of the World Agricultural Labour Force and Population 1965–2000: a Provisional Study', *Symposium on Population and Development*, Cairo, 4–14 June 1973. The non-agricultural labour force is computed simply by subtracting agricultural from total labour force.

the remaining period of the century, where the dependency ratio in these regions is expected to decline from 80 to 66 between the years 1980 and 2000. The trends of dependency ratios differ considerably among the major areas of the world as a result of the varying projected changes in the age structure of the population in these areas. Noteworthy in this respect is the substantial decline in the dependency ratio in East Asia because of the assumed early timing of high rates of decline in the level of fertility in this area. Africa, on the other hand, may experience an increase in its dependency ratio from 87 in 1970 to 92 in 1990, followed by a decline to 86 by the year 2000 (see Table 14.2).

Assuming that persons not in the labour force are non-productive whereas those in the labour force are productive, a more accurate index may be obtained by the ratio of economically inactive persons per 100 of the labour force. Calculated in this way, the dependency ratio for 1970 is 151 in the L.D.R.s and 123 in the M.D.R.s. The effect of the differentials among the two groups of regions in activity rates is reflected by the variation in the relative level of dependency as measured by the two indices mentioned above. Thus, the estimated level of dependency for 1970 in the L.D.R.s is 1·4 and 1·2 times that of the M.D.R.s according to the first and second indices respectively. In fact, the burden of dependency in the L.D.R.s is lightened to some extent by an early entry of children into the labour market and a delayed withdrawal of old persons from the labour force, particularly in the rural areas of these regions.[1] However, the expected decline in activity rates, especially among young and old persons, will more than offset the effects of the favourable changes in the age structure of the population in the L.D.R.s.[2] The net outcome will be an increase in the already heavy load of dependency (measured by the second index) from 151 in 1970 to 161 in the year 2000. Among the major areas, it may be noted that the extremely high levels of dependency in Latin America and Africa are brought about by the youthful age structure of the population as well as by the significantly lower female activity rates resulting from, among other things, the social customs prevailing in these regions.

In any case, the increasing burden of dependency in the L.D.R.s during the remaining period of this century may lead to the

[1] For details on differences between more or and less developed countries in the age pattern of activity rates, see United Nations, *Demographic Aspects of Manpower, Sex and Age Patterns of Participation in Economic Activities*, United Nations Publication, sales no. 61, XIII.

[2] It may be noted that even though the spread of education will contribute to the rise in the load of dependency through reducing activity rates among young age-groups, its potential positive effect on productivity in future years should not be ignored.

absorption of potential increases in productivity in these regions in meeting the needs of the dependent population, which, in turn, may impede their ability to create new job opportunities enough to secure productive employment for the growing labour force.

TABLE 14.2 DEPENDENCY RATIOS BY MAJOR AREAS, 1970–2000

Major area	1970	1980	1990	2000
A. *Number of persons below age 15 and those aged 65 and above per 100 of persons 15–64 years old*[a]				
World total	73	73	70	64
M.D.R.s	57	57	58	57
L.D.R.s	81	80	74	66
East Asia	66	61	56	51
South Asia	86	87	78	65
Europe	57	60	58	58
U.S.S.R.	57	54	57	58
Africa	87	91	92	86
Northern America	63	59	63	56
Latin America	86	85	82	77
Oceania	65	64	67	61
B. *Number of persons not in the labour force per 100 of the labour force*[b]				
World total	142	150	154	152
M.D.R.s	123	123	126	124
L.D.R.s	151	162	165	161
East Asia	118	120	119	115
South Asia	162	178	178	166
Europe	128	132	132	128
U.S.S.R.	98	92	99	105
Africa	161	177	192	196
Northern America	159	146	145	138
Latin America	222	234	240	236
Oceania	138	140	150	133

[a] *Source:* United Nations, 'World and Regional Population Prospects', Table 5.
[b] Computed from the data of Table 14.1.

In closing this section, it may be appropriate to throw some light on the components of labour-force growth. It has been stated earlier that the size of the labour force (LF) is the product of population size (P) and the crude activity rate (W); the latter being a weighted average of age-specific activity rates (w_x), where the proportions of the population in various age groups (c_x) are used as weights. In other words, the size of the labour force can be expressed as a function of these three variables, i.e. $LF = P \sum c_x . w_x$. Therefore, it is possible, by means of standardisation techniques, to decompose the change in labour-force size into these three components. Table

14.3 presents the estimates of these components for the world, the
M.D.R.s and the L.D.R.s during the period 1970–85 for which the
necessary data are available.[1] As would be expected, the results show
that the contribution of the anticipated changes in population size
to the growth of labour force overshadows that attributable to all
other factors reflected by the changes in the crude activity rate for
either sex in both the M.D.R.s and the L.D.R.s. The declining trend
of the crude activity rate is, of course, responsible for its negative
effect on the size of the labour force; the only exception is that of
females in the M.D.R.s. However, the negative effect of the crude
activity rate masks the opposing effects of the projected changes in
the age structure of the population and in the age pattern of activity
rates. Apart from the exceptional case indicated above, the anticipated developments in the age composition will have a positive effect
on the growth of the labour force in both the L.D.R.s and the
M.D.R.s. Nevertheless, the estimated negative effect of the changes
in the age pattern of participation in economic activities is significantly greater than the positive effect of the changes in the age
structure of the population in both groups of regions.[2]

It is to be emphasised that the estimated magnitudes of the
components of change should not be considered strictly as measures
of the causal effects of the corresponding factors on labour-force
growth, because of possible interrelations between these factors
directly or through intermediate variables. The estimated components may, however, be viewed as measures of the relative
influence which the given factors exert on the growth of labour-
force size.

III. URBANISATION AND THE
NON-AGRICULTURALISATION OF THE LABOUR FORCE

The problems of maintaining productive employment in the face of

---

[1] The equations employed for estimating components of growth are as follows:

Population size: $\frac{1}{2}(P_2 - P_1)(W_1 + W_2)$

Crude activity rate: $\frac{1}{2}(W_2 - W_1)(P_1 + P_2)$

Age structure: $\frac{1}{4}(P_1 + P_2) \sum (c_{x2} - c_{x1})(w_{x1} + w_{x1})$

Age-specific activity rates: $\frac{1}{4}(P_1 + P_2) \sum (w_{x2} - w_{x1})(c_{x1} + c_{x2})$

where 1 and 2 refer to the initial and terminal dates respectively. For details on the
method, see A. Nassef, 'Standardization as a Technique for Temporal Component
Analysis', *The Egyptian Population and Family Planning Review*, vol. 5, no. 1 (June
1972) pp. 79–90. The data used are those given in International Labour Office,
Labour Force Projections, Geneva, 1971.

[2] If the necessary data were available for the 1985–2000 period, the estimates
would have shown a more significant effect for the favourable changes in the age
structure anticipated during this period.

TABLE 14.3 ESTIMATES OF COMPONENTS OF LABOUR-FORCE GROWTH FOR THE WORLD, MORE DEVELOPED AND LESS DEVELOPED REGIONS, BY SEX, 1970-1985[a]

Components	Absolute numbers (000s)			As % of 1970 labour force			As % of total change		
	World	M.D.R.s	L.D.R.s	World	M.D.R.s	L.D.R.s	World	M.D.R.s	L.D.R.s
MALES									
Population size	353190	54922	298268	36·0	18·2	43·8	110·5	112·4	110·2
Crude activity rate	−33611	−6069	−27542	−3·4	−2·0	−4·0	−10·5	−12·4	−10·2
Age structure	26275	6677	19598	2·7	2·2	2·9	8·2	13·7	7·2
Age-specific rates	−59886	−12746	−47140	−6·1	−4·2	−6·9	−18·7	−26·1	−17·4
FEMALES									
Population size	169467	29211	140256	32·7	15·6	42·2	123·7	90·4	134·0
Crude activity rate	−32469	3094	−35563	−6·3	1·7	−10·7	−23·7	9·6	34·0
Age structure	7294	−1020	8314	1·4	−0·5	2·5	5·3	−3·2	7·9
Age-specific rates	−39763	4114	−43877	−7·7	2·2	−13·2	−29·0	12·8	−41·9
BOTH SEXES									
Population size	522657	84133	438524	34·8	17·2	43·3	114·5	103·7	116·8
Crude activity rate	−66080	−2975	−63105	−4·4	−0·6	−6·2	−14·5	−3·7	−16·8
Age structure	33569	5657	27912	2·2	1·2	2·8	7·3	7·0	7·4
Age-specific rates	−99649	−8632	−91017	−6·6	−1·8	−9·0	−21·8	−10·7	−24·2

[a] The data used are those of the population and labour force by age and sex which are available in the International Labour Office, *Labour Force Projections*, Pt V, Geneva, 1971, after grouping the data in the way stated in footnote 2. The estimating equations are given in footnote 6.

rapid population growth in developing countries are not confined to the growth of labour-force size. In fact, there is a general recognition that high rates of population growth may seriously impede the structural shifts of the labour force which are associated with the process of economic development.

Dovring has stated that the rate of change in the proportionate share of the non-agricultural sector is determined by the difference between the rate of increase of the population (or the total labour force) and that of the non-agricultural labour force.[1] Moreover, the pace of the redistribution of the labour force between these two broad sectors depends also on the relative share of the labour force initially in agriculture. That is, given the growth rate of the population, the higher the proportion of agriculture in the labour force, the greater the rate of increase in the non-agricultural sector that is required to achieve a given amount of decline in the agricultural share. In this simple model, however, agriculture is assumed to exhibit a 'surplus' of manpower which is viewed as 'residual'. The non-agricultural sector, on the other hand, is considered as the dynamic element whose expansion depends on the process of capital formation and on the development of complementary institutional arrangements.

Other writers have extended Dovring's framework by introducing the role of increasing labour productivity in economic transformation. Thus, they have shown that the conditions necessary for holding the size of the labour force in agriculture constant and for decreasing it may be expressed in terms of the rate of growth of the total labour force, the initial proportion of agriculture in the labour force, and the rates of increase in productivity and total product in the non-agricultural sector.[2]

[1] F. Dovring, 'The Share of Agriculture in a Growing Population', *Monthly Bulletin of Agricultural Economics and Statistics*, Food and Agriculture Organization of the United Nations, vol. VIII, no. 8/9 (Aug–Sep 1959) 1–11. Dovring has correctly pointed out that 'If the growth of labor force is different from that of the total population..., then it may be necessary to keep apart the rates of growth referring to manpower and total population' (p. 1).

[2] A. J. Jaffe and J. N. Froomkin, 'Economic Development and Jobs – A Comparison of Japan and Panama, 1950 to 1960', *Symposium No. 1, Population Problems in the Pacific*, 11th Pacific Congress, Tokyo, August 1966. According to the authors, the rate of increase in output of the non-agricultural sector (G_m) required to keep the numbers of agricultural workers constant may be estimated as follows:

$$G_m = \sqrt[n]{\left[\frac{(l+1)^n - a_1}{l - a_1} (l + p_m)^n - 1 \right]}$$

where l is the increase in the labour force, p_m is the labour productivity increase in non-agriculture, a_1 is the ratio of agricultural employment to the total labour force during the base period, and n is the length of the period.

There are a number of other models for economic transformation, a few of which incorporate demographic variables and, even then, the treatment of these variables is rudimentary. In a recent study based on Chenery's model, Blandy has estimated the effects of population growth on employment structure. He states that 'a reduction in population growth brings an acceleration in the transformation of the economy ...'[1]

Nevertheless, the following discussion makes use of the projections of agricultural labour force prepared by the Food and Agriculture Organization of the United Nations. These projections are based on explaining the changes in the relative shares of agriculture in the total labour force during 1950–60 in terms of changes in per capita gross domestic product (GDP), contribution of agriculture to GDP and differentials between the growth rates of GDP and the contribution of agriculture to GDP. Thus, in projecting changes in the proportions of agriculture in the labour force, the targets of these economic magnitudes available from international development studies such as those of the Second United Nations Development Decade and the F.A.O.'s Indicative World Plan of Agricultural Development are used as independent variables. By applying the projected proportions to the I.L.O. labour-force projections linked with the U.N. medium variant projections of the population, the absolute size of agricultural labour force is projected for each fifth year up to 1985. However, in the absence of estimates for the independent variables beyond 1985, another method using the rate of migration of labour force from the agricultural to the non-agricultural sector is applied for the period 1985–2000.[2]

According to these projections, considerable changes in the distribution of the labour force among the two broad sectors are expected

[1] R. Blandy, 'Patterns of Industrial Growth: An Introductory Empirical Exploration', *International Labour Review*, vol. 106, no. 4 (Oct 1972) 347–66, and references referred to therein. According to Chenery's model, employed in several studies, sector output per head of population (x_i/p) depends on income per head (y/p) and population size (P), whereas sector employment (L_i) depends on sector output (X_i). That is

$$\frac{X_i}{P} = x_i \left(\frac{Y}{P}, P \right) \tag{1}$$

$$L_i = l_i(X_i) \tag{2}$$

Blandy has introduced labour supply in the economy as a whole (L) as a factor effecting sector employment. Thus, equation (2) of Chenery's model becomes:

$$L_i = \phi_i(X_i, L)$$

[2] Food and Agriculture Organization of the United Nations, 'Projections of World Agricultural Labour Force and Population, 1965–2000: A Provisional Study', *Symposium on Population and Development*, Cairo 4–14 June 1973.

in M.D.R.s and L.D.R.s. For instance, the proportionate share of
agriculture in the total labour force of the L.D.R.s is projected to
decline from 66·2 to 43·5 per cent between the years 1970 and 2000;
compared to a decline from 20·7 to 3·5 per cent in the M.D.R.s
during the same period. Moreover, the projected proportion for the
major areas of the world in the year 2000 ranges between 1·6 per cent
in Northern America and 47·5 in Africa (Table 14.4).

TABLE 14.4 PERCENTAGE OF LABOUR FORCE IN
AGRICULTURE BY MAJOR AREAS, 1970–2000[a]

Major area	1970	1980	1990	2000
World total	51·4	45·0	39·0	33·5
M.D.R.s	20·7	13·9	8·3	3·5
L.D.R.s	66·2	58·5	50·8	43·5
East Asia	60·3	52·7	45·9	39·7
South Asia	68·3	60·5	52·5	46·2
Europe	21·6	15·1	9·4	4·5
U.S.S.R.	31·8	21·4	11·9	2·7
Africa	71·8	65·8	58·3	47·5
Northern America	4·4	2·7	2·0	1·6
Latin America	41·5	34·6	27·7	21·8
Oceania	23·7	19·9	16·8	14·3

[a] *Source:* F.A.O., 'Projections of the World Agricultural Labour Force and Population', op. cit., Table 2, p. 11.

These projections indicate that by the year 2000 the size of the
non-agricultural labour force in the L.D.R.s is expected to be 3·2
times its size in 1970. Compared with the past experience of the
more developed countries, the anticipated increase of 749 million in
the non-agricultural labour force of the L.D.R.s, with an average
annual rate of 3·9 per cent during the thirty-year period, appears to
be an ambitious target to achieve. The economically active population in the non-agricultural sector of the M.D.R.s, on the other
hand, is projected to increase by 1·6 per cent per year, a rate that is
less than one half of the corresponding rate for the L.D.R.s. The
projected growth rates of the labour force in the non-agricultural
sector show a wide range of variation among the major areas of the
world.[1] For example the annual rate is expected to be as high as
4·5 per cent in Africa between 1970 and 2000; while the lowest annual

[1] Since the method employed for the projections makes use of the structural
changes of the labour force during 1950–60, the F.A.O.s study notes that in some
areas, particularly U.S.S.R. and Eastern Europe, the rapid decrease in the agricultural
labour force is partly explainable by the unusually pronounced changes during the
base period (1950–60). Ibid., p. 13.

rate of growth is projected for Europe (1·3 per cent) during the same period (see Table 14.1).

It is equally important to take cognisance of the fact that together with the substantial growth rate of the labour force in the non-agricultural sector of the L.D.R.s, the expected high rates of population growth in these regions will allow for a sizeable increase in the economically active population in the agricultural sector as well. Thus, even though the relative share of agriculture in the labour force will decline considerably, the agricultural labour force in the L.D.R.s is projected to increase by 26 per cent, i.e. 173 million workers, between the years 1970 and 2000. The increase may reach 35 per cent under the 'high' and 'constant' variants of the United Nations projections, and 18 per cent under the 'low' variant.[1] By contrast, the agricultural labour force is expected to decrease at an annual rate of 5·1 per cent during the same period in the M.D.R.s.

The growth of the agricultural labour force in the L.D.R.s may give rise to different types of employment problems in the countries of these regions. In some of these countries such as India, Pakistan, Java and Egypt, the cultivated areas are densely populated and the prospects for their extension are very limited. Thus, the growth of the agricultural labour force will lead to an increase in the already high man/land ratio which may, in turn, aggravate the degree of underemployment prevailing among agricultural workers in these countries. In the other group of countries where land and water resources could be extended for agricultural use, the amount of capital required for the extension of these resources to absorb the increasing agricultural workers, together with the capital needed for the creation of new jobs for the fast growing non-agricultural workers and for the other social services (such as education, health, etc.) may turn out to be beyond the economic capacity of these countries.

A better understanding of the process of the non-agricultural-isation of economically active population may be reached by linking it with the process of urbanisation, and vice versa. It is to be emphasised first that urbanisation in modern times is inevitable and irreversible. In fact, rural-to-urban migration is an essential condition for economic development. However, it is widely recognised that the rate of urbanisation in the L.D.R.s in recent times has been higher than would be justified on the basis of the levels of their economic development. It has been stressed in the literature that the main reason for rural-to-urban migration in the L.D.R.s is the population pressure on land in the impoverished rural areas, rather than the increasing demand for labour in urban areas. Consequently,

[1] Ibid., pp. 15–17.

many of the migrants are unemployed or engaged in activities characterised by very low levels of productivity. Moreover, the growth of urban population has been too fast to secure the essential environmental conditions for decent urban life. In short, it is indicated that rural-to-urban migration in the L.D.R.s results in a transfer of poverty from rural to urban areas, although, in some studies, migrants claim that their living conditions in rural areas were even worse.

Nevertheless, it is estimated that a quarter of the population in the L.D.R.s and slightly less than two-thirds in the M.D.R.s lived in urban places in 1970. According to the United Nations Projections, the percentage of urban population is expected to rise to 43 in the

TABLE 14.5   ESTIMATED PERCENTAGE OF URBAN
POPULATION BY MAJOR AREAS, 1970–2000[a]

Major area	1970	1980	1990	2000
World total	37·2	41·5	46·1	51·1
M.D.R.s	65·7	71·4	76·4	80·7
L.D.R.s	25·0	30·4	36·3	42·6
East Asia	28·6	35·4	42·7	50·7
South Asia	21·2	24·9	29·1	33·7
Europe	63·2	68·1	72·8	77·0
U.S.S.R.	57·1	64·2	70·7	76·5
Africa	22·2	27·3	33·0	39·2
Northern America	74·2	78·3	82·0	85·1
Latin America	55·9	63·2	70·0	75·9
Oceania	67·9	69·8	71·0	71·7

[a] *Source:*   U.N., 'World and Regional Population Prospects', op. cit., Table 7.

L.D.R.s and to 81 in the M.D.R.s by the end of the century. The lowest projected percentage urban in the year 2000 for the major areas of the world is that of South Asia (34), while the percentage of Northern America (85) is the highest (Table 14.5).

The projections imply that urban population in the L.D.R.s will more than triple between the years 1970 and 2000, with an average annual rate of growth of 4·1 per cent. On the other hand, the urban population of M.D.R.s is expected to grow by 64 per cent, or by annual rate of 1·6 per cent. It is noteworthy that the projected tremendous amount of urban growth in the L.D.R.s during the thirty-year period (1·5 billion) is more than the anticipated size of the total population in M.D.R.s at the end of the period, or more than 1·5 times its size at the beginning of the period.

The projected annual rates of urban growth are around 4 per cent or more in Africa (4·7%), South Asia (4·0%) and Latin America

(3·8%), and 2 per cent or less in Europe (1·4%), Northern America (1·7%) and U.S.S.R. (2·0%). The rates for East Asia and Oceania are 3·3 and 2·2 per cent, respectively (Table 14.1).

Parallel to the rapid growth of urban population in the L.D.R.s the rural population is projected to increase by more than 50 per cent during the last thirty years of the present century, with an average annual rate of 1·4 per cent. In contrast, the M.D.R.s are expected to experience a decrease in the size of their rural population at the rate of one per cent per year.

The anticipated considerable growth (978 million) of the rural population in the L.D.R.s may exacerbate the current poor living conditions in the rural areas, especially when it is inferred that most of the expected growth of non-agricultural employment will occur in urban areas with little effect on the existing structure of the rural economy in these regions. Therefore, without real efforts to improve the conditions of rural life, the projected growth of rural population may lead to even higher rates of migration to urban areas than anticipated by the United Nations projections.

In short, the rapid growth of the population in the L.D.R.s during the remaining part of the century may pose serious employment implications. Suffice it to say that together with problems of the formation of the types of skills required for the projected economic transformation, it is estimated that the L.D.R.s 'need (investment) rates of 15 to 20 per cent *net*, as against the current 15 to 18 per cent *gross*, if they are to maintain equilibrium between the demand for and supply of jobs'.[1]

IV. CONCLUDING OBSERVATIONS

Considerable population growth is expected in the L.D.R.s during the remainder of the present century. As a result, there will be a substantial rise in the demand for new job opportunities, an issue that requires serious attention, together with appropriate measures for reducing the extent of underemployment of the existing labour force.

Moreover, the anticipated decline in activity rates, particularly among the young and old age groups, will more than offset the positive effects of the favourable changes in the age structure of the population of the L.D.R.s on the level of dependency. The result will be an increase in the already heavy load of dependency.

During the thirty-year period, it is projected that the non-

[1] W. A. Lewis, 'Summary: The Causes of Unemployment in Less Developed Countries and Some Research Topics', *International Labor Review*, vol. 101, no. 5 (May 1970) p. 553.

agricultural labour force (and the urban population) will more than triple. In addition, the rapid population growth in the L.D.R.s may also give enough room for a sizeable increase in the agricultural labour force (and rural population).

In meeting the needs of a large proportion of dependent population, preparing human skills required for the anticipated economic transformation, providing needed investment for creating additional jobs to secure productive employment for the growing labour force, and improving the environmental conditions in rural and urban areas during the remaining period of the twentieth century, the L.D.R.s will be facing a serious challenge which necessitates the formulation of comprehensive development plans in which population and manpower policies should be given an appropriate attention.

15 The Importance of Labour-force Structure in Relation to Employment and Unemployment in Less-developed Countries

Pravin Visaria

I. INTRODUCTION

During the past few years, the focus of most discussions on economic development has shifted from food production to poverty and unemployment. In many developing countries, the increase in the output of staple cereals like wheat, made possible by the availability of high yielding varieties of seeds responsive to chemical fertilisers under conditions of assured and controlled water-supply, has raised the welcome prospect of self-sufficiency in foodgrains, at least during normal weather conditions. However, for the non-cultivating households, work by at least the able-bodied males is the main source of purchasing power required for food consumption. The problem of providing productive employment opportunities to the growing labour force therefore assumes great importance.

There is widespread concern about the number of unemployed persons, who are presumed to be without any source of income during the period of their unemployment. Given the acute poverty, and the absence of any system of social security or unemployment insurance, the unemployed can hardly draw on the resources of other groups in the community and, therefore, they are presumed to suffer from acute stress, if not starvation. The substantial mental and material hardship involved in the non-availability of gainful employment is so obvious that the problem certainly deserves sustained attention of the planning authorities. However, most surveys and studies, using the internationally recommended or approved criteria, report much lower incidence of unemployment and visible underemployment, i.e. involuntary part-time work. The natural reaction of the politicians and the lay public is to doubt the tools and definitions used by the statisticians and survey planners.

The purpose of this paper is to examine these estimates in the light of the structure of the labour force in terms of its distribution by industry or occupation and by class of worker, which seem to have a significant effect on the results of various surveys or studies. Much of the discussion will be based on the data available for India, which, with its population of nearly 580 million, accounts for nearly 21 per cent of the total population of the developing countries (nearly 2·8 billion). It is likely that the Indian situation resembles in many respects the conditions prevailing in a number of other countries with a predominance of seasonal agriculture. The available information for Malaya, South Korea and Philippines is briefly discussed in the Appendix.

II. DISGUISED UNEMPLOYMENT: ITS LIMITED OPERATIONAL SIGNIFICANCE

Let me begin with the statement that the disguised unemployment or underemployment which is believed to be pervasive in the self-employed sector in agriculture, household industry, trade and other services, does not seem to be of much operational significance, at least in the near future. The mobilisation of savings potential inherent in this disguised unemployment has often been assigned a critical role in the development strategy advocated by economists since the end of the Second World War. Several attempts have been made to measure the quantum of disguised unemployment and the potential surplus manpower in agriculture, although it is recognised that the phenomenon exists in the non-agricultural or the urban sector as well. In this process, it has also come to be recognised that the quantum of 'removable' surplus persons, after allowing for fractional and seasonal components, would tend to be limited. As a result, the emphasis on the mobilisation of the savings potential inherent in or attributed to disguised unemployment appears to have been exaggerated.

In some sense, the problem of disguised unemployment and under-employment is equivalent to the problem of low productivity or poverty and therefore its elimination forms the core of economic development. However, in a democratic society, compulsory re-allocation of manpower resources among different activities is not possible. Therefore, the removal of the surplus manpower from agriculture would require either an authoritarian form of government, little concerned with the current preferences and attitudes of the people or, if the economic incentives are to be relied upon, a rate of growth of non-agricultural employment that is much higher than the rate of growth of the labour force. As we shall see below, at least in India, there has been little change during the past two decades in the proportion of the working force engaged in agriculture, which continues to be the 'residual' employment sector. In other words, the non-agricultural employment opportunities have not expanded at a rapid pace and there is little prospect that this situation will change in the near future. It is, therefore, appropriate to direct our attention first to those segments of the labour force which are openly unemployed or underemployed.

Such a choice seems justified also because of the uncertainty about the size of the labour force or the economically active population in developing countries like India. Admittedly, the measurement of the labour force engaged in agriculture, particularly the female labour force, is difficult even in the developed countries. Yet the difficulties seem to be more acute in a predominantly agricultural economy in which a majority of the working force is engaged in self-employment or unpaid work on small farms.

These problems have a vital bearing on the estimates of disguised unemployment or underemployment which seem to assume that persons classified as workers or members of the labour force would want to work on a full-time basis if only they had the opportunity to do so. The evidence to the contrary is not quite conclusive but there is a fair volume of literature which indicates that it would be erroneous to ignore, for example, the multiple responsibilities of the unpaid family workers, which restrict their ability to work on a full-time basis, and also their preferences about the nature and location of work they would like to perform. We shall now illustrate the points by reference to the Indian data.

III. SIZE OF THE INDIAN LABOUR FORCE

Until about 1952 the decennial censuses were the only source of information on the size and characteristics of the economically active population in India. Since then, the successive Rounds of the National Social Survey have helped to build up a large body of information on the various characteristics of the labour force which facilitate an intensive analysis of the different facets of the problem. Unlike the census, the N.S.S. data are generally available only for rural and urban India as a whole (although some state-level estimates are also possible).

Normally, the labour-force participation rates change only gradually but the post-independence Indian census data on the subject show very sharp fluctuations. When the worker population ratio increased from nearly 39 per cent reported by the 1951 census[1] (54 per cent for males and 23 per cent for females) to 43 per cent in 1961 (57 per cent for males and 28 per cent for females), it confirmed the earlier widespread belief that the workers were under-enumerated in 1951, particularly in the southern states of Andhra Pradesh, Tamil Nadu and Mysore and to a lesser, though not insignificant, extent also in other states such as Assam, Bihar, Bombay, Orissa and West Bengal. The 1961 worker rate[2] was higher particularly for rural females. But it has remained a moot point whether the fault lay with the 1951 census instructions which did not specifically note the need to record family workers as one category of workers or whether it was due to the liberal definitions of the 1961 census, according to which persons working in seasonal activities for 'at least one hour a day throughout the greater part of the working season' were to be recorded as workers. It is obvious that such a definition can hardly be applied with any mathematical precision in a large operation like the census conducted by essentially honorary enumerators. In effect, the 1961 census attempted to adopt the usual status approach and made a reasonably complete inventory of the economically active population.

To ascertain the extent to which marginal workers had been included in the 1961 count, the 1971 census attempted to distinguish between (a) those whose 'main activity' (i.e. the activity in which a person 'engages himself mostly') was work (i.e. participation in any economically productive work by physical or mental activity, involving not only actual work but effective supervision and direction of work) or in other words, full-time workers and (b) other 'not mainly working' persons whose 'main activity' was other than work. The instructions specifically laid down that persons engaged in household duties or studies, who participated in the 'family economic activity' on a less than full-time basis, should *not* be classified as having work as their 'main activity'. All persons who were recorded as non-workers according to the main activity were indeed to be

---

[1] The basic tabulation plan of the 1951 census had attempted to classify the entire population according to its main source of livelihood. The non-earning dependants were grouped with the self-supporting persons and earning dependants with a particular means of livelihood. Subsequently, the data relating to the self-supporting persons and the earning dependants – their principal and secondary means of livelihood – have been reworked to obtain data on the number of workers and their industrial classification. For a detailed bibliography on the Indian data on the subject, see Pravin Visaria, *A Survey of Research on Employment in India*, a report prepared on behalf of the Indian Council of Social Science Research, 1972 (in press).

[2] The 'worker rate' is used as a synonym for 'worker-population ratio'. Both these terms differ from the conventional 'labour-force participation rate' in so far as their numerator does not include the unemployed persons.

TABLE 15.1 WORKERS, UNEMPLOYED AND THE LABOUR FORCE ENUMERATED BY THE 1961 CENSUS AND THEIR PERCENTAGE IN THE POPULATION

Area	Workers		Unemployed			Labour force	
	('000)	as % of population	('000)	as % of population	as % of labour force	('000)	as % of population
MALES							
All India	129,114	57·12	1,293	0·57	0·99	130,407	57·69
Rural India	106,696	58·17	541	0·29	0·50	107,237	58·51
Urban India	22,418	52·40	752	1·76	3·25	23,170	54·15
FEMALES							
All India	59,458	27·95	126	0·06	0·20	59,578	28·02
Rural India	55,448	31·38	63	0·04	0·11	55,511	31·45
Urban India	4,010	11·09	57	0·16	1·40	4,067	11·25
PERSONS							
All India	188,572	42·98	1,413	0·32	0·74	189,985	43·30
Rural India	162,144	45·02	604	0·17	0·37	162,748	45·23
Urban India	26,427	33·48	809	1·02	2·97	27,237	34·51

Note: Sikkim is excluded.
Source: Census of India, 1961, vol. I, *India*, pt II-B(i) and pt II-B(iii), *General Economic Tables*, Tables B-I and B-IX.

TABLE 15.2 WORKERS, UNEMPLOYED AND THE LABOUR FORCE ENUMERATED BY THE 1971 CENSUS AND THEIR PERCENTAGE IN THE POPULATION

Area	Mainly working		Secondarily working[a]		Unemployed			Labour force	
	('000)	as % of population	('000)	as % of population	('000)[a]	as % of population	as % of labour force	('000)	as % of population
				MALES					
All India	149,075	52·50	123	0·04	2,768	0·97	1·82	151,966	53·52
Rural India	120,408	53·46	92	0·04	1,491	0·66	1·22	121,991	54·16
Urban India	28,667	48·82	30	0·05	1,277	2·17	4·26	29,974	51·05
				FEMALES					
All India	31,298	11·85	2,311	0·88	526	0·20	1·54	34,135	12·93
Rural India	27,966	13·09	2,137	1·00	328	0·15	1·08	30,431	14·24
Urban India	3,332	6·61	174	0·35	198	0·39	5·35	3,704	7·35
				PERSONS					
All India	180,373	32·92	2,433	0·45	3,294	0·60	1·77	186,100	33·96
Rural India	148,375	33·81	2,230	0·51	1,819	0·34	1·19	152,424	34·73
Urban India	31,999	29·33	204	0·19	1,475	1·35	4·38	33,678	30·87

[a] The figures are estimates based on the 1 per cent sample of the 1971 population.
Source: Census of India, 1971, ser. I, *India*, Paper 3 of 1972, Economic Characteristics of Population (selected tables).

asked whether they participated in *any* economic activity or work and such economic activity was to be recorded as 'secondary work'. In elaborating the instructions it was stated that even 'marginal' economic activity was to be recorded under the question on secondary work ('in addition to whatever' was recorded as the main activity in the preceding question). The total working force would include (a) all those who reported work as their 'main activity' *plus* (b) persons whose main activity was other than work but who reported some economic activity under the question pertaining to secondary work. However, the enumerators apparently failed to recognise the importance of recording the secondary economic roles.

The data summarised in Tables 15.1 and 15.2 show that according to the 1 per cent sample of the 1971 census, the number of mainly non-working but secondarily working persons was not more than 2·4 million, largely among rural women. As a result, the worker population ratios based on the 1971 census are substantially lower than those of 1961. The differences are much larger among the ratios for females than among those for males and much larger for rural females than for urban females.

To obtain labour-force participation rates, we have to add the unemployed persons to the workers. The 1961 census had provided two categories of non-workers to classify (a) the new entrants who were unemployed and (b) the experienced unemployed. The number of unemployed reported by it did not, however, exceed 1·4 million. This led to a widespread recognition of the limitations of the census for collecting data on a complex subject like unemployment.[1] In the 1971 census, except in the data collected on a self-enumeration basis from the scientific and technical personnel, no one was classified specifically as unemployed. However, the number of unemployed can be presumed to equal the residual category of 'others' among the non-workers, after the sorting out of (a) full-time students, (b) persons engaged in household duties, (c) dependants and infants, (d) the retired, rentiers and persons of independent means, (e) beggars, vagrants, etc. and (f) inmates of penal, mental and charitable institutions. On this presumption, the number of unemployed persons enumerated in 1971 appears to have been 3·29 million (2·77 million males and 0·52 million females) which is more than twice the number enumerated in 1961. Yet, even when we add them to the mainly and secondarily working persons, we obtain an estimate of

[1] For a comparative study of the data on unemployment provided by the census and the successive Rounds of the N.S.S. and the underlying definitions see: Pravin Visaria, 'Employment and Unemployment in India: A Review of Selected Statistics', Appendix II to the *Report of the Committee of Experts on Unemployment Estimates*, Planning Commission, Government of India, 1970.

the labour force at 186 million, i.e. about 34 per cent of the population.

The apparent sharp decline in the worker population ratios as well as the labour-force participation rates during 1961–71, suggested by the census data, is sometimes alleged to be due to the sharp increase in the level of unemployment. It is argued that while the population has increased by nearly 109 million from 439 million in 1961 to 548 million in 1971, the land area under cultivation has increased very slowly, at the rate of less than one million acres per year. The increase in the area under irrigation since 1961 and the improved possibilities of multiple cropping would not raise this figure to any significant extent. As a result, the scope for the absorption of additional workers in agriculture would obviously be limited and some substitution of male labour for female labour might also have taken place. While such reasoning might prima facie appear plausible, it is not consistent with the results of the latest available N.S.S. Round (21st) conducted during 1966–7. Of course, the N.S.S. data are based on a reference period of a week; and since the survey is spread over the entire year, they provide an average picture for the year as a whole. The resulting participation rates, shown in Table 15.3, were lower than those reported by the 1961 census but much higher than indicated by the 1971 census. Table 15.3 also shows the estimated rates that would have been observed in 1971, if the 1966–7 rates had continued to hold. It is most unlikely that the participation rates would decline so sharply within a five-year period and there-fore, the low participation rates reported by the 1971 census must be viewed largely as an artifact of the changes in definitions and/or their interpretation by the enumerators.

Such variations in the data on the labour force have been mentioned or noted in the literature. Particular mention is made of the need to evaluate the extent to which the unpaid family workers are included among or enumerated as workers.[1] Such problems are particularly acute in a one-point operation like the census.

I have argued that the 1971 census instructions advising the record of housewives, students, etc., as non-workers in terms of their main activity are likely to affect particularly the unpaid family helpers who have dual roles. The hypothesis that the unpaid family workers are not included among the 1971 provisional figures relating to full-time workers or mainly-working persons can explain adequately the 7 to 8 per cent difference between the full-time worker rate of 1971 and the worker rate of 1961 in respect of males, both in rural and urban

[1] United Nations, *Demographic Aspects of Manpower*, report 1, *Sex and Age Patterns of Participation in Economic Activities*, New York, 1972.

TABLE 15.3 LABOUR-FORCE PARTICIPATION RATES REPORTED BY THE 21ST
ROUND OF THE N.S.S. FOR RURAL AND URBAN INDIA DURING JULY 1966–
JUNE 1967 AND ESTIMATES FOR ALL-INDIA IN 1971, BASED ON THE N.S.S. RATES

	Rural India 1966–7	Urban India 1966–7	All India estimate for 1971
Males	53·96	50·66	53·28
Females	28·53	10·85	25·16
Persons	41·41	31·93	39·73

Note: The estimates for all India for 1971 show the rates that would have been observed if the rates for males and females in rural and urban India in 1971 were the same as in 1966–7.

areas. As for the corresponding rates for females, about 75 per cent of the differences can be explained by the above hypothesis.[1]

Further support for this hypothesis comes from the fact that the 1 per cent sample tables of the 1971 census relating to the distribution of non-cultivating workers by status or class of worker show a sharp increase in the proportion of employees. According to the figures shown below in Table 15.4, the increase was much faster

TABLE 15.4 PERCENTAGE OF EMPLOYEES AMONG WORKERS, OTHER THAN
THOSE ENGAGED IN CULTIVATION[a] ACCORDING TO THE CENSUSES OF 1961
AND 1971

	All India		Urban India		Rural India *	
	Males	Females	Males	Females	Males	Females
1961	46·29	25·10	59·59	43·09	35·17	18·93
1971[b]	56·25	52·52	63·96	48·59	47·17	58·97

[a] Cultivators and agricultural labourers are excluded. Workers engaged in household industry are included.
[b] The data pertain only to persons whose 'main activity' was work. They are based on the 1 per cent sample of the population enumerated by the 1971 census.
Sources: Census of India, 1961, vol. I, India, pt II-B(i), *General Economic Tables*, Tables B-IV-A and B; Census of India 1971, ser. I – India, pt II Special, *All India Census Tables (Estimated from One Per Cent Sample Data)* 1972.

among the female workers, particularly those in rural areas. Among farm workers also, the proportion of agricultural labourers has sharply increased and that of cultivators has declined. While such trends are not implausible, the magnitude of the increase in the proportion of employees is so large that it can be explained only in terms of the exclusion of non-employees from the 1971 census count

[1] Pravin Visaria, 'The Provisional 1971 Census Data on the Working Force', a paper presented at the seminar on the 'First Results of the 1971 Census of India' under the joint sponsorship of the Indian Association for the Study of Population and Institute of Economic Growth, Delhi, 22–3 November 1971.

of workers. Indeed, for employees, work has to be the main activity, receiving full-time attention; only the self-employed and the unpaid family workers can undertake economic activity as supplementary or secondary to their other roles.

The preceding discussion illustrates the need for extreme caution in accepting the available statistics on the labour force as the basis for making estimates of the volume of surplus workers or disguised underemployment. This issue is relevant also to the international comparisons of per worker productivity. As Simon Kuznets has shown, differentials in per worker productivity between the countries of the highest and the lowest 'economic level' (or income class) shrink substantially if unpaid family workers are excluded from consideration.[1] This result is a consequence of the high importance of unpaid family workers in the labour force in the predominantly rural or agricultural economics of underdeveloped countries and their limited significance in developed countries. However, these issues have been ignored in much of the discussions.

IV. SEASONAL FLUCTUATIONS IN THE SIZE AND COMPOSITION OF THE LABOUR FORCE

The distinction between unpaid family workers and other members of the labour force has important implications for employment policy. However, let me first discuss the seasonal variations in the size and composition of the labour force which form an important facet of the situation. The labour-force surveys that have been carried out in a number of developing countries during the past two decades have also drawn attention to the significant seasonal fluctuations in the size of the rural labour force. In India an attempt was made to obtain information on this subject during the 14th and 15th Rounds, when the selected households were visited six times during 1958–9 and three times during 1959–60. The reference period for the collection of data on economic activity was one week but the data for each sub-round, represent an average picture during two months of 1958–9 and four months of 1959–60. The data based on the 14th Round have been summarised in Table 15.5.

If we measure the degree of seasonality by relating the range to the average value for the Round as a whole, we observe during the 14th Round a variation of almost 20 per cent in the female labour-force participation rate and of 44 per cent in the proportion of unpaid household labour in the female population. In absolute terms, the

---

[1] Simon Kuznets, 'Quantitative Aspects of the Economic Growth of Nations: II Industrial Distribution of National Product and Labour Force', *Economic Development and Cultural Change*, vol. 5, no. 4, July 1957 (supplement).

variation in the percentage of unpaid household labour (5·23 points) is almost equal to the variation in the percentage of house workers (4·72 points); and the two are inversely related. The seasonal fluctuations in the various characteristics for males are much smaller although not altogether negligible.

TABLE 15.5 SEASONAL FLUCTUATIONS IN RURAL INDIA IN THE LABOUR-FORCE PARTICIPATION RATES, PERCENTAGE OF UNEMPLOYED, THE PERCENTAGE CLASSIFIED AS UNPAID HOUSEHOLD LABOUR, THE PERCENTAGE OF HOUSE-WORKERS, AND THE INCIDENCE OF UNEMPLOYMENT, BY SEX, ACCORDING TO THE 14TH ROUND OF THE N.S.S., 1958–1959

Sub-Round	Period	Percentage of population classified as				
		In the labour force	Unemployed	Unpaid household labour	House workers	Incidence of unemployment (%)
		MALES				
1	July–August	57·53	1·48	11·40	0·65	2·57
2	September–October	57·74	1·78	11·79	0·79	3·08
3	November–December	57·22	1·62	11·55	0·75	2·83
4	January–February	56·67	2·39	10·46	0·95	4·22
5	March–April	56·20	2·46	10·46	1·00	4·38
6	May–June	55·95	2·69	10·80	0·91	4·81
	Aggregate	56·88	2·07	11·24	0·84	3·64
	Range	1·79	1·21	1·39	0·35	2·24
	Range as % of aggregate	3·15	58·26	12·37	41·67	61·54
		FEMALES				
1	July–August	29·02	1·94	14·40	30·68	6·69
2	September–October	27·99	1·92	13·69	31·14	6·86
3	November–December	28·15	1·71	13·07	31·94	6·07
4	January–February	25·80	2·64	11·61	34·20	10·23
5	March–April	25·33	3·28	10·68	33·82	12·95
6	May–June	23·81	4·18	9·17	35·40	17·56
	Aggregate	26·66	2·66	12·08	32·89	9·83
	Range	5·21	2·26	5·23	4·72	11·49
	Range as % of aggregate	19·54	86·26	43·29	14·35	116·89
		PERSONS				
1	July–August	43·43	1·71	12·88	15·50	3·94
2	September–October	42·97	1·85	12·74	15·86	4·31
3	November–December	42·74	1·66	12·31	16·29	3·88
4	January–February	41·30	2·52	11·28	17·51	6·10
5	March–April	40·85	2·87	10·81	17·33	7·03
6	May–June	39·93	3·43	9·98	18·10	8·59
	Aggregate	41·86	2·34	11·66	16·77	5·59
	Range	3·50	1·77	2·90	2·60	4·71
	Range as % of aggregate	8·36	75·64	24·87	15·50	84·26

Source: The National Sample Survey, report no. 100.

Such seasonal fluctuations in the participation rates and the composition of the gainfully employed population by class of worker affect also the industrial and/or occupational composition of the rural workers. During the 14th Round, the proportion of population (*not* the working force or the labour force) occupied in agriculture showed a variation of 5 percentage points (or 11·4 per cent) among males and of 7·8 percentage points (or 39·3 per cent) among females.

In other words, during the slack agricultural season, the proportion of workers employed in the non-agricultural sector does indeed increase although it does not alter the basic fact that agriculture continues to be the primary source of employment in the rural economy. Such changes reflect responses to the magnitude of demand for different types of labour during different seasons. In all probability, the pattern of these fluctuations is almost uniform or regular during different years. The estimates of disguised unemployment or underemployment need to take account of these fluctuations. Even though the relative differences in such estimates may seem small, the point is noteworthy.

The literature on employment and unemployment makes frequent references to seasonal unemployment that is illustrated in Table 15.5 above as well as in the tables included in the Appendix, but it does not fully recognise the fluctuations in the size of the labour force itself. While the evidence suggests that the unpaid family workers who are unable to find work during the slack season of the year drop out from the labour force, we do not know whether any of them join the ranks of the unemployed. We also do not know whether persons who withdraw from the labour force during the slack season do so due to the compulsions of their non-economic roles or because of the paucity of demand for their labour. While there is little specific information available on this subject, other evidence suggests significant variations in the availability of different sections of the rural working force for additional work or for wage-paid employment. Before examining these data let us first review the composition of the working force according to status.

V. THE STATUS DISTRIBUTION OF THE
WORKING FORCE

The status or the class of workers shows the relationship of a worker to others in the enterprise, if any. The estimates of the distribution of the gainfully employed or the working population of India by class of worker or status are available from the various Rounds of the N.S.S. rather than from the census. These data based on the 15th Round in urban India and the 17th Round in rural India have been used to make an estimate for the country as a whole, for 1 March 1961 (i.e. the reference date of the 1961 census). These data are summarised in Table 15.6.

According to these data nearly 57 per cent of the male workers and 66 per cent of the female workers in the country in 1961 were either self-employed (i.e. own account workers) or unpaid family workers. The wage or salaried employment accounted for only 35 per cent

TABLE 15.6   THE PERCENTAGE DISTRIBUTION OF THE WORKING POPULATION
BY SEX AND BY CLASS OF WORKER

	Males			Females		
Class of worker	India[a] 1 March 1961	Rural India 17th Round (1961–62)	Urban India 15th Round (1959–60)	India[a] 1 March 1961	Rural India 17th Round (1961–62)	Urban India 15th Round (1959–60)
All workers	100·00	100·00	100·00	100·00	100·00	100·00
Employers	7·79	9·00	2·03	2·86	3·04	0·43
Own account workers	42·45	43·66	36·68	19·88	19·14	30·19
Employees	35·25	31·51	53·10	30·78	29·88	43·34
Unpaid family workers	14·51	15·83	8·19	46·46	47·94	26·04
Sample (persons)	—	72,976	9,367	—	26,383	1,791

[a] The figures for India for 1961 are estimated on the assumption that the status distribution of the gainfully employed reported by the N.S.S. for its 15th Round (1959–60) in urban India and the 17th Round (1961–62) in rural India was also valid for the workers enumerated by the 1961 census. The 1961 census tables do not report the status classification of cultivators.

Source: India, National Sample Survey, report no. 157, *Tables with Notes on Urban Employment and Unemployment*, 15th Round, pp. 25–7 and report no. 190, *Tables with Notes on Employment and Unemployment in Rural Areas*, 17th Round, pp. 14–5.

of the total. As might be expected, the proportion of employees was significantly higher among urban male workers than among their rural counterparts (32 per cent). A similar though smaller difference existed among female workers as well. The N.S.S. data from successive Rounds show some increase in the proportion of employees in the urban labour force but no such tendency is evident in the rural labour force.[1] As we shall see below, the high proportion of the self-employed and the unpaid family workers in the economy has important implications for estimates of unemployment obtained from various sources such as the N.S.S.[2]

VI. STATUS OF WORKERS AND THE ESTIMATES OF UNEMPLOYMENT

The Indian data on unemployment do not show the earlier occupation, activity or the status of unemployed persons who had worked before, i.e. the experienced unemployed. However, during the N.S.S. Rounds undertaken in 1956–60, persons classified as unemployed were asked whether they had 'a job or an enterprise at a future date'. Between 50 and 60 per cent of the rural males and between 46 and 54 per cent of the rural females classified as unemployed reported that they had some such job. No question was asked about

[1] See Pravin Visaria, 'Employment and Unemployment in India', op. cit., p. 82. As noted earlier, the census data on the subject are not quite reliable.

[2] Ibid., pp. 78–81. It might be noted that the estimated proportions of unpaid family workers among the gainfully employed in India, shown in Table 8, are not the highest on record, but they are substantially higher than those reported for the developed western countries.

the nature of the job or enterprise expected to be taken up so that we do not know how many of these persons were seasonally unemployed agricultural workers. While answers to a question about the intrinsically uncertain future must be viewed with some reservations, prima facie, the data were not implausible. It is likely that many of these persons might belong to the ranks of the self-employed or unpaid family workers.

Some supplementary information on this subject consists of answers to a question on availability for work. Questions on availability for work were introduced in the N.S.S. in recognition of the fact that in the absence of an organised labour market many persons might not actively seek employment even when they were without work, but that a specific question as to whether they were available for work would elicit an expression of their needs. Sometimes it is argued that the question on availability for work relates to a hypothetical situation which can hardly be comprehended by the respondents. Further, it may not be very meaningful without reference to the wage rate. However, N.S.S. definitions had indeed specified that the question about availability for work would relate to work at 'current rates of remuneration in prevailing conditions of work'. One may doubt whether such details of the definitions would be effectively conveyed to the respondents but it is unlikely that these issues would be overlooked by the respondents.

Since the 11th Round of the N.S.S., which began in 1956, persons not seeking but available for work, whom one might term the inactive unemployed, were included among the unemployed persons. Over the ten-year period 1956/7–1966/7, such inactive unemployed formed between 28 and 55 per cent of the unemployed males and between 42 and 62 per cent of the unemployed females in rural India. In urban areas, their proportion was smaller (between 8 to 14 per cent among the unemployed males and between 17 to 34 per cent of the unemployed females). While this change in the definition led to a certain raising of the estimates of incidence of unemployment, the figures have continued to remain low.

In Tables 15.1 and 15.2 above, we have shown the estimates of unemployment based on the 1961 and 1971 censuses. For various reasons, these estimates are not really comparable with those available from the N.S.S. The N.S.S. data have been based on a reference period of a week since the 14th Round conducted in 1958–9. According to the estimates provided by these Rounds, the highest figure of unemployment in rural India was reported during 1958–9, when the sample households were visited six times during the year. As shown earlier in Table 15.5, 5·6 per cent of the man-weeks were reported to be unemployed. For urban India, 5·3 per cent of the man-weeks of unemployment was the highest estimate, based on the 15th Round conducted during July 1959–June 1960. (During the 11th and 12th Rounds conducted during August 1956–August 1957, with a reference period of one day, 6 per cent of the man-days of rural labour force and 7·4 per cent of the man-days of urban labour force were unemployed.)

It can be argued that the impression of a low incidence of unemployment results from the particular choice of the denominator. Those classified as unemployed can be presumed to be seeking opportunities for wage-paid employment or work as hired labourers. Therefore, the proper denominator would be the 'unemployed plus wage and salaried employees' (or 'days of unemployment plus days of hired or wage and salaried work'). Such a procedure would be a better indicator of the extent to which opportunities for wage and salaried employment need to be augmented. This interesting approach was adopted in the analysis of the data collected under the Poona schedules of the N.S.S. during 1950–1 relating to labour time disposition during the three days preceding the date of interview. The results indicated that about 17 per cent of the available labour time (of adult males and females) for 'hired farm and non-farm labour' was utilised or unemployed.[1] A similar exercise for the recent Rounds of N.S.S. indicates that during 1960–1 and 1961–2, when the reference period was one week, the opportunities for wage employment for rural males needed to be augmented by about 4·8 to 6·4 per cent.

Sometimes the definitions used for the classification of persons according to their employment status are blamed for the low estimates of unemployment. It is argued that the procedure which assigns priority to the classification of a person as employed even if he works for only one day or for a nominal period during the reference week, leads to an understatement of the level of unemployment. In recognition of this point, the Committee of Experts on Unemployment Estimates appointed by the Planning Commission recommended in 1970 that even when the reference period is a week, the employment status should be recorded separately for each day of the week so that a man-day would become the unit of analysis.[2] However, these refinements make little difference to the estimates of

[1] V. M. Dandekar, *Second Report on the Poona Schedules of the National Sample Survey* (1950–1), Gokhale Institute of Politics and Economics, Poona, 1954.

[2] In the 25th and the 27th Round of the N.S.S., covering the period July 1970–June 1971 and September 1972–August 1973, respectively, a further refinement has been introduced to take account of the intensity of work in terms of the hours worked. Work for four hours or less is to be counted as half intensity whereas work for more than four hours would be considered as work with full intensity.

the level of unemployment among the wage earners. This has been confirmed by the Rural Labour Enquiry conducted during 1963–4 as well as the 25th Round of the N.S.S., which attempted to make a special study of the employment and living conditions of the weaker sections of rural India, i.e. small cultivators and the non-cultivating wage earners. More importantly, these same criteria and definitions, when applied in other countries of Asia, yield estimates of unemployment which are substantially higher. Reasons for these differences are difficult to explain. One surmises that they are related to the living conditions or the level of income, which affect the reservation prices of the potential job seekers. In India, the level of living is probably so low that sheer survival requires the acceptance of work irrespective of the level of remuneration or productivity.

It appears that the status distribution of the workers is an important relevant factor. The self-employed and the unpaid family workers do not always seek work outside their family farms or household enterprises. For women, it is obviously not possible to take up work far beyond their villages unless the entire family moves with them. There are also indications that either because of considerations of prestige or for other reasons, certain groups of people are unwilling to move out of their familiar vocations or villages in search of jobs.

The present author had collected some data on the willingness of cultivators to work outside their family farms in a survey of seven villages of the Ratnagiri district of Maharashtra and 14 villages of the Kutch district of Gujarat during 1966.[1] Over 54 and 65 per cent of the male and female farmers, respectively, in Ratnagiri district and almost 80 and 84 per cent of the male and female farmers, respectively, in Kutch district expressed an unwillingness to work outside their own farms. An analysis of data according to the caste of the respondents showed marked intercaste differentials, consistent with our expectations, although because of the small numbers in individual castes, one has to be cautious in their interpretation. Such preferences may break down in the face of economic compulsions; but their relevance to the programme of employment creation and amelioration of poverty is quite obvious.

Similarly, some recent surveys conducted during 1971–2 in a few villages of Rajasthan and Andhra Pradesh have suggested some significant differences in the reported availability for wage-paid employment among persons owning land and among those who were principally or mainly self-employed as distinguished from casual

[1] Pravin Visaria, 'The Farmers' Preference for Work on Family Farms', Appendix vi to the *Report of the Committee of Experts on Unemployment Estimates*, op. cit., pp. 185–94.

workers.[1] It is also reported that persons who take advantage of the special employment projects under the rural works programme belong mainly to the landless households with a low per capita monthly income. The *relatively* better-off do not avail themselves of such opportunities even when they have spare time on their hands.

Some supplementary evidence on the factors underlying the reported level of unemployment is available from the N.S.S. data on the availability of even the employed persons for additional work. We shall now examine these data at some length.

VII. VISIBLE UNDEREMPLOYMENT ACCORDING TO STATUS OF WORKERS

The N.S.S. had put the questions about availability for additional work also to persons who were classified as employed. Responses to these questions cross-tabulated according to the hours of work performed by the persons classified as working or employed have provided useful information on visible underemployment or involuntary part-time work. Data for the 16th and the 17th Rounds of the N.S.S. conducted during 1960–1 and 1961–2 have been tabulated according to the status of the employed persons. These data are summarised below in Table 15.7. The data suggest that contrary to the general impression, there is not much difference between the number of hours worked by the self-employed, the unpaid family workers and the employees among males. Among the gainfully employed females, the employees reported somewhat longer hours of work than the unpaid family workers and the self-employed but once again the differences do not indicate substantially reduced hours of work for the non-employee class of workers. Secondly, about 12 per cent of the male workers and between 27 and 30 per cent of the female workers in rural India reported having worked for 28 hours or less during the reference week. Among male workers, the proportion of such part-time workers did not vary according to status. Among female workers, however, the proportion of such part-time workers was the lowest among employees and the highest among the self-employed. Finally, the percentage of workers reporting availability for additional work was much lower among the unpaid family workers and the self-employed than among

[1] Kanta Ahuja, 'Rural Employment Survey 1971–72, Jhalawar District and an Evaluation of the Crash Scheme for Rural Employment', Department of Economics, University of Rajasthan, Jaipur, September 1972; G. Parthasarathy and G. D. Rama Rao, 'Employment and Unemployment of Rural Labour and the Crash Programme: A Study of West Godavari District', Department of Co-operation and Applied Economics, Andhra University, Waltair, 1972.

TABLE 15.7 SELECTED CHARACTERISTICS OF GAINFULLY EMPLOYED PERSONS IN RURAL INDIA, BY SEX AND STATUS, ACCORDING TO THE 16TH AND 17TH ROUNDS OF THE NATIONAL SAMPLE SURVEY

	Males		Females	
Status	*16th Round 1960–1*	*17th Round 1961–2*	*16th Round 1960–1*	*17th Round 1961–2*
(a) *Percentage distribution of the gainfully employed by status*				
Employers	11·22	9·00	3·95	3·06
Self-employed[a]	41·91	43·66	22·99	19·14
Unpaid family workers	16·26	15·84	43·67	47·90
Employees	30·61	31·50	29·39	29·90
All workers	100·00	100·00	100·00	100·00
(b) *Average number of hours of work during the reference week*				
Self-employed[a]	46·5	47·0	36·1	36·9
Unpaid family workers	46·8	46·8	36·7	38·6
Employees	46·7	46·7	39·5	40·1
All workers	46·6	46·9	37·4	38·6
(c) *Percentage of workers reporting work for 28 hours or less*				
Self-employed[a]	13·0	12·4	33·6	34·1
Unpaid family workers	12·1	11·9	31·3	25·9
Employees	11·2	11·9	23·7	23·3
All workers	12·3	12·2	29·7	26·9
(d) *Percentage reporting availability for additional work*				
Self-employed[a]	7·92	8·94	6·79	8·27
Unpaid family workers	5·28	6·11	6·07	5·04
Employees	16·43	16·05	25·54	24·44
All workers	10·11	10·74	11·99	11·55
(e) *Percentage of those not available for additional work among workers working for 28 hours or less*				
Self-employed[a]	74·2	71·4	87·5	84·8
Unpaid family workers	81·5	82·2	88·2	88·5
Employees	49·4	50·9	44·7	49·5
All workers	68·5	66·8	77·8	77·4
(f) *Sample (persons)*				
Self-employed[a]	17,149	39,116	3,536	5,979
Unpaid family workers	5,526	11,481	6,567	12,307
Employees	8,936	22,379	3,914	8,097
All workers	31,611	72,976	14,017	26,383

[a] Owner-operators and working partners hiring labour as well as those not hiring labour, i.e. employers, together with the self-employed, have been grouped together.
Note: For calculating the average number of hours of work, persons classified as working for more than 57 hours have been arbitrarily assumed to be working for 60 hours.
Source: The National Sample Survey, report no. 114 (pp. 184, 186); no. 190 (pp. 122–7).

employees. This is so in the case of both male and female workers. It appears, therefore, that the somewhat lower average hours of work for the unpaid family workers and the self-employed among females do not necessarily lead to their availability for additional work.

The preceding conclusion is supported by the data on the percentage of workers who reported work for 28 hours or less during the reference week but who reported themselves to be not available for additional work. Such persons can be considered 'voluntarily part-time workers', and their percentage was the highest among unpaid family workers (more than 80 per cent) and the lowest among employees (between 45 and 50 per cent). In other words, as noted earlier, the customary assumption that every member of the labour force would want a full-time job appears to be unrealistic. Admittedly, the validity of data on hours of work is limited by the possibility of work-spreading. Yet, those available for work (or additional work, if they are already working for some time) are the persons whose effort can probably be tapped immediately for productive activity, without any coercion.

VIII. UNEMPLOYMENT AMONG THE WEAKER SECTIONS IN RURAL INDIA

Some useful data on the level of unemployment and the availability for work of the weaker sections were also collected during the 25th Round of the N.S.S. conducted during 1970–1. The preliminary data pertaining to nearly 30,000 households from fourteen states of the country have been manually tabulated to provide information on the employment situation and work preferences of the non-cultivating wage earners as well as small cultivators (i.e. the lowest 10 per cent of the households having some cultivated land during the year preceding the 25th Round, July 1969–June 1970).[1] In this Round, the situation pertaining to employment and unemployment on each day of the reference week (with an attempt made to record the intensity of work)[2] was taken into account.

Except in Punjab, Haryana, Rajasthan and Assam, wage employment in farm and non-farm work was the major source of employment for the small cultivators. One would, therefore, be inclined to consider the small cultivators of most states as more or less on par with the non-cultivating wage earners. Yet, the data on the incidence of unemployment indicated that except in Kerala, Tamil Nadu and Bihar, the male members of the households of small cultivators were unemployed for less than 5 per cent of the man-days. The incidence of unemployment was relatively higher in the households of non-cultivating wage earners but less than 10 per cent in all states except

[1] For an analysis of the salient features of these data, see: Pravin Visaria and Leela Visaria, 'Employment Planning for the Weaker Sections in Rural India', *Economic and Political Weekly*, vol. VIII, nos. 4–6, Annual Number, pp. 269–76.

[2] See note 2 on page 425, above.

in Kerala, Tamil Nadu, Punjab and Bihar.[1] Evidently, the refined measurement of unemployment, taking into account the under-utilisation of available labour time within the reference week, did not make any substantial difference to the estimates of unemployment. Yet, to some extent, land ownership helps to mitigate the incidence of unemployment. One might be surprised that the estimates of unemployment for even the weaker sections of the population were so low. In all probability, the explanation lies in the fact that the poor cannot afford to remain without work; and in order to survive, they have to take up any work, however low the remuneration or productivity.

Further, it is significant that when asked about the willingness of at least one member of the household to take up regular full-time wage employment likely 'particularly in public works', between 37 and 60 per cent of the households of small cultivators and non-cultivators reported no one willing to take up such a regular job. A majority of them indicated that they had 'adequate' employment. While the data have not been cross-tabulated according to the per capita expenditure of the households, i.e. their living conditions, it appears that even the poor hesitate to move into unfamiliar surroundings. However, it is pertinent to note that a guaranteed job appears likely to induce a significant number of households (ranging between 11 and 27 per cent among small cultivators and between 14 and 47 per cent of non-cultivating wage earners) to send at least one member outside the village.

If we consider men willing to move out as a proportion of the adult male population, between 15 and 60 per cent were willing to take up employment outside the village. In many states, the percentage exceeded 30 and it was about 55 among non-cultivating wage earners in Kerala and Orissa. It cannot be denied that the provision of regular full-time employment to even those members of the weaker sections who are willing to take it up would meet with severe budgetary and organisational constraints. In fact, if the major premise of the hypothetical question is to be fulfilled, it would be necessary to develop something approximating a stable working force undertaking rural public works with a paid weekly holiday, as reportedly happens under the land-army scheme initiated in Mysore State in 1971.

VIII. PROSPECTS AHEAD AND THE POLICY IMPLICATIONS

It would be a serious error to infer from the data discussed above

[1] The figure for Punjab is not plausible. The data are probably affected by some errors.

that unemployment is not a serious problem in India. Like all problems, it is complex and has diverse facets. The reluctance or the unwillingness of the weaker sections to work on rural public works is related, for example, to the working conditions, the wage rates that are paid and the need for additional food consumption if they have to take up hard work like digging, etc. It is estimated that earth work requires an additional consumption of about 1,000 calories a day more than agricultural work and therefore it is regarded as hard work, which might affect the health or fitness of the workers. The experience of the workers about the promptness with which the wages due to them are paid also acts as a discouraging factor.

It is also likely that in view of the large expected additions to the size of the labour force in the years ahead, the status distribution of the working force would change progressively. The uncertainty about the size of the labour force discussed above affects also the industrial composition because those omitted from the count of workers are unlikely to be spread uniformly over the entire range of economic activities. Yet, according to the 1961 and 1971 censuses as well as the latest (21st) Round of the N.S.S. (1966–7), nearly 70 per cent of the male workers and over 80 per cent of the female workers are engaged in the primary sector. Agriculture continues to be the residual employment sector and those who cannot find work elsewhere have little option but to take to cultivation of owned or leased-in land, irrespective of the size of the holding, or to work as hired labourers on others' land.

According to the labour-force participation rates based on the 1961 census, which seem more appropriate to use, the total labour force (aged 10 and over) is expected to increase by nearly 52 million persons (35·3 million males and 16·5 million females) during 1971–81.[1] It seems unlikely that the industrial composition of the working force can be altered significantly during the current or the next decade to lessen the pressure of population on land. With limited prospects of bringing additional land under cultivation, an increase in the number of landless agricultural labourers and small cultivators appears almost inevitable. If so, the 'employee' class will increase even in rural areas and its unemployment and under-

---

[1] If the sex-age-specific proportions of unpaid family workers, estimated for 1961, continue to hold, nearly 10 million (3 million males and 6·8 million females) would be in the class of unpaid family helpers. For an attempt to distinguish between the unpaid family helpers and other members of the labour force, see Pravin Visaria, 'Estimates of Participation Rates and Labour Force, Including and Excluding Unpaid Family Workers, for India, 1961–81', Appendix v to the *Report of the Committee of Experts on Unemployment Estimates*, Planning Commission, New Delhi, 1970. The estimates presented above are based on the revised population projections, that take note of the difference between the earlier projection and the 1971 census count.

employment will be more open than that of the self-employed and the unpaid family workers. The extension of irrigation and the tapping of underground water resources, together with the evolution and spread of high-yielding varieties of seeds with a short maturity period, would help to raise the frequency of cropping and to mitigate the seasonal fluctuations in the demand for agricultural labour. Yet, seasonality of unemployment shown in Table 15.5 above is unlikely to disappear. The creation of supplementary employment programmes that would match the seasonality in the idle labour resources available for productive employment should therefore receive a high priority in the planning process. Due care must be taken also to ensure that these programmes result in technically sound and durable assets that raise the productivity of the rural economy. Given the availability of personnel trained in engineering, this should not be a difficult task; but our past record is not very satisfactory.

On the whole, raising the productivity of agriculture and household industries is one of the surest means of ameliorating the poverty of the millions of self-employed and unpaid family workers in rural India whose availability for additional work seems to be limited. Among the programmes that could play an effective role are the well-known subsidiary activities like dairying and poultry keeping. Most rural households are familiar with dairying; the skills required are not difficult to acquire or develop even for those who have never looked after milch cattle. Backed by a collective effort and cattle insurance, these activities can have an immediate impact on the underemployment of women, among whom the incidence of unemployment as well as involuntary part-time work appears to be greater, and also on their household incomes. The resulting improvement in the quality of employment would naturally lower their disguised unemployment and underemployment.

We have so far avoided any extended discussion of the nature and characteristics of unemployment in urban areas, which is to a considerable extent open. As noted earlier, a majority of the urban workers tend to be wage or salary earners. Partly as a consequence, between two-thirds and three-quarters of the unemployed in urban areas tend to be in the age group 15–24 (or 16–26) which are the ages of entry into labour force. The insistence of many employees on prior work experience particularly affects these new entrants into the labour force, whose number substantially exceeds (by 30 to 35 per cent) the net additions. While they look for a stable or 'permanent' job, with associated benefits in the form of earned leave and the employer's contribution to a provident fund or bonus, they also take up activities involving underutilisation of their skills or educational training. They suffer from disguised unemployment in its classical sense – the sense in which the term was used by Joan Robinson.

The urban and rural unemployment are, of course, interconnected through the channel of rural-urban migration and cannot be viewed in isolation. However, various characteristics of the structure of the rural labour force are to some extent valid also for the unorganised sector of the urban economy. Without adequate attention to these factors, both the macro and the micro policies aimed at the short or the long run are unlikely to attain their intended goals.

APPENDIX

In this Appendix we shall review some of the information on seasonal fluctuations in the size of the labour force, the incidence of unemployment and the structure or composition of the labour force that is available from the surveys conducted in Malaya, South Korea and the Philippines. The broad characteristics are similar to those reported for India in the body of the paper. The data presented below are essentially illustrative. They have been selected on the ground of their availability to the author and cannot be claimed to be either representative or exhaustive.

Malaya

Some interesting data on seasonal fluctuations in labour force and employment are available for Malaya from a survey conducted during 1962. Some data from this survey conducted during April and September have been summarised in Table 15.A. According to these data, even when attention was confined to persons in the age group

TABLE 15.A   SEASONAL FLUCTUATIONS IN LABOUR FORCE AND UNEMPLOY-MENT IN MALAYA, 1962

	Males			Females		
Characteristic	*Apr 1962*	*Sep 1962*	*Average*	*Apr 1962*	*Sep 1962*	*Average*
Labour-force participation rate	84·72	87·47	86·10	38·10	44·02	41·08
(a) Percentage of employed in population	79·86	83·40	81·64	34·75	40·85	37·82
(i) For 25 hours or more	75·37	80·46	77·93	30·54	37·09	33·84
(ii) For less than 25 hours	4·49	2·93	3·70	4·21	3·75	3·98
(Not available for additional work)	(2·02)	(1·72)	(1·87)	(2·65)	(2·81)	(2·73)
(b) Percentage of unemployed in population	4·84	4·05	4·45	3·33	3·15	3·24
(i) New entrants	2·04	2·07	2·05	1·72	2·29	2·01
(ii) Others	2·80	1·98	2·39	1·60	0·85	1·23
(c) Unemployed as percentage of the labour force	5·71	4·63	5·17	8·74	7·16	7·89

Source: Federation of Malaya, Department of Statistics, *Report on Employment, Unemployment and Under-employment, 1962*, Kualalumpur, June 1963.

15–70, the female participation rate was significantly higher in September than in April. The fluctuation in the male participation rate was, of course, smaller. Compared to April 1962, the incidence of unemployment (measured as percentage of the labour force or as percentage of the total population in the relevant age group) declined during September. The proportion of employed persons who reported work for 25 hours or more during the reference week was also higher in September than in April. Persons who entered the labour force during September were drawn largely from the ranks of the paddy farmers and the miscellaneous group of 'others'. Presumably, they participated in economic activity in response to the seasonal peak in the demand for labour in Malayan agriculture.

South Korea

The South Korean Economic Planning Board has also conducted seasonal sample surveys of employment by means of questionnaires and interviews. The surveys conducted during the period 1963–7 have provided interesting information on the seasonal fluctuations in the level and nature of employment in the farm and non-farm households. Data available to the author on some of the character-istics are limited to 1965. According to these data, summarised in Table 15.B the labour-force participation rate of males in farm house-holds fluctuated widely between 87·2 per cent in June and 62·4 per cent during December; the incidence of unemployment varied between 2·2 per cent in September and 5·7 per cent in December. Among females, the range of fluctuations was even higher with a labour-force participation of 50 per cent during June, when the incidence of unemployment was negligible (0·5 per cent) and 21·1 per cent during December, when the incidence of unemployment among them was 4·7 per cent.

Interestingly, there was little difference in the average labour-force participation rate of males in the farm and non-farm households during the year. The females from the non-farm households had a much lower average participation rate than their sisters in farm households. The incidence of unemployment was, however, much higher among non-farm households than among farm households. The seasonal fluctuations in participation rates were much smaller in the non-farm households than among farm households, for both males and females, but those in the level of unemployment were significant even in non-farm households.

Kwan Kim's analysis of the data covers the entire five-year period.[1] He does not distinguish between male and female workers;

[1] Kwan S. Kim, 'Labour Force Structure in a Dual Economy: A Case Study of South Korea', *International Labour Review*, vol. 101 (Jan 1970), 35–48.

but the average number of hours worked per week varied between
47·0 during June and 36·0 during December in 1963, when the
annual average was 42·9. The corresponding figures for 1967 were
47·6, 36·0 and 41·4 respectively. It is reported that according to the
average figures for 1963–7, the number of persons employed in the
farm households during the slack season in December was about
54 per cent of that during June. In terms of hours worked, the

TABLE 15.B SEASONAL FLUCTUATIONS IN THE LABOUR-FORCE PARTICIPA-
TION RATES AND THE INCIDENCE OF UNEMPLOYMENT FOR THE POPULATION
AGED 14 YEARS AND OVER AMONG FARM AND NON-FARM HOUSEHOLDS OF
SOUTH KOREA, 1965

	Labour-force participation rate			Incidence of unemployment (unemployed as percentage of labour force)		
	P	*M*	*F*	*P*	*M*	*F*
	Farm households					
1965 average	58·1	76·8	41·0	3·1	3·8	1·9
March	55·6	74·9	37·8	3·6	4·2	2·6
June	73·1	87·2	60·0	2·3	3·7	0·5
September	63·1	82·7	45·0	1·9	2·2	1·4
December	40·9	62·4	21·1	5·5	5·7	4·7
	Non-farm households					
1965 average	51·9	76·3	31·0	13·5	14·5	11·5
March	50·6	74·8	29·6	17·4	18·9	14·3
June	54·0	77·5	33·7	11·5	12·7	9·4
September	52·6	77·0	31·5	13·2	13·8	12·0
December	50·5	75·8	29·1	12·1	12·7	11·3

Note: The author is indebted to Mr D. B. Kim, a Fellow at the Demographic Training and Research
Centre, Bombay, during 1966–7, who supplied the above information.
Source: Republic of Korea, *Economically Active Population Survey*, vols 2, 3 and 4.

fluctuations were even wider, with the slack season input of work not
more than 40 per cent of that during June. Since employment
opportunities in paddy cultivation are limited during the off-
season, South Korea naturally faces a severe problem of seasonal
unemployment. Surprisingly, the seasonal migration of farmers to
urban areas is reported to be 'practically non-existent'. Obviously,
therefore, the unemployment rate would fluctuate seasonally and the
policies to encourage better utilisation of the available labour force
in farm households would require special programmes.

In the non-farm households (engaged in secondary and tertiary
industries) of South Korea also, the level of employment in terms of
persons employed as well as hours worked showed some seasonal

fluctuations but the range of fluctuations was much smaller (7 per cent in the number of employed persons and less than 11 per cent in hours worked). What is true of Korean agriculture is probably true also of other large numbers of underdeveloped countries with a predominance of seasonal agriculture.

Philippines

Somewhat similar information on seasonal fluctuations in the labour-force participation rates and the composition of workers in terms of status is available from the statistical survey of households conducted in the Philippines since May 1956. The data available to the author cover the period May 1956–April 1962 and have been summarised in Table 15.C. During the first year, the survey was conducted in three Rounds during May and October 1956 and March 1957. Thereafter, the frequency of the survey was restricted to two Rounds conducted each year during May or April and October or November.

The experience gained during the first Round is reported to have helped to exclude from the employed category a considerable number of women doing only odd jobs around the house, who were perhaps considered as working or employed part-time in May 1956. Similarly women who were primarily engaged in housekeeping and did not evince 'a sincere desire to work' or who were 'not serious about working' were eliminated from the category of unemployed. As a result, the high participation rate and a very high incidence of unemployment among women reported during May 1956 did not recur in any of the subsequent rounds.

In the rice-producing regions of the Philippines, the planting beginning in May is associated with a noteworthy increase in the participation rate. Interestingly, the incidence of unemployment is also reported to be somewhat higher during this month than during October. It suggests the possibility that some persons seek work or report availability for work (even though they do not seek it) when they expect better prospects of finding such work. More interestingly, the proportion of unpaid family workers among the employed also shows a marked increase during the peak season from about 24 per cent to 26 per cent during October–November to 30–34 per cent during April or May. Unfortunately, these data are not available separately for males and females but they suggest a resemblance between the Indian and the Philippine situations.

Other data (not shown in the Table) indicate that the proportion of unpaid family workers reporting work for 40 hours or more (i.e. on a full-time basis) during the survey week varied between 43 and 49 per cent during different rounds. The corresponding figures for

TABLE 15.C SEASONAL FLUCTUATIONS IN THE LABOUR-FORCE PARTICIPATION RATE, INCIDENCE OF UNEMPLOYMENT, THE PERCENTAGE OF EMPLOYED WANTING ADDITIONAL WORK AND THE DISTRIBUTION OF THE EMPLOYED BY CLASS OF WORKERS, PHILIPPINES, 1956–1962

Month/Year	Labour-force participation rate			Incidence of unemployment			Employed wanting additional work			Percentage of employed[a] classified as:		
	P	M	F	P	M	F	P	M	F	Employees	Self-employed	Unpaid family workers[b]
May 1956	65·1	80·3	50·3	12·5	7·7	19·8	n.a.	n.a.	n.a.	n.a.	n.a.	n.a.
October 1956	56·8	73·4	41·0	10·0	8·5	12·6	21·4	25·0	15·0	31·3	43·9	24·4
March 1957	56·1	74·2	38·8	7·0	5·7	9·5	19·9	22·2	15·6	25·2	43·4	30·9
May 1957	58·2	79·7	37·4	8·7	6·7	12·7	17·6	19·2	14·0	32·1	41·7	26·0
October 1957	56·9	74·9	39·7	7·1	5·8	9·5	n.a.	n.a.	n.a.	26·4	42·4	30·9
May 1958	61·2	80·4	42·9	9·1	6·7	13·3	21·1	22·3	18·9	31·3	41·7	26·7
November 1958	56·0	73·8	38·7	7·2	5·5	10·4	21·4	23·0	18·3	26·2	43·1	30·5
May 1959	58·9	78·5	39·9	7·7	6·4	10·3	20·0	21·3	17·5	31·7	43·0	24·9
October 1959	55·4	72·9	38·3	5·9	4·4	8·8	17·7	19·3	14·3	32·8	42·2	24·6
October 1960	53·8	71·9	36·0	6·3	5·1	8·8	21·9	23·2	19·1	28·3	40·7	30·1
May 1961	59·6	78·8	40·3	6·6	6·3	13·1	22·7	23·2	21·5	33·4	42·1	24·2
October 1961	55·6	72·1	39·5	6·4	4·8	9·1	24·5	25·8	22·0	29·4	40·4	30·1
April 1962	60·3	78·6	42·5	9·5	7·1	13·8	23·5	25·0	20·6			

[a] Figures may not add up to 100·0 per cent because for some persons the class of worker was not reported.
[b] Including employers.

Source: The Philippine Statistical Survey of Households, bulletin, ser. 1 (May 1956), 3 (Oct 1956 to Oct 1957), 5 (May and Nov 1958), 7 (May and Oct 1959), 9 (May 1961), 10 (Oct 1961), 11 (Apr 1962), Manila, various years.

the self-employed ranged between 54 and 72 per cent and those for the wage and salary earners between 73 and 80 per cent. Looked at in a different way, the average number of hours worked during the survey week was lower for unpaid family workers (around 35–6) than for wage or salary earners (around 45–6) and the self-employed (around 42–4).[1] Rather surprisingly, however, the Philippine data do not show any noteworthy seasonal fluctuations in the input of work by the employed persons, perhaps because the two survey rounds each year do not adequately reflect the actual seasonal fluctuations.

U.S.S.R.

Seasonal fluctuations in labour-force participation have been reported also for the collective farm members in the U.S.S.R.[2] Both in 1956 and 1959, the number of members working in July was 27 to 28 per cent higher than the average figure for the year. In December on the other hand, only about 70 to 80 per cent of the members participated in work. It is reported that these fluctuations were due to the entry of the family members in the working force during the peak season. The Soviet Union is reported to have planned programmes for the processing of agricultural raw material and the production of building material to reduce the seasonal underutilisation of labour.

[1] The average number of hours worked by all employed persons at work varied between 40·6 and 42·4 during May 1959–October 1961, i.e. the five rounds for which the information is available.

[2] International Labour Office, Employment and Economic Growth, Geneva, 1965, p. 78n.

Discussion of the Papers by
Dr Nassef and Professor Visaria

Professor Khachaturov said that Dr Nassef's paper discussed a very important problem, namely, how to maintain employment during rapid population growth up to the year 2000. It might be said that it was rather trite to discuss the so-called demographic explosion and that its consequences would not be so frightful as many sociologists and economists had forecast. The future would show who was right. However, he saw solid grounds for saying that, among the problems mankind faced, rapid population growth was one of the more serious.

Dr Nassef had used the projects of the United Nations, the International Labour Office, the Food and Agriculture Organization and the Population Division of the United Nations. Professor Khachaturov felt the data could not be accepted without criticism. There were inaccuracies, particularly for the Soviet Union. But assuming that the data were generally correct, people who would enter the working population (the 15–64 age group) before 1987 were already born. This facilitated further calculations. According to the paper, the population of the less-developed countries (L.D.C.s) would roughly double (a growth of 2·3 per cent per annum) during the next thirty years, to reach 77 per cent of the total world population, instead of the present 70 per cent. The population of working age in the L.D.C.s was expected to increase by 116 per cent to 1·6 billion people.

The author referred to the future size of the economically active population. This depended on the total population and the crude activity rate, which was the weighted average of age-specific activity rates. Differences in these rates between less-developed and more-developed countries were explained by differences in the age structure of the population and the age pattern of activity rates. However, the factors which determined the level of the activity rate for every age group were not considered. Professor Khachaturov therefore thought the question was open to further research. There was also the difference in age structure between less-developed and more-developed countries. This was a result of the considerably higher percentage of children in the population of an L.D.C. and the smaller percentage of adults and old people. Another peculiarity of the age structure of L.D.C.s was the heavy burden of dependency; the ratio of people below the age of 15 and over 64 to those of working age was 81 per cent in the L.D.C.s and 57 per cent in the more-developed countries. The burden of dependency had a negative effect, because it could absorb potential increases in productivity in these regions and emphasised their inability to create new job opportunities.

At the end of this section of the paper, Dr Nassef showed that the main factor leading to the growth of labour force was population growth. It overshadowed other factors reflected by the changes in the crude activity rate.

In the second part of the paper, Dr Nassef considered the possibility of maintaining employment in the face of rapid population growth, after taking into account the future decline in the proportion of the labour force which would be employed in agriculture. Referring to the work of Professor

Dovring and others, Professor Khachaturov said that to achieve a given decline in the share of agriculture in the labour force would depend on the growth rate of the population, the initial proportion of the labour force in agriculture, and the rate of increase in productivity in the non-agricultural sector. This meant that the higher the proportion of the labour force in agriculture, the greater the rate of increase required in the non-agricultural sector to achieve a given decline in the agricultural share.

According to projections by the U.N. organisations mentioned, the share of agriculture in the total labour force in L.D.C.s should decline from 66 to 43 per cent, and in more-developed countries from 21 to 3·5 per cent. By the year 2000 the absolute size of the non-agricultural labour force of the L.D.C.s should be three times greater, or 750 million more than in 1970. The agricultural labour force should increase by roughly 170 million, and total rural population by nearly one billion more. Dr Nassef did not suppose that such a redistribution of the labour force could be brought about easily, without special measures. He stated that in many L.D.C.s the cultivated areas were densely populated, and prospects for their extension very limited. On the other hand, the agriculture of the L.D.C.s would have to increase rapidly to meet the food needs of their doubled population. This could be done mainly through increased productivity, through mechanisation and through the use of fertilisers and the selection of seeds. But some increase in the agricultural population was also possible, and was indeed provided for in the projects – about 170 million additional rural population. Certainly this was small in comparison with the future growth of population, and such a redistribution of population was inevitable and not impossible. Professor Khachaturov could remember tremendous changes in the U.S.S.R. in the last fifty years where, during the process of industrialisation, the rural population fell from 84 per cent in 1922 to 41 per cent in 1973, and continued to drop each year.

The redistribution of the population required mastery of the situation. Without very careful management, it could lead to a rise in unemployment and underemployment in both agriculture and industry, and, as a result, to a reduction in living standards and, eventually, to social disturbances. He therefore agreed with Dr Nassef that L.D.C.s would face a serious challenge which necessitated comprehensive development plans to secure the normal solution of a very acute problem.

In conclusion, Professor Khachaturov made several short comments. (1) One could doubt the U.N. projections of the rate of growth of L.D.C. population. As a result of underemployment and unemployment, the rate was likely to decrease considerably in the next decade. (2) It was impossible not to take into account the rise in the level of culture and education in the remaining decades of the century, even among the backward rural population of L.D.C.s. This would lead to a decrease in the birth-rate. (3) Possible agrarian reforms in the L.D.C.s, and the redistribution of land to the poor, could slow down the process of the impoverishment of agricultural populations, and even restore and raise productivity. (4) It was necessary to consider the possibilities for industrialisation in L.D.C.s. This was the only way to secure the possibility of population redistribution without general disturbances.

Mr Boulier introduced the paper by Professor Visaria, who unfortunately could not attend the conference. He said it was difficult to summarise and criticise a paper when the author was not present. First, there was the possibility of misinterpreting his findings. Second, the conference would miss Professor Visaria's considerable expertise during the discussion.

Mr Boulier said the purpose of Professor Visaria's paper was to measure and analyse the evolving size and composition of the Indian labour force. The major points of the paper could be summarised as follows:

1. The measurement and size of the labour force and of unemployment were extremely sensitive to the definition and measurement of unpaid family workers. This was not surprising, since by one definition, in 1961, unpaid family workers accounted for 15 per cent of rural male workers and 8 per cent of urban male workers, and a much higher percentage of female workers – 48 per cent in rural areas and 26 per cent in urban areas. Variations in the definition in surveys over time made trend analyses difficult.

2. There were substantial seasonal variations in the size and composition of the labour force. This was to be expected, given the seasonal nature of agricultural work and the high volume of employment in agriculture. This variation led one to consider whether there were untapped pools of labour in the off-season.

3. No matter how unemployment was measured in various surveys, we obtained a statistical picture that implied very little unemployment, in contrast to casual observation which suggested substantial unemployment and underemployment. In 1971, for instance, the number of unemployed and unemployment rate were derived by a residual procedure. Workers were defined as those whose main activity was work, plus those whose main activity was not work but who did engage in economic activity. This seemed to him to be a very broad definition of the employed, but no definition of this latter category was given in Professor Visaria's paper. The number of unemployed was calculated as total population minus workers minus a portion of the non-working population – students, dependants, retirees, vagrants, persons engaged in household activities, and institutional inmates. Thus derived, unemployment rates were 1·2 per cent in rural India and 4·4 per cent in urban India.

Professor Visaria suggested that part of the reason for these low rates was, of course, that many of the non-working population were in reality unemployed, since many classified as non-working would seek work if it were available. He cited some evidence on this point and suggested that 28–55 per cent of the unemployed males fell into the category of persons not seeking work but not at work, as did 42–62 per cent of females. Professor Visaria stated that adjustment for this finding did not increase the unemployment estimates very much. No data were given, and Mr Boulier was somewhat surprised at this, but did not have the census data to verify his statement.

4. Unemployment rates as conventionally calculated did not incorporate measures of part-time employment. Roughly 5 per cent of males in rural areas who were at work would work additional hours if employment were available; 10–11 per cent of all workers would do so.

5. Unemployment, as commonly measured was low in India because the low level of income, near subsistence level, forced people to find employment or starve.

Mr Boulier had no direct criticisms of the paper, but raised two points which the paper brought to mind. The first was somewhat technical. For some purposes, trends in the size and composition of the labour force were of interest. Professor Visaria had made some ingenious and interesting adjustments to the data in his attempt to get at these trends. The adjustments were necessary because of changes in the definition of employment categories and of changes in instructions to interviewers. But adjustment after the event was less than perfect. Mr Boulier therefore wondered whether it would be desirable, at the time of the census or the survey, to ask questions on both definitions, the new and the old. This could be done by asking both questions in each household for a sub-sample of the survey, or by asking the old question only for a part of a sample and the new improved version for the remainder. This would facilitate data comparison. It entailed costs, but would these be worth while? Some study along these lines might be valuable.

His second point was whether we could design questions and collect data on unemployment and underemployment which would be more useful to economists and economic planners. There were several reasons why employment data were of value. Two important ones were a concern with the relationship of employment to income distribution; and a concern for the relationship of labour as a resource to the output which it produced.

Employment and unemployment were of interest because of their relationship to income distribution. The bulk of national income was received from direct labour, although there were tricky questions in measuring labour income when a high proportion of the labour force was self-employed. It seemed important, therefore, that we should collect income data at the same time as employment data. For example, suppose we had a group of workers and that each person worked ten months on average but that he had sufficient earnings to obtain a reasonable annual income. Suppose, further, that employment was randomly spread throughout the year. At any point in time we would find one-sixth of the labour force unemployed. But we would not be as concerned with this situation as with one in which five-sixths of the labour force worked all the year round but one-sixth was almost continually unemployed, barely earning subsistence. To determine the income and unemployment relationship, and the duration of unemployment, was important for rural areas where a high proportion of unemployment was seasonal. It was also important in urban areas where a substantial number of persons were petty traders and casual labourers. Employment and unemployment data would be more useful if data on income and on the duration of unemployment were collected to aid in their interpretation.

Mr Boulier had a further concern with employment. Labour was an important resource, and we were concerned with its full utilisation in order to maximise welfare. Our interest in employment, unemployment and underemployment was therefore an interest in the supply of labour and the uses to which it was put.

As economists, we were concerned with the supply of labour. Could we devise questions which would enable us to estimate the supply curve of labour? Of course, we could not expect sensible answers from asking: 'How much would you be willing to work at five rupees per hour, and how would that affect the hours worked by the rest of your family?' But this was important information, and Mr Boulier wondered how to obtain it.

In discussing labour as a resource, we were interested in how it was used or not used, since our concern with underemployment was partially that some people with skills were involuntarily unemployed, and could be used more efficiently. For instance, we observed particularly high rates of unemployment among educated manpower. Assuming that much of this was involuntary, we were led to a discussion of the appropriate level and structure of wage rates. Did we have enough studies to show the consequences for employment of rigid institutionally-determined or customarily-determined wage rates? If we could show that holding down wages would increase the demand for labour considerably, we should give valuable assistance to policy-makers, who would urge such policies. We also needed research to design policies which would alter wage-rate structures.

Professor Sovani explained that he could not really speak for Professor Visaria but would make comments where possible, particularly to correct misinterpretations of the Indian situation. For all he knew, Professor Visaria might disagree with him. With reference to Mr Boulier's comments about the shortcomings of the data on the labour force in India used by Professor Visaria, he thought one must begin by asking a basic question: were the categories and concepts implicit in 'labour force' as an analytical construct applicable to the Indian agricultural situation? In fact, they were not. Concepts like unemployment, underemployment, job, working hours, implicit in the idea of a labour force were not meaningful in the Indian agricultural milieu. These concepts just did not catch the reality of the Indian agricultural situation. Consequently, placing the Indian situation into these unrealistic categories tended not to reflect reality but a poor, inaccurate and distorted image of it. This was partially recognised by the attempts made, at successive censuses, to change definitions, concepts, etc. But these gave rise to non-comparable statistics from one census to another and painful attempts to adjust the data to overcome the problems of non-comparability. Professor Visaria's paper bore ample testimony to this.

Mr Boulier had, for example, suggested that data on workers' incomes should be collected along with data on the labour force. The suggestion was not new. It had already been made at the international level, and followed in some recent censuses. Apart from the infinitely greater difficulties of gathering data about the incomes of labour engaged in agriculture in developing countries, such suggestions missed a basic truth; the meaninglessness of the whole of the labour-force approach in regard to agricultural conditions in developing countries in general, and India in particular. This approach had been forced on the L.D.C.s by international bodies, dominated by international experts who came mainly from developed countries. The latter could understand situations in developing countries only in terms of concepts and categories relevant to the developed countries. Hence their anxiety and drive to press such approaches on developing countries. Unfortunately, the Western-trained economists and demographers in India and other developed countries were similarly oriented. The data they generated did not reflect the situation accurately and were consequently not of much help to policy-makers. It was necessary to discard entirely the labour-force approach and to adopt one better suited to reflect the reality of agriculture in India and other developing countries.

Professor Schultz, referring to Professor Khachaturov's comments, spoke about the underlying relationship determining changes in age-specific labour-force participation rates. He thought the key question about the change in the labour-force participation rates was whether one thought these were supply or demand phenomena. Particular rates for young and old were declining as development proceeded. If there were no employment oppor-tunities for these groups, and people were forced into inactivity, there was indeed a policy problem. Employment-generating policies were needed. On the other hand, labourers who received a higher income could now afford to retire earlier, and children were foregoing earnings longer to stay in school. So the size of the labour force was diminishing for different reasons. In this second case, there were greater opportunities facing people and no policy problem was implied.

What then was the fundamental technical relationship? Professor Schultz thought it was necessary to seek an understanding of the basic behaviour pattern, and find out what each particular type of unemployment meant. Was it induced by force of circumstance, or by a greater opportunity set? Unless we could distinguish between the opposing causal models, differences in rates of labour-force participation, and even unemployment, were meaningless.

Dr Jones referred to the labour-force survey and its usefulness for economic analysis. He said that there was a big drive in South-East Asia to make this survey more relevant. To him it seemed more important to get data on the family than on the individual. In urban areas there were more non-working dependants. Obviously, unemployment was far more serious for a father of five, none of whose dependants earned income from productive work.

On changing definitions, Dr Jones said that experience in Indonesia had been very similar to that quoted by Mr Boulier. He also said that there was a problem in asking the same thing in two ways. The answers tended to be closer than expected, either because the interviewer became embarrassed about repeating himself, or because the respondent got fed up with being asked the same thing twice!

In Indonesia, urban unemployment rates were lower among the poorer and less educated, because unemployment was in a sense a luxury in these countries.

Over the last thirty years, there had been a delicate balance in the Malthusian situation, which underlay any interpretation of labour-force data. Boserup and Clark had claimed that population pressure in the agricultural community could lead to rising productivity, by a sort of challenge and response mechanism. Unfortunately, in Java, the response had tended to be not innovations to increase productivity but an evolution of the social and economic structure. Greater and greater underemployment and continuing poverty could be tolerated, by social sharing, without increasing agricultural production per worker. Java had come very close to the limits, as evidenced by worsening erosion, etc.

The Green Revolution was based on better species, more fertilisers, more pesticides, and quicker harvesting to get the benefits of multiple cropping. Unfortunately, this interfered with the delicate balance established over the years. For example, the arrangements for planting and harvesting were breaking down in many areas. Formerly large numbers of people had been employed by the land-owning villagers at these peak labour periods, and this enabled them to survive. Now there was a need for quicker and more efficient methods so that, for example, the traditional technique for rice harvesting, using a small knife to cut individual blades of rice was replaced by the use of a sickle. Formerly, the landowner had been responsible for the harvesters; now he sold the crop, before the harvest, to someone who would organise the harvest. The latter would use a smaller, more efficient labour force, because he felt less obligation towards the land-less villagers. This was just one example of how very delicate socio-economic arrangements broke down under the Green Revolution, with serious implications for rural employment.

Dr Ridker had three points for Professor Khachaturov. First, could he spell out more fully the reasons for his optimism about the labour force and future employment trends? Where would the capital come from to bring about quick industrialisation or structural change which would overcome the population pressures?

Second, on the issue of low Indian unemployment which various speakers had covered, was it useful to use single-point estimates, from the O.E.C.D. data? He referred to a very interesting piece of work by David Turnham, who had attempted to correct for the bias in the Indian data, which resulted in an underestimate of the amount of unemployment. Turnham had leaned over backwards to compensate, and had succeeded in raising the level of unemployment to 5 or 6 per cent from 1 or 2 per cent. By most conventional standards this still meant that unemployment in India was low. In part, the explanation for these low figures, he suggested, was the fact that they measured only open unemployment. But another part of the explanation was the extreme poverty of the unemployed; they must do something, even if it was only standing on a street corner all day to sell one pair of shoe laces, to stay alive. For them, it was something of a luxury to be unemployed. Perhaps, for these poor countries, we needed a concept of involuntary employment, as well as the more familiar concept of involuntary unemployment. In other words, people would not work at many of menial, unrewarding activities if there were any other way of keeping alive. In this situation, it would not be surprising to find that an exogenous increase in the standard of living led to an increase in the unemployment levels, and, of course, this would not necessarily mean a worsening of the situation.

Professor Parikh intervened here to question the relevance of the whole hypothesis that there would be an increase in the consumption of leisure after an increase in the standard of living.

Dr Ridker, as his third point, questioned whether it was valuable to use the conventional income approach, or whether, as Dr Jones had suggested, we should use a family-income approach. All depended on what one was trying to measure. In the case that Dr Jones had mentioned, there was low unemployment at harvest time because the traditional method of harvesting in Java involved sharing labour. If one wanted to get at the welfare function, it was better to estimate family income than to look at the effort expended to get that income; whereas if one wanted to determine the surplus labour available for a new project, one would need to measure the time effort, or intensity. Even then, if this new project was of higher productivity and some people shifted to it, one could not measure this shift if one had a measure only of the hours worked.

Professor Robinson thought that, on pages 427–9, Professor Visaria was very unconvincing when he discussed the Indian situation. He had treated 28-hour-a-week workers as voluntary half-time unemployed. Was this a legitimate inference, bearing in mind the question that had been asked? For example, might one ask a man who had looked after bullocks for four hours a day in the place where he and his family lived, whether he was available for other work? One would not be surprised if he said 'no' if the extra work was in the next village, which was a four-mile walk away. On the other hand, if the Green Revolution meant more hours of work in the same job, at the same place, the answer would almost certainly be 'yes'. Elsewhere in the paper, there was a reference to the Philippines, where 74 per cent of self-employed males said they were not available for additional work, and 81 per cent of the male unpaid farm-workers said the same. Professor Robinson was not at all sure whether those who had been asked the question could envisage the different ways in which extra work could arise. Was there not a Parkinson's Law about spreading work, so that everyone appeared to be occupied, unless other work became available? It did not follow from Professor Visaria's data that extra work could not be done.

Professor Sovani agreed with this. A lot did depend on the specific situation. If it was a question of doing further work on one's own farm, 'yes', but if it was a question of work further away, 'no'. He added that he had not seen the data for this particular study and so wondered whether the questions asked were usually specific to the person being interviewed, to his farm, to his own village, etc. He shared Professor Robinson's scepticism about whether the evidence really indicated that more labour was not available in the Indian villages.

Professor Eastman made a related point, saying that it was very difficult to design meaningful questions. One had to think carefully about the phenomena expected or not expected. He would give an example of how data on unemployment could be affected by the social security system. Three years earlier, in Canada, the employment insurance system was altered to assume more .characteristics of the social welfare system. As a result of this, measured unemployment increased rapidly, despite an increase in economic activity. The explanation of the paradox was in part that persons in seasonal occupations were now considered unemployed, and received payments out of season; also, in part, people altered their behaviour so as to receive payments.

Professor Parikh argued that, although India might have a very low level of unemployment, it was important to remember that a very large proportion of the population (between 40 and 60 per cent) was still below the poverty line. If one were looking at policy issues, therefore, one must still worry about providing employment, at wage rates high enough to lift them from this subsistence level.

A number of people were doing careful farm-management surveys in many parts of India, and these should give detailed information on the timing and availability of labour for further employment. He endorsed the point that most people did not want to travel to work, and that when questions were asked, it was very important to specify the available alternatives. If Indians did not see the alternatives, then the questions were nonsense to them. Where Professor Visaria had talked about the difficulty of getting labour for rural works projects, there might be other relevant points, such as the time lag in the receipt of wages, and the fact that the extra food that could be purchased with the additional income did not cover the extra calories required to do the job. So one could not conclude from these studies that people were not available for work.

Perhaps economists should revise their techniques and criteria for looking at new opportunities for the rural poor. There was a need to include other variables, like the distribution of the income generated, as well as the existing criteria of the amounts of capital and labour required for the project. Redistribution of income by other means was always theoretically possible, but people avoided taxes in India. As an example, Professor Parikh quoted the dismissal of hand spinning as inefficient because it required more capital and more labour per unit of output. If one were to take account of the income distribution generated, with its associated welfare implications, then hand spinning might look to be a much better proposition.

M. Sauvy said that the title of Dr Nassef's paper showed that the main point under consideration was how to maintain employment in the face of rapid population growth. The details were of great importance – that he did not deny – but he did not have much hope of improving the situation. Before take-off in Europe, there had been substantial unemployment and very great disguised underemployment, suggesting that such a situation was normal at this stage. However, we were all now trying to improve employment levels, as was the International Economic Association. The difference in point of view was, of course, very threatening. It was questionable whether there was enough food to feed everyone, but he felt that it must be possible to find a theoretical solution which would give everyone a chance. In England in the seventeenth and eighteenth centuries, agricultural improvements and surpluses made it possible to pay and feed carpenters and other non-agricultural workers. But the first Soviet famine showed the other side of the coin.

The question of employment and overpopulation depended on the pattern of consumption. If most of a population consumed a great deal of food and natural produce, there would be unemployment and overpopulation. On the contrary, if most people consumed more elaborate products, or services, the circuit was lengthened, the numbers employed increased, and extra calories were available to provide remuneration for these employees. These elementary, but little known, views had recently been taken up for North Africa by the economist Samir Amin.

Professor Hicks observed that there had been a lot of talk about unemployment in a statistical sense, but people were only in the unemployment statistics if they were alive. To the question of how people kept alive if they were unemployed, there seemed to be several answers. Some people lived off the welfare state, as in Professor Eastman's example. This was quite important, but not in India. Others lived off their own savings, and in certain circumstances this also was important. One case was where people were seasonally unemployed and supported themselves by what they had earned in the rest of the year. Others were supported by private charity, including money from their own relatives and friends. He thought this classification covered all cases.

The three classes of unemployment were clearly different and should be given different names. Type 2 unemployment might be quite useful, in that it took time to find better employment. This was important in the advanced countries, and was clearly not an economic problem. The seasonal case, however, was a problem in countries like Indonesia and India. The third type of unemployment seemed to be the real problem in the countries that were being discussed, but one could understand when it was or was not as large as expected. Perhaps we needed to bear such a classification in mind to clarify our thinking.

Mr Kegan, referring to the U.N. data which Professor Khachaturov had mentioned, said that the paper used only one set of projections, whereas the U.N. data included three sets. Taking only the median estimate was a very serious problem, and it was sometimes helpful to look at the alternative models. He personally thought that the lower estimate was just not possible. There really was a serious problem, which had not been faced by Professor Khachaturov.

Mr Conde thought that, from his experience of Tanzania, the distance from the village to the city should be added as a variable in the Todaro model. He pointed out that the O.E.C.D., under the guidance of Mr Kanhert, had carried out a whole series of studies on employment.

Dr Nassef explained that the aim of his paper had been a simple one, i.e. to look at the size and structure of the labour force in the light of the potential growth of population in the last thirty years of the twentieth century. He had tried to put together efforts by different international organisations to look at the overall demographic consequences for the labour force. Using the medium projection, the total labour force would increase tremendously. There would be some reduction in the dependency ratio between 1970 and the year 2000 because of the assumed reduction in fertility. However, declining activity rates would more than offset the favourable effects of the change in the population age structure. Dr Nassef had tried to estimate the relative effects of different factors on the labour force, and it was clear that the increase in population size predominated. Employment problems associated with rapid population growth were probably related not only to the size but also to the structure of the labour force. He had therefore used the projection of the agricultural and non-agricultural labour force to see what jobs would be needed in the two sectors. Expécted growth in non-agricultural jobs was 4 per cent per year, which he thought was a very ambitious target. In the light of expected urban growth, the implications were that the rural economic structure would be little changed. Most of the changes in the structure of the total labour force would be in the urban sector, leaving the rural sector not significantly altered. Population growth would leave room for large increases in the labour force in both urban and rural areas. He had tried not to be too pessimistic, but there was a real challenge to those worried about the labour-force prospects, and he thought this must be approached by overall planning.

In response to Professor Khachaturov, Dr Nassef said he had not gone into detail on age-specific fertility rates, but we knew there were classical factors at work, and these factors were taken into account in the U.N. estimates used in his study. Second, he had not looked at policy measures, but had merely tried to quantify the relationship between population growth and the labour force. There were serious problems for the less-developed countries who must work on the demographic side by reducing fertility, and/or on economic variables to increase the economic growth rate.

On the prospect of actual rates being lower than the U.N. estimate, Dr Nassef said that most of his conclusions held true for the three or four estimates available. He had not really looked at policy measures, and was sure that the underdeveloped countries were tired of developed countries telling them what to do. He appreciated the various criticisms of labour-force concept, but was disappointed that there were no alternative suggestions.

Professor Khachaturov replied that he preferred optimism to pessimism, especially with regard to the social development of countries. He had tried to find some answers to the question of how the less-developed countries could resolve successfully the important problems posed by rapid population growth. He agreed with Dr Nassef that there were few possible solutions, but thought that one was industrialisation, and another the possibility of population growing more slowly than was expected.

Dr Shorter said that the rural/urban migration problem must be included in the discussion of policies for development. In the past, governments had found it necessary to introduce new amenities in urban areas as a fundamental part of the development plan. It was therefore not surprising that people had moved from rural to urban areas.

Professor Robinson found the issue fascinating because of the demographic background to the big debate in Asia. Did one plan for the maximum growth of GDP, or was employment one of the objectives to be weighed, along with GDP? This was a very real problem for the less-developed countries which had very low labour/capital ratios indeed, whereas a lot of the solutions suggested by economists were just not available.

Lady Hicks, as a postscript, said that as a general point, individual cities wanted to know for future planning purposes the intentions of migrants – whether they were going to return or settle. Obviously they would be a mixed group, but surely something could be discovered about motives. For example, the intra-European movement of Italians to Germany would be for a limited period, but the movement of Italians to Australia was very different. Italy must surely want to know the proportions of each.

She thought that in Africa some migration might be temporary, to learn a new craft, as in Nigeria. Then the migrant would aim to return to his village as an entrepreneur, while other migrants would stay in the city hoping for bigger incomes. Most Indians, on the other hand, migrated for the benefit of social services, without much job expectation. For cities such as Lagos, Bombay or Mexico City, it was important to know just why migrants came, so that the needed services could be provided. For example, Mexico City needed only to provide in the first place good shanty settlements for the Amerindians who came initially to marginal jobs. The Japanese pouring into Tokyo had no problem finding employment; therefore Tokyo had only to provide housing and water supply. The main point was that it should be possible to determine what the immigrants came for and how long they would stay.

Lady Hicks asked if one should try to stem the tide of immigration by attempting to raise the level of rural incomes to that of urban incomes. In the U.K., rural and urban wage levels were more or less even, and there was not the same propensity to move into the city. In India, a good part of migration seemed to be mere urban drift, but perhaps there would not be the same propensity to move if there were more opportunities in the villages. At a conference in New Dehli a few years ago, a very interesting suggestion had been made by a Unilever manager, namely, that the main problem was the lack of a proper marketing system in the country for agricultural products. He suggested growth-centre villages with facilities for the sale of produce, repairs to equipment and general shopping within twenty miles of all farms. Farmers would then have more incentive to maintain the standards of the Green Revolution, which would work in the right conditions, i.e. the right seeds, some work, and somewhere to buy and sell the crop. She thought this was a promising approach to raise the standard of farming and to make it worth while to stay in the country.

Part Seven

Migration and Employment Opportunities

16 Employment Opportunities, Family-building and Internal Migration in the Late Nineteenth Century: Some Swedish Case Studies

Sune Åkerman and Anders Norberg
UNIVERSITY OF UPPSALA

I. INTRODUCTION

Swedish migration studies focusing on the recent historical development have used two different approaches. One type of study has tried to reflect the effects of industrialisation and urbanisation on the population turnover and particularly the net migration on an aggregated level. Another type has concentrated on the individual in the same framework but with a stronger inclination towards psychological and social effects which follow the structural changes of a modernising society. In the actual research situation we feel more concerned about reporting from the last mentioned type of investigation. Well aware of the importance of the macro-level approach, we are inclined to stress the necessity of scrutinising the migration patterns related to the individual. It means that we have to use other types of interpretations than have traditionally been applied by economists, geographers and demographers. We are quite convinced that such research, concentrating on the individual, is necessary for our understanding the macro-level as well.

Before moving *in medias res* we have to stress that the younger generation of researchers still partially works in the same tradition as Gunnar Myrdal's research group from the 1930s. This group of international scholars tried to isolate the consequences of industrialisation on the total internal population movement. In particular the reallocation of the population was investigated. To that end some 2500 administrative units were classified according to their level of industrialisation. During the actual period of research, 1895–1930, a clear tendency appeared, indicating a shift from rural towards more industrialised areas. This shift implied, to a certain degree, a migration by stages. Myrdal's group could also establish a connection between business cycles and the extent and chronology of the net migration movements. As in France the Swedish demographers have found large regional differences. The western region had a stronger growth of the population in the middle of the nineteenth century. This strong natural increase was partially decimated by out-migration to the eastern region which was characterised by a slower natural increase in combination with a faster economic growth. The western region was also the most typical emigration area of Sweden.

In the near future the senior author will publish a more systematic study, partially based on the huge material of the Myrdal group, in a book entitled *Swedish and Scandinavian Population Movements* (Perspectives in American History, Harvard Press, 1973). This study is closely related to Dorothy Swaine Thomas's earlier work in the field of migration and it will particularly concentrate on the structural complexity of the migration patterns. The following special study has to be viewed against this general background. The importance of the sawmill industry for the process of industrialisation in Sweden can hardly be overestimated. This industry functioned as a leader particularly during the economic development of the period 1870–90, which means the take-off of Swedish industrialisation.

This strongly expansive export industry created very many employment opportunities. These opportunities made their impact on the patterns of migration and on social phenomena like family-building. By investigating the individual reactions we are able to shed light on the complicated interplay between economic and demographic components which is a classical field of controversy among scholars. This debate has been conducted on such a level of abstraction that almost everybody has been able to present an interpretation of his own. (For a good survey of this debate see Chambers, 1972.) Under such circumstances it is an urgent task for future research to connect these many interesting interpretation attempts with firmly based empirical evidence. We are convinced that this is the only method of furthering a systematic knowledge.

Previous research has dealt with the relationship between family structure and migration in many different contexts. It has discovered that increases in the size of families are accompanied by a diminished inclination to migrate. However, there have been exceptions to this rule: for example, the early emigration to America was to some considerable degree characterised by families connected with agriculture (Thomas, 1938, p. 76; Svalestuen, 1971, p. 43).

At the present time there is a growing interest among demographic historians the world over in the family unit as an object of study and research. It is only natural that this interest has been directed to a more in-depth analysis of the relatively complex relationship between migratory movements and the formation of families. The present paper will attempt to conduct an analysis of this type on the basis of the comparatively exhaustive and detailed Swedish national registration material. This source material also enables the researcher to make a rather thorough registration of the migratory movements for the individuals concerned. Our focus of attention is the way in which the formation of families is affected by migration and not, as has traditionally been the case, the way in which migration is affected by family structure.

II. AN HYPOTHESIS

In a more limited sense one can assert that in the case of many marriages a good deal of moving and shifting about by people is necessary if these marriages are ever to take place. It often happens that one or both of the partners contracting marriage are forced to migrate in order to establish a new household. This type of mobility has been given far too little attention by researchers into migration. However, such a study will not be the focus of the present paper. Our interest here is connected with the migratory movements which resulted from industrialisation and the way in which this migration affected the formation of families and associated phenomena. Our efforts have been directed to finding an isolated situation in which impulses from a newly created industrial centre find their mark in the surrounding agricultural area.

We have found just such a situation with the rise of the lumber industry in the northern provinces of Sweden in the middle of the nineteenth century. In order to establish a starting point for our study, we will make certain assumptions in the form of a systematised schema and then construct a hypothetical model of development which will later be set against the empirical evidence.

The following reactions are obtained in response to the creation of relatively heavy industry in a traditionally agricultural area:

(i) *There is an increase in the mobility of the population*; this mobility is measured in terms of in-migration and out-migration set against a calculation of the average total population for the area in question.

(ii) *The net in-migration increases* as a result of the fact that the pertinent area becomes more attractive to manpower than the surrounding areas.

(iii) *In the initial phase manpower is primarily recruited from the immediate vicinity*. This follows from the fact that the industry in question does not require any high degree of professional skills. In other words, it does not need to recruit specialists or highly skilled workers at considerable distances. The majority of migration studies have emphasised that most of the population transfer occurs at very short distances. Therefore, it appears likely that the establishment of industry primarily gives rise to in-migration from nearby administrative units. However, this pre-supposes that a certain, so-called 'population overload' has existed, something which we can assume was the case at this time in the Scandinavian countries, which were experiencing an explosive growth in population among farming communities.

(iv) *There is a preponderance of males among those migrating.* This of course is due to the fact that the overwhelming majority of job opportunities is essentially open to male labourers in a heavy industry. On the other hand, we can expect secondary effects in the form of in-migration by women to this area at a later phase.

(v) *This situation leads to a low degree of family-building.* This is a consequence of the disproportional distribution of sexes. It is only after a period of time that conditions become more normal in this respect.

(vi) ˙It is expected that there will be a *comparatively low marriage age among the relatively small number of women, while the marriage age for men can be anticipated to lie at the same level or possibly somewhat higher* in comparison with the surrounding area.

(vii) This leads to a *somewhat higher degree of fertility in the marriages* as a result of the prolonged nuptial period in the case of the women. The basic premise for this thesis is that family planning has not been applied previously within this densely populated area. We can apparently work with such an assumption for the actual period of history under study here, namely the middle and close of the nineteenth century.

(viii) The somewhat higher fertility in the marriages will be supplemented by a *low fertility for the entire population* in the newly built-up area. This is the natural consequence of the low level of family-building which has been assumed above.

(ix) *The number of extra-marital children tends to be high* as a result of the highly fluid milieu which has newly been created, with migrants freed from the conformity of social regulations and the authority of masters and overseers in the farming communities.

(x) *Infant mortality can be anticipated to lie at a higher level than it did in the rural community.* Cramped housing accommodation and the accompanying risk of infectious diseases, especially for small infants, can be expected to raise the mortality rate.

III. EMPIRICAL OBSERVATIONS

The documentary evidence presented on the following pages is based on the rise of the lumber industry districts in Norrland. These

MAP 16.1 Sweden.

districts are Rödön parish in Jämtland, Söderala parish in Hälsingland, and Timrå and Alnö parishes in Medelpad.

In Söderala, Timrå and Alnö most of the sawmills were founded during the period 1865–85, while the Hissmofors works in Rödön parish was founded at the end of the 1890s. The farming community surrounding the lumber mills in Söderala and Rödön is comparatively productive in terms of agricultural yields. On the other hand, the Medelpad parishes represent a type of agriculture which is common to the Norrland region, namely a rather insignificant productivity often combined with forestry, fishing, etc. Judged according to Swedish standards, the intermediate sized farms lie in Söderala and Rödön, while the small farms lie in the parishes of the so-called Sundsvall district. These underlying conditions are of importance for the interplay of economic and demographical factors between the industrial areas and their immediate surroundings discussed in this study (Fahlén, 1970; Hedman and Tjernström, 1970; Rondahl, 1972).

Change in the rate of population turnover

Map 16.2 clearly shows the progress of industrialisation for the two parishes in question here, Timrå and Alnö, as well as the remaining

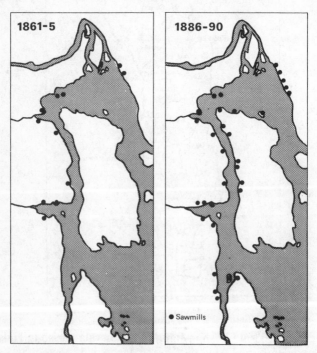

MAP 16.2 The Sawmills of the Sundsvall district, 1861–1865 and 1886–1890. *Source:* Wik, 1950, pp. 234 and 301.

parishes. The most dramatic transformation took place in Alnö which totally lacked any industrial enterprise up until the beginning of the 1860s. However, during the period 1886–90 no less than fifteen sawmills were in operation there. As expected, this new situation led to an increase in the rate of population turnover. Table 16.1 shows the way in which the total migratory movements in Alnö rose from 32 per cent of the average population during the five-year period 1865–9 to 69 per cent during the period 1880–4. As early as the first half of the 1870s the two movements had almost doubled and represented a turnover of almost 60 per cent.[1]

TABLE 16.1 THE RATE OF POPULATION TURNOVER OF ALNÖ PARISH, 1865–1899

Period	Average population	Inward migration	Outward migration	Total migration	Net migration	Turnover (%)
1865–9	1265	260	142	402	118	31·7
1870–4	1619	706	287	993	419	61·3
1875–9	2430	1009	421	1430	588	58·8
1880–4	3290	1461	794	2255	667	68·5
1885–9	4472	1429	1104	2533	325	56·6
1890–4	5305	1268	1403	2671	−135	50·3
1895–9	6098	1958	1365	3323	593	54·4

Source: The parish registers of Alnö.

This must of course be characterised as a drastic transformation, and there is little ground for doubt that industrialisation is the cause. However, it ought to be emphasised that the *annual* migration remains at the 10–15 per cent level, which by itself does not clearly distinguish this industrial area from the conditions prevalent in many agricultural regions in Sweden at this time. We will return to this matter in connection with migrations by seasonal labourers (Eriksson and Rogers, 1973).

There is a striking stability in the relative extent of the migration once it has reached the level dictated by the process of industrialisation. The situation becomes even more pronounced in the case of Timrå, as shown in Fig. 16.1. From 1865 until the end of the 1870s the out-migration actually remains at the same absolute level, while the in-migration rises slowly but steadily. No dramatic changes have taken place which might possibly have been anticipated. The stable net increase in the population each year – Timrå had a net out-migration only during a period of three years up to 1895 – still yielded strong, accumulated effects. At least in the case of certain

[1] The parish registers of Alnö.

areas there appear to be grounds for a de-emphasis of the rate of population turnover, which increased by leaps and bounds between the pre-industrial and industrial phases.

Increase in the net in-migration

As shown by Fig. 16.1, in-migration was consistently higher than out-migration. This assumption also proved to be the case for Timrå,

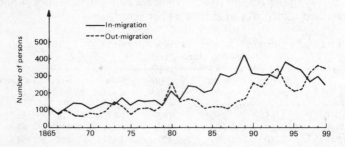

FIG. 16.1 In- and out-migration of Timrå parish.
 Source: Hedman and Tjernström, 1970, Appendix 3.

and the other areas taken up for study here were similar. The transformation is most pronounced in Rödön, which registered a net out-migration during the period in which the new industry was being founded. Thus, this net out-migration was transformed into a stable surplus of in-migrants at 5 per cent per year. At a later stage in this study the role played by family-building in population growth will be balanced against the effects of the net migration (Fahlén, 1970, Appendix 3).

The sharp contrast between the pre-industrial and industrial phases was to a certain extent not immediately obvious. However, it is clearly shown in the change of the net migration for the areas in question. It can be further illustrated by the migration statistics for Alnö, which show that the five-year net increase of migrants between 1865 and 1869 were numbered in hundreds, whereas the average figure proved to lie at a level of 500 persons during the two subsequent decades (see Table 16.1).

The predominance of short-distance migrations

This third point yields several surprises when it is seen against the empirical observations. Our first example is the village of Hägra, in the parish of Rödön, which was transformed into Hissmofors in connection with the industrialisation process. As previously mentioned, our basic starting point was the assumption that to a very substantial degree short-distance migrations normally dominate the movements of people from the countryside to densely settled areas within a country (internal migration). Furthermore, the creation of a host of new job opportunities primarily requires a flow of manpower from within the immediate vicinity of the new industrial areas (Fahlén, 1970, p. 20).

In 1895 the hamlet of Hägra had a population of 73 persons. This grew strongly during the subsequent decade, and in 1905 there were 651 registered residents. One decade later it had grown to the size of a densely populated area: in fact, it became a new centre in Rödön parish with almost 1000 persons. Thus, in terms of population the centre of concentration in the parish was shifted from the west, which was dominated by agriculture, to the east. From the standpoint of natural geography this proved to be somewhat more unfavourable, but nevertheless the Hissmofors works were founded in the eastern sector of the parish.

The Swedish source material also enables us to study migrations within the smallest administrative unit, namely the parish church district. The population transfer between Hägra–Hissmofors and the immediately surrounding area in connection with the rise of industry can be seen from Table 16.2.

TABLE 16.2 STATISTICAL SURVEY OF MIGRATIONS WITHIN PARISH BOUNDARIES DURING CONSECUTIVE FIVE YEAR PERIODS, 1890–1914

	1890–4	1895–9	1900–4	1905–9	1910–14
Inward migration	5	38	30	66	71
Outward migration	12	11	14	24	52
Net	−7	+27	+16	+42	+19

Source: Fahlén, 1970, p. 20.

At the beginning of the 1890s the population of the entire parish was 1700 persons. The net migration to the new industrial region was consistently five persons per year during the first five-year period. In the subsequent period there are only three persons annually who move into Hissmofors from the surrounding areas. Only then can we register a stronger reaction from the manpower within the church district.

Thus, the migration to Hägra-Hissmofors from within the parish boundaries does not reflect any 'shock' on the labour market which was closest at hand at the time the industry was being founded. On the contrary, the in-migration is greater towards the end of the period in question here. It is quite clear that short-distance migration within parish boundaries was only an insignificant cause of the explosive population growth in the industrial settlement.

Our hypothetical line of reasoning corresponds poorly with the empirical evidence in other ways as well. Only 35 per cent of the in-migration and out-migration during the period 1885–9 falls within a short-distance migration zone with a radius of 20 kilometres measured from Hissmofors (only migrations over parish boundaries have been included here). The corresponding figure for the period 1900–14 is a bare 25 per cent. A further zone drawn to a distance of 40 kilometres from Hissmofors accounts for 20–25 per cent. In other words, long distance migration represents almost 50 per cent of the entire population transfer over the parish boundaries. Not less than 20 per cent of the entire in-migration crossed over provincial boundaries. At a similar distance the net gains for Rödön parish were also significant. However, the net gains within the two immediate zones were very moderate. Thus, apart from the relatively small net gains obtained from migration within parish boundaries, it was primarily the migration from greater distances which gave Hissmofors its net gains.

On point after point the results from the Rödön survey correspond with the findings from the other regions in this study. The same is the case for Rödön's adjacent parish, Näskott, which has been the object of a similar study. The opposition to in-migration over short distances was, if feasible, even stronger in Söderala (Dryselius, 1970, p. 20; Rondahl, 1972, p. 263).

The male dominance in the migrations

We had counted upon a significant surplus of males in the in-migration to the regions in our study. However, even this thesis needs to be modified. The situation proved to be far more complicated than we assumed, and a simple, straightforward analysis of manpower is in no way sufficient as a means of explaining the migration pattern which we found in the case of the various parishes.

Timrå will serve as an example in this instance. In this rapidly expanding sawmill parish with a population of 1700 residents in 1865 and 5700 at the turn of the century, a total of 7700 persons were registered in the parish district during the same period of time. This highly extensive in-migration took place from all points of the compass and, as mentioned previously, partly at extremely long distances. There is an extremely significant distribution of sexes among those migrating in terms of the various distances involved and respective areas of origin (Hedman and Thernström, 1970, p. 9).

Long-distance migration from western Sweden, particularly the province of Värmland, showed a male surplus of 40 per cent, whereas women dominated the in-migration from the home province of Medelpad as well as the immigration from Finland. There was a 30–32 per cent surplus of women in these migrations.

In-migration by families accounted for 70 per cent of the in-migration from short distances within the province. Families also predominated in the migration patterns for the provinces of Ångermanland and Västerbotten during the initial phase of industrialisation. On the other hand, single persons dominated migrations over long distances. Men without families accounted for 42 per cent of the in-migration from Värmland, while families accounted for only 36 per cent of the entire in-migration. It was primarily unmarried women who migrated from Finland, and they accounted for 42 per cent of this immigration. They were mainly recruited from the Swedish-speaking parishes in Österbotten.

Despite these significant differences in the distribution of sexes, we obtain a set of interesting and thought-provoking statistics in this instance. The final results of the Timrå study show that women accounted for 50·2 per cent and men 49·8 per cent of the in-migration to the area during the period 1865–94.

We can draw an antecedent to our assertion that males predominate in the in-migration pattern and maintain that migrations by single persons should dominate the present phase of industrialisation. However, even this assertion lacks support in the Timrå findings. The same is the case for the findings of the other parish districts in this study. Migrations by families totally dominate the picture, even if their share of the migration fluctuates with the distance from the lumber industries.

It is important, however, to stress that these family movements to a high degree represented migration by stages which can be seen from Map 16.3. These movements were therefore the last link of a longer chain of movements comparable to long distance migration. Also this result accentuates how important the long-range migrations were for the sawmill industry during this period. At the same time this fact sheds light on our later discussion of the concept 'the rural–industrial barrier'.

IV. THE LOW LEVEL OF FAMILY-BUILDING

The results we have obtained from the sex structure of the migrations reverse our introductory premises. Thus, we find that the low degree of family-building which we expected earlier is altogether absent from the picture. We suspected that the lumber-industry areas under study would to a certain extent operate in the migration pattern as 'marriage markets' on the analogy of the term labour market.

We may observe this from the changes in the general marriage rate. In Alnö this was on a level of 7 per thousand in the 1960s, but

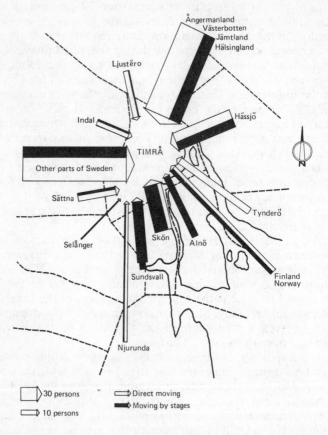

MAP 16.3 In-migration during the period 1865–1884 by persons in the age-cohort 20–24.
Source: Hedman and Tjernström, 1970, Appendix 21.

during the period 1871–85 it rose to more than 10 per thousand. This crude measurement indicates that we are dealing with a rapid increase in the inclination to marry.[1]

[1] Olsson, 1947, p. 228. Olsson finds in his investigation of the parish of Skön a marriage rate of 8 per thousand in the 1860s and 10 per thousand in the following decade. Norberg, The Alnö Investigation.

This observation gains reinforcement if we conduct a more in-depth analysis of family-building in connection with the in-migration to Timrå. This research has been conducted in the form of a cohort study covering the organisational phase of industry within the parish district. We have taken into account all registered in-migrants between the ages of 20 and 24 during the period 1865–84. These persons have then been followed over a fifteen-year period, i.e. until they reached the ages of 35–39, which in the case of women practically spans their full nuptial period (Hedman and Tjernström, 1970, p. 15).

TABLE 16.3 THE TWO COHORTS OF THE
TIMRÅ INVESTIGATION

	No. of in-migrants	No. of natives	Total
Cohort 1	181	81	262
Cohort 2	199	137	336
Total	380	218	598

Source: Hedman and Tjernström, 1970, Appendix 18.

There were 380 persons in the age group 20–24 years who moved into Timrå. These 380 persons were rather evenly divided, in proportional terms, between the 181 persons who in-migrated at an early stage during the years 1865–74 and the 199 persons who did so during the period 1875–84. The pronounced population transfer which we previously mentioned, naturally reduces the number of persons which can be studied throughout the entire research period with respect to Timrå. We find that only 31 per cent of those in the age group 20–24 who in-migrated to Timrå remained there for the duration of their fifteen-year period. Consequently, our study will be limited to 117 persons and their marriage partners as well as the children born to these marriages. The fact that these marriages were not completely terminated in so far as fertility is concerned is of lesser importance here. The control group used in this instance was constructed in such a way as to be completely applicable to comparisons we had in mind. At the outset this group consisted of 218 individuals originating from the Timrå district who reached the ages of 20 to 24 at the same time as the migrant group. The former group has a higher tendency to continued residence, which is a normal phenomenon for studies of this type. Those who have already moved on at least one occasion from a place of residence generally have a greater inclination to move again in the future.

As shown by Fig. 16.2 over the trend in persistence, the control group diminishes to 114 individuals. This means that 52 per cent of the original group remained in residence for the full duration of their fifteen-year period. The control group primarily reflects agricultural occupations. An ideal situation would have been our working with marriages in which both partners were entirely stationary in terms of residence. But even the agricultural population has been involved in a good deal of migratory movements, especially between the adjacent parish districts. This factor would have considerably reduced our control group. For this reason we have also

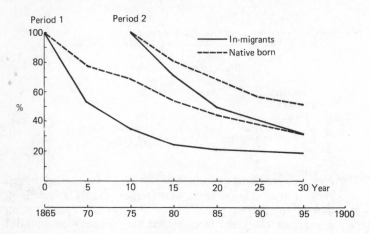

FIG. 16.2 The persistence trend for the two different groups in the two periods. *Source:* Hedman and Tjernström, 1970, Appendix 10.

included marriages in which one of the partners has in-migrated. This does not change the composition of the control group to any serious degree, inasmuch as the migrant working population appears to have had few contacts with the native population. This is something we will return to later on. Thus, 'mixed marriages' between industrial workers and the agricultural population have been rather uncommon.

We can calculate marriage frequency by means of registering the civil status of those persons in our study at the close of each respective fifteen-year period. In so doing we must also account for the fact that a small number of persons marry before reaching the ages 20–24 years. As far as the others are concerned, 74 per cent of the control group married, as did no less than 92 per cent of the in-migrant group. These figures must be revised in the case of remarriages, which in both instances amounted to 3 per cent.

Consequently, 89 per cent of the in-migrants and 72 per cent of the control group should have married for the first time. Statistically speaking, there is obviously a clear, significant difference between the two groups in our study.

By themselves, these percentage figures are high, and they would climb even higher if we were to follow the individuals until their fiftieth year or thereafter. However, the relationship between the time of in-migration and that of marriage is even more dramatic. Figure 16.3 shows how the absolute majority of marriages was already contracted during the first two years of residence in Timrå.

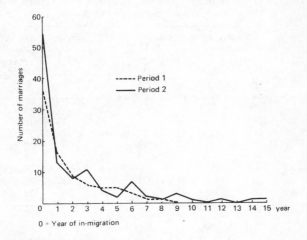

FIG. 16.3 The time between in-migration and marriage for the two cohorts.
Source: Hedman and Tjernström, 1970. Appendix 18.

As was also expected earlier, it is quite clear that the migrations were not only a labour market phenomenon but were to a great degree integrated with the building of families.

V. THE LOW MARRIAGE AGE OF WOMEN COMBINED WITH A COMPARATIVELY HIGH MARRIAGE AGE FOR MEN

Our prediction that the in-migrant women would marry early proved correct. However, this has nothing to do with our capacity for prophecy. The disproportional distribution of sexes did not prove to be a consequence of the extensive in-migration. In other words, the phenomenon must be explained in some other way.

In the in-migrant group under study here the median age of

women at the time of their marriage was 23 years. This must be considered as an extremely low median age. Of those in-migrants in the age group 20–24 years, 43 per cent had already reached the age of 23 at the time they registered in Timrå. Consequently, the low median age which we have obtained must have an underlying premise, namely that these persons married immediately upon or after their registration in the area. As for the younger in-migrants, they will to a great extent have had to marry in their early twenties.

TABLE 16.4   THE AGE AT MARRIAGE FOR MEN AND WOMEN FOR
TWO PERIODS, TIMRÅ PARISH

Age	Number of in-migrants				Number of natives			
	Period 1		Period 2		Period 1		Period 2	
	M	F	M	F	M	F	M	F
19	1	—	—	1	1	—	—	5
20–24	24	42	36	62	7	8	16	17
25–29	11	11	13	10	14	7	24	18
30–34	2	—	3	4	5	6	7	4
35–39	—	—	—	2	2	—	1	—
Unknown	—	—	1	—	1	—	—	—
Total	38	53	53	79	30	21	48	44
Median-age	24	23	24	23	26	26	25	24·5

Source: Hedman and Tjernström, 1970, Appendix 17.

This is precisely what has happened, and on several previous occasions we have been able to make the observation that in many instances the migration must have been a step in the direction of family-building (Hedman and Tjernström, 1970, p. 16).

In this light, the median marriage age of 24 years for in-migrant men is also extremely low. This must be seen as a natural consequence of the entire migration pattern and the circumstances associated with family-building. For both men and women in the control group family-building took place at a later stage as compared with the in-migrant group. The median age was 25·5 and 25 years respectively. In line with this thesis we ought to have raised the median age of the control group somewhat in order to make for a full range of comparisons at this point, inasmuch as this cohort is in itself somewhat retrograded in terms of age. As shown by Table 16.4, there was also a greater distribution of the pertinent five-year periods in the life cycle for members of the control group.

VI. HIGHER FERTILITY IN MARRIAGES

Even under this heading our faulty premises led us to the right conclusions relative to the conditions we were dealing with. In all circumstances the early marriage ages for the in-migrant women has led to a longer nuptial period. In and of itself, this factor might have been reduced by a greater degree of mortality among the in-migrant women, but this has in no way been the case. Furthermore, we have stated that the in-migrant men had a comparatively low marriage age.

There were 100 in-migrant parents in the group we are presently studying. Up to the point at which our study of these marriages terminated, 486 children had been born to these 100 persons. Our control group of 95 parents had 357 children. Thus, the ratio between the in-migrant and control group is 4·86 to 3·76. However, there was a lesser number of marriages among the in-migrant group, since these test subjects tended to intra-marry to a greater extent than the control group. Among other things, this was a consequence of the fact that those in the in-migrant group were on the average younger in age at the time of their registration in Timrå. Thus there were great possibilities that both men and women fell into the cohort studied here. As has been mentioned, only 20 per cent ($\frac{1}{5}$) of the control group married others within the same group. Despite the fact that we have not studied the women up until the age of 45, this statistic means that these families were larger in terms of size than the above ratios indicate. This especially ought to apply to the in-migrant group. Consequently, we should obtain an even sharper and more pronounced difference between the in-migrants and those who were residents of the immediate district.

The statistical material which we have at our disposal does not allow any closer specification of this difference. But we do have statistics from Alnö which make it possible for us to provide reinforcement for this discussion. On two occasions, namely 1875 and 1885, all of the families who acquired children during the course of the year were recorded in the registration statistics. We have subsequently studied these families over a ten-year period and even reconstructed their past history. The time period in question here is thereby limited to the years *c*. 1860–94, with the main focus of attention on the 1870s and 1880s. We have not limited the study to any set age group but rather included both younger and older families. We drew a sharper boundary line here between the in-migrant and control groups than was the case for Timrå. The control group consists only of those marriages in which both partners were born in Alnö. Furthermore a mixed group has been introduced which consists of marriages between an in-migrant and a native resident (Norberg, n.d.).

The three groups were compounded and arranged as shown in Table 16.5.

The difference between Group I and the in-migrant groups is clearly indicated: it amounts to nearly two children per family. In a fully logical manner, Group II falls in an intermediate position between the native residents and the in-migrants group.

It must be emphasised that the Alnö study not only registers fertility for the area in question but also reconstructs the way in which some of the families were established prior to in-migration.

TABLE 16.5　NUMBER OF CHILDREN PER FAMILY OF
THE THREE INVESTIGATED GROUPS

	Families	Children	No. of children born per family
Group I (native residents)	30	160	5·33
Group II (mixed group)	50	327	6·54
Group III (in-migrants)	114	808	7·08
Total	194	1295	6·67 (average)

Source: Parish registers of Alnö.

Consequently, the Alnö study is not entirely comparable with the results presented from Timrå. The statistics for the total number of children in these families show a greater comparability with the figures for the entire parish district than was the case in Timrå. Nonetheless, their actual level must still be regarded as somewhat lower.

On the other hand, these minimal figures are sufficiently high to provide a clear picture of the way in which the migration pattern, and particularly the net in-migration, effected a vitalisation of the population during the preliminary phase of industrialisation. What is especially striking from our standpoint is the difference between the in-migrant group and those already residing in the area. The in-migrant group shows a greater inclination for early marriages and the raising of rather large numbers of children.

In our introduction we raised the question as to whether some form of family planning might possibly have been prevalent in the industrial areas under study. Had there been any such family planning it would have ruined our line of argumentation, although it would of course have made for an interesting research finding. If we take into account that on the average the in-migrant families gave birth to seven children in the course of marriages which, to a certain extent, were not terminated in terms of fertility, the answer appears to be an obvious one. Family limitation can hardly have been practised.

If we turn to the native population, which was primarily engaged in agriculture, we find the same situation: the number of children born per family gives no indication of any use of family limitation. But this question cannot be answered simply in terms of a straightforward comparison between the number of families and the number of births. We must also take into account a significant child mortality, especially among small infants up to two years of age. This reduces the number of children per family to an average of 3·9 for Group I, 4·4 for Group II and 5·0 for Group III (in-migrants). Thus, there is a relatively limited number of children in every family in Group I (native residents). However, does this mean that we can speak in terms of family limitation? There are two factors which prevent our drawing such a conclusion. First of all, we have not followed the families throughout the entire reproductive period. Secondly, the source material studied here does not provide ready statistics on the number of children dead at birth (stillborn) and miscarriages. However, we can introduce such statistics in the course of this discussion.

Research meets with complicated problems in its attempt to detect the introduction of family planning in an historical source material. Several criteria must be worked with, for the number of children cannot provide the entire picture. The most important criterion is of course the interval between births. In analysing these intervals the researcher must consider the woman's nuptial period and the particular phase in this period at which the births occur. As mentioned previously, the researcher must make a calculation of infant mortality and the number of stillbirths which can have occurred. These statistics must be entered on the chart over the intervals between births, which illustrate the way in which the families have been formed. Moreover, in an ideal situation the researcher should also register additional statistics on the women, such as prolonged and malignant illnesses, etc. Such information should then be combined with relevant statistics on the men under study. It is important in this context that the researcher take note of the fact that infant mortality, for example, obviously affects different families with varying degrees of intensity. Consequently, the need for compensating the loss of children has varied greatly from family to family. The working framework for all of this information is of course an accurate record of the date for the marriage contract and any eventual dissolution of the marriage during the woman's period of fertility.

It is obvious that the best method of conducting an analysis of the way in which family planning was introduced is by studies of the individual family's behavioural pattern. This particular angle of perspective has not been taken up for examination by Swedish researchers in the field of demographical history.[1] For the present we can limit ourselves to making the assertion that the in-migrant population hardly appears to have shown a greater inclination for family planning than did the native population. It is possible that the situation was just the reverse.

VII. THE OVERALL LOW FERTILITY FOR THE AREAS OF STUDY

In many respects our prognosis of the results from our study of the source material has proved a total failure. This is particularly the case here: the empirical evidence is exceedingly severe on our introductory assumptions. It is clear that the significant net in-migration to the areas in our study combined with a favourable distribution of sexes among the in-migrant group led to a high marriage-frequency. This caused a comparatively high degree of fertility among this particular group.

But what effects did this have on the total fertility in the areas of study? This question is of course connected with the answer to another: what was the size of the in-migrant population, seen in relative proportion to the native population, during the various phases of industrialisation? Another important factor is the age distribution among in-migrants compared with that for the resident population. Of further importance here is a fact which we have already established, namely that on average the in-migrant group married somewhat earlier than the resident population. Finally, there is the significantly higher percentage of married persons among the in-migrants.

The Alnö study provides an answer to the question of the distribution of fertility among the in-migrant and resident populations.

Table 16.6 clearly shows how the in-migrant group (Group III) rapidly accounts for a two-thirds majority of the children born within the parish district. At the same time the corresponding figures for the resident population are reduced to one-tenth. As shown by the age-pyramid (Fig. 16.4), the industrial group still did not

[1] Compare Hofsten, 1972, who gives an interesting survey of fertility in various regions of Sweden.

TABLE 16.6 PERCENTAGE OF BIRTHS PER YEAR

	1860	1865	1870	1875	1880	1885
Group I	36·7	34·2	26·2	16·5	10·6	9·0
Group II	36·7	40·2	40·5	21·1	19·5	20·9
Group III	26·6	25·7	33·3	62·4	69·9	70·1

Source: Parish registers of Alnö.

represent a majority of the population by the middle of the 1880s (Norberg, n.d.).

Figure 16.4 also provides an answer to the question of the age distribution among the in-migrant and resident populations. It ought to be pointed out that it is only the industrial population which

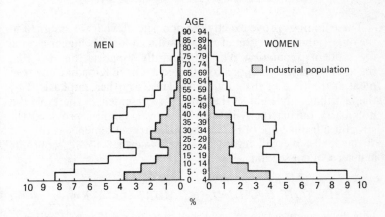

FIG. 16.4 Age distribution of industrial and total population of Alnö parish in 1883.
Source: Parish registers of Alnö.

has been recorded here, i.e. those persons residing in the sawmill regions. To a certain extent the industrial workers and their families found lodgings in the adjacent farming villages. Consequently, we are dealing here with minimal figures for the proportion of industrial workers among the total population. Nevertheless, the role played by Group III in the inherent growth of the population stands in sharp contrast to its more modest position on the population diagram. It is also clear that the age distribution for this sector of the Alnö population promoted a dynamic demographical development.

VIII. THE LARGE PROPORTION OF EXTRA-MARITAL CHILDREN IN LUMBER-INDUSTRY REGIONS

Even this assumption appears to be incorrect. The three groups in the Alnö study are distributed as shown in Table 16.7 with respect to extra-marital children.

TABLE 16.7 SHARE OF EXTRA-MARITAL CHILDREN OF THE THREE INVESTIGATED GROUPS

	No. of children	Extra-marital children	Percentage
Group I	164	12	7·3
Group II	336	17	5·1
Group III	1055[a]	43	4·1

Source: Parish registers of Alnö.

[a] Cf. Table 16.5, in which out-migrating women and children are excluded.

These findings prove exactly the opposite of what we assumed at the outset: the proportion of extra-marital children is higher among the resident population. The table hardly supports the idea that the lumber-industry regions constituted a type of Klondike environment at the time of their founding. This is further emphasised by the fact that only eight of the women represented in the table did not marry during their lifetime. Moreover, families provided the structural framework of the lumber-industry settlements at the end of the 1880s. We will return to these somewhat 'idyllic' concepts in a subsequent section.

IX. THE HIGH INFANT-MORTALITY RATE

This idyllic picture loses a great deal of its compelling attraction as soon as we focus on a study of infant mortality, especially in terms of infants who died shortly after birth. There was a total of 486 children among the in-migrant cohort in the Timrå study. Of these 486 children, 108 died before the age of 15, and 60 died as infants between the ages 0–2 years. The corresponding number of children for the control group is a total of 357. Mortality among children up to 15 years of age registered 69 deaths, and 28 infants died soon after birth. This means that for infants and children up to 15 years of age in the control group the infant-mortality rate accounts for 19·3 per cent. The corresponding figure for the in-migrant group was 22·2 per cent (Hedman and Tjernström, 1970, p. 20).

The difference is insignificant, but it verifies what we assumed at the outset. The contrast is greater if we isolate the deaths of infants up to 2 years of age. In this case, the figure for the number of children studied in the control group stands at 7·8 per cent, whereas the in-migrant group registers 12·3 per cent.

It is important for the purposes of our analysis that we recognise the fact that infant mortality affected the pertinent families on a varying scale of intensity. A relatively small number of these families accounted for the major share of deaths. Table 16.8 provides us with another important observation, namely that the highest infant-mortality rate in Alnö was registered for those villages with both a rural and an industrial population. If we narrow our focus to the families of industrial workers, i.e. families which consequently lived in the heart of the rural areas in the parish, we find that infant mortality there was as high as 54·5 per cent.

TABLE 16.8 INFANT MORTALITY IN A CHANGING RURAL ENVIRONMENT IN ALNÖ, 1875 AND 1885, BIRTH COHORT OF THE THREE INVESTIGATED GROUPS

	No. of children	Deaths before age 10	Percentage
Villages	67	22	32·8
Villages with an industrial population	69	31	44·9
Industrial population	(33)	(18)	54·5
Sawmill regions	88	32	36·4
Total	224	85	37·9

Source: Parish registers of Alnö.

This limited study justifies its original intentions. If the trends disclosed in our present findings hold true in future studies, it will have significant consequences for the interpretation of the results of subsequent research into the fluctuating levels of infant mortality.

X. INTERPRETING THE FINDINGS

In our introduction we constructed a series of hypothetical statements based on logical expectations from a given demographical development in connection with the establishment of an industry. Most of the statements were of such a nature that the reader could unconditionally accept them as reasonable and well in line with general conceptions of the course of development. The fact that population turnover, for example, may be expected to be larger in an industrial area than in the countryside ought not to contradict our preconceived ideas relative to the ways in which an area is measurably affected by the process of industrialisation.

However, the fact of the matter is that a different pattern emerges in case after case of study where our hypothetical theses have been subjected to the test of empirical data. We have already commented to some degree on the reasons for these differences, but it is now necessary to provide a more in-depth analysis for the most important points of our study. In so doing we will to some degree supplement the information given previously in terms of new data.

XI. RATES OF POPULATION TURNOVER

We have asserted that the rates of population turnover rose to a high level in connection with the initial extension of the sawmill industry into areas such as Alnö. Subsequently, the rates of turnover calculated on the basis of the mean population stayed at approximately the same level during the course of several decades. In this respect Alnö was typical of the entire Sundsvall district. These observations are well in line with what we thought we might expect under the given circumstances. However, we must stop at this point and give this matter a more thorough commentary. The situation here conceals technical as well as interpretative problems.

First of all, the registered migration does not account for the entire population turnover in the areas of study. A selective spot analysis of the Johannesvik sawmill in Alnö reveals that only 16 of approximately 80 workers were registered in the statistics. Similar results have been obtained previously for Ljusne in Söderala. This can be explained by the presence of a large number of seasonal migratory workers in the labour force. As a result, this means that we are dealing with a significantly higher degree of actual mobility in the population than that which emerges from a study of the parish church registers (Rondahl, 1972, ch. viii).

If these seasonal migrant workers are subsequently included in our estimates of the size of the population turnover, they accentuate our statistics tremendously. Immediately prior to the founding of the sawmills in Alnö the rate of population turnover lay at a level of 6 per cent. In a very short time it lay at the 15 per cent level, based solely on a tabulation of the registered migratory movements. If we were now to include the 70 per cent figure for the seasonal migrant workers in the labour force during the 1870s, the rate of turnover would climb to the 21 per cent level. This is a considerable increase, particularly in comparison with the 6 per cent figure for the 1860s. In this way we obtain a more appropriate means of measuring just how mobile the rising sawmill industry can have been at this time.

Yet in other ways the rate of population turnover is a rather rough standard of measurement. It has consequently been shown to lie at an even level over long stretches of time. In our opinion, this situation is partly due to the technical imperfection which is inherent in this statistical material. The intensity of population turnover is automatically reduced in an expanding population with a high birth-rate and a high degree of family-building. This is due to the fact that the rate of population turnover is subsequently set in contrast to the rapid growth in population. In order to maintain an even level of migratory movements, an environment of this type actually requires a continual rise in the flow of in-migration as well as out-migration. This is precisely what happened, for example, in the Sundsvall district during this particular period of the late nineteenth century.

What we obviously need here is a more appropriate means of measuring the population turnover. Such a standard of measurement must allow us to correct and adjust the effects of certain phenomena. For example, an extensive migration by families to an area with a relatively low number of children causes a disproportional increase in the rates of turnover. This can also be reversed: the actual significance of the turnover is unrealistically diminished in an area where movements of younger people disguise the effects of in-migration and out-migration by persons who represent the professionally employed age-group. It appears that the best solution is to construct *age-specific rates of population turnover*.[1]

In practical terms these rates of turnover can be constructed in such a way that children under the age of 15 are excluded from consideration both in terms of the migrant and the pertinent, stationary populations. One can also consider excluding the older individuals from the estimates. With regard to the present material under discussion, the line could be drawn at the age of 50. For a later historical period the age of 65 is usually considered as a line of demarcation between an active and passive adult population. In our study we have limited ourselves to excluding the ages of children.

If we now compare the rough rates of population turnover we find that in Alnö they lay at a level of 16·4 per cent in 1873 and at 15·4 per cent 10 years later. Consequently, it is possible to detect a moderate decline. Seen in terms of our age-specific estimates, these same figures actually prove to lie at a level of 14·3 and 16·0 per cent respectively, i.e. a clearly discernible upswing. It may appear as if the differences between these methods of calculation are not terribly great, but then it must be remembered that we obtain two entirely different trends.

Age-specific rates of population turnover are even more appro-

[1] Schofield, 1972, p. 261. Compare Schofield's concept 'age-specific mobility', which seems to be identical with our concept, but is not. He refers to the well-known fact that different age-groups show different inclination to migrate.

priate in making comparisons, for example, between a lumber
industry region and the Upsala-Näs area which was discussed above.
In this manner the exceedingly high rates of turnover obtained for
Upsala-Näs are scaled down, whereas the lumber-industry regions
receive a markedly higher population turnover. Moreover, if we take
the seasonal migrant workers into account we find that in 1883 the
rates of turnover in Alnö stand at an annual level of 40 per cent.[1]
Yet we must also take seasonal migrant workers into account for
the agricultural parishes in the Mälaren region, and for the period
of time we are presently discussing such migrations were probably
a considerable portion of the statistical picture. *We must draw the
conclusion that, unless one is prepared to qualify one's line of reasoning
and take into account the structural features of the migrational
flow, one cannot unconditionally assert that industrialisation generally
heightens the population turnover.* We are forced to this conclusion,
despite the fact that in our special study we have found a pronounced
rise in the rate of population turnover in connection with the initial
phase of industrialisation.[2]

XII. THE MARRIAGE MARKET

It is naturally an essential result of research to delineate the decisive
significance which the formation of marriages has evidently had
for the pattern of population turnover. This is especially the case in
light of the fact that research has given so little attention to the
matter. On the other hand, we ought not to over-dramatise the rapid
and extensive formation of marriages in Timrå. The *seasonal work
migrations* led to a disproportional balance between the sexes at
least during the warmer seasons of the year (March to October). This
was something we anticipated ahead of time but were not able to
discern in terms of the registered individuals. A heavy surplus of men
in relation to women usually gives rise to a situation in which the
latter marry on a large scale. Such was evidently the case in Timrå,
Alnö and elsewhere.

There is another important factor in this context, namely that
while the in-migration consisted of an equal proportion of men and
women, the out-migration from the area revealed a definite surplus

---

[1] During the period 1873–83 there were between four and nine sawmills located
in Alnö with approximately 70 seasonal workers at each mill. With four sawmills
there would have been about 250 seasonal workers and 500 migrations each year.
Approximately 230 adult migrations occurred each year. The mean adult population
for the period 1873–83 was 1400 plus 250 seasonal workers, or 1650. The rate of
turnover was $730/1650 = 41\cdot8$, or more than 40 per cent.

[2] Cf. Martinius, 1967, ch. 2, where a similar result is found.

of women. This factor reinforced the numerical share of married women in the in-migrant population, inasmuch as the single women who did not find a marriage partner within the course of a very few years of residence in our areas of study moved on to other regions. It ought to be emphasised that the structure of the in-migration and out-migration for the entire Sundsvall district was of a similar nature. Consequently, our observations concerning Timrå and Alnö have also applied to the other parishes. This means that in five cases we obtain a complicated equation of in-migration, one which miraculously enough can be solved and which reveals how important the marriage market evidently has been as a complement to the labour market (Tedebrand, 1972, p. 119).

XIII. IMPORTANCE OF THE FAMILY IN THE PROCESS OF ADJUSTMENT

Perhaps the most important result in our study appears to be *the fact that the family unit has obviously played a central role in the migrant's process of adjustment* in the new areas. There is good reason for emphasising that this observation completely contradicts the general conception that a city and industrial environment tends to dissolve the matrix of the family unit.[1] Moreover, the new population centres with their scores of in-migrants have, to all appearances, created certain substitutes for family life, for example dissenting religious sects, prohibitionist movements, trade unions, political organisations, and the like. Such activities as these were probably stimulated by the somewhat longer periods of free time enjoyed by workers in industry as contrasted with the situation facing workers in agriculture. However, our findings still clearly show that to a very high degree the individuals in our study aimed at building families and raising children while they were still very young. We also know by means of oral tradition that these newly-created households formed the basis for a great deal of the seasonal work migrations. The seasonal workers lived and were fed to a great extent in these households.

One interesting phenomenon which illustrates the situation of adjustment here is the significantly high number of instances in which persons from a certain region have married others from the same area. This phenomenon is of course well known on a larger scale, for example, from the course of immigration to America. This

[1] A similar criticism against the common idea about the declining role of the family in the urban environment is to be found with Allardt and Littunen, 1962, p. 70. Similar ideas have been investigated by Braun (1960, ch. 2) for an early period in Switzerland. Cf. Olsson, 1949, p. 85.

is naturally connected in part with the fact that in many cases eventual partners agreed to marry even before their migration to the lumber-industry area. Thus, they succeeded in preserving some degree of a social context despite the migration from a distant and at times very different environment. We have not conducted any further in-depth studies of this factor in terms of the internal migration, but we venture to assume that the phenomenon has been instrumental in simplifying the adjustment process for the in-migrants.

We also registered an extensive degree of migrations by families, especially in the introductory phase. This factor has been reinforced somewhat in that single migrants came to a sawmill and remained there for a period of time without filing their certificates of change of residence. It was not until after they married at some later date that they were entered in the registers over changes of residence (*flyttningslängd*) and the records of the parish catechetical meetings (*husförhörslängd*). The extent of migrations by families as well as the high birth-rate in the lumber-industry regions *must be seen in connection with the fact that child labour was a very common phenomenon in the sawmills and lumber yards*. This made it possible for several persons in each family to contribute actively as bread-winners (Olsson, 1949, pp. 59, 82).

We discovered that there was a higher frequency of extra-marital children among the agricultural population in Alnö than among the population in the densely-settled areas. This finding should give impetus to further studies of the family structure in the rural community. It is conceivable that such studies would lead us to discover that, all things considered, family ties have been weaker in the agricultural community than they were in the environment formed by the Sundsvall district. This would mean that our conceptions of the differences between a rural and urban environment are completely reversed.

XIV. THE RURAL–INDUSTRIAL BARRIER

We have discovered a surprising resistance among the rural population to the prospects of moving into a newly created industrial area. There are two factors at work here. The process of recruiting manpower to the lumber industries under study has to a very little extent focused on short distances from the agricultural sector of the population. Moreover, the scores of seasonal migrant workers showed a rather moderate numerical inclination to the prospect of moving on a definite basis to the sawmill districts. This factor naturally illustrates the resistance we have mentioned. We have called this phenomenon the rural–industrial barrier. This must be seen in light of the fact that wages were on the average higher in industry and that free time was somewhat longer. Other factors such as the relationship between workers and employers have not in any way been sufficiently studied to enable us to make any definitive statements on the eventual advantages or disadvantages which come into the picture during a population transfer into areas of industry. However, it appears as if the advantages clearly outweigh the disadvantages. Nonetheless, we do find this resistance to migration; such a result must be very carefully substantiated. This is what we tried to accomplish in a series of studies and especially in a doctoral dissertation by Björn Rondahl (1972, ch. vi).

It is of course imperative that we investigate and sort out a great many factors which can distort this result. First of all, we must have a clear idea of whether a surplus of manpower has actually existed in the pertinent, surrounding areas. This is admittedly not altogether necessary for our thesis, but it does give reinforcement to our conclusions. If we should happen to detect a shortage of manpower in the agricultural side of the picture, this would weaken our thesis to a corresponding degree.

We must not limit ourselves to a study of *the mobility between parish districts*, as has been the case in previous research. In a parish with such a sizeable population as Söderala (between 6000 and 10,000 residents during this period) a good deal of short-distance mobility might be concealed if we employed the usual method of analysis.

On the whole, we must also be able to exclude the possibility that *commuting* has taken place by manpower over short distances. The same is the case for the possibility that the agricultural population has been active on a *part-time basis* in the sawmill industry.

It is also important to clarify *the situation regarding our source material*. In other words, we must make certain that scores of persons have not managed to reside and work at the sawmills without having been officially registered and that, consequently, many of them might actually have belonged to the agricultural population which we must look for in the neighbouring vicinity.

It appears as if our findings are confirmed on all of these points. This even applies to the objection which might conceivably be raised that the industry in question can have been so specialised that the agricultural population, quite simply, could not carry out its work assignments without a certain degree of training.

It is altogether clear that the rural–industrial barrier says more to us about the majority of the population's reactions than any directed study we might make on those persons who actually migrated. We now discover a new way of stating the problem and one which is worth examining: *how was the resistance to migration overcome?* This is a matter to which we will return later.

XV. DIFFERENCES BETWEEN MIGRANTS AND RESIDENTS

As has been mentioned, the in-migration which proved to have the most significance for the growth of population in the lumber industry came from the effective long-distance migrations. These migrations originated in an area of Sweden which has been called *the main, western demographic region.* This region is characterised by a higher birth-rate than is the case for the eastern region, in which Söderala, Timrå, and Alnö were situated (Sundbärg, 1910, Appendix V, p. 4). Moreover, a good deal of the long-distance migrants came from Västerbotten in the northernmost part of Sweden and from Österbotten in Finland. Both of these provinces had a particularly high degree of fertility. It does not appear unlikely that the migrants can have carried with them to the new areas of settlement the behavioural pattern which was prevalent in their home districts. With regard to the question of the behavioural pattern of the migration, we have made findings in other studies which show that such a phenomenon may actually have been the case (Nilsson, 1970, ch. IV).

However, this is only one of many proposals for interpretation which we must analyse. Researchers in the area of international migration research believe they have detected that the migrant population is on the whole more energetic than the stationary, resident population. This consideration might possibly be introduced as an explanation for the pronounced differences we have discovered in comparing migrants with a control group consisting of a stationary population.

We have already caught a glimpse of a third possibility of explanation. The prevalent use of child labour might have induced the newly-formed families in industry to be more inclined to raise rather large numbers of children. We can hardly anticipate a similar propelling force in the agricultural communities, although they can to a certain extent have profited from the rapidly expanding industrial sector. In terms of our present field of knowledge it is impossible to arrange these proposals for interpretation in some order of precedence. We must take particular caution in ascribing a great deal of importance to the main demographical regions for the differences we have made note of before we have succeeded in carrying out more in-depth studies.

XVI. STAGES IN DEMOGRAPHICAL DEVELOPMENT

Other studies conducted by our research group have shown that an attempt to reconstruct the various *phases* in a migratory development proves highly effective. Research dealing with emigration to America has applied itself particularly well to this type of systematisation.

It is obvious that the migration to the lumber industry regions at the end of the nineteenth century can also be considered from the same angle of perspective. This means that we obtain a framework for the various results which have been presented (Fig. 16.5).

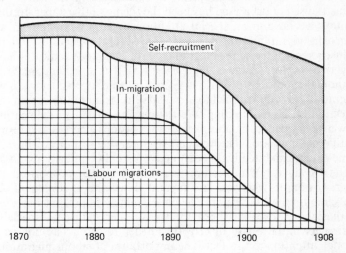

FIG. 16.5 Phases of labour recruitment in Ljusne sawmill district, 1870–1908.
Source: Rondahl, 1972, p. 264.

In Phase I, which formed the initial period, we find the following phenomena: a significant surplus of in-migration combined with extensive seasonal work migrations, an insignificant, local recruitment of manpower, as well as an unusually rapid trend in family-building with a high birth-rate.

Phase II exhibits a continual surplus of in-migration, although it lies at a considerably lower level than previously. The seasonal work migrations are still highly significant, although their formative role has diminished somewhat. At the same time local recruitment of labour appears on the scene as a result of the high fertility in the previous phase.

When we enter Phase III, the surplus of in-migration has been transformed into a definite surplus of out-migration, which reflects the fact that the period of expansion in the sawmill industry has come to an end. The seasonal work migrations are now a closed chapter, and the present recruitment of manpower has mainly taken the form of local contract of labour. It is possible that the rural–industrial barrier begins to break down in this phase for the agricultural population residing on the outskirts of the industrial areas.

XVII. CONCLUDING REMARKS

The implication of migration for an expansive region which was industrialised or urbanised has been the theme of this paper. In this context we have given special attention to family-building in an area of in-migrational movement, namely several expanding lumber-industry regions along the Norrland coast. This study indicates how sensitive the formation of marriages was to the general play of economic conditions at various points in time. It also shows how migration *per se* functioned to a great degree as an initial step in the direction of family-building. We thereby succeeded in delineating how a nearly perfect balance between sex groups emerges as a result of different migrational movements over varying distances which to some extent exhibited highly distinctive sexual compositions. In so doing we have not taken into account the large proportion of migrant workers who were less integrated into this environment. At the same time we have noticed how extremely important this part of the labour force has been for the lumber industry, especially during its initial phase of growth. Earlier research has not paid enough attention to this fact. The importance of labour migrations might apply to the first phase of industrial development in general. It is also possible that our delineation of the phases of labour recruitment of a growing industry represents a more or less general pattern (Cf. Mendels, 1972). In that context we have focused our interest on the reactions of a rural population to the influences of a growing industry. We have established a rural–industrial barrier.

From other studies by our Uppsala group we have noticed that in expanding rural areas there is a connection between a high proportion of males in the population and a high propensity to marry. As in the case of these studies the intense degree of marriage formation registered in our study was undoubtedly due to the heavy proportion of males in the population. During our period of study 90 per cent of the female in-migrants to these areas married within as short a time as two years after their arrival. Inasmuch as these women were on the average very young at the time of in-migration their nuptial period was very long. Subsequently, we can observe a particularly dramatic difference between the industrial labourers and the small farming and fishing populations in the adjacent rural community within the same administrative district.

In one of our areas of study industrial labourers represented only 30 per cent of the population, but during the 1870s and 1880s they accounted for no less than 80 per cent of the fertility figures. Such statistics give us an idea of the way in which a population was vitalised as a consequence of the scores of new employment opportunities available within the important sawmill industry. We have found that the lumber-industry labourers also had a greater number of children per family: this further accentuates the difference between them and the agricultural population. We could not establish any direct tendencies toward family limitation during this particular phase. However, the junior author has found, in an unpublished study, that the agricultural population evidently attempted to concentrate childbirths to a certain time of the year which would not interfere with the participation of the women in the harvesting of crops. Yet the major result of this study was essentially the following: the family unit generally assumed an important role in the adjustment process of industrial labourers to the environment of a region at a point in time when conditions have been presumed to resemble those of the Klondike gold fields. Our results also point to the effect that the often discussed dissolution of families appeared earlier in rural areas compared to more urbanised surroundings. In opposition to the general idea about the dichotomy, rural versus urban, we can suggest this interpretation, one of several results from this paper that we want to elaborate in forthcoming research.

REFERENCES

E. Allardt and Y. Littunen, *Sociologi* (Uppsala, 1962).
R. Braun, *Industrialiserung und Volksleben* (Stuttgart, 1960).
J. D. Chambers, *Population, Economy, and Society in Pre-industrial England* (London, 1972).
A. Dryselius, 'Emigrationen från Näskott 1881–1930 samt Näskotts omflyttning 1896–1909 och 1917–1930', unpub. paper, Department of History, Univ. of Uppsala (1970).
I. Eriksson and J. Rogers, 'Mobility in an Agrarian Community. Practical and Methodological Considerations'. In the present publication (Uppsala, 1973).
K. Fahlén, 'Rödöns socken, emigration och omflyttning åren 1885–1914', unpub. paper, Department of History, Univ. of Uppsala (1970).
I. Hedman and G. Tjernström, 'Migration och äktenskapsmarknadbefolknings-rörelsen i Timrå socken 1865–1899', unpub. paper, Department of History, Univ. of Uppsala (1970).
E. Hofsten, *The Swedish Population 1750–1970* (Stockholm, 1972).

S. Martinius, *Befolkningsrörlighet under industrialismens inledningsskede i Sverige*, summary in English, Meddelanden från Ekonomisk-historiska institutionen vid Göteborgs universitet, nr. 8 (1967).

F. F. Mendels, *Social Mobility and Phases of Industrialization*, paper delivered to M.S.S.B. Conference of International Comparisons of Social Mobility in Past Societies, Institute for Advanced Studies, Princeton (1972).

A. Norberg, 'Alnöundersökningen', unpub. papers, Department of History, Univ. of Uppsala (n.d.).

R. Olsson, *Ur Skönbygdens historia* (Sundsvall, 1947).

—— *Norrländskt sågverksliv under att sekel* (Sundsvall, 1949).

B. Rondahl, *Emigration, folkomflyttning och säsongarbete i ett sågverksdistrikt i södra Hälsingland 1865–1910. Söderala kommun med särskild hänsyn till Ljusne industrisamhälle*, summary in English (Uppsala, 1972).

R. Schofield, 'Age-specific Mobility in an Eighteenth Century Rural English Parish', *Annales de Démographie historique, 1970: Migration*.

G. Sundbärg, *Emigrationsutredningen*, Bilaga v (Stockholm, 1910).

S. Svalestuen, 'Nordisk emigrasjon – en komparativ oversikt', *Emigrationen fra Norden indtil 1. Verdenskrig*, rapporter til det nordiske historikermøde 9–12 Aug 1971 (Köpenhamn, 1971).

L.-G. Tedebrand, *Västernorrland och Nordamerika 1875–1913. Utvandring och återinvandring*, summary in English (Uppsala, 1972).

D. S. Thomas, *Research Memorandum on Migration Differentials*, Social Science Research Council, New York, bul. no. 43 (1938).

H. Wik, *Norra Sveriges sågverksindustri från 1800-talets mitt fram till 1937*, skrifter från Uppsala Universitets Geografiska institution, nr. 21 (Stockholm, 1950).

Discussion of the Paper by
Professors Åkerman and Norberg

Mr Black introduced the discussion. He said that, using registration data not often available in such detail, which permitted control-group measurement in an isolated laboratory area of Northern Sweden, the researchers had traced the effect of economic development on migration, family formation and fertility. They focused on how family formation was affected by migration, and this led to some insights into the classic demographic transition.

First, Mr Black pointed to some highlights of the study. Åkerman and Norberg had picked an area with intense migratory movement, with a turnover of up to 69 per cent, caused by latent overpopulation in low-productive agriculture, and by the magnet of a labour market. A reasonable working hypothesis provided the relatively surprise-free scenario. Mr Black pointed to the following conclusions: (1) Long-distance migration provided about half of total migration. (2) Migration was dominated by families already formed, or formed soon after the move. (3) There was therefore a high family-building rate and early marriage. (4) Migrants showed higher fertility than locals and there was no evidence that family planning was practised. (5) Migrants accounted for two-thirds of children born and provided a dynamic impact to the society and to the economy. (6) There were fewer illegitimate children in the migrant community. (7) There was surprisingly high infant mortality – up to 55 per cent. (8) The marriage market complemented the labour market.

Mr Black then indicated some issues for discussion. (i) The fact that there were seasonal migrant workers in the area complicated the data and inhibited the conclusion that industrialisation had led to turnover. (ii) The labour market had been a male one – would a female labour market have led to a different family formation and fertility pattern? (iii) Had the opportunities for employment for the children of migrants, or of agricultural workers, given an incentive to higher fertility, and therefore acted like high child mortality to stimulate fertility? (iv) What had happened to the empty farms when migrants left? Was there a population surplus to fill them? (v) Was not family preservation through high fertility normal in any 'frontier' settling movement, North Sweden being an industrial opportunity frontier? High productivity, dynamism and fertility were part of the pattern everywhere. (vi) Would the transition from high to stable turnover of population occur if there were not continual economic development, and opportunity for extended migration?

Finally, Mr Black suggested a general point for discussion. Was a micro-family investigation of this kind more relevant and more saleable to developing countries than the conventional macro-approach of demographers? There was the difficulty of how to fit a micro-study into the context of a total economy and society. We must know something about the push-pull forces affecting the movement of people, technology and capital in relation to the international division of labour before drawing policy conclusions.

Professor Åkerman said that he felt in one respect an outsider in the conference. He had not concentrated on economic variables alone, but had looked at the effect of migration on society and on the individual. He felt that some findings of his case study were interesting and intriguing in their implications for future research. He personally had found Dr Lesthaeghe's remarks on Limburg very interesting, and thought that the lessons from Sweden in the late nineteenth century and early twentieth century had relevance for developing countries in the same way. He thought there were links and parallels between different countries and different times with social, demographic and economic developments. Good historical data were available for the whole of Sweden and twenty or more studies of different areas were going on, although only one had been reported on this occasion.

Professor Hermalin was delighted that there had been greater emphasis on micro-studies for some time, but thought there were still some omissions. For one thing, migrants had not been compared with natives, so that we did not have a complete picture. He thought we were confounded by looking only at housing. He admitted that this was the most obvious and problematical area, but thought there were other areas of interest. A Mexico City case study had shown how important it was where migrants came from; for example, from rural areas or small towns. If the level of education were taken into account, his study showed that migrants were now better off than natives in terms of income, though he agreed that this might not be the case elsewhere. Researchers needed to be very specific and to use careful controls. Professor Åkerman had attempted to build in such controls, as well as using historical data. Migration might give positive benefit rather than just redistribute poverty. The discussion of the European migration, particularly the contrasted comments of Professor Hague and M. Leridon, had shown the need for more studies of France and Germany. He thought there was a further need, to broaden the narrow economic approach, to include other variables, and to make studies ranging across developed and developing nations.

Dr Hume reported that work was going on in Germany, the preliminary results of which he had seen. Migrants had been compared with their German socio-economic counterparts on the basis of income, saving, length of stay, and so on.

Professor Giersch asked two questions about the Åkerman study. (1) How far was migration from rural areas to the cities due to the push of rural unemployment rather than the pull of urban life and labour shortage? (2) What could we learn that would increase our understanding of the European migration discussed previously?

Professor Guitton was concerned with the relationship between micro- and macro-analysis and thought that the problems of migration, as studied, seemed to establish some links between global and partial methodology. Had the point been reached – though he thought not – where the variables explaining migration in Sweden were the same as those in the macro-models? Were we going too fast, and attempting to build a general theory too quickly? Earlier discussion had focused on longer-distance migration, and this usually involved crossing frontiers, whether linguistic, political, military or cultural: frontiers related to the way of life. Professor Guitton thought these movements were quite different from internal migrations, where the migrants were of the same mind, culture and background, so that no drastic change was involved. He thought the psychological, behavioural and motivation variables were very important. He was worried about the way global statistics were interpreted, and wondered how many elements in a complex reality were hidden in global data. In the Swedish study, he had been struck by the more human interpretation, using sociological and psychological variables. He did not wish to advocate one method of study to the exclusion of the other but rather a convergence, and he wondered if there was any threshold beyond which there was a fundamental change, making one or other approach more applicable. As M. Sauvy had also said, he considered it a great privilege to be able to meet in the Association to try to work together to produce better tools and concepts.

Professor Ohlin also wanted to make some methodological comments which probably stemmed from the fact that he was a non-demographer. He wondered why particular measures had been used in preference to others which he would have looked at. Professor Guitton had already raised the question of the age structure of the population, which could mean more people 'at risk' in the population, and therefore a rise in the rate of marriage. The authors of the paper had compared fertilities and found that the fertility rate of migrants was higher than that for residents. He, personally, was surprised to find no use of age-specific fertility ratios. Similarly, the data on numbers of children was given per family, not per completed family, which would have been preferable. Had such data simply not been available, or had the researchers chosen not to use it?

Mr Kegan reported that the Liège conference had discussed the model used by the I.L.O., which sought to relate employment, migration, fertility and other factors in tackling problems of the sort mentioned by Lady Hicks in the discussion of India.[1] The model which showed greatest population growth was the 'closed cities' model. These models told us something about the respective merits of micro- and macro-models, and about the links between development policy and population policy.

Professor Sovani said that the picture of urbanisation in India that Lady Hicks had implicitly painted was popular and stereotyped, but unreal. It was a picture of rural population pressure exploding into urban growth, through excessive migration to towns and consequent unemployment there. 'Rural population pressure' was an extremely nebulous concept and there was little evidence that rural population density and urban growth were positively correlated. Much of the increase in the urban population of India in recent decades was attributable to the natural growth of the urban population, and not mainly to in-migration. The incidence of unemployment in urban areas in India was also much lower among the in-migrants to the towns than among the autochthons. Rural-urban migration in India seemed to be a well-calculated move, and was not the result of a mere 'push' from the rural areas.

[1] See p. 449.

Professor Åkerman said he was astonished to find the ready acceptance of this rigid rural-urban dichotomy, instead of the gradation that existed in reality.

To Professor Ben Porath, he said that there was a huge body of potentially relevant knowledge that Professor Todaro seemed to know very little about; for example, in the fields of history, geography, etc. Professor Åkerman thought it should be possible to build a different model, using the findings of psychology, sociology, history, geography, as well as the findings of economic research.

Professor Giersch had commented that the strong desire of immigrants to bring their families with them was not very true for Germany. Professor Åkerman thought that if we wanted people to move and adjust, we must help them to bring their families with them, though he realised that there were other dimensions of international migration, particularly the political one.

Professor Åkerman said that Professor Guitton's point about amalgamating qualitative and quantitative models was very relevant, and that something must be done to make economic research in this field more realistic. He personally liked to think of migration as correlated to human beings. With this starting point, it was a better strategy for a researcher to begin work at the micro-level. In general, he thought it was impossible for economists to explain huge migrations, such as those to Canada and the U.S.A. in the nineteenth century, by using only four or five variables.

Finally, to Professor Ohlin, Professor Åkerman said that the whole study reported in the paper was age-specific, in that it looked at cohorts, though he admitted that it was time-consuming and technically difficult to produce such research. The migration research group at Uppsala University, however, had used this type of cohort analysis in several studies, to find more about the correlation between migration and social mobility.

17 Some Economic Aspects of Labour Migration in Europe since the Second World War*

Ian M. Hume

This paper examines some economic aspects of the third form of demographic movement, namely migration. The paper is specific rather than general. It examines the particular migration, involving mainly workers, from Southern and Eastern Europe into the industrial nations of Western Europe, particularly through the decade of the 1960s to the present.

The paper has five sections. The first, Section I, gives a general summary of facts and figures regarding the extent and scope of the migration. Sections II and III examine respectively its economic origins and consequences. Section IV suggests a means of viewing the costs and benefits of the migration to the participating countries.

I. THE SCOPE OF MIGRATION

While post-war Europe has experienced several different currents of migration including the exodus from Eastern Europe and the movements both to and from the colonies or ex-colonies, the migration discussed here concerns the movement of people, mostly workers, from the Mediterranean basin countries, plus Portugal, Turkey, Yugoslavia and some countries in North Africa, into the industrial countries of Western Europe. This is the major migration in post-war Europe. Although it began in the early 1950s or before, its principal growth was in the mid and late 1960s. It continues today at a significant pace and it has prospects for doing so through the rest of this decade.

Some facts and figures

There is no unique set of statistical information giving a true count of all foreign workers and their families now resident in Western Europe. The presence of East Germans in West Germany, of

*I am grateful to Ross Parish, Shankar Acharya, D. Kumar, Sudhir Anand and particularly to Fred Shorter for comments made on an earlier draft of this paper. Remaining errors are of course my own.

Algerians in France, of E.E.C. members in other member countries all confound the conceptual issue of who should be classed as a 'migrant'. There are, in addition, some reporting deficiencies attendant upon recording the arrival and departure of large numbers of

TABLE 17.1 DISTRIBUTION AND ORIGINS OF THE STOCK OF SURVIVING MIGRANT WORKERS IN 1971 (IN THOUSANDS)

	Receiving countries					
	Germany	France	Switzerland	Benelux	United Kingdom	Total
Migrant workers in:	2241	1957^a	624	300^b	655	5777
Percentage of total migrant workers in:	38·8	33·9	10·8	5·2	11·3	100·0
	Percentages from sending countries^c					Share of total (%)^d
Greece	12·7	1·0	0·8	2·7	—	5·1
Italy	24·8	17·9	60·7	31·2	—	28·0
Portugal	1·9	17·8	—	5·7	—	8·6
Spain	9·9	20·7	14·1	13·6	—	15·4
Turkey	15·5	0·5	1·0	8·4	—	6·3
Yugoslavia	16·5	3·0	2·7	1·5	—	7·5
Others	18·7	39·1	20·7	36·9	100·0	29·1
	100·0	100·0	100·0	100·0	100·0	100·0

^a Estimated to allow for underrecording of official statistics.
^b Estimated.
^c Based on 1969 figures.
^d Exluding the United Kingdom.

TABLE 17.2 EUROPEAN MIGRANT-WORKER FLOWS IN 1969 (IN THOUSANDS)

	Receiving countries							Germany 1970–71^a	
	Germany	France	Switzer-land	Benelux	United Kingdom	Total	% of total	(Thou-sands)	% of total
Sending country:									
Greece	65·1	—	—	—	0·3	65·4	7·1	31·1	9·7
Italy	136·2	6·5	57·0	—	2·3	202·0	21·9	29·9	9·3
Portugal	13·2	80·9	—	—	0·7	94·7	10·2	13·9	4·3
Spain	50·1	23·9	15·0	—	4·8	93·8	10·1	34·8	10·8
Turkey	121·5	2·6	—	—	0·2	124·3	13·4	95·4	29·7
Yugoslavia	192·2	11·3	—	—	0·7	204·2	22·1	78·6	24·4
Others	67·7	42·7	29·8	30·7	—	170·9	15·2	37·9	11·8
Total:	646·0	167·8	101·8	30·7	9·0	955·3	100·0	321·6	100·0

^a Recent figures for other countries not yet available.

foreigners, though these deficiencies have been minimised in recent years. Making allowance for these factors, and using information released by the receiving countries, estimates have been made to suggest that about 8·0 million foreign workers were resident in

Western Europe at the beginning of 1973.[1] Adding to this the number of family members would raise the total migrant population to between 9 and 10 million. Tables 17.1 and 17.2 give an idea of the main country breakdown of the sending and receiving countries both in terms of the migrants resident in the receiving countries in 1971 and of the gross inflow of new migrants in that year.

A figure of 8 million workers represents the equivalent of about 10 per cent of the domestic labour force in the receiving countries taken as a whole, though this proportion is very unevenly spread. In Germany, for example, foreign workers comprise about 7 per cent of the labour force while in Switzerland the proportion is about 28 per cent. The figure of 8 million corresponds to about 15 per cent of the total labour force in the major sending countries.

Significant changes have occurred in recent years in the mix of countries supplying and demanding the migrant workers. Whereas France and Germany historically had a roughly equal share of the migrants, Germany is now, with about 40 per cent of the total as against 34 per cent for France, by far the major country. This is even clearer in terms of current inflows of new migrants, about 70 per cent of which go to Germany. Switzerland accepted almost no new migrants in 1972. On the supply side, whereas the Latin countries were the major source of migrants until the mid sixties, now these countries supply declining shares while Yugoslavia and, more particularly, Turkey have become the major suppliers of labour. In 1970–1 Turkey supplied about 30 per cent of the gross inflow of migrants in that year with Yugoslavia adding 24 per cent.

II. ECONOMIC ORIGINS

Since the migration is essentially a migration of labour it seems logical that economic factors will provide an important part of its explanation. This is not to discount the importance of non-economic factors, least of all the influence of demographic variables which have been of central importance in contributing to the economic imbalances resulting in the migration. Economic factors, however, have probably been paramount. What is required, which as yet is only partly developed in the literature, is a suitable economic framework in which to discuss the origins and implications of the migration.

[1] Detailed factual information on the migration can be found in Livi-Bacci and Hagmann (1971). See also an I.B.R.D. working paper written by the current author (1970). The principal individual country data can be found from the *Bundesanstalt fur Arbeit*, Nuremburg; from the *Office Nationale de l'Immigration*, Paris; and from 'La Vie Economique', Government Printer in Berne.

At a very general level, the situation in Europe appears to have been one in which in the receiving countries, demographic deficiencies and other factors effecting the slow growth in the labour force, coupled with relatively abundant supplies of investment capital, have led to disproportions in factor availabilities as between labour and capital. To the extent that the pace of labour-saving, capital-deepening innovations in investment is not without limit, these countries have as a result faced a chronic excess demand for labour in domestic production. In this situation, the alternatives were to divert capital to foreign investments or to seek labour from abroad.

In the sending countries on the other hand, factor disproportionalities have been somewhat reversed. Historically, these have been capital-scarce countries with relatively elastic labour supplies, both in terms of demographic increase and on account of their having relatively large reserves of labour in traditional low-wage agriculture. Since wages in the receiving countries were generally much higher this gave the personal incentive for workers to move.

Neo-classical theory would tend to interpret this situation as one in which combinations of free trade, free factor movements and elastic rates of substitution between capital and labour would work to eliminate the imbalance and equalise factor prices between countries. In reality, however, disequilibrium rather than equilibrium models are required. There are obstacles to free trade and factor movements and substitution rates appear to have been insufficiently elastic. Consequently, labour markets have not been brought to equilibrium, factor-price differentials, specifically the wage differential, have not been eliminated.

Labour transfer models from development theory may also not be the most appropriate in this situation. This applies, for example, to attempts to discuss the migration in terms of a Lewis-type model which views the migration as an 'internal' movement in a two-sector, single labour market economy.[1] Receiving countries are viewed as high-wage 'labour demand' sectors, sending countries as traditional low-wage 'labour pool' sectors. Migration occurs through a combination of recruiting by employers and private decisions to migrate by income maximising workers. Labour transfers are equilibrating since the resulting relative movement of labour's marginal product in each country tends to narrow the wage differential.

Four sectors, not two sectors

What seems to be required in the European situation is a model which accounts not just for the 'between' country-labour market

[1] This is done, for example, by C. Kindleberger (1967).

but with the 'within' country markets as well. Each country has its own labour demanding and labour supplying sectors. Even though, on balance, the receiving countries are characterised by labour deficits for industrial growth they also have domestic labour supplies which, under different policies and pricing, could transfer from other sectors into industry. It is an often argued point that institutional pricing practices in these countries have harboured relatively large shares of the labour force in agriculture. Table 17.3 attempts to show the relocation of labour out of agriculture in the receiving countries has been relatively slow in comparison to the United States and the United Kingdom,[1] particularly when account is taken of the respective shares of labour in agriculture.

TABLE 17.3   PERCENTAGE SHARES OF LABOUR FORCE IN AGRICULTURE AND
THEIR TRENDS, 1958–1969

	1958	1965	1969	1969 (1958 = 100)	Reduction factor[a]
	(S_1)		(S_2)	(W)	
France	22·4	17·1	14·4	5·14	64·3	7·0
Germany	15·1	10·9	9·4	3·36	62·3	11·3
Switzerland	12·5	8·3	7·3	2·61	58·4	16·1
United Kingdom	4·3	3·3	2·8	1·00	65·1	34·9
United States	8·0	5·7	4·3	1·54	53·8	29·9

[a] Reduction factor = $S_1 - S_2/W$, where S_1 is the share of labour in agriculture in 1958, S_2 the share in 1969 and where W is a weighting factor for 1969 such that the United Kingdom = 1·00, the United States = 4·3/2·8 = 1·54, etc. The assumption is that the greater the share in agriculture the greater the scope for drawing on labour in that sector. The factor W therefore standardises for the differing proportions in agriculture.
Source: O.E.C.D., 'Labour Force Statistics', 1958–69.

Further, in the sending country, how is the 'labour surplus' defined? With respect to these economies per se it has to be defined in terms of the local labour market, rather than in terms of the numbers who might migrate abroad. These countries have themselves created a significant number of industrial jobs to which local workers have moved from agriculture. In fact, with the exception of Turkey, all sending countries have succeeded in creating more jobs than the growth in labour force (see Table 17.4).

A suggested framework

The evidence above suggests that an appropriate framework would need to take account both of the fact of latent labour supplies in the receiving countries and a significant labour demand in the sending countries. Analysis might then proceed in the context of

---

[1] This point is made more forcefully and comprehensively in the excellent study by L. Danieli (1971).

TABLE 17.4 GROWTH IN LABOUR FORCE AND NON-FARM EMPLOYMENT IN
THE SENDING COUNTRIES, 1958–1969

| | % Growth rates | | Absolutes (000) | |
	Labour force	Employment	Labour force	Employment
Greece	1·3	2·9	560	506
Italy	−0·4	1·1	−225	1629
Portugal	1·1	1·8	360	389
Spain	1·0	2·1	1362	1743
Turkey	1·2	3·8	1760	1276
Yugoslavia	1·0	3·5	627	1154
Total	—	—	6697	4444

Source: O.E.C.D., 'Labour Force Statistics', 1958–68.

these factors being insufficient in weight, other things considered, to offset the need for migration.

How could such a framework be annotated? One way would be to let labour price distortions serve as a reflection of disequilibrium labour markets. Thus, assume an equilibrium market is one in which the market wage (MW) equals both the supply price of labour (SP) from labour supplying to labour demanding sectors, and the social opportunity cost of labour (SOC). Inequalities between these variables can then be used to reflect imbalanced markets, as follows:

(i) *The receiving country* has a labour market characterised by excess demand for labour in industry, despite some potential supply in agriculture. The fact that this supply does not transfer to industry implies that it has a supply price (SP_r) higher than the market wage in industry (MW_r). Part of the reason for this may be institutional price support in agriculture which has arbitrarily maintained high incomes in this sector. To this extent there will have been a distortion between the social opportunity cost of labour (SOC_r) and the current wage in agriculture (AW_r) even if the latter reflects the marginal product in agriculture. Since the agricultural wage is observably less than the industrial wage, this implies the following set of inequalities in the receiving country:

$$SP_r > MW_r > AW_r > SOC_r \qquad (17.1)$$

from which $SP_r \gg SOC_r$, i.e. the supply price of domestic labour is much greater than its social opportunity cost.

(ii) *The sending country* has a labour market characterised by an excess supply of non-industrial labour, willing to work in industry for less than the going wage. Thus the supply price of labour in these countries (SP_s) is less than the market wage (MW_s). Assuming labour's marginal product in agriculture in these countries is less than the average income in agriculture (AW_s) then the social opportunity cost (SOC_s) will also be less, so that:

$$MW_s > SP_s > AW_s > SOC_s \qquad (17.2)$$

(iii)   At going exchange rates it is observable that market wages are higher in receiving countries, i.e. $MW_r > MW_s$. The relevant differential, however, is that between the market wage in the receiving country and the supply price of labour for foreign employment in the sending country. Assuming there are disutilities to migration this will be greater by some amount (d) than the supply price for local employment. The relevant inter-country differential is therefore:

$$MW_r > (SP_s + d)^1 \qquad (17.3)$$

Depending on the degree of excess demand for labour in the receiving country and the excess supply in the sending country, migration will at some point begin to reduce the inequality in (17.3) above, thus bringing a decline in the incentive for further migration. This could occur, as in the Lewis model, through an increase in the marginal product (and hence the wage and supply price) of labour in the sending country as surplus labour is drawn off.

This effect of the migration will serve to remove the distortions in the domestic labour market of the sending country. The rising marginal product of labour in agriculture moves the social opportunity cost of labour and labour's supply price towards the market wage.[2]

In the receiving country, on the other hand, domestic-labour price distortions tend to be perpetuated by the migration even though the supply of migrant labour may satisfy the excess demand for labour in industry. Depending on the dynamics of the production function, the migration may have a tendency to retard the growth of labour's marginal product in industry and hence in the industrial wage (MW_r).[3] Equally, by permitting industrial expansion without a transfer of labour out of agriculture the marginal product in agriculture remains unchanged. Since the supply price of domestic labour, institutionally determined, remains unaffected, the inequalities in (17.1) above are maintained.

[1] Depending on the degree of disutility in migration, ($SP_s + d$) may be higher or lower than the market wage in the sending country.

[2] Even if migrants in fact move from the industrial sector of the sending country, their places will be taken by internal migrants from agriculture, so the final adjustment is in the marginal product in agriculture.

[3] Thus perpetuating the distortion $MW_r < SP_r$.

Describing the migration in a setting such as this may serve not only to highlight the 'within' as well as the 'between' country distortions, and how these may be affected by the migration; it may also provide a useful framework in which to pose questions relating to the so-called costs and benefits of migration. A return is made to this subject in Section IV below.

'Pull' migration, not 'push-pull' migration

One important point about the dynamics of the European migration has to be emphasised. This is that within the context of the relative differentials and inequalities just described, the actual flow of migrants at any time depends essentially on labour demand in the receiving country, not at all on the pressure of excess labour supplies in the sending countries. This is determined institutionally by the fact that workers cannot legally migrate to the receiving country before having been recruited within the sending country by a receiving country employer.[1] Thus, excess supplies of labour for foreign jobs stack up on the waiting lists of recruiting offices in the sending country. This explains why there is not a disequilibrium over migration into the receiving countries possibly leading to rising unemployment, as occurs with the rural-urban drift in many developing countries. It also implies that 'push-pull' models of migration often applied in development economics cannot be applied to the situation in Europe without modification.[2]

III. ECONOMIC CONSEQUENCES

No paper of this sort could ever hope to give a full account of even the major economic consequences of the migration being discussed. Here the focus is on three major direct effects, namely labour supplies, incomes and remittances. In addition, a brief discussion is given on some of the indirect or external effects.

Labour supplies

The migration represents exogenous population growth in the receiving countries and corresponding declines in the sending countries. Since most migrants are workers this demographic shift has a direct effect on the relative labour supply-elasticities in each

---

[1] France provides some exception to this because some workers enter France as tourists and become 'regularised' migrant workers after having found employment.

[2] Since, in general, workers only migrate after having secured employment, theories of migration such as those developed by Harris and Todaro which hinge on an employment probability function, might also be inappropriate. See, for example, Harris and Todaro (1969, 1970).

country. The absolute numbers involved have already been discussed in the first part of the paper. Some idea of the impact of these flows on supply-elasticities in each country can be had from relating them to their respective growth in labour force. This is done in Table 17.5 below. What emerges is that the migration during the years in question served to double the growth rate in labour force in the receiving countries while reducing that in the sending countries almost to zero.

TABLE 17.5 RATES OF GROWTH IN THE LABOUR FORCE, 1958–1969 (PER CENT AVERAGE PER ANNUM)

	Before migration	After migration
Receiving countries[a]	0·2	0·4
Sending countries[b]	0·8	0·1

[a] France, Germany, the Netherlands, Switzerland, United Kingdom.
[b] Greece, Italy, Portugal, Spain, Turkey, Yugoslavia.
Source: O.E.C.D., 'Manpower Statistics, 1958–69' and 'Migrant Workers in Western Europe'; I.B.R.D., 1970.

It is not, of course, contended here that labour force increase is a final measure of changes in the elasticity of labour supply, only that it is an important component of the latter. Nor is it suggested that the reversal in relative growth elasticities was sufficient to bring each labour market into equilibrium. Zero growth in the labour force of the sending countries does not imply an elimination of labour surplus because of the backlog of underemployment. In Yugoslavia, the labour force actually declined in absolute terms over the intercensal period 1961–71, largely as a result of migration (see I.B.R.D. Economic Report, 1974, ch. III). However, labour surpluses persist in that country and migration abroad continues.

Equally, in the receiving countries, though migration boosted the supply of labour this was generally insufficient to meet the full extent of demand. Typical evidence of this is found in the German labour market where throughout the 1960s, despite the heavy employment of migrants, the number of unfilled vacancies far exceeded the numbers unemployed. From 1960–70 the number of unfilled vacancies averaged 566,000, i.e. about 4·5 per cent of the industrial labour force. With unemployment rates in Germany averaging less than 1 per cent in these years, this meant that there were about five unfilled vacancies for every registered work-seeker. Labour market disequilibria have thus persisted despite the migration.

Incomes

The employment of a migrant involves an increment in income for the migrant himself, for his employer and for both sending and receiving countries.[1] To measure the income gains to the employer and the receiving country is difficult without knowledge of the production function. This is also true of the sending country, though assessment of broad orders of magnitude are possible based on comparisons of internal wage data. For the migrant himself his income gain can be directly observed from wage data.

The following figures give some information on this. The data showing annual earnings are for 1966, converted at the 1966 official exchange rate:

TABLE 17.6 ANNUAL AVERAGE EARNINGS IN 1966

German industry (MW_r)	$2052
Yugoslav industry (MW_s)	$657
Yugoslav agriculture (AW_s)	$375[a]
Marginal production Yugoslav agriculture (SOC_s)	$169[b]

[a] Average product in Yugoslav agriculture.

[b] This is not an accurate estimate of the marginal product of labour in Yugoslav agriculture, but it represents the average income of a worker in the lowest income decile in this sector as revealed in the Yugoslav Household Budget Survey of 1968 (*Statisticki Bilten* no. 654, Federal Statistical Office, 1971). This surely gives a closer approximation to the marginal product than does the average income for the sector as a whole. It could, of course, be zero in some cases where departing workers are either fully unemployed (very rare in Yugoslavia) or where their erstwhile productive task is fully taken up by someone else (possibly quite common).

Source: Statistical Yearbooks, F.R. Germany and S.F.R. Yugoslavia.

These figures show that even if the migrant is employed in Yugoslav industry he will have enjoyed about a threefold gain in money income, at the official conversion, by moving to a job in German industry. Migrants leaving Yugoslav agriculture will have gained a fivefold increase. These magnitudes, even if they tend for various reasons to overstate the real differentials, nevertheless give a clear indication of the private gains to be had from migration. (Social gains are dealt with in Section IV below.)

[1] Strictly, the sending country gains income only under certain circumstances. These surely apply in the case discussed (see Berry and Soligo, 1970). The authors discuss *inter alia* the theoretical conditions for a country sending labour to enjoy a direct income gain. Generally, the sending country suffers a loss of average income. However, their model treats a full employment economy. In a labour surplus economy the more general result will be for the migration to raise the average income of those remaining behind because the departing migrants if underemployed release a claim on consumption greater than their marginal foregone output. Remittances can be added to this.

Remittances

The funds remitted by the migrants to their home countries, having grown to substantial magnitudes in recent years, are of major economic importance. In the period 1960–70 total remittances from Germany, France and Switzerland alone were about $13 billion. By 1972 annual remittance flows from these countries were around $2·3 billion. These payments, best viewed as factor payments rather than investment capital, serve to raise incomes in the recipient countries. In addition, since they are in hard currencies, the remittances contribute to the foreign exchange holdings of these countries allowing the purchase of imports needed to fuel economic growth. In both Turkey and Yugoslavia remittances now constitute the major single source of foreign exchange. Of course, the remittances also affect the balance of payments of the countries from which they are sent, having the effect of an invisible import payable in domestic currency.

Not much is known about the behaviour of remittances. This is important, not just intellectually but because those countries relying on remittances as a source of foreign exchange have no certainty that their future balance of payments might not be threatened if remittance flows turn out to be unstable.

Components of remittance flows

The flow of remittances can be formally described by the identity $R = M \cdot r$, where R is the total volume of remittances, M the number of migrants remitting and r the remittance per man. Table 17.7 below shows a decomposition of remittances from Germany to Yugoslavia into these components. It shows that the growth in remittances in the years studied has been due both to growth in migration and in changes in remittances per migrant, though the latter have been less than the former.

For given behaviour in the total number of migrants abroad, the analysis of remittances becomes an analysis of the behaviour of the remittance per man r. Examined in a behavioural sense, however, rather than as the residual in an identity, the r value is a complex variable whose main determinants have not yet been specified. Conceptually, r may be viewed as the outcome of the propensity to remit a given proportion (π) of a given wage (MW_r) such that $r = \pi \cdot MW_r$. Thus r may change either because of changes in π, i.e. in the propensity to remit, or because of wage increases. Table 17.7 shows that changes in r have been due to changes in both of these variables, though less in π than in MW_r.

What causes changes in the propensity to remit? Very few attempts have been made to answer this question. While some preliminary attempts have been made to specify a set of theoretical relationships which may provide an explanation for changes in π, these have not yet been tested against the facts (see I.B.R.D., 1974; Miller and Cetin, 1972). The basic assumption underlying these attempts has been that migrants find employment abroad specifically for a

TABLE 17.7 COMPOSITION OF REMITTANCES FROM GERMANY TO YUGOSLAVIA, 1963–1972

Annual average	(R) $(DM\,\mathrm{m.})$	(M) (000)	(r) $(DM/\mathrm{migrant})$	$(\pi)^a$	MW_r (DM/year)
I 1963–6	95·8	64·6	1·483	20·1	7342
II 1966–9	251·4	130·0	1·934	22·3	8689
III 1969–72	1216·3	380·1	3·200	26·7	11985
Growth					
II : I	2·62	2·01	1·30	1·11	1·18
III : II	4·84	2·92	1·65	1·20	1·38

[a] Remittance per man as percentage of average earnings.
Source: Remittances: National Bank of Yugoslavia.
Earnings: Statistical Yearbook of F.R. Germany.
Migrants: Bundesanstalt fur Arbeit, Nuremberg.

purpose of asset accumulation, generally for subsequent reinvestment in the home country. Remittance payments are seen as a drain on this accumulation, occasioned by obligations (the subsistence of family and dependants) in the migrant's home country.

In this situation, it is not immediately clear which variables should enter the specified equation, nor in some cases, what the specified sign of the variables should be. Does a migrant decide upon a given absolute payment to remit home or some proportion of his wage? What is his response to a wage increase – more savings, or more remittances, or some of each? Is the remittance payment responsive to money or real wage increases in the employing country? What is the migrant's response to a change in the exchange rate which devalues his home currency with respect to that of the employing country? For any individual migrant, does the propensity to remit tend to decline the longer he is employed abroad? Questions such as these are still outstanding in pursuit of some knowledge of the factors influencing the propensity to remit.

Some external effects

Of the many indirect effects, both economic and otherwise, which the migration has had, brief mention here will be made of only four. This is not intended necessarily to claim their pre-eminence, though they are issues frequently raised in discussions about the migration. They are, respectively, the demographic effects of the migration, the inflation issue, the question of technology and innovation and the issue of social overheads.

Demographic effects

While the age/sex selectivity of the migration has been well documented[1] there has been less work on its final demographic implications for either the sending or receiving countries. As yet unpublished results of work in progress in Yugoslavia[2] have shown significant correlations between outmigration from the regions of Croatia and declines in fertility rates. Since some of these regions are experiencing depopulation, these declines are of importance to their economic future.

A second issue, also clearly visible in the data on Yugoslavia (I.B.R.D., 1974), is that the migration has significantly raised the dependency ratios of the population remaining in Yugoslavia. This is particularly marked in the less-developed regions of the country. In principle this implies that the migration increases the burden on the productive workers remaining behind. However, so long as the net income effects of migration (either or both through remittances and the reduction of underemployment) are positive, this burden may not be a real one.

The inflation issue

It has been argued both that the migration has restrained inflation in the receiving countries and the reverse. The first argument (Kindleberger, 1967) holds that migrants provide added elasticity to the labour supply thus, all else equal, restraining wage increases and cost inflation. A second argument is that the employment of migrants contributed to demand inflation through the need to channel resources out of productive uses into the provision of social overheads for the migrants.[3] In view of the leakages caused by the migrants' high propensity to save and to remit funds home, demand inflation on the face of it seems implausible.

Further, the presence of a migrant labour pool has meant that the margin of the labour supply schedule to the receiving country lies

[1] See Livi-Bacci and Hagmann, 1971; Hume, 1970; and Baucic, 1970. Baucic has completed a similar work on Yugoslav migrants in France.

[2] In the Republic Institute of Statistics, Croatia.

[3] I have not seen a written account of this argument with reference to the European migration in question, but I have heard the argument raised by officials in Europe. For a general discussion of this argument see Lerner (1958).

beyond its own borders. This considerably eases the social problems – *à la* Phillips Curve approach – of combatting inflation by demand deflation. The down side of the Phillips Curve shows up not as rising domestic unemployment but as a decline in recruitment of foreign workers.

It is sometimes argued that remittances are inflationary in the countries receiving them. The argument here is that the remittance represents an injection of purchasing power for which there is no 'real' counterpart of goods, hence creating an inflation gap. In a smoothly (and rapidly) adjusting economy this situation will not result in price increases since the foreign exchange provided by the remittances can be used to buy imports to fill the gap. In practice, however, leads and lags in the system may leave room for some inflation to result during the adjustment process. This may be more marked where remittances are spent on non-tradeables, e.g. personal services.

Technological innovation

It is argued[1] that in the receiving countries the enhanced elasticity of labour supply allowed by the availability of migrant labour has the effect of retarding the development and adoption of labour-saving techniques. This is held to carry a social cost to the extent that it perpetuates low productivity uses of the scarce domestic factor, labour.

This hypothesis is not easily tested. In principle, evidence in support of this view would show up as relative declines in the pace of capital deepening during periods of high migration, coupled with relative declines in the growth of labour productivity. The evidence in Table 17.8 is ambiguous. It shows, in favour of the hypothesis, that productivity has grown less rapidly during the 1960s when migration was strongest. However, against this, capital deepening has been much more rapid in this than in the earlier decade.

It seems *a priori* to be reasonable that if simply no migrants were available then the pressure to innovate (or invest abroad?) would have been greater. However, there is an economic limit to the pace of capital deepening. Also, if the migration lessened, it probably did not completely eliminate the pressure to innovate – there has been a persistent excess demand for labour even with the migration. The question is, therefore, whether or not this residual pressure was sufficient or insufficient to press the pace of innovation

---

[1] For example, in Kade and Schiller (1972). This article contains useful references to some of the German literature on the migration issue.

TABLE 17.8 ANNUAL PERCENTAGE GROWTH RATES
IN CAPITAL, OUTPUT AND LABOUR COEFFICIENTS
IN THE GERMAN ECONOMY, 1952–1970

	Capital: Output	Capital: Labour	Labour Productivity
1952–60	−2·1	3·4	5·4
1960–65	1·2	5·8	4·4
1965–70	1·1	5·5	4·5

Source: 'Das Reproduzierbare Anlagevermongen in Preisen von 1962',
Wirtschaft und Statistick, Oct 1971.

to its limit. A difficult question indeed to measure against the facts.

The social overheads

It is clear that the use of foreign labour incurs costs for the receiving country which the use of domestic labour (were it available) would not do. The direct costs of transporting the migrants, of language training, special community centres, etc., would all feature in these costs. There is no point in detailing them here. From the point of view of economic evaluation the central question to be examined here is not what the *absolute* extent of the costs are but what the difference is between these amounts and what would have been necessary had some other solution to the labour shortage been found. The issue of overheads is seldom posed within the framework of this proposition.

IV. THE COSTS AND BENEFITS OF MIGRANT LABOUR

All discussions of the migration issue, not least of all at the current level of policy-making in European capitals, inevitably lead to questions of the ultimate costs and benefits, to all parties involved, of this practice of employment migration. The issues here are enormous. They are in fact essentially unsolvable because time horizons, personal and social objective functions, and social prices cannot really be stipulated. These issues are not gone into here.

In this last section of the paper a simple attempt is made to suggest a way of approaching the question of the assessment of costs and benefits to the sending and to the receiving countries respectively. Discussion of the private benefits (i.e. to the migrant and to the employer) is left to one side since these are generally assumed to be positive so long as migration continues without state intervention.

The approach taken is the following in each country. The costs and the benefits are each viewed as being comprised of (i) 'direct' components (*D*), i.e. those related to its most immediate effects and for which observable data are generally readily available and (ii) the 'external' effects (*E*) which are all the other consequences, some of which were discussed above. These are necessarily difficult to quantify. Adding the net direct benefits (i.e. direct benefits – direct costs) to the net external benefits (which may of course be negative) will give the total net benefits. Whether this benefit is socially optimal will depend on whether it is greater or less than the yield that could have been obtained in the next best use of all the resources required in the use of migrant labour. Thus, assuming *D* is a declining function of migration, and $-E$ a rising function then, for a given time *t* and number of migrants *n*, optimality is given by:

$$\sum_{t=0}^{n} \frac{D+E_t}{(1+a)} = 0 \tag{17.4}$$

The sending country

In the sending country the 'direct' components resulting from the migration of one worker can be thought of as (i) the remittance he sends home (i.e. $\pi.MW_r$), (ii) the income increment due to the reduction of underemployment in the sending country (y),[1] and (iii) his output foregone (SOC_s). The first two components (i) and (ii) are benefits, (iii) is a cost. These terms can be entered into the denominator of equation (17.4) above, which, to simplify, can be expressed in static rather than dynamic form. In this way, the statement of optimal sending country benefits, taking account of both direct effects and externalities, would be:

$$(\pi.MW_r + y) - SOC_s + E_s = 0 \tag{17.5}$$

Assuming net externalities are negative[2] this transforms to:

$$E_s = \pi.MW_r + AW_s - 2SOC_s \tag{17.6}$$

From income data for Yugoslavia and from remittance data from Germany to Yugoslavia, as discussed in earlier paragraphs, it is possible to give a magnitude to E_s in this equation. From page 500 above $SOC_s = \$169$ and $AW_s = \$375$ in 1966. Assuming an average value for π of 22·7 per cent and an average wage (MW_r) of \$2443

---

[1] As described in note 1 on page 500 above. As an approximation *y* can be thought of as the difference between the average income and marginal product in agriculture (i.e. $AW_s - SOC_s$).

[2] The case where they are positive makes the argument redundant.

in the period 1963–71 this gives a remittance value of \$555. Thus, from the equation, migration could still have been beneficial to the sending country under these conditions even had external costs for migrants approached \$592 per migrant year, a seemingly large sum.

The receiving country

Working on a similar basis in the receiving country, the key variables here seem to be the following. The 'direct' gain is the value added by the employment of the migrant, some portion (p) of which accrues to the employer, the remainder being the migrant's wage (MW_r). Some portion (π) of the migrant's wage is remitted home so $\pi . MW_r$ is a cost to the receiving country. Also, some portion (c) is consumed, so that cMW_r may also be seen as a cost. Adding externalities gives the following relationship:

$$p + MW_r - (\pi . MW_r + c . MW_r) + E_r = 0 \qquad (17.7)$$

which, under the assumption of negative net externalities, transforms to

$$E_r = p + MW_r - MW_r(\pi + c) \qquad (17.8)$$

Again, observed magnitudes can be applied, except that there are no direct data for p. Assume p is negligible. In this case if $\pi = 0.22$ and $c = 0.40$[1] then E_r has a value equal to 34 per cent of the market wage, i.e. \$831 per migrant in 1966 prices. Giving a positive value to p will have raised the margin of tolerable externalities even beyond this figure.

It is interesting to note that the use of migrant labour incurs no output foregone in the receiving country (this is incurred as SOC_s in the sending country). In terms of this principle, therefore, migrant labour has a zero opportunity cost to the receiving country. The use of labour from domestic agriculture, on the other hand, may incur some output loss. In the case when domestic labour is considered as an alternative to migrant labour the key questions are:

(i) Is the domestic output foregone (SOC_r) greater than the consumption and remittance costs of the migrant (i.e. $MW_r(\pi + c)$)? If consumption patterns can be assumed equal (migrants probably save more) then the question reduces to one of a comparison between the migrants' remittance and the local output foregone, i.e. migrants are cheaper if $\pi . MW_r < SOC_r$. Given working values of π around 0.20 the question to be answered is whether domestic

[1] As suggested by Yugoslav and German survey data.

output foregone would be as low as or less than 20 per cent of the market wage.[1]

(ii) How much greater are the negative externalities involved in the use of migrants?

V. SUMMARY AND CONCLUSIONS

These various manipulations are not intended to provide concrete proof of the benefits of past migration. Their purpose is rather to suggest a method of approach. However, the actual evidence for the relative levels of wages, remittances, etc., described in the earlier discussion of the economic framework, do suggest, when applied to the cost-benefits equations, that the net social benefits may have been substantial to both sets of countries. At least, this seems so in the case of data for Yugoslav migration to Germany. Of course, there has been no attempt in this paper to try and quantify the externalities nor to establish whether these have on balance been positive or negative.

The intention has simply been to show, at a time when much popular discussion about the migration seems to suggest that it incurs negative externalities for each country involved, what order of magnitude such external costs might have to reach before the social benefits to each country are eliminated. I leave to other economists the task of deciding whether the actual totality of net externalities falls short of or exceeds the limits suggested by this paper. As a final caveat, the observation has to be made that from the point of view of actual policy action to regulate migration flows much of this discussion may be academic if, as has already happened in some countries, purely political considerations serve to intervene as a barrier to further migration.

---

[1] I have no estimate of the social marginal product of agricultural labour in Germany. Average earnings in agriculture range in the region of 70 per cent of industrial earnings. This gives no real measure of the SOC_r, however, both because these earnings reflect institutional pricing in the sector and because there is no indication of how marginal labour reductions relate to average product.

REFERENCES

I. Baucic, *The Origin and Structure of Yugoslav Workers in Germany*, Institute of Geography (Univ. of Zagreb, 1970).

R. A. Berry and R. Soligo, 'Some Welfare Aspects of International Migration', *Journal of Political Economy* (Mar 1970).

L. Danieli, 'Labour Scarcities and Labour Redundancies in Europe by 1980: An Experimental Study', Departimento Statistico Matematico (Firenze, 1971).

R. Harris and M. Todaro, 'A Model of Labour Migration and Urban Unemployment in Less Developed Countries', *American Economic Review*, vol. LIX, no. 1 (Mar 1969).

——, 'Migration, Unemployment and Development: A Two Sector Analysis', *American Economic Review*, vol. LX, no. 1 (Mar 1970).

I. M. Hume, 'Migrant Workers in Western Europe', I.B.R.D. working paper no. 102 (Washington, D.C., Oct 1970).

I.B.R.D. Economic Report, *The Economic Development of Yugoslavia* (Johns Hopkins Press, Jan 1974).

G. Kade and G. Schiller, 'Foreign Workers – Development Aid by LDCs?', *Inter-economics*, no. 1, Verlag Weltarchiv GMBH, Hamburg (Jan 1972).

C. Kindleberger, *Europe's Postwar Growth*, Harvard Univ. Press, 1967.

A. P. Lerner, 'Immigration, Capital Formation and Inflationary Pressure', *Economics of International Migration*, ed. B. Thomas, I.E.A. conference proceedings (London, 1958).

M. Livi-Bacci and H. M. Hagmann, 'The Demographic and Social Pattern of Migrants in Europe, Especially with Regard to International Migrations', *Second European Population Conference*, Council of Europe, Strasburg (Sep 1971).

D. Miller and I. Cetin, 'The International Demand for Brawn Power and the Wealth Effect of Migration – A Turkish Case Study', mimeo, paper presented to the Middle East Studies Association Annual Meeting, State University of New York, Binghamton (Nov 1972).

Discussion of the Paper by Dr Hume

Professor Hague introduced the paper, saying there seemed to be at least three kinds of migration. What he would call Case 1 was permanent, or long-term migration, as with Irish or West Indians immigrating to the United Kingdom. Case 2, or the Amin case, was forced emigration. In Case 3 a migrant worker spent, say, two or three years abroad; perhaps Dr Hume could give the average stay in Case 3, and the range.

Dr Hume's paper studied Case 3 migration to Western Europe from Mediterranean lands, including Portugal and Yugoslavia, whose main period was the middle to late 1960s. The paper first presented the statistical evidence, pointing to problems of classification and recording. Table 17.1 identified some eight million Class 3 migrants in Dr Hume's countries; ten million if one included dependants. On average, for countries in Table 17.1 migrants represented about 10 per cent of the labour force in the receiving country and 15 per cent in the sender. There was considerable variation, from 7 per cent in Germany to 28 per cent in Switzerland. The pattern of Case 3 migration had recently altered, with Germany, not France, now the main receiver, and the main senders Turkey and Yugoslavia.

This part of the paper was factual, although participants were free to disagree with it if they believed that they had better, or different, facts. He would not disagree, but would like clarification about Switzerland. The proportion of 28 per cent seemed high. Were many migrants employed in seasonal work in hotels, going back to neighbouring countries when the 'season' ended? If so, was the 28 per cent 'in' or 'out of' season?

The paper saw Case 3 migration as mainly the result of economic factors, and Professor Hague agreed. Demographic factors might explain the low wages which caused emigration, but the motive force was economic – to escape them. We should make such links between economic, social and demographic analyses. Dr Hume saw economic disequilibrium as causing Case 3 migration, and perhaps it was the most important factor. But sociologists might legitimately be more interested in who emigrated and why; how the 'grapevine' told them about employment possibilities abroad; whether the more entrepreneurial migrated; where they went; whether they had difficulties of assimilation in the new country? And so on.

It had been suggested earlier in the conference that not all migrants from country to town found satisfactory employment. What about European migrant workers? Was their situation better because they were sought for specific purposes by specific employers? Of course, because receiving countries were prepared to cut off the supply of jobs if unemployment increased, there was never an excess supply of Case 3 migrants.

This left open what was the economic process. Dr Hume explained that in receiving countries capital was abundant relative to labour, but capital deepening was 'not without limit'. Could he be more precise? For sending countries, their capital was scarce relative to labour, but there were large labour reserves in agriculture. There were also large labour reserves in European agriculture which did not move to industry because of the common agricultural policy; continental Europe was not reducing its agricultural labour force as rapidly as the U.K. or the U.S.A., despite having a much higher percentage of population in agriculture. Only Turkey among Dr Hume's sending countries had been creating a smaller absolute number of jobs than the absolute increase in its labour force. Yet, while one could criticise European agricultural policy, it might benefit the underdeveloped world more for Europe to take in Class 3 migrants rather than move its labour from agriculture to industry. European countries would pay to keep their own nationals in agriculture, but might not contribute a similar amount in foreign aid to countries like Yugoslavia and Turkey, if the common agricultural policy were abolished.

Dr Hume went on to look at a disequilibrium model, using the wage rate and the supply price of labour in both the receiving and sending country, and the social opportunity cost in each. This was rather unsatisfying and Professor Hague preferred Dr Hume's later, more complex, cost-benefit model. One could see the value of explaining the flow of migrants by differences in wage rates and supply prices of labour, but to use social-opportunity cost imported a cost-benefit element which needed spelling out, as the later model did.

Essentially, the Case 3 migrant wanted to raise his family's standard of living and/or stock of savings. Professor Hague would call this stock of savings a 'nest egg'. An interesting conclusion was that the migrant had a wider choice than whether to consume or save his income. He had to choose how much income to remit to his dependants to cover support costs, as well as the size and location of the nest egg. Professor Hague did not think Dr Hume had thought enough about the location, as distinct from size, of the nest egg.

Participants had already doubted the ability of parents in underdeveloped countries to choose the size of family. Was it more or less realistic to see them choosing where to hold their growing nest eggs? In recent years, a profit-maximising migrant would have remitted the minimum amount from Germany and the maximum from the U.K., even if not to his country of origin. For example, a migrant to the U.K. would have been well advised to transfer his nest egg to Germany, unless his country of origin had a steadily appreciating currency. The recent rate of appreciation of the deutschmark meant that if we believed that consumption was significantly dependent on the rate of appreciation, the migrant should have reduced his consumption in Germany to build up a nest egg which could appreciate with the deutschmark, and the opposite in the U.K. In theory, the rate of currency appreciation, interest and inflation in the receiving and sending countries also came in and indeed in other countries to which funds could be sent. We then saw how complex the model needed to be.

Finally, Dr Hume gave his results. Migration seemed to double the rate of growth of the labour force in his receiving countries; in his sending countries, it reduced it almost to zero. Four parties benefited from migration; the migrant, the employer, the sending country, and the receiving country. Only the gains to the migrant were at all easy to measure. Professor Hague would have liked a more comprehensive comparison, but Dr Hume did show that emigration might give Yugoslav agricultural workers as much as a fivefold increase in income, and industrial workers as much as a threefold one. One problem was that exchange rates rarely reflected differences in standards of living, and most were floating at present. One should beware of remarks such as: 'These magnitudes, even if they tend for various reasons to overstate the real differentials, nevertheless give a clear indication of the private gains to be had from migration.' While this was probably true for Yugoslavia, it was not acceptable as a general statement. If one did not know the size of a difference in the purchasing power of two currencies, one could not argue that even a 100 per cent or 200 per cent difference in wages would cancel it out. This was true, even though, for Yugoslavia, one felt that a difference of 400 per cent was big enough. Professor Hague suggested that a rough measure of real income was the length of time a worker had to work to buy a basket of commodities and services. As Professor Rasmussen had said in a mealtime discussion during the conference, the labour theory of value must be at least 90 per cent right. This simply showed how badly, with floating exchange rates, we needed a new Gilbert-Kravis comparison of standards of living in different countries. Certainly, any precise study of the issues that Dr Hume raised needed it.

Professor Hague argued that if the main aim of the Case 3 migrant was to accumulate a nest egg, then remittances were the important variable. Unfortunately, as Dr Hume said, we did not know what determined their size, though the paper showed that, for Germany, about a quarter of the migrant's income was remitted.

This was a clear benefit to sending countries; remittances were now the main source of foreign exchange for Turkey and Yugoslavia. But it was a precarious benefit, although it would be some time before the total number of migrants fell far enough to have a serious effect on their balance of payments. For the receiving country, what happened would depend on the number of immigrants as well as their remittance pattern. With a constant immigrant labour force, and an unchanged remittance pattern, the aggregate nest egg and support payments would be constant, unless immigrants left funds to benefit from a revaluation of the receiving country's currency, or sent them out to avoid a devaluation. If immigration increased, remittances were likely to increase in proportion, but so would nest eggs left in the receiving country.

Professor Hague would have made three changes in Dr Hume's determinants of the propensity to remit. The first would have been to distinguish the nest-egg effect more clearly from the support effect. Second, he would suggest that a major determinant of the size of the support effect was the number of dependants, and especially where they were located. That would determine the standard of living they wanted and its cost. Third, the expected changes in the exchange rates would, in principle, influence any decision aimed at maximising the local currency value of the nest egg minus support payments. These were more hypotheses to test, but he hoped someone would test them.

Professor Hague said that, in introducing the discussion, he would skip the sections on the demographic and inflationary effects of Case 3 migration, but he did want to say something about the effect of migration on technical innovation.

Dr Hume's hypothesis here was that where migrant labour was available, this might hold back labour-saving innovations in the receiving country. While explaining that the hypothesis was not easily testable, Dr Hume cited evidence that labour productivity had grown more slowly in the 1960s when migration was greater, though capital deepening was also greater. This worried economists in the United Kingdom. Professor Hague argued that only if the United Kingdom rate of growth of GNP slightly exceeded that of productive potential were British businessmen sufficiently willing to instal labour-saving equipment. With more migrant labour, the reaction might well be to continue gratefully to invest in assets that saved too little labour. Every time the British economy approached full employment, labour scarcity led the government to slow down growth. In countries like the United Kingdom an increase in migration might simply delay the necessary introduction of more labour-saving plant. Technological change seemed to be the only significant benefit which migrants gave receiving countries.

Dr Hume pointed to the enormous problems of carrying out such an analysis, but suggested how it might be done. Professor Hague did not want to go into these issues, though others might wish to do so, but did want to explore the relationship of all this to the notion of national income. Suppose a migrant moved from Yugoslavia to Germany, and increased output in Germany. He consumed much of this output on the spot, and most of the rest went ultimately to the sending country. There seemed to be two major benefits to Germany. First, if the nest eggs were kept in Germany, a large number of migrants with even a modest nest egg per man could make a useful contribution to savings in Germany. Second, Germany would benefit to the extent that the migrant consumption expenditure went into profits. This suggested some interesting Marxian conclusions.

What seemed to be important for the receiving country was, first, the number of dependants of migrants and where they were located. This determined whether they would spend, save or remit, and the social costs that the receiving country would have to incur in providing housing, education, etc.

To sum up: the biggest benefits seemed to be, first, where the migrants' dependants stayed in the sending country, but where the aggregate of nest eggs in the receiving country was large and both consumption in the receiving country and remittances small. Migrants could then contribute significantly to savings in the receiving country. Second, if the side effects of migration, especially on technical change, were significant; and, third, if migrants' spending went to profits rather than wages, and so (presumably) increased savings.

None of this contradicted anything that Dr Hume had said, but Professor Hague hoped it took the argument a little further. Moreover, this did seem to throw light on the significance of the nation. If one's aim was to raise the real incomes of the initial population of the receiving country, the benefits from migration might be much smaller than one might suppose.

Dr Hume said he had no quarrel with the introduction, but did want to make it clear that, where he had looked at the direct and indirect effects of migration, he had not really measured the magnitude of externalities, but only their possible upper limits. We were not in a position even to list all the factors qualitatively. The point about separating direct from external effects was precisely that only direct effects were even vaguely capable of tangible measurement. By applying such data as we had for direct effects, we could get an idea of the net direct benefits from migration. This magnitude provided the limit of the extent to which net externalities could be negative without leading to an overall net loss from that migration.

Professor Giersch was very interested in this problem, coming as he did from one of the main recipient countries. He saw European migration as a move from the periphery to the centre. The growth of the Common Market had strengthened the locational advantage of Central Europe, so that there was now excess demand in the centre, but declining regional productivity and increasing unemployment towards the periphery. A possible explanation for the insufficient flow of capital towards the periphery was that real wages declined less than productivity as one moved from the centre.

In the 1950s, most immigrants to West Germany had come from Eastern Germany, and later from Southern Europe. The effect had probably been positive in the short run but would be negative in the long run, especially as far as labour productivity was concerned. In Western Germany the labour supply had become rather elastic, so that labour productivity had increased less than one might expect from looking at the share of investment in GNP. Without migration, GNP would have grown outside Germany rather than inside. Labour migration at the beginning of the 1960s had alleviated labour shortages, with immediate benefits for labour productivity and national growth in Germany. In the long run, migration might well slow innovation.

On the point made by Professor Hague, he felt that German entrepreneurs were probably different from those in the United Kingdom. In Germany, structural change had been delayed, and while he thought this had been beneficial in the short run, he was not so sure about the long run.

Immigration had also relieved wage pressure in Germany, thus reducing cost inflation and allowing the undervaluation of the deutschmark to persist. In consequence, between the revaluations of the deutschmark in 1961 and 1969, the marginal efficiency of capital in Germany had been artificially high, thus preventing the outflow of investment which would otherwise have occurred. The undervaluation of the deutschmark provided both a subsidy for exports and a tariff on imports. As a result, weak industries in Western Germany, including agriculture, were protected and prevented from shrinking. Professor Giersch said that this agreed with the points made by Dr Hume.

Manufacturing industry, he suggested, had gained most from the effects of immigration. This was supported by several pieces of evidence. For example, West Germany had a much higher proportion of manufacturing than one would have expected from cross-sectional analysis. The Rhine locations, especially, would have had much less attraction if there had been no immigration. The proportion of immigrants was highest in manufacturing, with hardly any in the tertiary sector except for a few employed in hotels. Among branches of industry with low requirements for human capital, one would have expected Germany to be at a disadvantage compared with less-developed countries. These types of industry would have been squeezed out under the influence of competition, had it not been for immigration and the related undervaluation of the deutschmark. In brief, Germany would have imported more labour-intensive products; instead, she had imported labour.

Professor Giersch noted that if we extrapolated present trends, the share of immigrants in the labour force would total 17 per cent in 1980, as against 11 per cent in 1972. This, if it was true, was low compared with Switzerland in 1970, but there were several other factors to consider. First, the level of qualification of immigrants was declining. Second, they were increasingly wanting to bring their families with them to settle in Germany, which would inevitably increase the burden on the infrastructure. Third, the average figure concealed the concentration of immigrants in urban agglomerations. There was a social risk that these concentrations of immigrants could not be integrated into the local population. Fourth, immigration had made the labour force in Germany much more mobile, so that there had been less compulsion for German industry to move to country districts where there were pockets of immobile labour; so this dis-equilibrium had been maintained. Fifth, immigrants tended to demand, or accept, low standards of housing which in Germany were no longer tolerable. Sixth, immigrants had recently been involved in a series of wildcat strikes, which had previously been quite unusual in Germany.

Professor Giersch concluded with a policy suggestion: to promote capital investment in the peripheral regions of Europe.

M. Leridon made one or two suggestions for extending work on migration. How did such movements take place? How often did migrants return home? Did we know how long they stayed in the host country? It seemed to him that there was little information available on such questions, but they were important for the policies of both receiving and sending countries. He referred to Puerto Rico, an example of a culture that had for many years experienced the positive effect of migration to the U.S.A. These positive effects (the return of skilled workers) could be important where a country was in process of economic development. Southern Europe constituted another area where technical progress was important for development.

The transfer of earnings was an important aspect of migration. M. Leridon said it was important to find out what happened to remittances. To what sector did they go? Were they used productively? Remittances from France to Black Africa often remained unproductive, and were therefore of little use to the sending country.

Professor Khachaturov understood that there had been little attempt to quantify the costs and benefits of migration, but was it not possible to classify the positive and negative effects? For the sending countries, there would be a decrease in unemployment, and a fall in productivity, or even production. For the receiving countries, there would be an increase in production and a fall in wage levels. Even if we had no figures, such a classification would be useful.

Professor Ben Porath followed up the point about the cost and benefits of migration and said he did not agree with Professor Hague. He preferred to think in terms of the old-fashioned theory of trade, using Mill rather than Hume. The basic point was that there were gains from trade when factors were traded. If imported labour was paid its marginal product, this was because it paid the employer to do so, and, under reasonable assumptions, there were gains to the country that received migrants as well as to the migrants themselves. A fairly simple analysis was to be found in a recent paper by Berry and Soligo in the *Journal of Political Economy*. He was a bit puzzled about the complaint about the effect of migration on labour-saving technical change. Labour saving was not an end in itself.

Professor Ohlin made a similar point about not forgetting fundamental economic analysis. It seemed odd that when a migrant worker moved across an international frontier, it was supposed to be an entirely different matter from internal migration. He found this hard to swallow, and was reminded of the difficulty of defining national gains and losses when there was any factor movement, whether of capital or labour. There was a simple theoretical explanation in the textbooks; in the absence of a policy to deal with them, we could expect excessive factor movements. In other words, countries were not using their excessive monopoly and monopsony power, since otherwise policy based on national interest could easily restrain immigration and emigration.

Professor Ohlin felt that it was too easy to evolve *ad hoc* and casual ideas in the field and one could, in fact, turn round the argument that had been presented. One might suggest that in the short run immigration acted as a considerable brake on the process of capital substitution, but that in the long run it would make for expansion of the economy. The hypotheses were equally *ad hoc* and thus equally plausible. The fact that we did not know showed that the step from economic theory to policy was particularly great in this field.

Mr Lengyel referred to Professor Giersch's point about inward migration providing an alternative to capital investment in the peripheral regions. When the skill of a labour force was falling, and the residual pool of labour becoming less qualified, these regions were even less attractive to capital investment. This seemed to be the typical situation when a pool of labour was creamed off, as illustrated by the Irish example in the nineteenth century. The urban/rural problem was of a similar nature. Mr Lengyel wanted to know if there were any answers to this problem.

Mr Boulier questioned the size and nature of these skills. He cited the case of Yugoslav workers who moved into the French construction industry and learned no skills which they could not have acquired at home. Had we a measure of the skills acquired and how important they were later on?

Dr Hume replied to the discussion. Data on returning immigrants was very flimsy, but some work had been done in Germany on Turkish and Yugoslav immigrants. An attempt had been made to find the percentage of Yugoslavs in Germany who were engaged in extracurricular learning, and this proved to be as low as 5 per cent. However, the measures used did not take account of informal learning, and therefore understated the position. He felt he had to agree with the conventional wisdom, which was that learning was minimal. Most workers seemed to return to a different job at home from the one they had held as migrants.

In answer to the questions of Professor Hague and M. Leridon on the length of stay of migrants, Dr Hume said that work had been done in 1970 on Yugoslavs in Germany, which showed an average stay of three years. The data was not very good, particularly since this type of migration had only really gathered momentum in 1955–6.

The figure of 28 per cent for the proportion of the Swiss labour force that was immigrant was much higher than the percentage of the Swiss population that was foreign. Seasonal migration in Switzerland represented only 10 to 12 per cent of total immigrants.

As for the location and size of the 'nest eggs', there was again some data on Yugoslavs in Germany. Sample surveys had shown that about 20 per cent of the average wage was remitted, and 30 to 40 per cent consumed in West Germany. The balance (i.e. 40–50 per cent) was saved. The total accumulated was therefore substantial, bearing in mind that the total number of migrants in Germany was four to five millions.

Dr Hume explained that his concern with migration reflected that of the World Bank, which was interested in the size of migrant remittances and their possible effects on the balance of payments of several countries. Remittances might be a stable function of some variable, as indeed studies seemed to indicate. But what would happen if migration went down towards the end of the decade? When would the long-term migrants take their nest eggs back home? To the extent that return migration was accompanied by a repatriation of these savings, the foreign exchange receipts of labour-sending might increase in the 1970s.

On the determinants of the propensity to remit, Dr Hume said very little work had been done. He pointed out that, for Yugoslavia and Turkey, the successive devaluations of their currencies relative to the deutschmark had caused sharp increases in the flow of remittances. Indeed, the Turkish authorities had instituted a preferential exchange rate for remitters. This indicated the importance of such flows, and of the rational choice-behaviour of remitters.

Dr Hume replied to the argument that the pressure for capital deepening in receiving countries would have been greater had there been no migration. Even with migration, there was still excess demand for labour in Germany, as evidenced by unfilled vacancies of some 600,000 per year, with almost no unemployment. This was enough in itself to put pressure on employers to pursue labour-saving technical innovation.

Dr Hume's next point was that his paper had focused primarily on the economic aspects of migration. He could not really comment on the point about wildcat strikes, but thought that political factors might well be overriding and would eventually stop migration.

In response to Professor Khachaturov, Dr Hume said that the classification of direct and indirect costs and benefits of migration had been done quite well some time ago by Peter Scott. That paper, however, did not attempt a synthetic treatment of all the points, whereas he himself had tried to bring them all together in one calculation.

Finally, Dr Hume replied to the suggestions by Professors Ben Porath and Ohlin that his analysis had not been rigorously founded in neo-classical theory. While this was true, no general equilibrium theory of migration had been written, in the main, and he was aware of it. He had started to look at magnitudes and, in the light of marginality considerations which were consistent with the general economic theory, to try to grope towards the policy parameters involved.

Part Eight

Demographic Variables and Education

18 Demographic Variables in the Economics of Education*

Richard Stone
CAMBRIDGE UNIVERSITY

I. INTRODUCTION

In this paper I shall try to trace associations between certain demographic, educational, economic and social variables and to examine the form of these associations. The method I shall use is a cross-section analysis of country data which, despite differences in definitions and in reliability, has the merit of enabling a wide range of variation to be studied. My first effort in this direction was set out in a paper (1972) in which I made exclusive use of log-linear relationships. Clearly this form could only be approximate since most of the relationships with which I am concerned must, in principle, be sigmoid: for instance, the proportion of the population under 15 or illiterate must lie between 0 and 1. Accordingly, in this paper, besides repeating and extending the results of (1972), I have experimented with several other forms of relationship and displayed the results in a series of diagrams.

The order of the paper is as follows: in the next section I discuss the various kinds of relationship I have considered and the way in which I have used graphical analysis in trying to determine which is likely to provide the best approximation given the data available; in Sections III–IX the various analyses are set out. The main topics are: the association of the proportion of children in the population with the gross reproduction rate and with the growth rate of the population and the G.N.P. per head; the association of life expectancy with the G.N.P. per head; the association of the dependency ratio with the growth rate and the G.N.P. per head; the association of the illiteracy rate with the growth rate and the G.N.P. per head; the association of the structure of educational systems, that is the proportion of total enrolments in the elementary stages of these systems, with the illiteracy rate and the G.N.P. per head; the

* I should like to thank my friend and colleague Angus Deaton for many interesting discussions in connection with the preparation of this paper and for programming and carrying out the calculations relating to the sigmoid relationships. He is not, of course, responsible for any errors or ambiguities that may be found in what I have written.

association of the coverage of educational systems, that is the proportion of the relevant age-groups enrolled at the primary and secondary levels, with the G.N.P. per head and the urban ratio; and the association of the proportion of the G.N.P. spent on public education with the G.N.P. per head. In most of these cases I have examined a number of other possible associations and I have mentioned only those that turned out to be significant.

The paper ends with some conclusions, a table setting out, with short notes, the data I have used and a list of works cited.

II. FORMS OF RELATIONSHIP

The data used in this paper represent a number of simple measures relating to countries all over the world whose population exceeded one million in the mid-1960s. The demographic, educational, economic and social systems which generate these data cannot be supposed to be in any kind of stable equilibrium and so it is not to be expected that the data will conform closely to relationships based on equilibrium assumptions, although it would be very useful to know what form such relationships would take. Furthermore, the data show very large differences: for instance, the G.N.P. per head expressed in dollars varies through two orders of magnitude and the ratio of the population growth rate to the G.N.P. per head varies through four. Finally, the quality of the data is likely to be highly variable.

In these circumstances a preliminary graphical analysis seemed desirable, and the question was what scales to use on the axes of the diagrams. I have made use of the following variants although, of course, they are far from exhaustive.

(a)   *Linear scales.* If we suppose that two variables are related linearly, a scatter diagram with linear scales on the two axes will at once show if the observations conform to this assumption. If they do, to some degree of approximation, we can formalise our supposition in the regression equation

$$y = Xb + e \qquad (18.1)$$

where: y denotes a vector whose elements are the observations on the dependent variable; X denotes a matrix, one of whose columns is the unit vector (to allow for a constant term) and the other contains the observations on the determining variable; b is a vector of parameters; and e is a vector of disturbances. If we feel justified in assuming that e is distributed independently of X with mean zero and variance σ^2, then we can use the method of least squares to obtain an estimator, b^* say, of b given by

$$b^* = (X'X)^{-1}X'y \tag{18.2}$$

where X' denotes the transpose of X and $(X'X)^{-1}$ denotes the inverse of $X'X$. The calculated value of y, y^* say, is given by

$$y^* = Xb^* \tag{18.3}$$

The estimator in (18.2) can readily be adapted to allow the observations to be given unequal weights but I have not made use of this device because I have no information about the relative accuracy of the observations.

The above equations do not need to be rewritten if it is thought that the dependent variable is linearly related to more than one determining variable; all that happens is that the number of columns in X and the number of elements in b and b^* are increased.

As I have said, many of the relationships we expect to find in this area are sigmoid; that is to say they have a lower and an upper bound between which the observations lie. A particularly simple form of sigmoid curve is the logistic which in its simplest, standard, form can be written as

$$\eta = \frac{1}{1+e^{-\xi}} \tag{18.4}$$

where η and ξ denote respectively individual values of the dependent and determining variables. This equation results from integrating

$$\frac{d\eta}{d\xi} = \eta(1-\eta) \tag{18.5}$$

when the constant of integration is equal to 1. The dependent variable rises symmetrically from a lower bound of 0 towards an upper bound of 1, passing through a point of inflection corresponding to $\eta = 1/2$, $\xi = 0$.

The standard form can be elaborated as follows. First, if we wish to change the lower bound from 0 to, say, δ we must add δ to the right-hand side of (18.4) and, at the same time, change the numerator of that expression to $1-\delta$. Second, if we wish to change the upper bound from 1 to, say, γ, we must replace $1-\delta$ by $\gamma-\delta$. Third, if we wish to change the speed of the adjustment process from 1 to, say, β, we must multiply the exponent, $-\xi$, in the denominator of (18.4) by β. And, finally, if we wish to change the value of ξ corresponding to the point of inflection from 0 to α/β we must add α to the exponential term. If all these changes are made (18.4) is replaced by

$$\eta = \delta + \frac{\gamma - \delta}{1 + \exp(\alpha - \beta\xi)} \qquad (18.6)$$

and if we define two transformed variables, η^* and ξ^* say, where

$$\eta^* = (\eta - \delta)/(\gamma - \delta) \qquad (18.7)$$

and $$\xi^* = \beta\xi - \alpha \qquad (18.8)$$

then it can be seen that η^* and ξ^* are connected by the standard form, (18.4).

The simple logistic generalises easily to a multivariate function. All that is necessary is to replace $\beta\xi$ in the denominator of (18.6) by $\beta_1\xi_1 + \beta_2\xi_2 + \ldots$. This enables us to make η a logistic function of any ξ_j for fixed values of the remaining ξ's.

None of these changes alters the symmetry of the relationship. In practice we frequently have to deal with sigmoids that are positively skewed and defined only for positive values of ξ. The logistic can be adapted to this case by replacing ξ by $\log \xi$. If this is done the standard form, corresponding to (18.4), is simply

$$\eta = \xi/(1 + \xi) \qquad (18.9)$$

Many methods have been proposed for estimating the parameters of the logistic function. In choosing a method it is necessary to consider how an error term should be introduced into (18.6). If, as seems natural, it is simply added on to the right-hand side of (18.6), the method of maximum likelihood can be applied to the untransformed equation; in this case estimation is equivalent to non-linear least squares. This method is used throughout this paper. If, however, it were thought preferable to add the error to the exponential term in the denominator, the estimating equations would take a different form.

(b) *Semi-log scales.* By this term I mean that the vertical scale is linear while the horizontal scale is logarithmic. A scatter of points which cluster round a straight line indicate that in this case η is linearly related to $\log \xi$. The term semi-log was used to describe such a relationship by Prais and Houthakker (1955): hence its use in the present context.

A scatter of points which, on these scales, cluster round a symmetric sigmoid curve suggest that η is related to $\log \xi$ by a logistic curve, or that η is related to ξ by a relationship that might be termed log-logistic. If the variables are drawn on linear scales this relationship is positively skewed.

Somewhat similar results would be obtained by using a relationship, the log-normal integral, which certainly deserves to be considered in this context though I have not so far made use of it. A variable, ξ, is log-normally distributed if log ξ is normally distributed and the log-normal integral is the integral of the log-normal distribution function. This distribution has been fully analysed by Aitchison and Brown (1957), where they show that it and its integral have many applications, particularly in the social sciences. Whenever I have found a log-logistic relationship, it would be worthwhile to consider this alternative, which can be examined graphically by using logarithmic probability paper.

(c) *Double-log scales.* If η and ξ are both plotted on logarithmic scales a linear connection between them indicates a constant-elasticity relationship, that is one in which $\xi\, d\eta/\eta\, d\xi = $ a constant. In my experience this is the most promising relationship to start from, especially if the data show a wide range of variation. It is for this reason that I used it exclusively in my paper (1972).

A scatter of points around a regular sigmoid curve when the variables are plotted on logarithmic scales, suggests that log η is connected to ξ by a log-logistic relationship.

Before embarking on the various analyses, there are two points I should like to make.

In the first place, the reason that I have put so much emphasis on sigmoid relationships is that I hope eventually to build a model into which these relationships can be fitted. For this purpose, it seems desirable, to say the least, that the individual relationships used should be incapable of leading to impossible results, such as more than the whole population being either under 15 years of age or illiterate. Simple linear or log-linear relationships may describe observations very well but in abnormal circumstances they are capable of getting completely out of hand.

In the second place, and this is an entirely different point, I should emphasise that in the following sections I am concerned with association and with forms of association rather than with causality; to take the economists' favourite example, I do not always know whether I am talking about a supply or a demand curve. For instance, at one point I am concerned about the association between the illiteracy rate, the rate of population growth and the G.N.P. per head and, in one analysis, I summarise my results by showing that the illiteracy rate is approximately proportional to the ratio of the other two variables. This can hardly be a causal relationship since the illiteracy rate relates to the population over 14 years of age and this cannot depend on the current rate of population growth or the current G.N.P. per head. From a causal point of view, it would be more reasonable to say that an illiterate population with a fast rate of growth, and therefore a lot of children to be educated, could hardly be expected to produce a high G.N.P. per head. But I doubt if this kind of explanation would satisfy most economists; they would probably want to talk about primary inputs, technology and effective demand. No doubt the two views can be reconciled, but perhaps I have said enough to indicate that what follows in this paper deals with association rather than causality.

III. THE PROPORTION OF CHILDREN IN THE POPULATION

In an educational context the proportion of children (defined as persons under 15 years of age) in a population is obviously important since it is mainly children that have to be educated. The well-known, but nevertheless striking, fact is that in the countries of the world this proportion ranges from 20 to 50 per cent; and, in exceptional circumstances, both these bounds are exceeded.

The age composition of a population depends on fertility, mortality and migration, but mainly on fertility. If, under stable conditions, age-specific mortality rates fall uniformly, the age composition of the population will be unchanged once a stable equilibrium has been regained. For large countries, migration is usually a secondary influence. Consequently, the first association to be considered would seem to be that between the proportion of children in the population and fertility.

In most fields ideal measures are rarely available widely, but acceptable proxies for them often are. In the present case, the gross reproduction rate is acceptable. If we define the proportion of children as the percentage of the population under 15 years of age, then with $v = 70$, where v denotes the number of countries for which this proportion, η_1 say, and the gross reproduction rate, ξ_1 say, are available, their association can be expressed by the semi-log relationship

$$\eta_1^* = 23 \cdot 038 + 19 \cdot 444 \log \xi_1 \qquad (18.10)$$
$$(0 \cdot 714) \quad (0 \cdot 875)$$

where η_1^* denotes the estimated value of η_1 and $\bar{R}^2 = 0 \cdot 876$. The symbol $\bar{R}^2$ usually denotes the square of the multiple correlation coefficient adjusted for degrees of freedom but I shall use it in this sense even in the case of simple correlation between two variables. The figures in brackets are the standard errors of the regression estimates which, in this case, are both highly significant. The observations and the regression line, (18.10), are illustrated in Fig.

18.1. In this figure, as in all that follow, the observations are distinguished according as they relate to Africa, America, Asia or Europe (together with the U.S.S.R., Australia and New Zealand).

If this diagram were redrawn with a linear horizontal scale, the straight line would be replaced by a rising curve of diminishing slope but no upper asymptote.

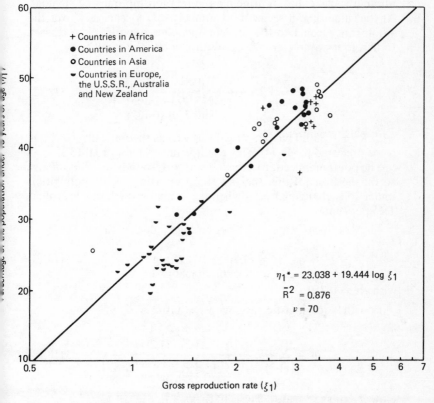

FIG. 18.1 The association between the proportion of the population under 15 years of age and the gross reproduction rate (semi-log relationship).

Having seen that there is a fairly close association between the percentage of the population under 15 years of age and the gross reproduction rate, let us now see what can be said about the association between this proportion, η_1, and the annual rate of growth of the population, ξ_2 say. Here I have tried a number of possibilities.

First, a simple linear regression with $v = 110$, gave

$$\eta_1^* = 21 \cdot 79 + 7 \cdot 748 \xi_2 \qquad (18.11)$$
$$(0 \cdot 89) \ (0 \cdot 878)$$

with $\bar{R}^2 = 0 \cdot 792$.

Second, while (18.11) shows a reasonably high degree of association, it is clear that in principle the relationship must be sigmoid. At the same time it seems most unlikely that η_1 can vary over the whole range from 0 to 100 per cent and, consequently it is necessary to fit a four-parameter logistic. With $v = 110$, the result is

$$\eta_1^* = 21 \cdot 2 + \dfrac{45 \cdot 3 - 21 \cdot 2}{(0 \cdot 8) \quad (2 \cdot 3)} \qquad (18.12)$$
$$(2 \cdot 3) \quad 1 + \exp[3 \cdot 200 - 2 \cdot 205 \xi_2]$$
$$(0 \cdot 799) \ (0 \cdot 422)$$

with $\bar{R}^2 = 0 \cdot 830$. Thus, empirically as well as theoretically, (18.12) is to be preferred to (18.11). This result is illustrated in Fig. 18.2.

The point of inflection of the logistic corresponds to $\xi_2 = \alpha/\beta$ and so on the basis of this analysis the proportion of the population under 15 is changing fastest when the annual growth rate is around $1 \cdot 45$ per cent.

Third, a linear regression of η_1 on $\log \xi_2$ gave, with $v = 110$,

$$\eta_1^* = 31 \cdot 807 + 10 \cdot 595 \log \xi_2 \qquad (18.13)$$
$$(0 \cdot 526) \quad (0 \cdot 586)$$

with $\bar{R}^2 = 0 \cdot 759$.

Fourth, a log-logistic gave, with $v = 110$,

$$\eta_1^* = 23 \cdot 4 + \dfrac{46 \cdot 4 - 23 \cdot 4}{(1 \cdot 3) \quad (1 \cdot 2)} \qquad (18.14)$$
$$(1 \cdot 2) \quad 1 + \exp[1 \cdot 559 - 3 \cdot 598 \log \xi_2]$$
$$(0 \cdot 358) \ (0 \cdot 669)$$

with $\bar{R}^2 = 0 \cdot 832$. This result is illustrated in Fig. 18.3.

In this case the point of inflection corresponds to an annual population growth rate of around $1 \cdot 44$ per cent, which is almost the same as the value of $1 \cdot 45$ per cent obtained from the simple logistic.

Fifth, a linear regression of $\log \eta_1$ on $\log \xi_2$ gave, with $v = 110$,

$$\log \eta_1^* = 3 \cdot 423 + 0 \cdot 3278 \log \xi_2 \qquad (18.15)$$
$$(0 \cdot 015) \quad (0 \cdot 0167)$$

with $\bar{R}^2 = 0 \cdot 778$.

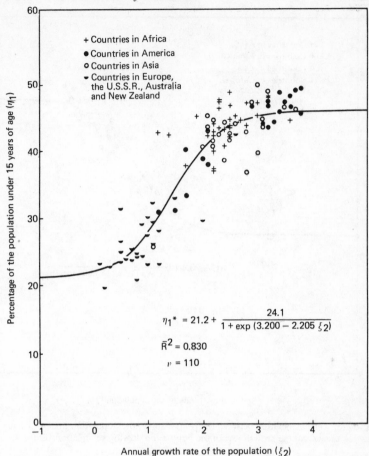

$$\eta_1^* = 21.2 + \frac{24.1}{1 + \exp(3.200 - 2.205\,\xi_2)}$$

$$\bar{R}^2 = 0.830$$

$$\nu = 110$$

Annual growth rate of the population (ξ_2)

FIG. 18.2 The association between the proportion of the population under 15 years and the growth rate of the population (logistic relationship).

Reflection on the following lines suggests that a possibly important factor may have been left out at all the above analyses. Consider a poor country and a rich country whose populations happen to be growing at the same rate. Since the expectation of life is low in poor countries and, up to a certain level, rises sharply with income, the poor country will necessarily have a larger proportion of its population under 15 than does the rich country. Thus if we introduce G.N.P. per head, ξ_3 say, into the regressions we may expect to find a

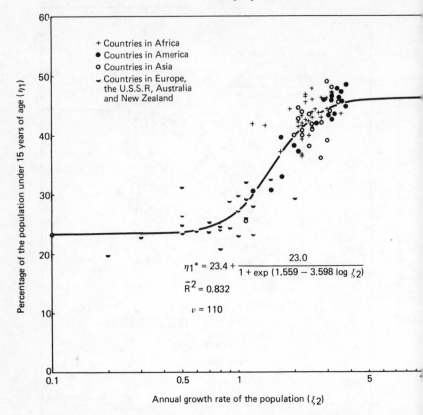

FIG. 18.3 The association between the proportion of the population under 15 years of age and the growth rate of the population (log-logistic relationship).

negative effect. In fact, this effect is clearly marked, as the following four analyses show.

If we introduce ξ_3 as a further determining variable in (18.11) we obtain, with $v = 107$,

$$\eta_1^* = 27{\cdot}57 + 6{\cdot}112\xi_2 - 0{\cdot}003563\xi_3 \qquad (18.16)$$
$$(1{\cdot}07)\ (0{\cdot}380)\quad (0{\cdot}000484)$$

with $\bar{R}^2 = 0{\cdot}858$. If we compare this result with (18.11) we can see that: $\bar{R}^2$ is raised from $0{\cdot}792$ to $0{\cdot}858$; the coefficient of ξ_2 is somewhat reduced but greatly increased in accuracy (the standard error falls from $0{\cdot}878$ to $0{\cdot}380$); and the coefficient of ξ_3 is negative and significant, being over seven times its standard error.

If we introduce ξ_3 into (18.12), again with $v = 107$, we obtain the bivariate logistic surface

$$\eta_1^* = 22\cdot2 + \cfrac{\underset{(1\cdot0)\quad(1\cdot7)}{46\cdot5 - 22\cdot2}}{1 + \exp[\underset{(0\cdot490)\,(0\cdot290)}{1\cdot914 - 1\cdot598\,\xi_2} + \underset{(0\cdot00018)}{0\cdot00075\,\xi_3}]} \quad (18.17)$$

with $\bar{R}^2 = 0\cdot832$. If we compare this result with (18.12) we can see that: $\bar{R}^2$ is raised from $0\cdot830$ to $0\cdot832$; the coefficient of ξ_2 is reduced in absolute magnitude and somewhat improved in accuracy; and the coefficient of ξ_3 is positive (indicating that η_1 falls as ξ_3 increases) and is significant, being over four times its standard error.

If we introduce $\log \xi_3$ into (18.14), with $v = 107$, we obtain the bivariate log-logistic surface

$$\eta_1^* = 23\cdot1 + \cfrac{\underset{(1\cdot8)\quad(1\cdot2)}{47\cdot7 - 23\cdot1}}{1 + \exp[\underset{(0\cdot627)\,(0\cdot514)}{-1\cdot637 - 2\cdot478 \log \xi_2} + \underset{(0\cdot105)}{0\cdot456 \log \xi_3}]} \quad (18.18)$$

with $\bar{R}^2 = 0\cdot896$. If we compare this result with (18.14) we can see that: $\bar{R}^2$ is raised from $0\cdot832$ to $0\cdot896$; the coefficient of ξ_2 is reduced in size but somewhat improved in accuracy; and the coefficient of ξ_3 is positive, as it should be, and over four times its standard error.

Finally, if we introduce $\log \xi_3$ into (18.15) we obtain, with $v = 107$,

$$\log \eta_1^* = \underset{(0\cdot064)}{3\cdot910} + \underset{(0\cdot0171)}{0\cdot2580 \log \xi_2} - \underset{(0\cdot00980)}{0\cdot07642 \log \xi_3} \quad (18.19)$$

with $\bar{R}^2 = 0\cdot851$. If we compare this result with (18.15) we can see that: $\bar{R}^2$ is raised from $0\cdot778$ to $0\cdot851$; the coefficient of ξ_2 is somewhat reduced but with no increase in accuracy (the standard error rises from $0\cdot167$ to $0\cdot171$); and the coefficient of ξ_3 is negative and significant, being nearly eight times its standard error.

Equations (18.17) and (18.18) enable us to draw the sigmoids connecting η_1^* with ξ_2 (or ξ_3) for fixed values of ξ_3 (or ξ_2). For purposes of illustration (18.18) has been used and Fig. 18.4 below shows the curves connecting η_1^* and ξ_2 for values of ξ_3 equal to \$50, \$500 and \$5000 per head.

Figure 18.5 below shows the curves connecting η_1^* and ξ_3 for values of ξ_2 equal to $0\cdot1$, 2 and 4 per cent a year.

While all these curves lie within the same bounds, it can be seen that η_1^* varies greatly over the ranges of ξ_2 and ξ_3 which are encountered in practice.

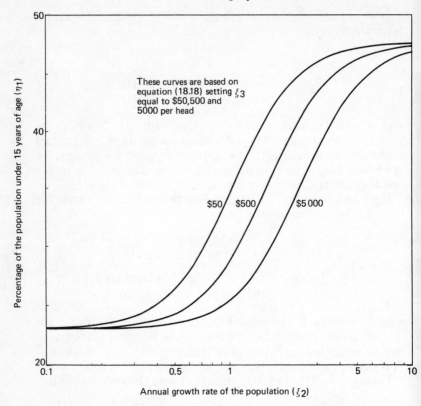

FIG. 18.4 The association between the proportion of the population under 15 years of age and the growth rate of the population for three values of the G.N.P. per head.

The fact that there is a significant association between the proportion of the population under 15 and the G.N.P. per head seems to warrant brief digressions on the associations of the expectation of life at birth and the dependency ratio with the G.N.P. per head.

IV. THE EXPECTATION OF LIFE AT BIRTH

Estimates of the expectation of life at birth, for the average of both sexes, range from a little under 30 to somewhat over 70 years. If these estimates, η_2 say, are plotted against the G.N.P. per head, ξ_3, on linear scales, it appears that at low levels of G.N.P. per head the expectation rises fast but at a falling rate and that little further

FIG. 18.5 The association between the proportion of the population under 15 years of age and the G.N.P. per head for three values of the annual growth rate of the population.

improvement is experienced after a figure of about $1000 has been reached.

Several log-logistic analyses were carried out and some of the results are shown in Fig. 18.6

The curves shown are fitted with $v = 104$, the observations contained in the cartouche in the south-east part of the diagram having been omitted. The solid curve represents the unconstrained relationship

$$
\eta_2^* = 32\cdot9 + \frac{72\cdot9 - 32\cdot9}{1 + \exp[8\cdot308 - 1\cdot546 \log \xi_3]} \quad (18.20)
$$
$$
\quad (3\cdot8) \quad (1\cdot7) \quad (3\cdot8)
$$
$$
\quad (1\cdot832) \ (0\cdot317)
$$

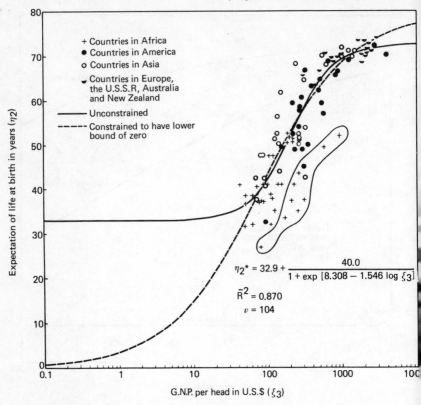

FIG. 18.6 The association between the expectation of life at birth and the G.N.P. per head (log-logistic relationship).

with $\bar{R}^2 = 0.870$. The dotted curve represents a relationship constrained to have a lower bound of zero and given by

$$\eta_2^* = \frac{\underset{(6\cdot6)}{79\cdot7}}{1 + \exp[\underset{(2\cdot439)}{3\cdot106} - \underset{(0\cdot352)}{0\cdot713}\log\xi_3]} \tag{18.21}$$

with $\bar{R}^2 = 0.859$.

The high lower bound of (18.20) is probably a reflection of the fact that we do not know, and cannot know, much about the lower end of this relationship since no society can survive at a level of income below some minimum of subsistence. The constraint in (18.21) was introduced to provide a more plausible lower end to the curve but it is of doubtful statistical validity. It might be thought that the relationship would be better approximated by a hyperbola but this is not the case: the fit is worse and the parameters are badly determined.

In (18.20) the point of inflection is reached with $\xi_3 = \$215$ a year per head and $\eta_2^* = 52.9$ years. When $\xi_3 = \$1000$ a year per head $\eta_2^* = 69.5$ years compared with the upper bound of 72.9 years.

It may be wondered why this analysis is based on only 104 countries. The eleven others, which have been excluded, all show relatively low life expectancies and relatively high incomes. One of the more extreme cases is South Africa, and it can easily be seen that such multi-racial societies are likely to call for special treatment, as are societies which, while not multi-racial, have acquired great mineral resources the ownership of which is concentrated in a few hands. An example will make it clear that in such societies it is especially necessary to recognise heterogeneity and treat the separate groups separately. Suppose that group A in a society has a life expectancy of 35 years and a G.N.P. per head of $50; and that another group, B, has a life expectancy of 70 years and a G.N.P. per head of $2500. These differences, a ratio of 1 to 2 in the case of life expectancy and a ratio of 1 to 50 in the case of income per head are representative of national extremes in the case of fairly homogeneous societies. If, however, 80 per cent of the population of a society comes from group A and 20 per cent comes from group B, the average life expectancy will be 42 years and the average income will be $540. In other words, the presence of a small proportion of Bs raises the life expectancy relatively little and the average income relatively much compared with the standards achieved by the As.

This suggests that either the average measures should be abandoned in favour of measures for more homogeneous groups or that a new variable (or variables), such as race, should be added to the analysis. Had (18.20) been fitted to all available observations ($v = 115$), the parameter estimates would not have been much changed but they would have been less well determined and the value of $\bar{R}^2$ would have fallen substantially.

V. THE DEPENDENCY RATIO

Education is likely to create problems not only if there is an excessive number of children but also if there is a deficiency in the economically active age groups. Some light can be thrown on this problem by calculating the dependency ratio, that is the ratio of the economically inactive to the economically active. Conventionally, the age group 15–64 is deemed to be economically active and the remainder of the

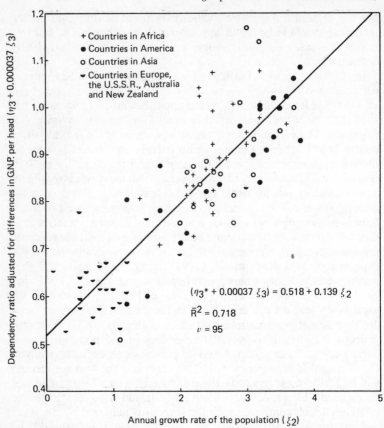

FIG. 18.7 The association between the dependency ratio adjusted for differences in G.N.P. per head and the growth rate of the population (linear relationship).

population to be economically inactive. This definition says nothing about the extent to which the active age group is in fact occupied and the choice of age groups would seem better suited to a population with a life expectancy of 70 years than to one with a life expectancy of 35 years; nevertheless, it will be used in what follows.

Fast-growing countries (which are usually poor) tend to have a relatively large proportion of children and slow-growing countries (which are usually rich) tend to have a relatively large proportion of old people. It is not clear from these considerations which type of country will tend to have the higher dependency ratio. To examine this question I worked out the regression, with $v = 95$, of the dependency ratio, η_3 say, on ξ_2 and ξ_3 with the result

$$\eta_3^* = 0.518 + 0.139\xi_2 - 0.000037\xi_3 \qquad (18.22)$$
$$\quad (0.032)\ (0.011)\quad (0.000014)$$

with $\bar{R}^2 = 0.763$. The scatter of $\eta_3 + 0.000037\xi_3$ is plotted against ξ_2 in Fig. 18.7 together with the partial regression line $\eta_3^* = 0.518 + 0.139\xi_2$. This linear relationship cannot be improved by transforming the variables to semi-log or double-log scales; the only consequence is to diminish such linearity as appears in the figure. Thus the semi-log variant of (18.22) has $\bar{R}^2 = 0.657$ and the double-log variant has $\bar{R}^2 = 0.691$.

So far I have confirmed what is probably general knowledge, namely that fast-growing, poor countries tend to have a high proportion of children to educate and a small proportion of economically active people to support not only education but everything else. Let us now turn to analyses dealing with specifically educational variables, beginning with illiteracy.

VI. ADULT ILLITERACY

As was shown in my paper (1972) there is a fairly close linear association between the logarithms of the percentage illiterate in the population aged 15 and over, η_4 say, the percentage of the population under 15 years of age, η_1, and the G.N.P. per head ξ_3. With $v = 107$, the regression estimates are

$$\log \eta_4^* = -4.257 + 3.318 \log \eta_1 - 0.807 \log \xi_3 \qquad (18.23)$$
$$\quad\ (2.067)\ (0.446)\qquad (0.097)$$

with $\bar{R}^2 = 0.811$. Thus there appears to be a significant degree of association between the three variables.

We have already seen in (18.15) that there is a fairly close association between $\log \eta_1$ and $\log \xi_2$, the logarithm of the growth rate of the population. If we replace $\log \eta_1$ by $\log \xi_2$ in (18.23) we obtain, with $v = 114$,

$$\log \eta_4^* = 7.988 + 1.058 \log \xi_2 - 0.958 \log \xi_3 \qquad (18.24)$$
$$\quad (0.499)\ (0.138)\qquad (0.076)$$

with $\bar{R}^2 = 0.803$. Since the coefficients of $\log \xi_2$ and $\log \xi_3$ are similar in magnitude but opposite in sign, we can simplify (18.24) by replacing the two variables on the right-hand side by $\log(\xi_2/\xi_3)$. In this case, again with $v = 114$, we obtain

$$\log \eta_4^* = 8.214 + 0.990 \log(\xi_2/\xi_3) \qquad (18.25)$$
$$\quad (0.245)\ (0.046)$$

with $\overline{R}^2 = 0.804$. On this formulation the illiteracy rate is approximately proportional to the population growth divided by the G.N.P. This result is illustrated in Fig. 18.8 below.

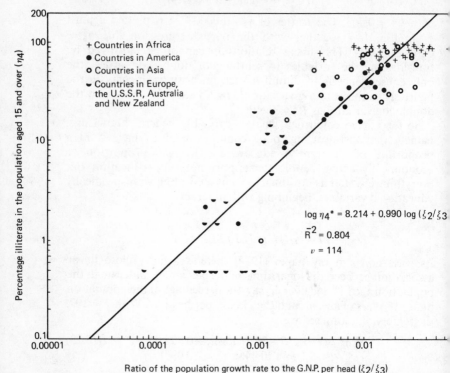

FIG. 18.8 The association between the percentage illiterate in the population aged 15 and over and the ratio of the population growth rate to the G.N.P. per head (Double-log relationship)

Despite the high value of $\overline{R}^2$, it is impossible to be much satisfied with this result. Not only does the regression line exceed 100 per cent illiteracy well within the range of the observations but there is a visual impression of curvilinearity which would perhaps be accentuated if the row of observations indicating 0·5 per cent of illiteracy were left out. These observations were taken from Ehrlich (1970) and indicate not precise measurements but the generally accepted view that illiteracy in North-West Europe, Australia and New Zealand is negligible.

In these circumstances it seemed useful to fit a sigmoid curve in place of the unacceptable straight line. The result, with $v = 101$, is

$$\log \eta_4^* = -1 \cdot 021 + \frac{\underset{(0 \cdot 088)\ (0 \cdot 426)}{4 \cdot 230 + 1 \cdot 021}}{1 + \exp[\underset{(2 \cdot 446)\ (0 \cdot 224)}{-14 \cdot 006 - 1 \cdot 054} \log \xi_2 + \underset{(0 \cdot 376)}{2 \cdot 041} \log \xi_3]} \quad (18.26)$$

with $\bar{R}^2 = 0 \cdot 887$. If, for simplicity but with less justification than before, we take $\log(\xi_2/\xi_3)$ as the determining variable, we obtain

$$\log \eta_4^* = -0 \cdot 849 + \frac{\underset{(0 \cdot 102)\ (0 \cdot 398)}{4 \cdot 236 + 0 \cdot 849}}{1 + \exp[\underset{(2 \cdot 169)\ (0 \cdot 354)}{-11 \cdot 065 - 1 \cdot 645} \log(\xi_2/\xi_3)]} \quad (18.27)$$

with $\bar{R}^2 = 0 \cdot 871$. This relationship is illustrated in Fig. 18.9 below.

There are always difficulties in assessing the results shown in diagrams with a logarithmic vertical scale since, in such cases, a discrepancy between 50 and 100 per cent counts for no more than a discrepancy between 5 and 10 per cent or between 0·5 and 1 per cent. Although the analyses illustrated in Figs. 18.8 and 18.9 succeed in accounting for a substantial part of the variation in illiteracy rates, it has to be admitted that there are many countries which depart substantially from each relationship. Compared with their values of ξ_2 and ξ_3, a number of countries, such as Burma, Thailand, South Korea, Ceylon and Japan, show a surprisingly high degree of literacy; while other countries, such as Libya, South Africa, Singapore, Portugal, Greece and Italy, show a surprisingly low degree. This suggests that there are many factors, cultural, religious, racial and so on, which ought to be taken into account. So far, I have been unable to allow for these particular factors but I have introduced two others into the log-linear analyses set out in (18.23) and (18.25) above. Although in both cases the new variables added nothing significant, they are perhaps worth reporting.

It might be supposed that the more a country was urbanised the lower would be its illiteracy rate since it is presumably easier to provide education if children are assembled in towns than if they are scattered over the countryside. If we denote the urban ratio by ξ_4 and introduce $\log \xi_4$ into (18.23) above, we obtain, with $v = 101$,

$$\log \eta_4^* = \underset{(2 \cdot 236)}{-3 \cdot 535} + \underset{(0 \cdot 478)}{3 \cdot 161} \log \eta_1 - \underset{(0 \cdot 160)}{0 \cdot 930} \log \xi_3 + \underset{(0 \cdot 167)}{0 \cdot 162} \log \xi_4 \quad (18.28)$$

with $\bar{R}^2 = 0 \cdot 815$. Thus the inclusion of the urban ratio makes almost

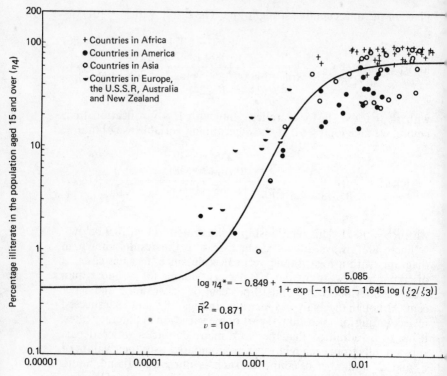

FIG. 18.9 The association between the percentage illiterate in the population aged 15 and over and the ratio of the population growth rate to the G.N.P. per head (Double-log logistic relationship)

no difference and, furthermore, its coefficient is positive and less than its standard error.

It might be supposed that the higher the expenditure on education per child (reckoned at comparable prices) the lower would be the illiteracy rate. There is a difficulty here since it is the expenditure per child in the past that is relevant to adult illiteracy and my only series relates to the mid-1960s. Since educational systems have changed very differently it cannot be assumed that the expenditure per child at any given date bears a constant relationship to expenditure at the relevant period in the past. Besides this, my series relates to expenditure on public education only. If we denote public expenditure on education as a percentage of the G.N.P. by η_5, then my series for expenditure per child is derived as $\eta_5 \xi_3 / \eta_1$. This series is probably not very reliable and is not shown in Table 18.A (pp. 549–51).

If this measure is included in (18.25) we obtain, with $v = 102$,

$$\log \eta_4^* = 8\cdot272 + 0\cdot982 \log(\xi_2/\xi_3) - 0\cdot0314 \log(\eta_5 \xi_3/\eta_1) \quad (18.29)$$
$$\quad (0\cdot330) \quad (0\cdot136) \qquad\qquad (0\cdot1348)$$

with $\bar{R}^2 = 0\cdot808$. Once more, nothing is gained.

It would be interesting to take a more dynamic view of illiteracy, linking the changes in illiteracy rates over time with the progression of school systems. But such a work is beyond anything I have been able to contemplate so far.

VII. THE RELATIVE IMPORTANCE OF ELEMENTARY EDUCATION

It is reasonable to suppose that poor countries with high illiteracy rates will devote most of their educational resources to the conquest of illiteracy and that, as a consequence, by far the greater part of their enrolments of pupils and students will be at the primary and pre-primary levels. On the other hand it is sometimes suggested that underdeveloped countries tend to give too much weight to education at higher levels, if not in their current practice at least in their plans for future development. This point has been made by Dougherty (1971) with respect to the position in Columbia and by Bowles (1969) with respect to the position in Northern Nigeria. Bowles contrasts the distribution of pupils by levels derived from plans based on the manpower requirements approach to educational planning with his own estimates derived from a multi-stage linear programme based on maximising the future economic return to present educational activity. He reaches the conclusion that the plans underestimate the importance of elementary education and give too much weight, from a purely economic point of view, to advanced education.

I have tried to throw some light on this issue by working out the association between structure measured by the proportion of enrolments at the elementary (primary and pre-primary) levels, η_6 say, with G.N.P. per head, ξ_3, and the per cent illiterate in the population aged 15 and over, η_4. From a linear relationship connecting the logarithms of these variables we obtain, with $v = 114$,

$$\log \eta_6^* = 4\cdot512 - 0\cdot049 \log \xi_3 + 0\cdot046 \log \eta_4 \quad (18.30)$$
$$\quad (0\cdot118) \quad (0\cdot016) \qquad (0\cdot010)$$

with $\bar{R}^2 = 0\cdot622$. Since the coefficients of $\log \xi_3$ and $\log \eta_4$ are similar in magnitude but opposite in sign, (18.30) can be simplified by taking

$\log(\eta_4/\xi_3)$ as the determining variable. If we do this we obtain, again with $v = 114$,

$$\log \eta_6^* = 4\cdot497 + 0\cdot047 \log(\eta_4/\xi_3) \qquad (18.31)$$
$$ (0\cdot013) \ (0\cdot003)$$

with $\bar{R}^2 = 0\cdot625$. This result is illustrated in Fig. 18.10.

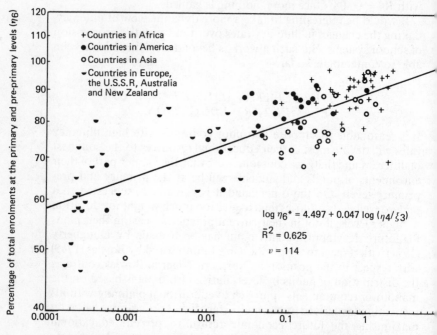

FIG. 18.10 The association between the percentage of total enrolments at the primary and pre-primary levels and the ratio of the per cent illiterate in the population aged 15 and over to the G.N.P. per head (Double-log relationship).

Figure 18.10 brings out the fact that poor countries with high rates of adult illiteracy tend, as we should expect, to have high ratios of elementary to total enrolments. It also shows that there is a considerable scatter around the regression line at all levels of $\log(\eta_4/\xi_3)$ so that it can always be said that for some countries η_6 is relatively low and for others that it is relatively high. The question is: why should this be so?

I have not yet found the answer to this question, but I have considered two possible influences: the urban ratio, ξ_4, and the percentage of the G.N.P. spent on public education, η_5. If these variables are introduced, logarithmically, into (18.30) we obtain, with $v = 99$,

$$\log \eta_6^* = 4\cdot604 - 0\cdot063 \log \xi_3 + 0\cdot040 \log \eta_4$$
$$\quad (0\cdot134) \ (0\cdot025) \qquad\quad (0\cdot011)$$
$$\qquad\qquad\qquad - 0\cdot008 \log \xi_4 + 0\cdot025 \log \eta_5 \quad (18.32)$$
$$\qquad\qquad\qquad\quad (0\cdot022) \qquad\quad (0\cdot025)$$

with $\bar{R}^2 = 0\cdot640$. Once more, nothing is gained.

VIII. THE COVERAGE OF EDUCATIONAL SYSTEMS

Let us turn now to the question of coverage, that is to say the percentage enrolled, at primary and secondary levels combined, of the population of school age as defined in different countries. This variable, η_7 say, appears to be associated not only with the G.N.P. per head, ξ_3, but also with the urban ratio, ξ_4, which, it will be remembered, did not play a significant role in connection with illiteracy. Using a logarithmic formulation, we obtain, with $v = 104$,

$$\log \eta_7^* = 1\cdot580 + 0\cdot152 \log \xi_3 + 0\cdot438 \log \xi_4 \quad (18.33)$$
$$\quad (0\cdot189) \ (0\cdot055) \qquad\quad (0\cdot074)$$

with $\bar{R}^2 = 0\cdot664$. The partial association between η_7 and ξ_4 is illustrated in Fig. 18.11 below in which $\log \eta_7 - 0\cdot152 \log \xi_3$ is plotted against $\log \xi_4$.

As in other cases, I have tried to improve on the results of (18.33). The additional variables I introduced were the percentage of the population under 15, η_1, and the percentage of the G.N.P. spent on public education, η_5. With these two variables added to (18.33) we obtain, with $v = 97$,

$$\log \eta_7^* = 1\cdot846 - 0\cdot077 \log \eta_1 - 0\cdot027 \log \eta_5$$
$$\quad (1\cdot051) \ (0\cdot225) \qquad\quad (0\cdot085)$$
$$\qquad\qquad\qquad + 0\cdot121 \log \xi_3 + 0\cdot501 \log \xi_4 \quad (18.34)$$
$$\qquad\qquad\qquad\quad (0\cdot076) \qquad\quad (0\cdot078)$$

with $\bar{R}^2 = 0\cdot687$. In both cases, the regression coefficients of the added variables are far less than their standard errors. Once more, nothing is gained.

IX. EXPENDITURE ON EDUCATION AS A PERCENTAGE OF THE G.N.P.

I have now introduced eleven variables of which one, η_5, represents the percentage of the G.N.P. devoted to public education. From the

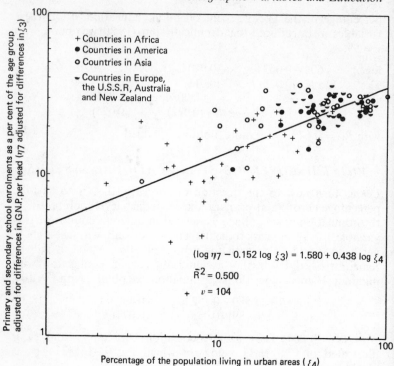

FIG. 18.11 The association between primary and secondary school enrolments as a percentage of the age group (adjusted for differences in G.N.P. per head) and the percentage of the population living in urban areas (Double-log relationship).

point of view of demand, we might suppose that this percentage would be associated with the G.N.P. per head, the relative price of educational services and some indicator of tastes, compounded perhaps of objective needs and the priority attached to education relative to other types of expenditure. Out of this list, I have no information about the relative price of educational services in different countries or about priorities attached to education. From the point of view of supply, we might suppose that the percentage would depend on the G.N.P. per head, relative prices, priorities and since, because of statistical limitations, we must restrict ourselves to public education, the budgetary position of public authorities and the role played by private education. Out of this list, apart from relative prices and priorities, I have no information on the role played by private education, except in a few countries, and I have not extracted the information available about educational expenditures in relation to the incomes of public authorities.

With so many gaps in information, I have not succeeded in tracing any significant associations of η_5 other than that with ξ_3, the G.N.P. per head itself. With $v = 107$, a linear regression between logarithms yields

$$\log \eta_5^* = -0.031 + 0.215 \log \xi_3 \qquad (18.35)$$
$$(0.222) \quad (0.037)$$

with $\bar{R}^2 = 0.223$. This result is illustrated in Fig. 18.12 below.

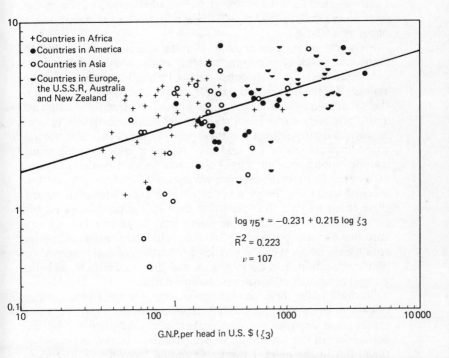

FIG. 18.12 The association between the percentage of the G.N.P. spent on public education and the G.N.P. per head (Double-log relationship).

The only comfort we can extract from this result is that the regression line is significant and upward-sloping since this is at least consistent with the assumption, generally made, that education is income-elastic.

The introduction of such plausible variables as η_1, η_6, η_7 and ξ_4 does nothing to improve the analysis: in every case the regression coefficient is less than its standard error. Thus, with $v = 97$, we obtain

$$\log \eta_5^* = -1.756 + 0.082 \log \eta_1 + 0.290 \log \eta_6$$
$$(2.125) \quad (0.293) \qquad (0.425)$$
$$-0.043 \log \eta_7 + 0.226 \log \xi_3 + 0.082 \log \xi_4 \quad (18.36)$$
$$(0.128) \qquad (0.097) \qquad (0.115)$$

with $\bar{R}^2 = 0.198$. Once more, nothing is gained.

X. CONCLUSIONS

In this section I shall not repeat the detailed results of the earlier sections but shall restrict myself to general conclusions based on the paper as a whole.

First, although there must be considerable inaccuracies and, in many cases, lack of true comparability in the body of data I have used, nevertheless a fairly consistent and plausible picture seems to emerge. It is the fast-growing countries that tend to be poor and it is these that tend to have a high proportion of children to be educated and a relatively small proportion in the economically active ages as conventionally defined. It is these poor countries that tend to have a low expectation of life and this increases quickly with rising incomes, though beyond a level of income, modest by the standards of Western Europe, the increase is very small. Fast growth and low incomes tend to be found in countries with high illiteracy rates and these countries tend to concentrate their educational forces largely on elementary education. They also tend to have relatively low enrolment rates, particularly if they are little urbanised. Poor countries tend to spend a smaller proportion of their income on public education than do rich ones and this is consistent with the general belief that education is income-elastic.

Second, while these tendencies emerge clearly enough, there remain in every case substantial departures from them. To some extent these departures could probably be accounted for by imperfections in the basic data or shortcomings in my treatment of them. But in the main, I think, we should look elsewhere and, in particular, to the influence exerted by history and traditions, cultural attitudes, religion and race. It is highly plausible that such factors should play a role and not to be expected that everything can be accounted for in terms of simple demographic and economic indicators. As we saw in the analysis of the expectation of life, heterogeneity, as usual, raises special problems.

Third, the bounded nature of relationships in this area suggests that we should try, wherever possible, to replace linear and other unbounded approximations by bounded ones. The possibility of generalising the logistic and other sigmoid relationships so as to provide boundedness in any number of dimensions seems highly promising.

APPENDIX: THE BASIC DATA

The data used in this paper are set out in Table 18.A below. They are taken from United Nations statistical publications (see References), supplemented in a few cases by information provided by P. and A. Ehrlich (1970). The population growth rates are calculated for the period 1963–70 and other series relate to 1966 or to the closest year possible. The data in Table 18.A, with two exceptions, were set out for a wider range of countries in Table 5 (Stone, 1972) in which the date or period to which they relate was also listed. The two exceptions are: (i) the gross reproduction rates which are taken from U.N. *Demographic Yearbook* (1969 ed.); and (ii) the expectations of life at birth which were obtained by averaging the estimates for the two sexes in Stone (1972) in all cases where a single figure was not available.

Eleven series are listed in Table 18.A below. The countries shown are those with a population of one million or more for which the information available enabled them to contribute to one or more of the analyses. The order of the countries follows the list in U.N. *Demographic Yearbook* (1970 ed.) p. 23. The sources of the series are as follows.

Percentage of the population under 15 years of age, η_1: these estimates are based on the data set out in U.N. *Demographic Yearbook* (1970 ed.) Table 6.

Expectation of life at birth in years, η_2: taken from U.N. *Demographic Yearbook* (1970 ed.) Table 20.

Dependency ratio, η_3: based on the data set out in U.N. *Demographic Yearbook* (1970 ed.) Table 6.

Percentage illiterate in the population aged 15 and over, η_4: mainly taken from U.N. *Demographic Yearbook* (1970 ed.) Table 11 supplemented by Ehrlich (1970). Similar information is given in UNESCO *Statistical Yearbook* (1970 ed.) Table 1.3 but this is incomplete and only intended to supplement the data given in the 1965 edition.

Public expenditure on education as a percentage of G.N.P., η_5: mainly taken from UNESCO op. cit., Table 2.19. In a number of cases this source has been replaced as far as the G.N.P. is concerned by the sources described below in the paragraph on G.N.P. per head.

Percentage of total enrolments at the primary and pre-primary levels, η_6: based on a sequence of issues of U.N. *Statistical Yearbook* from the 1965 edition onwards, the Table number in the 1969 edition being 201. The reason for this procedure was to obtain, as far as possible, data for 1966 or an adjacent year.

Percentage of the relevant age group enrolled in primary and secondary education, η_7: taken from UNESCO, op. cit., Table 2.5. This table gives a new set of enrolment ratios, in calculating which the different national systems of education and the duration of schooling at the first and second levels are taken into account.

Gross reproduction rate, ξ_1: taken from U.N. *Demographic Yearbook* (1969 ed.) Table 31.

Annual growth rate of the population, ξ_2: taken from U.N. *Demographic Yearbook* (1970 ed.) Table 2. For various reasons growth rates are not given for some countries and, where possible, these gaps have been filled by similar estimates from Ehrlich (1970).

G.N.P. per head in U.S. \$, ξ_3: mainly taken from U.N. *Yearbook of National Accounts Statistics,* vol. II (1969 ed.), Table 1C and from U.N. *Statistical Yearbook* (1970 ed.) Table 183. The 1970 edition of the *Yearbook of National Accounts Statistics* was little used since it does not provide estimates of the G.N.P. explicitly. The estimates relating to the U.S.S.R. and to most other communist countries are taken from Ehrlich (1970) and are based on data supplied by the International Bank for Reconstruction and Development.

Urban population as a percentage of total population, ξ_4: based on U.N. *Demographic Yearbook* (1970 ed.) Table 6.

TABLE 18.A THE BASIC DATA

	η_1	η_2	η_3	η_4	η_5	η_6	η_7	ξ_1	ξ_2	ξ_3	ξ_4
AFRICA											
Western Africa											
Dahomy	46·0	37·3	0·99	95·4	4·1	92·0	19	—	2·5	81	9·3
Ghana	44·5	37·5	0·91	72·5	4·6	86·3	54	—	3·0	314	23·1
Guinea	42·1	27·0	0·83	85·0	—	87·7	18	—	2·2	80	8·3
Ivory Coast	42·7	35·0	—	88·5	5·0	90·9	38	—	2·3	256	—
Liberia	37·2	37·4	0·70	91·1	2·8	89·3	43	—	1·7	210	—
Mali	42·3	37·2	0·83	97·8	3·6	96·6	14	—	2·1	88	11·2
Mauritania	43·3	41·0	0·85	93·5	4·1	91·9	4	—	2·2	155	6·7
Niger	43·8	41·0	0·89	97·0	1·4	94·1	7	—	2·7	88	—
Nigeria	43·0	37·0	0·82	88·5	2·3	91·9	19	—	2·5	76	16·1
Senegal	42·5	41·0	0·86	92·5	3·1	83·5	23	—	2·4	227	22·7
Sierra Leone	36·7	41·0	0·72	93·3	3·3	84·7	18	—	2·2	155	—
Togo	47·9	35·1	1·07	85·0	2·0	91·9	32	—	2·5	124	14·9
Upper Volta	41·6	31·6	0·81	88·5	2·6	91·6	7	—	2·1	49	·5·3
Eastern Africa											
Burundi	46·8	36·6	1·04	88·5	1·9	95·7	16	—	2·3	50	2·2
Ethiopia	44·4	38·5	—	92·5	1·2	84·5	8	—	1·9	62	8·1
Kenya	46·3	47·5	—	72·5	4·6	94·7	35	—	3·0	119	7·8
Madagascar	46·5	37·9	1·02	66·5	5·8	90·9	40	3·30	2·3	114	12·7
Malawi	43·9	38·5	0·92	77·9	4·1	96·9	21	—	2·5	63	5·0
Mozambique	42·0	41·0	—	92·5	—	95·0	30	—	1·2	100	—
Rwanda	—	41·0	—	87·5	2·1	97·6	38	—	2·8	42	3·5
Somalia	—	38·5	—	92·5	—	69·6	5	—	2·2	50	—
Southern Rhodesia	47·1	51·4	0·97	72·5	3·7	97·5	56	—	3·2	219	16·9
Uganda	41·4	47·5	0·77	74·9	2·0	85·0	32	—	2·5	104	5·0
Tanzania	44·4	40·5	0·89	85·0	3·5	96·2	22	—	2·6	71	5·5
Zambia	44·5	43·5	—	52·6	6·2	94·2	42	—	3·0	265	20·2
Northern Africa											
Algeria	47·3	50·7	1·07	81·2	4·9	90·0	39	3·42	3·2	220	38·8
Libya	43·7	52·1	0·93	78·3	3·4	86·1	52	3·30	3·6	932	24·6
Morocco	44·4	50·5	0·94	88·8	4·1	80·0	32	—	3·0	185	29·3
Sudan	43·0	47·6	—	95·6	4·1	78·7	14	3·37	2·8	105	8·3
Tunisia	46·3	51·7	1·00	67·8	5·0	85·5	64	3·42	2·8	199	40·1
Egypt	42·8	52·7	0·86	73·7	4·7	71·5	52	3·19	2·5	188	38·0
Middle Africa											
Angola and Cabinda	41·7	33·5	0·80	93·5	—	88·4	26	—	1·4	170	10·6
Cameroon	36·4	41·0	—	94·0	2·5	94·4	48	3·06	2·2	139	16·1
Central African Republic	41·6	32·0	0·79	97·9	3·2	96·2	36	—	2·2	110	27·3
Chad	45·6	32·0	—	94·4	3·9	95·0	17	2·40	2·3	62	6·9
Congo Democratic Republic	39·4	38·8	.	84·6	4·4	93·5	52	—	2·2	110	22·0
Southern Africa											
South Africa	40·1	49·5	0·78	67·5	3·4	80·2	68	—	2·4	578	46·7
NORTHERN AMERICA											
Canada	32·9	72·0	0·68	1·5	7·2	68·2	88	1·37	1·7	2677	73·6
United States	30·5	70·3	0·66	2·2	5·3	57·8	101	1·34	1·2	3874	69·9
LATIN AMERICA											
Tropical South America											
Bolivia	41·9	49·7	0·83	60·0	3·7	83·3	55	—	2·6	151	33·9
Brazil	42·8	60·7	0·83	38·9	2·3	80·1	59	2·62	3·2	291	46·3
Columbia	46·6	45·1	0·99	27·1	2·3	81·4	56	2·71	3·2	307	52·8
Ecuador	45·0	52·4	0·93	32·5	3·0	85·2	60	3·22	3·4	219	36·0
Peru	43·3	54·1	0·89	38·9	4·3	79·0	76	3·10	3·1	271	47·4
Venezuela	45·7	66·4	0·93	36·7	3·8	79·2	70	2·95	3·6	879	67·4

TABLE 18.A (continued)

	η_1	η_2	η_3	η_4	η_5	η_6	η_7	ζ_1	ζ_2	ζ_3	ζ_4
LATIN AMERICA (continued)											
Middle America (mainland)											
Costa Rica	48·4	63·4	1·07	15·7	4·1	83·2	79	3·11	3·8	406	34·5
El Salvador	44·8	58·5	0·92	51·0	2·8	86·7	53	3·17	3·8	276	38·5
Guatemala	46·0	49·0	0·95	62·1	2·1	87·5	36	3·17	2·9	298	34·0
Honduras	47·8	49·0	1·01	55·0	2·9	91·7	49	3·12	3·4	237	23·2
Mexico	46·3	62·4	0·98	34·6	2·5	86·4	62	3·19	3·5	493	50·7
Nicaragua	48·2	49·9	1·05	50·2	2·7	87·3	50	2·92	3·7	355	40·9
Panama	43·5	59·3	0·89	26·7	4·2	76·2	74	2·56	3·3	546	41·5
Temperate South America											
Argentina	30·8	66·0	0·57	8·6	3·6	75·2	76	1·50	1·5	849	73·8
Chile	40·0	57·2	0·80	16·4	3·9	88·0	77	2·01	2·4	576	68·2
Paraguay	45·9	59·4	0·99	25·5	1·7	89·2	62	3·18	3·2	220	35·8
Uruguay	28·2	68·6	0·56	9·6	3·7	72·0	80	1·46	1·2	664	80·8
Caribbean											
Cuba	37·3	66·8	0·72	22·1	7·5	83·1	74	2·20	2·1	320	51·4
Dominican Republic	47·3	57·9	1·01	35·5	2·6	87·9	61	3·49	3·6	278	30·3
Haiti	38·3	32·6	0·71	89·5	1·3	90·8	22	—	2·0	92	12·2
Jamaica	46·0	64·7	1·02	18·1	2·6	89·2	66	2·48	2·3	519	23·4
Puerto Rico	39·6	69·5	0·83	19·4	5·6	62·7	95	1·75	1·7	1252	44·2
EAST ASIA											
Mainland region											
China (mainland)	—	50·0	—	45·0	—	89·3	—	—	1·8	—	14·2
Hong Kong	40·8	70·0	0·77	28·6	2·1	76·1	78	2·39	2·2	560	76·6
Mongolia	30·4	57·7	0·66	5·0	—	—	68	—	3·2	—	40·8
Japan	25·6	71·7	0·47	1·0	4·4	48·5	91	0·77	1·1	1027	68·1
Other East Asia											
China (Taiwan)	43·3	68·1	0·85	27·6	2·9	72·5	75	2·34	2·6	245	58·2
Korea, Democratic Republic of (North)	—	57·7	—	—	—	—	—	—	2·8	—	—
Korea, Republic of (South)	43·5	52·4	0·88	29·8	2·0	77·9	73	2·59	2·4	134	33·6
SOUTH ASIA											
Middle South Asia											
Afghanistan	—	37·5	—	90·0	—	86·1	12	—	2·4	70	—
Ceylon	41·8	61·7	0·83	24·9	4·4	68·4	74	2·44	2·3	154	19·1
India	41·0	41·3	0·79	72·2	2·6	87·1	41	—	2·5	86	18·0
Iran	46·1	50·0	1·00	77·2	3·3	77·7	39	—	2·9	263	39·1
Nepal	40·0	40·6	0·75	91·2	0·5	83·2	18	—	2·0	93	3·6
Pakistan	44·5	51·4	—	81·2	1·2	70·6	31	3·74	2·1	125	13·1
South-East Asia											
Burma	40·0	42·3	—	35·0	3·0	78·3	31	—	2·2	69	—
Cambodia	43·8	43·8	0·87	59·0	4·2	89·1	44	—	2·2	147	10·3
Indonesia	42·1	47·5	0·81	61·0	0·7	87·8	44	—	2·8	86	14·9
Laos	—	47·5	—	75·0	2·6	94·3	22	—	2·4	82	15·0
Malaysia	44·0	64·6	0·92	75·0	4·1	73·7	59	2·64	3·1	314	38·2
Philippines	45·7	51·3	0·94	28·1	2·8	77·5	87	—	3·5	269	29·9
Singapore	42·7	68·2	0·84	52·0	3·9	71·7	85	2·26	2·1	620	100·0
Thailand	43·2	56·2	0·85	32·3	2·8	91·4	56	3·20	3·1	137	18·2
Vietnam, Democratic Republic of (North)	38·0	50·0	—	35·5	—	—	—	—	2·4	—	—
Vietnam, Republic of (South)	—	50·0	—	—	1·1	79·2	55	—	2·6	142	9·5

TABLE 18.A (continued)

	η_1	η_2	η_3	η_4	η_5	η_6	η_7	ξ_1	ξ_2	ξ_3	ξ_4
SOUTH ASIA (continued)											
South-West Asia											
Iraq	48·0	51·6	1·13	85·6	6·0	77·5	49	3·48	3·2	269	38·8
Israel	36·1	71·0	0·70	15·8	7·1	77·6	81	1·89	2·8	1498	77·9
Jordan	45·4	52·3	0·99	67·6	3·6	75·1	70	3·44	3·7	264	43·9
Lebanon	—	—	—	45·0	1·5	74·8	62	—	2·9	517	—
Saudi Arabia	—	42·3	—	90·0	5·5	88·8	16	—	2·7	324	—
Syria	49·0	52·8	1·16	69·2	4·6	75·3	58	3·46	3·0	214	36·9
Turkey	41·9	53·7	0·85	54·0	3·6	80·6	51	—	2·5	326	34·4
Yemen	—	42·3	—	92·5	—	97·0	4	—	2·7	90	—
Yemen, Democratic Republic of	—	42·3	—	—	—	75·7	22	—	2·7	—	93·3
EUROPE											
Western Europe											
Austria	23·6	69·9	0·59	0·5	4·1	68·0	84	1·30	0·5	1383	33·4
Belgium	23·9	70·6	0·58	1·5	5·0	61·6	93	1·23	0·6	1919	66·4
France	24·4	71·8	0·59	1·5	4·2	65·2	88	1·35	0·9	2194	70·0
Germany, Federal Republic of	23·1	70·6	0·54	0·5	3·5	61·4	89	1·23	1·0	2056	71·1
Netherlands	28·1	73·7	0·61	0·5	6·6	59·7	79	1·41	1·2	1672	78·4
Switzerland	23·3	71·4	0·52	0·5	4·1	51·2	70	—	1·2	2463	51·3
Southern Europe											
Albania	39·1	66·0	0·82	28·5	—	89·9	80	2·75	3·0	300	27·5
Greece	25·4	69·1	0·53	19·6	2·3	65·3	85	1·12	0·7	759	43·3
Italy	24·4	69·8	0·53	9·3	4·7	62·5	72	1·22	0·8	1226	47·7
Portugal	28·9	63·6	0·60	37·2	1·4	71·0	72	1·45	0·9	441	22·7
Spain	27·4	69·6	0·55	14·4	1·6	73·1	77	1·40	1·0	770	42·9
Yugoslavia	29·3	66·9	0·57	19·7	4·6	77·9	77	1·28	1·1	510	28·4
Eastern Europe											
Bulgaria	23·8	70·8	0·48	9·8	4·4	75·4	99	0·97	0·7	620	46·5
Czechoslovakia	24·9	70·5	0·54	2·5	5·0	82·4	79	1·08	0·5	1010	47·6
East Berlin	19·8	—	0·56	0·5	—	—	—	1·13	0·2	—	—
Germany, Democratic Republic of	23·3	71·2	0·61	0·5	5·0	80·5	96	1·18	0·1	1220	73·2
Hungary	22·8	69·4	0·50	2·6	5·2	84·8	79	0·91	0·3	800	41·8
Poland	29·9	69·9	0·59	4·7	5·5	76·0	92	1·17	1·0	730	48·3
Rumania	26·0	68·5	0·51	11·4	—	83·2	82	0·92	1·1	650	31·3
Northern Europe											
Denmark	23·8	73·0	0·55	0·5	6·3	57·9	82	1·27	0·7	2317	46·2
Finland	26·5	69·0	0·53	0·5	6·0	46·4	78	1·14	0·5	1861	45·3
Ireland	31·2	70·0	0·74	0·5	4·1	71·4	80	1·91	0·5	1025	49·2
Norway	24·7	73·5	0·59	0·5	5·6	58·2	85	1·39	0·8	2040	41·3
Sweden	20·9	74·2	0·51	0·5	6·8	47·3	92	1·15	0·8	2918	77·4
United Kingdom	23·5	71·5	0·55	0·5	5·3	58·0	88	1·33	0·5	1952	77·9
OCEANIA											
Australia and New Zealand											
Australia	29·4	71·1	0·61	0·5	3·6	60·9	92	1·40	2·0	2165	83·3
New Zealand	32·6	71·1	0·69	0·5	4·1	72·8	85	1·58	1·5	2020	68·3
Melanesia											
New Guinea	42·3	46·8	0·77	—	—	95·2	43	—	2·1	—	4·7
U.S.S.R.	32·0	70·0	—	12·0	7·4	78·8	95	1·19	1·1	890	53·7

REFERENCES

J. Aitchison and J. A. C. Brown, *The Lognormal Distribution* (Cambridge Univ. Press, 1957).

S. Bowles, *Planning Educational Systems for Economic Growth* (Harvard Univ. Press, 1969).

C. R. S. Dougherty, 'Optimal Allocation of Investment in Education', *Studies in Development Planning* (Harvard Univ. Press, 1971).

P. R. Ehrlich and A. H. Ehrlich, *Population, Resources, Environment* (San Francisco, 1970).

S. J. Prais and H. S. Houthakker, *The Analysis of Family Budgets* (Cambridge Univ. Press, 1955; 2nd impression, abridged, 1971).

R. Stone, 'Demographic Growth and the Cost of Education', mimeographed (Cambridge, 1972).

UNESCO, *Statistical Yearbook* (Paris, annually).

U.N. Statistical Office, *Demographic Yearbook* (New York, annually).

U.N. Statistical Office, *Statistical Yearbook* (New York, annually).

U.N. Statistical Office, *Yearbook of National Accounts Statistics*, 2 vols (New York, annually).

19 The Influence of Demographic Variables on Development via their Impact on Education[*]

Gavin W. Jones

DEMOGRAPHIC INSTITUTE, UNIVERSITY OF INDONESIA

I. INTRODUCTORY

Rising educational levels amongst the labour force are generally considered to constitute a very significant source of the increase in a country's output over time.[1] From the individual's point of view, schooling and post-school training appear to explain a substantial share of the difference in earnings between individuals (35 per cent in a recent study by Mincer, 1974). Demographic trends, in so far as they affect the pace and pattern of educational development in a country, will therefore affect both the rate of growth of output and the pattern of income distribution. Population trends will, of course, have a variety of complex effects on both growth of output and the pattern of income distribution, quite apart from those linked to educational development, and population growth will in turn be influenced by trends in output and income distribution. But this paper confines itself to the narrower task of identifying some of the ways in which population trends influence the growth of output through their effects on the development of schooling, in the developing countries.

II. THE EDUCATIONAL CONTEXT

Despite very impressive achievements in bringing a larger proportion of children into the formal education system and, as a result, gradually raising literacy levels, the developing countries still lag well behind the West in terms of both 'quantity' and 'quality' of education. Various measures of the 'quantity' of coverage of education are available. One example is the ratio of secondary school

[*] The writer wishes to thank Jeremiah Sullivan and Marli Melton for their incisive comments on an earlier draft of this paper. However, sole responsibility for any shortcomings in the paper rests with the writer.

[1] For example, Denison ascribes 23 per cent of the growth rate of real national income in the U.S. in the 1929–56 period to education. See O.E.C.D. Study Group, 1964.

enrolments to the age group 10–19, which was 37 per cent in the developed countries in 1969, compared with 7 per cent in the developing countries.

During the past decade, there has been a definite, and measurable, improvement in the coverage of education almost universally in the developing countries. Primary-school enrolments have risen, on average, by 5·6 per cent per annum and secondary school enrolments by 9·3 per cent per annum. Such increases have resulted in substantial improvement in the proportion of children in school, though this increase is less impressive than the absolute increase in school enrolments. About half of the increase in primary-school pupils has been necessary merely to keep pace with the growing numbers of children due to continued high birth-rates; only the remaining half has been broadening the coverage of the school system.

It is more difficult to generalise about the quality of education, or indeed to devise a suitable index of educational quality. Nevertheless, however quality of education is defined, there is general agreement that throughout the less-developed world it leaves a great deal to be desired. Poor physical facilities, poorly trained teachers, rote learning and irrelevant courses are only too common. High repeater rates, rates of non-attendance and drop-out rates during the early years mean that a substantial proportion of educational effort and expenditure is devoted to children who do not become even functionally literate. In Asia as a whole[1] in the 1960s, less than half of the pupils who entered Grade 1 completed Grade 4. Yet recent research in Thailand has shown that the majority of Grade 4 graduates either never attained functional literacy or had lapsed into illiteracy three years after leaving school.

What about *trends* in educational quality? There is very little hard evidence. For example, data on trends in educational wastage are virtually non-existent. On the whole, pupil-teacher ratios appear to have risen slightly in the developing countries, with the exception of the more advanced countries of Latin America, during the 1960s. On the other hand, teacher qualifications have definitely improved in Asia (data were not available to the writer for the other regions).

Educational expenditures per pupil in the developing countries of Asia, expressed in current prices, rose only from U.S. $17·2 in 1960 to $18·7 in 1968 (Jones, 1975, ch. 3, Table 6). Allowing for inflation and for the tendency for the share of enrolments in the more expensive second and third levels of education to rise, these figures appear to imply an actual decline in real expenditure per pupil at each level of education. In Africa and Latin America, it would appear that during the same period, more than a third of the major countries

[1] Excluding Japan and China.

(those with populations exceeding one million) had constant or declining real expenditures per pupil at the first or second levels of education or both.[1]

Trends in educational quality, then, remain something of a mystery. But one's general impression is that during the past two decades, the tremendous drive to expand educational coverage in the face of rapid population growth has on the whole been at the expense of improvement in educational quality. The implications of this are sobering. With the continued rapid increase in the school-age population in the developing countries, it will require an increase of 50 per cent in schooling facilities in about fifteen years just to maintain the enrolment rates at the existing level. If we add to this the extra facilities needed to raise enrolment rates, it becomes clear that even with a rise in the proportion of education expenditure in the G.N.P., expenditure per student can rise, if at all, only marginally in the coming years.

III. DEMOGRAPHIC STRUCTURE AND EDUCATIONAL DEVELOPMENT

The demographic structure of the less-developed countries is highly unfavourable to rapid educational development. When the countries of the world with populations exceeding 5 million were divided into three groups according to their level of educational development in 1965,[2] the rate of natural increase of population in the less and least educationally developed countries (2·4 per cent in both groups, as a mean weighted by the populations of the countries concerned) was far above that in the most educationally developed countries (0·8 per cent). Not one of the educationally least advanced countries had a rate of natural increase as low as the *highest* rate recorded in any of the educationally most advanced countries.

The main cause of these striking differences was the high fertility rate in the less-developed countries. Again, there was an almost complete dichotomy between the most developed countries and the other two groups; only for a few countries in the middle (less-developed) group had birth-rates fallen to levels as low as the *highest* birth-rates recorded in the educationally developed countries.

For educational planning, the implications of these differences in

[1] This estimate is very rough, and is based on an examination of Table 2.26 of *UNESCO Statistical Yearbook*, 1971, allowing for the fact that figures in that table are expressed in current prices.

[2] The division was according to the two criteria of literacy rates and proportion enrolled of the population of primary and secondary-school age as defined by each country. See Jones, 1975, ch. 3.

population structure are twofold. Firstly, the growth of the school-age population is much more rapid than in the developed countries, necessitating much faster educational expansion merely to prevent enrolment rates from falling. Secondly, the population structure resulting from a history of high birth-rates makes for a greater burden of educational expenditure in these countries, because the ratio of school-age population to working-age population is much higher. In the educationally developed countries, 16 per cent of the population was aged 5–14 in 1965; in the other two groups of countries, the proportion was around 27 per cent.

The countries with furthest to go in terms of educational development, then, are precisely those whose demographic structure is least favourable to achievement of universal and high quality education. The demographic barrier to educational progress in these countries can be demonstrated by an example: a comparison of Thailand with the countries of Europe – which will seek to isolate the effects of age structure on the burden of education by simulating to some degree the dynamics of the situation.

Thailand's crude birth-rate in 1970 was approximately 41 per 1000, compared with 17 per 1000 in Europe, and the rate of population growth approximately 3·0 per cent compared with 0·8 per cent in Europe. Twenty-seven per cent of Thailand's population was aged 5–14, compared with 16 per cent in Europe. Thailand is still far from its stated goal of achieving seven years' compulsory primary education for all children, but a pattern of educational development is

TABLE 19.1 EDUCATION COSTS PER WORKER IN EUROPE AND THAILAND, ASSUMING THAILAND'S ENROLMENT RATES AND COSTS PER STUDENT APPLY IN BOTH CASES [1] (U.S. $)

	(1)	(2)	(3)	(4)	(5)
		Educational cost per worker			
Year	Europe	Thailand (assuming rapid decline in fertility after 1970)	Excess cost in Thailand (2) / (1)	Thailand (assuming only slight decline in fertility after 1970)	Excess cost in Thailand (4) / (1)
1970	7·2	13·3	1·84	13·3	1·84
1980	9·2	16·5	1·79	16·7	1·83
1990	11·1	16·6	1·50	19·1	1·72
2000	11·9	15·5	1·30	19·4	1·63

[1] Age-specific labour-force participation rates were held constant after 1970.

hypothesised in this example which would lead to attainment of near-universal primary education, and significant improvement at higher levels of education, by the year 1990.

Let us suppose that we can put the educational clock back in Europe, to the extent that Europe had achieved exactly the same enrolment rates for the various levels of education in 1970 as in Thailand. Suppose further that the recurrent costs per child in school[1] at the different levels were exactly the same in Europe as in Thailand. Using actual European labour-force participation rates for Europe and South Asian rates for Thailand, we find that the costs of education *per worker* would be 84 per cent higher in Thailand (see Table 19.1).[2]

For simplicity, assume that labour-force participation rates and educational costs per child in school at each level do not alter after 1970, but that enrolment rates are improved. Table 19.1 shows the resulting trends in costs per worker, given expected population trends in Europe[3] and two alternatives for population growth in Thailand: one assuming a rapid decline in fertility after 1970, the other assuming only a slight decline.[4]

Costs per worker in Europe would rise from $7·2 to $11·9, mainly because of the improvement in enrolment rates; the population structure in Europe would alter very little during the thirty-year period. In Thailand, costs per worker would also rise, but if fertility declined rapidly, these costs would level off by 1990 and then begin to fall. If a slower decline in fertility took place, costs per worker would continue to rise, but proportionately not as much as in Europe. This is because, over time, the population structure in Thailand would be shifting in favour of the working-age as compared with the school-age population.

Columns 3 and 5 show the ratio of educational costs per worker in

[1] Educational costs are defined for our purposes to include government expenditure for public education and a slightly lower cost per student for private secondary schools, which provide approximately half of secondary education in Thailand. Costs do not include payments by students for uniforms, books, etc., or the opportunity costs of schooling.

[2] Use of the South Asian participation rates for both Europe and Thailand would make very little difference; the excess cost per worker would rise to 89 per cent. South Asian rates were used in preference to Thai rates because the recorded female rates in Thailand are exceptionally high for Asian countries. If Thailand's recorded participation rates are used for Thailand, the excess cost per worker would fall to 42 per cent.

[3] The United Nation's medium projections were used (see United Nations, 1970).

[4] In the former example, the general fertility rate was approximately halved in thirty years; in the latter, the general fertility rate declined by a quarter in thirty years, very slowly at first. Both projections assumed a slow but steady decline in mortality.

Thailand to those in Europe. The ratio falls over time, but even after thirty years of declining fertility in Thailand, educational costs per worker would still be 30 per cent higher than in Europe. If only a slow fertility decline took place, costs per worker in Thailand would still be 63 per cent higher by the year 2000.

If this example were applied to most developing countries, we would need to make further allowance for the fact that unemployment rates are higher than in the West. Hence the educational cost per *employed* worker would compare even less favourably with Europe. Since unemployment rates are not very high in Thailand, this factor has been ignored in the present example.

The two conclusions to be drawn from this example are that a decline in fertility in the developing countries would make for a population structure more favourable to rapid educational development, but that the legacy of the present high-fertility, heavily dependent age structure cannot quickly be removed.

A word should be added about the effect of mortality changes. Although mortality declines have a rather limited effect on the age structure, they have two other effects of importance to educational planners: they increase the rate of population growth and they lead to lowered wastage of educational investments due to the death of students before they complete their education. The acceleration in population growth in developing countries in the past quarter century has been primarily due to lowered mortality; the 'baby boom' was a matter of increased *survival* of babies rather than a rise in the frequency with which they were born to mothers. The mortality revolution has not yet spent itself and some developing countries (in Africa and South Asia, especially) could still face considerable increases in growth rates of population and of potential school children through the halving of infant mortality rates currently at levels of 150 per thousand or above, and parallel mortality declines at other ages.

Aside from raising the growth rate of the school-age population, such mortality declines would have the beneficial effect of reducing the mortality wastage of children who have received some education. How important will this effect be? If we assume a country's mortality changes from roughly the level now experienced in Indonesia to roughly the level now experienced in Malaysia,[1] then the proportion of children aged 5 who will die before they reach age 15 will fall from about 4·8 per cent to about 1·2 per cent.[2] This would appear to be

[1] That is, from a crude death-rate of about 19 (expectation of life at birth about 45 years) to a crude death-rate of about 7 (expectation of life at birth about 65 years).

[2] This was calculated by comparing levels 11 and 19 in the Coale and Demeny model life tables west.

a rather marginal contribution to the lowering of educational wastage compared with the size of the wastage problem as a whole. However, it must be borne in mind that the educational expenditure on pupils who die is completely lost, whereas the productivity of those who drop out for other reasons is no doubt raised to some extent by their educational experience. Moreover, improvements in mortality at least to some extent reflect a decrease in morbidity, which is itself one of the factors responsible for high absenteeism and drop out of pupils. The effects of the decline in mortality and morbidity, taken together, may be quite large.

IV. FERTILITY DECLINE AND THE COST OF EDUCATION

(a) *Effect on enrolments and teacher requirements*

It is obvious to even the casual observer that a decline in fertility should, with a lag, reduce the costs of providing given amounts of education to any given proportion of the nation's children. The decline in fertility will reduce the ratio of potential students to labour force, and since there is no obvious reason why output per worker should rise more slowly in the medium term when fertility declines, the fertility decline implies a chance to raise enrolment rates and achieve given improvements in educational quality at a lower cost in terms of available resources than would otherwise have been the case.

In this section I would like to present the results of three country case-studies – Ghana, Thailand and Ceylon – (Jones, 1972, chs 6, 7) which indicate that this effect is large enough to be taken into serious account in determining population policy. In each of these studies, enrolments, teacher requirements and costs were projected according to a variety of assumptions about future population trends and trends in the proportion of children in school at different levels of education. The Thailand and Ghana studies used a simple projection of trends in enrolments at each level as a proportion of the age group from which these enrolments are normally drawn.[1] The Ceylon study used the more complex grade-cohort approach, whereby an 'entry cohort' of pupils is traced through the system according to different assumptions about annual progression rates from grade to grade.

The demographic assumptions of these studies are summarised briefly in Table 19.2. In all studies, a gradual increase in expectation

[1] Because of the problem of over-age pupils, the age group selected in most cases was a little wider than the 'official' age range for that level of education, but not wide enough to cover the extreme cases. This does not affect the validity of the results.

of life at birth was assumed in all population projections. In Ghana, a state of constant fertility was compared with a steady decline in fertility, whereas in Thailand and Ceylon fertility was assumed to decline in all projections, but at different speeds. The fertility declines assumed for all three countries are not unrealistically rapid; they lie within the realm of the possible.

TABLE 19.2 DEMOGRAPHIC ASSUMPTIONS, COUNTRY CASE STUDIES

Country and projection	Fertility assumption	Mortality assumption
GHANA		
High projection	Total fertility rate remains constant	Expectation of life at birth rises by 0·5 years per annum
Low projection	Total fertility rate declines linearly from 6·9 to 3·0 in 40 years	
THAILAND		
High projection	General fertility rate declines by a quarter within 30 years	Expectation of life at birth rises by a third of a year per annum
Medium projection	Accelerating fertility decline, totalling 47·5 per cent in 25 years	
Low projection	More rapid fertility decline, totalling about half in 30 years	
CEYLON		
	Gross reproduction rate falls from 2·6 to 1·2 in 35-year period according to three paths:	
Projection 1	Rapid, then decelerating, decline	Female expectation of life at birth rises 12 years in a 35-year period
Projection 2	Steady decline	
Projection 3	Slow, then accelerating decline	

The onset of a fertility decline will not have any effect on primary-school enrolments for 6 years, and no substantial effect for 8 or 9 years. The effect on secondary enrolments is even more delayed: the lower secondary students of 1984 are already born. Over time, however, fertility decline sharply affects the numbers requiring schooling. For example, if we assume a rise in the primary-school enrolment rate in Ghana from 73 per cent in the base year to 87 per cent 20 years later and a slightly faster rise in Thailand, then the percentage increases in enrolments in five-year periods will differ as follows, according to whether fertility rates remain high or decline:

	1st 5 years %	2nd 5 years %	3rd 5 years %	4th 5 years %
GHANA				
High fertility	23·9	28·2	28·3	24·4
Declining fertility	23·9	23·7	14·2	17·2
THAILAND				
High fertility[1]	28·6	23·6	19·9	18·8
Declining fertility	29·0	18·4	7·3	7·7

The saving in enrolments resulting from a decline in fertility is translated directly into savings in requirements for teachers if teacher/pupil ratios are left unchanged. It is here that the major savings in educational costs are effected, because teacher salary costs typically constitute 60 to 80 per cent of the total recurrent costs of an educational system.

Fertility changes will also have important effects on educational costs through their influence on teacher training requirements. In the Ceylon study, after estimating annual enrolments and teaching force required, needed enrolments in teacher training institutions each year were projected backwards, using various assumptions about attrition rates, rates of re-entry of former teachers, etc. The results of this exercise are shown in Fig. 19.1. The goal was to ensure that all new primary-school teachers after 1971 should be two-year trained, implying the gradual elimination of uncertificated teachers, who at the beginning of 1970 constituted 25 per cent of all primary-school teachers. The influence of the alternative paths of fertility is very pronounced. For example, in the ten-year period 1975–85, well over four times as many teachers would need to be graduated from Teacher Education Institutes in projection 3 as in projection 1 (124,000 as compared with 26,000). The reason for these marked differences is that teacher-training requirements are heavily influenced by *changes* in the number of pupils, and alternative paths of fertility have a much sharper effect on the increment to the student population than on the absolute size of that population.

(b) *Effect on expenditures*

By making reasonable assumptions about trends in certain key components of educational costs (e.g. teacher salaries for various categories of teachers, non-teacher recurrent costs per pupil) it is possible to project the costs of meeting given educational goals, according to different trends in population growth. Increases in the dollar costs of education have little meaning in isolation; the key variables of interest are the projected trends in educational costs

[1] Slight fertility decline.

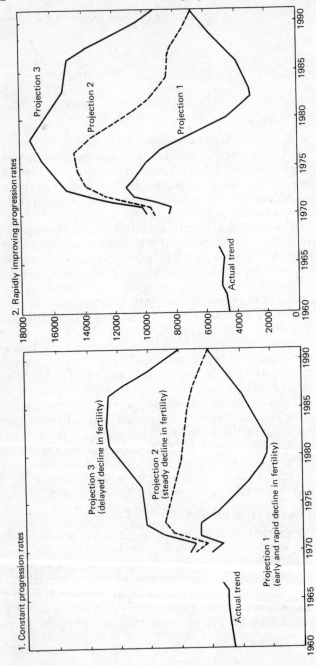

FIG. 19.1 Ceylon: Required enrolments in Teacher Education Institutes, 1970–1991, to ensure that all new primary-school teachers after 1971 are fully trained.

as a proportion of government budgets or of G.N.P., and the projected savings resulting from lowered fertility, also as a proportion of budgets and of G.N.P.

The results of the Thailand study are given in Table 19.3. In this study it was assumed that the growth of total G.N.P. would not be affected by the trend in fertility. This implies that per capita income will grow faster in the projection with more rapid fertility decline, and is consistent with the results of macro-economic models which make due allowance for the major linkages between population trends and the other key determinants of the growth of output;[1] however, other assumptions could also be used without greatly

TABLE 19.3 THAILAND: TOTAL EXPENDITURE ON ALL LEVELS OF EDUCATION[a] AS A PERCENTAGE OF G.N.P., 1970–2000, ALTERNATIVE ASSUMPTIONS

Year	Constant enrolment rates			Improving enrolment rates		
	High projection	Medium projection	Low projection	High projection	Medium projection	Low projection
1970	3·5	3·5	3·5	3·5	3·5	3·5
1975	3·8	3·8	3·8	3·8	3·8	3·8
1980	3·4	3·4	3·1	3·9	3·9	3·7
1985	3·3	3·1	2·7	4·1	3·9	3·5
1990	3·1	2·9	2·5	4·1	3·8	3·3
1995	3·0	2·6	2·3	4·1	3·5	3·1
2000	2·9	2·3	2·1	4·1	3·3	3·1

[a] Includes both recurrent and capital expenditure. Capital expenditure includes replacement expenditures.
Source: Jones, 1975, ch. 6.

affecting the results. Another questionable assumption was that the growth of total G.N.P. would not be affected by the trends in school enrolment rates.

It must be borne in mind that the population projections for Thailand all assumed a decline in fertility. Therefore the savings shown in Table 19.3 result from the *more rapid* decline in fertility assumed in the low population projection, not from a comparison of declining fertility with a state of constant fertility.

Table 19.3 highlights the considerable lag (of about a decade) before fertility trends have a substantial effect on educational costs; nevertheless the savings build up, over time, to very significant proportions. In Thailand, the projected increases in enrolment rates would require an increase of a quarter in education's share of the G.N.P. by the mid-1980s if the high population projection obtains, but of only 10 per cent if the low projection obtains. By the end of

[1] The results of a number of such models are summarised in Ruprecht and Wahren, 1970, ch. II.

the projection period (the year 2000) education's share of the G.N.P. in the high projection exceeds that in the low projection by 32 per cent, a difference amounting to more than 1 per cent of the total G.N.P., of which the public sector share probably amounts to almost 4 per cent of the total government budget.[1] Yet in both these projections, the proportion of the school-age population enrolled at the different levels of education is identical.

The Thailand case-study's results are consistent with those of the other case-studies. Given the aim of gradually improving school enrolment rates, annual educational costs were higher by the following percentages in the higher fertility projection in the various studies:

	After 15 years	After 25 years
	%	%
Ghana	7	25
Thailand	16	33
Ceylon	17	54

The wide differences in these figures are caused primarily by differences in the assumed speed of the fertility decline in the respective 'low' projections.

V. RELATIVE IMPORTANCE OF POPULATION GROWTH AMONG FACTORS RAISING EDUCATIONAL COSTS

Out of all the factors leading to an increase in educational costs, just how important is rapid population growth? There can be no hard and fast rules on this. If a stationary population has been reached in which the school-age population does not increase from year to year, then population increase contributes nothing at all to the rise in educational costs. On the other hand, with a growing population that has pushed enrolment rates as high as it wants them to go, is not altering the qualification structure or average length of tenure of its teacher force and is not raising teacher pay scales, population growth is the *only* cause of rising educational expenditures. In between these zero and 100 per cent limits lies the real world.

It is possible to set the limits more narrowly if we recall that almost all developing countries have a rate of population growth exceeding 2 per cent per annum (i.e. doubling in less than 35 years) and in many of them the growth rate exceeds 3 per cent per annum (i.e. doubling in 23 years). Consider a country with a

---

[1] Education in recent years has constituted about 14 per cent of total government expenditures in Thailand, which in turn have constituted about 19 per cent of total domestic expenditures.

youth population of one million, increasing at 3 per cent per annum, which raises its school enrolment rate from 50 per cent to 70 per cent in 10 years. If the new pupils are accommodated at the same recurrent cost per head as existing pupils, then population growth will be responsible for more than half the total increase in costs. But what if other cost-raising influences are also present? Table 19.4 supplies some answers. On the assumption that the million school-aged children are all in the primary-school ages, the first section shows what will happen to the total recurrent costs of primary education when, in addition to the sharp rise in enrolment rates, pupil/teacher ratios are lowered somewhat and teacher salaries and other recurrent costs raised. Column 8 indicates, not surprisingly, that the more cost-raising factors are added, the smaller the proportion of the total increase in costs that can be attributed to population growth. This proportion ranges from 55 per cent if school enrolment rates are raised but no other changes are made down to 43 per cent when the other cost-raising factors are added.

Some developing countries have population growth rates below 3 per cent but almost all are above 2 per cent, so to set a lower limit to the estimates of the importance of population growth in cost increases, columns 3, 5 and 7 of Table 19.4 repeat the same calculations for a population growth rate of 2 per cent. In this case population growth is responsible for 32 per cent of the total increase in costs, when all the cost-raising factors are included, and its share ranges up to 43 per cent if school enrolment rates are raised but no other changes are made.

These simple examples deal with only one level of education. An effort to raise enrolment rates more rapidly at the second and third levels than at the primary level would greatly affect the cost relationships, since costs per student at these levels are much higher than at the primary level. But *within* each level of education, the general considerations already discussed in the primary education example apply, as the second section of Table 19.4 shows. Because of the assumption of rapid progress in secondary education, costs are raised dramatically (more than trebled in the example with 3 per cent population growth) and the contribution of population growth to the total increase somewhat less than at the primary-education level. The result, when the two levels of education are combined, is that the contribution of population growth to the increase in costs – 40 per cent in the 3 per cent population growth example and 30 per cent in the 2 per cent example – lies between the very high figure at the primary level and the lower figure at the secondary level.

One further point clearly emerges from Table 19.4. Column 5 shows that the relative saving in costs of education after a given

TABLE 19.4 EFFECT OF POPULATION GROWTH ON INCREASE IN RECURRENT
ENROLMENT RATES, LOWERING PUPIL/TEACHER

Assumption	Variable measured	Year 0 (1)
PRIMARY EDUCATION		
	Population at school-going age	1,000,000
Enrolment rate rises from 50% to 70% after 10 years	Enrolments	500,000
In addition to this assumption,		
(a) Pupil/teacher ratio constant at 35/1	Teachers	14,286
(b) Average teacher salary raised 20%	Cost of teachers	$1,428,600
(c) Pupil/teacher ratio lowered to 32/1	Teachers	14,286
(d) (b) and (c)	Cost of teachers	$1,428,600
(e) In addition to (d), non-teacher salary cost per student raised 40%	Total recurrent costs	$1,928,600
SECONDARY EDUCATION		
	Population at school-going age	400,000
Enrolment rate raised from 15% to 25% after 10 years	Enrolments	60,000
In addition to this assumption,		
(a) Pupil/teacher ratio constant at 30/1	Teachers	2000
(b) Average teacher salary raised 25%	Cost of teachers	$500,000
(c) Pupil/teacher ratio lowered to 25/1	Teachers	2000
(d) (b) and (c)	Cost of teachers	$500,000
(e) In addition to (d), non-teacher salary cost per student raised 40%	Total recurrent costs	$680,000
BOTH LEVELS OF EDUCATION		
	Population at school-going age	1,400,000
Enrolment rates raised	Enrolments	560,000
In addition to this assumption,		
(a) Pupil/teacher ratios constant	Teachers	16,286
(b) Average teacher salaries raised at each level	Teacher costs	$1,928,600
(c) Pupil/teacher ratios	Teachers	16,286
(d) (b) and (c)	Teacher costs	$1,928,600
(e) In addition to (d), non-teacher salary costs per student at each level raised 40%	Total recurrent costs	$2,608,600

length of time if population does not grow as independent of trends in cost-related factors such as pupil/teacher ratios, average teacher salary levels, and non-teacher cost per student. Viewed in this light, a rapid rise in enrolment rates and a variety of other quality-related changes do not 'wash out' even slightly the savings from reduced fertility. The relative savings resulting at any given time from the decline in fertility can be altered only by altering the speed of that decline.

It is conceivable that cost increases sharper than the 10·5 per cent per annum in Table 19.4[1] could be encountered in the real world,

[1] For both levels of education, in the example with population growth of 3 per cent per annum.

COSTS OF EDUCATION IN A HYPOTHETICAL COUNTRY THAT IS RAISING RATIOS AND RAISING TEACHER SALARIES

Year 10			After 10 years: ratio of case with population growth to case with no population growth		Percentage of total increase attributable to population growth	
0%	Population growth 2%	3%	$\frac{(3)}{(2)} \times 100$	$\frac{(4)}{(2)} \times 100$	$\frac{[(3)-(1)]-[(2)-(1)]}{(3)-(1)}$	$\frac{[(4)-(1)]-[(2)-(1)]}{(4)-(1)}$
(2)	(3)	(4)	(5)	(6)	(7)	(8)
1,000,000	1,218,994	1,343,916	121·9	134·4	100	100
700,000	853,296	940,741	121·9	134·4	43	55
20,000	24,380	26,878	121·9	134·4	43	55
2,400,000	2,925,600	3,225,360	121·9	134·4	35	46
21,875	26,665	29,398	121·9	134·4	39	50
2,625,000	3,199,800	3,527,760	121·9	134·4	32	43
3,605,000	4,394,414	4,844,797	121·9	134·4	32	43
400,000	487,598	537,567	121·9	134·4	100	100
100,000	121,899	134,392	121·9	134·4	35	46
3333	4063	4480	121·9	134·4	43	46
$1,041,562	1,269,687	1,400,000	121·9	134·4	30	40
4000	4876	5376	121·9	134·4	30	41
$1,250,000	1,523,750	1,680,000	121·9	134·4	27	36
1,670,000	2,035,726	2,244,446	121·9	134·4	27	37
1,400,000	1,706,592	1,881,483	121·9	134·4	100	100
800,000	975,195	1,075,133	121·9	134·4	42	53
23,333	28,443	31,358	121·9	134·4	42	53
3,441,562	4,195,287	4,625,360	121·9	134·4	33	44
25,875	31,541	34,774	121·9	134·4	37	48
3,875,000	4,723,550	5,207,760	121·9	134·4	30	41
5,275,000	6,430,140	7,089,243	121·9	134·4	30	40

though it rarely happens in practice over an extended period.[1] Even so, a second example has been computed, parallel to that shown in Table 19.4, but assuming a more rapid rise in enrolment rates and

[1] When a sharp increase in enrolments is achieved, pupil/teacher ratios are unlikely to fall, and the government is likely to resist sharp across-the-board salary increases in a situation in which educational expenditures are being forced up rapidly without them, though of course teacher salaries must be kept roughly in line with those in similar occupations if recruitment difficulties are to be avoided. Another factor tending to hold down average salary levels will be the heavy recruitment of young teachers to cope with the enrolment expansion; these young teachers will come in at the bottom levels of the pay scale, probably more than counteracting the tendency for their salaries to be higher because their level of training exceeds that of the existing teaching force.

teacher salary costs and a more rapid fall in pupil/teacher ratios. In this example, the contribution of population growth to the rise in the costs of education for both primary and secondary levels is 26 per cent if population is growing at 2 per cent per annum and 35 per cent if it is growing at 3 per cent per annum. Both figures are around 4 or 5 percentage points lower than the contribution of population growth in the previous example, because of the sharper influence of the other cost-raising factors.

A number of more detailed country case-studies conducted by the author and by the International Institute for Educational Planning (Ta Ngoc Châu, 1972, Table 19) show that when population increases rapidly, recurrent costs of primary education after 20 years will be almost double, and in some studies more than double, their level in a situation of no population growth.[1] The percentage contribution of population growth to the increase in costs over the 20-year period varies from 56 per cent to 68 per cent. This is higher than the contribution of population growth to the rising costs of primary education shown in column 8 of Table 19.4, no doubt because of the longer time period considered.

Bearing in mind (1) that in Latin America and the more educationally advanced Asian countries enrolment rates at the primary level are close to 100 per cent and therefore cannot be raised much higher; (2) that population growth in most less-developed countries exceeds $2\frac{1}{2}$ per cent per annum, we can conclude from this discussion that in the less-developed countries, the contribution of population growth to the increase in educational costs during the next decade is likely to be in the range of 30 to 50 per cent. It could go even higher if strong efforts are not being made to improve the coverage and quality of the total school system. Moreover, the contribution of population growth to the rise in educational costs tends to become greater the longer the time period considered.

This section must be ended with a note of warning. Although the role played by population growth in raising the cost of attaining given education goals needs to be understood, the practical consideration is not the advantage of switching immediately from a state of 3 per cent to zero annual population growth in the school-going age groups, but rather the benefits to be derived from a gradual deceleration of population growth. As shown in the previous section, these benefits, though real and cumulative, are substantially delayed, particularly when all levels of education are considered and not just the primary level.

---

[1] In these studies enrolment rates are assumed to be rising and a number of other cost-raising factors operating.

VI. FERTILITY DECLINE AND EDUCATIONAL COSTS: THE FEEDBACK INTO THE DEVELOPMENT PROCESS

We have demonstrated that a significantly higher share of national resources will be needed to achieve the same improvements in the average educational level of the young adult population in a higher-fertility situation, other things being equal. In the context of a strong commitment by governments of most developing countries to broaden the coverage and improve the quality of their educational systems, an important result of a decline in fertility is to widen the options available to the planners. The resources saved in achieving a given improvement in the coverage and quality of the school system could be used to improve further that coverage and quality, or be diverted to other development activities, or some combination of both.

However, given the way that budget allocations tend to be decided (basing each Ministry's allocation on the previous year's allocation with a decent, but restrained, mark-up), it is probably unrealistic to expect that fertility decline in most developing countries will lead to much diversion of resources from education to other activities. (Nor perhaps should it, when viewed from a strictly cost-benefit vantage point.) More likely, the gain from fertility decline will be through faster attainment of enrolment rate goals and qualitative improvements. This implies that the feedback from the fertility decline into the process of economic development via its effects on education will probably be a faster rise in the proportion, but not number, of trained people in the young groups entering the work-force and an improvement in the quality of the education which they (or some of them) are receiving.

There are few opportunities to check this claim against empirical data, but a comparison between recent educational experience in Thailand and Singapore is suggestive (see Table 19.5). Both countries achieved rapid economic growth during the 1960s, enabling a sharp increase in educational expenditures. But population trends were quite different.

In Thailand, population growth during the 1960s averaged approximately 3·0 per cent per annum. Fertility levels were high and apparently rather steady, with the result that the annual number of births probably increased by about one third over the decade; the proportion of these babies surviving was also rising. Thailand had virtually achieved universal compulsory four years' education by the beginning of the decade; expansion of enrolments at this level had therefore to cope 'only' with population growth. Early in the decade, however, the government committed itself to the expansion

TABLE 19.5   A COMPARISON OF EDUCATIONAL DEVELOPMENT IN THAILAND AND SINGAPORE, 1960–1970

	1960	1965	1970	% increase 1960–5	% increase 1965–70
THAILAND					
1. Primary-school enrolments ('000)	3935·5	4630·4	5604·2	18	21
2. Secondary-school enrolments ('000)	289·0	357·6	563·7	24	58
3. Tertiary-level enrolments ('000)	50·6	53·4	71·0	5	33
4. Ratio of above primary to total enrolments	7·9 %	8·2 %	10·2 %		
5. Recurrent government educational expenditures (current prices) (Bt. mill.)	1409 (1963)	1696	2716 (1969)	59[a]	80[b]
6. Recurrent government educational expenditures per pupil (Bt.)[c]	350 (1963)	395	563 (1969)	35[a]	56[b]
7. Recurrent government expenditures on primary education per primary school pupil (Bt.)[c]	236 (1963)	287	408 (1969)	62[a]	55[b]
8. Percentage of current education expenditure on primary school	63·3 (1963)	68·3	67·6 (1969)		
SINGAPORE					
1. Primary school enrolments ('000)	291	363	366	25	1
2. Secondary school enrolments ('000)	59	115	146	93	27
3. Tertiary-level enrolments ('000)	8	14	14	69	–1
4. Ratio of above primary to total enrolments	18·8 %	26·2 %	30·3 %		
5. Recurrent government educational expenditures (current prices) (Singapore $'000)	57,100	112,806	184,492	98	63
6. Recurrent government educational expenditures per pupil ($)	159·5	229·6	350·9	44	53
7. Recurrent government expenditures on primary education per primary school pupil ($)	128·2	179·6	210·5	40	17
8. Percentage of current education expenditure on primary school	65·3	57·7	44·4		

Note: Although educational expenditures are expressed in current prices, trends in inflation were roughly comparable in both countries. In Singapore, the consumer price index rose 12 per cent over the decade, compared with approximately 20 per cent in Thailand.

[a] 1963–5 trend extrapolated to five-year period.
[b] 1965–9 trend extrapolated to five-year period.
[c] In these rows government expenditures are related to the number of pupils in government schools.

Sources:
Thailand: Bennett *et al.*, 1972.
Singapore: Tan Peng Boo, 1970, Tables 3A, 12A and 14A; unpublished data supplied by Ministry of Education.

of compulsory schooling from 4 to 7 years of education. As a result, tremendous efforts went into expansion of the upper primary level of education, where a 125 per cent enrolment increase was achieved. Even so, the goal of 7 years' compulsory education is still far from being reached: in 1969/70 the overall progression rate from 4th to 5th grade was still only about 44 per cent (Bennett *et al.*, 1972), and in 1970 the ratio of upper primary enrolments to the numbers of children aged 11–13 was only 30 per cent.[1] Repetition rates in the primary schools have remained rather high, but the average educational qualification of the teaching force has risen, and this may be partly responsible for the surprisingly large rise in the expenditure per pupil at the primary-school level.

Secondary-school enrolments almost doubled during the 1960s, most of the increase occurring towards the end of the decade, when the policy of restricting the growth of secondary enrolments appeared to break down under increasing pressure from the public. (The ratio of secondary-school enrolments to the numbers aged 14–18 was still only $12\frac{1}{2}$ per cent in 1970.) Enrolments in teacher training institutions increased rapidly, particularly toward the end of the decade, though in other institutions of higher education enrolments expanded at only about 6 per cent per annum, again due to deliberate restrictions on university entrance.

Singapore started the decade with a more advanced education system than Thailand; for example, the goal of universal six-years' primary education was almost reached, and enrolment ratios for the primary and secondary levels of education combined were 78 per cent of the relevant age groups compared with 59 per cent in Thailand.[2] Population trends during the 1960s contrasted dramatically with those in Thailand. In Singapore, a decline in fertility dramatic enough to halve the gross reproduction rate in 12 years began in 1957. The absolute number of births fell from almost 62,000 in 1960 to less than 45,000 in 1969, and this decline was reflected, with a lag of six years, in primary school entrants. However, numbers of prospective secondary-school pupils will not begin to decline until the mid-1970s. By the mid-1960s, primary school enrolments had levelled out and by the end of the decade they were actually starting to decline. It was therefore possible to put strong

[1] This does not mean that 30 per cent of 11–13 year olds were in school, because not all upper primary students are drawn from exactly this age group, and some 11–13 year olds are still in lower primary schools. But it does give a rough idea of the proportion of the target population currently enrolled in upper primary schools.

[2] That is, total enrolments at primary and secondary levels were 59 per cent of the age groups from which these enrolments are officially supposed to be drawn (7–18).

efforts into the secondary and higher levels of education;[1] secondary-school enrolments were raised 146 per cent during the decade, and primary education's share in total educational expenditures over the decade declined from 65 to 44 per cent.

Apart from documenting the long lead time between a fertility decline and its effect on enrolments, what are the main implications of the Singapore-Thailand comparison?

One is that rapid population growth cannot be considered an insuperable barrier to educational progress. Thailand has made modest, but real, progress in extending the coverage and improving the quality of its education system. However, there has been a good deal of 'static expansion' to cope with rapidly-increasing numbers of school-age children, and the basic structure of the school system has altered little. A roughly similar increase in public education expenditures in Thailand and Singapore has been associated with little increase in the ratio of post-primary to total enrolments in Thailand, but a sharp increase in Singapore.

A second implication would appear to be that it is unrealistic to expect a decline in fertility, even one as sharp as in Singapore, to lead to any considerable deceleration in the rise in educational expenditures. Certainly there has not yet been any slackening of educational expenditures in Singapore and none in prospect, because along with the downturn in primary school enrolments there are plans for a marked expansion of secondary education, mainly through expansion of technical and vocational education to take those pupils who are not fitted for the academic stream, and of post-secondary education, through opening new vocational institutes, a technical institute and a junior college. In addition, expenditures *per pupil* at each level of education have been increasing sharply, due to replacement of inadequate buildings, upgrading of the educational standards of the teaching force, and so on.

In other words, the main contribution of fertility decline to educational development in Singapore has been not in slowing the rise in educational expenditures, but rather in rapidly increasing the average educational attainment of young people and in improving the quality of the educational system.

VII. THE EMPLOYMENT AND PRODUCTIVITY GOALS OF POPULATION AND EDUCATION POLICIES

It is generally taken for granted that further expansion of the

---

[1] Higher education enrolments did not increase in the 1965–70 period, but by 1965 these enrolments already constituted five times as high a proportion of the relevant age group as in Thailand.

proportion of children proceeding further through the school system will be conducive to economic growth in the developing countries. On the whole, the faith in the value of investment in education would appear to be soundly based. McLelland, for example, has shown that, within groups of countries starting at approximately the same level of economic or technological development, countries which invest more heavily in education have tended to develop more rapidly than other countries (McLelland, 1966). Then there is all the work showing the importance of education in the 'residual's' contribution to economic growth. And of the rather limited number of studies on the rates of return to education in developing countries, most show higher returns than the average return on capital. But others do not; in Malaysia, for example, social rates of return on both primary and tertiary education appear to be quite low (Hoerr, 1973). The same goes for vocational secondary and higher education in Thailand (Blaug, 1971, Table 20).

Therefore, even if we accept as valid the findings of rates of returns studies, there is reason to doubt that a drive towards Western educational levels across-the-board will always be a desirable investment of a developing country's scarce resources. The uncertainty is compounded when we allow for some of the well-known weaknesses in the rate-of-returns approach to evaluating educational investment.[1]

Nevertheless, the 'educational imperative' is very much a fact of life, and the concern in this paper has been to demonstrate the implications of population trends, given the context of often sacrosanct educational goals with which they will interact.

If, as suggested earlier, the major developmental effect of fertility decline via the education system is to raise more rapidly the proportion of each young cohort who proceed further through the school system and to raise the quality of the education they receive, the effect on output will be felt only after these cohorts have entered the labour force. What kind of lags are involved, and are there offsetting argument in favour of maintaining fertility at a high level?

[1] See, for example, Merrett, 1966; Taubman and Wales, 1972. Particularly worrying, to my mind, is the projection of future trends from cross-section evidence in a rapidly changing situation in which it will often (probably normally) be invalid to assume a close relationship between recent and future rates of return. Developing countries are concerned not with marginal changes, but with massive structural changes both in the economy and the educational system itself. To this is added the problem of especially high unemployment rates among the secondary educated in many countries, which often are taken into account neither in calculating rates of return to education (though they can be) nor in realistically facing the political dangers to economic progress of an overly rapid expansion of certain kinds of education, well illustrated by the 'insurrection' in Sri Lanka in 1971.

In seeking to answer this question, we must begin by considering the dynamics of labour force replacement.

VIII. EFFECT OF POPULATION GROWTH AND EDUCATIONAL DEVELOPMENT ON THE EDUCATIONAL COMPOSITION OF THE LABOUR FORCE

The labour force in developing countries is much more youthful than in the West. In most Asian countries with relevant data, more than 40 per cent (and in some countries, half) of the labour force around 1960 was aged less than 30. In Western countries, by contrast, these young workers typically constituted less than 40 per cent of the labour force, and in many countries, less than 30 per cent. Although qualifications as to the quality and comparability of the data are in order, this basic difference in the age structure of the labour force is real enough. Since trends in both fertility and schooling have their initial impact on the youthful sector of the labour force, they can have a substantial impact on labour-force size and composition earlier in the developing countries than would be possible in the West.

Because of the rapid expansion of education in the post-war years, in most developing countries the average educational attainment of younger people is much higher than that of older people. Therefore, over time, there is a steady rise in the average educational attainment of the labour force, as younger, better-educated workers replace older, less-educated workers. If rising levels of education of the labour force do in fact contribute powerfully to the growth of output, then it can be argued that the quicker the older, less-educated workers are replaced by younger workers, the better (see Leibenstein, 1971). Such a replacement can be accelerated in two ways: firstly, by keeping fertility high and hence ensuring that the ratio between young labour-force entrants and older labour-force withdrawals is high; secondly, by expanding the educational system as rapidly as possible so that the educational level of young entrants will exceed that of older withdrawals by as wide a margin as possible.

But it is not as simple as this. Rapid population growth will not necessarily lead to a more rapid rise in the educational attainment of the labour force if it holds back the percentage of young people in school (which it does). Nor will rapid expansion of enrolments in post-primary education necessarily lead to a more rapid rise in the educational attainment of the labour force if it delays the entry into the labour force of those who are staying on longer in school (which it does). The interactions, then, among population trends, educational development and the educational composition of the labour force are highly complex, and an infinite variety of scenarios can be devised, in which trends in the educational composition of the labour force will vary according to the assumed trends in population and educational expansion, and the assumed strength of the above-mentioned factors which work to offset the positive effects of those trends on labour-force composition.

Despite the clear need to understand these interrelationships and the relative strength of the various factors affecting the dynamics of labour-force replacement in any broadly-based strategy for man-power development, little work has been done in this field. We can nevertheless muster some evidence relating to the argument that the dynamics of labour-force replacement is a possible reason to maintain high fertility in the developing countries. This is a naive sugges-tion, which fails to recognise four important facts. If we compare two initially identical populations, in one of which fertility remains high and in the other of which it steadily declines, then after, say, 30 years (i) the higher fertility population will have lower capital/labour ratios, because there is no reason to suppose that the faster growth of population (initially faster *only* in the dependent age groups) will result in accelerated capital accumulation. (ii) The labour force will be growing more rapidly in the high fertility population, an un-desirable prospect in view of the high unemployment levels generally prevailing in the developing countries. Moreover, unemployment rates are highest in the young age groups and typically among those with a high-school education.[1] (iii) It will in fact be substantially harder to raise the average educational attainment of new labour-force entrants as rapidly in the high-fertility population as in the declining-fertility population (as this paper has already shown). (iv) *Even if* the high fertility population succeeds in raising school enrolment rates as rapidly as the declining fertility population, the higher fertility will in fact make very little difference to the time taken to replace the poorly-educated labour force with a group of better-educated workers. (See Appendix for further elaboration.)

Therefore there is no valid case, from the point of view of raising

[1] (For evidence, see Turnham, 1971, Table III.3; and University of Indonesia, 1974.) There are two possible interpretations of these facts. One is that the higher unemployment among the young and better-educated is simply a structural thing; these groups *always* have higher unemployment rates than other groups because they are the groups still trying to find their niche in the job market. The other interpreta-tion is that the high unemployment rates in these groups reflect a worsening unemployment situation due to the massive influx of young workers, which will be reflected later in rising unemployment rates at older ages as these cohorts age and are followed by successively larger cohorts. Clearly, the 'structural' explanation is the main one; but there is very little time-trend evidence on which to decide whether the 'worsening unemployment' explanation is also applying. If it is applying, of course, it would support even more strongly the case for lowered fertility.

the educational attainment of the labour force, for perpetuation of high fertility in the developing countries. The issue is rather that of determining the *optimum mix* of fertility decline and educational advance for improving labour-force composition. Rapid expansion of school enrolment will certainly have effects on labour-force growth and structure which might support or weaken the case for lower or higher investment in education built on the findings of conventional rate of return analysis. This is a very complex issue, however. The growth of the labour force will be slowed as a result of a rapid expansion of school enrolments. In a country with an initial fairly high level of unemployment, this will presumably result in both lower unemployment rates and lower total employment. Unless marginal productivity of labour is zero, lower employment will mean lower total output and lower output per head of population. Against this negative short-run effect, it is necessary to balance both the positive short-term effect of lower unemployment and the positive longer-run effect of presumably higher output, as those who stay on in school subsequently enter the labour force with more education than they would otherwise have had. The relative weighting given to these short-term and medium-term effects will depend on many factors, including the original level of unemployment, the original skill mix of the labour force, the sensitivity of employment prospects and earnings to educational attainment, expected trends in the size of the labour-force age groups, and the general prospects for the economy.

The importance of the interactions of population growth, educational expansion and labour-force composition in the development process, and our primitive state of knowledge in this field, singles it out as a fruitful area for co-operation between demographers, educational planners, economic model-builders and sociologists in the future. Any adequate treatment must recognise that population growth, often treated as a *deus ex machina* by economists, is itself profoundly affected by educational development and social and economic progress.

The modest contribution of the present paper to the elaboration of a more satisfactory population-education-development model is simply to demonstrate that a decline in fertility is likely to have decidedly positive effects in the medium term at a number of key points of interaction with the development of education and the subsequent productivity of the labour force.

APPENDIX
Relationship between fertility, educational progress and educational attainment of the labour force

Given the rate of advance in raising school enrolment rates, a decline in fertility makes little difference to the time taken to replace a developing country's poorly-educated labour force with a group of better-educated workers. If we compare two populations, originally identical but with constant and declining fertility respectively, and assume that both raise school enrolment rates at exactly the same rate, the trends in the educational composition of the labour force will differ very little.

The reason for this somewhat surprising conclusion hinges on two facts. (For the evidence in detail, see Jones and Gingrich, 1968; and Jones, 1975, ch. 11.) Firstly, the extreme youthfulness of the base-year, high fertility population ensures the rapid replacement of the bulk of the existing labour force *whether or not* fertility declines. Even when children are being held longer in school as a result of improving educational levels, the constant fertility population takes only 18 years to replace half of the original labour force with new workers; the declining fertility population also takes 18 years. The constant fertility population takes 31 years to replace three-quarters of the original labour force with new workers; the declining fertility population takes only one year longer.

Secondly, the average educational attainment of cohorts when they are young (aged 10–14 and 15–19) is lower than it will be when they reach ages beyond 20, because many of these young people have still not completed their education. Moreover, those who enter the labour force at these ages have lower educational attainment than the cohort as a whole, because they tend to be the early school drop-outs. Although these facts are rather obvious, they are often overlooked, and it is therefore perhaps worth emphasising them with an example. Take a country with a stable population growing at a little above 2·9 per cent per annum and a birth-rate of 43 per thousand. Assume that educationally it is rather more advanced than Thailand. More specifically, assume that every child begins school on his or her sixth birthday, but that only 40 per cent complete seven years' primary education, and that on average it takes them eight years to do so. Further, assume that half of those who complete primary education (i.e. 20 per cent of all children) enter secondary school, that half of these (10 per cent of all children) complete secondary education five years later, and that half of these proceed to tertiary education. Figure 19.2 shows the educational attainment of a cohort

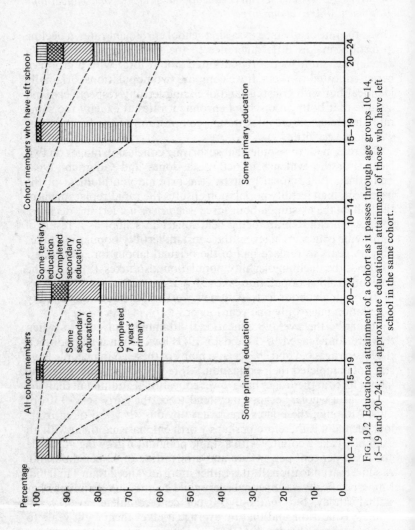

FIG. 19.2 Educational attainment of a cohort as it passes through age groups 10–14, 15–19 and 20–24; and approximate educational attainment of those who have left school in the same cohort.

whose educational experience conforms to this pattern. The educational attainment of the cohort is continually improving as it passes through the teenage years into the twenties. Furthermore, at any given time, the educational attainment levels of those who have left school and are therefore available to participate in economic activities are below those of the cohort as a whole. As a result of these two factors, the educational attainment of those who participate in the labour force at ages 15–19 is well below the educational attainment of those from the same cohort who will engage in economic activity at ages 25–29.

It follows that if educational levels are not improving over time, young members of the labour force (aged 10–19) will have a *lower* level of educational attainment than the remainder of the labour force. Since the 10–19 group is a larger component of the labour force in the high fertility projection, the average educational attainment of the labour force will be somewhat lower in this projection than in the declining fertility projection. However, in the more realistic case in which educational levels are improving, the improving educational level of each succeeding cohort passing through the ages 10–19 approximately counterbalances the effects just mentioned. The net result of these effects in the Jones-Gingrich study was that given the rate of educational advance, the educational attainment of the labour force differed insignificantly over time between the constant and declining fertility projections.

Although further simulation studies are needed to verify the conclusions reached, it seems clear that the high-fertility population's relative advantage in terms of educational attainment of the labour force over time is so small, if it exists at all, that very little weight should be given to it in assessing the relative merits of high versus falling fertility.

REFERENCES

N. Bennett *et al.*, 'Problems of Financing the Thai Educational System During the 1960s and 1970s', mimeo, Educational Planning Division, Ministry of Education, Bangkok (June 1972).

M. Blaug, 'The Rate of Return to Investment in Education in Thailand', mimeographed (Bangkok, 1971).

O. D. Hoerr, 'Education, Income and Equity in Malaysia', *Economic Development and Cultural Change*, vol. 21 (Jan 1973).

G. W. Jones, 'Educational Goals in Tropical Africa', *Population Growth and Economic Development in Africa*, ed. S. H. Ominde and C. N. Ejiogu (London, 1972).

—— *Population Growth and Educational Planning in Less Developed Countries* (Appleton Century Crofts, 1975).

G. W. Jones and P. Gingrich, 'The Effects of Differing Trends in Fertility and of Schultz, T. P., *cont.*

Educational Advance on the Growth, Quality and Turnover of the Labor Force',
Demography, vol. 5, no. 1 (1968).

H. Leibenstein, 'The Impact of Population Growth on Economic Welfare – Non-
traditional Elements', *Rapid Population Growth: Consequences and Policy
Implications*, National Academy of Sciences (Johns Hopkins Press, Baltimore,
1971).

D. C. McLelland, 'Does Education Accelerate Economic Growth?', *Economic
Development and Cultural Change*, xiv, 3 (Apr 1966).

S. Merrett, 'The Rate of Return to Education: A Critique', *Oxford Economic
Papers*, 18, no. 3 (Nov 1966).

J. Mincer, 'Schooling, Age and Earnings', *Human Capital and Personal Income
Distribution*, National Bureau of Economic Research (New York, 1974).

O.E.C.D. Study Group in the Economics of Education, *The Residual Factor and
Economic Growth* (Paris, 1964).

T. K. Ruprecht and C. Wahren, *Population Programmes and Economic and Social
Development*, O.E.C.D. Development Centre (Paris, 1970).

T. N. Châu, *Population Growth and Costs of Education in Developing Countries*,
International Institute for Educational Planning (Paris, 1972).

T. P. Boo, 'Education in Singapore', Educational Publications Bureau, Ministry of
Education (Singapore, 1970).

P. Taubman and T. Wales, 'The Inadequacy of Cross-Section Age-Earnings Profiles
when Ability is not held Constant', *Annals of Economic and Social Measurement*,
1/3 (1972).

D. Turnham, *The Employment Problem in Less Developed Countries*, O.E.C.D.
Development Centre (Paris, 1971).

United Nations, *World Population Prospects, 1965–2000, as Assessed in 1968*,
ESA/P/WP.37 (17 Dec 1970).

University of Indonesia, Demographic Institute, *Report on the Urban Unemployment
Survey, 1972* (1974).

Discussion of the Papers by
Dr Jones and Professor Stone

Professor Ohlin raised three points for discussion from Dr Jones's paper. The author wanted to identify ways in which population trends influenced the growth of output, but rather failed to do so. The purely formal calculation of changes in age distribution was irrefutable but how the potential saving in educational costs were used, and what the effect was, would all depend on the particular case.

There was also the question whether the magnitude of the potential saving was sufficient to constitute a very striking argument in favour of fertility reduction. It might seem considerable at first sight, but on second thought one might find it trivial. In Thailand, the author thought one might find it trivial. In Thailand, the author estimated that educational costs in the year 2000 might, on a high fertility assumption, amount to 4·1 per cent of G.N.P. With the low fertility hypothesis, they would be 3·1 per cent of G.N.P. This was a difference of some 25 per cent, but 1 per cent of G.N.P. thirty years from now did not seem impressive in view of the enormous changes in G.N.P. and other variables that would occur before then and completely overshadow this minor difference.

Second, the author had considered only public expenditure. The cost to parents, including earnings foregone, might also have been included, and this would have had a much greater effect of fertility reduction. Such total costs, however, came close to the cost of rearing children at all, and we then had something more like a regular Coale-Hoover model.

On the other hand, if the author wished to focus on public expenditure, perhaps because it might be expected to be of special concern to policy-makers, why not include health expenditures and other welfare costs?

The reason was probably that the author would like to think of education as an input which promoted economic growth. If low fertility meant more education per pupil, there was then the prospect of further benefits. But the returns to education were by no means established. Professor Schultz's estimate that some 35 per cent of the variance of incomes in the U.S.A. could be imputed to education was quite irrelevant to growth economics. The author cited studies from developing countries which failed to establish great returns, and was aware of the criticism of school systems, which all too often failed to create functional literacy, even among those few who attended them for a couple of years. In view of the present search for relevant, cheap educational systems, was it worth while extrapolating costs on the basis of past experience?

Of course, no matter how education was pursued, it would cost something. The author's main point remained valid. But it seemed more interesting to focus on the cost to parents, and the deterrent effect on fertility it was likely to have, at least in some circumstances. Whether the cost to the public purse induced governments to adopt population policies, and whether such policies had any effect, was far more dubious.

Professor Machlup introduced Professor Stone's paper on 'Demographic Variables in the Economics of Education', saying that it examined possible associations among eleven variables.

1. The percentage of the population under 15 years of age.
2. The gross reproduction rate of the population.
3. The annual growth rate of the population.
4. The life expectancy at birth.
5. The dependency ratio, i.e. the ratio of the economically inactive to the economically active, the latter being those between 15 and 64 years.
6. The illiteracy rate within the population aged 15 and over.
7. The percentage of total enrolments at the primary and pre-primary levels.
8. The percentage of the relevant age group enrolled in primary and secondary education.
9. The urban population as a percentage of total population.
10. The gross national product per head (in U.S. dollars).
11. Public expenditure on education as a percentage of the gross national product.

Professor Machlup saw the first nine of these variables were demographic, inasmuch as they dealt with relative numbers of persons in a variety of groups; the last two variables were economic, inasmuch as they dealt with the national product and its use for public educational efforts. The data used were chiefly those published in the Yearbooks of the U.N. Statistical Office, supplemented by two or three other sources. Only countries with a population exceeding one million people were included in the analysis.

Professor Machlup said that Professor Stone found, confirmed or re-confirmed twelve 'associations' among his variables:

1. There was a fairly close association between the percentage of the population under 15 years and the gross reproduction rate.
2. The proportion of the population under 15 was rising fastest when the annual growth rate of the population was around 2·55 per cent on the basis of a 'simple logistic', or 2·42 per cent on the basis of a 'log-logistic'.
3. There was a significant association between the proportion of the population under 15 and the G.N.P. per head.
4. The association of life expectancy at birth with G.N.P. per head showed that at low levels of G.N.P. per head life expectancy rose rapidly with rising G.N.P. per head but at a falling rate, and that little further improvement was experienced after a figure of about $750 per year had been reached. The increase in G.N.P. per head exercised its maximum effect on life expectancy at a figure of $72 per year.
5. For plural societies, either because of differences in race or because of extreme concentration of wealth, the average measures of these variables must be abandoned in favour of measures for more homogeneous groups, or one or more new variables must be added to the analysis.
6. An analysis of the association between the dependency ratio adjusted for differences in G.N.P. per head and the growth rate of the population reconfirmed that poor countries with fast-growing populations tended to have a high proportion of children to educate and a small proportion of

economically active people to support education as well as everything else.

7.   The illiteracy rate was approximately proportional to the population growth divided by the G.N.P. per head, if a double log relationship was assumed; by fitting a sigmoid curve, however, the association appeared to be problematical. Large differences in the literacy rates among different groups of countries suggested that many factors, cultural, religious, racial, etc. ought to be taken into account.

8.   The hypothesis that the degree of urbanisation could make a significant difference – because education was more easily provided for children assembled in towns than for children scattered over the countryside – was not confirmed. The inclusion of the urban ratio made almost no difference.

9.   The hypothesis that the expenditure on education per child would make a significant difference was examined, but – perhaps because present expenditures told little about past expenditures when the present adults went to school, or perhaps because the data were only for public education, not for private – the inclusion of this variable made no difference.

10.   The association between the proportion of enrolments at the elementary level with G.N.P. per head, and the illiteracy rate among adults, showed a considerable scatter around the regression line, indicating wide variations among countries. For an explanation of the variations, two possible influences suggested themselves: the urban ratio and the percentage of G.N.P. spent on public education, but the inclusion of these variables made no difference.

11.   A variable called 'coverage of the educational system', measuring the percentage enrolled at primary and secondary levels, appeared to be associated not only with G.N.P. per head but also with the urban ratio. The inclusion of further variables, such as the percentage of the population under 15 and the percentage of the G.N.P. spent on public education, made no difference.

12.   Since for most of the variables which one would expect to determine the supply of education and the demand for education statistical information was unobtainable, the association between G.N.P. per head and the percentage of G.N.P. spent on public education was used as a substitute for more comprehensive sets of variables. The regression line was significant and upward-sloping, reconfirming that the provision of public education was income-elastic. The inclusion of other variables, such as the percentage of the population under 15, the percentage of total enrolments at the primary and pre-primary levels, and the percentage of the relevant age group enrolled in primary and secondary schools, made no difference.

At the end of his paper, Professor Stone selected for special emphasis the following 'general conclusions':

It is the countries with fast-growing populations that tend to be poor and it is these that tend to have a high proportion of children to be educated and a relatively small proportion in the economically active ages as conventionally defined. It is these poor countries that tend to have a low expectation of life and this increases quickly with rising incomes, though beyond a level of income, modest by the standards of Western

Europe, the increase is very fast. Population growth and low incomes tend to be found in countries with high illiteracy rates and these countries tend to concentrate their educational forces largely on elementary education. They also tend to have relatively low enrolment rates, particularly if they are little urbanised. Poor countries tend to spend a smaller proportion of their income on public education than do rich ones and this is consistent with the general belief that education is income-elastic.

Professor Machlup said that, in a second paragraph, Professor Stone explained the substantial departures which he had found from the stated tendencies by a) imperfections in the basic data; b) shortcomings in his treatment of the data; and c) influences exerted by history and traditions, cultural attitudes, religion and race. Finally, he restated that 'the bounded nature of relationships in this area suggests that we should try, wherever possible, to replace linear and other unbounded approximations by bounded ones'. He found the possibility of generalising the logistic and other sigmoid relationships highly promising.

Professor Machlup then submitted that none of the associations stated by Professor Stone could be regarded as findings of hitherto unknown relationships. To the extent that Professor Stone's findings confirmed or re-confirmed formerly known propositions, he doubted whether confidence in their validity or probability value was much increased by the results of the regressions. The numerical estimates of coefficients on the basis of notoriously poor data, and in view of the large differences among individual countries, were hardly of more than impressionistic value. He suspected that the value of Professor Stone's study lay in his proposals of statistical techniques for application to data of the sort presented, not in the specific numerical findings; but he himself was not competent to judge the merit of these statistical techniques.

Professor Stone's disclaimer that he was concerned not with causal relationships, but only with statistical associations and their form, called for some remarks. We could be sure that he was not interested in nonsense correlations. He looked at statistical associations between certain variables only because he entertained hypotheses regarding causal relationships. Indeed, at least ten times in his paper, Professor Stone stated his expectations of such causal relationships. Thus, he was, in fact, concerned with causality both at the outset when he selected his variables and at the end when he delivered his results.

Professor Stone disclaimed any concern with causality because the statistical data were poor proxies for the theoretical constructs which a proposition on cause and effect employed. For example, the illiteracy rate surely had something to do with education. Expenditures on education tended to reduce illiteracy, and a more literate society tended to become more interested in more education. Likewise, causal connections were likely to exist between education and G.N.P., again in both directions. But it should be clear that the statistical data for one and the same year were not acceptable as proxies for the theoretically relevant variables. Professor Stone was quite explicit in explaining this in his paper. If education contributed to greater literacy, and increased national product per head, via greater efficiency and perhaps also via reduced reproduction rates, the time lag was substantial. Expenditures for the education of the young could not have any of these effects on the achievements and attitudes of adults, except after several years. The literacy rate and G.N.P. per head now might be causally connected with education several years ago. For the causal relationship in the opposite direction, the time lag might be smaller but still considerable. Demand for education was a politically expressed demand which translated itself into public expenditure in subsequent years.

Thus, the statistical data of any one year could be regarded as empirical proxies for the causally relevant variables, at best, if they were taken as telling us something also about past or future magnitudes. The associations among the simultaneous magnitudes were therefore not by themselves good indicators of causal relationships, and perhaps this was what moved Professor Stone to disclaim any concern for causality.

Professor Stone's actual concern with causal relationships induced him several times in his paper to include additional variables in his functions. Undoubtedly he did so because he believed that there were more causally relevant factors than those whose associations he had exhibited. Repeatedly, the figures defeated his efforts, and Professor Stone had to conclude that nothing was gained by their inclusion.

Professor Machlup thought that the refusal of Professor Stone's equations to produce significant regression coefficients would not persuade him to give up his commonsense beliefs in the operation of the unconfirmed causal relationships. He would try again and again until his data and his equations would at last behave and perform according to strong beliefs, warranted thus far only on the basis of theoretical arguments. We did not often allow statistical facts to spoil our theories, economic or otherwise!

Dr Gavin Jones thought Professor Ohlin's comments were fair, but contained some slight misrepresentations. His paper was not aimed at the advocacy of reduced fertility, and he did not intend to show missionary zeal, though he had possibly been guilty of this in the past. He believed he had simply presented the facts, but said that if missionary zeal was evident, he must apologise. He admitted that his approach was partial and that it could have been broadened to deal with costs of health, etc. but insisted that the topic was chosen for the conference and that he had accepted the brief. The subject was big enough, even as delimited, and he felt no guilt at ignoring these other points.

Professor Guitton was not against missionary zeal so long as different hypotheses were used in that zeal. It was for the politicians to decide which hypothesis to listen to. Professor Machlup's comments on the paper by Professor Stone should come in here, because they went to the very heart of causality, which would always be relevant.

Professor Stone said that the 'concern' that had been picked up by Professor Machlup was not really appropriate, but that it was impossible to talk about causality, or to make claims on the basis of this data, in the work he had done. He wanted to say something on technical problems later.

Professor Demeny argued that Dr Jones's main proposition was that education cost money, so that, if fertility was lower, the burden of education would be correspondingly lower. He agreed that this was undoubtedly true. But why should fertility be low? A family decision on fertility was not connected to the social system. There was no signal from the public finance system to parents, so there was no incentive to parents to do anything about the source of the burden, which was carried by the state. Significant elements of cost were carried by parents, if only implicitly. If we took an imaginary village in a less-developed country, and if the elders could cut fertility by 50 per cent, and also reduce the educational budget by 50 per cent, there would still be the problem of educational quality. Substitution between quantity and quality of children was removed from the decision-making unit. We had another example of bad advice, or the copying of things not relevant to their own situation. Even in the relatively centralised system in Eastern Europe, with educational standards imposed from the centre, decisions were decentralised even if they were not on the shoulders of the family. Interests and arguments meant that there was a far closer link between the cost of education and the decision to increase the family than there was in developing countries. Educational finance tended to be regressive, in that income was transferred from the poor to the rich. There was also the mistaken belief that parents did not value the education of their children, and this led to taking educational control from the parents. It would perhaps be better if parents influenced the quality of education, and if there were also a feed-back system to give an incentive to parents to limit their families, because of their concern for the quality of education.

Professor Hermalin said that the question of policies to influence fertility had been raised. There had been studies of the connection between educational aspirations and fertility behaviour. An incentive scheme – the educational bond programme – based on such studies, was being carried out in Taiwan on a small scale. Women with two or three children received credits to encourage them to prevent further children, and the bond would help them procure secondary education for their children if there were no further births. This experiment was built on the knowledge that interest in education was part of the culture, as established by a previous survey. Schemes for other cultures would probably have to be different. For example, Dr Ridker's work on the tea estates in India suggested this.

Professor Coale also wanted to take up the issue of policy implications. There was a widespread commitment to education in developing countries. Maybe more education was being attempted than could be justified by G.N.P. improvements that might result. Education was wanted for its own sake, and as an educator, he had to agree; a literate population was seen as valuable in its own right. Anyhow, developing countries had this view; in fact, it was often written into the constitution, which indicated the strength of that belief. Economists who advised caution had great difficulty in persuading less-developed countries that further investment in education would be wasted, so that these commitments were not likely to change. Dr Jones's analysis was important because, in many developing countries, despite the growth in enrolment of 4 per cent, the numbers not in school were still increasing. How did we influence politicians? It might be important for ministers of education and other government ministers to appreciate that current demographic trends made it impossible to reduce the proportion of children not in primary school.

Professor Rasmussen wanted to make a footnote on methodology, particularly the opposed viewpoints of Professors Machlup and Stone. Professor Stone was concerned only with associations; Professor Machlup with theory and causality. Professor Stone looked for relationships which *a priori* made sense and therefore overdid his modesty. Professor Rasmussen felt that Professor Machlup exaggerated the immutability of theory in the face of facts. So both overdid their points of view.

Professor Schultz said he was pleased with Dr Jones's paper and its challenge to Liebenstein's thesis that rapid population growth yielded benefits, by permitting a society to re-educate a large fraction of its labour force each year.

Evidence that university education yielded a low private rate of return was not well-documented for most countries, although some studies in Africa and South Asia had found unusually high levels of unemployment among the highly-educated. If the returns to education were generally found to decline after primary and secondary schooling, rather than investing in the further over-production of university graduates. But this was an issue for much further empirical study.

A point made by Professor Kuznets many years ago, and frequently misinterpreted, appeared to come up in Dr Jones's paper. The delayed entry of students into the labour force, because they remained in school, should not necessarily be seen as a social cost of expanding the educational system. This private cost – the opportunity value of the student's time – was presumably offset by the private returns the student thought he would obtain from his education when he did enter the labour force. This element of private cost was usually considered when one was estimating private rates of return to education, from cross-sectional data. As for the proposal that education should be financed more heavily by direct charges against the parent, it should be obvious that such a change in the financing of education would, in most instances, redistribute resources away from the poor and disadvantaged. This was an outcome that should be avoided if at all possible.

Referring to the techniques using sigmoid curves in Professor Stone's paper, and the related need to analyse appropriately dichotomous dependent variables (those which took on a value of either zero or one, yes or no, etc.), Professor Schultz thought that these non-linear estimation techniques had an important role to play in the analysis of demographic phenomena. Where dependent variables were constrained within bounds (i.e. the zero-one interval), linear regression and correlation analysis, and the linear probability function this often implied, were at best only first approximations, and exhibited many undesirable statistical properties.

Dr Jones responded to the objection by Professor Schultz about whether the delayed entry of children into the labour force should be considered as a net cost. Dr Jones said he had not said this, but in the short run would expect delayed entry to hold down per capita income, even if there was a bigger increase later. On the question of returns to education at the primary and higher levels, he was not confident that rates of return were lower for higher education, because there was not enough data. Some studies showed social returns from primary education to be greater than for secondary, but there was no final proof.

On the equity and efficiency of publicly-financed education, *Professor Eastman* said that it might redistribute income mainly within income groups rather than between them as was often assumed. He also said that the economic models of educational expenditures typically made use of the family welfare function, which was a rather shaky construct. The parents made the expenditure and the child got the yield. The former were likely to underspend, with the result that there might not be overinvestment in education in a public system.

Mr Kegan referred to the comments by Professor Ohlin and Professor Coale. He accepted Dr Jones's findings that an increased educational burden would result from the dependency ratio and continued population growth. He would accept this as independent of productivity. He commented on the work by Dennison and Mintzer, connecting education to productivity, and to the work by Ted Seeley and Fritz Machlup on education in developed countries, though he thought that the latter was not relevant for the developing countries today, where there was often high unemployment and underemployment of the labour force. He also referred to the content of education and the distinction that had been made between education and instruction. It was important to focus on education for literacy, for certain trades, for adults, and on sex education. There were policy implications for the objectives we were concerned with, and there should be more attention to the *content* of education.

The question of employment of women was relevant. We were concerned with the education of women for the most part, including sex education, so that all these effects were associated. Women did have a new status and a new role, which would help to reduce fertility. There were therefore influences in the training and use of women in relation to the population programme itself which would result in redistribution of income. Advances in education increased literacy and maybe productivity as well.

Mr Conde commented on the African situation in the light of Dr Jones's paper. At a UNESCO meeting in Addis Ababa, education by 1980 was envisaged for all children of school-going age. The results were not satisfactory because they did not take account of population growth. The African countries which came nearest to the goal were those in Central Africa with lower population growth. West African countries, with higher rates of growth, were less far forward.

He also raised the question of what education or instruction was for. All too often it seemed that education so far had produced people with no job to go to, so that they migrated to the towns. There was a need to study the content of education and its role in development. It was all very well to carry out mathematical regression analysis of population, but would it not be more interesting to look at the association between school education and the growth rate, and the effect that the education ratio had? In other words, we should tackle the problem from the other end.

Dr Hume noted Dr Jones's references to the magnitude of savings. He suggested that the paper underestimated the social value of savings, because it was not just income that was saved, but money in the public fisc. The social value of money in the fiscal system was often greater than its nominal value. Dr Jones claimed his low fertility projections resulted in a saving of 1 per cent of G.N.P. over thirty years, but there would be savings for each year, not just for the thirtieth year. This implied that total savings would be about 4 per cent instead of the 1 per cent calculated by Dr Jones.

Professor Parikh commented on Professor Stone's paper. He was impressed by its technical sophistication, but wondered what its purpose was. In Fig. 18.1, for example, if one knew the gross reproduction rate over the past fifteen years, one could easily calculate the percentage of population under 15 years of age. Similar comments could be made about the other diagrams in Professor Stone's paper, so why go to all this complexity?

Professor Létinier asked Mr Conde about the unemployment of children with secondary education in Africa. Was it children with primary or secondary education who became unemployed?

Mr Conde replied that it was both.

Professor Létinier then asked why. Did not primary education give the ability to read, as well as cultural improvement? Could this not be used to improve agricultural productivity? Did education not help to become a motor mechanic? Was there no psychological explanation, for example, why these children felt certain work to be not worthy?

M. Sauvy said that education was now extremely practical and that books had been written, for example, by engineers. Were we referring to classical education or to the new education? There was obviously a need for very practical schooling more related to the real situation.

Professor Robinson said that Dr Jones seemed to be engaged on comparative statics in his paper, in looking at the implications for annual costs of larger population size, higher school enrolment, different age distributions, and so on, all on the basis of existing methods. This was an important first step, but there were several other major issues. Dr Jones had not brought in the capital cost of building schools, which, of course, was very important. One had to remember that Indonesia was experimenting with do-it-yourself provision of schools. He would like again to take the case of Bangladesh. What were the real opportunity costs of educational policy? Could one throw on the village all the costs of the village school, including the building? It was not obvious that one could not. But the major question was what teachers should be paid. There was the question of early graduate unemployment. Was it possible to employ all graduates for a year or two in a national social service, either as teachers or in a medical service? And what must one pay them? Did it have to be middle-class incomes to attract them to work in rural areas? Dr Jones assumed that teachers would be paid as at present, but the opportunity cost seemed to an economist extremely small, unless middle-class incomes and middle-class standards must be provided.

A second issue, again to quote Bangladesh, was the 15 per cent literacy level, with roughly 50 per cent of adults illiterate. There was much talk about a direct attack on adult literacy, and he wanted to know whether the same buildings and teachers could not be used for adults and children. He saw these as the real problems facing developing countries, and thought we had to be very careful about the type of analysis carried out, and about thinking we had done a cost/benefit analysis when we had done only a half-study, on wrong assumptions.

Dr Jones replied to Professor Robinson, saying that the main part of his study was basically one of dynamics, not comparative statics, and included the investment cost of education as well as the operating cost. He agreed that there was a percentage of teachers on lower wages, but the potential group of teachers was small in relation to the size of the group to be educated, though we did need unconventional measures. The experiments in Iran seemed to have been successful, but he still felt that it was hard to get people to do things for nothing.

Professor Parikh agreed with Professor Robinson that it was difficult to work out the cost of education, because it varied so much with quality. It tended to be income-elastic, and one got as good an education as one could afford. For example, in Bombay City, the cost of the best education available was three, four or even five times the cost of public-school education. The children of the rich might be more successful because they were rich, not because they had an expensive education. How did one then work out the costs and benefits of education? Developing countries did not see the need to do cost/benefit analysis; they wanted the best education possible, because they believed it to be good in itself.

Professor Ben Porath asked Professor Demeny, in the light of his opening comments, what stock-taking he could now do on the policy implications of the discussions. Could we at least identify the critical problems, and attempt an answer? We knew something of steady states and of demographic processes, and had some elements of capital and growth models. We should be able to find some qualitative relationships between income per capita and other variables. We knew that in order to keep up steady state-educational capital, we should get a low income per capita with higher rates of population growth. But we also needed quantitative content.

The crucial policy issue was that of educational financing. If the demand for education was not price elastic, shifting cost to the population would not have much effect on demand for education, but might reduce the number of children, and hence have implications for reducing population growth. If both the demand for children and for education were not price-responsive, this would be resolved elsewhere. People would object to shifting the cost, because there would be no effect on the birth-rate and nothing would be achieved. We were back to individual responses which turned out to be crucial for the choice of policy instruments.

Professor Perlman admired the neatness of Professor Machlup's method of analysis of Professor Stone's paper, but thought we needed a similar analysis on Dr Jones's paper. He noted that Professor Coale had said that education was good for its own sake, even if it did not pay off. This in itself did not make it non-economic. Education might be a final as well as an intermediate good. There were other things, such as increasing returns on the consumption side. And what happened when girls were educated? Maybe the interval between generations increased, so that instead of having a first child at 18 years, a woman had her first child at 25. The educational burden diminished rapidly. One of Professor Perlman's doctoral students (Dr Manharlal Vyne), had looked at the Addis Ababa programme in terms of performance against target. The target date had been set too soon, but from the Kenyan responses, he discovered that if the target were set for 20 years, costs were very much greater than if it were set at 10 years. With a smaller number of people to educate, one could transfer funds to other social purposes which might not be internationally desirable, for example, war. On the other hand, the funds could be used to increase the quality of education. As education was seen as only an intermediate product, the countries did not educate girls. We might be missing the key point of the Jones argument.

Professor Guillaumont came back to the consequences of greater or lesser fertility on the educational process, as evidenced by West African and Central African experience. There were great differences in the quality of education, depending on whether classes were large or not. Qualitative aspects made the whole issue very debatable and many speakers had expressed the need for more specific educational policy. What did Dr Jones think about these qualitative aspects? Was lower fertility a good factor in this respect? We did not have enough empirical data.

Professor Schultz wished to underline some of the things Professor Perlman had said, and agreed with Professor Ohlin's comments about the inappropriateness of treating children simply as goods.

Mr Boulier made some comments on the voucher system for higher education, which he thought was a good plan. The idea was to push the costs of higher education on to the family, so that family decision-making would incorporate those costs.

Professor Stone wished to make two comments. The first was in answer to Professor Parikh. There was no need for his type of analysis if we were concerned only with one country. But standard techniques identified coherent relationships in the collected data for a number of countries, and this seemed to him a reasonable thing to do. Other relationships he had studied were complex and he wanted to see if anything came out if one took a world view. He did find elementary coherence even if the same analysis had been done before. If one wished to probe deeper, it was not difficult to find further ways of accounting for the observed variation. One could go on to suggest attitudes, religion, history, race, etc. but it was difficult to get data, or even to form the variables required; but he thought the analysis should be pursued.

His second point related to sigmoid curves. All growth was sigmoid, but most simple economic models led to exponential growth. He felt that such exponential models needed an opponent. What were the technical problems with this type of model? His original paper for the conference had been needed too soon, and he had had to use an approximate method, and badly at that! He now knew how to do the sums. For example, if we looked at the proportion of the population under 15, as against the rate of population growth, the full maximum likelihood treatment gave smaller limits than in the original calculations. Taking the world-wide view, the lower limit would now be 22 instead of $17\frac{1}{2}$ per cent, and the upper limit 45 instead of 65 per cent. He had used simple assumptions, but thought members of the conference would have views on what these limits were likely to be. Did 65 per cent sound ridiculous? Or 45 per cent? Professor Stone did not know, but members of the conference might. If one used maximum likelihood estimate methods, one would fit the average observations in the absence of further information. Obviously, one would not give an *a priori* illiteracy of greater than 100 per cent. On the basis of UNESCO data however, one would probably give one very near to 100 per cent. In studying illiteracy, there might well be data that could be taken into account. On the proportion of the population under 15, which Professor Machlup mentioned, Professor Stone had found that the maximum effect of the rate of population growth came at $2\frac{1}{2}$ per cent under the original method, which seemed very high; and $1\frac{1}{2}$ per cent under the revised method. Once again his methods really were inefficient but there was the possibility of generalising to give sigmoid curves which had been done in other fields for years. The paper was only an exploration, but this seemed to be an area of interest. Taking the world view, whatever the data problems, gave quite a lot of variation for comparison.

Professor Coale said that, since Professor Stone had only just mentioned his methodology, he wished to make a couple of points. With reference to the proportion of the population under 15, an upper limit of about 50 per cent seemed plausible to him. His objection, on reading the paper, had been that the exploration would have been more valuable and convincing if Professor Stone had been more careful about the data he used, for example, in Africa, where his data showed growth rates for all countries, but gross reproduction rates for only a few countries. The facts were the reverse of this, as far as Professor Coale knew. He would have been happy to see a whole column of data on gross reproduction rates but with growth rates for only a few countries. The transformations suggested, before the tests were carried out on the data, were the same as those suggested in John Tukey's work. There, transformations were suggested to make the data more symmetrical, irrespective of the context of the problem.

Dr Jones made several points in reply. The first was about the importance of the things he was trying to measure. In Mr Leridon's terms, was this a mere 'hiccup', a small saving of development funds, or something more important – a contribution to the on-going development process? Dr Jones thought the importance attached to the relationships outlined in his paper would depend on the criteria applied to evaluate it. The conference would have to draw its own conclusions.

His second point was to emphasise that, in the next decade, we could expect population growth to contribute 30 to 50 per cent of the increase in the cost of education in developing countries.

Third, he wished to say that the last few pages of his report were the most important, and the key question to emphasise there was: what would be done with the savings? It was most unlikely that there would be a great reduction in educational spending (compared with the high-fertility situation); rather the savings would be used for increasing the enrolment rate more rapidly, or improving educational quality. This, in turn, would effect productivity by improving the subsequent quality of the labour force.

Professor Guitton was struck by the rigour of Professor Stone's approach and by his modest attitude – surely the sign of a great scientist, who would not make claims beyond his findings. Professor Stone did not want to become involved in causality problems, but if we looked at the future, Professor Guitton did not see how we could do away with a concern for causes. We must walk very cautiously, despite Dr Jones's talk of a mission. Perhaps in developing countries one should not take risks. History looked to the past, but economists must look to the future. Even if we limited our analysis to the past, knowledge was very difficult to acquire. We had a duty towards the future and therefore we should be interested in further work, as well as in what we had achieved so far.

Index

Entries in **bold type** under the names of participants in the conference indicate their papers or discussions of their papers; entries in *italic* indicate contributions by participants to the discussions.